CATHOLIC SOCIAL PRINCIPLES

CATHOLIC SOCIAL PRINCIPLES

The Social Teaching of
The Catholic Church
Applied to American Economic Life

BY

REV. JOHN F. CRONIN, S.S., Ph.D.

ASSISTANT DIRECTOR, DEPARTMENT OF SOCIAL ACTION
NATIONAL CATHOLIC WELFARE CONFERENCE
DIRECTOR, INSTITUTE OF CATHOLIC SOCIAL STUDIES
CATHOLIC UNIVERSITY OF AMERICA

THE BRUCE PUBLISHING COMPANY
MILWAUKEE

Nihil obstat: JOSEPH T. BECKER, S.J., Censor Deputatus
Imprimatur: ✠ PATRICK A. O'BOYLE, Archiepiscopus Washingtoniensis
February 1, 1950

To the Memory of the Great Pontiff
POPE PIUS XI,
WHOSE SOCIAL ENCYCLICALS
INSPIRED THE STUDIES EMBODIED IN THESE PAGES,
THIS VOLUME
IS JUSTLY AND GRATEFULLY DEDICATED

INTRODUCTION

One of the chief obstacles to an effective presentation of Catholic social teaching has been its doctrinaire approach to the problems of economic life. Exponents of the teaching of the social encyclicals have for the most part been men well versed in social philosophy and the science of morals, but not always equally well versed in the science of economics. As a result their analysis of the causes of the social problem and their corrective recommendations for the establishment of a sound social order have been frequently too abstract. They have failed to correlate their exposition of principles with a sufficient understanding of practical situations so that the man of action who must deal with problems in the concrete and seek solutions in the practical order of administration was not greatly impressed.

This new book by Dr. Cronin is happily free from such limitations. It was designed not only for general use among students of social science, but was particularly directed to the needs of our colleges and seminaries which have heretofore lacked an adequate textbook. The authoritative text of the papal encyclicals is presented at the opening of each chapter in such comprehensive fashion and so pertinently correlated with the immediate subject under consideration that there is no need for the student to search out the references on his own responsibility. The interpretation and application of the papal doctrine are clearly stated without injecting personal opinions into the text so as to mar their objective value. When there is doubt or obscurity in respect to the correct interpretation or application of the principles involved the author gives not only his own view but also a careful and unbiased presentation of differing attitudes and positions. An illustration of this scholarly approach is found in his treatment of the much discussed and much misunderstood "Industry Council System."

Dr. Cronin not only sets forth the distinctive papal doctrine concerning the organization of economic life, namely the principle of co-operation by labor, management, and ownership for the common good, but he makes clear that neither good will alone, nor individual action is sufficient to accomplish the necessary reforms. Group action with governmental sanction of new institutional forms is required to implement these principles. His exposition definitely makes room for governmental responsibility, but definitely rejects the idea that government should make the chief economic decisions. He makes allowance for the principle of competition under social control and thus avoids the paralyzing effects of comprehensive national planning with priorities, allocations, and the various devices used to establish domination by the state.

Catholic scholars have been agreed that social legislation will not alone be effective in bringing about the necessary improvements of our economic system, but that new agencies or institutions must be created to solve such urgent problems as unemployment, depressions, increased productivity, wider distribution of income, and the expanded investment necessary to promote a higher standard of living. They have not been agreed as yet on the full definition of the function to be performed by the "Industry Councils" — as these new institutions are rather inadequately called in current terminology. Some think that prices, profits, investments, as well as wages and working conditions should be determined by these "Industry Councils." Dr. Cronin rejects this extension of responsibility as unwarranted and dangerous. While giving due weight to the argument of those who differ with him, he makes out a very convincing case for his own interpretation.

One of the areas in which this new work makes a distinctive contribution is that of fiscal policy in its relation to the social teaching of the encyclicals. There has been a tendency among many to concentrate attention on labor problems exclusively and neglect the very important fields of monetary policy, credit, investment, savings, and similar problems, all of which have a definite relation to the common good and the improvement of social conditions. None of these aspects of the social problem are overlooked by Dr. Cronin.

This new text is a welcome addition to our literature on social problems. It is comprehensive in its treatment, well balanced in its judgments, and practical in its application to the current economic scene. The thorough scholastic training of Dr. Cronin both in sociology and economics as well as his daily contact with concrete problems in the fields of management and labor make him particularly well qualified to serve as a reliable guide in this most complicated subject.

MOST REVEREND KARL J. ALTER, D.D.
Bishop of Toledo

PREFACE

This book offers an explanation of Catholic social principles in the light of American economic life. The social teaching of the Church is basically a mixture of ethics, moral theology, and prudent judgment as applied to the field of social economics. It is called Catholic because of its immediate source. But its principles are so founded in human nature that men of all creeds can readily see its truth and wisdom. While it has been presented authoritatively by various statements of recent popes, its roots go back to the inspired words of Holy Writ.

There is an unavoidable ambiguity in the use of the term *social* in these pages. A more exact usage would favor such expressions as socioeconomic or social-economic, since many questions normally called social are not treated here. Yet, historically, the impact of economic structure and function upon society has been called "the social problem." When the papal encyclicals treat of the social question, they deal with problems similar to those discussed here. Inasmuch as the present volume is based upon these "social" encyclicals, their language is followed where American usage permits.

The primary sources used are the social writings and addresses of Popes Leo XIII, Pius X, Benedict XV, Pius XI, and Pius XII. Occasional reference is made to other authoritative documents. Among these are the teachings of St. Thomas Aquinas, statements by the hierarchies of various countries, and the carefully prepared *Code of Social Principles,* issued by the International Union of Social Studies. But the papal statements above all crystallize and apply to modern conditions the social principles developed from Scripture teachings and natural law.

Little effort is here made to trace the historical development of main social principles. Lack of space precludes the pursuit of this fascinating study. The interested reader will find references in the Appendix to books dealing with the social message of the Gospels, the flowering of Catholic social thought during the Middle Ages, and its revival during the nineteenth and twentieth centuries.

In presenting Catholic social teaching, textual excerpts from authoritative sources are reprinted in each chapter. This practice gives the reader convenient opportunity to study the documents which are being explained and applied. Several reasons suggested this practice. In the first place, many of the papal writings are not available in any English collection. This is particularly true of the writings of the present Holy Father, Pius XII. Again, allusions to a given topic may be scattered through three or four encyclicals, with a number of different references in each encyclical. The task of checking back would be tedious. Finally, the instant availability of sources gives the reader an opportunity to compare the views presented here with the actual writings of the popes, bishops, and theologians.

The use of quotations has been selective rather than exhaustive. Where there is duplication, the better texts are quoted, with references given to the others. In a few instances, very lengthy treatments are summarized rather than quoted. In such cases, the pope may be dealing at length with conditions no longer relevant in all their details. Nevertheless, excerpts are usually generous, to avoid the danger of taking material out of context. Needless to say, the author hopes that readers will be inspired to read the major encyclicals in their original sequence. With this in mind, quotations have been largely drawn from a few generally available books and pamphlets. An exception to this rule is the use of discourses, messages, and letters of the present Holy Father, even when the texts are not available in any current English source. The directives of Pope Pius XII, in the light of postwar problems, are so timely that their inclusion was mandatory, even though many readers may not have access to the original documents for study in context.

Each set of excerpts is then explained in the light of general ethical and moral principles. Where useful, background material is supplied. This is sometimes necessary where the full meaning of writings destined for the entire world may not be immediately evident in terms of our language and customs. Moreover, there are many important points where the encyclicals are either silent or not conclusive. In these cases moralists often differ in their views. Thus, we find divergent points of view on the question of a worker's obligation to join a union. Again, authors are not agreed whether the duty of paying a living wage is an obligation of commutative or of social justice.

On controversial questions, different points of view are presented and references given for further study. Moreover, the best available experts have been consulted. In this way, a distinction is made between what is clear or generally agreed upon and what is still the subject of serious discussion.

The ethical commentary is accompanied by an application of principles to current American economic conditions. Here is one of the major justifications for the writing of the present book. We have many good commentaries on the ethical aspects of one or more social encyclicals. But only one American book has appeared during the 1940's to apply papal social principles to economic life today. The author of that book chose to confine his treatment to one major encyclical, *Quadragesimo Anno*. While this is a worthy undertaking, there is also need to note both previous and subsequent papal statements, particularly those dealing with postwar developments.

Economic application is especially needed as a service to the great body of Catholics, clergy and laity, who are already familiar with the broad principles of social ethics. Unfortunately, these principles are not easily applied in the complex world of economic life. In many cases, it is even difficult to learn the facts to which principles pertain. Even when the facts are known, there may be disputes as to the relevant economic laws governing the situation. Yet, unless moral norms are applied properly, they remain abstract and indefinite.

Two perennial controversies illustrate this point. One concerns the obligation to pay a "living wage" to workers. The other involves the proper level of industrial profits. In both cases, there are disputes as to the facts. Difficult questions arise when we determine the size of the "normal" family and the level of living which could be called suitable. Likewise, there is controversy over the actual amount of business profits. Some economists argue that present accounting methods exaggerate profits in times of inflation and minimize them under depression conditions.

Even where there is agreement as to facts, the problem remains of applying economic laws so as to serve the common welfare. A highly complex set of techniques may be needed to bring about the payment of a universal living wage. Again, the level of business profits today is more than a matter of determining the proper return to investors. Profits are closely tied in with the questions of business expansion, full employment, and general economic health.

These are but a few of the cases where extreme difficulties are encountered in applying social principles to actual life. Yet these problems must be faced, or we will be reduced to uttering generalities which will be quickly dismissed as impractical idealism. We have not hesitated in other fields, such as medical ethics, to face delicate issues in applying principles. There is even greater need in the social field for concrete application, since the popes, dealing with world-wide problems, must necessarily speak in general terms. But time and again they have urged Catholic social scientists to apply principles to the problems of their day and age.

Practical application is likewise needed if our teachings are to be honored by the non-Catholic world. Too often Catholics are secretly apologetic about their social teachings. They act as if they were an *arcana disciplina,* truths too sacred to be bandied about. Such diffidence is largely unwarranted. On the contrary, when our principles are presented in language and contexts familiar to Americans, they usually meet with enthusiastic acceptance. An illustration of this is the current emphasis upon "human relations" in industry. Thirty great universities, several large societies and major periodicals, and hundreds of books have devoted attention to this subject. Yet the field of "human relations" is a rediscovery, by way of psychology, sociology, and practical experience, of truths enunciated in detail by Popes Leo XIII, Pius XI, and Pius XII. What we have been timidly hiding is a major discovery in modern industry.

In presenting our social ethics, the order of treatment involves a progression from general principles to fields of more limited application. There are three main parts to the present book. In the first, the social problem is outlined in relation to the broad bases of human nature. The general social teachings of the Church are given. Judgment is passed upon other social philosophies prevalent in the modern world. In the second part, the focus is narrowed to special fields, such as capital, labor, property, the state, international economic life, and the means for social reform. Finally, there is an appraisal of the major schools of thought which affect American Catholics. This would include both authoritative statements by our hierarchy and views of individuals or schools which have molded segments of American Catholic thought. An annotated and topically arranged reading list is offered as an aid for further study.

Various classes of readers were considered in the preparation of this book. It was designed to be read and used as a reference by all Catholics interested in the critical social problems of our times. In this light, it is nontechnical in approach. For those not familiar with ethics or economics, source references are given for consultation. Since statistics in the economic field become rapidly dated, suggestions are offered for obtaining current figures and facts. In this regard, the reader is also urged to consult the final chapter and the appendix material in the author's *Catholic Social Action*.

Special consideration was given to the needs of the Catholic laity interested in adult social education or in social action. With the growth of study clubs and discussion groups connected with the Confraternity of Christian Doctrine and of social action committees under Catholic lay organizations, there is definite demand for a single text which presents both encyclical teaching and its application to American life. It is hoped that our increasingly alert Catholic laity will find in these pages an answer to a need.

The clergy should also find this book useful. It contains in one volume material which may be needed for sermons, talks to various organizations, labor-school courses, forums, and discussion groups. Many who use the more modern books in teaching religion will find background material here. In this light, the present book could well be used in formal courses to be given in secular and religious seminaries. It could also supplement the moral theology treatment on justice. Many of the existing texts on moral theology treat this subject with few references to modern conditions.

There will be an increasing need by teachers in our elementary and high schools for a reference work on Catholic social principles. As the process of integrating these principles with our curricula continues, more and more teachers of religion, history, and the social sciences will need background material to explain allusions in the texts which they are using. This volume offers the convenience of giving original texts, ethical explanation, and concrete application in a single book.

Not many Catholic colleges or universities today offer formal courses in Catholic social principles. Undoubtedly this will be changed in view of the importance of the subject and the emphasis given it by recent popes. Pope Pius XII, in his letter to the Catholic University at Washington, stressed the key position of the school which treats Catholic social principles. Because of the evident need, it is expected that the present volume will be used as a text in many schools.

Finally, this work is offered for the careful consideration of men of good will, of all faiths, who may wish to know the ideals of our Church. The problems of the world today are too serious for men to be divided through ignorance of others' principles. Too often the social teaching of the Church has been misunderstood, when its existence is even acknowledged. Perhaps its moderation will bring it a hearing today, now that the folly of extreme positions has been shown in so many nations.

In conclusion, the present study does not pretend to be a research treatment or the last word upon the subject. Although it was eight years in preparation, and a mimeographed version was used at the Institute of Catholic Social Studies for six years, the subject is too broad for one author to master fully. Use has been made of excellent earlier commentaries, most of them concentrating upon ethical principles rather than concrete application. The topical gathering of texts and the economic application are original to this book. At the same time, special mention should be made of two outstanding works which appeared while this book was in manuscript form: R. Kothen, *L'Enseignement social de l'Église,* and J. Messner, *Social Ethics.* Both volumes were consulted in the final preparation of the text. The present author is happy to acknowledge the service rendered by these scholarly studies.

There are frequent cross references to other works by the present author, namely, *Catholic Social Action* and *Economic Analysis and Problems.* The books on Catholic social principles and action are naturally complementary, with the former furnishing the philosophy and the latter giving techniques for application. In this connection, the encyclical references in Chapter XIV are especially pertinent, since they furnish lengthy papal directions for social action. The economics text is likewise complementary, in the sense that it offers a more detailed explanation of points which are mentioned briefly here. It also contains additional references for further study. At the same time every effort was made to make the present book reasonably complete. It is hoped that all important material is treated adequately here, so that reference sources will be needed only for further study rather than for clarification of major issues.

REV. JOHN F. CRONIN, S.S.

ACKNOWLEDGMENTS

The author is deeply grateful to the many experts who assisted by reading the manuscript and offering criticisms. Special thanks are due to the Most Reverend Karl J. Alter, D.D., Bishop of Toledo. Not only did Bishop Alter kindly consent to write the introduction to the book, but it was due to his encouragement that the work was started. The author is equally grateful to the Most Reverend Patrick A. O'Boyle, D.D., Archbishop of Washington. Archbishop O'Boyle succeeded Bishop Alter as Chairman of the Department of Social Action and likewise gave his endorsement to the project of writing this book. Nor could the work have been completed without the generous assistance of Rev. Raymond McGowan, director, and Rev. George Higgins, assistant director of the Department. Both accepted without complaint the additional burdens involved in releasing the author for this time-consuming task.

Several experts were kind enough to read the entire manuscript and offer their criticisms. These included: Rev. Leo Brown, S.J., and Rev. Joseph Becker, S.J., of St. Louis University; Dr. Goetz Briefs, of Georgetown University; Dr. Alphonse Clemens, of the Catholic University; Rev. Vincent O'Connell, S.M., of Notre Dame Seminary, New Orleans; and Rev. Joseph Donnelly, social action director, Diocese of Hartford.

The chapter on communism was criticized by Mr. Karl Baarslag, of the American Legion, and Mr. Benjamin Mandel, of the House Committee on Un-American Activities. Mr. Robert Dixson, of Johnson & Johnson, read the chapters on capital and labor. Msgr. John Donovan, of the Archdiocese of Detroit, offered useful suggestions concerning Chapters XI and XIX. Rev. James

Vizzard, S.J., of Georgetown University, commented on Chapters XII and XVII. Helpful observations on farm problems were also offered by the Rev. Martin Schirber, O.S.B., of St. John's University, Collegeville. Rev. Leo R. Ward, C.S.C., studied the chapter on distributism and the co-operative movement. Rev. Paul H. Furfey and Rev. Edward A. Keller, C.S.C., were more than kind in reading sections often critical of their own viewpoints. Mr. Eugene Willging, librarian of Mullen Library, Catholic University; Mr. Phillips Temple, librarian of Riggs Memorial Library, Georgetown University; and Miss Agnes Collins, librarian of the N.C.W.C., were generous and helpful in bibliographical matters. Special mention is due to Rev. John Sherbno, of the Diocese of Toledo, for his permission to use the manuscript of his compilation of social encyclicals. Brother Gerald Schnepp, S.M., of St. Louis University, arranged to secure criticisms of Chapter VII from his committee on industry councils. Many staff members of the N.C.W.C. helped in their specialized fields. Finally, a large number of persons sent in suggestions as to the scope and contents of the book.

The author is grateful for editorial and proofreading assistance from his sister, Miss Margaret Cronin, and from Misses Alma Jane Hale and Merle Nolde. The burden of typing and retyping was generously carried by Miss Patricia Kelly, Mrs. Jane Reno, and Mrs. Eileen Lynam.

Problems connected with social pathology were discussed with two practicing social workers, Miss Mary Vivian Fu, of Catholic Charities, Brooklyn, and Miss Mary Jane FitzGerald, of Bellevue Hospital, New York.

To these, and many others unnamed but not forgotten, the author expresses deep gratitude.

AUTHORITATIVE REFERENCES

The following list names the major documents used as authoritative sources in the text. They are listed in chronological order in each main heading. After each document, a key is given which indicates the source used for the text cited. Where possible, English-language sources were used.

POPE LEO XIII
Quod Apostolici Muneris, December 28, 1878 (Husslein)
Diuturnum Illud, June 29, 1881 (Husslein)
Immortale Dei, November 1, 1885 (Husslein)
Libertas Praestantissimum, June 20, 1889 (Husslein)
Sapientiae Christianae, January 10, 1890 (Husslein)
Rerum Novarum, May 15, 1891 (N.C.W.C.)
In the Midst of Solicitudes, February 16, 1892 (G.E.L.)
Letter to Bishop of Grenoble, June 22, 1892 (C.C.)
Longinque Oceani, January 6, 1895 (G.E.L.)
Graves de Communi, January 18, 1901 (Husslein)
Letter to Italian Bishops, December 8, 1902 (A.S.S., Vol. 35, p. 263)

POPE PIUS X
Il Fermo Proposito, June 11, 1905 (P.Pe.) (P.P.)
Letter on Sillon, August 25, 1910 (A.A.S., Vol. 2, p. 607)
Singulari Quadam, September 24, 1912 (C.L.)

POPE BENEDICT XV
Letter to Bishop of Bergamo, March 11, 1920 (C.L.)

POPE PIUS XI
Ubi Arcano, December 23, 1922 (Husslein)
Mens Nostra, December 20, 1929 (Husslein)
Divini Illius Magistri, December 31, 1929 (Husslein)

Casti Connubii, December 31, 1930 (Husslein)
Quadragesimo Anno, May 15, 1931 (N.C.W.C.)
Non Abbiamo Bisogno, June 29, 1931 (Husslein)
Caritate Christi Compulsi, May 3, 1932 (Husslein)
Ad Catholici Sacerdotii, December 20, 1935 (Husslein)
Mit Brennender Sorge, March 14, 1937 (Husslein)
Atheistic Communism, March 19, 1937 (N.C.W.C.)
Firmissimam Constantiam, November 23, 1939 (Husslein)

POPE PIUS XII

Summi Pontificatus, October 20, 1939 (P.P.)
Sertum Laetitiae, November 1, 1939 (P.P.)
La Solennità della Pentecoste, June 1, 1941 (P.P.)
Nell' Alba, December 24, 1941 (P.P.)
Christmas Broadcast, 1942 (P.P.)
Address to Italian Workers, June 13, 1943 (C.M., July, 1943)
Christmas Message, 1943 (C.M., February, 1944)
Radio Address, September 1, 1944 (C.M., October, 1944)
Letter to French Episcopate, January 6, 1945 (D.R., Vol. 7, p. 3)
Address to Italian Workers, March 11, 1945 (C.M., December, 1947)
Address to College of Cardinals, June 2, 1945 (C.M., August, 1945)
On Women's Duties, October 21, 1945 (C.M., December, 1945)
Christmas Broadcast, 1945 (C.M., January, 1946)
Discourse to Members of Italian Electric Industry, January 24, 1946
    (D.R., Vol. 7, p. 349)
Letter to Semaines Sociales, July 10, 1946 (C.M., November, 1946)
Discourse to Italian Farmers, November 15, 1946 (N.C.R.L.C.)
Address to Members of Renascita Cristiana, January 22, 1947
    (C.M., July, 1947)
Allocution to Sacred College of Cardinals, June 2, 1947
    (C.M., August, 1947)
Letter to Semaines Sociales, July 18, 1947 (C.M., November, 1947)
Discourse to Catholic Action Men, September 7, 1947 (*London Tablet*,
    September 13, 1947)
Allocution to International Union of Leagues of Catholic Women, September 12, 1947 (*London Tablet*, September 20, 1947)
Address to Small Craftsmen, October 20, 1947 (D.R., Vol. 9, p. 295)
Christmas Broadcast, 1947 (C.M., February, 1948)
Address to Congress of International Exchange, March 7, 1948
    (C.M., July, 1948)
Discourse to International Institute for the Unification of Private Rights,
    May 20, 1948 (D.R., Vol. 10, p. 89)

Allocution to Sacred College of Cardinals, June 2, 1948
  (C.M., August, 1948)
Discourse to Christian Association of Italian Workers, June 29, 1948
  (C.M., October, 1948)
Address to Young Men, September 12, 1948 (C.M., January, 1949)
Discourse on Public Finance, October 2, 1948 (C.M., March, 1949)
Address to Representatives of Fiat Automobile Plant, October 31, 1948
  (C.M., May, 1949)
Christmas Message, 1948 (C.M., March, 1949)
Address to Catholic Employers, May 7, 1949 (C.M., July, 1949)
Address to Minister from India, July 6, 1949 (*New York Times,* July 7,
  1949)
Address to Women of Italian Catholic Action, July 24, 1949
  (C.M., December, 1949)
Letter to Semaines Sociales, 1949 (N.C.W.C. News Service, August 1, 1949)
Message to German Catholics, September 4, 1949 (C.M., November, 1949)
Allocution to Belgian Workers, September 11, 1949 (C.M., January, 1950)

AMERICAN HIERARCHY

Social Reconstruction (N.C.W.C.)
Pastoral Letter, 1919 (N.C.W.C.)
Bishops' Statement, 1933 (N.C.W.C.)
The Church and Social Order, 1940 (N.C.W.C.)
Secularism, Statement of American Hierarchy, November, 1947 (N.C.W.C.)
The Christian in Action, 1948 (N.C.W.C.)
The Christian Family, 1949 (N.C.W.C.)

OTHER AUTHORITIES

Summa Theologica, St. Thomas Aquinas
Sacred Congregation of the Council to the Bishop of Lille, June 5, 1929
  (A.A.S., Vol. 21, p. 494)
Socialization, Australian Hierarchy, 1948 (C.M., May, 1949)
Peace in Industry, Australian Hierarchy (A.N.S.C.A.)
Pattern for Peace, Australian Hierarchy (A.N.S.C.A.)
Congregation of the Holy Office, July 13, 1949 (*New York Times,* July 14,
  1949)
Code of Social Principles (Oxford: Catholic Social Guild)
Pastoral Letter, French Cardinals, September 8, 1949
  (C.M., December, 1949)
Pastoral Letter, Hierarchy of Quebec, February, 1950 (S.E.)

Key

A.A.S.: *Acta Apostolicae Sedis* (Rome: Typographia Vaticana, 1909–)

A.S.S.: *Acta Sanctae Sedis* (Rome: Typographia Vaticana, 1878–1908)

A.N.S.C.A.: Australian National Secretariat of Catholic Action (Melbourne, Australia)

C.C.: *Le Canoniste Contemporain*

C.L.: Ryan, J. A., and Husslein, J., *The Church and Labor* (New York: Macmillan, 1920)

C.M.: *Catholic Mind*

D.R.: *Discorsi e Radiomessagi di sua Santità Pio XII* (Rome: Tipographia Poliglotta Vaticana, 1939–)

G.E.L.: *Great Encyclical Letters of Pope Leo XIII* (New York: Benziger, 1903)

Husslein: Husslein, J. (ed.), *Social Wellsprings* (Milwaukee: Bruce, 1940–1942)

N.C.R.L.C.: "The Pope Speaks on Rural Life" (Des Moines: National Catholic Rural Life Conference, 1948)

N.C.W.C.: National Catholic Welfare Conference

P.P.: Koenig, H. (ed.), *Principles for Peace* (Milwaukee: Bruce, 1943)

P.Pe.: *The Pope and the People* (London: Catholic Truth Society, 1937)

S.E.: *Service extérieur d'éducation sociale,* Quebec

CONTENTS

PART I · THE CHRISTIAN SOCIAL ORDER

PART I
_____

THE CHRISTIAN SOCIAL ORDER

Chapter I. THE SOCIAL QUESTION

Leo XIII, Rerum Novarum

5. In any event, We see clearly, and all are agreed that the poor must be speedily and fittingly cared for, since the great majority of them live undeservedly in miserable and wretched conditions.

6. After the old trade guilds had been destroyed in the last century, and no protection was substituted in their place, and when public institutions and legislation had cast off traditional religious teaching, it gradually came about that the present age handed over the workers, each alone and defenseless, to the inhumanity of employers and the unbridled greed of competitors. A devouring usury, although often condemned by the Church, but practiced nevertheless under another form by avaricious and grasping men, has increased the evil; and in addition the whole process of production as well as trade in every kind of goods has been brought almost entirely under the power of a few, so that a very few rich and exceedingly rich men have laid a yoke almost of slavery on the unnumbered masses of nonowning workers.

66. For the violence of public disorder has divided cities into two classes of citizens, with an immense gulf lying between them. On the one side is a faction exceedingly powerful because exceedingly rich. Since it alone has under its control every kind of work and business, it diverts to its own advantage and interest all production sources of wealth and exerts no little power in the administration itself of the state. On the other side are the needy and helpless masses, with minds inflamed and always ready for disorder.

Pius XI, Quadragesimo Anno

3. For toward the close of the nineteenth century, the new kind of economic life that had arisen and the new developments of industry had gone to the point in most countries that human society was clearly becoming divided more and more into two classes. One class, very small in

number, was enjoying almost all the advantages which modern inventions so abundantly provided; the other, embracing the huge multitude of working people, oppressed by wretched poverty, was vainly seeking escape from the straits wherein it stood.

5. The same feeling those many Catholics, both priests and laymen, shared, whom a truly wonderful charity had long spurred on to relieve the unmerited poverty of the nonowning workers, and who could in no way convince themselves that so enormous and unjust an inequality in the distribution of this world's goods truly conforms to the designs of the all-wise Creator.

54. Property, that is, "capital," has undoubtedly long been able to appropriate too much to itself. Whatever was produced, whatever returns accrued, capital claimed for itself, hardly leaving to the worker enough to restore and renew his strength. For the doctrine was preached that all accumulation of capital falls by an absolutely insuperable economic law to the rich, and that by the same law the workers are given over and bound to perpetual want, to the scantiest of livelihoods. It is true, indeed, that things have not always and everywhere corresponded with this sort of teaching of the so-called Manchesterian Liberals; yet it cannot be denied that economic-social institutions have moved steadily in that direction. That these false ideas, these erroneous suppositions, have been vigorously assailed, and not by those alone who through them were being deprived of their innate right to obtain better conditions, will surprise no one.

58. Gravest evils due to the huge disparity between the few exceedingly rich and the unnumbered propertyless.

59. These commands have not lost their force and wisdom for our time because that "pauperism" which Leo XIII beheld in all its horror is less widespread. Certainly the condition of the workers has been improved and made more equitable especially in the more civilized and wealthy countries where the workers can no longer be considered universally overwhelmed with misery and lacking the necessities of life. But since manufacturing and industry have so rapidly pervaded and occupied countless regions, not only in the countries called new, but also in the realms of the Far East that have been civilized from antiquity, the number of the nonowning working poor has increased enormously and their groans cry to God from the earth. Added to them is the huge army of rural wage workers, pushed to the lowest level of existence and deprived of all hope of ever acquiring "some property in land," and, therefore, permanently bound to the status of nonowning worker unless suitable and effective remedies are applied.

60. Yet while it is true that the status of nonowning worker is to be

carefully distinguished from pauperism, nevertheless the immense multitude of the nonowning workers on the one hand and the enormous riches of certain very wealthy men on the other establish an unanswerable argument that the riches which are so abundantly produced in our age of "industrialism," as it is called, are not rightly distributed and equitably made available to the various classes of the people.

62. All these things which Our Predecessor has not only suggested but clearly and openly proclaimed, We emphasize with renewed insistence in Our present Encyclical; and unless utmost efforts are made without delay to put them into effect, let no one persuade himself that public order, peace, and the tranquillity of human society can be effectively defended against agitators of revolution.

83. Nevertheless, as the situation now stands, hiring and offering for hire in the so-called labor market separate men into two divisions, as into battle lines, and the contest between these divisions turns the labor market itself almost into a battlefield where, face to face, the opposing lines struggle bitterly. Everyone understands that this grave evil which is plunging all human society into destruction must be remedied as soon as possible.

105. In the first place, it is obvious that not only is wealth concentrated in our times but an immense power and despotic economic dictatorship is consolidated in the hands of a few, who often are not owners but only the trustees and managing directors of invested funds which they administer according to their own arbitrary will and pleasure.

109. Free competition has destroyed itself; economic dictatorship has supplanted the free market; unbridled ambition for power has likewise succeeded greed for gain; all economic life has become tragically hard, inexorable, and cruel. To these are to be added the grave evils that have resulted from an intermingling and shameful confusion of the functions and duties of public authority with those of the economic sphere — such as, one of the worst, the virtual degradation of the majesty of the state, which, although it ought to sit on high like a queen and supreme arbitress, free from all partiality and intent upon the one common good and justice, is become a slave, surrendered and delivered to the passions and greed of men.

112. All the more gravely to be condemned is the folly of those who neglect to remove or change the conditions that inflame the minds of peoples and pave the way for the overthrow and destruction of society.

132. Hence arises that unquenchable thirst for riches and temporal goods, which has at all times impelled men to break God's laws and

trample upon the rights of their neighbors, but which, on account of the present system of economic life, is laying far more snares for human frailty. Since the instability of economic life, and especially of its structure, exacts of those engaged in it most intense and unceasing effort, some have become so hardened to the stings of conscience as to hold that they are allowed, in any manner whatsoever, to increase their profits and use means, fair or foul, to protect their hard-won wealth against sudden changes of fortune. The easy gains that a market unregulated by law opens to everybody attracts large numbers to buying and selling goods, and they, their one aim being to make quick profits with the least expenditure of work, raise or lower prices by their uncontrolled business dealings so rapidly according to their own caprice and greed that they nullify the wisest forecasts of producers. The laws passed to promote corporate business, while dividing and limiting the risk of business, have given occasion to the most sordid license. For We observe that consciences are little affected by this reduced obligation of accountability; that furthermore, by hiding under the shelter of a joint name, the worst of injustices and frauds are perpetuated; and that, too, directors of business companies, forgetful of their trust, betray the rights of those whose savings they have undertaken to administer. Lastly, We must not omit to mention those crafty men who, wholly unconcerned about any honest usefulness of their work, do not scruple to stimulate the baser human desires and, when they are aroused, use them for their own profit.

134. Thus it came to pass that many, much more than ever before, were solely concerned with increasing their wealth by any means whatsoever, and that in seeking their own selfish interests before everything else they had no conscience about committing even the gravest of crimes against others. Those first entering upon this broad way that leads to destruction easily found numerous imitators of their iniquity by the example of their manifest success, by their insolent display of wealth, by their ridiculing the conscience of others, who, as they said, were troubled by silly scruples, or lastly by crushing more conscientious competitors.

135. With the rulers of economic life abandoning the right road, it was easy for the rank and file of workers everywhere to rush headlong also into the same chasm; and all the more so, because very many managements treated their workers like mere tools, with no concern at all for their souls, without indeed even the least thought of spiritual things. Truly the mind shudders at the thought of the grave dangers to which the morals of workers (particularly younger workers) and the modesty of girls and women are exposed in modern factories; when we recall how often the present economic scheme, and particularly the shameful housing conditions, create obstacles to the family bond and normal family life; when we re-

member how many obstacles are put in the way of the proper observance of Sundays and Holy Days; and when we reflect upon the universal weakening of that truly Christian sense through which even rude and unlettered men were wont to value higher things, and upon its substitution by the single preoccupation of getting in any way whatsoever one's daily bread. And thus bodily labor, which Divine Providence decreed to be performed, even after original sin, for the good at once of man's body and soul, is being everywhere changed into an instrument of perversion; for dead matter comes forth from the factory ennobled, while men there are corrupted and degraded.

Pius XI, On Atheistic Communism

8. . . . in an age like ours, when unusual misery has resulted from unequal distribution of the goods of this world.

47. But when on the one hand we see thousands of the needy, victims of real misery for various reasons beyond their control, and on the other so many round about them who spend huge sums of money on useless things and frivolous amusement, We cannot fail to remark with sorrow not only that justice is poorly observed, but that the precept of charity also is not sufficiently appreciated, is not a vital thing in daily life.

Pius XI, Caritate Christi Compulsi

2. Even those, very few in number, who appear to have in their hands, together with enormous wealth, the destinies of the world, even those very few who with their speculations are in the first part the cause of so much woe, are themselves quite often the first and most notorious victims [of depressions]. Together with themselves, they drag down into the abyss the fortunes of countless others. . . .

3. Is it not that lust of earthly goods that the pagan poet called with righteous scorn "the accursed hunger for gold," is it not that sordid egoism which too often regulates the mutual relations of individuals and society, is it not, in fine, greed, whatever be its species and form, that has brought the world to a pass which we all see and deplore? From greed arises mutual distrust, that casts a blight on all human dealings; from greed arises hateful envy, which makes a man consider the advantages of another as losses to himself; from greed arises narrow individualism, which orders and subordinates everything to its own advantages without taking account of others, on the contrary cruelly trampling underfoot all rights of others. Hence the disorder and inequality from which result the accumulation of the wealth of nations in the hands of a small group of individuals who manipulate the market of the world at their own caprice, to the immense harm of the masses. . . .

28. In place of moral laws, which disappear together with the loss of faith in God, brute force is imposed, tramping on every right. Old-time fidelity and honesty of conduct and mutual relations, extolled so much even by the orators and poets of paganism, now give place to speculation in one's own affairs, as in those of others, without reference to conscience.

Pius XII, Nell' Alba

1748. For the human spirit, overwhelmed in the confusion of this moral abyss, by its alienation from God and Christian practices, no other course remained but that of turning all its thoughts, purposes, and enterprises and every evaluation of men's possessions, actions, and labor and directing them to the material world, striving and sweating with might and main to spread out in space, to surpass all previous accomplishments in the attainment of riches and power, to engage in a competition of speed, to produce in greater quantity and quality everything that material advancement and progress seemed to require. These very symptoms appear in politics as an unlimited demand for expansion and political influence without regard to moral standards. In economic life they are represented by the predominance of mammoth concerns and trusts. In the social sphere it is the agglomeration of huge populations in cities and in the districts dominated by industry and trade, an agglomeration that is accompanied by the complete uprooting of the masses who have lost their standards of life, home, work, love, and hatred. By this new conception of thought and life, all ideas of social life have been impregnated with a purely mechanico-materialistic character.

1749. With the increasing lack of restraint, outward compulsion and domination founded purely on power seemed to prevail over the forces of order, which established the relations of law and charity in their natural and supernatural foundations as they had been laid down by God. To the detriment of human dignity and personality as well as society, the conception makes headway that it is might which creates right. Thus private property is being abused on the one hand as a means of exploitation; on the other hand, as a reason for envy, revolt, and hatred. The situation ensuing therefrom is being exploited by a struggle of interests which is being waged without any restraint.

Pius XII, Radio Address, September 1, 1944

Accordingly where, for instance, "capitalism" is based on such false concepts and arrogates to itself an unlimited right over property, without any subordination to the common good, the Church has condemned it as contrary to the natural law.

In fact, We see the ever increasing ranks of the workers frequently confronted with this excessive concentration of economic goods which, often hidden under anonymous titles, are successfully withdrawn from contributing, as they should, to the social order and place the worker in a situation where it is virtually impossible for him effectively to acquire private property of his own.

We see the small and medium holdings diminish and lose their value in human society, and constrained to join in a conflict ever more difficult and without hope of success.

On the one side, We see immense riches dominating public and private economic life and often even civil life; on the other, the countless number of those who, deprived of every direct or indirect security of their own livelihood, take no further interest in the true and higher values of the spirit, abandon their aspiration to genuine freedom and throw themselves at the feet of any political party, slaves to whoever promises them in some way bread and security; and experience shows of what tyranny, under such circumstances, human nature is capable even in our times.

Pius XII, On Women's Duties

. . . can a woman . . . hope for her real well-being from a regime dominated by capitalism? . . . You know its characteristic signs and you yourselves are bearing its burden: excessive concentration of population in cities; the constant, all-absorbing increase of big industries; the difficult and precarious state of others, notably those of artisans and agricultural workers; and the disturbing increase in unemployment.

Pius XII, Christmas Broadcast, 1942

1839. But the Church cannot ignore or overlook the fact that the worker, in his efforts to better his lot, is opposed by a machinery which is not only not in accordance with nature, but is at variance with God's plan and with the purpose He had in creating the goods of earth.

Economic life exists to furnish the material basis for man's cultural and spiritual interests. It should minister to the fundamental rights of man, both individual and social. For this purpose, it should be organized in the light of the common welfare. Actually, things have been quite otherwise. There have been times when man's rights have been trampled underfoot in an orgy of exploitation and oppression. A greedy and avaricious materialism has perverted economic life from its divinely ordained purpose. The lives and welfare of millions have been pawns in gigantic struggles for power. In the words of Pope Pius XI, "all economic life has become tragically hard, inexorable, and cruel." Such is the social question, the existing state of economic life, as contrasted with the ideal.

Insofar as the social question springs from human greed and avarice, from pride of life and lust for power, it will be always with us. Man, blinded in intellect and weakened in will, is prone to evil as well as to good. There will always be selfish men, ambitious for power and material success, whatever the means used to accomplish their ends. But there is another aspect to the social question, the problem of *social institutions*. Men, even the most individualistic among them, do not act in a social vacuum. They are influenced by the laws, customs, and habits of their day. The sanctions of society are powerful compelling forces which have a strong impact on the wills of individuals. To the extent that social institutions change, the intensity of the social question will vary from age to age. In this light, it may be apposite to glance into history, so as to furnish a background for studying the social problem today.

THE MEDIEVAL PATTERN

A Christian Social Order. The story of poverty and oppression goes back to the beginnings of recorded history. Organized societies of older days had economic crises, not too dissimilar to those of modern times. Indeed, philosophers of history often find disturbing parallels between the decline of Rome and the tensions of our day. There are gloomy forebodings in the writings of Spengler, Toynbee, Sorokin, and others. However, such a study, interesting and enlightening as it is, is not pertinent to the immediate question. Our problem rather is to trace the Christian influence in society, particularly in the strains which affect the dominant culture of the Occidental world. For such a quest, it is natural to begin with the Middle Ages. Before the eleventh century, it would be futile to look for extensive Christian penetration of organized society. By the time that the Church was an effective force in the Roman empire, the empire was in hopeless decline. During the Dark Ages, the Church kept burning the flickering light of Graeco-Roman culture, but social life was not organized to any extensive degree. It was only with the eleventh century that we find a revival of a complex economic, political, and social life. This life was strongly influenced by Christian ideals.

Space does not permit a description of economic and political life in medieval and early modern times.[1] Rather, stress will be laid upon social institutions and their effect upon the social question. In this regard, we note significant differences between medieval and modern times. Faults can be found with medieval society. There were wars and oppression. The countless sermons against usury testify to the prevalence of human greed. But the important point is that wrongdoing was recognized as such and not canonized as progress. Economic and political life was considered as subordinate to man, not his master.

The Church in medieval times did not hesitate to formulate a social moral code. It had specific teachings on the purpose of man's life and the place of material things in this over-all picture. The doctrine of justice was applied in detail to the market place. While the institution of private property was upheld, the social obligations of ownership were also stressed. The prime importance of the common welfare, as contrasted with individual selfish aims, was insisted upon.

The significance of medieval Church teaching on social problems was greater then than it would be today. The best comparison in modern terms, anomalous as it may seem, is with Soviet Russia. Americans are beginning to understand the influence of ideology among Communists. They act in terms of a creed, however perverted and grotesque may be such teachings. Likewise, in the Christian society of the Middle Ages, the teaching of theologians and the sermons of preachers were more than mere exhortations. They laid down binding rules of conduct, accepted as moral obligations upon the consciences of individual

---

[1] For a summary, with extensive references, see J. F. Cronin, *Economic Analysis and Problems* (New York: American Book Company, 1945), Chaps. 1, 2, 5, and 26.

Christians. Hence medieval religious teachings on justice, political life, property, the social virtues, avarice, and usury were effective in influencing individuals. Of course, men could disregard the moral law then, as they do now. But it is one thing to have all the pressures of religious and social sanctions directed against a line of conduct, and an entirely different thing to remove economic life in its entirety from the moral sphere, as happened in modern times.[2]

Medieval Social Institutions. So powerful was the influence of religion in the medieval world that the social teaching of the Church could be called in itself a significant social institution. Nevertheless, its influence went beyond its direct effect upon the consciences of individuals. It also led to the establishing or the modification of important social institutions. Some of these factors warrant further analysis.

Among the basic characteristics of medieval life was the system of feudalism. Feudalism was a complex phenomenon whose origins are disputed. It probably arose from the disordered political life of the Dark Ages, in which peasants were compelled to associate themselves with a powerful lord for the sake of personal protection. At any rate, it involved personal and economic service to a lord in return for a grant of land. Here an important social concept was introduced: the idea of the mutuality of rights between classes of society. The serf was unfree; but he was not a slave, for the precise reason that he had rights as well as duties. Political machinery existed to enforce these rights. Serfs were bound to the service of the lord who owned or held the land from which they lived, but they had a right to their livelihood and to protection against violence and injustice.

It has long been the custom to look down upon feudalism as a form of society little better than slavery. True, from a purely political point of view, men in modern democratic states enjoy

---

[2] In this regard, R. H. Tawney, *Religion and the Rise of Capitalism* (New York: Harcourt, 1926), and A. Fanfani, *Catholicism, Protestantism, and Capitalism* (New York: Sheed, 1936), offer superb analyses. See also *Economic Analysis and Problems,* Chap. 26. On the general influence of ideology, see R. M. Weaver, *Ideas Have Consequences* (Chicago: Univ. of Chicago Press, 1948).

greater freedoms. But for a society just emerged from the anarchy of the Dark Ages, the idea of mutuality of rights and a social order organized in terms of interdependence represents a significant advance. No one was too mean to be beneath the protection of law, or so powerful as to be above it. "All powerful custom determined every man's rights and obligations. This fact alone was enough to prevent the pitiless severity to which the free exercise of economic supremacy gives rise under the spur of profit."[3] While the modern world does not accept the idea of status as governing the position of the individual, it should not overlook the definite moral and social principles embodied in feudalism.

In industrial life, the guild system introduced social ideals into the economic order. The craft guilds were organizations of masters, journeymen, and apprentices in the various skilled trades. They regulated in considerable detail all phases of production and exchange. In general, they discouraged monopoly, insisted upon uniform high quality, and protected the rights of workers. During the height of the medieval period, these craft guilds were quite democratic. The path from apprenticeship to mastership was open for all who met the not too difficult requirements. Thus, standards of justice and concern for the common welfare were imbedded in industrial life. However, from the fourteenth century on, grave abuses intruded into the guild system. As religious ideals became less influential in society, ordinary workmen were exploited by the master in a fashion not unlike the worst abuses of capitalism.

Guilds flourished in commercial life as well, and here also ethical norms were given an institutional framework. Merchants in a locality organized into protective associations. These groups determined prices, set up standards of quality, and prevented both monopoly and unfair competition. In the early Middle Ages,

[3] H. Pirenne, *Economic and Social History of Medieval Europe* (New York: Harcourt, 1937), p. 64. Many historians hold that the power of law and custom, involving the consent of the governed, made medieval society democratic in a real sense. For an extensive documentation from non-Catholic sources, see R. W. and A. J. Carlyle, *A History of Medieval Political Teaching in the West* (New York: Putnam, 1903–1936).

merchant guilds were likewise fairly democratic. Toward the
fourteenth century they lost their earlier principles and became
powerful oligarchies, often dominating over their communities.
Indeed, the rise to power of the cities and their merchant groups
was to be a potent factor in the breakdown of feudalism.

The ethical norm determining the conduct of the guilds was
the common good, an expression of which was the just price.
Basically this involved an equality in exchange. The price of an
article must conform to its true value, as determined by public
authority or common estimate. It would be immoral for either a
buyer or seller to exploit a monopoly position in order to lower
or raise the price. The price should not be so low as to impoverish
workers, artisans, or merchants; nor should it be so high as to
deprive the poor of the necessities of life. The significant point
is that this ethical norm was accepted by the commercial and
industrial community and institutionalized in the guilds.[4]

Ethics also entered into the sphere of finance. The condemnation of usury was bound to affect economic life. While a return
from rent and partnership was permitted, pure interest was considered an unjust exaction. Many of the considerations which
enter into the modern interest rate, such as a charge for the risk of
loss, were allowed, but a fee for the use of money as such was
outlawed. The basic reason for this was that money, in contrast
to real property, was considered unproductive. Hence a charge
for its use was an exploitation of another's needs, not a participation in a productive venture. The result of this was the
channeling of small-scale lending into the non-Christian community, although powerful Italian bankers, the Lombards, did
carry on large-scale financial operations. But the influence of
Church teaching was so great that, even in the late Middle Ages,
the powerful Antwerp Bourse and the House of Fugger sent
couriers to Rome for moral rulings on their transactions.

Above all these particular practices was a concept of property.

---

[4] The best English treatment of medieval ethical ideas is contained in E. G. O'Brien,
Essay on Medieval Economic Teaching (New York: Longmans, 1920). For other
references, see *Economic Analysis and Problems*, Chaps. 1 and 26.

Private ownership was considered to be in accord with the nature of man. Private property is a normal expression of man's right of ownership. But property should be used in such a way as to promote the common interest of all. Right laws and customs would lead to such a happy situation that the advantages of both private and common ownership would be preserved. Moreover, actual ownership would be diffused, since possession of property is an important distinction between the slave and the free man. The property owner has resources which minister to his freedom. Moreover, the social virtues, such as liberality, should guide the individual in the use of his property.[5]

Thus there emerges a picture of a theocentric society, with economic life governed by moral obligations embodied in social institutions. At its peak, this society combined a large measure of justice with economic stability. Yet it was not adverse to progress, as is testified by the great growth of commerce and industry during the medieval period. Such a society offers a striking contrast to modern notions, in that economic life was then strictly subordinate to cultural, moral, and religious considerations.

Transition to Modern Times. The system was to fail, although not from any inherent weakness in the approach. A combination of events served to sharpen man's acquisitive instincts, at the very time that a decline in religious fervor and observance was taking place. The fearful catastrophe of the Black Death (1347) in itself would have been sufficient to disrupt even the most stable of societies. Not only did it depopulate much of Europe, but its impact was hardest upon the leaders of society who ministered to the sick and dying. Records show that deaths among the clergy were proportionately much greater than among the population as a whole. The best-educated and most idealistic members of the community were taken from it.

Religious fervor declined for other reasons as well. Many abuses grew within the Church. Schisms and heresies became more common. Even the papacy itself had unworthy members,

---

[5] See W. J. McDonald, *The Social Value of Property According to Thomas Aquinas,* (Washington: Catholic University, 1939).

while the period of exile at Avignon (1309–1317) was weakening
and disruptive. These trends culminated in the Protestant Revolt.
The influence of the Church upon society declined as it engaged
in a terrific struggle for internal reform and the return of its lost
members. It could be said that, from the sixteenth until the mid-
nineteenth century, the Church was preoccupied with the hard
core of doctrinal orthodoxy and moral reform.

The newly formed Protestant churches, after an uncertain
beginning, were to turn away from the idea of organized social
morality. Both Luther and Calvin accepted much of the economic
morality of the Church. But the branches springing from Lu-
theranism were to carry religious individualism to its logical
conclusion. With religious belief left largely to personal conscience and private interpretation of the Scriptures, there was
little chance for a widely accepted social morality to be imposed
on the institutions of society. At the same time, the Calvinist
root of Protestantism was to develop the concept of "calling."
The sign of predestination to heaven was God's blessing upon
one's "vocation." In the minds of many, this led to an equation
between material success and divine approval.[6]

As the influence of religious and moral sanctions lessened, other
factors were to offer positive stimulus to business enterprise.
Among these was the revival of commerce which began with
the Crusades. Commerce expanded until the quest for supplies
and markets led to the discoveries of new-world colonial opportunities in the fifteenth and sixteenth centuries. The growth of
merchant power in turn brought about a clash between the
medieval city and the feudal nobility. This struggle gradually
developed into the broader contests which led to modern nationalism. An alliance between merchant groups and ambitious
lords led to the consolidation of national power, particularly in
France and England. These new states then used every means
to stimulate economic growth as an instrument for political

---

[6] This point is treated in detail by Tawney and Fanfani, cited earlier. See also
E. Troeltsch, *The Social Teaching of the Christian Churches* (London: Allen & Unwin,
1949).

power. By the seventeenth century, France under Louis XIV was even to impose a form of statism upon business, in order to regulate it in the interest of national strength.

While commerce expanded, both of its own momentum and as a result of state encouragement, businessmen were growing restive under government controls. They turned eagerly to the theories formulated by the great pioneer economists of the eighteenth century. These theories are now known as *laissez-faire* individualism. It was held that economic life was regulated by its own natural laws, which should not be subject to interference by the state or any other group. These laws are based on the human desire to maximize pleasure and minimize pain. Man is considered basically selfish in his economic pursuits. But by the benevolent designs of Providence, man's selfishness actually leads to the greatest common good. In the struggle for survival, each man produces to the best of his ability. The sum of such efforts would be maximum production at the highest quality possible. Hence, the good of all would be served. Any interference with this process, through state or private intervention, would only lead to decreased production and increased misery. Free competition must be the sole guiding rule of economic life. Such were the policies which many justified on the basis of the teachings of Turgot, Adam Smith, Malthus, and Ricardo. Ricardo further held that by virtue of competition workers must always remain at a subsistence level (the iron law of wages), even though he conceded that this level might gradually rise. Such limited optimism was not shared by Malthus in his study of population. This author held that workers would reproduce faster than the economy could grow and hence would always press toward a state of poverty.[7]

By the eighteenth century, the social institutions of earlier ages, embodying a moral and religious code in their practices, were largely gone. Their ideological base was destroyed as a

---

[7] For details on this position, see L. H. Haney, *History of Economic Thought* (New York: Macmillan, 1930), Chap. 10 ff.; and E. Whittaker, *A History of Economic Ideas* (New York: Longmans, 1940), Chaps. 1 and 3.

result of the factors noted above. Moreover, the very process of commerical and industrial growth and change was important in breaking up social organizations founded under different conditions. Great movements of population, the subdivision of labor as a result of new processes, and the enlargement of the market necessarily outmoded the guilds and their customs. Even if society had not changed in its moral and ethical framework, economic developments would have called for profound modification of existing institutions. By the eighteenth century, however, the temper of society was such that earlier organizations were destroyed without being replaced. As a result, the masses of workers in the newly expanded cities became a proletariat, a formless group without internal coherence, security, or direction in economic life.

It would not be accurate, however, to assert that earlier ideals were abandoned without being replaced. The concept of liberty itself became the *leit motif* of the age. Man exulted in the idea of freedom as the guiding principle of life. Freedom was symbolized in the religious sphere by the Reformation, in political life by the rise of democracy, and in the economic world by the idea of a *laissez-faire* economy. Thus an all-pervasive liberalism affected society in the eighteenth and nineteenth centuries, the culminating result of the ferment originating in the fourteenth century.

The external changes in economic life followed a pattern familiar to all students of history. Commerce expanded rapidly during the postmedieval period. The growth of commerce in turn led to a demand for better and more efficient methods of production. This need was met by the Industrial Revolution, commencing with the late eighteenth century. The advent of steam power made possible the development of the machine. Subsequently the discovery of electrical power, the internal combustion engine, and now the vista of atomic power were to multiply unbelievably the resources available to man. Chemical and metallurgical advances led to better machines, while electronics gave these machines a skill often surpassing the trained

senses of man. Progress moved in its triumphant march. But
social institutions failed to progress as rapidly as did technical
skill. The social problem arose, with all its appalling features of
calloused cruelty and exploitation.

THE RISE OF THE SOCIAL PROBLEM

Early Conditions. The beginnings of the social problem coincide with the first revolts against medieval moral restraint
upon business and industry. When the guilds decayed, starting
with the fourteenth century, the masters became oppressive. Both
merchant and craft guilds intensified and abused their monopoly
positions. In the crafts, advancement to mastership was made
almost impossible, except for sons of masters. The journeymen
and apprentices were cruelly exploited and subject to periodic
unemployment. Riots and revolts, particularly in Flanders, became common during the fifteenth century. Merchants often
sold shoddy goods at monopolistic prices.

The next step in exploitation was the enclosure movement in
England. While city workers were becoming proletarians, the
sturdy yeoman of England was driven off the land. The growth
of commerce made sheep raising profitable, since woolen goods
were in high demand. The feudal conception that the serf and
vassal had a right to the land was lost in the nationalistic states,
where the landowners possessed political power. The displaced
yeomen migrated to the cities, adding to the masses of workers
competing for the available jobs. Poverty and wretchedness
reached unbelievable levels. Theft became so common that
punishment was made drastic, without stopping the practice fed
by desperation.

Parallel to the gigantic growth in commerce was an orgy of
speculation. When these speculative bubbles burst, thousands
of businessmen were ruined. Their workers were thrown out of
jobs, thereby intensifying the problem of destitution. The burden
of periodic unemployment, often caused by speculative excesses,
was to grow with the Industrial Revolution. To meet this the
factory worker married early, raised a large family, and sent

his children into the mills. But such methods only added to the misery, since they increased the competition for jobs and beat down the wage level. Hours were long and working conditions atrocious. Workers became so demoralized that drunkenness and vice became commonplace in factory towns.

Pauper children were sent to work at the age of five or six. They were chained to the machines during the day and locked in sleeping huts at night. They worked from five or six in the morning until nine or ten at night. If they faltered, they felt the whip of the overseer. This happened at a time when the "better classes" in England were disturbed by the plight of the Negro slave in the United States, but were often blind toward even worse exploitation at home.

Conditions in France were no better. The seventeen-hour day was normal in the early nineteenth century. Four-year-old children worked in the shops of Lille. Children were starved, dwarfed, and deformed in body and spirit as a result of this torture. In the mines of England, women were harnassed to carts to pull up the coal, since the tunnels were too narrow to permit the use of animals. Such were the fruits of *laissez-faire* individualism. "Man's inhumanity has gone to greater excesses in the passion of war; men have been harsher under the spell of primitive savagery; but Christian nations have rarely, if ever, practiced the callousness which was an offshoot of the industrial revolution."[8]

The nadir of oppression and exploitation was reached by the

---

[8] J. F. Cronin, *op. cit.,* p. 18. For a detailed study of the social problems consequent upon the growth of modern capitalism, see: J. W. Thompson, *Economic and Social History of Europe in the Later Middle Ages* (New York: Appleton-Century, 1931); L. B. Packard, *The Commercial Revolution* (New York: Holt, 1927); W. J. Ashley, *An Introduction to English Economic History and Theory* (New York: Putnam, 1908); W. Cunningham, *Growth of English Industry and Commerce in Modern Times* (Cambridge: Cambridge Univ. Press, 1915); F. C. Dietz, *The Industrial Revolution* (New York: Holt, 1927); A. Toynbee, *Lectures on the Industrial Revolution in England* (New York: Longmans, 1896) and *Industrial Revolution of the Eighteenth Century in England* (New York: Longmans, 1920); J. L. Hammond and B. Hammond, *The Village Laborer* (New York: Longmans, 1927) and *Rise of Modern Industry* (New York: Harcourt, 1926); and P. Mantoux, *The Industrial Revolution in the Eighteenth Century* (New York: Harcourt, 1927).

mid-nineteenth century. By that time, corrective forces were springing up in most capitalistic countries. Sensitive souls were revolted by the by-products of the new industrialism. Thus, in England the Tory landlords were among the sponsors of the first social legislation. In France, the beginnings of a Catholic social movement were manifest by the 1830's. Germany was in ferment by the following decade. The currents of reform were many, often moving in contradictory directions. In a few cases, wealthy factory owners attempted to set up ideal patterns for their brethren. There were also occasional examples of labor unionism as an upward step. But much of the corrective movement arose in the intellectual world, dividing into two camps: the various schools of socialism, and the Christian social reformers. The former group advocated state ownership of the means of production, while many of the latter concentrated upon social legislation.

As a result of these forces for reform, a pattern of social legislation was set up in Europe. Child labor was regulated and gradually reduced. The hours of work were shortened and pay was increased. Conditions in factories and mines were improved. There was some tendency toward a more equitable distribution of income. Slums remained, but even in this regard there was improvement. The trend was toward justice, although the catastrophe of two world wars in the twentieth century was bound to set back social progress. Nevertheless, much remained to be done. The powerful indictments by Pope Pius XI, quoted earlier in this chapter, show that by 1931 there were still grave evils. We might summarize his attitude in this fashion: social legislation and other improvements, while welcome, are basically palliatives so long as the institutions of economic society are themselves deeply infected with injustice. More fundamental reforms are necessary. These may be studied in the light of American conditions.

The Social Problem in the United States. Social conditions in the United States were both better and worse than those of Europe. They were better, in that the exploitation of individuals never plumbed the depths reached in Europe. But they were worse, to the extent that the fundamental evils scored by Pope Pius XI were more prevalent. The ever beckoning frontier, with its offer of opportunity for men of zeal and energy, prevented all-out exploitation here. Until 1890, men could readily move into new land if conditions became intolerable at home. Indeed, the great migrations to California during the 1930's and 1940's were, in effect, continuations of the frontier spirit. Even at this date, large-scale population shifts are not unheard of in the United States. On the other hand, industrial concentration and periodic depressions took a recurring toll in terms of human misery. Selfish individualism persisted long after Europe had enacted comprehensive social legislation.

The American farmer has been burdened with an excessive share of economic problems. Periodic agrarian crises have been standard features of our national life. The farmer has been beset by debt, exploitation by middlemen, fluctuating markets and uncertain prices, and an unfavorable ratio between prices received for farm goods and those demanded for manufactured products. Even as late as the early 1930's, our farming community was virtually bankrupt.

The fortunes of labor were equally uncertain. Hours of work were long, factory and mine conditions hazardous and often nearly intolerable, and pay was low. There was much child labor and work by women in unsuitable jobs. The autocratic employer, particularly in the large factory, was more the rule than the exception. Discrimination for reasons of race, religion, and national origin was common. Efforts to improve conditions through unionism were bitterly fought. As recently as 1937, major segments of American industry waged all-out war against the formation of labor unions, and in 1947 a Labor Management Relations Act was passed which had many antiunion features. As a result of low pay, America has its share of slums, with all the evils which they foster.

The scandal of American capitalism, however, has been primarily financial. From the beginning of our industrial growth, the specter of greed, speculation, and titanic struggles for power has haunted our economy. The network of railroads which ribbon our land was constructed in an atmosphere of graft, bribery, and stock manipulation which was shocking to the conscience. The exploits of the "robber barons" of the middle and late nineteenth century would seem incredible, were they not so thoroughly documented. Ruthless competition led to periodic crises, dramatized by the two "Black Fridays" which paralyzed the financial community. In the course of these struggles, banks collapsed, losing the savings of millions and throwing more millions into the quagmire of unemployment.

Starting with 1880, unbridled competition gave way to consolidation, the "economic dictatorship" referred to by Pope Pius XI. At first, mergers and trusts were often forced upon small businessmen by unprincipled giants, such as Standard Oil. Independents either sold out or they were forced out of business by unscrupulous methods. Later, J. P. Morgan gave the process a gentler touch. Persuasion rather than pressure accomplished the mergers of the early 1900's. Finesse was also the overtone during the 1920's. But in the course of these mergers, stocks were manipulated and market values often lost all touch with reality. Speculation contributed powerfully to the boom and bust sequence which followed with sickening regularity. The debacle of 1929 was but the most recent and devastating in a long series. The toll in human tragedy surpasses the imagination. It is against this background that one must read the indictments quoted in the first part of this chapter.[9]

A Pattern of Improvement. In the United States, political power was used to counter the grave abuses noted briefly above. When the two relatively exploited and colonial areas of the South and West could unite, they were politically stronger than the financial and industrial North. Moreover, when labor's political power increased, it also was a strong influence. Usually these

---

[9] For reference material, see M. Josephson, *The Robber Barons* (New York: Harcourt, 1934), and F. L. Allen, *The Lords of Creation* (New York: Harper, 1935). Other references are given in J. F. Cronin, *op. cit.*, Chaps. 2 and 5.

forces were not united, since their differences seemed more important than their common fight against entrenched finance. But crises did bring about temporary alliances, and during these periods (around 1890, 1904, 1914, and 1932–1938) many fundamental reforms were effected.

The first reform movements were directed against industrial concentration and financial irresponsibility. These include the Interstate Commerce Act of 1887, to regulate the railroads; the Sherman Act of 1890 and the Clayton Act of 1914, to prevent combination in restraint of trade; and the Federal Reserve Act of 1914, which was an attempt to strengthen the banking system. That none of these reforms was adequate was proved by subsequent experience, culminating in the crash of 1929.

Really basic social reform in the United States was concentrated in the six years of the New Deal, 1932–1938. At this time, a thorough and comprehensive effort was made to remedy the great abuses which had prostrated the nation. Thus, various devices were used to bring about farm stability. The aim was an equating of food supply with demand at prices which would enable farmers to buy the industrial products they needed. The debt problem of the farmer was also considered.[10] The right of labor to organize was guaranteed by the federal government in areas under its jurisdiction. In these same areas, minimum-wage legislation led to some immediate improvement. Child labor was restricted. An extensive social-security program was instituted. The consumer was further protected from fraud and obnoxious products through better regulation of food sale and some forms of advertising.

Among the basic and lasting reforms of the New Deal were those connected with finance. Strong measures were taken to curb fraud in the original sales of securities and subsequent speculation in these stocks and bonds. Public-utility holding companies were regulated. Far-reaching financial reforms were instituted, with the result that the banking system achieved a

---

[10] For details of this and other New Deal social legislation, consult the relevant chapters of J. F. Cronin, *op. cit.*

degree of strength and flexibility never before attained. Further protection was given to the depositor in the form of deposit insurance. Various attempts were made to meet the problem of depressions, culminating in the post-New Deal period in the Employment Act of 1946. By this law, the federal government undertakes to watch over general economic conditions and to take suitable measures to stave off depressions and conditions which lead to the boom and bust cycle.

In the light of these developments, it is natural to ask: Do the strictures of Pope Pius XI apply to the United States today? Undoubtedly there have been great improvements which render certain passages in *Quadragesimo Anno* matters of historical interest only. But the optimism expressed in many widely read publications seems excessive. It is not true that the areas of social pathology in the United States are negligible, even if we restrict ourselves to fields strictly economic. Some of the basic disorders noted in *Quadragesimo Anno* still persist. Nor can it be asserted that the many statements of Pope Pius XII apply only to conditions outside the United States. In this light, it would be useful to examine the social problem today.

THE SOCIAL PROBLEM TODAY

Economic Society. The basic trouble with American economic life is that it is disorganized, in the sense explained subsequently in Chapter VII.[11] It lacks a basic unity and coherence, an organic character, which would be expected in an ideal social order. The system as a whole is disorganized, because it is vainly expected that a sound and consistent order will result from conflict. Conflict is too often considered either desirable or unavoidable. On the production level, there is much strife between capital and labor. In selling and distribution, we have both extreme competition, to such an extent that it is wasteful of resources and a source of economic insecurity, and concentration of economic power, leading to monopoly and closely held control of economic life

---

[11] As a convenience, in this section there will be allusions in parentheses to the subsequent chapters which explain more fully the problem under discussion.

(Chapters V and XII). Above all there is the problem of depressions and underemployment which plague modern economic life. This leaves all groups insecure: business, labor, farmers, financiers, and professional men (Chapter X). All these problems stem from an excessive reliance upon individualism and free competition, and the consequent reaction toward statism or struggles for power. Strife, instead of co-operation for the common good, is enthroned as a central principle.

Disorganization also characterizes individual industries and professions. The basic reason why our living standards are not higher is a lack of adequate production. This in turn involves intricate price relationships and problems of cost and efficiency. In a well-organized society, the more we produce, the better will be the condition of all. But, with limited resources and labor supply, increased production is largely a matter of greater efficiency and mechanization. This brings in questions of labor security, proper tax methods, and investment and profit incentives. A haphazard, class-conflict approach to these problems is inhibiting our economic growth and preventing both full production and full employment (Chapters VIII, X, and XII).

In the effort to solve such problems, we have turned to state intervention and social legislation. Such an approach is undoubtedly legitimate and was necessary in the historical circumstances of our growth. But it also involves the danger of further concentration of power to the detriment of individual freedom. The world today is beset with giantism. First, industrial and financial power was concentrated in the United States. Then, by reaction, there arose a tendency to give more power to the state. Large labor unions and farmer organizations also countered industrial and financial power, but at the risk of further giantism and increased social tension. While the individual is made to live in society, we may rightly fear that society is losing sight of its mission to aid the individual and is becoming an excessively autonomous force in present-day life.

What is needed badly is a return to freedom springing from real personal independence. This must be based primarily on effective ownership or control of one's economic life. Both wide-spread ownership of productive property and greater security for wage earners should contribute to this result. But really basic reform would change the entire direction of economic life by restoring a large degree of self-government to lesser economic groups. These in turn would co-ordinate their activities for the common good. Government would protect and foster individual freedom by encouraging ownership and diffusion of economic power. It would then be relieved of multitudinous details and be free to perform its sovereign function of guiding and encouraging subordinate groups in the light of public economic welfare (Chapters III, VII, XII, and XIII). Likewise, it could perform its duty, in concert with other nations, of restoring a healthy international economic life. Nations should have both security at home, access to raw materials, fair conditions of trade, and reasonable freedom for population movements (Chapter XIII).

There are many roots to the social problem today, but its moral and spiritual causes are fundamental. A philosophy of secularism, materialism, selfish individualism, greed, avarice, limitless ambition, and denial of social interests is bound to make society unhealthy. If social justice and social charity are not practiced, disorder and insecurity are sure to result. Man cannot live without God and remain conscious of his basic duties. Unsound moral and spiritual attitudes lead to a denial of human dignity and of social responsibility. Too often American economic groups — business, industry, finance, labor, farmers, and professions — have sought selfish gains to the neglect of both public interest and private rights. This is the more tragic, since such attitudes are self-defeating, even for the parties who mistakenly pursue them on the grounds of self-interest. Monopoly, greed for excessive profits, unwarranted strikes, and struggles for power only lead to a misfunctioning economic system which penalizes both the guilty and the innocent. Hence we need spiritual and moral reform as the foundation of a soundly organized economic life (Chapters IV, VIII, XI, and XIV).

While the American economic system has accomplished technical wonders, it has not achieved a form of smooth social organization comparable to its mechanical and engineering triumphs. It will not obtain secure prosperity until co-operation replaces group hostility, unsocial forms of competition, and struggles for economic power. This is a deep, underlying malady of our social life. Only when it is cured can we hope for a society organized in accordance with Christian principles.

The Family. As a result of faults in economic life, there are social problems which menace the stability of our families. Here the basic need is a living wage, for all male workers, which would support a normal-sized family in decent comfort. We must admit frankly that one reason for the high living standards enjoyed by millions of Americans is the fact that there are many childless and one-child families. It is difficult for the average worker to have a family of more than two children and provide adequate food, housing, clothing, medical care, education, and some minimum comforts of life. We have at our disposal sufficient statistics as to the cost of living, average wages, income distribution, and total income received by both city and rural families to know that the problem of raising even a moderately large family is very great. About one third of our four-person families and over half of six-person families living in large cities receive incomes inadequate for decent living. The average wage received by male workers permits moderate comfort for a nonworking wife and one child, if they live in large cities. Thus, there are grave economic obstacles to decent family life (Chapters X and XII).

With inadequate incomes, it is only natural that we should have a housing problem. The cost of housing is too high, particularly if one keeps in mind the minimum needs of large families. It is difficult either to rent or buy housing accommodations adequate for three or more children. But this is not merely a problem of inadequate incomes. Our housing industry is so badly organized that the cost of building is excessive in comparison to costs of other goods produced by modern methods.

This vital industry is using techniques not basically different from those of the eighteenth century, and that in a nation famous for its development of mass production and technological efficiency (Chapter X).

A similar problem of disorganization leads to lack of adequate medical care. Normal medical costs are not too high. As a nation we spend more for tobacco and liquor than we do for medical attention. But we have not done enough to meet the problem of unusual and unpredictable medical costs. Prepayment plans of hospitalization are partial answers to this problem, but little has been done on the economics of chronic illness, exceptional cases involving complicated and expensive diagnosis, and the consequent medical and surgical fees. Most families can meet ordinary needs through hospital prepayment, but the family which is burdened with many operations and one or more cases of chronic illness becomes economically prostrate. In addition, the cost of maternity care is a further obstacle to normal family life. Moreover, many regions of the country lack sufficient doctors, nurses, clinics, and hospital facilities. All this adds to the difficulties of family life and often forms an economic incentive for family limitation (Chapters X and XIII).

At the present writing, many family problems have been lessened through various forms of social insurance, particularly unemployment insurance and old-age pensions. But the income levels set in 1938 are quite inadequate in the light of the war inflation, which almost halved the purchasing value of the dollar. Moreover, the system of state, in contrast to national, control of unemployment insurance leads to many hardships. States where poverty and need are greatest are often least able to give adequate grants to unemployed workers. Many refinements and improvements are still needed in our social security system (Chapter X).

A final result of inadequate incomes for some families is the practice of unsocial forms of child labor and employment of women. Many children still work in occupations which endanger their health, morals, or educational opportunities. About 30 per

cent of our working force consists of women and half of them
are married. The fact that married women work outside the
home is a definite obstacle to family life. Moreover, the reason
for such work in most cases is lack of adequate income supplied
by the male wage earner (Chapter IX). Thus, faulty economic
life reflects back upon family stability.

The Individual. Modern economic life affects the individual
in many ways. Here the fundamental problem is the danger to
freedom and the lack of respect for human dignity. The lack of
freedom is a result of the giantism mentioned earlier. Often the
individual can exercise economic freedom only through the
political and economic pressure of large political, business, labor,
professional, or farmer organizations. Such organization is in
itself good. Man is a social animal and economic life should be
social. But the danger arises from the size rather than from the
fact of organization. The single individual in a very large group
has little voice in its detailed policies. He is swallowed up in the
mass. Hence society, instead of ministering to the individual, is
tending to control his life (Chapters III, VII, XII, and XIII).

This is particularly the case with ownership of productive
property. Concentration of control (a basic factor in ownership)
is characteristic of large areas of manufacturing, transportation,
mining, finance, power production, and communications in the
United States. It has even spread to the fields of distribution and
farming. Moreover, the obstacles to small business make it
difficult for an individual to achieve productive ownership. Various factors have contributed to a shortage of funds available for
such enterprises, among them a tax system which discourages
investment. The result is that the giant corporation is growing
in power through internal expansion and through mergers, while
smaller groups are finding it difficult to survive (Chapter XII).

The worker who has no chance to achieve independent ownership of a business is to that extent less a master of his own
destiny. Moreover, the giant size of modern industry often makes
for situations which injure his human dignity. He is but a cog
in a vast machine. Recent developments in "human-relations"

programs by industry are bettering this condition somewhat, but we are still far from fully recognizing individual human dignity. Labor unions have also protected many rights of the worker and given him a greater sense of participation in economic life. But their size has paralleled the size of industry, so that often the individual union member feels he has little voice in his great organization. There are also problems arising from the nature of mass production: speed-up of the tempo of production, routine and monotonous work, and the lack of creative incentive. All this offers a real challenge to restore conditions which minister to human dignity, without losing the effectiveness of machine production and efficient organization (Chapters III, IX, and XI). There are ways for giving the worker a greater say in his economic life, without disturbing the basic control over economic decisions by the owners. The present Holy Father adverted to this fact in his address of May 7, 1949.[12]

Finally, there are many specific problems which affect individual dignity. Most important among these is discrimination in employment for reasons of race, religion, national background, or cultural inheritance. The treatment of Negroes, Jews, Mexicans, and Orientals has often been grossly unjust. It is not surprising that communism should have its greatest appeal to such minority groups. It is true that communism here has manifested its greatest danger in the political field through espionage, penetration of government, and deception of public opinion. Nevertheless, we should not overlook the economic factors and social discrimination which give effective arguments to such enemies of God and man (Chapters VI and IX).

Thus, we might conclude that there exists a basic social problem in the United States today. It is not so grave in the matter of gross abuses as was the case in the 1920's or the nineteenth century. But the difficulties which remain are by no means minor. Insecurity in economic life, concentration of power, dangers to individual freedom, and the many obstacles to family life are serious threats to our civilization. Certainly the Church cannot

---

12 This important address was reprinted in the July, 1949, issue of *The Catholic Mind*.

remain indifferent to conditions which endanger the freedom of man and the sound bases of human society. The social problem is at the same time a moral and a religious problem (Chapters II and XIV).

In working out solutions to these problems, we should keep in mind the purposive character of economic life, as outlined in the papal address of June 3, 1950. The ultimate purpose of a sound economy is the production of useful goods. Rational consumption, not production viewed as an end in itself, should control the markets. In our economic systems, we should avoid "Neo-Kantian critiquism," that is, an abstract and mathematical approach which prescinds from both reality and purposiveness in economic activity. We should likewise eschew the purely formalistic approaches to full employment, which view this desirable goal in purely quantitative terms, ignoring the usefulness of the jobs secured and the possible dangers inherent in the means used. Here, as everywhere, man must remain the center of economic life.

READINGS*

J. Messner, *Social Ethics,* pp. 249–280.
E. Cahill, *Framework of a Christian State,* Chaps. 1–15.
E. G. O'Brien, *Essay on Mediaeval Economic Teaching.*
A. Fanfani, *Catholicism, Protestantism, and Capitalism.*
R. H. Tawney, *Religion and the Rise of Capitalism.*
E. Troeltsch, *The Social Teaching of the Christian Churches.*
K. Polanyi, *The Great Transformation.*

---

*For further readings, see Lists Nos. 1 and 3 in the Appendix. Publishers, dates of publication, and descriptive data on books listed above may also be found in the Appendix.

Chapter II. THE CHURCH AND THE SOCIAL PROBLEM

Leo XIII, Graves de Communi

10. For it is the opinion of some, which is caught up by the masses, that the social question, as they call it, is merely economic. The precise opposite is the truth. It is first of all moral and religious, and for that reason its solution is to be expected mainly from the moral law and the pronouncements of religion.

Leo XIII, Rerum Novarum

24. We approach the subject with confidence and surely by Our right, for the question under consideration is certainly one for which no satisfactory solution will be found unless religion and the Church have been called upon to aid.

25. Assuredly, a question as formidable as this requires the attention and effort of others as well, namely, the heads of the state, employers and the rich, and finally, those in whose behalf efforts are being made, the workers themselves. Yet without hesitation We affirm that if the Church is disregarded, human striving will be in vain. Manifestly, it is the Church which draws from the Gospel the teachings through which the struggle can be composed entirely or, after its bitterness is removed, can certainly become more tempered. It is the Church, again, that strives not only to instruct the mind but to regulate by her precepts the life and morals of individuals, that ameliorates the condition of the workers through her numerous and beneficent institutions, and that wishes and aims to have the thought and energy of all classes of society united to this end, that the interests of the workers be protected as fully as possible. And to accomplish this purpose she holds that the laws and the authority of the state, within reasonable limits, ought to be employed.

42. But it must not be supposed that the Church so concentrates her energies on caring for souls as to overlook the things which pertain to

mortal and earthly life. As regards the nonowning workers specifically, she desires and strives that they rise from their most wretched state and enjoy better conditions.

Pius XI, Ubi Arcano

60. For, although from her divine mission the Church is directly concerned with the spiritual and not with the temporal, still, as all these things aid one another and are closely intertwined, the Church fosters the temporal prosperity of individuals and society as effectively almost as if she had been instituted for that purpose alone.

Pius XI, Firmissimam Constantiam

19. . . . Catholic Action should never take responsibility in matters that are purely technical, financial, or economic, because such matters lie outside the scope and purpose of Catholic Action.

Pius XI, Quadragesimo Anno

41. Yet before proceeding to explain these matters, that principle which Leo XIII so clearly established must be laid down at the outset here, namely, that there resides in Us the right and duty to pronounce with supreme authority upon social and economic matters. Certainly the Church was not given the commission to guide men to an only fleeting and perishable happiness but to that which is eternal. Indeed "the Church holds that it is unlawful for her to mix without cause in these temporal concerns"; however, she can in no wise renounce the duty God entrusted to her to interpose her authority, not of course in matters of technique for which she is neither suitably equipped nor endowed by office, but in all things that are connected with the moral law. For as to these, the deposit of truth that God committed to Us and the grave duty of disseminating and interpreting the whole moral law, and of urging it in season and out of season, bring under and subject to Our supreme jurisdiction not only the social order but economic activities themselves.

42. Even though economics and moral science employ each its own principles in its own sphere, it is, nevertheless, an error to say that the economic and moral orders are so distinct from and alien to each other that the former depends in no way on the latter. Certainly the laws of economics, as they are termed, being based on the very nature of material things and on the capacities of the human body and mind, determine the limits of what productive human effort cannot, and of what it can attain in the economic field and by what means. Yet it is reason itself that clearly shows, on the basis of the individual and social nature of things and of men, the purpose which God ordained for all economic life.

43. But it is only the moral law which, just as it commands us to seek our supreme and last end in the whole scheme of our activity, so likewise commands us to seek directly in each kind of activity those purposes which we know that nature, or rather God the Author of nature, established for that kind of action, and in orderly relationship to subordinate such immediate purposes to our supreme and last end. If we faithfully observe this law, then it will follow that the particular purposes, both individual and social, that are sought in the economic field will fall in their proper place in the universal order of purposes, and We, in ascending through them, as it were by steps, shall attain the final end of all things, that is God, to Himself and to us, the supreme and inexhaustible Good.

104. We have in mind the good not only of those who dwell in regions given over to "capital" and industry, but of all mankind.

125. It is certainly most lamentable, Venerable Brethren, that there have been, nay, that even now there are men who, although professing to be Catholics, are almost completely unmindful of that sublime law of justice and charity that binds us not only to render to everyone what is his but to succor brothers in need as Christ the Lord Himself, and — what is worse — out of greed for gain do not scruple to exploit the workers. Even more, there are men who abuse religion itself, and under its name try to hide their unjust exactions in order to protect themselves from the manifestly just demands of the workers. The conduct of such We shall never cease to censure gravely. For they are the reasons why the Church could, even though undeservedly, have the appearance of and be charged with taking the part of the rich and with being quite unmoved by the necessities and hardships of those who have been deprived, as it were, of their natural inheritance. The whole history of the Church plainly demonstrates that such appearances are unfounded and such charges unjust. The Encyclical itself, whose anniversary we are celebrating, is clearest proof that it is the height of injustice to hurl these calumnies and reproaches at the Church and her teaching.

130. Yet it is not rash by any means to say that the whole scheme of social and economic life is now such as to put in the way of vast numbers of mankind most serious obstacles which prevent them from caring for the one thing necessary; namely, their eternal salvation.

144. Certainly there is the greatest need now of such valiant soldiers of Christ who will work with all their strength to keep the human family safe from the dire ruin into which it would be plunged were the teachings of the Gospel to be flouted and that order of things permitted to prevail which tramples underfoot no less the laws of nature than those of God.

The Church of Christ, built upon an unshakable rock, has nothing to fear for herself, as she knows for a certainty that the gates of hell shall never prevail against her. Rather, she knows full well, through the experience of many centuries, that she is wont to come forth from the most violent storms stronger than ever and adorned with new triumphs. Yet her maternal heart cannot but be moved by the countless evils with which so many thousands would be afflicted during storms of this kind, and above all by the consequent enormous injury to spiritual life which would work eternal ruin to so many souls redeemed by the Blood of Jesus Christ.

Pius XI, On Atheistic Communism

34. The Church does not separate a proper regard for temporal welfare from solicitude for the eternal. If she subordinates the former to the latter according to the words of her divine Founder, "Seek ye first the Kingdom of God and His justice, and all these things shall be added unto you," she is nevertheless so far from being unconcerned with human affairs, so far from hindering civil progress and material advancement, that she actually fosters and promotes them in the most sensible and efficacious manner. Thus even in the sphere of social economics, although the Church has never proposed a definite technical system, since this is not her field, she has nevertheless clearly outlined the guiding principles which, while susceptible of varied concrete applications according to the diversified conditions of times and places and peoples, indicate the safe way of securing the happy progress of society.

Pius XII, La Solennità della Pentecoste

1675. He [Leo XIII] had no intention of laying down guiding principles on the purely practical, we might say technical, side of the social structure; for he was well aware of the fact — as Our immediate Predecessor of saintly memory, Pius XI, pointed out ten years ago in his commemorative Encyclical, Quadragesimo Anno — that the Church does not claim such a mission.

1676. It is, on the other hand, the indisputable competence of the Church, on that side of the social order where it meets and enters into contact with the moral order, to decide whether the bases of a given social system are in accord with the unchangeable order which God, our Creator and Redeemer, has shown us through the natural law and Revelation, that twofold manifestation to which Leo XIII appeals in his Encyclical. And with reason: for the dictates of the natural law and the truths of Revelation spring forth in a different manner, like two streams of water that do not flow against one another but together, from the same divine Source: and the Church, guardian of the supernatural Christian Order in which nature and grace converge, must form the consciences even of those who are called upon to find solutions for the problems and the duties imposed by social life. Upon the form given to society, whether conforming or not to the divine law, depends and emerges the good or ill of souls, depends the decision whether men, all called to be revived by the grace of Christ, do actually in the detailed course of their life breathe the healthy vivifying atmosphere of truth and moral virtue or the disease-laden and often fatal air of error and corruption. Before such a thought and such an anticipation, how could the Church, loving Mother that she is, solicitous for the welfare of her children, remain an indifferent onlooker in their danger, remain silent or feign not to see or take cognizance of social conditions which, whether one wills it or not, make difficult or practically impossible a Christian life? . . .

Pius XII, Christmas Message, 1943

Undoubtedly, the poverty of the stable in Bethlehem is a condition which He chose for Himself only, and it does not therefore imply any condemnation of the economic life as far as it is necessary for the physical or natural development and perfection of man.

But that poverty of the Lord and Creator of the world, deliberately willed by Him, a poverty which will accompany Him in the workshop of Nazareth and throughout His public life, signifies and portrays the command and the dominance he had over material things; and thus it shows with striking efficacy the natural and essential subjection of material goods to the life of the spirit and to a higher cultural, moral, and religious perfection which is necessary for man endowed with reason.

Those who looked for the salvation of society from the machinery of the world economic market have remained thus disillusioned because they had become not the lords and masters but the slaves of material wealth, which they served without reference to the higher end of man, making it an end in itself.

Pius XII, Address to Members of Renascita Cristiana, January 22, 1947

To wish to draw an exact line of separation between religion and life, between the natural and the supernatural, between the Church and the world, as if they had nothing to do with each other, as if the rights of God were valueless in all the manifold realities of daily life, whether human or social, is entirely foreign to Catholic thought and is positively anti-Christian. The more, therefore, the powers of darkness bring their pressure to bear, the more they strive to banish the Church and religion from the world and from life, the more there is need on the part of the Church itself of steadfast and persevering action in order to reconquer and to place all fields of human life under the most sweet empire of Christ, so that His spirit may breathe more abundantly, His law reign with a more sovereign sway, and His love triumph more victoriously. Behold what we must understand by the Kingdom of Christ!

This task of the Church is indeed arduous, but they are simply unwitting deserters or dupes who, in deference to a misguided supernaturalism, would confine the Church to the "strictly religious" field, as they say, whereas by so doing they are but playing into the hands of their enemies.

Pius XII, Allocution to Sacred College of Cardinals, June 2, 1947

By disposition of Divine Providence, the Catholic Church has formulated and promulgated its social doctrine. She points out the path to be followed, and no hope of achieving temporal gain, or fear of losing possessions, or of appearing less in harmony with modern civilization, or less national or social, could authorize true Christians to deviate even a hair's breadth from this path.

Pius XII, Letter to Semaines Sociales, 1949

There can be no incompatibility between a realism, healthfully nourished by facts, statistics, and economic laws, and a social order quite legitimately imbued with aspirations for more justice and humanity. These two aspects of the same problem are complementary; to them can be applied the words of the Gospel, *Haec oportuit facere et illa non omittere*. Social Catholics have sometimes been accused of pursuing an ideal too high to be applicable.

The Lille Social Week will prove that they are inspired no less by real and positive facts, grounded in which the social doctrine of the Church presents a unified whole as practical as it is harmonious. Their concern with economics in its relation to social progress places them at an equal distance from unrestrained liberalism and from the tyranny of atheistic materialism. For them the economy remains in the service of man, of his freedom and Christian dignity, at the same time that it serves the common good.

Pius XII, Address to Young Men, September 12, 1948

The social question, beloved sons, is undoubtedly an economic question also, but even more than that it is a question which concerns the ordered regulation of human society. And, in its deepest sense, it is a moral and therefore a religious question. As such, it may be summed up thus: have men — from the individual to the people, and right through to the community of peoples — the moral strength to create such public conditions that in the life of society there will not be any individuals or any peoples who are merely objects, that is to say, deprived of all right and exposed to exploitation by others, but all instead will be subjects, that is, having a legitimate share in the formation of the social order and able, according to their art or profession, to live happily and tranquilly with sufficient means of support, protected effectively against the violence of an egoistic economy, in freedom defined by the general welfare, and with full human dignity, each respecting his neighbor as he respects himself? Will humanity be capable of generating and possessing the moral strength to realize such a social order?

Pius XII, Message to German Catholics, September 4, 1949

The social program of the Catholic Church is based upon three powerful moral pillars: truth, justice, and Christian charity. To deviate, even for a little, from the requirements of these principles would have been impossible for the Church, even if for this she had to renounce temporary propaganda successes and to delude the fervor of the strife, either on one or the other side.

The Church has always favored those who seek the right and need help, but by principle she has never been contrary to any group, rank, or social class, and aims at the common welfare of all members of the people and of the state.

The Church and Social Order

9. First, let it be made clear that the Church is concerned only with the moral aspects of trade and industry and does not enter into the field of business in matters that are purely material or technical. The Church is not concerned with the accuracy of economic surveys or the resultant data, nor with the problems of scientific organization, production, cost-accounting, transportation, marketing, and a multitude of similar activities. To pass judgment on their aptitude and merit is a technical problem proper to economic science and business administration. For such the Church has neither the equipment nor the authorization. We frankly declare that it would be unwise on her part to discuss their operation except insofar as a moral interest might be involved.

18. Who can deny the close relationship between economic injustice and a long train of evils, physical, social, and moral? Unfair wages due to greed for excessive profits and insecurity due to false and immoral economic principles lead directly to undernourishment, bad housing, inadequate clothing, and indirectly to irregular family relations, child delinquency, and crime. Excessively long hours in some industrial areas and

in some industrial processes create danger to life and limb, impair the health of workingmen, and impoverish whole families through infection, disease, and premature death. Because human beings and not animated machines toil in industry, therefore the Church cannot abdicate her right and duty to speak out in defense of the rights of human personality nor fail to declare uncompromisingly the moral obligations of industrial and economic life.

Code of Social Principles

7. Economic science observes, describes, and classifies the human relationships of joint labor, exchange, and distribution, which necessarily arise as soon as man desires to be master over matter and to satisfy his needs. It both describes and lays down rules: it describes phenomena; it prescribes the order which should be applied for the better management of life on this earth, in the successive human acts of joint labor and exchange.

8. Between economics and ethics there are necessary relations and real co-ordination. For the human relationships of which political economy treats (between landlord and tenant, master and man, taxer and taxpayer, buyer and seller, producer and consumer) are subject to the control and judgment of our moral conscience. A consequence derives from this principle: the Church, the guardian of morals, exercises a lawful control over economic life.

70. Economic laws, properly so called, relate to human acts. These laws are discovered through the study of psychology and history and the observation of facts. Economic laws can produce certain evil or unjust consequences according to the conditions under which they are allowed to act. Too great a supply of goods and services, for instance, has the result of depreciating them. It is therefore often necessary to provide by suitable organization for the working of this or that economic law. Monetary inflation has unavoidable results, but the inflation itself can be avoided.

72. Since economic phenomena relate to human affairs, the interpretation which is put upon them calls for an exact knowledge of human nature and of the imponderable factors in the psychological and moral order which react upon human activities, and depends upon the use of a multitude of other than statistical data. Into this work of interpretation necessarily enter metaphysical ideas, regarding human nature, its origin, its destiny, the relative values of men, and their mutual relations. The Catholic economist must seek these ideas in Christian philosophy, if he desires to be logical and consistent with himself.

73. Besides, the Church herself has here both the competence and the right to intervene, not in the technical sphere, but in all that touches the

moral law. For, if the Church has received the mission to lead mankind to eternal happiness and not merely to a transient prosperity, she can never forget that economic activity must be subject to the moral law and that the temporal end is subordinate to the eternal.

As the social problem worsened, the Church was not inactive. During the first part of the nineteenth century, a powerful Catholic social movement arose in France and Germany. Christian principles were applied to the pressing questions of the hour. At the same time, a need was felt for the authoritative directions of the Holy See. This was first given in regard to socialism. Popes Pius IX and Leo XIII showed how this system was a false and insidious road to social reform. Pope Leo XIII then offered in 1891 his great encyclical, *Rerum Novarum,* dealing with the labor question, property, and socialism. Forty years later, Pope Pius XI issued his masterful work, *Quadragesimo Anno,* and, in 1937, *Divini Redemptoris.* These letters covered in a comprehensive manner the entire social problem, and offered the outlines for a Christian solution. In 1941, Pope Pius XII issued a solemn discourse, *La Solennità della Pentecoste,* which reaffirmed and clarified the teachings of his predecessors. Thus, the Church in modern times applies the principles of social morality to the economic world.

While these pronouncements were widely greeted as profound analyses of current problems, and while their solutions were acclaimed for their depth and wisdom, there were also questioning voices raised in many lands. It was asked: By what right does the Church intrude into secular affairs? Is not the Church lowering its dignity by descending from the altar and moving into the market place? Nor were these questions confined to those who professed no religious belief or who did not acknowledge the authority of the pope. Many Catholics were shocked by these encyclicals, as if the ancient Church, custodian through the centuries of divinely revealed truth, were bringing in new doctrines and strange teachings. A few summarily rejected the words of the popes. Others said that they did not apply to conditions in their countries. Many simply ignored these great documents, making no effort to study them or to apply them to the world about them.

RIGHT AND DUTY TO INTERVENE

American Attitudes. In view of the attitudes just noted, it is opportune to study the right and duty of the Church to intervene in the social problem. This is a special need in view of American conditions. The Church in the United States, with outstanding exceptions, was slow to react to *Rerum Novarum*. Organized Catholic social action did not begin here on a national scale until 1919. Systematic programs for introducing Catholic social teaching into our school system were not undertaken until 1939, with the formation of the Commission on American Citizenship. Millions of American Catholics know little of the social encyclicals. Occasionally the remark is heard that these letters are not binding doctrinal teaching, or that they do not apply to American conditions.

Until recently, many American businessmen had little use for Church intervention in matters of industry, business, and finance. Some labor leaders have been equally abrupt in bidding the Church to keep its place. Statements like these are made: Business and politics should be kept out of the pulpit; We do not tell you how to run your Church, you should not tell us how to run our business; and, You never had to meet a payroll, how can you talk of our problems? To these strictures, the Church replies that there is a moral as well as a technical aspect to business. The Church has a right and duty to speak out on moral matters. Clergymen seek business advice in financial affairs connected with their churches. They ask assistance in accounting and bookkeeping, construction of churches and schools, insurance, and similar "practical" matters. At the same time, they insist upon their right to discuss ethical problems connected with the market place. Moreover, they hold that the Church can make a definite contribution to social reform, since motivation is of the highest importance in matters of social policy. The insistence by the

Church on the demands of social justice furnishes a needed incentive for a better social order.

It was noted earlier that the posing of such questions is a relatively new development. In the Middle Ages, it was taken for granted God's law applied to the totality of life. The idea of a double standard of morality, with a strict code for private life and a minimum of moral obligation for business and public life, is an innovation based on philosophical and religious individualism of the eighteenth century. With the growth of secularism in our age, there is still greater conflict between the attitude of the Church and that of the unbelieving world. The time is ripe to reopen the question and to face squarely the nature and end of man, in accord with God's purposes and laws as known through faith and reason.

Social Problems Are Human and Moral Problems. While there are technical and economic aspects to social problems, we dare not overlook their human and moral aspects. They concern human beings and affect their lives intimately. What is more, those participating in economic life make decisions in which they are bound by moral law. Morality enters into business decisions in at least three ways: the object sought, the motives of the doer, and the result in terms of human values.

Certain business problems involve a purely objective morality. Thus, a promotion venture which is permeated with fraud would be dishonest of its very nature. The same would be true if economic force were used to compel another to do something wrong. Abuse of a monopoly position by the charging of clearly exploitive prices would be contrary to the virtue of justice. Stealing does not become right, merely because it is accomplished in the course of large-scale business transactions. On the other side of the picture, certain business practices could be called morally good by their nature. Thus the inventor who markets a new process which will create useful employment renders a service to society. The industrialist who gives an example of fine human relations in his plant is acting according to sound ethics.

In other cases, motives will influence the morality of a transaction. While good motives will never make right out of wrong,
it is possible to do something morally good or neutral for unsound motives. It is not wrong in itself to amass wealth, but
greed and avarice are sinful. The acquisition of economic power
may be a normal result of shrewd and successful business
operations, but it may also be the product of pride and disordered
ambition. A labor leader may often be morally justified in calling
a strike, yet it is not inconceivable that personal pique or like
unworthy motives may enter into his decision. Thus, he could
be guilty through unethical motives.

Finally, circumstances and especially the impact upon others
enter into the morality of business operations. Actions may not
be judged in isolation. A factory which gives out obnoxious fumes
might legitimately be constructed in a remote region. If the same
factory were constructed in a residential neighborhood, it would
lower property values and make homes useless for living purposes.
Again, factory waste dumped into a river could ruin its drinking
and recreational values. An industrial process which would poison
the workers in the plant would be wrong. A pace of operations
which would burn out a worker's energy in a few years would
do him an injustice. Thus, the moral nature of a transaction may
not be judged in the abstract. The total picture must be considered, particularly the social effect of a given operation.

In recent centuries, practically all these aspects of business
morality have been obscured and minimized. Generally speaking,
the religious conscience revolted against outright fraud and injustice. However, there were some who held that all was fair in
business. The motto, *caveat emptor,* was by no means an empty
phrase. There were even cases of men, apparently genuinely
religious, who were among the worst of the "robber barons" of
the last century. In other cases, sincere men appealed in vain for
moral advice on business transactions. Our moral theology texts
were, in general, hopelessly out of date in applying moral principles to economic life. Apparently few moralists knew enough
about economic facts to work out a realistic and complete solu-

tion. Hence moral teaching generally confined itself to obvious justice and injustice and clearly defined motives. Even in the sphere of motives, sermons on greed, avarice, selfishness in business matters, unwarranted ambition, and unsocial conduct are as rare today as they were common in medieval times.

The real lack, as emphasized in the social encyclicals, was in the overlooking or denying of the social aspect of business life. It was widely held among all groups in economic life — business, labor, industry, finance, and farming — that each person should look out for himself alone. If, in his striving for personal gain, others were injured, he should not be concerned, provided there was no violation of law or strict justice. In the United States, the idea of social responsibility was largely imposed from without the business community, by law, political pressure, or the economic power of some affected group, such as organized labor. It was not accepted as a personal obligation binding the individual conscience. The virtues of social charity and social justice were ignored. There is a definite need for Americans to recover a strong sense of social morality.

The Price of Injustice. The moral nature of economic life can be shown from the fact that it deals with human beings. Human acts are subject to moral review in terms of object, motive, and circumstances. Because of this the Church, as guardian of the moral order, has the right and duty to pronounce on the moral aspects of economic life. It would not be faithful to its teaching mission, were it to remain silent concerning such a vital sphere of activity. But there is another aspect to the economic order which affects the Church, this time in its religious as distinct from its teaching mission. The Church has found, through experience, that an unsound social order contributes to the ruin of souls. This is true both of individuals and of whole societies.

In regard to the individual, he suffers when economic life departs from its true purpose. The economic order should be essentially subordinate to the cultural and spiritual orders. When, on the contrary, economic life becomes supreme and all-absorbing, the dignity of human nature is outraged. Such an outrage may be imposed on an individual when, through no fault of his own, he is crushed by a grinding poverty. Poverty of this sort is not the Gospel detachment from worldly goods; it is the precise opposite, since it forces men to concentrate unduly upon the problem of mere survival. Insecurity likewise brings about an unhealthy preoccupation with material goods. At the other extreme, greed, avarice, and lust for power involve excessive attachment to material things. These latter faults are not imposed upon the individual by external constraint, but a materialistic and secularistic society does make such lapses more probable. Public opinion and the moral tone of a community are powerful forces affecting individual conduct.

There is a loss of souls connected with the desperate poverty of slum areas. It can be shown that a definite correlation exists between slum conditions and a high incidence of crime, vice, disease, and ignorance. The reasons for this are obvious. When the home is cramped and unlovely, it is difficult to have a normal family life. Children play in crowded city streets. In doing this, they irritate many people and thus are driven from place to place. This tends to bring about an antisocial attitude. Storekeepers, the police, and "solid citizens" become their enemies. Many find it easy to drift into delinquency, crime, and vice. Their parents likewise tend to desert the home. Their social clubs are often neighboring taverns. In the effort to eke out their small income, they may indulge in betting, particularly the "numbers game," which will accept the pennies of the poor.[1]

When both parents must work to bring in an adequate income, it often happens that children are neglected and forced to roam the streets. Again, economic stringency leads many to the practice of birth control. Moreover, extreme strains and anxieties often bring about quarrels and cruelty in the home. In this way, economic conditions produce an atmosphere adverse to the practice of religion and morality. Nor should it be said that such poverty and its results are the fault of the individuals involved. Some poverty does spring from shiftlessness and irresponsibility, but

[1] See C. Dirksen, *Economic Factors of Delinquency* (Milwaukee: Bruce, 1948).

much destitution arises from a faulty economic system. Again, some families have the moral strength to rise above adverse circumstances. But the great majority are average in abilities and character and, as such, are deeply affected by the conditions under which they live. Heroic virtue is the exception in all walks of life.

Sometimes religious persons justify their inaction in regard to social problems by quoting the Gospel saying: The poor you shall always have with you. They say further that you cannot change human nature, so you will inevitably have oppression and injustice. But it seems strange to quote the Saviour as condoning a form of poverty which, so far as we can know, leads to the loss of souls. And the overworked excuse that human nature does not change would, if followed logically, lead to an utter abdication of religion and morality. We are trying constantly, as we should, to control our instincts by reason in the matter of sexual morality. Since the passions which lead to economic injustice and disorder are relatively weak as compared with sex desires, there is even less excuse for apathy in regulating them. Furthermore, while some aspects of human nature may not change, men are profoundly influenced by their environment and the institutions of society. On the premise that most of us swim with the tide, it makes a real difference how economic life is organized. Strong men, whether good or evil, make their way independently. The Harmels worked out a good social program for their factories in spite of the ideas prevalent in *laissez-faire* France during the nineteenth century. Jacques Coeur acquired vast wealth by unsocial means in the medieval society which condemned his acquisitions. But most men merely try to live up to the customs and expectations of their age. In this light, it is clearly the mission of the Church to seek out ways of making society an influence for good rather than for evil.

The Overthrow of Society. Not only does an unsound social order affect adversely both individuals and families, but it also may hurt severely both the Church and sound civil society. Thus, in modern times the Church has suffered greatly from anticlericalism. This has ranged from extreme hatred in countries such as France and Italy to milder forms of resentment which do not affect basic loyalty to the Church. Of course, it would be unfair to assume that anticlericalism arises mainly from the faults of churchmen. At times we are resented for preaching a stern moral law in an age which seeks laxity and license. Some Catholics today rebel against our marriage laws and our teaching on birth control. But in other cases we are at fault, and frequently the fault is indifference to socioeconomic problems.

There were countries in Europe in which extreme disparity existed between the very wealthy and the poor. Rightly or wrongly, the Church was accused of favoring the rich. In some cases, the charge was unjust. It was superficially plausible insofar as the Church may have opposed violent revolution and hence, in fact, appeared to be on the side of the rich. But such charges would not have been made if churchmen had been active in the cause of social reform. The excesses of the last century in Spain, Italy, France, and Mexico might have been mitigated had churchmen been more vigilant in promoting social justice.

We mention the failings of our fellow Catholics, not with the pharisaical attitude that we are without fault, but merely because the opportunities were greater in the Latin countries. Catholics are a minority here, so we have some excuse. Yet, in fact, we have been remiss in using the opportunities we have. The strong and enlightened stands taken by the bishops and their representatives have been slow to permeate through the entire Catholic body. At the same time, we have among the faithful a very large percentage of workers and city dwellers, most affected by economic injustice. Our relations with the workers have been good, but not entirely adequate. We have lived among them and shared their personal problems. During the depression of 1929, we strained our resources to help the unfortunate. The Department of Social Action, National Catholic Welfare Conference; the National Catholic Rural Life Conference; the Catholic labor-school movement; the Association of Catholic Trade Unionists; and others have been most helpful in spreading our social message. But much still remains to be done. Only when all Catholics realize that the Church has a deep and intelligent interest in all their problems can we be safe from the evil of anticlericalism. We may not load burdens upon others, without lifting a finger to help.

Anticlericalism, serious as it is, is mild compared to other evils suffered by the Church as a result of economic injustice. Since 1916, the Church has been beset by a virulent form of statism which threatens its organized survival in some parts of the world. Fascism, National Socialism, and finally the spread of Soviet Communism loomed as embodiments of the antichrist. It is not necessary to detail the evils done to religion by totalitarianism. The supreme state is, by its very nature, the mortal enemy of the Church. It knows that it must root out religion from the hearts of its subjects, or it will be unable to claim the total allegiance it demands. Mussolini sniped against the Church; Hitler tried to destroy it; and the rulers of Soviet Russia would eradicate God from the minds of men. The Church must fight totalitarianism as the greatest evil of all history.

The total state, once it has been established, is hard to destroy. Revolt is out of the question; internal dissolution is unlikely; and war against it is an extreme and desperate measure. It is far better to prevent the evil than to seek to remedy it after it has arisen. To prevent it, it is necessary to remove its causes. And an important part of the cause is economic, the failure to solve the social question. Communism openly professes its dependence upon economic injustice for its origin. Indeed, in this case, it is necessary at times to play down the economic claims, so as to make proper allowance for political factors, propaganda and organization, and military conquest. But with these adjustments, it is still true that communism uses the social question as its main weapon.

The origin of National Socialism was even more complex. There were considerations of national pride, political ineptitude on the part of the victors in World War I, and the fanatic mysticism of Hitler. Yet, it is too often forgotten that "socialism" was an integral part of the Nazi movement. This was the appeal used to win the millions of the unemployed, the middle classes who were being crushed, and even some wealthy industrialists who wanted an organized society at the time when the nation was in danger of anarchy. The social problem was real and urgent in the Germany of 1933. The definite economic progress made under Hitler strengthened his hold on the people. Again, Mussolini was a former socialist. When he marched on Rome, Italy was verging on economic collapse. His restoration of the nation's economy caused many to support him.

The bitter fact is that, when given the choice between freedom and bread, many will sacrifice freedom. Political freedom is often an empty phrase to the man on the park bench, without a job or assurance that he will eat. Desperate men can always convince themselves that things will be different in their country, just as today French or Italian Communists (in the lower ranks) try to reconcile communism with love of country and of Church. In the face of such a menace, can anyone say that the Church should confine itself to worship and keep out of the market place? Under these conditions, indifference to the social problem would be inviting a persecution so drastic that millions may apostatize rather than face it. Nor should it be said that we must fight this evil with spiritual weapons only. Not only is the social question a moral question, and hence a problem for the Church, but the exclusively spiritual approach to any material problem is of doubtful doctrinal orthodoxy. We do not seek to cure epidemics by prayer alone; we use our God-given intelligence to discover causes and remedies. We should be no less zealous in facing the social problem.

To summarize, the Church has the right to discuss social problems because they are at the same time moral problems. It has the duty to enter this field, because its teaching mission includes the moral law as well as dogmas of faith. This duty is reinforced by the urgency of modern problems. Failure to solve them may lead to the loss of souls, the more so if it brings about the totalitarian state. This much conceded, it is important to define the precise scope and nature of intervention by the Church.

THE SCOPE OF SOCIAL TEACHING
BY THE CHURCH

Economic Law and Moral Law. There are three pertinent phases of economic life, with their respective laws. First, the technical phase of production and distribution leans heavily upon the physical sciences and is in turn governed by physical law. Next, organization of resources is an economic problem, regulated by the laws of economics. Finally, the direction of organization and the use of physical instruments can often be a moral problem, subject to the dictates of ethics and religion. When these three sets of guiding principles are properly co-ordinated and subordinated, we have a smoothly running economic system.

The purely technical phase of economic life certainly includes the fields governed by physical law. Thus, the important synthetic fiber industry is mainly a product of chemistry. The proper use of soils, particularly in regard to fertilizer, crop rotation, choice of crops, and irrigation is also dependent upon physics, chemistry, and biology. Physical facts, such as the availability of resources, power, and water transportation, can influence economic decisions. Even phases of economic organization can be affected by technical considerations. Thus, if we wish low-priced automobiles, we must have mass production with its consequent form of factory organization.

Since physical law is unchanging, it is clear that neither economic nor moral considerations can affect its working. However, the choice of technical means can be subject to both economic and moral judgments. As an illustration, two types of raw material might be equally suitable for a chemical process. But economics would incline us to use the material which is relatively abundant and easily available. Ethics might also enter into the choice, insofar as the decision might influence human welfare. The fact that a problem is technical does not imply that it is *merely* technical and hence excluded from moral judgments. Examples of the purely technical might be the choice between two honest systems of cost accounting, or two processes for making synthetic gasoline from abundant resources. But when the common good or human welfare is involved, even technical decisions have their moral aspects.

Economic law consists of generalizations from experience, based largely on psychology. Thus we know that, other factors remaining unchanged, an increase in the money supply, while production of consumer goods is not increased (as during a war), will bring about inflation. Again, when the demand for a product does not change greatly at different price levels, a large increase in supply will bring prices down rather sharply. Laws of this nature work with a constancy which permits accurate prediction, provided all the factors are known. It is true that our state of knowledge is not sufficiently advanced to allow us to predict complex events, such as depressions. Nevertheless, it would be accurate to say that there are economic laws, even though we do not know all of them. Even those we know, we cannot always use because of limitations in factual knowledge. But limited knowledge is real, although inadequate.

Economic laws, soundly established, may not be flouted. Thus a country which depends upon exports could not, without suffering greatly, set a monetary exchange level which would price its goods out of the market. An industry which prices its products at too high a level will lack customers. Accordingly ethical demands must be framed within the limits of economic as well as physical possibility. For instance, to use an extreme example, if taxi drivers were to set their wage standards at three hundred dollars a week, they would soon be out of work. They could discourse at length on the ethical demands for a living wage and full employment, but the economic organization of their industry simply could not give them work at such wage levels. No one is morally bound to the impossible, and this demand would be impossible under the present type of economic life.

On the other hand, the existing form of economic organization is not in itself unchangeable. Granted the constancy of some economic laws, it is still possible to adapt these laws to various forms of social organization. This point is obvious from the varying economics of modern states. In our times, capitalism, communism, socialism, National Socialism, and fascism have organized economic life in different patterns. Even among the capitalist states, some countries are much more successful than others. Hence it would be more accurate to say that economic life is governed both by laws and by patterns of organization. The former may often be constant, but the latter are subject to experimentation and change.

In the concrete, it may often happen that ethical aims may be unrealizable under a given form of organized economic life. Thus, the terrible exploitation of the last century may have been inevitable under atomistic competition. But a better organization of society and the use of machinery did lead to sharply improved wages and working conditions. This fact explains the stress laid by Pope Pius XI upon the reform of the *institutions* of society. With proper organization, our physical resources and economic knowledge could lead to a level of production which would permit decent wages, secure employment, and good working conditions. Thus the impact of ethical obligation is manifold. It affects immediately the individuals involved, to the extent that conditions are under their control. But when they are unable to fulfill their obligation under existing circumstances, they are not thereby released from all responsibility. The question still remains: Can the conditions be changed which led to a result undesirable from a moral viewpoint? If they can, through appropriate group action or social adjustments, the individuals have the duty to participate, as conditions permit, in organizing such changes.

Two conclusions seem evident. First, there are no hard and fast lines between what is purely technical or economic and what may be moral. The point of distinction is the impact upon the human person and the common welfare. Secondly, there is a real sense in which moral law takes precedence over economic or physical laws. While we cannot ignore genuine laws in the economic field, we often can alter circumstances and conditions so that, under the same laws, different results will ensue.

The Task of the Moralist. In the light of these conclusions, there devolves upon the moralist a twofold task when he considers economic matters. His first and primary duty is to define rights and obligations, as deduced from the nature of man, the function of society, and the purpose of economic life. But his other charge, even though it is somewhat extrinsic to his field, is not less important. This is the burden of applying general ethical principles to the world of business. True, this does not devolve upon the moralist as such. But if ethical principles are to be accepted and applied, they must be shown in the language of economic life.

In theory, it might be held that the moralist should enunciate principles and the men of affairs should put them into practice. Actually, he must go more than halfway to meet the world of business, or his views will not meet acceptance. The first reaction of the businessman, when confronted with ethical principles, is the feeling that they are impractical or even impossible to work out in everyday life. If he knows any ethics, he can take refuge in the maxim: No one is held to the impossible. Hence the moralist, working in the economic field, should know enough of the laws and facts of economic life to enable him to speak in the language of business.

This obligation, of course, does not devolve upon the Church or its official teaching body. We would look in vain, and this is as it should be, in the encyclicals for an economic system or a minute blueprint for social reform. The Church teaches moral law, not economics. But those who are applying the Church teaching will be largely ineffectual if they do not advance beyond this position. At the same time, in making such concrete applications, they must know their place. They can no longer speak unequivocally for the Church. There is always a margin of error, due to the limitations of their own prudential judgment. On this level, there is room for disagreement between Catholics applying identical principles. Disputes at this stage cannot normally be resolved by an appeal to authority, but must be settled on the merits of the concrete issues.

Some Catholics are mildly shocked at public arguments between authorities discussing the social question. Actually, such differences are a healthy sign. They indicate that we have progressed from the abstract treatment of principles to the more difficult, but vitally necessary, application to daily life. We can be sure that out of such controversies a gradually growing area of agreement will rise. Thus, the *Code of Social Principles,* quoted here as a quasi-authoritative document, evolved from such discussions among experts. We may well hope that the Catholic moralists and economists in the United States will eventually reach agreement on an even more detailed and concrete application than is had in the *Code.*

The goal to be sought is an ever closer liaison between moralists and men of affairs. This involves a thorough study of economics by competent theologians. Conversely, Catholic economists should know the social principles of the Church. Then, as our programs of adult and school education along social lines progress, Catholic businessmen, industrialists, labor leaders, and farmers will reach a greater understanding of social principles. At this stage, discussions among all the groups will bring about a detailed and workable application of the social encyclicals to American life.

Binding Force of the Encyclicals. There has been considerable discussion among Catholics as to their religious obligations in regard to the social encyclicals. At first glance, it might seem to some that teachings on the social question would not come under the heading of faith, morals, or Church discipline. Actually, the Church has held that socioeconomic problems are in part moral and religious problems. To this extent they certainly are within the competence of Church teaching. This point was made clear earlier in the chapter. Once this is granted, however, there have been further objections on two grounds. It has been held that, because the social encyclicals are not infallible pronouncements, they may be accepted or rejected at will by Catholics. Others, not willing to go that far in defiance of papal authority, held that these encyclicals do not apply to American conditions. They maintained that the encyclicals, even though addressed to the entire world, were formulated in view of conditions which do not obtain here. Both these attitudes are in error. The first indicates a serious misunderstanding as to the religious duties of Catholics. The second shows a basic misconception of the social encyclicals. They enunciate moral principles which are universal in application.

In the first place, the teaching mission of the Church is not confined to infallible pronouncements by the pope or ecumenical councils. Christ's injunction to teach all nations was not limited by any qualifications. The Church has been commissioned by God to teach with authority on matters of faith and morals. It has been promised the guidance of the Holy Spirit. In rare cases, the fullness of this guidance is invoked in a solemn definition of an article of faith. But the great bulk of Church teaching is had through the normal channels of pronouncements by the popes, bishops, and theologians. In regard to the pope, the type of teaching varies in solemnity and urgency. At times, the pope instructs directly and formally. On some matters, he is content to speak through the Sacred Congregations. Again, positions may be urged as a matter of prudence, rather than faith. Thus, for a long period, the Church took a reserved attitude toward the use of "higher criticism" in explaining the Holy Scriptures. With the progress made in this field, Pope Pius XII decided that the use of such material was now opportune and desirable. But prior to this decision, Catholic writers were bound to give first place to the Vulgate text and traditional interpretations based on that text. Accordingly, a "minimist" attitude of accepting only infallible pronouncements is simply un-Catholic.

A careful perusal of the papal writings themselves will show the great authority attached by the popes to encyclicals and other documents. It is a common practice for one pope to quote from the writings of another pontiff, and this in such a way as to indicate that these writings are considered binding upon the faithful. This is particularly noticeable during the pontificates of Popes Pius X and Benedict XV, both of whom referred frequently to the encyclicals of Pope Leo XIII. The latter pontiff likewise has been often used as a source by Popes Pius XI and Pius

XII. In the famous letter of the Sacred Congregation of the Council, June 5, 1929, sent to the Bishop of Lille on the occasion of an industrial dispute in his diocese, the seven principles given as a basis for settlement were all buttressed by quotations from papal documents. Again, the instruction on interfaith meetings, issued by the Sacred Congregation of the Holy Office under the date of December 20, 1949, notes the binding force of the encyclicals, even though "not all things are of faith."

No Catholic who has examined the entirety of papal social literature from 1890 to the present date could hold that the bulk of these documents were other than binding teachings directed for world-wide use. This statement applies even when the original document was addressed to a particular country. Thus, in *Quadragesimo Anno* Pope Pius XI refers to *Singulari Quadam,* orginally addressed to the German bishops. Likewise, the present Holy Father has referred in other contexts to *Sertum Laetitiae,* a letter to the bishops of the United States. Indeed, it has often been the practice of Pope Pius XII to use special occasions or audiences to particular groups as media for broad moral pronouncements.

As a second point, the form of teaching is relatively unimportant. Rather it is the solemnity and definiteness as determined by the text itself. It is true that the very nature of an encyclical, addressed to the entire world, implies a certain solemnity. But a broadcast, a papal letter, an allocution, or even an address to a particular group may, under certain circumstances, involve important and binding teachings on some matters. The intention as manifested in context is more important than the external form of teaching. Thus, Pope Pius XI is frequently solemn and formal in his pronouncements given in *Quadragesimo Anno.* We may quote one passage as an illustration: " . . . the deposit of truth that God committed to Us and the grave duty of disseminating and interpreting the whole moral law, and of urging it in season and out of season, bring under and subject to Our supreme jurisdiction not only the social order but economic activities themselves" (No. 41). At other times, the pope may indicate that he merely counsels, not commands, a given line of action. An example of this is his judgment on the wage contract: "We consider it *more advisable,* however, *in the present condition of human society* that, *so far as is possible,* the work-contract be *somewhat modified* by a partnership-contract . . ." (No. 65). The italicized words show a form of qualification which indicates a desire rather than binding teaching.

In regard to the social encyclicals in particular, their historical context clearly shows their binding force. They are part of a series issued by Popes Leo XIII, Pius XI, and Pius XII, to deal with the grave and urgent problems of the times. The issues were so serious that Rome felt constrained to give guidance and leadership to the faithful. Here both the external circumstances surrounding their issuance and the internal notes of solemnity and urgency indicate beyond doubt that the popes were commanding the faithful on important moral questions. This point was also stressed in the 1949 instruction of the Holy Office, concerning interfaith meetings. In discussing gatherings on the social question, the Congregation stated: "Even in these assemblies, as is evident, Catholics are not allowed to approve or concede anything that is not in accord with Divine revelation and with the Church's teaching, including her teaching on the social question."

Theologians all agree on the broad teaching authority of the pope. This point is well summarized by a French author: "In regard to directives given in an encyclical, while they are not infallible, they nevertheless oblige in conscience, because every Catholic owes an unrestricted and unreserved submission to the exercise of supreme jurisdiction over the universal Church. The Supreme Pontiffs, as is their right, have never used an ordinary encyclical to promulgate an absolute and definitive doctrinal decision. But it does not follow, may we repeat, that the encyclicals do not give directives binding in conscience. When the pope, in his position as supreme teacher and pastor of the universal Church, condemns, for example, the error of socialism and offers instead the social teaching of the Church, such teaching is binding upon the faithful. The obligatory nature of such assent is particularly serious when the pope declares that he has, not only the right, but the duty to pronounce with supreme authority the social teaching of the Church. 'Respectful silence, which consists in neither rejecting nor criticizing the given teaching,' is inadmissible in this matter."[2] The Sacred Congregation of the Council, in its letter of June 5, 1929, clearly defended the right of the Church to speak on socioeconomic matters, quoting both *Rerum Novarum* and *Singulari Quadam* (Pius X) in support of this position.

In the light of such authority, it is hardly possible for a Catholic to justify by-passing of the social encyclicals, much less rejection of their contents, on the grounds that they are not infallible. Where the pope is clearly teaching on a matter of divine revelation or natural law, he is acting under the general guidance of the Holy Spirit. His pronouncements may not be solemn definitions, yet it is the part of prudence to assume that this guidance has protected him from error. If a particular teaching appears difficult to accept, there is always the possibility that the reader may have misunderstood the pope. Expert interpretation by competent theologians may be necessary to clarify certain terms and to integrate a given text with other related teachings. Even on doctrinal matters, such theologians may seek to reopen questions which have not been defined in infallible pronouncements or their equivalent. But the average Catholic priest or layman should accept doctrinal and moral teachings of the popes.

The second objection of the "minimist," that they do not apply to American conditions, has been answered in part in the preceding chapter. Some general principles on this point might be added here.

The social encyclicals and addresses contain various levels of teaching. At the highest level are the references to revealed

---

[2] G. C. Rutten, O.P., *La doctrine sociale de l'Église* (Liège: La Pensée Catholique, 1932), pp. 20–21. See also E. Mangenot, "Encycliques," in the *Dictionnaire de théologie catholique;* R. Kothen, *L'Enseignement social de l'Église* (Louvain: Warny, 1949), pp. 29–35, 130; and L. Choupin, *Valeur des décisions doctrinales et disciplinaires du Saint Siège* (Paris: Beauchesne, 1907).

teaching as embodied in the Scriptures. From this source alone, it would be possible to derive broad principles for social life. Scripture references to justice, charity, and unworldliness; the condemnation of greed and avarice; and the stress upon the dignity of the human person give us the basic points of a social message.[3] In addition, the popes make frequent allusions to matters contained in natural law. Conclusions derived from the nature of man and of society belong in this category. Again, we could formulate a social ethic from these points alone. Hence there are two levels of teaching in papal documents which by their very nature are universally binding.

On a third level, there are applications of these teachings to historical situations, either past or current at the time of writing. Numerous examples of this nature were given in the preceding chapter. In such cases, it would be legitimate to note that a given encyclical may not apply to this country or that certain sections are no longer applicable. This is purely a factual question. However, as was noted before, it would be rash to conclude that there is no social problem in the United States. We are not yet ready to assume a pious mien and cast stones at others.

A fourth level of teaching involves prudential recommendations for reform of economic life. In such cases, the pope is usually clear as to the nature of his teaching. For example, he merely recommends a change from the wage contract to a form of partnership contract. He suggests that a firm which is unable to pay a living wage consider going out of business. But he asserts flatly the duty of such employers to support and promote institutions organized to prevent competition incompatible with fair treatment for the workers. He is no less solemn in his repeated insistence upon a form of social organization called in America "The Industry Council Plan."[4] At the same time, in

---

[3] See J. Schumacher, *Social Message of the New Testament* (Milwaukee: Bruce, 1937), and I. Giordani, *The Social Message of Jesus* (Paterson: St. Anthony's Guild, 1944).

[4] The term "Industry Council Plan" is explained more fully in Chapter VII. It refers to a papal program based on social collaboration. This same term has been used in the United States by the Congress of Industrial Organizations (C.I.O.) for its project of social planning. Needless to say, the papal program was formulated before

making such prudential recommendations, the popes have stressed that they are not setting up a rigid framework or detailed blueprint. Rather they are issuing general moral directives, to be applied in each country according to conditions and circumstances prevailing there. In making such applications, Catholics may and do differ. But they differ within the framework of papal teaching, even on prudential matters. Should they, by chance, conclude after careful and prolonged study that a certain instruction would not be salutary for their country, the remedy would be a request to Rome for clarification, not a summary disregarding of the pope's teaching. Such situations are highly improbable, given the flexibility and general nature of papal statements on prudential matters.

The Encyclicals and the Non-Catholic World. The reception given the encyclicals by the non-Catholic world has been good. Those who have read them and understood them have generally acclaimed their wisdom and insight. Unfortunately, many do not understand their full meaning because they are unfamiliar with the language of theology and ethics. When the same ideas are presented in popular terms, they receive a much wider acceptance. This should not be surprising, since there is little in the social encyclicals which is exclusively Catholic. They are based to such a degree upon general Scripture teachings and the principles of natural law that practically all who believe in God and in human dignity should welcome them.

In recent years, Protestant and Jewish church groups have worked out an elaborate social code. Thus, the World Assembly of Churches pronounced in 1948: "The Christian churches should reject the ideologies of both Communism and *laissez-faire* capitalism, and should seek to draw men away from the false assumption that these extremes are the only alternatives. . . . It is the responsibility of Christians to seek new creative solutions which never allow either justice or freedom to destroy the other."

---

the C.I.O. came into existence. Neither proposal has been given a definitive and authoritative application to American economic life, so that comparisons between them at this time would be premature.

The Federal Council of Churches of Christ in America sponsored a series of studies on "Christianity and the Economic Order," in the effort to apply Christian principles to American life. This group accepts the principle that both individual reform and the change of institutions are necessary to procure social justice. Its detailed comments on property, labor, prices, and profits are not dissimilar from much that is found in Catholic social teaching. There should be little conflict on social principles between Catholics and Protestants who accept the Federal Council Report. Futhermore, Jewish groups have been equally active in promoting a social message.[5]

On the other hand, those who hold that the economic system is a self-sufficient unit, subject to no laws outside its sphere, must logically reject the intervention by the Church in social matters. The same is true for those who admit the imperfections of our present system, but hold that it is better than any conceivable alternative. The former attitude overlooks the facts that economic life embodies changeable institutions as well as constant laws. The latter approach shows a deep pessimism in regard to the improvement of human institutions, or else a shallow optimism concerning our achievements thus far.[6] But to most men, economic life exists to serve the needs of all, and should be changed when it fails to fulfill its purpose.

Economic life must meet the needs of man and be based on man's nature, which is both individual and social. It must take its important but subordinate place in human society. In this way, it will function properly and minister to the common good of the entire community. Economics will then be the servant of man, not his master.

---

[5] See "The Churches Speak to Business," *Fortune,* Dec., 1948; W. A. Orton, "Business and Ethics," *Fortune,* Oct., 1948; and J. F. Cronin, *Economic Analysis and Problems,* Chap. 24. In this regard, the noted Protestant theologian, Reinhold Niebuhr, stated: "This consensus of Protestant thought is the more remarkable in that it approaches the main emphases in the social teachings of the Catholic encyclicals since *Rerum Novarum.*" (Quoted in *Time,* April 10, 1950, p. 89.)

[6] For a debate on this subject, see F. H. Knight and T. W. Merriam, *The Economic Order and Religion* (New York: Harper, 1945).

READINGS*

J. Messner, *Social Ethics,* pp. 697–947.
G. Clune, *Christian Social Reorganization,* pp. 3–6, 266–267.
G. C. Rutten, *La doctrine sociale de l'Église,* Chap. 1.
E. Cahill, *Framework of a Christian State,* Chap. 29.
O. von Nell-Breuning, *Reorganization of Social Economy,* pp. 79–89.
R. Kothen, *L'Enseignement social de l'Église,* pp. 128–140.

---

* For further readings, consult Lists Nos. 1 and 4 in the Appendix.

Chapter III. MAN AND ECONOMIC LIFE

Pius XI, On Atheistic Communism

27. Man has a spiritual and immortal soul. He is a person, marvelously endowed by his Creator with gifts of body and mind. He is a true "microcosm," as the ancients said, a world in miniature, with a value far surpassing that of the vast inanimate cosmos. God alone is his last end, in this life and the next. By sanctifying grace he is raised to the dignity of a son of God, and incorporated into the Kingdom of God in the Mystical Body of Christ. In consequence he has been endowed by God with many and varied prerogatives: the right to life, to bodily integrity, to the necessary means of existence; the right to tend toward his ultimate goal in the path marked out for him by God; the right of association and the right to possess and use property.

Pius XII, Christmas Broadcast, 1942

1831. The origin and the primary scope of social life is the conservation, development, and perfection of the human person, helping him to realize accurately the demands and values of religion and culture set by the Creator for every man and for all mankind, both as a whole and in its natural ramifications. A social teaching or a social reconstruction program which denies or prescinds from this internal essential relation to God of everything that regards man, is on a false course; and while it builds up with one hand, it prepares with the other the materials which sooner or later will undermine and destroy the whole fabric. And when it disregards the respect due to the human person and to the life which is proper to that person, and gives no thought to it in its organization, in legislative and executive activity, then instead of serving society, it harms it; instead of encouraging and stimulating social thought, instead of realizing its hopes and expectations, it strips it of all real value and reduces it to an utilitarian formula which is openly rejected by constantly increasing groups.

1832. If social life implies intrinsic unity, it does not, at the same time, exclude differences which are founded in fact and nature. When we hold fast to God, the Supreme Controller of all that relates to man, then the similarities no less than the differences of men find their allotted place in the fixed order of being, of values, and hence also of morality.

1844. First: He who would have the star of peace shine out and stand over society should co-operate, for his part, in giving back to the human person the dignity given to it by God from the very beginning; should oppose the excessive herding of men, as if they were a mass without a soul; their economic, social, political, intellectual, and moral inconsistency; their dearth of solid principles and strong convictions, their surfeit of instinctive sensible excitement and their fickleness.

1845. He should favor, by every lawful means, in every sphere of life, social institutions in which a full personal responsibility is assured and guaranteed both in the earthly and the eternal order of things.

1847. Second: He who would have the star of peace shine out and stand over society should reject every form of materialism which sees in the people only a herd of individuals who, divided and without any internal cohesion, are considered as a mass to be lorded over and treated arbitrarily; he should strive to understand society as an intrinsic unity, which has grown up and matured under the guidance of Providence, a unity which — within the bounds assigned to it and according to its own peculiar gifts — tends, with the collaboration of the various classes and professions, toward the eternal and ever new aims of culture and religion.

Pius XII, Address to Representatives of Fiat Automotive Plant, October 31, 1948

The Church does not promise that absolute equality which others are proclaiming because she knows that life in human society always and of necessity produces a whole range of degrees and differences in physical and mental traits, in inward dispositions and inclinations, in occupations and in responsibilities. But at the same time she assures you full equality in human dignity, as also in the Heart of Him who calls unto Himself all those who labor and are heavily burdened, and invites them to take upon themselves His yoke and find peace and rest for their souls; for His yoke is sweet and His burden light (cf. *Matt.* 11, 28–30).

Leo XIII, Rerum Novarum

26. There are truly very great and very many natural differences among men. Neither the talents, nor the skill, nor the health, nor the capacities of all are the same, and unequal fortune follows of itself upon necessary inequality in respect to these endowments.

Code of Social Principles

1. Man is immortal — not human society, but each individual man created in the image and likeness of God. It is each man personally whom God loves and Christ has redeemed.

Individualism is not merely this acknowledgment of man's personality and individual end. That grave error tends, under a pretense of individual development, to relieve man of every kind of dependence.

2. It is not true that the individual is sufficient unto himself. No one, however gifted, can maintain his existence or perfect his mind and heart save in that society in which he is called to live.

3. If individualism exaggerates individual rights, other systems, on the contrary, overrate collective rights. While individualism deifies the individual, socialism deifies the state, and positivist sociology deifies society.

Between these extremes the Christian philosopher firmly grasps the two ends of the chain, i.e., the outstanding dignity of the human person and his need of society for his complete development.

4. In the legal order, individualism betrays itself in a radical subjectivism which attributes absolute independence to the human person, and unconditional value to individual rights. The constitutions of the nineteenth century have fallen more than once into this extreme.

5. Reciprocally, positivist sociology betrays itself in the legal order by a radical objectivism. It is pretended that society is a reality higher than and antecedent to its members, so that the latter have no rights but such as social solidarity may require. Such objectivism results in a misunderstanding of the personality of man and in denying the rights which flow from human nature. It makes society the end, man the means.

The truth is exactly contrary. Man has a personal destiny, society is for him the necessary means that helps him to attain his proper end. His rights flow from his nature, but they are subject, on the part of society, to certain limitations which community life imposes. For instance, there is an individual right to work, but this right must conform to the organization of labor in a given occupation or locality.

MAN IN SOCIETY

The Social Nature of Man

Pius XI, Mit Brennender Sorge

35. Real common good ultimately takes its measure from man's nature, which balances personal rights and social obligations, and from the purpose of society, established for the benefit of human nature. Society was

intended by the Creator for the full development of individual possibilities, and for the social benefits which, by a give-and-take process, everyone can claim for his own sake and that of others. Higher and more general values, which the collectivity alone can provide, also derive from the Creator for the good of man, and for his full development, natural and supernatural, and the realization of his perfection. To neglect this order is to shake the pillars on which society rests, and to compromise social tranquillity, security, and existence.

Pius XI, On Atheistic Communism

29. But God has likewise destined man for civil society according to the dictates of his very nature. In the plan of the Creator, society is a natural means which man can and must use to reach his destined end. Society is for man and not *vice versa*. This must not be understood in the sense of liberalistic individualism, which subordinates society to the selfish use of the individual; but only in the sense that by means of an organic union with society and by mutual collaboration the attainment of earthly happiness is placed within the reach of all. In a further sense it is society which affords the opportunities for the development of all the individual and social gifts bestowed on human nature. These natural gifts have a value surpassing the immediate interests of the moment, for in society they reflect the divine perfection, which would not be true were man to live alone. But on final analysis, even in this latter function society is made for man, that he may recognize this reflection of God's perfection, and refer it in praise and adoration to the Creator. Only man, the human person, and not society in any form is endowed with reason and a morally free will.

34. Thus authority is reconciled with liberty, the dignity of the individual with that of the state, the human personality of the subject with the divine delegation of the superior; and in this way a balance is struck between the due dependence and well-ordered love of a man for himself, his family and country, and his love of other families and other peoples, founded on the love of God, the Father of all, their first principle and last end.

Leo XIII, Sapientiae Christianae

2. For nature has not formed society in order that man might look to it as an end, but in order that in it and through it he might find fitting help to his own perfection.

Private and Public Societies

Leo XIII, Rerum Novarum

71. The end of civil society concerns absolutely all members of this

society, since the end of civil society is centered in the common good, in which latter, one and all in due proportion have a right to participate. Wherefore, this society is called public because through it "men share with one another in establishing a commonwealth." On the other hand, societies which are formed, so to speak, within its bosom are considered private and are such because their immediate object is private advantage appertaining to those alone who are thus associated together. "Now a private society is one which is formed to carry out some private business, as when two or three enter into association for the purpose of engaging together in trade."

72. Although private societies exist within the state and are, as it were, so many parts of it, still it is not within the authority of the state universally and *per se* to forbid them to exist as such. For man is permitted by a right of nature to form private societies; the state, on the other hand, has been instituted to protect and not to destroy natural right, and if it should forbid its citizens to enter into associations, it would clearly do something contradictory to itself, because both the state itself and private associations are begotten of one and the same principle, namely, that men are by nature inclined to associate.

Pius XI, Quadragesimo Anno

37. Leo's learned treatment and vigorous defense of the natural right to form associations began, furthermore, to find ready application to other associations also and not alone to those of the workers. Hence no small part of the credit must, it seems, be given to this same Encyclical of Leo for the fact that among farmers and others of the middle class most useful associations of this kind are seen flourishing to a notable degree and increasing day by day, as well as other institutions of a similar nature in which spiritual development and economic benefit are happily combined.

Civil Society

Leo XIII, Diuturnum Illud

7. And indeed nature, or rather God who is the author of nature, wills that man should live in a civil society; and this is clearly shown both by the faculty of language, the greatest medium of intercourse, and by numerous innate desires of the mind, and the many necessary things, and things of great importance, which men isolated cannot procure but which they can procure when joined and associated with others. But now, a society can neither exist nor be conceived in which there is no one to govern the wills of individuals in such a way as to make, as it were, one will out of many, and to impel them rightly and orderly to the common good; therefore God has willed that in a civil society there should be some to rule

the multitude. And this also is a powerful argument, that those by whose authority the state is administered must be able so to compel the citizens to obedience that it is clearly a sin in the latter not to obey. But no man has in himself or of himself the power of constraining the free will of others by fetters of authority of this kind. This power resides solely in God, the Creator and Legislator of all things; and it is necessary that those who exercise it should do it as having received it from God.

8. Those who believe civil society to have arisen from the free consent of men, looking for the origin of its authority from the same source, say that each individual has given up something of his right, and that voluntarily every person has put himself into the power of the one man in whose person the whole of those rights has been centered. But it is a great error not to see, what is manifest, that men, as they are not a nomad race, have been created, without their own free will, for a natural community of life. It is plain, moreover, that the agreement which they allege is openly a falsehood and a fiction, and that it has no authority to confer on political power such great force, dignity, and firmness as the safety of the state and the common good of the citizens require. Then only will the government have all those ornaments and guarantees, when it is understood to emanate from God as its august and most sacred source.

9. Whence it will behoove citizens to submit themselves and to be obedient to rulers, as to God, not so much through fear of punishment, as through respect for their majesty; nor for the sake of pleasing, but through conscience, as doing their duty.

Leo XIII, Immortale Dei

2. Man's natural instinct moves him to live in civil society. Isolated, he cannot provide himself with the necessary requirements of life, nor procure the means of developing his mental and moral faculties. It is, therefore, divinely ordained that he should lead his life — be it domestic, social, or civil — in contact with his fellow men, where alone his several wants can be adequately supplied. But no society can remain united without someone in command, directing all to strive earnestly for the common good. Hence, every civilized community must have a ruling authority, and this authority, no less than society itself, has its source in nature, and consequently has God for its author. It follows, then, that all public power must proceed from God: for God alone is the true and supreme Lord of the World.

Pius XI, On Atheistic Communism

30. Man cannot be exempted from his divinely imposed obligations toward civil society, and the representatives of authority have the right to

coerce him when he refuses without reason to do his duty. Society, on the other hand, cannot defraud man of his God-granted rights, the most important of which We have indicated above. Nor can society systematically void these rights by making their use impossible. It is therefore according to the dictates of reason that ultimately all material things should be ordained to man as a person, that through his mediation they may find their way to the Creator.

33. Both man and civil society derive their origin from the Creator, who has mutually ordained them one to the other. Hence neither than be exempted from their correlative obligations, nor deny or diminish each other's rights. The Creator Himself has regulated this mutual relationship in its fundamental lines. . . .

THE PURPOSE OF ECONOMIC LIFE

Pius XI, Caritate Christi Compulsi

30. No leader in public economy, no power of organization will ever be able to bring social conditions to a peaceful solution, unless first in the very field of economics there triumphs moral law based on God and conscience. This is the underlying value of every value in the political life as well as in the economic life of nations; this is the soundest "rate of exchange." If it is kept steady, all the rest will be stable, being guaranteed by the immutable and eternal law of God.

Pius XI, Quadragesimo Anno

33. Thus associations of this kind have molded truly Christian workers who, in combining harmoniously the diligent practice of their occupation with the salutary precepts of religion, protect effectively and resolutely their own temporal interests and rights, keeping a due respect for justice and a genuine desire to work together with other classes of society for the Christian renewal of all social life.

42. Even though economics and moral science employ each its own principles in its own sphere, it is, nevertheless, an error to say that the economic and moral orders are so distinct from and alien to each other that the former depends in no way on the latter. Certainly the laws of economics, as they are termed, being based on the very nature of material things and on the capacities of the human body and mind, determine the limits of what productive human effort cannot, and of what it can attain in the economic field and by what means. Yet it is reason itself that clearly shows, on the basis of the individual and social nature of things and of men, the purpose which God ordained for all economic life.

43. But it is only the moral law which, just as it commands us to seek our supreme and last end in the whole scheme of our activity, so likewise commands us to seek directly in each kind of activity those purposes which we know that nature, or rather God the author of nature, established for that kind of action, and in orderly relationship to subordinate such immediate purposes to our supreme and last end. If we faithfully observe this law, then it will follow that the particular purposes, both individual and social, that are sought in the economic field will fall in their proper place in the universal order of purposes, and We, in ascending through them, as it were by steps, shall attain the final end of all things, that is God, to Himself and to us, the supreme and inexhaustible Good.

75. The various occupations will combine and coalesce into, as it were, a single body and like members of the body mutually aid and complete one another. For then only will the social economy be rightly established and attain its purposes when all and each are supplied with all the goods that the wealth and resources of nature, technical achievement, and the social organization of economic life can furnish. And these goods ought indeed to be enough both to meet the demands of necessity and decent comfort and to advance people to that happier and fuller condition of life which, when it is wisely cared for, is not only no hindrance to virtue but helps it greatly.

110. Since the present system of economy is founded chiefly upon ownership and labor, the principles of right reason, that is, of Christian social philosophy, must be kept in mind regarding ownership and labor and their association together, and must be put into actual practice. First, so as to avoid the reefs of individualism and collectivism, the twofold character, that is individual and social, both of capital or ownership and of work or labor must be given due and rightful weight. Relations of one to the other must be made to conform to the laws of strictest justice — commutative justice as it is called — with the support, however, of Christian charity. Free competition, kept within definite and due limits, and still more economic dictatorship, must be effectively brought under public authority in these matters which pertain to the latter's function. The public institutions themselves, of peoples, moreover, ought to make all human society conform to the needs of the common good; that is, to the norm of social justice. If this is done, that most important division of social life, namely, economic activity, cannot fail likewise to return to right and sound order.

Pius XII, La Solennità della Pentecoste

1685. Likewise the national economy, as it is the product of the men who work together in the community of the state, has no other end than to secure without interruption the material conditions in which the individual life of the citizens may fully develop. Where this is secured in a permanent way, a people will be, in a true sense, economically rich because the general well-being, and consequently the personal right of all to the use of worldly goods, is thus actuated in conformity with the purpose willed by the Creator.

1686. From this, beloved children, it will be easy for you to conclude that the economic riches of a people do not properly consist in the abundance of goods, measured according to a purely and solely material calculation of their worth, but in the fact that such an abundance represents and offers really and effectively the material basis sufficient for the proper personal development of its members.

Pius XII, Nell' Alba

1751. Nobody should think that by indicting the materialism of the nineteenth and twentieth centuries We intend to blame technical progress. No. We do not indict what fundamentally is a gift of God; for, as the Lord God makes wheat to grow from earth and soil, thus, when He created the world, He hid for us in the depth of the earth treasures, metals and precious stones, so that they may be mined by man for his needs, for his works, and for his progress. The Church, the mother of so many European universities, attracts today, as she always did, the most prominent scientists; but she is well aware that man can use every good entrusted to him, even the freedom of will, either for good or for evil. Thus the spirit and the direction in which technical progress has been used has now resulted in science having to expiate its own errors. Science has been misused for destruction, and, in fact, today it destroys the very buildings that it yesterday proudly erected.

Pius XII, Christmas Broadcast, 1942

1851. Those who are familiar with the great Encyclicals of Our Predecessors and Our Own previous messages know well that the Church does not hesitate to draw the practical conclusions which are derived from the moral nobility of work, and to give them all the support of her authority. These exigencies include, besides a just wage which covers the needs of the worker and his family, the conservation and perfection of a social order which will make possible an assured, even if modest, private property for all classes of society, which will promote higher education for the children of the working class who are especially endowed with intelligence and good will, will promote the care and the practice of the social spirit in one's immediate neighborhood, in the district, the province, the people, and the nation, a spirit which, by smoothing over friction arising from privileges or class interests, removes from the workers the sense of isolation through the assuring experience of a genuinely human, and fraternally Christian, solidarity.

Pius XII, Radio Address, September 1, 1944

For the same purpose small and medium holdings in agriculture, in the arts and trades, in commerce and industry should be guaranteed and promoted; co-operative unions should ensure for them the advantages of big business; where big business even today shows itself more productive, there should be given the possibility of tempering the labor contract with a contract of co-ownership (Encyclical, *Quadragesimo Anno*).

And it should not be said that technical progress is opposed to such a scheme and in its irresistible current carries all activity forward toward gigantic business and organizations, before which a social system founded on the private property of individuals must inevitably collapse. No. Technical progress does not determine economic life as a fatal and necessary factor. It has indeed too often yielded timidly to the demands of rapacious, selfish plans calculated to accumulate indefinitely; why should it not then yield also the necessity of maintaining and ensuring private property for all, that cornerstone of social order? Even technical progress, as a social factor, should not prevail over the general good, but should rather be directed and subordinated to it.

Pius XII, Address to Italian Workers, June 13, 1943

(*Summarized.*) The salvation of the workers is not to be found in revolution, but rather in the evolving of a just social order. Even if revolution were to bring about material progress, the price in terms of human liberty would be too great. In fact, revolution does not bring about progress, even in the material sense. We should not abolish private property, but rather extend real ownership. We should not dissipate capital; instead we should regulate it for the common welfare. No class in society should be favored exclusively. The ideal would be to bring all into harmony. Moreover, technical progress should not aim merely at increasing profits. It should bring leisure and comfort to the workers as well. Finally, we should not make individuals completely dependent upon the state. Rather we should promote institutions which make them really self-sufficient.

THE NATURE OF MAN

Under God, man is the center of the universe. Man has an inner dignity, based on his nature, origin, and destiny, which all must respect. This nature is the immediate source of rights and duties. It confers upon man an aura of sacredness which is not shared by the animals of the field or by purely material things.

But man does not live alone. To realize fully his powers and aspirations, he must live in the society of his fellow man. This fact, to a degree, modifies the rights and duties which spring from the nature of the individual. It also adds new rights and duties.

Such in a nutshell is the foundation of Catholic social theory. The detailed spelling out of man's prerogatives and obligations is but an amplifying of these fundamental principles. Time and again, the great encyclicals of recent popes have come back to this bedrock upon which a sound social order must rest.

The Dignity of Man. The dignity of man springs from his nature. It is not conferred by society, nor is it merely a product of law or custom. Certain rights are inalienable. They may not be abridged or taken away by any man. Long before the Christian era, sound philosophers reached this conclusion, however imperfectly. Man has a soul. He has reason and free will. This spiritual nature raises him above the animal kingdom, and even higher above lifeless matter. Man is thus lord of the universe. Lesser things are made to serve his needs. He may use them in accordance with the law of his nature and nature's God.

In addition, Christian revelation teaches us of an even higher status of man. We know that man is destined, provided he is worthy, for an immortal life with God. Even in this world, the Christian in the state of grace shares in the life of God. He is "an adopted son of God," "a temple of the Holy Spirit," "a brother of Christ," and "a member of the mystical body of Christ." This special and wholly gratuitous solicitude of God toward the creature made in His image and likeness confers a unique dignity upon every man. Christ teaches that what is done to the least of the little ones is done to Him.

Even among those who do not accept the full Christian revelation, there is often a traditional respect for the dignity of man. In much of the world, human life is held to be sacred. The taking of life, or even the doing of violence to the human person, is considered a crime. Men will risk their own lives to avoid even the involuntary killing of another. Thus, when an automobile driver sees a child dart into the street in front of him, he applies the brakes and swerves at the risk of fatal injury to himself. When a person falls overboard from a ship, an effort is made to rescue him, though this may involve great danger to the seamen concerned. In such circumstances, there is no calculation of cost or of the relative talents and achievements of the individuals in danger.

A great portion of Christian social ethics could be derived from this one principle of man's worth. It could be the basis of a philosophy of labor. The right to work at a decent wage, the right to fair and just treatment, and many similar rights follow from the dignity of man. Man is more than a machine or a commodity.

Because of man's nature, the great modern heresy of statism stands condemned. Any system which holds that man's rights are conferred by the state, and that they may be modified or taken away at the whim of a despot, is unnatural and grossly immoral. Communism is wrong, not primarily because of its economic tenets, but because it makes a slave of men. National Socialism and fascism were wrong, not in the first place because of their wars of aggression, but because they made man a tool in the hands of a dictator. Wherever the state arrogates to itself supreme power, disregarding the law of God and man's inalienable rights, it is a monstrosity contrary to all reason.

The evil roots of statism are many. But in the United States, we should particularly note the influence of Auguste Comte and his philosophy of positivism. His sociology holds that the state is antecedent to man and is the source of man's rights. We are fortunate indeed to have escaped the full implications of this theory. But we should not ignore the fact that this system is taught and accepted in many American universities. It has infected our intellectual world with an empiricism and experimentalism which denies the idea of natural rights and basic moral principles. This fact undoubtedly explains in part the sympathy of some intellectuals toward collectivism and communism. With others, it leads to secularism and pragmatism. Thus, we have a rapidly shifting society, based on expediency, not principle.

A sound social philosophy also repudiates materialism. Man has a spiritual soul, and this is the source of human nobility. A concentration upon material achievement, to the detriment of the spiritual, is a perversion of right order. The material world is to be the servant of man, not his master. Economic life is not an end in itself; it must be subordinated to higher and nobler laws. Here again, we Americans must be vigilant in regard to our values. We have achieved such wonders of material progress that we are prone to exaggerate its importance. The cultivation of the mind and the soul is, after all, man's greatest boast.

More controversial is the assertion made by some that modern industrialism, with its assembly-line techniques, does violence to the dignity of man. It is held that repetitive labor is degrading, whereas creative and responsible labor is ennobling. This point will be discussed in more detail subsequently. There is, at least, this truth to be observed: that the conditions surrounding work do have an influence upon man's character and personality.

The Rights of Man. Upon man's nature there are founded certain inalienable rights. A right is generally defined as an inviolable moral power which a person has to do something, or to have, acquire, or dispose of something. A duty is a moral obligation of doing or not doing something. Rights and duties are interconnected. One man's right imposes upon another the duty of respecting his prerogatives. Nevertheless, rights and duties may conflict in practice. Hence there is vital need for classifying rights and determining their relative priorities.

One method of evaluating rights is in terms of their origin. Thus, some rights spring directly from nature, whereas others are conferred by law or by man. The rights to live and to marry are natural; the right to a government job may derive from law; and the right to use another's house may come from a contract made between men. These examples also illustrate the priority of rights. Those rooted directly in human nature are fundamental and may not be abrogated by law or by agreement among men. On the other hand, just laws, enacted in the interest of the common welfare, take precedence over private contracts. Divine law is higher than the law of man. Of man's natural rights, those involving directly the spiritual side of his nature would be more vital than those connected with his physical well-being. Hence it would not be sound to treat all rights equally, not distinguishing between the higher and the lower.

A second basis for evaluation is the relative necessity of rights for their intended purpose. Thus, the right to possess property is closely connected with the natural right to live. But not all property would minister equally to the right to live. The meager stock of food and clothing of the very poor would be more necessary for them than the millions possessed by a wealthy man. In the one case, the goods described are needed for the welfare of the human person. In the second instance, many of the possessions are superfluous in terms of survival. The urgency of a right deepens as it goes closer to its source and justification.

A final classification pertinent here concerns the relative priority of community rights in contrast to individual rights. Here Catholic thinking takes a turn which may surprise many. The common good has precedence over individual rights *in the same sphere*. Even with the most fundamental rights, this is true. An illustration of this point is war, in which individuals risk their lives for the welfare of the nation and the lives and liberties of others. At first glance, this point might seem to be a concession to statism. However, when the term "common good" is correctly defined, the apparent conflict will vanish. The more detailed explanations given in subsequent chapters will make this point clear.

Confusion in regard to rights and duties can be avoided when the universe is considered in relation to the master plan of the Creator. There are two profound philosophical truths in particular which should not be overlooked in discussing the foundations of social ethics. First, the world is purposive. All nature strives toward determined ends. Man, however, seeks the ends of his being consciously and freely. Secondly, reality is pluralistic, with gradations of being and consequently of value. Spiritual being is of a higher nature than material; living being is "more real" than nonliving being. While every grade of being tends to seek its own ends, it is at the same time subordinate to higher forms of reality. Thus, animals serve man and nonliving matter is assimilated and often transformed by living beings. In man the needs of the body are subsidiary to those of the soul.

When metaphysics is applied to the field of ethics, we have a sound basis for a distinction among various types of rights. Thus, rights essential for the basic ends of man's existence are more important than and have priority over nonessential rights, even of a higher order. For example, a man should not risk his life to protect a work of art from vandals. His right to one type of cultural perfection, though higher in nature than the right to bodily survival, is relatively nonessential, whereas the latter is essential. On the other hand, among rights equally necessary for the ends of man's nature, the higher would take precedence over the lower. In times of persecution, men rightly die rather than apostatize from their religious faith. Essential values of the spirit are more important than bodily survival.

In line with this reasoning, the economic order exists to minister to the human person. When economic institutions become perverted, so that essential ends of man's nature are not adequately realized, a change in economic life is morally justified. This point is fundamental to the present study.

These general principles will take on life and vigor when they are applied to concrete problems. Indeed, most of the field of social ethics is concerned with the classifying of relative rights and duties. Delicate balances must be struck between conflicting rights in the same sphere and in different spheres. The basic dignity of the individual must be interpreted in the light of his duties to society. Then a clear picture will emerge of a social order, conformable to man's nature, as seen in terms of sound reason and divine revelation.

Fundamental Rights. Recent encyclicals have enumerated nearly a score of basic rights, but those connected with socioeconomic problems are apposite here.[1] In this sphere, the right to live is most fundamental. This conforms with the deep-rooted instinct of self-preservation, which is so clearly a part of man's nature. Negatively this right is expressed in the commandment "Thou shalt not kill." Positively, it involves the right to the necessary means for existence. This means not only a minimum of food, clothing, and shelter, but the obtaining of this minimum in a manner conforming with human dignity. It demands a socioeconomic order which affords men the opportunity to live as human beings. Mere animal survival is not living in a human sense.

Family rights are closely connected with the right to live. The physical, emotional, and spiritual needs of man are normally satisfied only in a family environment. The instinct to propagate the race is deep-rooted in our nature. Futhermore, we know from divine revelation, reason, and experience that monogamous family life is the only acceptable way for preserving the human race. Accordingly, a sound social order must minister to the needs of family life.

The right to possess property is also fundamental. Individual and family living in a human way would not ordinarily be possible otherwise. If all goods were in common, we would face an intolerable choice between two evils. On the one hand, there could be a disorderly struggle for immediate needs. Organized economic life would be impossible, and strife and contention the normal course of events. On the other hand, the community could control all wealth. But this would place in the hands of the collective group, and its ruler, absolute power over the individual

---

[1] For a lengthy enumeration, with many quotations from the popes, see Robert Kothen, *L'Enseignement social de l'Église*, pp. 166–214. J. A. Messner, in his volume *Social Ethics* (St. Louis: Herder, 1949), pp. 222–226, lists fourteen basic rights.

and the family. Neither way of life meets the demands of human nature.

The right of association likewise springs from man's nature. We are social creatures, intimately dependent upon one another. The full powers of the individual are realized only in conjunction with others. In the economic sphere, organization is normally necessary for efficient and orderly production. So universal is this instinct for association that it can be called a basic human trait. Hence man has the natural right to form groups or teams for lawful ends.

Finally, the social order should be so organized that higher rights, not enumerated here, should be protected. Man has spiritual and cultural needs in addition to the physical. Rights in this sphere are generally of a higher order than those connected with bodily needs. The lower should minister to the higher; certainly it should not impede or conflict with nobler ends.

The Equality of Man. On the basis of man's nature and fundamental rights, we can say that "all men were created equal." Men are equal in origin, nature, and destiny. All are created alike by God. All possess the same basic human qualities of reason and free will. All have immortal souls destined to eternal life. All are called to the higher destiny revealed in the teachings of Christ.

While men have a moral equality, at the same time they have individual differences which may not be ignored. Not all have the same talents or dispositions. There are varying degrees of intelligence among individuals. Characters differ, as do tastes and aptitudes. In addition to inborn variations, circumstances and environment affect people deeply. Family care, the degree of education, and economic status are bound to make a difference.

As a result, it would be contrary to human nature to expect or to demand absolute equality among men. There is nothing inherently wrong in the distinction between leaders and followers, the well-to-do and those less endowed with material goods, the educated and the uneducated. These distinctions could be wrong, however, if their source were vitiated or their unnecessary continuance were contrary to the common good. Leadership based on force and violence could be unjust. Unequal distribution of wealth could proceed to extremes which would be harmful to society.

An intriguing question concerns political equality. The Church has been traditionally reluctant to pronounce judgment upon forms of government. Its concern has rather been that governments be just, that they rule under law, and that this be in conformity with the law of God. Because of the inequalities of men, some Churchmen have even been hesitant in past centuries to espouse the idea of popular sovereignty. In this light, it is interesting to note the observation made by Pope Pius XII in his Christmas broadcast of 1944: "If then, we consider the extent and nature of the sacrifice demanded of all the citizens, especially in our day when the activity of the state is so vast and decisive, the democratic form of government appears to many as a postulate of nature imposed by reason itself."

On the same line of reasoning, there are current demands for greater industrial democracy. Granted the inequalities among men, it is still true that modern economic life is so pervasive in its influence and so exacting in its demands, that those partaking in it should have a greater voice in directing its course. In earlier societies, life was so organized that men could keep a basic independence, even though economically subject to another. There was more opportunity to shift from one job to another, to become an independent craftsman or to own a small enterprise. Today even the directors of huge factories are often subordinate officials, taking orders from a central office or from financial groups who control the company. It may well be questioned whether all inequalities existing today spring from unequal ability, or whether some come from a form of social organization which is encroaching upon the basic rights of the individual.

A problem of inequality which, while not strictly economic, has important social and economic overtones involves racial and religious discrimination, particularly against Negroes. There is hardly any need to elaborate upon the un-Christian nature of such practices. A conception of life which would deny basic rights to a whole race merely because of the accident of color is essentially barbaric. By contrast, a true Christian social order calls for the harmonious integration of all groups into the social body. It does not reject the fact of diversity, but it achieves an organic union of various groups into the body politic and economic.

While the principles enunciated here are by their nature universal, it is useful to state explicitly that justice and right must be given to minority groups. Indeed, many of our social problems exist in heightened form among exploited peoples. Thus, Negroes and Mexicans suffer more than others from poverty, inadequate housing, insufficient facilities for medical care and education, and poor working conditions. Hence the obligations outlined in these pages apply especially where the abuses are greater. This is particularly true of the need for *organized* social action, as demanded by the virtue of social justice. Education, laws, and other forms of community influence and pressure should be used to counter these evils. Indeed, broad programs for social reform are not likely to be successful, if one group can be exploited with impunity. The competitive pressure from such underpaid workers would lower standards for all.

It is shameful that the most vocal proponents of racial justice have been the American Communists. It speaks well for the basic good sense of minorities that Communists have found so few recruits from their midst. Nevertheless, there is no assurance that Negroes and others will always remain unresponsive to the pleas of agitators. Moreover, in the present world struggle Americans would be indeed shortsighted were they to overlook the propaganda value for the Soviet Union derived from American discrimination. The great peoples of the Orient, especially, feel bitter about racial slurs. It would be tragic were our domestic prejudices to drive them into the Soviet orbit, while we were spending billions for an anticommunist foreign policy.

MAN IN SOCIETY

The discussion of rights thus far has centered primarily upon the individual and only incidentally upon society. In a sense, this emphasis is correct. Society exists for the individual, and not the reverse. But in another sense the approach just taken needs completion. Man is a social animal, as well as a person with rights and duties based upon his individual nature. Indeed, social living is essential to the full development of the human personality. Moreover, it is an aspect which needs stress in the United States, since our traditions have been heavily individualistic. Only recently has our Catholic educational system begun to emphasize the requirements of social living. Again, we have the reputation of being a nation with many laws, but yet restive under law and occasionally defiant of law. Our frontier tradition of resourcefulness and individual initiative has persisted long after the frontier has been closed, and has been felt in fields where social co-operation is also needed.

The Social Nature of Man. Man's physical and psychological being shows that he is social. Physically, man is helpless without society. At birth, he is weak and puny. He needs the fostering care of the family to survive. He matures slowly, in contrast to the animal kingdom, where the young are rarely dependent for more than a few months or a year. In the struggle for survival, man does not have the physical resources to meet the challenge of savage nature. He has not the strength of the lion or tiger, the fleetness of the antelope, the cunning and sensitiveness of the fox, the natural defenses of the porcupine, the protective coloration of the rabbit, the agility of the squirrel, or other of the qualities, refined senses, or instincts which nature gives to animals for their self-protection. Without society, the child would freeze in the winter, starve for lack of food, or be the easy prey of any predatory animal.

Psychologically, man needs society. In contrast to the animal, we are born with few instincts. We do not sense dangers, nor do we realize what natural foods are good and what poisonous. We only learn from others in these vital matters. Moreover, our rational nature develops only in society. Men who live isolated lives rarely become fine personalities, and often lose their sanity. Even the family is too small a unit for the full development of personality. Introverted, ingrown families are not adapted for living in this complex world. The overprotected and excessively sheltered child becomes a problem. Our minds, wills, and characters grow and become strong only in the give and take of social living.

Man has strong aspirations for social living. He seeks the company and values the esteem of his fellow man. The desire to love and to share in the love of others is among the deepest traits of our nature. Hence it is only to be expected that a rich social life characterizes human existence. Even our relationships to lower orders of being tend to be social. Thus, man the worker is exercising dominion over the world. He performs, as it were, a task of creation in changing and ennobling lesser goods. But he has found that work must be performed as part of a harmonious pattern of social life, if it is to be fully effective.

Society is almost essential for economic life and the physical survival of the race. It may be just possible for a single family in a suitable environment to meet its economic needs. By heavy and unceasing toil, it could obtain the bare minimum of food, clothing, and shelter necessary to survive. Only a few families could be maintained under such conditions. Even the primitive farming, hunting, grazing, and nomadic societies afforded a living to but a relatively few. For the large population of modern times, social organization is essential.

Economic Society. In economic life, organization permits specialization, division of labor, and large-scale production, with consequent multiplication of skill and efficiency. When men specialize, they acquire great skills in their particular fields. By division of labor, a large operation can be broken down into many simple tasks, which each worker can perform more efficiently. As individual tasks become simpler, they are subject to mechanization, whereby human skills can be multiplied greatly.

The machine takes over the skill of the individual worker, and power resources concentrate in a small factory energies which could be supplied only by thousands of workers. Thus, the essentials of living can be obtained for large populations with relatively small effort, and time is made available for luxuries, cultural living, social relationships, and other characteristically human occupations.

It is true that complex economic organization brings its own problems. Some result from abuses; others are probably inherent in the system. But it is rather hazardous to condemn industrialism in its entirety, as is the fashion among some Catholic writers and others who are not Catholic. The population of the modern world is a fact, and it is likewise a fact that it could not survive on the basis of older forms of production. Moreover, granted the virtues of craftsmanship and individual ownership of productive property, it is still possible to overemphasize both the qualities of simpler ways of economic life and the tedium of assembly-line production. Tedium is not a modern invention. There is much routine and repetitive work in farming. Even intellectual tasks, such as teaching, involve the bore of grading hundreds of papers periodically. The scribes who copied out medieval manuscripts would probably have welcomed a typewriter, even if it meant a stint at the assembly line to produce one. Likewise, the silversmiths who turned out beautiful vessels by hand would hardly have objected to modern polishing and grinding tools.

Political Society. Finally, man is destined for political society. Given our social nature, it is normal for us to live in communities. But if community life is to function smoothly, there must be an inherent principle of unity. A mere aggregation of individuals, without order or purpose, would not meet man's social needs. Order and purpose in turn can only come from some directing principle, from some one or group in authority. St. Thomas, Suarez, and Bellarmine all use the example of the human body, composed of many members, but centrally directed for the common good of all. These great philosophers and theologians held that society and political authority are natural to man. And, since

God created human nature, political authority derives ultimately from God.

The notion of the divine origin of civil power flatly contradicts the theory of the "social contract," popularized by Rousseau and widely held today. The modern world swings between two extremes: statism, which makes society a law unto itself, independent of divine law and political control by its citizens; and political individualism, which considers society as the temporary depository of powers surrendered for a time by the citizens. One extreme exaggerates civil power; the other so minimizes it as to lead to the danger of anarchy. The middle position upholds the authority of government, at the same time maintaining the right of citizens to choose their rulers and to instruct them in their policies. Whatever the form of government, it must rule justly, for the common good, and in conformity with natural law and divine positive law.

While Catholics abhor statism and American Catholics are strongly prodemocratic, we are not always so careful to avoid political individualism. Too often we share the common attitude that government is something apart from us which imposes unwelcome restrictions which we evade when we can. We stress the corruption and inefficiency of government, as if we were not responsible for the condition of democratic government. Many times our moral theology texts teach a casuistry in regard to law, taxes, and the social obligations of citizens which is ill-suited for modern times. Possibly such casuistry was applicable in other circumstances to nondemocratic governments, where evasion and passive resistance were often the citizen's only recourse against state tyranny. But in modern times, where the citizen has the right to participate in lawmaking and where social obligations are so diverse and vital, casuistry and negativism are out of place. Likewise, where citizens can pick their rulers, it is unseemly to be carping against political corruption and inefficiency. We have a duty to do something about it, and not to withdraw by way of purely negative criticism.

Man's Social Rights and Obligations. Since social living is part of man's nature, this fact is bound to modify our concept of rights and duties based on the individual person. Not only are individual rights qualified by the impact of equal or even superior rights of others, but specific rights and duties arise from the fact of social living.

Among the more fundamental rights is the right of association mentioned earlier. What man's nature impels him to do is clearly a right, provided it is exercised within the bounds of reason. The associations of interest here are those connected with the economic order. They would include business partnerships and corporations, labor unions, various forms of co-operatives, industrial councils, and similar natural groupings. The functioning of these societies should, of course, be governed by the laws of justice and the common good. Within these bounds, they have a right to exist peaceably. Any effort by a more powerful society to destroy them is morally wrong. Such would be the case with the totalitarian state, which permits only organs under its absolute control to survive. Again, if a corporation were to use its economic power to dissolve a labor union desired by its workers, it would be acting unjustly.

Basic among the social duties of man is the obligation to contribute, according to his position, to the common good. Since society is natural to man, he must share the responsibilities as well as the privileges of social living. Of course, not all societies are equally necessary. Some, such as the state or the family, flow from nature itself. Others, such as choral groups or bridge clubs, are purely matters of taste and convenience. There is a third group which occupies an intermediate position which is difficult to classify today. This would comprise associations which are virtually indispensable to achieve some necessary good. Thus, some would argue that in modern society the labor union is a practical necessity in order to achieve some basic rights of man. This point will be discussed subsequently, but it illustrates the complex nature of the common good. However, the principle is clear: when a society is necessary to achieve some basic end springing from man's nature, we are not privileged to be neutral.

88 THE CHRISTIAN SOCIAL ORDER

These ideas are relevant to another school of thought among Catholics, which will be treated in Chapter XVIII. This is the attitude that the evils of society can be cured only by radical abstention from modern economic life. The economic world is considered to be so fundamentally evil that withdrawal and nonparticipation are the only remedies. This theory comes dangerously close to a denial of man's social duties. It involves a considered refusal to accept responsibility for the common good. It seems quite foreign to the spirit of the social encyclicals and pronouncements of Popes Pius XI and Pius XII. Thus, in the political sphere, Pope Pius XII gave, as his answer to political corruption, increased participation in political life by men of high principles.[2] Pope Pius XI has often stated the duty of all to seek the common good of society.

While society exists to serve man, it is also necessary for his welfare. By using society for the welfare of all, each individual secures his own well-being. This means that a proper balance must be struck between individual rights and social responsibility. The working out of this formula in detailed problems is not easy, but it is a task which may not be shirked. In facing this problem, the principles given earlier in regard to the priority of rights will enable us to secure results fully consonant with human nature.

THE PURPOSE OF ECONOMIC LIFE

The type of society most germane to the present study is the economic order, with all its ramifications among other social institutions. One of the major problems of modern times is the reorientation of economic life, so that it may conform to God's purpose in creating material things.

Goals Sought. Of first importance is the realization that economic life is subordinate to higher values. It deals with the material order, and this by its nature is inferior to matters cultural and spiritual. The lower should minister to the higher. Hence the basic purpose of economic life is to provide man with the

---

[2] Christmas Broadcast, 1944.

necessities for survival, and the foundations for cultural and spiritual life. It will achieve this when every willing and able worker can earn at least a stable decent wage for himself and his family. This wage will provide necessities, a minimum opportunity for comfort and leisure, and some chance to realize nonmaterial aspirations according to the interests and talents of the individual.

Economic life should furnish, insofar as possible, opportunity for individuals to develop and utilize their personal talents. It should be the material foundation of an educational system which will bring out abilities and skills. For those whose aptitudes are mechanical, this would mean at least adequate vocational training. Where abilities tend toward the intellectual or the professional spheres, there should be sufficient opportunities for advanced study. In general, the trend should be toward an increase in leisure, so that man can be freed from excessive preoccupation with material things.

An important step toward this goal would be the wider distribution of wealth, particularly the actual ownership of property. In this way, individuals would have greater independence. They would be able to exercise personal choice as to the use of their resources for themselves and their families. There would also result a greater stability in economic life, to the extent that a smaller proportion of individuals would depend upon giant economic organizations. In principle, this method of securing cultural benefits is preferable to organized efforts by the state to provide for many of the needs of its citizens. Of course, we should not condemn social insurance, grants-in-aid for education, or civic recreational and cultural developments. In modern times these are necessary. But it is still desirable that individuals have the greatest possible freedom to direct their own lives in these fields. A more equitable distribution of resources would bring this about.

Although widespread diffusion of ownership is the most desirable foundation for individual freedom and economic stability, it is nevertheless a fact that many will remain in the status

of wage earners. Under these circumstances, a goal of social
policy must be the preservation and enhancement of human
dignity under conditions of economic dependence. The wage
earner must at the minimum be accorded his basic rights and
treated as befits a human being. Above this level of essential
rights there are opportunities for giving the worker greater
participation in the economic process. He could be given a more
definite voice in matters which greatly affect his welfare. In this
way, to use the language of Pope Pius XII, he would no longer
be a mere object — a passive factor in the economic planning
of others — but he would be a subject, a person exercising some
control over his own destiny. Society would not be mechanical
— a mass held together by external force — but it would be
organic, based on the intelligent co-operation of free men and
independent but colloborating social groups.

In attaining material wealth, technical progress can be a
substantial help. The popes have insisted that, in condemning
certain abuses in the socioeconomic sphere, they were not
minimizing the value of modern technology. Wisely used,
these processes can bring about the abolition of want. They can
make food, clothing, and housing abundant for the needs of all.
Moreover, they can provide leisure and comfort for many, and
ultimately for all. Such goals are in themselves desirable from the
viewpoint of Christian virtue. Excessive poverty brings a preoccupation with material things which injures the dignity of
human nature and is contrary to the law of God. Of course, this
wrongful solicitude about material things can come from an opposite extreme, when men seek wealth for its own sake and become preoccupied with amassing riches. Greed, vanity, and lust
for power are also contrary to the law of God.

Economic Stability. Most important today is the need for
stability in economic life. Alternations between boom and bust,
between high prosperity and the depths of depression, are upsetting to higher values. Family life is strained. Men cannot
make reasonable plans for the future. They are unhappy in good
times for the fear of what is to come. The result is strife between

capital and labor, between farm and city, and between citizen and government. The fabric of social life is torn asunder. Great evils, such as communism or statism, are threatened. Indeed, instability is the prime economic disorder in modern times.

Stability is mainly a problem of organization. It is obvious that we have the natural resources, technical skill, power, machines, labor supply, and managerial talent to abolish want and produce a high standard of living. It is equally obvious that we have not so organized these factors that we are able to utilize them fully. This is the problem and challenge of our age.

Organization in turn is a social problem. It involves the harmonious working together of individuals and groups. This is a twofold task. In part, it is technical, in that certain economic and social laws must be explored. Sound science and experience must contribute rules and policies. But, above all, social organization is a moral and ethical problem. Thus, goals must be set which harmonize with the general purposes of the universe as shown by nature and divine law. Under these broad goals, particular ends for economic life will be chosen. Then individuals and groups, actuated by a sense of social responsibility, will organize to secure these ends. The many organizations and institutions needed to effectuate policy will vary in different times and places. Economic science, prudential judgment based on experience, and social ethics will work together in bringing about the desired result. This would be the Christian social order, the restoring of all things in Christ.

Reform of Institutions. The first steps toward this goal will be the infusion of Christian principles of justice and charity into the various classes of society. Four great groups are important in this connection: capital, labor, the farming community, and government. By capital is meant, not merely finance, but the ownership of all productive property. This would include industry, business, and the service trades. The aim would be the spread of social justice and charity among each of the four groups so that each would seek the common welfare as well as individual goals. This would not be primarily a matter of forming a Christian conscience among individuals, important as this is. Rather it would involve a reform of the *institutions* of society. If the institutions of society tend toward wrong ends, the efforts inspired by personal good will are likely to be nullified. On the other hand, if the institutions of society are sound, they will contain and constrain men of ill will, preventing them from doing serious harm.

It would be premature to detail here the institutions which should be reformed. But to anticipate points to be developed later, some basic premises of modern economic life are questionable. Thus, the idea that strife between capital and labor is inevitable or even desirable does not fit in with the Christian ideal. Furthermore, it is not self-evident that our economic system functions best in terms of unlimited competition. The problem of depressions, among others, challenges the thesis that the automatic working of economic laws leads to the highest social ends. Finally, the acceptance of selfishness as a basic trait in economic life is hardly Christian, nor is it even good economics. The social responsibility of capital, labor, and the farming community is a fundamental point of sound ethics. Economics also testifies to the disruptive force of selfish tactics, especially when they are reinforced by monopoly powers.

The work of reform is committed to all classes of society. In one sense, the state, as the supreme social group, should take the lead in seeking to reform social institutions. The common good is its very reason of being. But at the same time, the state itself may often be in need of reform. In modern times, it has reacted from a *laissez-faire* individualism, where it stood by impotently in the face of great injustice, to some approximation of statism, where it absorbed powers which should be committed to lesser groups. The state best seeks social justice by aiding subordinate groups to perfect institutions which bring about harmonious and prosperous economic life. Other groups in turn, inspired by Christian principles, should endeavor to correct evils in their spheres of action, and to direct their aims in the light of justice and charity. Thus we would achieve a basic reorientation of society.

Clearly this is an immense task. But it is made easier by the fact that other alternatives are being rejected. In much of the world, the old order has been cast aside. But some of the newer forms, such as communism, are worse than those which they supplanted. As extremes are shown to be unsound, men are bound to respect the moderation and sanity of the Christian social ethic. If we can formulate it in detail, and show its applicability to a complex society, it may well be received as were the first good tidings of the Gospel.

READINGS *

J. Messner, *Social Ethics*, pp. 1–122, 188, 207, 222–226, 908–911.
G. Clune, *Christian Social Reorganization*, Chaps. 10–12.
E. Cahill, *Framework of a Christian State*, Chaps. 16, 17, 23.
R. Kothen, *L'Enseignement social de l'Église*, Chap. 3.
H. F. Trehey, *Foundations of a Modern Guild System*, Chap. 2.
Kerby Foundation: *Democracy, Should It Survive?*

---

* For further readings, see Lists Nos. 1 and 4 in the Appendix.

Chapter IV. THE SOCIAL VIRTUES

JUSTICE

Commutative Justice

Pius XI, Quadragesimo Anno

47. That justice called commutative commands sacred respect for the division of possessions and forbids invasion of others' rights through the exceeding of the limits of one's own property; but the duty of owners to use their property only in a right way does not come under this type of justice, but under other virtues, obligations of which "cannot be enforced by legal action."

110. . . . the twofold character, that is individual and social, both of capital or ownership and of work or labor must be given due and rightful weight. Relations of one to the other must be made to conform to the laws of strictest justice — commutative justice, as it is called, with the support, however, of Christian charity.

Pius XI, On Atheistic Communism

31. . . . the salary due in strict justice to the worker for himself and for his family.

Pius XII, Sertum Laetitiae

37. Now if the rich and prosperous are obliged out of ordinary motives of pity to act generously toward the poor, their obligation is all the greater to do them justice. The salaries of the workers, as is just, are to be such that they are sufficient to maintain them and their families.

Distributive Justice

Leo XIII, Rerum Novarum

49. Consequently, among the numerous and weighty duties of rulers who would serve their people well, this is first and foremost, namely, that they protect equitably each and every class of citizens, maintaining inviolate that justice especially which is called distributive.

Pius XI, Quadragesimo Anno

25. The function of the rulers of the state, moreover, is to watch over the community and its parts; but in protecting private individuals in their rights, chief consideration ought to be given to the weak and the poor.

Pius XII, Address to Catholic Employers, May 7, 1949

It would be just as untrue to assert that every particular business is of its nature a society, with its personal relationships determined by the norms of distributive justice to the point where all without distinction — owners or not of the means of production — would be entitled to their share in the property, or at the very least in the profits, of the enterprise. Such a conception stems from the assumption that every business belongs naturally within the sphere of public law. The assumption is inexact. Whether the business is organized in the form of a corporation or an association of all the workmen as part owners, or whether it is the private property of an individual who signs a wage contract with all his employees, in the one case as in the other it falls within the competence of the private-law discipline of economic life.

Social Justice — The Common Good

Leo XIII, Immortale Dei

22. Nevertheless, as We have laid down, to take no share in public matters would be equally as wrong (We speak in general) as not to have concern for, or not to bestow labor upon, the common good.

Leo XIII, Rerum Novarum

14. . . . however the earth may be apportioned among private owners, it does not cease to serve the common good of all. . . .

48. For the state is bound by the very law of its office to serve the common interest.

50. . . . all citizens, without exception, are obliged to contribute something to the sum-total common good.

52. It is not right, as We have said, for either the citizen or the family to be absorbed by the state; it is proper that the individual and the family should be permitted to retain their freedom of action so far as this is possible without jeopardizing the common good and without injuring anyone.

Pius XI, Quadragesimo Anno

25. . . . Just freedom of action must, of course, be left both to individual citizens and their families, yet only on condition that the common good be preserved and wrong to any individual be abolished.

49. It follows from what We have termed the individual and at the same time social character of ownership, that men must consider in this matter not only their own advantage but also the common good.

57. Therefore, the riches that economic-social developments constantly increase ought to be so distributed among individual persons and classes that the common advantage of all, which Leo XIII had praised, will be safeguarded; in other words that the common good of all society will be kept inviolate. By this law of social justice, one class is forbidden to exclude the other from sharing in the benefits.

58. To each, therefore, must be given his own share of goods, and the distribution of created goods, which, as every discerning person knows, is laboring today under the gravest evils due to the huge disparity between the few exceedingly rich and the unnumbered propertyless, must be effectively called back to and brought into conformity with the norms of the common good, that is, social justice.

71. Every effort must therefore be made that fathers of families receive a wage large enough to meet ordinary family needs adequately. But if this cannot always be done under existing circumstances, social justice demands that changes be introduced as soon as possible whereby such a wage will be assured to every adult workingman.

74. Hence it is contrary to social justice when, for the sake of personal gain and without regard for the common good, wages and salaries are excessively lowered or raised; and this same social justice demands that wages and salaries be so managed, through agreement of plans and wills, insofar as can be done, as to offer to the greatest possible number the opportunity of getting work and obtaining suitable means of livelihood.

84. That common good, to achieve which all Industries and Professions together ought, each to the best of its ability, to co-operate amicably.

85. The most important among these interests is to promote the co-operation in the highest degree of each industry and profession for the sake of the common good of the country.

88. Loftier and nobler principles — social justice and social charity — must, therefore, be sought whereby this dictatorship may be governed firmly and fully. Hence, the institutions themselves of peoples and, par-

ticularly, those of all social life, ought to be penetrated with this justice, and it is most necessary that it be truly effective, that is, establish a juridical and social order which will, as it were, give form and shape to all economic life.

101. But it does violate right order when capital hires workers, that is the nonowning class, with a view to and under such terms that it directs business and even the whole economic system according to its own will and advantage, scorning the human dignity of the workers, the social character of economic activity and social justice itself, and the common **good.**

110. The public institutions of themselves, of peoples, moreover, ought to make all human society conform to the needs of the common good; that is, to the norm of social justice.

Pius XI, On Atheistic Communism

51. In reality, besides commutative justice, there is also social justice with its own set obligations, from which neither employers nor workingmen can escape. Now it is of the very essence of social justice to demand from each individual all that is necessary for the common good. But just as in the living organism it is impossible to provide for the good of the whole unless each single part and each individual member is given what it needs for the exercise of its proper functions, so it is impossible to care for the social organism and the good of society as a unit unless each single part and each individual member — that is to say, each individual man in the dignity of his human personality — is supplied with all that is necessary for the exercise of his social functions. If social justice be satisfied, the result will be an intense activity in economic life as a whole, pursued in tranquillity and order. This activity will be proof of the health of the social body, just as the health of the human body is recognized in the undisturbed regularity and perfect efficiency of the whole organism.

53. It happens all too frequently, however, under the salary system, that individual employers are helpless to insure justice unless, with a view to its practice, they organize institutions the object of which is to prevent competition incompatible with fair treatment for the workers. Where this is true, it is the duty of contractors and employers to support and promote such necessary organizations as normal instruments enabling them to fulfill their obligations of justice.

54. If, therefore, We consider the whole structure of economic life, as We have already pointed out in Our Encyclical *Quadragesimo Anno,*

the reign of mutual collaboration between justice and charity in social-economic relations can only be achieved by a body of professional and interprofessional organizations, built on solidly Christian foundations, working together to effect, under forms adapted to different places and circumstances, what has been called the Corporation.

Pius XII, La Solennità della Pentecoste

1685. Hence, it follows that the care of such a common good does not imply a power so extensive over the members of the community that in virtue of it the public authority can interfere with the evolution of that individual activity which We have just described, decide directly on the beginning or — excepting the case of legitimate capital punishment — the ending of human life, determine at will the manner of his physical, spiritual, religious, and moral movements in opposition to the personal duties or rights of man, and to this end abolish or deprive of efficacy his natural rights to material goods. To deduce such extension of power from the care of the common good would be equivalent to overthrowing the very meaning of the word common good, and falling into the error that the proper scope of man on earth is society, that society is an end in itself, that man has no other life which awaits him beyond that which ends here below.

Pius XII, Christmas Broadcast, 1942

1833. The whole political and economic activity of the state is directed to the permanent realization of the common good.

Pius XII, Summi Pontificatus

1419. Hence, it is the noble prerogative and function of the state to control, aid, and direct the private and individual activities of national life that they converge harmoniously toward the common good.

Code of Social Principles

160. Along with commutative justice which governs contracts and distributive justice which regulates social burdens and benefits, due place must be given to social and legal justice. This relates to the common good, of which authority has the care and which each individual member of the social body is bound to serve and enrich. The individual, as the beneficiary of the common good, is in some measure its guardian, although it is the rulers who are primarily responsible.

Social justice should permeate the institutions and the entire life of the people. Its efficacy should be especially manifest in the creation of a legal and social order which informs the entire economic life.

St. Thomas Aquinas, Summa Theologica

The common good is the end of each individual member of a community, just as the good of the whole is the end of each part (II, II, 58, 9, ad 3).

The good of the individual is subordinate to the good of the many (II, II, 47, 11, ad 3).

The common good . . . and the particular good of the individual differ not only in respect of the many and the few, but also under a formal aspect (II, II, 58, 7, ad 2).

The common good takes precedence over the private good if it be of the same genus (II, II, 152, 4, ad 3; *see also*, I, II, 113, 9, ad 2).

Every law is directed toward the common good . . . any command toward a particular object does not have legal effect, except insofar as it is directed toward the common good (I, II, 90, 2).

The common good is to be preferred to private good (II, II, 32, 6).

Right reason . . . judges that the common good is better than the good of an individual (II, II, 47, 10).

He who seeks the common good of the many consequently seeks his own good as well . . . private good cannot exist without the common good of the family, or the city, or the state (*ibid.*, ad 2).

Among human goods, the public good is pre-eminent over private good (II, II, 117, 6).

SOCIAL CHARITY

Leo XIII, Graves de Communi

11. By the law of mutual charity, which, as it were, completes the law of justice, we are bidden not only to give their due to all and interfere with the rights of none, but also to practice kindnesses one to another "not in word nor in tongue, but in deed and in truth" (*1 John* iii, 18), remembering what Christ most lovingly said to His disciples: "A new commandment I give unto you, that you love one another, as I have loved you, that you also love one another. By this shall all men know that you are my disciples, if you have love for one another" (*John* xiii, 34, 35). Such zeal in the performance of deeds of charity, though it ought to be first of all solicitous about the eternal good of souls, should nevertheless not neglect what is good and useful for this life. And in this regard it is worthy of note that Christ, when asked by the disciples of the Baptist: "Art thou he that is to come, or look we for another?" singled out His works of charity to bear evidence to the office entrusted to Him among mankind, recalling the words of Isaiah: "The blind see, the lame walk, the lepers are cleansed, the deaf hear, the dead rise again,

and the poor have the gospel preached to them" (*Matt.* xi, 5). So, again, in reference to the last judgment and the rewards and punishments to be then adjudged, He declared that He would examine in particular the charity men had practiced toward one another. It is indeed wonderful how in this discourse Christ left unmentioned that aspect of compassion which ministers to the soul and spoke only of the offices of bodily compassion, and of these as rendered to Himself: "I was hungry, and you gave me to eat; I was thirsty, and you gave me to drink; I was a stranger, and you took me in; sick, and you visited me; I was in prison, and you came to me" (*ibid.*, xxv, 35, 36).

Leo XIII, Rerum Novarum

83. Certainly, the well-being which is so longed for is chiefly to be expected from an abundant outpouring of charity; of Christian charity, We mean, which is in epitome the law of the Gospel, and which, always ready to sacrifice itself for the benefit of others, is man's surest antidote against the insolence of the world and immoderate love of self; the divine office and features of this virtue being described by the Apostle Paul in these words: "Charity is patient, is kind . . . is not self-seeking . . . bears with all things . . . endures all things."

Pius XI, Quadragesimo Anno

4. Quite agreeable, of course, was this state of things to those who thought it in their abundant riches the result of inevitable economic laws and accordingly, as if it were for charity to veil the violation of justice which lawmakers not only tolerated but at times sanctioned, wanted the whole care of supporting the poor committed to charity alone.

88. Social charity, moreover, ought to be as the soul of this order, an order which public authority ought to be ever ready effectively to protect and defend. It will be able to do this the more easily as it rids itself of those burdens which, as We have stated above, are not properly its own.

90. If the members of the body social are, as was said, reconstituted, and if the directing principle of economic-social life is restored, it will be possible to say in a certain sense even of this body what the Apostle says of the mystical body of Christ: "The whole body (being closely joined and knit together through every joint of the system according to the functioning in due measure of each single part) derives its increase to the building up of itself in love."

137. But in effecting all this, the law of charity, "which is the bond of perfection," must always take a leading role. How completely deceived, therefore, are those rash reformers who concern themselves with the

enforcement of justice alone — and this, commutative justice — and in their pride reject the assistance of Charity! Admittedly, no vicarious charity can substitute for justice which is due as an obligation and is wrongfully denied. Yet even supposing that everyone should finally receive all that is due him, the widest field for charity will always remain open. For justice alone can, if faithfully observed, remove the causes of social conflict but can never bring about union of minds and hearts. Indeed all the institutions for the establishment of peace and the promotion of mutual help among men, however perfect these may seem, have the principal foundation of their stability in the mutual bond of minds and hearts whereby the members are united with one another. If this bond is lacking, the best of regulations come to naught, as we have learned by too frequent experience. And so, then only will true co-operation be possible for a single common good when the constituent parts of society deeply feel themselves members of one great family and children of the same Heavenly Father; nay, that they are one body in Christ, "but severally members one of another," so that "if one member suffers anything, all the members suffer with it." For then the rich and others in positions of power will change their former indifference toward their poorer brothers into a solicitous and active love, listen with kindliness to their just demands, and freely forgive their possible mistakes and faults. And the workers, sincerely putting aside every feeling of hatred or envy which the promoters of social conflict so cunningly exploit, will not only accept without rancor the place in human society assigned them by Divine Providence, but rather will hold it in esteem, knowing well that everyone according to his function and duty is toiling usefully and honorably for the common good and is following closely in the footsteps of Him, who, being in the form of God, willed to be a carpenter among men and be known as the son of a carpenter.

Pius XI, On Atheistic Communism

46. Still more important as a remedy for the evil we are considering, or certainly more directly calculated to cure it, is the precept of charity. We have in mind that Christian charity, "patient and kind," which avoids all semblance of demeaning paternalism, and all ostentation; that charity which from the very beginning of Christianity won to Christ the poorest of the poor, the slaves. And We are grateful to all those members of charitable associations, from the conferences of St. Vincent de Paul to the recent great relief organizations, which are perseveringly practicing the spiritual and corporal works of mercy. The more the workingman and the poor realize what the spirit of love animated by the virtue of Christ is doing for them, the more readily will they abandon the

false persuasion that Christianity has lost its efficacy and that the Church stands on the side of the exploiters of their labor.

47. But when on the one hand We see thousands of the needy, victims of real misery for various reasons beyond their control, and on the other so many round about them who spend huge sums of money on useless things and frivolous amusement, We cannot fail to remark with sorrow not only that justice is poorly observed, but that the precept of charity also is not sufficiently appreciated, is not a vital thing in daily life.

48. There is a divine regenerating force in this "new precept" (as Christ called it) of Christian charity. Its faithful observance will pour into the heart an inner peace which the world knows not, and will finally cure the ills which oppress humanity.

49. But charity will never be true charity unless it takes justice into constant account. A "charity" which deprives the workingman of the salary to which he has a strict title in justice, is not charity at all, but only its empty name and hollow semblance. The wage earner is not to receive as alms what is his due in justice. And let no one attempt with trifling charitable donations to exempt himself from the great duties imposed by justice. Both justice and charity often dictate obligations touching on the same subject matter, but under different aspects; and the very dignity of the workingman makes him justly and acutely sensitive to the duties of others in his regard.

54. . . . . the reign of mutual collaboration between justice and charity. . . .

Pius XII, Summi Pontificatus

1437. . . . the re-education of mankind must be, above all things, spiritual and religious. Hence, it must proceed from Christ as from its indispensable foundation; must be actuated by justice and crowned by charity.

The Church and Social Order

63. Unfortunately there has been a tendency among too many to dissociate the virtue of justice from the virtue of charity, with the result that life has been made even more selfish and heartless. Charity is no substitute for justice, but it cannot be ignored or derided without failing utterly to comprehend its meaning and its potent influence in regulating and sublimating our social relations and responsibilities. We need justice without doubt or equivocation, but we also need charity if we are to put our lives in harmony with God's plan and promote that spirit of benevolence which will lift the burdens not only from the backs but also from the souls of men.

Code of Social Principles

161. But justice is far from exhausting the whole of one's duty toward others. Over and above its requirements, there is a limitless field for that brotherly love which men owe to each other as sons of the same Heavenly Father and descendants of the first parents; a field of initiative and personal sacrifice for the common good. Charity thus finds a most important part to play in economic life. . . .

As for social charity, it ought to be the soul of that legal and social order, which is the care of the public authorities and which ought to inform the entire economic life, as has been said above.

SUBSIDIARY VIRTUES

Pius XI, Quadragesimo Anno

47. . . . . the duty of owners to use their property only in a right way does come under this type of justice [commutative], but under other virtues, obligations of which "cannot be enforced by legal action."

50. The Sacred Scriptures and the Fathers of the Church constantly declare in the most explicit language that the rich are bound by a very grave precept to practice almsgiving, beneficence, and munificence.

When the Church confronts the social problem, she acts through moral teaching, not through political or economic means. Her purpose is to teach individuals sound principles, which they will put into effect in the practical order. Men of good will, imbued with these teachings, are to reform the institutions of society in accordance with God's will.

The first level of Church teaching concerns the dignity of man, his place in society, and the purpose of economic life. We realize that, under God, man is the center of the world. Material things are created to serve him. Man in turn is a social creature. He realizes his full powers and aspirations only in conjunction with his fellow man. When these principles are applied to economic life, it is evident that economic society should be organized to minister to the dignity of man. Its institutions, that is, enduring social habits, should be organized in view of the general welfare.

On the second level of Church teaching in the socioeconomic field, we find the social virtues. These are habits of action which respect the dignity of the human person, the nature of society, and the purposes of economic society. The most important of these virtues are justice and charity, although there are others which complete and perfect social life. When these virtues are observed, men act in accordance with God's law and the soundest rules for human nature.

JUSTICE

Kinds of Justice. Justice ministers directly to human dignity, since it is concerned with the rights and duties of persons. It could be called a constant habit or intention of giving each person his due. It involves a relationship of equality between two persons, in virtue of which one is bound to give the other his due. Accordingly, in treating of justice, we might distinguish three elements: equality, otherness, and something due.

The fact of equality is based on the dignity of the human person, since persons alone have rights. We are bound to respect the human nature of others and the rights which accrue to that nature. Again, there is the aspect of otherness. In contrast to such virtues as temperance or fortitude, which perfect the individual alone, justice involves a relationship with other persons. Finally, and this is the distinctive element in justice, there is the idea of something due. Justice is the respecting of rights, not merely proprieties or things that are fitting. Thus, it may be fitting or desirable that a wealthy man endow a particular hospital or university. But he is bound in justice to pay his chauffeur a living wage.

We ordinarily speak of three kinds of justice. The first is general or legal justice, which calls for giving society its due. Under this virtue we are bound to consider the common good as well as our particular aims in all our actions. Some writers do not consider legal justice as a strict virtue, in the sense that it commands us to do certain acts which are proper to it alone. Rather, according to their point of view, it gives an overtone and direction to other virtues, directing their exercise in the light of the general welfare. Thus, almsgiving is commanded under the virtue of charity, but in helping the unfortunate legal justice binds us to consider the common good. Legal justice would incline us to one form of charity in preference to another. Other authors, however, do speak of specific actions commanded by legal justice in its own right. This is particularly true of the aspect of legal justice which is called social justice. Whichever view is held, legal justice involves the duties of the individual in regard to the community. He is obliged to seek the common good.

In contrast to general justice are the more particular forms of this virtue, called distributive and commutative justice. Distributive justice deals with the obligations of the community and its leaders toward the individual members. It calls for an equitable and proportional distribution of benefits and burdens to the members of society. Thus, legislators must be fair in giving out benefits (such as social insurance) or burdens (such as taxes). A father must be equitable in treating his children. Equity in such cases does not necessarily mean equality, since the needs of one may be greater than those of another. The socialist maxim: "From each according to his ability, to each according to his needs," is a fair approximation of distributive justice. If we could use mechanical terms to apply to virtues, we might say that the direction of flow is reversed when one compares legal and distributive justice. The one involves the individual's duty to society; the other, the rights of the person in connection with a given society.

Finally, there is strict justice, called commutative justice, which involves clearly defined rights and duties between two or more persons. It might be called exchange justice, since it usually embodies the idea of a *quid pro quo*. In this case, equality between the persons is definite in regard to the debt in question. Furthermore, the word "persons" could mean a moral person as well as an individual. If Mr. Jones buys a car from a large corporation, he owes a strict debt for the price of the car. Even the societies considered under the headings of legal and distributive justice can be parties to an obligation in commutative justice. A government could sell property or a son could enter into a binding contract with his father. Here the societal relationship does not enter into the obligation. Hence we might define commutative justice as a relation of equality between two fully distinct persons in virtue of which each is bound to render the other his due.

Each of these forms of the virtue has important implications in regard to the social problem. There are cases in which strict justice is involved. In some instances one person is clearly defrauding another. In other situations, society enters in, as either the subject of a right or of a duty. Unfortunately, the full problem of justice has been too often overlooked. In the past, there has been a tendency to concentrate only upon strict or commutative justice, and even this has been defined much too narrowly. More recently, there has been some recognition of the need for distributive justice as applied to the social problem. It remained for Pope Pius XI to define clearly and apply fully the virtue of social justice, although he did not originate the term. Accordingly, it is necessary to note in some detail the social aspects of each type of justice.

Commutative Justice. When strict justice is considered, we have a definite obligation, clearly defined, between two or more persons, including moral persons. A good noncontroversial example would be a debt. When Mr. Jones borrows two hundred dollars from a finance company to buy a washing machine, he is obliged in justice to repay this sum of money. If he willfully fails to do so, he sins. He can be forgiven only if he promises to make restitution, provided he is morally able to do this. The same situation would apply when he is charged a fair price for services, such as doctors' or dentists' bills. An element of equality and debt is involved; he has received something and promised to repay its equal value.

Two of the most publicized social teachings in the Middle Ages rested upon strict justice, namely, the doctrines of usury and the just price. In the example of borrowing from the finance company, we noted Mr. Jones's obligation to repay the principal in full. Medieval theologians would not acknowledge the full interest payment as being due in justice. They held that equality was served when the principal was restored, and that any charge for the use of money as such was an unfair exaction. In the actual interest payment to the finance company, part would be allowed by these theologians, such as collection charges and insurance for risk. But they held money as such to be nonproductive (in contrast to land, property, or a business) and hence any charge for its use (in absence of loss to the lender as a result of the loan) to be unjust. Modern theologians hold a different view, considering money the virtual equivalent of productive capital and hence entitled to a return. Even when the loan is not for productive purposes, there is the possibility that the lender could have used it for such ends, so that he is incurring a loss by making the loan.

In the matter of the just price, the seller and buyer should consider the fair value of the object. Any raising or lowering of price, simply to take advantage of another's need, would be contrary to justice. In medieval writings, value was determined either by authority or the common estimate of a reasonable charge. This would include fair wages for the workers, an equitable price to suppliers, and a suitable profit for the seller. The norm for estimating equity for these factors would make allowance for the dignity of the human person, the technical state of economic life, and the demands of the common good. Market value, as determined under conditions of competition, monopoly, or in-between situations would not necessarily be the same as a fair value.

The value of the just-price teaching under modern conditions is somewhat limited. There are clear cases where it applies. Such would be instances of fraud, deception, or obvious exploitation of the need of another. The fraudulent issuance of securities or the selling of a virtually useless product (through deception) would be definitely unjust. The abusing of a monopoly position by charging what the market will bear in the effort to secure exorbitant profits would likewise violate strict justice. On the other hand, the major social problems of today spring primarily from faulty institutions of society. Economic society may be so organized that an individual is forced into practices which are materially unjust. Thus, under competition, a manufacturer may be compelled to beat down his suppliers by paying unfair prices. The alternative would be to go out of business. To say that he should go out of business in such cases would be to deprive the economic community of leaders who have sensitive consciences (the others would pay no attention to moralists). A more realistic solution would be to invoke social justice, that is, the obligation to change the institutions of society so that they would foster justice.

A more modern example of theological application of commutative justice to economic life is the obligation to pay a living wage. Pope Pius XI has stated that the duty to pay the worker a wage which will afford decent support to himself and his family is a matter of strict justice. It is true that some theologians still argue that the duty is a matter of social rather than commutative justice. Accepting the majority view, however, that strict justice is involved, we are confronted again with a mixed problem. There are cases where employers can pay a living wage without excessive hardship. But in very many instances, the situation involves the recurring question of economic institutions. Only by a better organization of economic society will it be possible for many employers to pay a decent wage. We must use to the full our technical resources and managerial skill to turn out the products needed for a comfortable standard of living for all workers.

In summary, it would be inaccurate to say that strict justice has no place in solving the social problem. On the contrary, there are many and important instances where it applies. Nevertheless, there are even more vital issues where the broader approach of social justice is needed. Individual good will and rectitude are not enough to solve the pressing problems of insecurity and disorganization in economic life. Society itself is sick, and remedies should be sought which will get to the root of social ills.

Distributive Justice. In the traditional usage, the term distributive justice was applied to rulers of states. It obliged them to secure for each citizen his due and proportionate share of both the advantages and the burdens which are involved in the conduct of civil society. The older theologians talked of the fair distribution of public offices, on the one hand, and of taxes on the other. A more modern example would be social legislation or public subsidies. Benefits thus distributed are not given on a basis of arithmetical equality, but rather in consideration of need and other special circumstances. Thus, a federal subsidy for education which would be based only on the tax contributions of the states would be self-defeating. The states which were able to pay the most taxes would be least in need of subsidies. In this regard, Pope Leo XIII stated that governments should look out especially for the needs of the poor, since the rich can often take care of themselves.

More recently, the idea of distributive justice has been applied to other societies than the state. Thus, the masterly volume by the late Monsignor John A. Ryan, *Distributive Justice,* dealt with the fair distribution of the products of industry to the factors involved in production. The reasoning of the eminent author dealt mainly with the equitable sharing of the benefits of modern industry. This was particularly noticeable in his rating of relative claims to the national product, where he valued considerations of need and human dignity above the claims of imputed productivity. Another illustration could be found in the canons of taxation, where the fact of ability to pay was considered decisive. A system of progressively higher rates of income taxes for those with larger income could well be in accord with distributive justice.

In both the narrow and the broad usages, distributive justice is pertinent to the solution of the social problem. Benefits distributed by the state can be very important in modern economic life. Examples of this would be subsidies for low-cost housing; subsidies for farmers or high-cost producers of needed goods; justified tariffs; distribution of social insurance benefits in view of needs as well as contributions; contributions for public hospitals in rural areas; and grants to special groups, such as reasonable pensions for soldiers. The same observation applies to the sharing of burdens. On the basis of distributive justice, it is fair that the wealthy should pay proportionately higher taxes than the poor. Taxes on luxuries would be more equitable than taxes on necessities. In these cases, it is to be noted that distributive justice seeks, not directly the common good of society, but rather the proportionate sharing among the members of society of the benefits and burdens included in the common good. In fact it is conceivable that a practice favored by distributive justice might not be prudent in the light of the common good. Thus, in a period of inflation caused by an excessive money supply, the common good might demand a tax policy with a broad base, rather than one concentrated on those most able to pay. In such a case, social justice, which seeks the common good, would take precedence.

In the broad use of distributive justice, it is likewise applicable to modern problems. Distribution of the product of industry should consider needs as well as contribution. Thus, on the basis of strict justice, the claims of a bondholder and a wage earner might be equally sound. But distributive justice would favor the worker, as having the greater need. An even better example derives from the progressive increases in living standards afforded the American worker during the last fifty years. This happened in spite of the fact that, on the whole, he works for less hours and expends less energy per hour of work than was the case at the turn of the century. The reason for the difference is primarily the increased mechanization of industry, or the increase in the amount of capital invested per worker. Yet, in many instances, the worker has benefited proportionately more than the investor. During the past fifty years, the real wages of the average worker have increased threefold, although he works less hours. At the same time, the real return per dollar invested has remained stationary or declined. Such a situation might well be sanctioned by distributive justice, however, in view of the needs of the worker and his human dignity. The increase was bringing him up to living standards which were his due as a human person, whereas the average investor already possessed comfortable living conditions.

At the same time, great caution should be used in applying the canons of distributive justice to private industry. In the strict sense of the term, distributive justice pertains to government and indicates the duties of the sovereign. It concerns the equitable distribution of things which belong to the community. In the case of tax money, for example, the funds to be dispensed are owned by the citizens. Obviously these same principles could not be applied to a private fortune, owned by an individual. Nor is it clear that they can be used in the case of business profits, considered abstractly. Thus, if an owner paid a fair wage to workers and charged consumers a just price (both matters of commutative justice), it would not seem that distributive justice could be applied to his use of the resultant profits. The present Holy Father has warned against indiscriminate application of distributive justice to private spheres. It may well be that many Catholic moralists have erred in this respect. If this is true, it does not necessarily follow that their conclusions are invalid. Undoubtedly in many cases, a re-examination of problems in terms of social justice and the common good will lead to the same conclusions, this time based on a sounder foundation.

Granting the real value of distributive justice, it is still an ineffectual weapon for a complete conquest of the social problem. It deals with distribution of the products of the existing civil and industrial system. But it may well be true that the existing system is structurally inadequate. A fair distribution of an insufficient national product could only mean an alleviation of extreme poverty, not an advance to good standards for all. Measures which aim merely at equalizing incomes, lowering the number of hours worked per week (when they are not currently excessive), and the like would fall under this indictment of insufficiency. Indeed, if a broad historical generalization might be permitted, this was one of the major gaps in the Roosevelt New Deal. There was an emphasis upon distributive justice, which was good so far at it went. But the vision of social justice, which would lead to a thorough reorganization of economic society for the common good, was not always clearly seen.

Even Catholic writers, fortified by the wisdom of *Quadragesimo Anno,* have been slow to capture the powerful dynamism of social justice. Older works treat of the social problem mainly in terms of strict justice. More recent treatises have given play to the implications of distributive justice. But the one is too narrow and the other too vague to serve as the exclusive bases of a social ethic. Furthermore, neither reaches to the root of the problem, the disorganization of society. The basis for a total solution can be found only in the works of that strong and fearless apostle of social justice, Pope Pius XI. Without social justice, we are seeking to remedy symptoms, while leaving untouched the basic causes of social ills. This point simply cannot be overstressed.

Social Justice: Definition. Legal justice has been defined as the virtue binding every member of the state to contribute his due share to safeguarding and promoting the common good. It applies to rulers as well as subjects, obligating each to do his part for the general welfare. This concept was broadened and clarified when Pope Pius XI gave his description of social justice.

Social justice deals with reciprocal rights and duties of social groups and their members in relation to the common good. It might be described as the obligation upon individuals to participate, according to their ability and position, in *group action,* designed to make the *institutions of society* conform to the *common good* in the socioeconomic sphere. The italicized phrases indicate the important aspects of social justice: organization, institutions, and the common good.

The theoretical aspects of social justice, particularly in relation to legal and distributive justice, are subject to considerable controversy. Some writers consider it a fully distinct virtue, with its own material and formal aspects, inasmuch as it organizes individuals for the common good. Other authors hold that it is merely a special form of legal justice, with no distinct material object, but merely the formal aspect of directing actions toward the common good. The great German Jesuit, Heinrich Pesch, speaks of contributive and distributive social justice, thus making distributive justice but one phase of social justice. No effort is made here to resolve these theoretical questions, especially since there is fairly wide agreement as to the practical implications of social justice. The following analysis emphasizes aspects of social justice stressed in *Quadragesimo Anno*.[1]

Social Justice: Organization. The first significant contribution in the notion of social justice is the idea of organized effort. Commutative justice deals largely with individuals. Distributive justice applies to existing organizations, especially the state; it does not necessarily deal with new ones. But social justice can call for the forming of new groups, as well as the proper directing of existing ones.

It is necessary to face frankly the relative impotence of the isolated individual in modern life. Giving due credit to the power of example and leadership, it nevertheless happens that this is an organized age, particularly in the economic sphere. Markets are often national and international. Giant corporations dominate over vital phases of industrial life. Huge labor unions set the pace for labor policies. When the individual is confronted with such power situations, he is virtually helpless. To make himself felt, he must generally act as a member of a group.

There is nothing inherently wrong in this penchant for organization. On the contrary, it fits in with man's social nature. Cooperative effort is the logical way to get great tasks done. Hence any social reform program which aims to restore man's freedom by breaking up all power organizations and atomizing society into a mass of isolated individuals is foredoomed to failure. It is essentially anarchic. Existing groupings may be unsound. There

---

[1] One of the most recent studies of the problem is *La Giustizia Sociale* by A. Brucculeri (Rome: La Civiltà Cattolica, 1948). Father Brucculeri holds that social justice is not really distinct from legal justice. A different position is advocated by W. Ferree in *The Act of Social Justice* (Washington: Catholic University of America, 1942) and J. Messner in his article "Soziale Gerechtigkeit" in *Staatslexikon* (Freiburg in B.: Herder, 1931). Pesch's position is given in his *Lehrbuch der Nationalökonomie* (Freiburg in B.: Herder, 1905), I, p. 165, and II, pp. 272–275. The present treatment follows Ferree and Messner.

is definite need for more buffer groups and a greater decentralization of power in the interests of individual freedom. All this would restore the proper balance, so as to make society serve man rather than rule him. But the answer is sounder organization, not no organization.

The need for organized effort has been implied in several of the analyses given earlier. Thus, we noted the individual employer, given unrestricted competition, is often helpless in the matter of setting just prices. He follows the market practice or goes out of business. The same is true when the question of a living wage arises. It is true that some employers have been able to fight existing trends. By a combination of exceptional managerial skill and higher productivity arising from the good will of their workers, they have been able to pay more than the going rate of wages. But, in general, the individual acting alone cannot do the task.

Even if, to visualize the improbable, all employers and all workers practiced commutative and distributive justice to the full, the social problem would not be solved. Society would still lack organization designed to use natural resources and technical skill so as to insure the utmost production. Some major defects in economic life, such as insecurity and depressions, would not be met. Hence the theory, often expressed, that if all employers had sound human-relations programs, there would be no need for labor unions, is radically incomplete. It is individualism on a higher plane. It does not tackle the broader problems of modern business. Because of this, some moralists even argue that in present-day American society, all workers have an obligation to belong to a labor union or a comparable organization. Such an argument is not without merit.

This aspect of social justice is directly contrary to the individualism honored in theory if not always in practice by American business. The theory of atomistic individualism is that competitive strivings of isolated units will lead each to do his best. This in turn will lead, in the aggregate, to maximum output at highest quality and lowest price. In practice, it has often dragged the mass down to the level of the most unscrupulous competitor. The actual groupings of both businessmen and workers show that pure individualism contradicts man's social nature. Business and labor have both been forced to organize.

Yet, these existing forms of organized economic life in America are inadequate. After the era of nineteenth-century individualism, first we had business concentration, then a building up of the powers of the state, and lastly powerful groupings of labor, farmers, and like classes. At times their tendency has been to seek control of the state and through its power to effect needed changes. While legislation is a vital part of social reform, present trends have submerged the individual in powerful groups which he cannot effectively control. As was noted above, organized action is necessary and, at times, this action must be on an extensive scale. But the use of wide powers can be effectively controlled only if there exists a multitude of lesser groups, also having real power, which serve as a buffer between the individual and giant power groups. Hence social legislation and joint action by national organizations are but partial answers to the problem.

In fine, most socioeconomic problems can be met only by organized action. This is demanded by the nature of the problems and man's social nature. But societies exist to serve and protect individual human dignity. Hence they must be of such a nature that they do not get out of hand and become laws unto themselves.

Social Justice: Institutions of Society. Organization is but a first step. If the present tone of society were basically good, it might be enough to have suitable groups to utilize its resources. But, unfortunately, we cannot be complacent about our social medium. Too often it works adversely to the aims of social justice. The moral atmosphere of the day still tends toward selfish individualism.

Basic to this analysis is a view on the influence of environment. Experience has shown that the collective pressures generated by the thousands of forces which constitute a social situation have an enormous effect upon individuals. Customs, styles, habits, and even prevailing points of view often have the force of law. An obvious example is style in clothes. The ideal dress or hat is one that is pleasantly different within a framework of generally accepted lines. Provided there is basic conformity, there is a place for minor expressions of individuality. But the limits of individual freedom are relatively narrow. Convention and custom are all powerful for most persons. In every society there are a few strong individualists who can defy custom, but such persons are in a minority. The great majority of mankind conforms to the customs of its group.

Beyond the level of custom, there are even more rigid patterns which we call institutions. An institution might be described as a relatively stable social pattern which governs actions in a given medium. In this sense, we could call civil society, the Church, the family, the neighborhood, or one of the learned professions institutions. They are groups with fairly fixed laws influencing and even governing the actions of individual members of the group. The life of the individual is affected by scores of institutions impinging upon every phase of his life. Even informal groups, such as a "gang" of boys or a social set, can have rigid codes to which members must conform. The nonconformist is usually ostracized, a penalty which is quite severe for most people.

In the economic sphere, there are similar pressures. Some are informal and almost intangible, constituting the general atmosphere of life. Businessmen in any community have a common loyalty which expresses itself in certain conventions. Professional men have their "codes of ethics," which as often express proprieties and customs as strict ethical obligations. Workers in a factory develop a body of custom which they enforce in an informal but highly effective manner. All these influences add up to a tone of society which may be good or bad, but which is usually controlling upon the individual.

The more formal institutions of economic life are practices and customs so widely accepted that they are often considered as economic law. For example, the philosophy of individualism which prevailed in the eighteenth and nineteenth centuries was profoundly influential. It expressed itself in unregulated competition in business and a *laissez-faire* attitude of government in the face of social abuses. It led to a pattern of business organization — some would call it disorganization — which deeply affected the whole economic community. When individualism was replaced by a trend toward concentration in the twentieth century, new patterns were set up. But their influence was equally great. They forced conformity upon unwilling businessmen and led to titanic struggles with labor which was challenging the dictatorial power of industry and finance.

Those who are interested in the reform of society must assess accurately the influence of customs and institutions. In the first place, the great majority of persons in any group are usually unwilling to challenge the social pattern of their community. They do not have the moral strength to be nonconformists. Hence any effort to bring about social reform merely by preaching individual obligations is bound to fail. Religious-minded individuals will observe the more obvious demands of commutative justice and charity. But, when confronted by such complex obligations as the living wage or the just price, they will plead inability to act differently from their competitors. Racial discrimination is another striking example of a strong, but vicious, institution.

In the second place, there are problems which could not be solved even by widespread individual good will. These are cases where the institutions of society are essentially inadequate. Thus, if every businessman in the United States agreed to practice commutative and distributive justice, it would be quite unlikely that this step would prevent depressions. The grave social evil of unemployment springs primarily from faulty institutions: the acceptance of customs and practices which make periodic disorganization inevitable. Complete social reform will be had only when economic institutions lead to general prosperity and the common good.

It does not follow from this that individual effort is wasted

or that leadership is not of vital importance. If the individual
has the moral courage to swim against the current and set an
example of justice, these efforts will often bear fruit. Thus, an
employer who would break a united front against unions and
sign a union contract would be acting courageously. He might
face social ostracism. But eventually his example might prove an
excellent influence in his community. On the other hand, an
employer who would try to pay a living wage in a badly disorganized industry might go bankrupt. He would be unable to
withstand competition based on lower prices made possible by
exploitive wages elsewhere. Such a vain effort might be called a
social waste, since the business community would lose a highly
conscientious employer. His efforts would have been better
directed had he tried to organize the industry so that all could
pay a living wage.

There is a definite place for leadership in bringing about
social reform. At times this leadership can furnish notable examples of just conduct. It can be a protest against customs and
conventions which are wrong or inadequate. But at other times
the function of leadership demands more than individual good
example. It may call for patient persuasion and education of
others in the same social medium, so that basic institutions may
be changed. Thus, a strongly entrenched labor leader might be
able to set up a pattern of sound collective bargaining within
his industry in defiance of a general union trend which he considers unsound. Individual leadership might be effective in this
case. But a less secure leader would only lose his job by fighting
the trend. He would be more successful were he to try to persuade
union members and fellow officials that their current proposals
would, in the long run, do them more harm than good. In this
way, he would change his social medium so that it fostered the
common good rather than immediate selfish interests of
individuals.

These points are important in view of certain attitudes not
uncommon in Catholic circles. Thus, the view is sometimes expressed that, if we preached religion, we would not need to

worry about social problems. Such a position badly underesti-
mates the influence of institutions upon individual conduct. It
places an impossible burden on the man of good will. Others
stress individual leadership and example, as is the case with the
Christopher movement. Emphasis upon leadership is good, but
there are limitations to the power of example alone. Organized
effort is often indispensable. Finally, there are Catholics who
preach a spiritual isolationism. Their answer to the evils of
society is a revolt through nonparticipation. The Catholic is to
live up to the counsels of perfection and concentrate upon
personal spiritual progress. But this individualism would be an
abandonment of social justice, since it leaves society untouched.
It is essentially selfish and nonapostolic. Our mission is to change
the world, not abandon it to its fate.

Accordingly, social justice directs that the institutions and
the moral atmosphere of a community be such that they promote
the common good. Laws, customs, and attitudes should influence
individual conduct in view of the welfare of all. Such institutions as government, business organizations, trade unions, farmer
associations, lobbies, schools, and media for molding public
opinion should seek general interests as well as particular ends.
It is the duty of individuals to influence their groups in this
direction. At times it may be their obligation to form organizations or to try to create customs for the same purpose. If these
things are done, the social environment of the community will
be healthy.

Social Justice: The Common Good. Sound organizations and
institutions should promote the common good. This common
good may be described as the conditions of social life which favor
the proper ends of the individual members of a society. In the
economic sphere, it would include established arrangements of a
public nature which lead to prosperous production and equitable
distribution of material goods. The relationship of common good
to particular goods, like that of society to the individual, is somewhat like that of the whole to the part. There are certain private
ends which can best be obtained only in a well-functioning com-

munity. Here, however, careful distinctions must be made to avoid the opposite errors of statism and individualism.

Statism exaggerates the rights of society. It correctly holds that there can be social ends apart from and superior to the private aims of members of society. There is a valid distinction between acts of a community and the sum of the individual actions of members of a community. But statism misconceives the function of society. It considers the community as an end in itself, to be fostered by all means, even at the expense of the basic rights of the individual. By contrast, sound ethics hold that society exists for the purpose of aiding its individual members. While it has superior rights, it must use its powers for the good of its components. Moreover, the common good has precedence over private goods only in the same moral sphere. Thus, where material things are concerned, the state would have a right to regulate property for the public welfare. But it could not rightly impair spiritual goods for material ends. If, for instance, a government were to forbid the training of students to the priesthood, on the grounds that material progress would be enhanced if such candidates became factory workers, it would be acting wrongly. The essential spiritual good furnished by the ministrations of the clergy is of a higher order than material aims. Even in the material sphere, it would be wrong for the state to take over functions already performed efficiently by individuals or lesser societies. Here the state would be considering itself an all-sufficient end, instead of a means for promoting the good of all.

By contrast, individualism errs in treating the common good as the mere sum of individual goods. It holds that if each person seeks his own interest in competition with his fellows, the net result would be a higher total of satisfaction than would be otherwise possible. This viewpoint is profoundly antisocial and hence contrary to human nature. It overlooks the fact that social organizations can contribute to the welfare of individuals. This is particularly true in the economic sphere, where organized action is often necessary to secure the general good. Thus, in a hilly country there may be a number of farms. The farmer whose land is highest up might suffer only slightly from water erosion and hence not be disposed to take steps to prevent it. But, as various streams converge, they form a torrent which could ruin a low-lying farm. The common good would demand that all farmers take antierosion measures, in order to safeguard the low-level lands. If we were to consider obligations from an individual viewpoint only, this duty would be in charity, and heavy expense to the high-level farmers might excuse them from personal obligation. Here social justice applies and binds them to take group action, possibly to obtain government subsidy for the nonproductive expenses of the farmers on higher ground.

The examples given in terms of state intervention do not mean that the state is the only guardian of the common good. Some Catholic writers in the social field leave a false impression on this matter. There are many common goods, just as there are many societies. The family, the factory, the trade union, the city, the state, and the national government each have their own ends and corresponding areas of common good. The national government is only the highest among these societies. It should seek the general welfare of all, whereas particular societies seek the welfare of their own members, in subordination to the general good of all. In terms of individual obligations, the individual is bound to procure the common good in all societies of which he is a member.

The various relations in this hierarchy of goods correspond to the hierarchy of ends and purposes in the universe. God is the supreme end of all. In regard to Him, everything else can be called a means to an end. Under Him are the spiritual and material orders, with the spiritual in a position of predominance. Man's nature partakes of both orders, and he is also a member of society as well as an individual. Hence, man must balance the claims of spiritual and material goods, and individual and social ends in both spheres. Society exists to serve the individual, but it has its own rights which must be acknowledged if it is to fulfill its function. Hence, the common good, rightly conceived, comprises those conditions of society which are necessary means for attaining individual goods. Since the individual cannot function normally without society, he must see that necessary and useful societies attain their proper ends. In acting socially, the individual does not lose his personality, but rather develops it in a way which would be impossible through solitary action. There is no denial of human personality in the statement that the common good has precedence over particular goods.

Briefly, the common good is served if each particular society is so organized that it serves both the welfare of its members and the entire community. The supreme co-ordinating society is the state, which directs lesser groups so that the common interest is secured. The extent of such intervention is controlled by the public interest; it would be wrong for the state to intervene when a smaller social organization is serving both the particular and the general common goods.

These abstract statements will take on more point and effectiveness when they are applied to particular problems in later chapters. But, even at this stage, it is clear that American life does not meet the ideal outlined here. Many of our economic societies are mere pressure groups, aiming to gain the most for their own members, whether or not the common good is obtained. There are even cases — racketeers in a few labor unions are an example — when they do not even seek the interests of their members. Because of this basic disorganization of economic life, there is terrific pressure for the state to force justice and morality upon the social order. While the state is doing its duty in meeting this need, the situation is not ideal. Excessive state intervention curbs initiative and destroys freedom. Social justice would envision a hierarchy of societies, each sentitive to the needs of the common good, with the state directing, stimulating, guiding, and co-ordinating such activities to the extent that the public interest demands.

What Social Justice Demands. Many conclusions follow from the study of social justice. The most important of them have been summarized by the Rev. William Ferree in his excellent doctoral dissertation, *The Act of Social Justice,* and his briefer pamphlet

study, "Introduction to Social Justice." Since his order of treatment differs from that used here, the present study will only
high-light a few of his points not sufficiently emphasized
hitherto.

Social justice demands that each individual or group be prepared to act appropriately so as to realize the common good.
This involves first a willingness to subordinate private goods, or
the common interests of lesser groups, to the general welfare.
Secondly, it calls for both organization and co-operation to
achieve this end. The realization of the common good will not
come about by chance, much less by struggle and conflict between social groups. To secure this organization and unity, there
must be freedom of association in a society. Men must be able
to form into groups natural for the attaining of legitimate ends.
Closely connected with this is the so-called principle of subsidiarity, holding that a higher and more powerful group
should never arrogate to itself functions and powers which are
being used properly by a smaller group. All this harmonizes with
the nature of society, which is to serve man, not to crush him.
Since smaller groups are generally closer to the individual, and
more easily controlled by him, they should have a favored position. But this is not to derogate from the other principle that
the common good, at the highest level, has priority over lesser
goods. As was noted above, the common good, rightly understood, brings about the greatest realization of particular goods.

It is evident from the nature of society that the work of
social justice must be continuous. A given obligation in strict
justice may be discharged and the transaction is concluded. But
the problem of organizing the institutions of society for the
common good is never done. Problems change. Leaders and
rulers of groups are being constantly replaced. Hence there
is no place for complacency, indifference, or neutrality. We are
born into a complex world and must take our appropriate place
in its societies, especially when they are necessary groups closely
connected with the general good of all. The urgency of this duty
is the greater because the problems of modern life are so mo-

mentous. No man may shirk his share of the common burden.

The implications of social justice have often been expressed in terms of certain principles which should govern group action. Thus, Father Trehey, in his dissertation, *Foundations of a Modern Guild System,* writes of the principles of liberty, organic structure, subsidiarity, self-government, graded structure, public-legal status, general welfare, and state intervention in regard to "modern guilds." These principles are basically applications of social justice to the institutions of society. While they are often expressed as separate canons of social conduct, in reality they can be justified primarily in terms of the demands of social justice. They belong in two general categories insofar as they concern the structure of society and its functioning, particularly in relation to government. Structurally, an organic society best meets the demands of the common good. This involves a multitude of hierarchically graded and interrelated social institutions, each with relative autonomy but subject to the overriding demands of the common good. Thus, from the economic aspect, an organic society would involve organized groups of business, industry, finance, labor, the professions, and the farming community, substantially solving their own problems but co-operating with others for the common welfare, under the supreme authority of the state. As these social groups function, they should be accorded full freedom to work out their own ends, provided that this does not conflict with the common good (principle of subsidiarity; principle of autonomy). On the other hand, the state has the right and duty to intervene where the public welfare demands (principle of intervention). These points will be treated more at length in subsequent chapters, particularly Chapters VII and XIII.

SOCIAL CHARITY

The distinction between social justice and social charity is not easy to express, since both incline the individual to seek the common good. Justice emphasizes what is due to another. This aspect of "otherness" and "debt" is a necessary emphasis, particularly in a society which tends toward the extremes of individualism. But at the same time, it is vital to stress the "oneness" of mankind. In seeking the common good, under social justice, we are also working for those bound to us in the charity of Christ. Social charity, as a generous concern for the good of the community, is a unifying principle over and above the organizing force of social justice. For this reason, the task of rebuilding the social order cannot be accomplished by justice alone.

Justice cannot bring about the complete union and harmony which will make society a smoothly functioning body. It cannot procure the generosity, patience, and tolerance needed in the slow years of transition between a disorganized society and one that is united in the interest of the common welfare. In fact, due to the frailty of human nature, it often happens that the vigorous quest for justice may actually drive men asunder. In theory, we can condemn injustice and yet not pass judgment on the motives of those who perpetrate injustice. In practice, we do not always separate the man from his deeds. Hence, were we content to limit ourselves to denouncing social injustice, we might actually divide society into warring classes. Thus, if organized labor were to attack some business practices, the effect might be to produce a united front of one group against the other. Even those who do not condone injustice might feel a sense of solidarity with their group which is being attacked. We might have a form of the class struggle occasioned by the pursuit of justice.

From this, of course, one should not conclude that the fight for justice should be slackened. Rather, it must be completed by the kindly bonds of charity. This is the more true since much social injustice is not necessarily a product of individual malice. Where the institutions of society are unsound, it is possible for well-meaning individuals to be caught in the snares of a bad system. Conventions, customs, and institutions lead them to practices which they may deplore, but feel helpless to remedy by themselves. Unless we take the pessimistic attitude that most men are evil, we should be willing to appeal to the better instincts even of those who are enmeshed in objective evil. Without such attitudes, it is difficult to see how we can achieve the co-operation and organization postulated by social justice.

Charity, in this sense, might be called benevolence toward one's fellow man in society. It is quite distinct from the form of the virtue most frequently associated with the word, namely, aid to the poor and distressed. Almsgiving and related practices are but one form of the Christian virtue of charity. Moreover, in the present context, charity toward the distressed must be subject to careful scrutiny. Good as it is in itself, it can never substitute for justice. We may not give to the worker as alms what is his due in justice. It is unfortunate that the English language does not give us a word which expresses accurately the full Christian virtue of charity. Catholics generally use the word "charity," but to the general public this often means assistance to the unfortunate. Protestant divines prefer the term "love," but this has an emotional content in ordinary usage which is not necessarily inherent in the virtue of charity. Other terms, such as brotherhood, benevolence, and solidarity, likewise have their limitations. It may be possible that the phrase "social charity," used by Pope Pius XI, will gain acceptance as a technical description of the virtue in its present context.

Social charity fits in well with the demands deriving from the dignity of the human person. Many of these obligations, it is true, hold in terms of justice. But the recognition of a man's individual worth also calls for a certain good will toward him as a person. He does not then feel that he is submerged in a large group, whether this be civil society, a labor union, or a factory working force. Rather he senses the bonds of human relationship between himself and others, whether they be his fellow workers or his employer. Indeed, the prolific literature currently produced on human relations as a key to industrial labor relations is mainly an effort to implement the Christian virtue of charity. Personnel experts speak of the need for communication, participation, and teamwork in the factory. They stress individualized treatment of a worker's problems in the plant and elsewhere. Such techniques are said to be the key to the building of a happy and efficient working force. Yet we do not exaggerate in saying that these human-relations programs could well be implementations of the commandment second only to the law of love for God.

Just as human-relations programs are the employer's expression of charity, so also we might call union-management harmony efforts the union's way of living up to this virtue. When a union seeks to meet with the employer on terms of co-operation rather than enmity, it is acting in a Christian fashion. The idea of essential class struggle is Marxist, not Christian. There is no inherent conflict between a worker's loyalty to his union and his loyalty to his company. Even granting the historical fact that many unions were formed to remedy injustice and hence often grew up in an atmosphere of bitterness, it is not necessary to perpetuate such attitudes. With intelligence and good will on both sides, relations of genuine friendliness are possible. Indeed, they are more common in American industry than is generally realized. Furthermore, personal contacts between union officials and industrial leaders, particularly in solving common problems, can bring about a mutual respect which is the prelude for deep co-operation. Such a phenomenon was observed in various joint government committees during World War II, such as the War Labor Board or the War Production Board.

In the socioeconomic field, co-operation is often facilitated by referring to issues as problems, which they often are, rather than immediately denouncing them as injustices. A problem offers a challenge to the participants to reach a solution. Discussions may be had as to feasible methods of meeting the issue. After much give-and-take, it is often possible to reach a sound conclusion. By contrast, denunciations and the proposal of ready-made solutions often stir up resentments. A man who is condemned for practicing injustice often feels bound to defend his position and yields only reluctantly and with poor grace. But if the same man is asked to co-operate in meeting a problem, even though it is mainly of his own making, he often shows more good will. Furthermore, he can thus save face without difficulty.

There are two aspects to social problems which are often over-looked. The first is that in most controversies both parties have legitimate interests which they are trying to safeguard. It is rare that social conflict arises from injustices so clear that right is completely on one side or the other. Most problems involve intricate relationships and delicate balancing of rights. Justice itself compels us to make this distinction, but social charity makes it easier to practice this type of justice. Moreover, a second and interrelated point must be considered in matters of social reform: the fact that change is normally a slow process of adaptation of the old to the new. A situation which may seem ideal from the viewpoint of abstract theory may be quite impractical in terms of prudent policy. In our complex society, a change in one sphere may involve thousands of changes in related spheres. Hence conservatism is a natural human trait and should not necessarily be denounced as reactionary. Here again social charity, by inducing understanding of motives, permits pressure for needed change without causing revolutionary disruption.

These reflections may be helpful to Catholics who are concerned with problems of social justice. Too often we are prone to denounce the evil and propose a solution, forgetting completely the human problem involved in reaching this solution. Resounding denunciations may give some persons psychological satisfaction, but they are not always constructive. It is frequently better to approach the individuals concerned and work out with them a program which meets the needs under discussion. If this fails, and patient persuasion seems vain, then it may be appropriate to unlimber the weapons of condemnation. But our first task is to bring social groups together, and this point must always be considered in facing a particular issue.

The virtue of charity is the unique contribution of the Christian. Justice is so clearly a natural virtue that all right-thinking men acknowledge its worth. Many who have no religion have become stanch defenders of justice in the social field. But the benevolence which unites does not come so easily to the non-religious man. Generous good will which goes beyond rights and seeks to bring people together is best promoted by religion. It is true that a case could be made for social unity merely in the interests of more efficient production. But somehow human beings do not react well to this type of "enlightened selfishness." This fact explains the checkered history of many "welfare schemes" in industry. Some firms have been successful with profit-sharing and like devices, while others have found them to be failures. In all likelihood, one of the most important factors in their success or failure has been the degree of real benevolence which permeated them. Men respond to genuine good will. But they suspect benefits if they do not trust the motives of those who confer them. Human hearts are won by virtues in others, not by clever schemes and ingenious programs. The charity of Christ triumphs where cold "realism" fails.

SUBSIDIARY VIRTUES

There are many other virtues which could affect economic life. Insofar as they affect primarily the spiritual welfare of the individual, they will be noted later in Chapter XIV. At that point, the stress is upon spiritual reform as a means of bringing about social reform. But where a virtue is more significant for its effect upon the social order, rather than in terms of individual perfection, it would be more appropriate to consider it in this general chapter. St. Thomas mentions four such virtues: beneficence, almsgiving, liberality, and munificence; and three of these are noted by Pope Pius XI.

Beneficence is the doing of good to others. It is an act of friendship and kindness. Technically, it is but a phase or manifestation of the greater virtue of charity. However, it is especially valuable in the socioeconomic field, since it spurs men to seek the welfare of others. It makes them more willing to bring about the reign of justice, while at the same time it tempers the harshness of justice with kindness and good will. Beneficence can be contagious. Good will is often returned in kind whereas justice alone often leaves men unfriendly and cold.

Almsgiving involves giving to the needy for motives of compassion and love of God. Again, it is technically a phase of charity, with the special aspect of mercy. We are commanded to help the needy with our superfluous goods.[2] The definition of "super-fluous" is relative, not absolute. Obligations of family and position in life would make the area of superfluous income different in various situations. A wealthy and aged bachelor would have fewer relative necessities than a younger family man receiving the same income. From the broad social aspect, however, two observations must be made about almsgiving. First, it should never be a substitute for justice. An employer who pays miserable wages would not even matters by donating generously to a community hospital. His first duty is to his own workers. In the second place, intelligent giving of wealth can contribute in a modest but definite manner to the easing of social tensions. The fact that the wealthy use their superfluous income for sound community projects removes some of the ill feeling which might arise from too great disparity in the distribution of incomes. The poorer groups would feel that the wealthy have a certain sense of trusteeship in regard to their money. Less envy or resentment would be felt under such circumstances. Moreover, intelligent philanthropy can bring public benefits not otherwise possible. Many projects, worthy in themselves, might not be suitable for government support. Nor could they exist on the basis of general public contributions. Private donations in substantial amounts have done much good in this borderline field.

Liberality is a virtue connected with the right use of external goods, particularly in the economic field. It manifests itself mainly through giving, on the basis of the Scriptural maxim that it is more blessed to give than to receive. This virtue calls for a middle position between prodigality and avarice. These extremes manifest unsound attitudes toward wealth, with the prodigal

---

[2] St. Thomas asks the question whether we are obliged to contribute from things which are necessary for our own existence. He denies that such an obligation exists, but states that such an action would be praiseworthy if it were done for some public person, eminent in either civil or ecclesiastical society. In such a case, a man might expose himself or his family even to the danger of death, "since the common good is to be preferred to one's particular good" (II, II, 32, 6). This is another illustration of St. Thomas' stress on the primacy of the common good.

overlooking its useful function, while the avaricious man exaggerates its worth. Money should be considered a means to secure higher ends, not a goal in itself. It should be used for the good of the owner and his family, with superfluous funds freely expended in a way that will help one's neighbor. Liberality thus might at times lead to almsgiving, and at other times to risking funds in investments which would be a service to the community. This second field has the greatest social implications today. In our present economic system, there must be a continual flow of new investments to maintain job opportunities for an expanding population. New enterprises also absorb workers displaced by more efficient machines or methods of production. At the same time, existing American tax laws make such investments more hazardous financially than was formerly the case. Wealthy persons are tempted to put their funds into government bonds, taking a small but certain return. By contrast, the virtue of liberality would incline the wealthy to assume the risk involved in financing new job-producing enterprises. At the same time, it would not preclude their pressing for more skillful tax laws, which could encourage investment without giving up the principle of distributive justice which considers ability to pay an important factor in setting tax rates.

A special form of liberality is munificence, or the parting with great sums of money. This indicates a great freedom of spirit in regard to possession of external goods and a notable devotion to the common welfare. A common form of this virtue is the establishing of foundations with large fortunes as their bases. Many worth-while community enterprises have been fostered in this manner. Substantial donations to hospitals, schools, and universities, works of charity, and religious enterprises would belong in this category. An interesting example with socioeconomic implications is the setting aside of a fund to promote new enterprises involving unusual financial risk but holding great promise for the community. A wealthy American family is currently supporting such a project. Another illustration would be the giant limited-dividend and relatively low-cost housing programs sponsored by a large insurance company. Such use of wealth could promote social goals and mitigate the evils which might otherwise be expected from large concentrations of funds and of economic power.

From the examples given, it is clear that these so-called subsidiary virtues can bring about good results in the socioeconomic field. In this context, they are far less important than the great virtues of justice and charity. But they involve attitudes toward wealth which could lessen social tensions and develop enterprises not otherwise attainable. So long as we have large fortunes, especially if they are accumulated without injustice, it is good that they should be used for the common welfare. Today the trend is away from large personal fortunes. Many factors, but primarily tax laws, make it difficult for an individual to accumulate great wealth. The result is that nonprofit organizations, which must be subsidized to survive, are turning more and more to seek government help. The state is thereby increasing its already large area of power and influence. Perhaps this trend is inevitable, in view of the great changes wrought by wars and depressions. But to the extent that private subsidies, by individuals, corporations, labor unions, and the like, are possible, they tend to enlarge the area of freedom and diminish centralized control.

READINGS*

J. Messner, *Social Ethics,* pp. 122–235, 793–794.

St. Thomas Aquinas, *Summa Theologica,* II, III, p. 32, 33, 58, 61, 117, 134.

W. Ferree, *The Act of Social Justice.*

———— "Introduction to Social Justice."

J. A. Ryan, *Distributive Justice.*

E. Cahill, *Framework of a Christian State,* Chaps. 24–27.

G. C. Rutten, *La doctrine sociale de l'Église,* Chap. 4.

V. Michel, *Christian Social Reconstruction,* Chap. 1 and Appendix.

J. B. Desrosiers, *Soyons justes,* Vol. 1.

W. J. McDonald, *The Social Value of Property According to St. Thomas Aquinas,* Chap. 2.

H. F. Trehey, *Foundations of a Modern Guild System,* Chap. 3.

* For further readings, consult Lists Nos. 1 and 4 in the Appendix.

Chapter V. UNSOUND PHILOSOPHIES OF ECONOMIC LIFE

THE CHURCH AND GOVERNMENT

Leo XIII, Immortale Dei

23. But in matters merely political, as for instance the best form of government, and this or that system of administration, a difference of opinion is lawful. Those, therefore, whose piety is in other respects known, and whose minds are ready to accept in all obedience the decrees of the Apostolic See, cannot in justice be accounted as bad men because they disagree as to subjects We have mentioned; and still graver wrong will be done them, if — as We have more than once perceived with regret — they are accused of violating, or of wavering in, the Catholic faith.

Leo XIII, Graves de Communi

6. For the precepts of the natural law and the Gospel, for the very reason that they transcend the vicissitudes of human existence, must necessarily be independent of any particular form of civil government and adapt themselves to all forms so long as these are not opposed to what is right and just. In themselves, they therefore are and remain completely outside of party rivalries and political changes, so that, under any kind of government, people may and ought to abide by those precepts, which bid them love God above all and their neighbors as themselves. This has ever been the morality of the Church. By it the Roman Pontiffs have constantly dealt with states, whatever might be their form of government.

Leo XIII, Libertas Praestantissimum

32. Of the various forms of government, the Church does not reject any that are fitted to procure the welfare of the subject; she wishes only — and this nature itself requires — that they should be constituted without involving wrong to anyone, and especially without violating the rights of the Church.

Leo XIII, In the Midst of Solicitudes

In this order of speculative ideas, Catholics, like all other citizens, are free to prefer one form of government to another precisely because no one of these social forms is, in itself, opposed to the principles of sound reason nor to the maxims of Christian doctrine.

INDIVIDUALISM

As a Philosophy

Pius XI, Quadragesimo Anno

10. He [Leo XIII] sought no help from either Liberalism or socialism, for the one had proved that it was utterly unable to solve the social problem aright, and the other, proposing a remedy far worse than the evil itself, would have plunged human society into greater dangers.

14. For it boldly attacked and overturned the idols of Liberalism.

25. With regard to civil authority, Leo XIII, boldly breaking through the confines imposed by Liberalism, fearlessly taught that government must not be thought a mere guardian of law and of good order, but rather must put forth every effort so that "through the entire scheme of laws and institutions . . . both public and individual well-being may develop spontaneously out of the very structure and administration of the state."

27. And while the principles of Liberalism were tottering, which had long prevented effective action by those governing the state, the Encyclical *On the Condition of Workers* in truth impelled peoples themselves to promote a social policy on truer grounds and with greater intensity, and so strongly encouraged good Catholics to furnish valuable help to heads of states in this field that they often stood forth as illustrious champions of this new policy even in legislatures.

78. Things have come to such a pass through the evil of what we have termed "individualism," that, following upon the overthrow and near extinction of that rich social life which was once highly developed through associations of various kinds, there remain virtually only individuals and the state.

133. Strict and watchful moral restraint enforced vigorously by governmental authority could have banished these enormous evils and even forestalled them; this restraint, however, has too often been sadly lacking. For since the seeds of a new form of economy were bursting forth just

when the principles of rationalism had been implanted and rooted in many minds, there quickly developed a body of economic teaching far removed from the true moral law, and, as a result, completely free reign was given to human passions.

Pius XI, On Atheistic Communism

32. The lamentable ruin into which amoral Liberalism has plunged us.

38. There would be today neither socialism nor communism if the rulers of the nations had not scorned the teachings and maternal warnings of the Church. On the bases of Liberalism and laicism they wished to build other social edifices which, powerful and imposing as they seemed at first, all too soon revealed the weakness of their foundations, and today are crumbling one after another before our eyes, as everything must crumble that is not grounded on the one cornerstone which is Christ Jesus.

As an Economic System

Pius XI, Quadragesimo Anno

88. Just as the unity of human society cannot be founded on an opposition of classes, so also the right ordering of economic life cannot be left to a free competition of forces. For from this source, as from a poisoned spring, have originated and spread all the errors of individualistic economic teaching. Destroying through forgetfulness or ignorance the social and moral character of economic life, it held that economic life must be considered and treated as altogether free from and independent of public authority, because in the market, i.e., in the free struggle of competitors, it would have a principle of self-direction which governs it much more perfectly than would the intervention of any created intellect. But free competition, while justified and certainly useful provided it is kept within certain limits, clearly cannot direct economic life — a truth which the outcome of the application in practice of the tenets of this evil individualistic spirit has more than sufficiently demonstrated. Therefore, it is most necessary that economic life be again subjected to and governed by a true and effective directing principle. This function is one that the economic dictatorship which has recently displaced free competition can still less perform, since it is a headstrong power and violent energy that, to benefit people, needs to be strongly curbed and wisely ruled. But it cannot curb and rule itself.

105. In the first place, it is obvious that not only is wealth concentrated in our times but an immense power and despotic economic dictatorship

is consolidated in the hands of a few, who often are not owners but only the trustees, and managing directors of invested funds which they administer according to their own arbitrary will and pleasure.

106. This dictatorship is being most forcibly exercised by those who, since they hold the money and completely control it, control credit also and rule the lending of money. Hence they regulate the flow, so to speak, of the lifeblood whereby the entire economic system lives, and have so firmly in their grasp the soul, as it were, of economic life that no one can breathe against their will.

107. This concentration of power and might, the characteristic mark, as it were, of contemporary economic life, is the fruit that the unlimited freedom of struggle among competitors has of its own nature produced, and which lets only the strongest survive; and this is often the same as saying, those who fight the most violently, those who give least heed to their conscience.

108. This accumulation of might and of power generates in turn three kinds of conflict. First, there is the struggle for economic supremacy itself; then there is the bitter fight to gain supremacy over the state in order to use in economic struggles its resources and authority; finally there is conflict between states themselves, not only because countries employ their power and shape their policies to promote every economic advantage of their citizens, but also because they seek to decide political controversies that arise among nations through the use of their economic supremacy and strength.

109. The ultimate consequences of the individualist spirit in economic life are those which you yourselves, Venerable Brethren and Beloved Children, see and deplore: free competition has destroyed itself; economic dictatorship has supplanted the free market; unbridled ambition for power has likewise succeeded greed for gain; all economic life has become tragically hard, inexorable, and cruel. To these are to be added the grave evils that have resulted from an intermingling and shameful confusion of the functions and duties of public authority with those of the economic sphere — such as, one of the worst, the virtual degradation of the majesty of the state, which although it ought to sit on high like a queen and supreme arbitress, free from all partiality and intent upon the one common good and justice, is become a slave, surrendered and delivered to the passions and greed of men. And as to international relations, two different streams have issued from the one fountainhead: on the one hand, economic nationalism or even economic imperialism; on the other, a no less deadly and accursed internationalism of finance or international imperialism whose country is where profit is.

Bishops' Statement, 1933

The social philosophy prevailing during recent centuries has carried human society far from its safe moorings. That philosophy — if, indeed, it be worthy of the name — which has ruled governments, groups, and individuals for the past three hundred years has not taken as its guide the moral law, has not considered the rights of man. Money, not man, has been the supreme consideration and the justifying end. That philosophy has aroused opposition and has given rise to errors and exaggerations that are anti-Catholic and anti-Christian.

The same demoralizing philosophy defended, and defends today, unrestrained individual economic freedom and the economic dictatorship that has succeeded it. That philosophy permits individuals, corporations, and nations to accumulate as much wealth as they can, according to the unfair methods of modern business, and to use such accumulated wealth as they see fit. It honors and proclaims as sovereign rulers of economic empires men who have succeeded in amassing unjustly these fabulous fortunes.

That philosophy has broken down or forbidden the establishment of protective organizations. It has broken down or forbidden an organized economic life to administer the production of wealth and its distribution in accordance with social justice and the interdependence of economic relations. It has denied Government its right to guard justice and the common good. It has given greed a free hand.

That philosophy denied and denies, in reality, the oneness and the solidarity of mankind. In its light, wealth, business, and the power that material prosperity gives are in themselves supreme ends. Human rights must be sacrificed to those ends, and humanity itself must become the mere instrument in the production of wealth, not the master controlling it. Such a philosophy has always been and will ever be false and unChristian in principle and application. It has literally taken God out of the world.

This extreme of individualism has led to the extreme of communism.

SOCIALISM

Leo XIII, Diuturnum Illud

17. Hence we have reached the limit of horrors, to wit, communism, socialism, nihilism, hideous deformities of the civil society of men and almost its ruin.

Leo XIII, Rerum Novarum

7. To cure this evil, the Socialists, exciting the envy of the poor toward the rich, contend that it is necessary to do away with private possession of goods and in its place to make the goods of individuals common to all, and that the men who preside over a municipality or who direct the entire state should act as administrators of these goods. They hold that, by such a transfer of private goods from private individuals to the community, they can cure the present evil through dividing wealth and benefits equally among the citizens.

8. But their program is so unsuited for terminating the conflict that it actually injures the workers themselves. Moreover, it is highly unjust, because it violates the rights of lawful owners, perverts the functions of the state, and throws governments into utter confusion.

9. Clearly the essential reason why those who engage in any gainful occupation undertake labor, and at the same time the end to which workers immediately look, is to procure property for themselves and to retain it by individual right as theirs and as their very own. When the worker places his energy and his labor at the disposal of another, he does so for the purpose of getting the means necessary for livelihood. He seeks in return for the work done, accordingly, a true and full right not only to demand his wage but to dispose of it as he sees fit. Therefore, if he saves something by restricting expenditures and invests his savings in a piece of land in order to keep the fruit of his thrift more safe, a holding of this kind is certainly nothing else than his wage under a different form; and on this account land which the worker thus buys is necessarily under his full control as much as the wage which he earned by his labor. But, as is obvious, it is clearly in this that the ownership of movable and immovable goods consists. Therefore, inasmuch as the Socialists seek to transfer the goods of private persons to the community at large, they make the lot of all wage earners worse, because in abolishing the freedom to dispose of wages they take away from them by this very act the hope and the opportunity of increasing their property and of securing advantages for themselves.

Pius XI, Quadragesimo Anno

10. He [Leo XIII] sought no help from either Liberalism or socialism, for the one had proved that it was utterly unable to solve the social problem aright, and the other, proposing a remedy far worse than the evil itself, would have plunged human society into greater dangers.

113. The other section, which has kept the name socialism, is surely more moderate. It not only professes the rejection of violence but modifies

and tempers to some degree, if it does not reject entirely, the class struggle and the abolition of private ownership. One might say that, terrified by its own principles and by the conclusions drawn therefrom by communism, socialism inclines toward and in a certain measure approaches the truths which Christian tradition has always held sacred; for it cannot be denied that its demands at times come very near those that Christian reformers of society justly insist upon.

114. For if the class struggle abstains from enmities and mutual hatred, it gradually changes into an honest discussion of differences founded on a desire for justice, and if this is not that blessed social peace which we all seek, it can and ought to be the point of departure from which to move forward to the mutual co-operation of the Industries and Professions. So also the war declared on private ownership, more and more abated, is being so restricted that now, finally, not the possession itself of the means of production is attacked but rather a kind of sovereignty over society which ownership has, contrary to all right, seized and usurped. For such sovereignty belongs in reality not to owners but to the public authority. If the foregoing happens, it can come even to the point that imperceptibly these ideas of the more moderate socialism will no longer differ from the desires and demands of those who are striving to remold human society on the basis of Christian principles. For certain kinds of property, it is rightly contended, ought to be reserved to the state since they carry with them a dominating power so great that it cannot without danger to the general welfare be entrusted to private individuals.

115. Such just demands and desires have nothing in them now which is inconsistent with Christian truth, and much less are they special to socialism. Those who work solely toward such ends have, therefore, no reason to become Socialists.

116. Yet let no one think that all the socialist groups or factions that are not communist have, without exception, recovered their senses to this extent either in fact or in name. For the most part they do not reject the class struggle or the abolition of ownership, but only in some degree modify them. Now if these false principles are modified and to some extent erased from the program, the question arises, or rather is raised without warrant by some, whether the principles of Christian truth cannot perhaps be also modified to some degree and be tempered so as to meet socialism halfway and, as it were, by a middle course, come to agreement with it. There are some allured by the foolish hope that Socialists in this way will be drawn to us. A vain hope! Those who want to be apostles among Socialists ought to profess Christian truth whole and entire, openly and sincerely, and not connive at error in

any way. If they truly wish to be heralds of the Gospel, let them above
all strive to show to Socialists that socialist claims, so far as they are just
are far more strongly supported by the principles of Christian faith
and much more effectively promoted through the power of Christian
charity.

117. But what if socialism has really been so tempered and modified
as to the class struggle and private ownership that there is in it no longer
anything to be censured on these points? Has it thereby renounced it
contradictory nature to the Chrisian religion? This is the question that
holds many minds in suspense. And numerous are the Catholics who
although they clearly understand that Christian principles can never
be abandoned or diminished, seem to turn their eyes to the Holy See
and earnestly beseech Us to decide whether this form of socialism ha
so far recovered from false doctrines that it can be accepted without the
sacrifice of any Christian principle and in a certain sense be baptized
That We, in keeping with Our fatherly solicitude, may answer their
petitions, We make this pronouncement: Whether considered as a doc
trine, or an historical fact, or a movement, socialism, if it remains truly
socialism, even after it has yielded to truth and justice on the point
which we have mentioned, cannot be reconciled with the teachings of
the Catholic Church because its concept of society itself is utterly foreign
to Christian truth.

118. For, according to Christian teaching, man, endowed with a social
nature, is placed on this earth so that by leading a life in society and
under an authority ordained of God he may fully cultivate and develop
all his faculties unto the praise and glory of his Creator; and that by
faithfully fulfilling the duties of his craft or other calling he may obtain
for himself temporal and at the same time eternal happiness. Socialism
on the other hand, wholly ignoring and indifferent to this sublime end of
both man and society, affirms that human association has been instituted
for the sake of material advantage alone.

119. Because of the fact that goods are produced more efficiently by a
suitable division of labor than by the scattered efforts of individuals
Socialists infer that economic activity, only the material ends of which
enter into their thinking, ought of necessity to be carried on socially
Because of this necessity, they hold that men are obliged, with respect
to the producing of goods, to surrender and subject themselves entirely
to society. Indeed, possession of the greatest possible supply of things
that serve the advantages of this life is considered of such great im
portance that the higher goods of man, liberty not excepted, must take
a secondary place and even be sacrificed to the demands of the most
efficient production of goods. This damage to human dignity, undergon

n the "socialized" process of production, will be easily offset, they say, by the abundance of socially produced goods which will pour out in profusion to individuals to be used freely at their pleasure for comforts and cultural development. Society, therefore, as socialism conceives it, can on the one hand neither exist nor be thought of without an obviously excessive use of force; on the other hand, it fosters a liberty no less false, since there is no place in it for true social authority, which rests not on temporal and material advantages but descends from God alone, the Creator and last end of all things.

120. If socialism, like all errors, contains some truth (which, moreover, the Supreme Pontiffs have never denied), it is based nevertheless on a theory of human society peculiar to itself and irreconcilable with true Christianity. Religious socialism, Christian socialism, are contradictory terms; no one can be at the same time a good Catholic and a true socialist.

NONCOMMUNIST STATISM

Pius XI, Non Abbiamo Bisogno

49. And here We find Ourselves confronted by a mass of authentic affirmations and no less authentic facts which reveal beyond the slightest possibility of doubt the resolve (already in great measure actually put into effect) to monopolize completely the young, from their tenderest years up to manhood and womanhood, for the exclusive advantage of a party and of a regime based on an ideology which clearly resolves itself into a true, a real pagan worship of the state — the "statolatry" which is no less in contrast with the natural rights of the family than it is in contradiction with the supernatural rights of the Church.

57. A conception of the state which makes the rising generations belong to it entirely, without any exception, from the tenderest years up to adult life, cannot be reconciled by a Catholic either with Catholic doctrine or with the natural rights of the family.

Pius XI, Quadragesimo Anno

(Summarized.) 91–96. The pope describes the syndicalist and corporative organization of production in Italy, whereby all economic activity is directed by state-controlled syndicates. Workers and employers are represented in these groups, but the state has the final word. The advantages of this system are class collaboration and a unified economic life. Its disadvantages follow from the state's substituting itself for the free activity of the parties, political and involved administration, and the serving of particular political ends rather than the reconstruction and promotion of a better social order. These evils may be overcome if moral and religious principles are integrated with the system. There should also be a broader participation in the control of the system on the part of those who could contribute technical, occupational, and social knowledge and experience.

Pius XII, Address to Sacred College of Cardinals, June 2, 1945

He [Pius XI] proclaimed to the world on Passion Sunday, 1937, in his encyclical *Mit Brennender Sorge* what National Socialism really was: the arrogant apostasy from Jesus Christ, the denial of His doctrine and of His work of redemption, the cult of violence, the idolatry of race and blood, the overthrow of human liberty and dignity.

Pius XII, Summi Pontificatus

1420. To consider the state as something ultimate to which everything else should be subordinated and directed, cannot fail to harm the true and lasting prosperity of nations. This can happen either when unrestricted dominion comes to be conferred on the state as having a mandate from the nation, people, or even a social class, or when the state arrogates such dominion to itself as absolute master, despotically, without any mandate whatsoever. If, in fact, the state lays claim to and directs private enterprises, these, ruled as they are by delicate and complicated internal principles which guarantee and assure the realization of their special aims, may be damaged to the detriment of the public good, by being wrenched from their natural surroundings, that is, from responsible private action.

1429. The idea which credits the state with unlimited authority is not simply an error harmful to the internal life of nations, to their prosperity, and to the larger and well-ordered increase in their well-being, but likewise it injures the relations between peoples, for it breaks the unity of supranational society, robs the law of nations of its foundation and vigor, leads to violation of others' rights, and impedes agreement and peaceful intercourse.

The two preceding chapters laid the foundation for a Christian answer to the social problem. We assert the dignity of man and his social nature, with all the rights and duties springing therefrom. We note that economic life exists to serve the needs of man, and that it must harmonize with the total nature of human society. To realize these ends, the great virtues of justice and charity must be practiced. In this respect, commutative and distributive justice minister primarily to the dignity of the individual. Social justice and social charity, on the other hand, are directed toward realizing man's social nature and the purpose of economic life. If all these virtues are practiced in the world of affairs, then material things will serve man's needs and economic society will function smoothly. Moreover, this harmonious working of the economic order will bring prosperity to nations and a full use of natural resources, technical skills, and the organizing powers of capital and labor.

Against this general background, it is now fitting to examine the institutions and customs of social life, weighing them in the light of sound ethics and Christian teachings. The present chapter and the one to follow will consider the main forms of organized economic life as they exist in the modern world. In view of their defects, in Chapter VII there will be given the outline of an ideal economic order based on ethical principles.

The various social systems considered in the encyclicals do not fall into any single pattern. Some, such as fascism and National Socialism, are primarily political philosophies. Any economic element is secondary and derivative. By contrast, individualism is mainly an economic philosophy, with minor political overtones. Finally, socialism and communism are basically economic, but with very important political consequences deriving from economic premises. To add to the complexity of the pattern, some systems are currently practiced (individualism, communism); others are matters of history (fascism, National Socialism), while socialism has not yet been fully tried in a modern industrial nation of any size.

If we are to make valid comparisons between systems so diverse, certain standards of judgment must be set up. Accordingly, in addition to the ethical norms thus far established, the scope of treatment will be determined by two principles: the present status of a system, and its current impact on American life. Purely historical matters will not be examined for their own sake. The history of a system will be noted only insofar as it has present significance. Moreover, only those aspects of economic philosophies which have present value for American readers will be stressed. As a result, there will be a certain distortion of perspective. A program about which volumes have been written may be dismissed in a paragraph. Even systems which have been the subject of major emphasis in the social encyclicals may be treated lightly, if they are no longer of current interest. This limitation is dictated by the purposes of the present study, which is primarily an explanation and application of Catholic social principles in the light of American conditions, rather than an historical commentary upon the social encyclicals.

THE CHURCH AND GOVERNMENT

The emphasis upon political systems is, in the present context, largely negative. Political forms, as such, do not enter into the scope of this treatment. The actual type of government, taken by itself, is an indifferent matter in relation to economic life. Often it has no inherent bearing upon most of the rights and freedoms of man. Such statements may seem startling in this age of totalitarian governments. Yet there is a valid distinction, by no means too subtle or refined, between the form of political life and the philosophy which pervades the rulers of states. The total state has the political form of dictatorship or authoritarianism. But in addition it has a philosophy of absolutism, and this is the precise element of evil in the system. Throughout the centuries there have been hundreds of authoritarian states, such as monarchies or dictatorships. Many times their rule has been just and benign, winning the enthusiastic support of their citizens. It is for this reason that political philosophers distinguish between the type of a government and its basic philosophy.

It is vital to secure the perspective of history when considering the form of governments. Modern Americans have heard so much about the virtues of democracy and the evils of dictatorship that they tend to consider the one inherently good and the other essentially bad. History does not bear out such a sweeping generalization. For a democracy to be successful, its citizens must be informed, reasonably literate, and interested in their government. Otherwise demagogues may rise to power or political machines may wallow in corruption and misrule. With all the forms of democracy, it is still possible for entrenched political machines to rule with almost absolute power over cities, states, and even entire nations. Sometimes such abuses have been so extensive and prolonged that democracy has broken down and been replaced by authoritarian rule, and this with the enthusiastic approval of the citizens.

These observations are not made to belittle the democratic way of life. On the contrary, in the complex modern world, where the state has such great powers and where revolt by citizens is so difficult, it is probably the best guarantee of man's liberties. But historical perspective does explain many Church attitudes and passages in papal encyclicals which might otherwise be confusing. The Church has been and is neutral in regard to forms of government. She has lived under monarchies, party dictatorships, and democracies. In her philosophy, the functioning of government is more important than its form. No system of government can readily be labeled as either inherently bad or essentially good. The best is subject to abuse, while the worst could govern justly and benignly. Thus, most observers concede that the Portuguese dictatorship of Salazar is not despotic. On the other hand, friends of democracy have often been in despair at the functioning of French parliaments.

This attitude of neutrality has subjected the Church to criticism, when it tried to work out a *modus vivendi* with a bad government. American liberals, who are the first to criticize alleged Church intrusions into politics, were vocal in denouncing Vatican concordats with Hitler and Mussolini. Because we did not oppose these rulers politically, we were alleged to have favored them. Liberals have been less fluent in regard to Church efforts to survive behind the Iron Curtain, even though Catholic attitudes on communism are well known. Actually, the Church has patiently adjusted itself to all forms of civil rule, even the worst, while keeping the freedom to denounce injustice and tyranny.

It may be argued that certain forms of government, by their nature, lend themselves to abuse. Thus, dictatorship may be judged by the maxim of Lord Acton: power corrupts, and absolute power corrupts absolutely. Yet, there are so many historical factors which enter into the choice of a government, that valid generalizations are few and limited in scope. Of course, totalitarianism is essentially wrong, but this is an abuse of a particular form of government. It is not inherent in the theory of dictatorship. Subtle distinctions of this nature do not rest well with the average American, who considers the existing historical situation in its concrete setting. Those who differentiate between the form and the functioning of a government are considered to be defending an actual state which they may in fact deplore. Nevertheless, if we are to base our conduct on principle rather than expediency, we must make the necessary distinctions.

In the present context, primary emphasis is laid upon the economic impact of a system. Political elements are introduced only to the extent that they either affect economic life or bear upon man's basic rights and duties. Of course, in the modern world the influence of business and industry is so great that it is bound to affect political life to some degree. Politics and economics are becoming more closely intertwined. Yet, to revert to earlier distinctions, such relationships involve the functioning rather than the form of governments. The real test of a government is its ability to meet the needs of its citizens. It must consider the dignity and the social nature of man. It must rule in accord with the common good. It must serve its subjects, and not be an end in itself. These are the cardinal principles which should govern political life.

INDIVIDUALISM

The Philosophy of Individualism. Among the major economic attitudes stressed in the encyclicals is individualism, or the theory that each man is a law unto himself in the world of business.

This system has had tremendous impact in the modern world. For nearly two centuries, it has been the prevailing attitude in the large industrial nations. It has been particularly honored in the United States, where the phrase "rugged individualism" has, until recently, evoked feelings of pride and admiration. We consider ourselves a nation of self-made men, where the successful have forged ahead in a fair struggle among equals. Before 1932, it was a generally accepted principle that business was largely autonomous, governed by neither political nor social considerations. Events since that time have modified this view somewhat, but it still has many powerful defenders. Hence it is useful to pass judgment upon this system in the light of the basic ethical principles laid down in the preceding chapters.

Individualism, in contrast to fascism and National Socialism, is not bound up with any form of government. It could flourish in a democracy, a monarchy, or even a dictatorship. Indeed, some of the worst current abuses of individualism are found in Latin American dictatorships. It is, of course, profoundly opposed to totalitarian forms of dictatorship, but otherwise it is politically neutral.

Individualism is primarily a philosophy of economic life. It has both its negative and positive aspects. Negatively, it abhors all forms of state intervention in economic affairs. It was developed in the eighteenth century as a revolt against the current statism of France and England. During this period, these powerful nations considered economic growth as a necessary factor in augmenting national strength. As a result, particularly in France, economic life was subject to strict political controls. Detailed regulations were laid down in the attempt to co-ordinate the national economy and increase production. Businessmen grew restive under these controls and led a successful revolt against them. The pendulum then swung to the other extreme, so that government was considered an intruder and usurper if it attempted to intervene in economic affairs. It was supposed to be neutral or at most mildly helpful in certain matters, such as police protection for property owners. The motto: *Laissez faire, laissez passer,* which may be paraphrased: "Leave business alone," was accepted as the rule of the day.

In France, the philosophy of individualism was part of the general theory that man was by nature good and society should let nature take its course. If man acted according to his nature and the natural laws of economics, there would be prosperity. If these were interfered with, chaos and confusion would result. The cry was: "Give us freedom." Property rights should be protected and freedom of contract insured. Nothing more was needed. This emphasis upon freedom, *libertas,* gave the movement the name of Liberalism. In the encyclicals, Liberalism is used in this classic sense. Needless to say, it is almost the exact opposite of current American liberalism. American liberalism generally holds that individual freedom is best secured by state and labor-union intervention in economic life.

English writers developed a more positive philosophy for individualism. They held that the free and selfish strivings of individuals would bring about the highest degree of economic prosperity. Enterprisers and workers, competing among themselves, would work their hardest and turn out the most products of the highest quality. They could not do otherwise in a free and competitive market. The slacker or the producer of shoddy goods would be by-passed by the buyers of labor service or commodities. Hence there was every incentive for each to do his best. But if each did his best, the total would be the maximum output in the light of available resources. Moreover, this output would be distributed fairly by these same forces of competition. A worker who was not paid the real value of his contribution could find another employer who would recognize his worth. A producer who was making abnormal profits would soon find new competitors underselling him. Once these premises are accepted, it logically follows that any outside interference, whether by law, labor unions, or business organizations, would lead to lowered output and economic distress. Such was the philosophy of Adam Smith, David Ricardo, and John Stuart Mill. In the encyclicals, they are referred to as the Manchester School.

Other historical factors contributing to the rise of individualism were noted in Chapter I. Thus, the religious individualism in Protestantism and the rejection of medieval social ethics were important elements in its success. The fact that individualism unleashed tremendous economic forces and coincided with and influenced the Industrial Revolution added to its prestige. At the same time, it brought about the social problem, as noted earlier. Regardless of historical developments, however, and even prescinding from its success or failure, individualism must first be judged as an ethical system.

The Immoral Nature of Individualism. On ethical grounds, individualism is untenable, since it flows from a distorted view of man and his nature. It is based on false philosophy, both in its French and English forms. If we stress its more optimistic aspect, we have the theory that man is good and society is evil. Hence the less that man is oppressed by society, the better. Yet, calm consideration will show that both phases of this argument are deficient. Man is not unblemished in his nature. He has faults and limitations. Nor is society necessarily an external imposition upon him. Man by his nature needs society at various levels, from the family to civil government. As was noted before, he cannot reasonably develop his abilities apart from social living. Accordingly, since individualism is basically antisocial, it is in fundamental conflict with human nature.

There is a more pessimistic argument for individualism, the theory of Hobbes that man is by nature the enemy of his fellow man: *homo homini lupus*. It is held that greed and selfishness are predominant in human nature. Hence it is useless to expect co-operation based on religious motives. We are fortunate, it is said, in having an economic system which, through competition, transforms these selfish drives into results consonant with the general welfare. Justice, equality, and efficiency are produced out of the antagonistic strivings of warring individuals. In fact, however, unqualified pessimism is as false as naïve optimism. Man is neither so bad nor so good as held by these differing schools which support individualism. It is indeed a morbid view of human nature which canonizes greed, selfishness, and strife as the ruling principles of human relations. Class war and giant struggles for power are the inevitable fruits of this evil tree. While selfishness and greed exist, Christian principles demand that they be held in check and not be glorified as creative and constructive forces.

In contrast to individualism, sound ethics hold that man is social as well as individual. He has rights and duties in relation to others which he may not ignore. The laws of charity would preclude the cold egoism postulated by Liberalism. Social and distributive justice bar the notion of a fully automatic economic system, as formulated by the Manchester School. Economic life must be organized for the common good, in harmony with the higher aims of man's existence. It is not an end in itself, much less a cruel game in which only the fittest may survive. Wealth and property are not absolute; rather they are limited by definite social obligations. The evil fruits of individualism, as noted in Chapter I, abundantly prove that this system could not be in accord with God's purpose for the material world. Material things were created to serve all men, not to contribute to the ambition and greed of the conscienceless few.

In particular, the doctrine of *laissez faire* is a derogation of the rights and duties of the state. Civil government has both the power and the obligation to seek the common good of all. It is to direct the resources available to the community so that they produce the maximum general welfare. Regardless of practical results, it would be wrong for the state to abandon all interest in such a vital field as economic life. Given the terrible abuses of the nineteenth and early twentieth centuries, it was even more shameful that states stood impotently by while millions of citizens were degraded and irreplaceable resources squandered. Even less justifiable is the struggle by economic groups to capture control of the state, to use its supreme powers for their own selfish interests. This was too often the real effect of *laissez-faire* policies, regardless of professions that the state should be neutral in economic affairs.

Many proponents of individualism might concede its undesirable ethical overtones, yet justify the system by its results. It removed many senseless and troublesome restrictions on business. They would further argue that it produces a better functioning economic system than any available alternative. Hence they ask that it be accepted at least as the lesser evil. Even this argument has serious deficiencies.

The Economics of Competitive Individualism. There is a direct antithesis between the theory of competitive individualism and the statement by Pope Pius XI that competition may not be the ruling principle of economic life. This theory holds that not only does competition bring about initiative and zeal in production and justice in distribution, but it also leads to a smoothly functioning and efficient economic system. We may concede at the outset that competition does lead to initiative and zeal in production. It is probable that no alternative device can stimulate men so effectively to turn out their best efforts for material success. It is not so evident that these best efforts necessarily lead to better products and more efficient enterprise.

Even granting the real and important virtues of competition, there are economic defects which must also be noted. Thus, it has often led to the wasteful exploitation of natural resources. Competitive policies in the use of forests and oil resources have wasted huge reserves of invaluable and often irreplaceable wealth. In the domain of agriculture, competition has encouraged wasteful use of land, soil erosion, and similar abuses. In industry, it has led to unnecessary duplication of facilities, inefficient distribution, and many "social costs." Illustrations of social costs would be the loss caused by excessive industrial smoke or the moving of whole industries from a town or region. Again, instead of better products, we often have goods made less durable so that future sales will not be impaired. Frequent style changes are made so as to make existing products esthetically obsolescent. At times these style changes interfere with function, as happened with some automobiles and typewriters. All this does not negate the real virtues of competition, but it does show its inadequacy as the "ruling principle of economic life."[1]

The greatest defect of competition as a guide to economic life is its inability to meet the need for basic security. It is argued that the free price system would lead to a full use of resources. If any factor of production, such as labor, land, enterprise, or money, were temporarily idle, the free market would automatically correct this evil. When the available supply is greater than the demand at the going price, it is held that prices would drop until this resource became attractive again. Hence there would never be any prolonged unemployment of men, land, machines, or money. Actually, there are more complex laws which govern economic life. During the early 1930's, men could have offered to work for nothing and still not have found jobs in some industries. Interest rates dropped to zero and even below (at one time during that period a short-term government loan was made at negative interest, i.e., the total principal and interest received by the lender was less than his original investment) and yet there was no substantial demand for investment funds. Without going into a detailed economic analysis of depressions, it is nearly universally conceded that a competitive market would not bring security in present-day economic life.[2] Moreover, the structure of our economy is such today that universal competition would be impossible, even if it were conceded to be desirable.

Nor is it clear that justice in distribution is achieved by the free workings of competition. Much of the argument here is circular, since it assumes that economic value, as determined by present-day markets, is real value. There is something specious in the claim that men of equal skill, working just as hard, were worth only half as much in 1932 as they were in 1929. It is true that the market valued the product imputed to their efforts at this lower figure. But does not this show a faulty organization of economic life? If economic life is to serve man and to produce goods for his needs, a market surplus at the time when there are

[1] For details, see J. F. Cronin, *Economic Analysis and Problems,* Chaps. 12, 14, and 15.
[2] For details, see J. F. Cronin, *op. cit.,* Chaps. 17–19.

countless real needs unsatisfied and millions of men able, willing, and even anxious to work so as to meet these needs is an anomaly.

These arguments do not prove the worthlessness of the competitive system. On the contrary, it does have great merit as an automatic regulator of many phases of economic life. It apportions resources, determines rewards, and stimulates output better than would be possible under the wisest of human planning. It has a function, as Pope Pius XI noted when he called it "justified and certainly useful provided it is kept within certain limits," but it fails badly as the sole regulating principle in the business field.

The determining of the proper limits of competition is a prudential matter, to be handled under the principles of social justice. The organized economic groups seeking their own just interests and the common good, and the state as the supreme guardian of the common good, should determine in detail what should be the function and boundaries of free competition. Thus, the avoidance of depressions, the securing of full employment, the wise use of natural resources, and the payment of living wages are goals which will not be met by competition alone. Yet they are among the primary aims of a sound economic system. Higher directing principles are needed to supplement competition if economic life is to meet the needs of man.

Economic Dictatorship Under Individualism. Pope Pius XI uttered a powerful condemnation of the economic dictatorship which has often supplanted free competition. He held that free competition was frequently suicidal, leading to gigantic struggles for power from which a few ruling groups emerged. The Pontiff called this economic concentration a characteristic note of contemporary economic life. He noted both its origins in the realm of high finance and its evil effects. Three of these were singled out: the struggle for power; the effort to capture the state as a pawn of economic interests; and finally, international effects, either in the forms of nationalism and imperialism or as a conscienceless internationalism "whose country is where profit is."

This is a strong indictment. Apparently it is too strong for the stomachs of some American Catholic writers, who hold that it does not apply to the United States. Actually, there were few countries in the world where it was more applicable at the time of *Quadragesimo Anno*. We, together with England, France, Germany, and Japan, showed the characteristics so well described by the Pope. It would take too long to document this thesis here, but abundant references are available.[3]

It is true that many of the serious abuses described by the Pope no longer obtain here. But the fact of economic concentration remains unchanged, limited only by the new attitudes and powers of government and the might of organized labor and farmers. It is particularly important to repeat that economic concentration persists. The argument that certain kinds of wealth are widely distributed does not invalidate this fact. Ownership may be scattered but control is tightly held. There are three bases for this statement, elaborated in the references given: large corporations have dominant power in American economic life; through various devices a small group controls these corporations; and giant financial institutions, especially banks and life-insurance companies, have billions in funds at their disposal. Within this oligarchy there may be serious differences and even warring factions. But, subject to limitations imposed by government, trade unions, and farmers, it is a fact that a relatively few persons have dominant control over the important segments of American industrial and financial life.

In addition to concentration of power, there is the ability to set prices at noncompetitive levels and the tendency to make these prices too high for the general good. Leaving aside the more subtle refinements of the economist, we may distinguish in American economic life three major price situations: competition, imperfect competition, and monopoly. Competition obtains when

---

[3] For a relatively brief analysis, with full documentation, see J. F. Cronin, *op. cit.*, Chaps. 2, 5, 6, 11, and 12. For book-length treatments, see M. Josephson, *The Robber Barons;* F. L. Allen, *The Lords of Creation;* and A. R. Burns, *The Decline of Competition* (New York: McGraw-Hill, 1936). Many facts are given in R. Miller, *Forty Years After* (St. Paul: Radio Replies Press, 1948), pp. 240–244.

there are so many sellers and buyers of a roughly identical product that no single seller or buyer, or feasible group of either, can control the market. The market is open and flexible and there are no outside controls. New producers may enter the field at will.

By contrast, the monopolist has complete control over production and sales in his market. He is able to fix price so as to produce maximum revenue for himself. He has no present fear of competition. In addition to this strict monopoly, there are monopolistic situations, in which many producers act in concert to achieve a single policy of price and production control. Such policies are illegal in the United States today, but they are not uncommon.

Imperfect competition is a blend of the first two. It might be called restricted competition among producers who have some ability to monopolize a market. There are two important types: monopolistic competition and oligopoly. We have monopolistic competition where there is a brand or product differentiation achieved for a roughly similar item. Automobiles, typewriters, cigarettes, breakfast foods, and brands of aspirin would be examples. In the case of aspirin, the product is identical. Breakfast foods differ markedly. The other examples are in between. But in each case a product serves a similar purpose and is practically interchangeable. Yet, through advertising or minor perfections a quasi-monopoly is achieved. With oligopoly, on the other hand, the important element is that there be only a few producers of the same goods. Some examples here would be steel, glass, farm equipment, chemicals, typewriters, and business machines. The fact that there are only a few producers does not exclude active competition (the tire and tube business is highly competitive), but it does make "live-and-let-live" situations more feasible.[4]

These distinctions are important in understanding the actual economic situation in America. We have areas of competition and of monopoly, but great segments of business belong in an intermediate position. This parallels the field of economic control, where we have a dozen or more financial empires, at times

---

[4] For further details, see J. F. Cronin, *op. cit.*, Chaps. 7, 10, 11, 12.

distinct in their interests and occasionally fiercely antagonistic one to the other. There is concentration and power interests rather than unified control.

In passing ethical judgment upon economic concentration, it is necessary to dwell upon the actual situation today. There is no question about the unsocial nature of past abuses, so eloquently described in *Quadragesimo Anno*. But, regardless of abuses, the fact of centralized economic power is in itself a danger. It confers upon a small group, responsible only to itself, almost absolute power over the community. The influence of economic life in the modern world is so great that those who control business, finance, and industry virtually control the body politic. If the only alternative to such control is the setting up of opposed huge power groups, such as labor unions, farmer organizations, and government boards, we have a battle between giants. In such a contest the individual is likely to be submerged. This is the main danger in the present American situation. Currently the struggles between the power groups have quieted somewhat into an uneasy truce. But it is definitely not desirable that our biennial elections develop into a contest by economic groups to control the state. The principle of subsidiarity is ill-served by such concentrations of power and struggles for control.

The growth of economic power is harmful to the interests of small business. In many fields, the independent owner is being swallowed up by great chains or large producers. This contributes to the depersonalization of the economy, already too far advanced. The human person is being dwarfed by growing conglomerations. We do not hold to an individualism which denies the social nature of man. But likewise we do not accept a trend toward social concentration which submerges the individual in giant groups. Rather we need buffer groups, small enough to be influenced by individuals, but powerful enough in the aggregate to stand up to such large organizations as may be compatible with the common good.

Again, the price policies of these powerful groups have, on the whole, been adverse to the common good. There has been too much of a tendency toward high prices which restrict consumption and hence employment. An unhealthy rigidity has often crept into certain fields of our economy. Of course, not all unsocial price policies are products of bigness. On the contrary, bands of small producers have secured fair-trade laws which lead to price-setting at rather high levels. All these restrictions interfere with the healthy and legitimate workings of competition.

In summary, the situations which led to economic dictatorship persist, although the worst abuses have been regulated or removed through the setting up of even greater counterforces. This reform was natural in the circumstances and good to a certain extent. But a real change in the institutions of economic society would bring about a greater diffusion of both power and control. The steps needed for such fundamental reform will be discussed in several subsequent chapters.

SOCIALISM

The Theory of Socialism. In contrast to individualism, socialism exalts the state in the economic sphere. Socialism has taken so many forms within the last century that it is difficult to specify its exact meaning today. Generally speaking, socialism calls for community owership of the means of production. On the theory that private property in productive goods is the basis of economic exploitation, and the premise that free enterprise varies between wasteful competition and antisocial monopoly, it is held that drastic remedies are needed. Nothing less than community ownership of productive property would permit planned production without exploitation.

The degree of proposed socialization varies among the several schools of Socialists. The system has moderated somewhat from an earlier position which would take over all forms of productive property. Some Socialists would exempt land held by small farmers and even small business firms. They would concentrate upon large, dominant enterprises. Likewise, there is variety in the type of control advocated. Some would have direct state ownership. Others would favor independent state corporations.

Finally, there is a school which would have smaller groups, such as guilds of workers, taking over enterprises.

Most modern socialism holds for democratic methods of seizure, with fair compensation for the former owners. Likewise, it professes that control of the seized property should be democratic, at least through popular participation in a socialist government. In some cases the tendency toward class warfare has been mitigated. Socialists attack the inefficiency of present owners rather than their alleged exploitation of workers. These moderating trends were noted in *Quadragesimo Anno*.

A formal distinction must be made between socialism and nationalization. This latter question will be treated in Chapter XIII. It would be possible to achieve socialism through progressive nationalization of enterprises, but it is also feasible to have considerable state ownership without socialism. A similar distinction can be made between socialism and economic planning, although not all would admit this. In theory, it is possible to have private enterprise with a substantial degree of state control. Some writers would contend that such a situation would inevitably lead to socialism or worse. This, however, is a debatable point.

Socialism has never been a formidable movement in the United States. We have a Socialist Party, with only a small group of followers and minor influence. It had some appeal before 1930 when the progress toward social reform here was slow and halting. But the New Deal gave all but the most doctrinaire Socialists a chance to bring about improvements in economic life without drastically changing our society. At the other extreme, the growth of communist Russia tended to attract radical Socialists into the Communist Party. Accordingly, because of this attrition from both sides, the Socialist Party has become noninfluential and relatively respectable. Its current leader, Norman Thomas, has been held in rather high esteem even by many whose economic philosophy is conservative.

A Critique of Socialism. Pope Pius XI observed the great changes which have come about in socialism. He even stated that many of its concrete proposals do not differ greatly from the just demands of Christian social reformers. He noted with approval its recession from positions regarding the class war and revolutionary violence. Nevertheless, he stated that true socialism, based on its historical principles, is incompatible with Christian teaching.

One basic objection to socialism is its inherent materialism. It would organize social life exclusively in the interests of economic efficiency. With greater and greater production the main aim of society, it is evident that higher values would be sacrificed for the sake of material goods. It may be objected that capitalism is likewise materialistic. But capitalism is not identical with civil society. Moreover, it would hardly be a reform of capitalism to take over and intensify one of its less desirable features.

Socialism would likewise endanger human liberties. If all economic power were concentrated in the hands of the state, such a state would have absolute power. Even if it were organized along democratic lines, there would be great pressures toward absolutism. Here would be a concentration of power much more extensive than under the most dictatorial forms of capitalism. Such centralization is inherently dangerous, no matter what safeguards against abuse are established. Moreover, there are persuasive arguments that central control of economic life is possible only by totalitarian methods. When other incentives are removed, compulsion remains as a last resort. It is not unlikely that a socialist government must either put down resistance by workers or lapse into anarchy. But if it acts against the group which gives it political support, it must either yield power to the opposition or consolidate it by dictatorial methods. There is no easy escape from this dilemma.

There are also strong economic reasons against the practicability of socialism. The idea that a planned economy is more efficient than a well-functioning free economy is a fallacy. Central planning imposes the decisions of the few upon the many. Under a free economy each consumer through his purchases participates in planning. Businessmen through their investments likewise plan. Their activities are co-ordinated in the market through the price mechanism. In this way the quantity and quality of goods, the distribution of labor and capital, and the rewards to producers are calculated in terms of consumer needs and available resources. It is true that defects exist in the actual functioning of our market economy, as was noted earlier in this chapter. But the remedy is a free economy working for sound social ends, not a controlled economy which squanders the initiative and planning of the many only to replace it with the plans of the few. Quite apart from the elements of compulsion inherent in socialism and central planning, it is quite doubtful that centralism can use human and material resources as efficiently as a free economy. To repeat, the issue is not between planning and anarchy, but between the planning of the few and the decisions of the many.[5]

It is for these reasons that the Pontiff states that no Catholic may be a Socialist. He calls the term "Christian Socialism" a contradiction. However, this stricture applies only to socialism in the literal sense of the term. Too often, in the United States, the term socialism is loosely applied to any proposed reform measure which would extend government authority in the economic field. Thus, health-insurance measures are sometimes mislabeled socialism or socialized medicine. Obviously, socialism in the technical sense has a very definite meaning. Even extensive nationalization is not of necessity socialism, although it may be undesirable for other reasons. Only if such measures are part of a pattern leading to complete state ownership of industry or control over services can we call them socialist.

NONCOMMUNIST STATISM

While socialism is the antithesis of individualism by virtue of state ownership of productive property, there are other forms of statism where control rather than ownership is the distinguishing feature. Thus, National Socialism and fascism did not take over private industry, but they subjected economic life to strict state

---

[5] For a succinct treatment of this problem, see J. Messner, *Social Ethics,* pp. 818–823, and L. von Mises, *Human Action* (New Haven: Yale Univ. Press, 1949), Chap. 26,

control. The system of ownership was undisturbed, but the owners were by no means their own masters in running their businesses. Prices were often regulated, production quotas set, and rigid patterns of working conditions imposed. The owners were allowed to receive profits, but they were often told how these must be invested in terms of economic expansion. Like every other phase of life in a totalitarian economy, business was forced to accept state dictatorship.

In discussing these varieties of statism, a sharp distinction must be made between state control of economic life and totalitarian control of all phases of life. This distinction is vital in appraising many modern government systems. Totalitarianism is essentially evil. By its very nature, it embodies a false concept of society. It denies basic rights to individuals. The total state intrudes in fields where government has no normal authority to enter. It probes deeply into family relationships, ignores parental authority in education, suppresses vital individual freedoms, and thus makes the citizen the slave of the state. It is unnecessary to elaborate in detail how all this perverts the notions of individual dignity, the function of society, and the true nature of the common good.

By contrast, complete state control over economic life, while generally wrong, is not such an absolute evil. It could be justified in times of war or national emergency. It is conceivable that in certain historical situations drastic measures of this nature might even be demanded by the common good. Furthermore, the degree of state control may vary considerably. It is even possible that dictatorships might organize economic life in such a way that its components have a large area of control over much of its functions. The state might be a co-ordinating agency rather than a bureaucratic colossus reaching into every detail of the economy. Hence some forms of statism might present only a potential rather than an actual evil. They might violate the principle of subsidiarity, but not necessarily to a greater degree than obtains in some capitalistic countries. This distinction explains the varying Church reactions toward modern authoritarian states. There is definite condemnation of totalitarian elements, but a more reserved and aloof reaction to states where political power is centralized and to some degree in control of the economic system.

In Italy, for example, Pope Pius XI was quick to attack any totalitarian tendencies in fascism. He denounced its attempts to take over control of youth and to dissolve religious organizations of the laity. His encyclical, *Non Abbiamo Bisogno,* was aimed at such abuses. But when, in *Quadragesimo Anno,* he discussed the fascist economic system, he was rather cautious in his appraisal. He noted both good points and abuses. In particular, he conceived the possibility that state control could be only in terms of general organization, with a high degree of autonomy left to the worker and employer groups in the corporative system. Even at best, such a situation might not be ideal. But in a world where capitalism was currently sunk in a deep economic crisis, a strong program to put order and purpose into economic life might have been considered a lesser evil.

In Germany, the totalitarian elements were more apparent, although not necessarily so at the time of the signing of the concordat. When Hitler showed his true colors, this same Pontiff issued the powerful encyclical, *Mit Brennender Sorge.* He denounced racism, state control over youth and education, violations of basic individual rights, and interference with religion. This same theme was further elaborated by Pope Pius XII, who called National Socialism "the arrogant apostasy from Jesus Christ . . . the cult of violence, the idolatry of race and blood, the overthrow of human liberty and dignity."

The situations in Spain and Argentina are more confused. They are roughly similar to the early phases of fascism, where totalitarian elements were apparently lacking. There is one-party dictatorship and suppression of political opposition. But, on the other hand, there are large areas of individual freedom. Interferences with religion, while annoying, do not clearly fit into a pattern of opposition to the Church. Business and labor have considerable autonomy, while some desirable social reforms have been instituted. Except for political dictatorship, there are few abuses which could not be paralleled in many democratic countries,

If the Church were to attack Franco and Perón, it would have to be on grounds that political dictatorship is either intrinsically evil, dangerous because of potential abuses, or unjust in view of the tremendous powers of the modern state. The Church has never taken the first stand. As was noted earlier in this chapter, it has been neutral in regard to forms of governments and concerned only with their functioning. Catholic writers have never held the right to suffrage to be an unqualified right. Indeed, if one were to hold that modern democracy is the only political expression of human dignity, one would then condemn practically all governments prior to the eighteenth century. Even today, it is widely held that not all peoples are yet capable of self-government. Those who accept it as an ideal still admit that some nations have not been educated to this level.

That dictatorships are potentially dangerous is a much more plausible argument. The military power of a modern state is such that popular revolt is rarely feasible. Hence, if a dictatorship becomes unjust and tyrannical, it is no longer practical for a people to rise against it. Likewise it might be contended, as Pope Pius XII noted, that the demands of the modern state upon its citizens are so great that they should rightly have a voice in controlling this state. It may be that Catholic writers will increasingly hold that, under modern conditions, only democratic government can effectively secure the common good. We Americans are rightly proud of the achievements of democracy. But, when the popes write for the entire world and survey the perspective of all history, they naturally take a more flexible position.

The case of Portugal illustrates the need for caution in pronouncing on forms of government. In that nation, democracy became so corrupt and inept during the 1920's that the nation was threatened with disaster. Complete economic collapse and political chaos were in the offing. It was under these conditions that Salazar assumed dictatorial powers. He gave the nation a well-administered and honest government. There are practically no totalitarian elements in his regime. Economic life is controlled in a corporative fashion, with an economic assembly as one of the organs of government. The nation has enjoyed comparative prosperity and progress under these conditions, and that in times when world trade was disrupted first by a depression and then by World War II.[6]

RECAPITULATION

So many complex distinctions have been introduced in this chapter that a summary of the main points seems desirable. The basic purpose has been to judge noncommunist economic systems in the light of the principles elaborated in the two chapters preceding. Do these systems pass muster in the light of human dignity, the nature of society, the purpose of economic life, and the demands of justice and charity?

Individualism in its various forms has been found wanting because it misconceives the nature of society and the common good. It exalts greed, selfishness, and lust for power. It denies to the state the power to intervene in economic matters when the common good demands it. Under the form of unregulated competition it produced great social evils. Matters were not improved when economic dictatorship took over. Rather a new threat was developed to the freedom and dignity of the individual.

Socialism as a remedy swung to the other extreme. It concentrated such immense powers in the state that freedom was likewise threatened. Moreover, it adopted an essentially materialistic view of economic life. As to other forms of statism, a distinction must be made between their political and their economic aspects. Politically, they were fundamentally wrong to the extent that they were totalitarian. As to an authoritarian political regime, the Church has remained neutral, although many writers feel that today democracy is the best safeguard for essential human liberties. The economic aspects of such systems are to be judged in the light of historical facts. An authoritarian government could

---

[6] For a brief summary of the Portuguese experiment and further references, see J. F. Cronin, *op. cit.*, Chap. 23.

leave the necessary autonomy to economic groups, intervening only to the extent demanded by the common good. Only the facts in each case will determine the answer. Individualism and socialism are basically economic philosophies and can be judged as such. Authoritarianism, when it is not totalitarian, is a political philosophy compatible with several different economic systems. No general pronouncement can be made in such cases.

The ideal economic system would balance both individual rights and social responsibilities. Its customs and institutions would lead to the common good of all. In such a society, government would be the supreme co-ordinating force, directing all else in the interests of the general welfare. But it would serve its citizens, not dominate over them for the sake of a class or party. Utmost freedom would be left to lesser groups and to individuals, provided only that their actions fitted in with the pattern dictated by the common good. This would be real economic democracy, directing the use of material goods for the best interests of all.

READINGS*

On Individualism and Socialism:

J. Messner, *Social Ethics,* pp. 543–565, 816–823, 927–930, 935–943.
E. Cahill, *Framework of a Christian State,* Chap. 11.
C. Clune, *Christian Social Reconstruction,* Chap. 6.
O. von Nell-Breuning, *Reorganization of Social Economy,* Chaps. 14–15.
G. C. Rutten, *La doctrine sociale de l'Église,* Chap. 10.
J. Husslein, *Christian Social Manifesto,* Chaps. 5, 9, 11, 12.
R. Miller, *Forty Years After,* pp. 200–265.
G. Bruehl, *The Pope's Plan for Social Reconstruction,* Chaps. 13–14.
J. F. Cronin, "Rugged Individualism."

On Statism:

J. Messner, *Social Ethics,* pp. 566–579.
R. Kothen, *L'Enseignement social de l'Église,* Chap. 7.
C. Dawson, *Religion and the Modern State.*
H. A. Rommen, *The State in Catholic Thought.*
H. W. Metz and C. A. H. Thomson, *Authoritarianism and the Individual.*

* For further readings, see Lists Nos. 1, 4, 6, and 12 in the Appendix.

Chapter VI. COMMUNISM

Pius XI, Quadragesimo Anno

62. All these things which Our Predecessor has not only suggested but clearly and openly proclaimed, We emphasize with renewed insistence in our present Encyclical; and unless utmost efforts are made without delay to put them into effect, let no one persuade himself that public order, peace, and the tranquillity of human society can be effectively defended against agitators of revolution.

112. Communism teaches and seeks two objectives: unrelenting class warfare and absolute extermination of private ownership. Not secretly or by hidden methods does it do this, but publicly, openly, and by employing every and all means, even the most violent. To achieve these objectives there is nothing which it does not dare, nothing for which it has respect or reverence; and when it has come to power, it is incredible and portentlike in its cruelty and inhumanity. The horrible slaughter and destruction through which it has laid waste vast regions of eastern Europe and Asia are the evidence; how much an enemy and how openly hostile it is to Holy Church and to God Himself is, alas, too well proved by facts and fully known to all. Although We, therefore, deem it superfluous to warn upright and faithful children of the Church regarding the impious and iniquitous character of communism, yet We cannot without deep sorrow contemplate the heedlessness of those who apparently make light of these impending dangers, and with sluggish inertia allow the widespread propagation of doctrine which seeks by violence and slaughter to destroy society altogether. All the more gravely to be condemned is the folly of those who neglect to remove or change the conditions that inflame the minds of peoples and pave the way for the overthrow and destruction of society.

Pius XI, On Atheistic Communism

8. The communism of today, more emphatically than similar movements in the past, conceals in itself a false messianic idea. A pseudo-ideal

of justice, of equality and fraternity in labor impregnates all its doctrine and activity with a deceptive mysticism, which communicates a zealous and contagious enthusiasm to the multitudes entrapped by delusive promises. This is especially true in an age like ours, when unusual misery has resulted from the unequal distribution of the goods of this world. This pseudo-ideal is even boastfully advanced as if it were responsible for a certain economic progress. As a matter of fact, when such progress is at all real, its true causes are quite different, as for instance the intensification of industrialism in countries which were formerly almost without it, the exploitation of immense natural resources, and the use of the most brutal methods to insure the achievement of gigantic projects with a minimum of expense.

9. The doctrine of modern communism, which is often concealed under the most seductive trappings, is in substance based on the principles of dialectical and historical materialism previously advocated by Marx, of which the theoreticians of Bolshevism claim to possess the only genuine interpretation. According to this doctrine there is in the world only one reality, matter, the blind forces of which evolve into plant, animal, and man. Even human society is nothing but a phenomenon and form of matter, evolving in the same way. By a law of inexorable necessity and through a perpetual conflict of forces, matter moves toward the final synthesis of a classless society. In such a doctrine, as is evident, there is no room for the idea of God; there is no difference between matter and spirit, between soul and body; there is neither survival of the soul after death nor any hope in a future life. Insisting on the dialectical aspect of their materialism, the Communists claim that the conflict which carries the world toward its final synthesis can be accelerated by man. Hence they endeavor to sharpen the antagonisms which arise between the various classes of society. Thus the class struggle with its consequent violent hate and destruction takes on the aspect of a crusade for the progress of humanity. On the other hand, all other forces whatever, as long as they resist such systematic violence, must be annihilated as hostile to the human race.

10. Communism, moreover, strips man of his liberty, robs human personality of all its dignity, and removes all the moral restraints that check the eruptions of blind impulse. There is no recognition of any right of the individual in his relations to the collectivity; no natural right is accorded to human personality, which is a mere cogwheel in the communist system. In man's relations with other individuals, besides, Communists hold the principle of absolute equality, rejecting all hierarchy and divinely constituted authority, including the authority of parents. What men call authority and subordination is derived from the com-

munity as its first and only font. Nor is the individual granted any property rights over material goods or the means of production for, inasmuch as these are the source of further wealth, their possession would give one man power over another. Precisely on this score, all forms of private property must be eradicated, for they are at the origin of all economic enslavement.

12. What would be the condition of a human society based on such materialistic tenets? It would be a collectivity with no other hierarchy than that of the economic system. It would have only one mission: the production of material things by means of collective labor, so that the goods of this world might be enjoyed in a paradise where each would "give according to his powers" and would "receive according to his needs." Communism recognizes in the collectivity the right, or rather, unlimited discretion, to draft individuals for the labor of the collectivity with no regard for their personal welfare; so that even violence could be legitimately exercised to dragoon the recalcitrant against their wills. In the communistic commonwealth morality and law would be nothing but a derivation of the existing economic order, purely earthly in origin and unstable in character. In a word, the Communists claim to inaugurate a new era and a new civilization which is the result of blind evolutionary forces culminating in a humanity without God.

14. Such, Venerable Brethren, is the new gospel which Bolshevistic and atheistic communism offers the world as the glad tidings of deliverance and salvation! It is a system full of errors and sophisms. It is in opposition both to reason and to divine revelation. It subverts the social order, because it means the destruction of its foundations; because it ignores the true origin and purpose of the state; because it denies the rights, dignity, and liberty of human personality.

15. How is it possible that such a system, long since rejected scientifically and now proved erroneous by experience, how is it, We ask, that such a system could spread so rapidly in all parts of the world? The explanation lies in the fact that too few have been able to grasp the nature of communism. The majority instead succumb to its deception, skillfully concealed by the most extravagant promises. By pretending to desire only the betterment of the condition of the working classes, by urging the removal of the very real abuses chargeable to the liberalistic economic order, and by demanding a more equitable distribution of this world's goods (objects entirely and undoubtedly legitimate), the Communist takes advantage of the present world-wide economic crisis to draw into the sphere of his influence even those sections of the populace which on principle reject all forms of materialism and terrorism. And

as every error contains its element of truth, the partial truths to which we have referred are astutely presented according to the needs of time and place, to conceal, when convenient, the repulsive crudity and in- humanity of communistic principles and tactics. Thus the communist ideal wins over many of the better-minded members of the community. These in turn become the apostles of the movement among the younger intelligentsia who are still too immature to recognize the intrinsic errors of the system. The preachers of communism are also proficient in ex- ploiting racial antagonisms and political divisions and oppositions. They take advantage of the lack of orientation characteristic of modern agnostic science in order to burrow into the universities where they bolster up the principles of their doctrine with pseudoscientific arguments.

17. There is another explanation for the rapid diffusion of the com- munistic ideas now seeping into every nation, great and small, advanced and backward, so that no corner of the earth is free from them. This explanation is to be found in a propaganda so truly diabolical that the world has perhaps never witnessed its like before. It is directed from one common center. It is shrewdly adapted to the varying conditions of diverse peoples. It has at its disposal great financial resources, gigantic organizations, international congresses, and countless trained workers. It makes use of pamphlets and reviews, of cinema, theater, and radio, of schools and even universities. Little by little it penetrates into all classes of the people and even reaches the better-minded groups of the com- munity with the result that few are aware of the poison which increasingly pervades their minds and hearts.

22. For the first time in history we are witnessing a struggle, cold blooded in purpose and mapped out to the least detail, between man and "all that is called God." Communism is by its nature antireligious. It con- siders religion as the "opiate of the people" because the principles of religion which speak of a life beyond the grave dissuade the proletariat from the dream of a Soviet paradise which is of this world.

23. But the law of nature and its Author cannot be flouted with impunity. Communism has not been able, and will not be able, to achieve its objectives even in the merely economic sphere. It is true that in Russia it has been a contributing factor in rousing men and materials from the inertia of centuries, and in obtaining by all manner of means, often without scruple, some measure of material success. Never- theless we know from reliable and even very recent testimony that not even there, in spite of slavery imposed on millions of men, has communism reached its promised goal. After all, even the sphere of

economics needs some morality, some moral sense of responsibility, which can find no place in a system so thoroughly materialistic as communism. Terrorism is the only possible substitute, and it is terrorism that reigns today in Russia, where former comrades in revolution are exterminating each other. Terrorism, having failed despite all to stem the tide of moral corruption, cannot even prevent the dissolution of society itself.

57. In the beginning communism showed itself for what it was in all its perversity; but very soon it realized that it was thus alienating the people. It has therefore changed its tactics, and strives to entice the multitudes by trickery of various forms, hiding its real designs behind ideas that in themselves are good and attractive. Thus, aware of the universal desire for peace, the leaders of communism pretend to be the most zealous promoters and propagandists in the movement for world amity. Yet at the same time they stir up a class warfare which causes rivers of blood to flow, and, realizing that their system offers no internal guarantee of peace, they have recourse to unlimited armaments. Under various names which do not suggest communism, they establish organizations and periodicals with the sole purpose of carrying their ideas into quarters otherwise inaccessible. They try perfidiously to worm their way even into professedly Catholic and religious organizations. Again, without receding an inch from their subversive principles, they invite Catholics to collaborate with them in the realm of so-called humanitarianism and charity; and at times even make proposals that are in perfect harmony with the Christian spirit and the doctrine of the Church. Elsewhere they carry their hypocrisy so far as to encourage the belief that communism, in countries where faith and culture are more strongly entrenched, will assume another and much milder form. It will not interfere with the practice of religion. It will respect liberty of conscience. There are some even who refer to certain changes recently introduced into Soviet legislation as a proof that communism is about to abandon its program of war against God.

58. See to it, Venerable Brethren, that the Faithful do not allow themselves to be deceived! Communism is intrinsically wrong, and no one who would save Christian civilization may collaborate with it in any undertaking whatsoever. Those who permit themselves to be deceived into lending their aid toward the triumph of communism in their own country, will be the first to fall victims of their error. And the greater the antiquity and grandeur of the Christian civilization in the regions where communism successfully penetrates, so much more devastating will be the hatred displayed by the godless.

Pius XII, Christmas Broadcast, 1945

Consequently, this totalitarianism fails by what is the only measure of progress, namely, the progressive creation of ever more ample and better conditions in public life to ensure that the family can evolve as an economic, juridic, moral, and religious unit.

Within the confines of each particular nation as much as in the whole family of peoples, state totalitarianism is incompatible with a true and healthy democracy. Like a dangerous germ it infects the community of nations and renders it incapable of guaranteeing the security of individual peoples. It constitutes a continual menace of war.

Pius XII, Address to Minister From India, July 6, 1949

It is a sorry characteristic of our times that there prevails in not a few places a concept of life and society that is vitiated by an excess of materialism or perverted by an outright denial of spiritual values. Hence it becomes all the more necessary and urgent that the rulers of states and peoples who recognize in the supremacy of the spirit over matter one of the fundamental laws of their existence and of the individual and the groundwork of their hopes for the future should join their forces of individual and collective vigilance to stem the tide of materialism, which must needs overflow in a spirit of violence and servitude, by erecting the barricade required to keep the moral patrimony of mankind intact.

Congregation of the Holy Office, July 13, 1949

The Supreme Sacred Congregation of the Holy Office has been asked: (1) Whether it is lawful to enlist in or show favor to the communist party? (2) Whether it is lawful to publish, read, or disseminate books, newspapers, periodicals, or leaflets in support of communist doctrine and practice or write any articles in them? (3) Whether Catholics who knowingly and freely perform actions as specified in Nos. 1 and 2 above may be admitted to the sacraments? (4) Whether Catholics, who profess and particularly those who defend and spread, the materialistic and anti-Christian doctrine of the Communists, ipso facto, as apostates from the Catholic faith, incur excommunication reserved especially to the Holy See?

The most eminent and reverend fathers, charged with the defense of matters pertaining to faith and morals, after having previously heard the opinion of the consultors at a plenary session held on Tuesday, the 28th day of June, 1949, decreed that the above-mentioned questions be answered as follows:

To No. 1 — In the negative, for communism is materialistic and anti-Christian. Besides, communist leaders, although they sometimes verbally assert that they are not opposed to religion, show themselves nevertheless, both by doctrine and by action, to be in reality enemies of God, of the true religion, and of the Church of Christ.

To No. 2 — In the negative, inasmuch as this is prohibited by law itself (of Canon 1399, *Corpus Juris Canonici*).

To No. 3 — In the negative, in accordance with the common principles governing refusal of the sacraments to those not having proper dispositions.

To No. 4 — In the affirmative.

And on the following Thursday, the 30th of the same month and year, His Holiness Pope Pius XII, when informed of the decision in the usual audience granted to His Excellency, the Most Reverend Assessor, approved and ordered to be published the above answers in the *Acta Apostolicae Sedis*.

Like the other systems examined thus far, communism offers a complete program in the socioeconomic field. It claims its own solution for the social problem. It is thorough, far-reaching, and drastic. There is a finality about communism which may explain part of its appeal. It is like a drug or a surgical operation, admittedly dangerous, which will either kill or cure completely. To many who suffer from chronic disease, there is a fascination in a remedy which will offer them complete relief, if it does not kill them. They are impatient with slow and tedious medication. They want immediate results, even at some risk.

Unquestionably, communism has developed a dynamism similar to that which individualism had at its beginning. Like individualism, it is simple in its approach and total in its promises. Individualism taught that business, if left alone, would work out a perfect economic order. It failed. Communists would then discard every element in individualism and abolish free enterprise and private property. For them, there would be no compromise as involved in statism or moderate socialism. There is no question of perfecting what is good and discarding what is evil in private capitalism. It has failed, so it must be liquidated.

This total approach of communism, considered in the light of human nature, explains well both its attraction and its fatal weakness. Solutions which are simple and complete will always have their followers. Some of these persons are idealists, who dream of a formula which will make the world perfect. Others are fanatics, who drive to a goal ruthlessly, regardless of the obstacles. Yet history, which is but a projection in time of psychology, shows the essential weaknesses of total solutions. Men change but slowly. Progress is evolutionary, not revolutionary. We adapt and perfect; we rarely discard the past completely. When idealists and fanatics have the power to act, they try to remake human nature in a day. They will fail, as communism will fail. But, at the present, it has immense and growing power. Hence it is necessary to examine in detail its theory, tactics, and practice.

The Theory of Communism. Communism is a system of dialectical materialism. It is based on the premise that matter is the only reality, with God, the soul, and spiritual values but fictions. Material forces dominate the evolution of the world. Most important of these are economic forces, since they determine man's ability to survive. In any society, the organized methods of production are the absolute determinants of that culture. Civil government, the family, the Church, and other social groups are merely by-products of economic organization.

This materialism is dialectical in the sense worked out by the German philosopher, Hegel. History is seen as a dynamic process, whereby groups of forces dominate a given period of time. But every action leads to an equal and opposite reaction. The thesis (the existing system) creates its antithesis, which is its direct opposite. The conflict between the two leads to a merged balance of forces, called the synthesis. Hegel would not consider this resolution of forces to be stable, but would call the synthesis the starting point for a new dialectical process. Marx, however, the philosopher of communism, did not go beyond the stages which he said would lead inevitably to communism.

Applying dialectical materialism to the nineteenth-century world, Marx considered capitalism to be the dominant economic system which determined contemporary history. The heart of capitalism is the institution of private property, which enables a few persons to secure control of economic life. Property, of course, is fundamental, since it furnishes the means of existence for man. When property is in private hands, its owners thereby control the lives of other men, who are nonowners. They can force others to work for them at whatever wages the owners choose. That such wages would be the minimum level needed for subsistence was proved by the capitalist economist, Ricardo. Hence private property is essentially a means of exploitation. Economic value is created only by work, but the owners return to the workers only a fraction of what they produce. The remainder, the surplus value, is retained for the immense profits of the capitalists.

To safeguard this system of exploitation, owners have developed two institutions for repressing the proletariat, the nonowning workers. The first is the state, which through its various powers protects the property owner. Most important of these powers is the police force which cows the workers. The courts, law, and such institutions are but elaborate developments of police and military power. Moreover schools, the bourgeois press, and other opinion-forming agencies are tools of the capitalists. Even the family, in its present form, embodies the capitalist mentality. Monogamy and parental control of children are but extensions of the ownership principle. Hence civil society is but a protective integument for monopolistic owners.

The second institution created to defend property is organized religion, the opiate of the people. Religion is an anodyne which deadens the frustrations of the workers by promising them justice in another world. In the crude language of the Industrial Workers of the World (I.W.W. — Wobblies), it offers "pie in the sky, instead of pie on earth." Religion sanctions property ownership in its command: Thou shalt not steal. It teaches to its votaries meekness and submission. The other-world mentality robs them of the ambition to remedy abuses here and now. It is an ideal tool for the capitalists.

Nevertheless, the dialectical forces of history may not be denied. The process of exploitation creates the weapons whereby it will ultimately be abolished. First, it arouses in the workers an ever increasing sense of anger and resentment. They become embittered at their lot, the more so when they contrast it with the wealth and luxury secured by others with the fruits of their labor. The next step naturally follows. The workers are "disciplined, united, organized, by the very mechanism of the process of capitalist production itself." These workers, given solidarity by their oppressors, unite in a revolutionary upsurge. "Centralization of the means of production and socialization of labor at last reach a point where they become incompatible with their capitalist integument. This integument is burst asunder. The knell of capitalist private property sounds. The expropriators are expropriated."[1]

The Communist Party exists to aid in the class struggle and thereby accelerate processes of history. It must educate the workers to realize their oppression and the means of deliverance. It must take advantage of poverty and exploitation, but especially it must capitalize on the recurring depressions and imperialist wars which are inevitable in the existing system. The unemployed offer a fertile field for recruits. In pursuing this aim, the Communists must not be deviated by the prospects of short-term reforms. While they may agitate for reforms, so as to win the allegiance of the workers, their demands must be insatiable, so that issues will always remain. This point is vital. Proletarian reform groups which would be satisfied with anything less than total revolution are traitors to the working class. They are more dangerous enemies than the capitalists themselves. The class struggle must be intensified, not mitigated.[2]

---

[1] Karl Marx, quoted in H. Laski, *Communism* (New York, Holt, 1927), p. 108.

[2] This element of communist theory is of vital importance for understanding communist tactics. Communists want issues, not reforms. An outstanding recent example was the sabotaging of the prodemocratic party in Portugal in 1949 by giving it the "kiss of death." American labor leaders and liberal legislators can cite scores of instances where our native Communists killed reforms by making impossible demands or through propaganda which alienated middle-of-the-road groups. Yet, thousands of other American liberals blindly persist in thinking of Communists as social reformers. They consider them extreme, but are willing to co-operate with them. This inexcusable blindness has set back the cause of social reform in countless cases. Noncommunist

Since the struggle is world wide, communist organization must be international. From the beginning, communism organized its international movements. Because of internal dissensions, moderates and deviationists were sloughed off. The latest authentic international movement is the Third International, formed by the Bolshevik government of Russia.[3] This organization, called the Comintern, controls all communist parties throughout the world. Ostensibly it was dissolved in 1943, but espionage activities and the world-wide unanimity of communist tactics prove that it persists in an underground manner. Its function is to aid in the formation of local communist parties and to direct their activities in accord with the current party line of the Soviet Politburo. It has enjoyed extraordinary success in welding together a world communist movement, slavishly subject to the discipline of the communist fatherland, the Union of Soviet Socialist Republics. The original purpose of the international was to create internal revolutions and sabotage in capitalist and colonial countries. With the growth of Soviet power, particularly after World War II, its function has now been modified. The Comintern has not given up the idea of internal revolutions, but it subordinates this aim to the more powerful weapon of Soviet foreign policy. Current emphasis is upon espionage, encouragement of pacificism and isolationism in capitalist countries, and preparation for ultimate communist military or political moves in regions adjacent to the Iron Curtain.

The original Marxist-Leninist theory envisioned a series of revolutions by workers united by the communist parties and the Comintern. The Communist Party would act as agent of the workers in setting up an interim dictatorship of the proletariat. This dictatorship would liquidate private property and the own-

---

leftist movements, such as Social Democracy, understand this tactic and are far more bitter enemies of Communists than are liberals or even conservative capitalists.

[3] Trotskyite and, more recently, Titoist groups talked of forming a Fourth International. But splinter communist groups which have broken from Stalinist discipline are not usually important in terms of world power. Frequently, however, they are more faithful to the teachings of Marx and Lenin than is the case with Comintern-controlled Communists.

ing class. It would destroy the institutions which protected property, including the Church. When property was socialized, production would then be organized in the interests of the workers. In this classless society, there would soon be abundance for all. The interim dictatorship could then be abolished, formal government would be unnecessary, and workers' soviets would control production. In such an ideal society, all would give according to their abilities, and each would receive according to his needs.

Communist Tactics. Karl Marx was the theorist of communism, but Vladimir Lenin was the evil genius of its tactics. He perfected all previous tactics into a synthesis which has produced remarkable results. Above all he understood the requirements for revolutionary seizure of power. Experts claim that communist tactics enable them to exert an influence far beyond the power of their numbers. While it is difficult to reduce such intangibles to mathematical terms, there is good evidence to show that in the United States, at least, a single Communist has at times the power of a thousand ordinary citizens. This figure is based upon detailed analyses of their influence in labor unions, political affairs, and propaganda campaigns.

The organization of the Communist Party is basically secret and dictatorial. Secrecy was often imposed upon it by government repression, but it has served party purposes so well that it is kept even where the Party has a legal right to function. Membership lists are not revealed; at times, no central lists are even maintained. Meetings are normally closed to outsiders and are rarely given much publicity. Decisions reached are absolutely binding upon all members, under penalty of expulsion. Lenin permitted considerable discussion prior to the reaching of decisions, but under Stalin there is little pretense of democracy in the "democratic centralism" of the Party. Major changes in the Party Line may be ordered by the Comintern and all members are expected to make an immediate *volte face*. Top leaders, such as Earl Browder, may be removed and disgraced in a day if Comintern interests demand. Deviationists are arbitrarily and ruthlessly purged, at times merely to dramatize a change in the line. In any country subject to Comintern discipline, leaders and policies must be approved by its delegate (called the CI-Rep).

Under such strict control, recruiting is naturally a slow and careful process. There is no one type which could be called characteristic material for communism. Most of its recruits, however, would fall into one of three groups: the seriously disgruntled, misled idealists, and ambitious opportunists. The first type is obvious material for a revolutionary movement. It includes victims of economic, racial, national, and religious or cultural discrimination. Many workers who become Communists do so because of crass exploitation or bitter class-struggle experiences in trying to better economic conditions. In the United States, recruitment for this reason alone has not been too successful.[4] The American Party has achieved better results among middle-class and even occasional well-to-do persons who are victims of racial, religious, or cultural discrimination. Certain foreign-language groups are considered good prospects. Of the average sixty thousand American Communists, about 80 per cent belong in minority groups of one type or other. This is also true of non-Party fellow travelers, who outnumber actual Communists here by a ratio of about fifteen to one.

The idealists who become Communists are often intellectuals. Their interest may be either negative, revulsion against oppression; or positive, attraction for a planned society or some features of Soviet Communism. Published material in the Canadian espionage cases, and unpublished material about the American spy rings, indicate that misguided idealists play an important part in communist plans. The initial appeal is made in terms of social justice, freedom of science, peace, or some other idealistic consideration. The victim is gradually led to believe that his ideals can be realized only under communism. This explains, in part,

---

[4] The common assumption that economic factors alone produce Communists does not stand up for the American Communist Party. Its appeal along strict economic lines has not been fruitful, at least as regards the actual victims of exploitation and mistreatment. Exploitation has been more of a factor in attracting liberal idealists than workers.

why high-paid and respected scientists and other intellectuals joined the Soviet espionage apparatus in England, Canada, and the United States.

A third class of recruits includes ambitious persons who feel that the Communist Party would be a vehicle for advancement in their chosen sphere of life. Obvious examples are the former Nazis, Fascists, and collaborators in Europe who quickly joined their respective communist parties to gain immunity and power. This fact was notorious in postwar Europe. Surprisingly, however, secret communist membership or sympathy with the Party could bring real returns in the United States. From published and highly reliable unpublished sources these facts are known: a communist patronage ring operated in Washington from about 1935 which pushed Communists or sympathizers into high office; prior to 1948, there was sufficient communist influence in branches of the C.I.O. to make the Party attractive to some ambitious labor leaders; and communist influence in the broad literary field, including screen, radio, and book and magazine writing, was such as to mean advancement, good reviews, and organized public acclaim for Party favorites. The same opportunities obtained for screen, stage, and radio actors who were sympathetic to the Communists.

When a subject is brought into the Party, he is given a thorough indoctrination in the principles of Marx, Lenin, and Stalin. What is even more important, he is hermetically isolated from the capitalist world. He is led to distrust all bourgeois sources of information and to cut off friendly contacts with non-Communists. With such complete dependence upon the Party, even for his thoughts, he soon becomes a fanatic. This explains in part the fanatical zeal which provokes admiration even from the enemies of communism. Another explanation of communist fanaticism is in terms of Darwinian selection: only persons who are zealots would be attracted to such an extreme system and survive its rigorous demands upon its members.

Much of the secret of communist success lies in its strict organization and iron discipline. It is axiomatic that an organized, disciplined minority can usually outmaneuver a disorganized majority. Another element is the power of massive deceit, the principle of the "big lie." Most persons do not know or care enough about many national and world issues to delve deeply into them. If the Communists can raise a smoke screen on any issue, the general public will be confused and indecisive, if not actually convinced by them. Examples of the successful application of these methods include propaganda about Loyalist Spain, Red China, and, until Soviet aggression became too patent, the Soviet Union itself. But the same tactics are applied on a small scale in struggles for control of union locals or similar immediate communist objectives.

The small Communist Party multiplies its influence by many tried and proved devices. It acts openly in the "united-front" approach, whereby it joins with other organizations for common action for a special objective. It is hoped that in such campaigns the Party would be able to take over the movement and thus lead the larger groups. As a minimum result, it would gain good will, contacts, and respectability. Moreover, it is then in a position to press for ever higher demands, precluding real reform but embittering other participants in the process.[5]

A second approach is the method called "boring-from-within." In these cases, secret Communists secure places in influential organizations, such as government, labor unions, representatives of minorities, and organs for propaganda, such as press, radio, the screen, publishers, and book-review publications. Here the minimum aim is influencing policy along communist lines. The maximum objective is capture and control of such groups.

A third tactic is the formation of "front organizations," or groups apparently noncommunist but secretly organized and controlled by the Party, which aim at ostensibly sound objectives. The method used here involves the determining of a high-sounding aim, such as peace, democracy, or some social reform.

[5] The united-front tactic is explained by the Comintern agent, J. Peters, in *A Manual on Organization* (New York: International Publishers, 1936), a valuable document which reveals much of communist mentality and methods. Successful results are described in Eugene Lyons, *The Red Decade* (New York: Bobbs-Merrill, 1942).

Then a core of names of prominent but naïve persons is secured as the organizing committee. On this basis, more names are obtained and fund-raising is started. With funds and names, it is possible to secure publicity, pressure upon government, and like objectives. The success of this tactic is amazing. While it has been exposed time and again, and individuals involved have realized their error in particular cases, its remains a reliable device for multiplying communist effectiveness. There seems to be an inexhaustible fund of prominent persons, who feel that they must be on record in favor of every worthy cause, but too busy to look into the real control of the group or to take any active part in the administration of the movement.

In addition to these broad programs, special approaches are developed for various interest groups, such as labor, Negroes, youth, women, consumers, tenants, the unemployed, pacifists, religious organizations, scientists, lawyers, doctors, teachers, social workers, librarians, book readers, and even businessmen. Thousands of such organizations have been listed by American investigative agencies. The amount of time, energy, and money which goes into such work is unbelievable in relation to the small size of the Communist Party, U.S.A.[6]

Communist tactics have achieved results which are almost beyond belief. In scores of nations they have reached positions of real power. They can influence public opinion and government policy, even when they are a small minority. Often they achieve political success through balance-of-power tactics, siding with the group which offers them the most promises. Even more remarkable is their tenacious hold upon their spheres of influence, even after public opinion has been revolted by Soviet expansionist tactics. Their power of adaptation and deception is unique.

Soviet Communism. Communist theory was put into practice, for the first time on a large scale, in Russia. In 1917, the Russia of the Tsars gave way to a democratic government, which was

---

[6] An excellent description is available in Eugene Lyons, *op. cit.* For communist labor-union tactics, see J. F. Cronin, *Catholic Social Action* (Milwaukee: Bruce, 1948), Chap. 7.

then overthrown by the Union of Soviet Socialist Republics. At its very beginning, the Communists put into effect their theories both of violent revolution and of contempt for moderate or even mildly radical reform. The actual communist revolt was not against the Tsars, but against the moderate Social Democratic government of Kerensky which had earlier replaced the monarchy. The well-disciplined communist forces under Lenin instigated the second or "October" revolution.

Soviet conduct may be viewed under three aspects: economic organization, internal political conduct, and foreign policy. In each of these three spheres the general principles of Marx have been observed, but with strategic and tactical modifications by Lenin and Stalin. The path toward their ultimate goal has at times been brutally direct, but at other times devious and roundabout, with many diversions and even retreats.

In the economic sphere, after five years of militant communism failed, the policy became one of retreat. Lenin felt the need for foreign capital and technical advisers. Hence for a period he permitted some private capitalism and encouraged outside aid. With the death of Lenin and the gradual coming to power of Josef Stalin, the New Economic Policy was scrapped and the Soviet Union moved in the direction of a self-contained economy. Collectivization was forced in the field of agriculture, with the brutal liquidation of the private owners (*kulaks*). Industry was regimented by a series of five-year plans, which concentrated upon the heavy industry suitable both for war and also for long-range economic growth. During this entire period, the needs of consumers were largely ignored. Housing, clothing, and even food were inadequate. In retrospect, it seemed that the people of the U.S.S.R. were being exploited by a communist ruling class, bent on the consolidation of its power. But, at the time, outside observers often waxed lyrical at the great and far-reaching plans for building a powerful nation with a group of untrained peasants operating only the most primitive machinery. Others subsequently justified these sacrifices as showing farsighted preparation for the Nazi attack in 1941. But the preponderance of evidence shows that Soviet leaders were building for future power at the expense of the ordinary citizen of Russia.

Variations in Soviet economic techniques make generalizations difficult. But, as a normal condition, all production both in industry and in agriculture is under strict state control. Productive property is owned either by the state or by collective groups controlled by the state. In industry, most production is in accord with the plans worked out by the central planning agency (*Gosplan*). Production quotas and prices are set by this board. State banks finance the factory managers who have to produce under the plan. Since all prices are controlled, the only flexible element left to the discretion of factory managers is labor productivity. As a result, extensive exploitation of workers is common. The factory manager is compelled to meet his quotas or be charged with counterrevolutionary sabotage, with death or exile to Siberian slave labor camps his punishment. By contrast, success can mean a life of relative luxury, with advancement in the communist hierarchy probable. Most managers take the easy way of exploitation, denouncing "slackers" as saboteurs. On the other hand, the penalties for failure prevent many talented persons from seeking positions of responsibility.

The Soviet worker does not enjoy any great degree of freedom. While he is technically able to leave his job, housing shortages and food-rationing methods keep him fixed. Even lateness for work can be penalized by exile to slave labor. Wages are largely tied up with productivity, with speed-up systems being the normal condition. Exceptional workers receive high wages and other rewards, but their pace soon becomes the standard which others are expected to meet. Labor unions are integrated with this system. They are mainly instruments for disciplining the worker and increasing production. Strikes are practically nonexistent.

In addition to the technically free workers, from twelve to twenty millions are slave laborers. They are concentrated in large camps, mainly in Siberia. The slaves build huge canals, level forests, and embark on other massive construction projects. They are treated abominably, working twelve or more hours a day, with inadequate clothing and poor food. They are considered expendible, since new political prisoners can be secured as the need arises. A small portion of slave laborers are common criminals, but the vast majority are intellectuals, victims of purges, scapegoats for production deficiencies or politically unreliable groups.

Farm production is forcibly collectivized, either in the form of state farms or ostensible collectives controlled by the Party. Collective farmers may keep some of the crops for their own use or black-market trading, but heavy government quotas have first claim on their output. Since peasant resistance to collectivization was strong, drastic measures were used to force compliance. Millions of recalcitrants were deported to slave labor. In the Ukraine, organized resistance was met in 1931 by a food blockade which caused millions to starve to death.

The economic results of these policies have been mixed. Some gains were realized at an immense cost, but the toll of bureaucratic inefficiency was high. Since the penalty for sabotage was so severe, there was a tendency to refer even the most routine decisions to top authorities. The result was frequent breakdowns in production. Experts generally hold that the achievements reached at untold cost in human misery did not exceed the levels probable had normal growth in the Tsarist period been continued. Accomplishments were more dramatic and spectacular than sound and evenly distributed.

In the internal political sphere, conditions deteriorated with the death of Lenin. While Lenin was ruthless toward enemies of the Party, he did permit considerable freedom within the Party and even for ordinary citizens not hostile to the regime. However, as Stalin consolidated his power, iron discipline pervaded the entire economy. The notorious secret police (its latest initials are M.V.D.) forced millions to be spies and informers. Stalin achieved power by purging rival leaders, especially Trotsky, and subsequently by gigantic purges of their alleged followers. M.V.D. "justice" is summary, with torture, secret trials, and death or slave labor the normal process. Soviet citizens have practically no political rights. The Communist Party controls the government and the Party in turn is a select club to which only a few are admitted (about 3 per cent of the population). The Party controls, not only the political state, but practically every sphere of life. Most factory managers, high army officers, teachers, and similar functionaries are now Party members.

Soviet rulers have not been content merely to deprive citizens of the basic rights to freedom of speech and of assembly. Their freedom even to think is controlled by state monopoly of press, radio, and education. Propaganda and indoctrination are normal features of Soviet life. Religious teaching has been particularly handicapped, with little freedom even of worship the general rule. A state church was revived during the recent war and has been continued as an adjunct to Soviet foreign policy. Current communist policies then emphasized total state control of religion rather than its complete suppression. The revival of persecution proved, as all but the naïve knew at the time, that this was but a gradual method of destroying religion rather than a change of communist policy. It was a tactic of divide and conquer, striking first at an independent clergy, with long-range educational programs used to root out the idea of God from the minds of the faithful.

Soviet communism is undoubtedly the most complete system of regimentation and total exploitation recorded in history.[7] Literally no phase of human life is free from state control. Even the family is the subject of experimentation. At first both divorce and abortion were common. More recently, the desire for a larger population has led to restrictions on both abuses. But the family has no more rights than the individual citizen. Children are trained to be loyal to the state rather than to their parents. There is even discussion of state nurseries to train all children from birth, so that their parents may both work on farms or factories.

While Soviet policy is subject to tactical changes, certain trends

---

[7] Documentation of this statement is given fully in the books listed in the Appendix.

seemed to have crystallized sufficiently to be called characteristic. Thus, the economic pattern described above seems likely to persist. Its efficiency may be questionable, but it fits in well with the pattern of total control. Much of it has been forced upon countries recently taken over by Communists. It is even more likely that the internal methods of police-state control will be retained. They are of the essence of totalitarianism, and communism is by nature a total system dominating the entire lives of its subjects.

The Soviet Union and World Communism. The Soviet Union has dominated over the Communist International, but its policies have been subject to many strategic and tactical changes. At the beginning, there was considerable disagreement as to the likelihood of further communist gains and the methods for achieving them. One school held that socialism in one country alone was impractical and, accordingly, that major attention should be given to fomenting revolutions elsewhere. Another school maintained that emphasis should rather be on developing the Soviet Union, so that its example would foster communist growth in other lands. This was part of the ostensible difference between Stalin and Trotsky, although subsequent events indicated that Stalin was really aiming to seize power, using alleged differences only as grounds for controversy.

The policy generally followed was one of concentrating upon the Soviet Union, while keeping alive the international apparatus of the Comintern. But Soviet policy was predominant. Thus, when Hitler's threat was apparent in 1935, communist parties everywhere were ordered to concentrate upon political matters, particularly by forming united fronts to meet the danger of fascism. Fascism was considered the ultimate form of capitalist degeneration, so that when it was removed there would be no obstacle remaining to prevent the advent of communism. An abrupt and humiliating reversal was ordered in 1939 when Hitler and Stalin agreed to divide the spoils of the forthcoming war. The invasion of Russia in 1941 brought about another dramatic change. A startling tactical maneuver was the ostensible dissolution of the Comintern in 1943 and the orders given to the American Communist Party to make its peace with capitalism. These tactics aimed at lulling the democracies into complacency, so that the Soviet Union could gain maximum concessions in the peace settlements. With the conclusion of the war, this tactical maneuver was reversed with the ousting of Earl Browder and the changing of the American communist line. Fortunately, from the communist viewpoint, American officials missed the significance of these changes in 1945 with the result that the U.S.S.R. gained two valuable years to extend and consolidate its power.

Current Soviet policy has identified the aims of world revolution with those of Soviet nationalism. Soviet military power has extended the field of communist control so that it embraces much of Europe and Asia. At the same time, the Politburo insists that native communist regimes subject themselves to strict control from Moscow. At this writing, three major policies are discernible in international communism. The first involves the consolidation of gains acquired by force through the war. Foci of resistance are stamped out, and budding elements of nationalism in the local communist parties are ruthlessly suppressed. The second policy calls for political penetration of noncommunist nations. All the weapons in the communist panoply are used for this stage: propaganda, bribery, exploitation of domestic discontent, and even sheer intimidation by the Soviet Union. The third program calls for weakening of states which may serve as the gathering point for anticommunist opposition. Local communist parties act as espionage and potential sabotage agents within these countries. Moreover, they attempt to break up any entente against communism by stirring up distrust and suspicion among the member states of the alliance.

It seems probable that future communist international programs will dovetail closely with the foreign-expansion potential of the Soviet Union. The world is rapidly dividing into two spheres, based on broad attitudes toward human freedom. The Soviet sphere is, on the whole, closely knit. Its policies are drawing together many of the free nations of the world into a defensive alliance. There is less likelihood that Soviet penetration into the free sphere will go unresisted. On the contrary, the free world is likely to unite on political and economic measures to support weaker members and to preserve a united front against communist aggression. Soviet strategists in turn feel that such an alliance is essentially temporary. It does not have the internal cohesion possessed by the Communists. They expect two factors to weaken the "freedom front." One is economic, the possibility that severe depressions under capitalism will break down international agreements and cause dissension among the opponents of Soviet power. The second weapon is political. It is felt that at a proper time the tension which unified the noncommunist states could be relaxed. Then tempting concessions could be made to some states, either in the economic or the political sphere. They would be drawn away from the alliance and the common front would be broken. By virtue of this reasoning, it is concluded that time will work in favor of Comintern policies.

In addition to direct Comintern operations on the international front, the Communist Party, U.S.S.R., has used other international organizations as its tools. Thus, for years the *Profintern* was the organ for uniting world labor. It had been replaced by the World Federation of Trade Unions, which is a propaganda organ for the Soviets in the labor sphere. Other international groups and congresses have been formed for youth, women, and intellectuals. They have enjoyed some success in convening world meetings of the groups affected. In reality, such groups are projections on a larger sphere of the tactics of the united front, boring-from-within, and the use of front organizations.[8]

Communism in the United States. The American Communist Party has been a faithful member of the Comintern. It has consistently accepted Moscow domination in terms of policies and even choice of leadership. As a regular policy, Comintern rep-

---

[8] For a thorough documentation from original sources of the ideology of world communism, see the scholarly article, "Stalin on Revolution," written by Historicus, *Foreign Affairs*, Jan., 1949. See also the report of the Subcommittee of the House Committee on Foreign Affairs, entitled "The Strategy and Tactics of World Communism." This has been reprinted as *Communism, Its Plans and Tactics* (Washington: Infantry Journal Press, 1948).

resentatives "advise" American Party leaders. The Party furnishes subjects for underground work, particularly where espionage is concerned. It employs standard tactics to gain power and influence, which it uses for the benefit of the Soviet Union.

The American Communist Party has never been large, with a membership generally ranging from 60,000 to 75,000. Its numbers are swelled by fellow travelers and dupes who can be counted upon for consistent support of Party policies. Thus, when the New York City Party membership was 25,000, about 400,000 votes could be polled by the communist-controlled American Labor Party. Nationally, the Progressive Party in 1948 counted over a million voters, maintaining the rough fifteen-to-one ratio which exists between fellow travelers and Party members. About 80 per cent of American Party members come from minority groups in the population. About half of the Party is classified as working class, with the other half being professional, artist, white-collar, and governmental. On the basis of trade-union infiltration, it could be concluded that nearly half the worker members are employed by relatively high-wage industries. In the United States, at least, the economic factor does not seem to be predominant in determining Party membership.

The Communist Party, U.S.A., was relatively noninfluential until the mid-1930's. At that time a combination of circumstances and policies multiplied its influence enormously. It gained in both prestige and power. The main factors were the rise of Soviet prestige through the glamour of the five-year plans and, subsequently, American government-fostered propaganda designed to enhance war-partnership solidarity; exploitation of the 1929 depression; the coincidence of the united-front policy of 1935 with a liberal American government which sympathized with many of the new communist objectives; and the rise of a mass labor movement which used communist organizers in its bitter, underground stage forced on it by corporation antilabor policies.

Communist gains through reflected Soviet glory were mainly among intellectuals, although a few labor leaders were deceived in this way. Planning was a gleaming symbol to many economists and social reformers, the more so since the Soviet Union appeared to be gaining while the United States was bogged in its greatest depression. Liberal reaction toward communism often varied between friendly toleration and enthusiastic admiration. This reaction facilitated penetration into the government, universities, and the literary and artistic world. Communists gained footholds in these power centers which they subsequently exploited in a highly successful manner.

The united-front policy, although motivated for different reasons, was admirably adapted to exploitation of the gains mentioned above. Hitler's racial and militaristic policies were causing wide alarm in the United States. Communists spearheaded antifascist moves and at the same time toned down their own extreme positions. They now supported the New Deal, which previously they had denounced as a Wall Street tool. Thus, they gained many popular issues at the very time they were shedding their less palatable programs. As a result, they had little difficulty in boring into liberal groups, forming united fronts and front organizations, and gaining considerable influence and prestige. Most liberals accepted them as friendly collaborators, although a few fell away when the purge trials were instituted in 1937. More were alienated by the Stalin-Hitler pact of 1939, but nearly all were ready to forgive and forget during the war period. Soviet adulation then swept the nation, partly in spontaneous tribute to Russian heroism and partly as a result of government-sponsored wartime propaganda. Since postwar Soviet imperialism became evident even to the blind, more liberals have been rejecting communist collaboration.

In the labor movement, Communists were extremely active during the 1920's. They got an early foothold in the Congress of Industrial Organizations, an advantage which they held until 1948. Two factors led to this situation: a shortage of trained union organizers and bitter corporation reprisals which called for skilled and fearless underground recruiting. President Lewis of the C.I.O. accepted communist help with the conviction that it could be discarded when the unions were organized. To his dismay, Communists entrenched their power in many key unions and in the national office. This control was extended during the war, until many feared that Communists would achieve unquestioned domination of this great labor organization. Fortunately, the postwar revulsion against communism rescued the C.I.O. But, for many years, its influence was abused by high appointive officials, who pushed through pro-Soviet resolutions in conventions and used labor's prestige to aid Communists in government positions.

The net result of these combined factors was a tremendous growth in communist power here, particularly in the periods 1935–1939 and 1941–1947. Communist officials reached high posts in government where they were often able to influence policies and aid the Comintern espionage apparatus. During the critical years 1945–1947, American foreign policy consisted in appeasing the Soviet Union and thus enabling the Soviets to expand their power to an alarming degree. Critical and wrong decisions in regard to China, Argentina, and Germany were made in accord with the communist line. It is difficult to apportion blame for such results, but each of the areas of penetration contributed to the outcome. Officials within the government; pressure from labor unions; and public opinion manipulated by front organizations, fellow-traveler news commentators, friendly publishers and book reviewers, all contributed to the final result. Thus, a small group almost dominated a nation which should have been a world leader.

One indication of communist success in propaganda has been the common attitude of applying a double standard to domestic and foreign communism. After 1947, American policy has been one of opposition to communist intrigues abroad. At the same time we have been often hesitant and apologetic about restricting communist activities at home. The Marshall Plan and the Atlantic Pact committed us to great sacrifices in the attempt to stem foreign communism. Yet there was no general domestic policy consonant with the position of Communists as agents of a hostile foreign power. Liberals continued to defend Communists when they were ousted from government jobs or university teaching positions, apparently blind to the essentially reactionary nature of communism. Such attitudes indicate the persistent power of communist propaganda and the deft character of their infiltration programs.

On the other hand, the character of anticommunist measures improved considerably in the postwar period. There was less tendency to confuse communism and liberalism, and particularly to label advanced measures of social reform as communist. Opponents of communism gradually realized that the aspects of foreign control and Soviet subservience were the really dangerous phases of American communism. There was decreasing stress upon its economic positions, and a more realistic attitude in regard to its likelihood of overthrowing the government by force. Countermeasures emphasized exposure of communist infiltration rather than mere defense of free enterprise and the "American way of life." Accurate information was given by a score of books and by several good periodical publications. Particularly notable was the improved attitude of many industrialists toward anticommunist labor leaders who but a few years back were tarred as "Reds." Labor leaders in turn learned from firsthand experience the essential opposition between sound trade unionism and communism. The combination of better information and the growing realization of Soviet aims produced a reaction which decidely set back communist programs. Americans were no longer the innocents of the 1930's. They were becoming experienced and sophisticated in dealing with secret and conspiratorial groups.

An Appraisal of Communism. It is hardly necessary to argue at length the evils of communism. It is fallacious as a theory and indescribably vicious in practice. The heart of Marxian economic analysis is the essentially exploitive nature of property ownership and the theory of surplus value. A century of experience has completely disproved his thesis. During the hundred years after the publication of the *Communist Manifesto,* the lot of labor improved greatly, and particularly so in the most capitalistic countries. Standards of living were continually raised and the worst abuses were mitigated if not wiped out. This was especially the case in the United States, which is the most highly developed capitalist nation. It is true that many abuses persisted and that insecurity became an increasing problem, but the fundamental Marxist thesis that labor would be kept at the level of mere subsistence was decisively refuted. Indeed, a new capitalist approach emphasized the position of workers as consumers and the need for securing better living standards so as to absorb the products of industry.

Equally fallacious is the communist denial of man's spiritual nature and inalienable rights. No system which would do without God could achieve a correct view of human nature. But communism went to the other extreme and denied rights which even unbelievers are wont to concede. So drastic has been its rejection of basic human rights that no considerations of economic progress could justify the system. Man does not live for bread alone. The animal-like existence under Soviet communism would be unendurable even if their economic standards exceeded our own. In fact, however, living standards under communism have been at the very level of exploitation attributed by Marx to the capitalists. Rarely in any system has the disparity between the privileged few and the exploited many been so extreme. In practice, communism has combined the terror of a police state with the exploitation of a slave economy.

Apart from the question of distribution, the economic gains which many expected from state planning have largely failed to materialize. Some giant enterprises were erected at tremendous cost but, on the whole, centralized control produced a cumbersome bureaucracy. When police methods were used to spur production, the result was often further decline, as managers sought to evade responsibility by referring all decisions to higher authorities. Inefficiency reached such extremes that it was not uncommon to have four workers in a Soviet factory to every one needed by an American factory for comparable tasks. When the comparison is made in terms of man-hours of work needed to earn funds for the purchase of specified necessities, the disparity often reached as high as ten to one. Communism has failed by any standard but one: the power of a police state to impose its rule upon the exploited masses.

In spite of these facts, communism is extending its sway in many parts of the world. It is vital that the reasons for this growth be discovered and that counterremedies be devised. This is a complex problem, since the factors prevailing in the growth of communism have varied from time to time and nation to nation.

Since 1940, there has been a considerable expansion of communism by military means. The armies of the Soviet Union and its political maneuvers brought communism to the Baltic States and the Balkans. Armed force was also a major element in the spread of Chinese communism. At times, military aid is combined with political strategy, as when Communists support liberation movements in colonial countries. In strife-ridden regions they may give financial help to dissident groups, aiding them to come to power. Situations in this category hardly come under the purview of the present treatise. Where communist gains are the result of purely military or political factors, the remedies in turn are likely to be military or political. It would be rare that socioeconomic measures would apply in such situations.

A second basis for communist gains is the broad field of social distress. Primarily this involves poverty and exploitation, but other forms of discrimination also breed resentment upon which communism feeds. In normal times, Communists stress the inequalities and injustices which are found under capitalism. Since World War II, they have also been able to exploit the distress resulting from war destruction and disrupted economic conditions. They have pressed their claims even in countries which have moved considerably in the direction of socialism. In this connection, it must be noted that it is not merely the victims of injustice who are converted to communism. Many intellectuals and liberals have been won over through their sympathy for the oppressed. Indeed, it is not uncommon to find that communism appeals more to intellectuals than to workers.

The answer to this appeal is twofold. First, of course, as Pope Pius XI noted in his encyclical, "On Atheistic Communism," the vigorous prosecution of social justice and social charity must remove the injustices which furnish excuses for communist propaganda. Where real oppression drives its victims into radical remedies, the only lasting cure is the elimination of the root evil. In taking this approach, we Catholics are not being "frightened" into social reforms by fear of communism. On the contrary, our basic principles demand such reform, and the effect on communism is but a by-product of something which we must do for its own sake. At the same time, it is usually essential to accompany social programs with counterpropaganda directed against communism. This serves several purposes. Reasonable reforms may often take time, particularly in lands impoverished by war. It is essential that those who tend to be impatient learn the realities of communism as contrasted with its promises. Again, it is practically impossible to outpromise communist propaganda. If a nation seeks needed reforms, Communists will ask for ever greater concessions. This accords with their basic tactic of prolonging strife and impeding real solutions to the social question. Accordingly, the oft-repeated statement that "the only answer to communism is social reform" oversimplifies the problem. It overlooks two major points: some of the most vital communist activities today are in the political and propaganda fields and, even in social matters, Communists will so distort our programs and outpromise the most optimistic reformer that a direct answer to their effusions is usually necessary.

These qualifications are especially applicable to American communism. Here there is only a slight connection between communist achievements and economic exploitation. As was noted earlier, half the American Communists are middle-class, and their influence among the very poor workers is almost negligible. One of the most oppressed groups in the United States is our Negro population. Yet, only 14 per cent of communist membership here is Negro, and the annual turnover among Negro Communists is nearly 100 per cent. Moreover, in recent years, the

Communist Party, U.S.A., has been largely preoccupied with political issues. It has aimed to promote the foreign policies of the Soviet Union. It has been more interested in penetrating into government positions and fields which influence public opinion than in converting workers. Even its infiltration into labor unions has been largely for political ends. It was this lack of mass support in the unions which made the fight against communist control in the labor movement so thoroughly successful, once it was made in earnest.

In this light, it is unfortunate that many American Catholics have erected a false dichotomy between the "positive" approach to fighting communism (by social justice) and the "negative" approach (which is merely against communist aims). Thus one who fights communism by exposing its methods and answering its propaganda is at times considered almost a slacker in the struggle for social justice. Actually, there is no conflict between the two methods. Even where Communists are concentrating on social issues, it is necessary to answer their propaganda and to counter their purely political maneuvers. A "positive" program will not stop their efforts to seize control of some reputable liberal group or to take over a labor union by machine-politics methods. Then there are the broad fields of foreign policy, espionage, penetration into government positions, infiltration into opinion-forming media, front organizations, and similar activities remote from the social question. Yet these latter activities are the ones which give significance to the American Communist Party. Its impact in the social field has been unimportant.

A careful reading of the encyclical "On Atheistic Communism" will show how keenly aware the Pontiff was of the tactical phase of communism. It was in this light that he laid down the rule of noncollaboration, forbidding Catholics to join in united-front maneuvers with Communists. The soundness of this command is even more evident today than it was in 1937. It does not mean, however, that Catholics should automatically withdraw from any sound enterprise, such as a labor union, once communist penetration is discovered. Such a policy would only aid the Communists. Rather, the path of duty may often involve the more arduous task of remaining in the group so as to challenge and defeat communist efforts to seize control. But where an organization is a strict communist front, formed by them for their own ends and under their unshakable control, nothing would be gained by joining. Our names would merely be exploited for their ends. The ban on such membership, imposed by the Holy Office in 1949, merely formalized a position that was inherent in Catholic teaching.

Summary. Communism is world-embracing in its philosophy and program. No simple method can be devised to meet such a comprehensive evil. It must be fought on many fronts, some of which are relevant to the present study, but also on others which are not pertinent here. Any program must meet both an attractive ideology and a subtle and extensive conspiratorial technique.

To the extent that communism is a diabolical attack on God and the Church, weapons of prayer and penance must be used. Incarnate evil must be fought with the aid of divine grace. At the same time, the moral faults in our own system, which give comfort to its enemies, should be removed.

Where communism grows through military and political means, it must be contained through the united action of free nations. The United Nations and regional defense pacts to protect those exposed to Soviet penetration are logical devices to meet this menace. Economic aid to nations weakened by war is also of great importance. In the sphere of geopolitics, it is vital that the great resources of skilled labor, engineering excellence, managerial experience, technical arts, and industrial capacity contained in Western Europe be denied to communism. Without these resources, it is doubtful that the Soviet Union would have the military strength to expand to world domination. Likewise, genuine independence and aid to colonial regions would lessen the appeal of communism to those seeking nationhood. A sane and Christian solution of the German problem is likewise a political imperative.

To the extent that communist influence is achieved by propaganda, the answer is the presentation of twofold truth: the facts about life under communism and the disparity between its promises and achievements; and the real achievements of free men, in spite of all their imperfections and failures. This is essential both on the international and the domestic front. Expert propaganda organs should be created when necessary, or supported and expanded where they already exist. Within our country, the truth must be taught through the schools, radio, lecture platforms, the press and publishing outlets, special interest groups, and like opinion-forming agencies. Secret communist propaganda devices should be exposed by factual publicity.

While government agencies should do their full share in disseminating truth, it is also essential that extensive private efforts be made along such lines. It would be dangerous for government to take a major part in influencing public opinion, even along sound lines. In view of the urgency of the communist problem, one would expect one or more national nonpartisan groups, with irreproachable and broadly representative sponsorship, as well financed as research for lesser evils such as cancer or heart disease, to bring to the country and the world the truth about communism. Such a group would use and co-ordinate real experts in detecting communist maneuvers and issue thoroughly documented exposés of the current Party Line, secret fronts, dangerous areas of infiltration, and similar underground activities of the Communist Party. It should be so competent and well directed that its findings will be automatically received by the nation's press, radio, lecturers, teachers, and like molders of opinion. Undoubtedly, failure of America's top citizens to perceive such a need and meet it earlier has cost the nation billions of dollars and much of its world prestige. It has subjected hundreds of millions to communist rule when wise statesmanship, guided by enlightened public opinion, could have prevented such gains. The world suffers when men who have power lack the qualities of leadership.

There are many answers to the social appeal of communism. It is not enough to remove festering sores which embitter men. Discrimination and injustice, whether they be in the economic, racial, or other fields, must go. But it is even more important to abolish the spirit of hatred and class strife upon which Communists thrive. Hence, in seeking reforms, our methods must be constructive when at all possible. It rarely pays to criticize in ways which embitter the subject and hinder real reform. It is better for capital and labor, Negro and white, Jew and Christian, native born and foreign born to work out their differences and problems in common. This is not always possible. But it should be the first approach attempted, with recourse to denunciation and economic or political pressure held in reserve as a last resort.

In every field, however, the urgency of the problem should not be overlooked. If Pope Pius XI, in 1937, could call communism the greatest menace to Christian civilization, how much more urgent is the danger today. Well did Pope Pius XII say that this is no time for neutrality, that the slacker is in the camp of the enemy, and that timid hearts and shaking knees do not befit the fortitude of the Christian.

READINGS*

J. Messner, *Social Ethics,* pp. 106–109, 930–934.
A. J. Osgniach, *Must It Be Communism?*
J. P. Lerhinan, *A Sociological Commentary on "Divini Redemptoris."*
F. J. Sheed, *Communism and Man.*
C. J. McFadden, *The Philosophy of Communism.*
J. F. Cronin, "Communism, A World Menace."

---

* For further readings, see Lists Nos. 1, 4, and 7 in the Appendix.

Chapter VII. THE IDEAL SOCIAL ORDER

CO-OPERATION, NOT CONFLICT

Leo XIII, Rerum Novarum

28. It is a capital evil with respect to the question We are discussing to take for granted that the one class of society is of itself hostile to the other, as if nature had set rich and poor against each other to fight fiercely in implacable war. This is so abhorrent to reason and truth that the exact opposite is true; for just as in the human body the different members harmonize with one another, whence arises that disposition of parts and proportion in the human figure rightly called symmetry, so likewise nature has commanded in the case of the state that the two classes mentioned should agree harmoniously and should properly form equally balanced counterparts to each other. Each needs the other completely: neither capital can do without labor, nor labor without capital. Concord begets beauty and order in things. Conversely, from perpetual strife there must arise disorder accompanied by bestial cruelty. But for putting an end to conflict and for cutting away its very roots, there is wondrous and multiple power in Christian institutions.

Pius XI, Quadragesimo Anno

39. Rather did our Predecessor draw from the Gospel and, therefore, from an ever living and life-giving fountain, teachings capable of greatly mitigating, if not immediately terminating, that deadly internal struggle which is rending the family of mankind.

Pius XII, Address to Catholic Employers, May 7, 1949

We have just made reference to the preoccupations of those who are engaged in industrial production. Mistaken and disastrous in its consequences is the prejudice, alas! too widely held, which sees in these problems an irreducible clash of rival interests. The opposition is only apparent. In the economic domain management and labor are linked in a community of action and interest. To disregard this mutual bond, to strive to break it, can only betray a pretension to blind and preposterous despotism. Employers and workers are not implacable adversaries. They are co-operators in a common task. They eat, so to speak, at the same table, seeing that they must live, in the last analysis, from the gross or net profits of the national economy. Each receives his income, and in this regard their mutual relations do not in any way imply that one is at the service of the other.

To receive one's wage is a prerogative of the personal dignity of anyone who makes his productive contribution in one form or another, as employer or laborer, toward the output of the nation's economy. In the accounting of private industry salary totals may be listed under costs to the employer. But in the national economy there is only one type of costs, which consists in the national resources utilized with a view to national production, and which must, in consequence, be constantly replenished.

From this it follows that both parties are interested in seeing to it that the costs of national production are in proportion to its output. But since the interest is common, why should it not manifest itself in a common outward expression? Why should it not be allowable to assign to the workers a just share of responsibility in the establishment and development of the national economy? Especially today when the scarcity of capital and the difficulty of international exchange are paralyzing the free flow of expenditure on national production?

ORGANIZED ECONOMIC LIFE

Pius XI, Quadragesimo Anno

81. First and foremost, the state and every good citizen ought to look to and strive toward this end: that the conflict between the hostile classes be abolished and harmonious co-operation of the Industries and Professions be encouraged and promoted.

82. The social policy of the state, therefore, must devote itself to the re-establishment of the Industries and Professions. In actual fact, human society now, for the reason that it is founded on classes with divergent aims and hence opposed to one another and therefore inclined to enmity and strife, continues to be in a violent condition and is unstable and uncertain.

83. But complete cure will not come until this opposition has been abolished and well-ordered members of the social body — Industries and Professions — are constituted in which men may have their place, not according to the position each has in the labor market but according to the respective social functions which each performs. For under nature's guidance it comes to pass that just as those who are joined together by nearness of habitation establish towns, so those who follow the same

Industry or Profession — whether in the economic or other field — form guilds or associations, so that many are wont to consider these self-governing organizations, if not essential, at least natural to civil society.

84. Because order, as St. Thomas well explains, is unity arising from the harmonious arrangement of many objects, a true, genuine social order demands that the various members of a society be united together by some strong bond. This unifying force is present not only in the producing of goods or the rendering of services — in which the employers and employees of an identical Industry or Profession collaborate jointly — but also in that common good, to achieve which all Industries and Professions together ought, each to the best of its ability, to co-operate amicably. And this unity will be the stronger and more effective, the more faithfully individuals and the Industries and Professions themselves strive to do their work and excel in it.

85. It is easily deduced from what has been said that the interests common to the whole Industry or Profession should hold first place in these guilds. The most important among these interests is to promote the co-operation in the highest degree of each industry and profession for the sake of the common good of the country. Concerning matters, however, in which particular points, involving advantage or detriment to employers or workers, may require special care and protection, the two parties, when these cases arise, can deliberate separately or as the situation requires reach a decision separately.

97. What We have taught about the reconstruction and perfection of social order can surely in nowise be brought to realization without reform of morality, the very record of history clearly shows. For there was a social order once which, although indeed not perfect or in all respects ideal, nevertheless, met in a certain measure the requirements of right reason, considering the conditions and needs of the time. If that order has long since perished, that surely did not happen because the order could not have accommodated itself to changed conditions and needs by development and by a certain expansion, but rather because men, hardened by too much love of self, refused to open the order to the increasing masses as they should have done, or because, deceived by allurements of a false freedom and other errors, they became impatient of every authority and sought to reject every form of control.

Pius XI, On Atheistic Communism

32. The means of saving the world of today from the lamentable ruin into which amoral liberalism has plunged us, are neither the class struggle nor terror, nor yet the autocratic abuse of state power, but rather the

infusion of social justice and the sentiment of Christian love into the social-economic order. We have indicated how a sound prosperity is to be restored according to the true principles of a sane corporative system which respects the proper hierarchic structure of society; and how all the occupational groups should be focused into a harmonious unity inspired by the principle of the common good. And the genuine and chief function of public and civil authority consists precisely in the efficacious furthering of this harmony and co-ordination of all social forces.

54. If, therefore, We consider the whole structure of economic life, as We have already pointed out in Our Encyclical *Quadragesimo Anno,* the reign of mutual collaboration between justice and charity in social-economic relations can only be achieved by a body of professional and interprofessional organizations, built on solidly Christian foundations, working together to effect, under forms adapted to different places and circumstances, what has been called the Corporation.

Pius XII, Letter to Semaines Sociales, 1947

The same is true of Our position with respect to professional or "corporative" organization, which has also been made the object of sundry and conflicting interpretations in public disputes — in some cases, perhaps, because of misunderstanding. Here also Our position is identically that of the Encyclical *Quadragesimo Anno,* safely above all reproach of interference in the purely political affairs of our times. But this social doctrine may well provide our generation with a highly pertinent object lesson and orientation.

Over and above the distinction between employer and employee, which threatens more seriously every day to become a pitiless separation, there is human labor itself: the work to be done, the job to which every man contributes something vital and personal, with a view to supplying society with goods and services adequate to its needs. It lies in the very nature of labor, understood in this sense, to draw men together in a genuine and intimate union, and to restore form and structure to a society which has become shapeless and unstable. This in turn would infuse new life into the relations between society and the state.

By contrast, those who would make of society and state a mere conglomeration of laboring men, disregard the fundamental nature of labor and civil society. Labor is emptied of its real meaning and denied its inward unifying power. In the last analysis, these people are not here planning to organize men — laborers considered as men — but to heap up a gigantic sum of incomes in the form of salaries or wages. The danger that economic forces may control the state, to the serious detriment of the general welfare, is every bit as serious in this instance, as when the state is subject to the dominating influence of capital.

Pius XII, Address to Italian Workers, March 11, 1945

As for "the democratization of economy," it is equally endangered by monopolies — that is, by the economic tyranny of an anonymous conglomeration of private capital — and by the preponderant power of organized masses, ready to use their power to the detriment of justice and the rights of others.

The time has come to repudiate empty phrases, and to attempt to organize the forces of the people on a new basis; to raise them above the distinction between employers and would-be workers, and to realize that higher unity which is a bond between all those who co-operate in production, formed by their solidarity in the duty of working together for the common good and filling together the needs of the community. If this solidarity is extended to all branches of production, if it becomes the foundation for a better economic system, it will lead the working classes to obtain honestly their share of responsibility in the direction of the national economy. Thus, thanks to such harmonious co-ordination and co-operation; thanks to this closer unity of labor with the other elements of economic life, the worker will receive, as a result of his activity, a secure remuneration, sufficient to meet his needs and those of his family, with spiritual satisfaction and a powerful incentive toward self-improvement.

Pius XII, Letter to Semaines Sociales, 1946

In Our judgment the establishment of associations or corporate groups in all the branches of the national economy would be much more conducive both to the realization of the end which you pursue and at the same time to the greater success of the enterprises. At any rate, this was certainly true wherever, as it was up to this time, the concentration of enterprises and the disappearance of small independent producers were working only in favor of capital and not in favor of the public economy. There is no doubt, besides, that, in the present circumstances, the corporative form of social, and especially of economic, life is, in practice, favorable to the Christian doctrines regarding the person, the community, labor, and private property.

Pius XII, Allocution to Sacred College of Cardinals, June 2, 1948

It is not a question today of merely distributing the products of the social economy more equitably in closer correspondence with the labor and the needs of individuals. Important as this requirement may be, still under present conditions, especially in view of the enormous destruction and fluctuation caused by the war, every social reform is strictly bound up with the question of a prudent organization of production.

The relations between agriculture and industry within the single natural economies, and of those latter with the economy of other nations, the manner and extent that each nation is to share in the world market — all these difficult problems present themselves today afresh and under aspects different from those of previous times. Upon their rational solution depends the productivity of the several nations, and consequently the welfare of individuals as well; for it is clear that there can never be sufficient distribution where there is not sufficient production.

Pius XII, Address to Catholic Employers, May 7, 1949

Our Predecessor of imperishable memory, Pius XI, had suggested the practical and timely prescription for this community of interest in the nation's economic enterprise when he recommended in his Encyclical *Quadragesimo Anno* "occupational organization" for the various branches of production. Nothing, indeed, appeared to him more suited to bring economic Liberalism under control than the enactment, for the social economy, of a public-law statute based precisely on the common responsibility which is shared by all those who take part in production. This feature of the encyclical stirred up a host of objections. Some saw in it a concession to modern political trends, while for others it meant a return to the Middle Ages. It would have been incomparably more sensible to lay aside the flimsy prejudices of the past and to get down to work sincerely and courageously to make the proposal, with its many practical applications, a living reality.

The owner of the means of production, whoever he be — individual owner, workers' association, or corporation — must always — within the limits of public economic law — retain control of his economic decisions.

The Christian in Action, American Hierarchy, 1948

Christian principles should be put into action in economic life. It is not enough to find fault with the way our economic system is working. Positive, constructive thought and action are needed.

The secularist solutions proposed by eighteenth-century individualism or twentieth-century statism issue either in perpetual conflict or deadening repression. Christian social principles, rooted in the moral law, call insistently for co-operation not conflict, for freedom not repression in the development of economic activity. Co-operation must be organized — organized for the common good; freedom must be ordered — ordered for the common good. Today we have labor partly organized, but chiefly for its own interests. We have capital or management organized, possibly on a larger scale, but again chiefly for its own interests. What we urgently need, in the Christian view of social order, is the free organization of capital and labor in permanent agencies of co-operation for the common good. To insure that this organization does not lose sight of the common good, government as the responsible custodian of the public interest should have a part in it. But its part should be to stimulate, to guide, to restrain, not to dominate. This is perfectly in line with our Federal Constitution which empowers government not only "to establish justice" but also to "promote the general welfare."

Catholic social philosophy has a constructive program for this organic development of economic life. Pope Pius XI, rounding out the social principles formulated by Leo XIII, laid down the broad outlines of this program seventeen years ago. In line with that constructive program we advocate freely organized co-operation between the accredited representatives of capital and labor in each industry and in the economy as a whole under the supervision but not the control of government. The agencies of this freely organized co-operation have been called by various names: Occupational Groups, Vocational Groups, or more recently, Industry Councils. American Catholic students of the social encyclicals have expressed their preference for the name "Industry Councils" to designate the basic organs of a Christian and American type of economic democracy into which they would like to see our economic system progressively evolve. This evolution can come only as the fruit of painstaking study and effort to safeguard, in justice and charity, the rightful interests of property and the rightful interests of labor in the pursuit of the dominant interest of all, which is the common good.

Such a constructive program of social order seems to us to be the answer to the questionings of high-minded leaders of industry and to the explicit proposals of sound and responsible leaders of organized labor. We bespeak for it in these critical times dispassionate consideration and calm, open discussion in an atmosphere of good will, and in a disposition to seek solutions by agreement rather than by force, whether political or economic. We call upon men of religious faith and principle, both in management and labor, to take the lead in working out and applying, gradually if need be, a constructive social program of this type. For the moral and social ideals which it would realize are their heritage.

The Church and Social Order

58. The state however cannot be relegated to the position of a mere policeman or umpire. It has the responsibility of providing for the common good. On the other hand it may not and should not become totali-

tarian in attempting to fulfill all social functions in the way of economic planning and direction. It should leave to the smaller vocational groups the settlement of business of lesser importance. It will then be free effectively to accomplish its real function of "directing, watching, stimulating, and restraining, as circumstances suggest or necessity demands."

59. The primary duty of the state and of all good citizens is to abolish conflict between classes with divergent interests. This may at first sight appear to be purely negative. There is however a positive responsibility to foster and promote harmony between the various ranks of society and that by specific means. "The aim of social legislation," says Pope Pius XI, "must therefore be the re-establishment of vocational groups."

60. The remedy for the class conflict which makes the labor market an arena where the two armies are engaged in combat, is to be found precisely in the reintegration of the social body by means of vocational groups, "which bind men together not according to the position they occupy in the labor market, but according to the diverse functions which they exercise in society." The chief qualifications of these vocational groups or guilds, as noted by Pius XI, are that they are autonomous, embrace whole industries and professions, are federated with other constituent groups, possess the right of free organization, assembly and vote, and that they should dedicate themselves to the common good and with governmental protection and assistance function in the establishment of justice and the general welfare in economic life.

The state itself in the manner described above and the existing free organizations of economic life should prepare the way for the ideal type of vocational groups or that sane corporative economic system of which the Pope so frequently speaks, which he so ardently desired to see realized, and toward which rightly conducted activities of these organizations can lead.

Pastoral Letter, 1919

In his pronouncement on Labor [*Rerum Novarum*] Pope Leo XIII describes the advantages to be derived by both employer and employee from "associations and organizations which draw the two classes more closely together." Such associations are especially needed at the present time. While the labor union or trade union has been, and still is, necessary in the struggle of the workers for fair wages and fair conditions of employment, we have to recognize that its history, methods, and objects have made it essentially a militant organization. The time seems now to have arrived when it should be, not supplanted, but supplemented by associations or conferences, composed jointly of employers and employees, which will place emphasis upon the common interests rather than the divergent aims of the two parties, upon co-operation rather than conflict. Through such arrangements, all classes would be greatly benefited. The worker would participate in those matters of industrial management which directly concern him and about which he possesses helpful knowledge; he would acquire an increased sense of personal dignity and personal responsibility, take greater interest and pride in his work, and become more efficient and more contented. The employer would have the benefit of willing co-operation from, and harmonious relations with, his employees. The consumer, in common with employer and employee, would share in the advantages of larger and steadier production. In a word, industry would be carried on as a co-operative enterprise for the common good, and not as a contest between two parties for a restricted product.

Australian Bishops: Pattern for Peace

The functions of the Industrial Council will vary, of course, according to its scope and jurisdiction. But the system could be applied to the following ends:

(a) To determine wages and industrial conditions throughout the industry. Co-ordination of wage rates and relativity of conditions should be preserved by means of a provision for appeal to the Arbitration Court from the decisions (original or by way of review) of the National Industrial Council.

(b) To control the prices, wholesale and retail, of the products of the industry.

It may be necessary to constitute some reviewing authority for such fixations.

(c) To control the maximum rates of dividends from year to year.

(d) To plan the amount and quality of production from year to year.

(e) To plan the marketing of the product.

(f) To control, with due regard to the demand and to the interests of all concerned, the number of enterprises operating in the industry.

(g) To determine conditions for the entry of workers into the industry and to ensure their efficient training.

(h) To arrange for pensions, insurance schemes, and other social benefits within the industry.

(i) In general to exercise complete control over the policy and development of the industry, including, in the case of a secondary industry, the supply of raw materials to other enterprises.

(j) To enable workers to suggest improvements and modifications which would improve productivity and lessen class hostility.

209

Code of Social Principles

57. Just as nature leads men brought together by dwelling in the same neighborhood to found cities, so does it induce members of the same calling to establish corporative groups.

In fact any calling — be it handicraft or liberal profession — creates by its very nature a community of interests among those who follow it.

58. When based upon vocational associations, human society is in a condition conformable to its natural structure. If built upon hostile classes it is in a condition of violence and instability. In the light of Christian social philosophy then, vocational associations may be considered as natural organs of civil society, if they are not essential organs of the same insofar as they are autonomous bodies enjoying true authority.

59. The principle of unity binding together the members of the same calling is to be found in the production of goods and the rendering of services resulting from their common activity.

60. The principle of unity for the totality of occupations lies in the common good to which all must tend, each in its own way, by co-ordinated effort.

61. Individual activity in industry cannot, without risk of anarchy, be left entirely to itself. The exercise of rights and the fulfillment of mutual duties in view of the common good of the profession and of society demand, in the vocational group itself, an authority whose chief function is to regulate internal disputes which might arise, to establish suitable regulations, to manage and to direct the activity of the profession.

62. If authority is necessary in the profession to regulate the activity of its members, it is still more necessary that there be a supreme authority over all industries, with power to regulate their mutual relations and to direct their activity toward the common good. Social justice therefore requires interprofessional organization on regional, national, and even international lines.

63. Experience shows that such corporations are exposed to a grave danger: induced by a certain group-selfishness they are prone to forget and to neglect their chief duty, which is to work as effectively as possible for the general welfare of the country. Hence a just relationship of dependence should be established and maintained between the state, guardian of this welfare, and the vocational groups. Vocational organization should relieve the state of many tasks which at present weigh heavily upon it, without however either absorbing or weakening it, but rather perfecting and strengthening it.

64. Once the vocational bodies have been established, three tasks will

remain to be accomplished: (1) the uniting of kindred associations and the creation of at least two federations, one for the trades and the other for the liberal professions; (2) the uniting of the corporations and federations under a supreme professional authority; (3) the integration of this supreme authority into the political structure of the nation and by this the attainment of the highest point toward which corporative organization tends and in which it ought to find its full realization.

65. Corporative organization is not of its very nature bound up with any particular form of state or government. On the contrary, just as in the political order, different forms of government are legitimate, providing they make for the common good, so in the professional order, the forms of corporative organization are likewise left to the preferences of the parties concerned.

66. Chief among the various duties of the corporative groups must be placed the technical training of the future members of the profession. This belongs primarily to each corporative group and in this matter the state retains only a subsidiary function. It is likewise the function of the authority within the profession to maintain services for vocational direction and placing in employment.

67. It may happen that divergent interests arise among members of the same vocational body, notably as regards the special interests of employers and employed. Corporative organization ought then to guarantee to either party the possibility of independent deliberation in order to safeguard its legitimate interests and prevent abuses which the other might cause by the advantage of its position.

68. For the perfect realization of the corporative order, institutions should draw their inspiration from principles of social justice and be mindful that each group has but a subsidiary function in the social hierarchy, and should not crush the activity of those subordinate to it. It may then be hoped that economic activity, that very important function of social life, will recover rectitude and balance in order.

A FLEXIBLE PROGRAM

Leo XIII, Rerum Novarum

76. Furthermore, if citizens have free right to associate, as in fact they do, they also must have the right freely to adopt the organization and the rules which they judge most appropriate to achieve their purpose. We do not feel that the precise character in all details, which the afore-mentioned direction and organization of associations ought to have, can be determined by fast and fixed rules, since this is a matter to be decided rather in the light of the temperament of each people, of experiment and practice,

of the nature and character of the work, of the extent of trade and commerce, and of other circumstances of a material and temporal kind all of which must be carefully considered.

Pius X, Il Fermo Proposito

A certain freedom of organization should be allowed them, for it is not possible when many persons meet together, that all should be modeled on the same pattern or follow one single direction. Their organization should spring spontaneously from the works themselves; otherwise they will be like buildings of fine architecture, but without solid foundations, and therefore quite unstable.

It is also necessary to take into account the natural disposition of separate populations. Different usages and tendencies are found in different places. The important thing is to have a good foundation of solid principles, maintained with earnestness and constancy, and if this be the case, the method and form of the various works will be only accidental.

Pius XI, Quadragesimo Anno

86. The teaching of Leo XIII on the form of political government, namely, that men are free to choose whatever form they please, provided that proper regard is had for the requirements of justice and of the common good, is equally applicable in due proportion, it is hardly necessary to say, to the guilds of the various Industries and Professions.

87. Moreover, just as inhabitants of a town are wont to found associations with the widest diversity of purposes, which each is quite free to join or not, so those engaged in the same industry or profession will combine with one another into associations equally free for purposes connected in some manner with the pursuit of the calling itself. Since these free associations are clearly and lucidly explained by Our Predecessor of illustrious memory, We consider it enough to emphasize this one point: People are quite free not only to found such associations which are a matter of private order and private right, but also in respect to them "freely to adopt the organization and the rules which they judge most appropriate to achieve their purpose." The same freedom must be asserted for founding associations that go beyond the boundaries of individual callings. And may these free organizations now flourishing and rejoicing in their salutary fruits, set before themselves the task of preparing the way, in conformity with the mind of Christian social teaching, for those larger and more important guilds, Industries and Professions, which We mentioned before, and make every possible effort to bring them to realization.

THE PRINCIPLE OF SUBSIDIARITY

Leo XIII, Rerum Novarum

20. Wherefore, assuming, of course, that those limits be observed which are fixed by its immediate purpose, the family assuredly possesses rights, at least equal with those of civil society, in respect to choosing and employing the things necessary for its protection and its just liberty. We say "at least equal" because, inasmuch as domestic living together is prior both in thought and in fact to uniting into a polity, it follows that its rights and duties are also prior and more in conformity with nature.

Pius XI, Quadragesimo Anno

79. Just as it is gravely wrong to take from individuals what they can accomplish by their own initiative and industry and give it to the community, so also it is an injustice and at the same time a grave evil and disturbance of right order to assign to a greater and higher association what lesser and subordinate organizations can do. For every social activity ought of its very nature to furnish help to the members of the body social, and never destroy and absorb them.

80. The supreme authority of the state ought, therefore, to let subordinate groups handle matters and concerns of lesser importance, which would otherwise dissipate its efforts greatly. Thereby the state will more freely, powerfully, and effectively do all those things that belong to it alone because it alone can do them: directing, watching, urging, restraining, as occasion requires and necessity demands. Therefore, those in power should be sure that the more perfectly a graduated order is kept among the various associations, in observance of the principle of "subsidiary function," the stronger social authority and effectiveness will be and the happier and more prosperous the condition of the state.

Pius XII, Letter to Semaines Sociales, 1947

On the other hand, it is clearly our bounden duty today, when the former propensity for the "hands-off" system of laissez faire shows serious signs of weakening, to beware of plunging to the opposite extreme. In organizing production, we must guarantee full weight and directive influence to the principle, advanced time and again in the social teaching of the Church, according to which the activity and services of society must play a merely "subsidiary" role, aiding or supplementing the activity of the individual, the family, and the profession. We trust that the third part of your Semaines Sociales may be developed within the clear perspective of this concept of production and of its just regulation.

The preceding chapters painted a twofold picture. On the one hand, they stressed the inadequacy of present socioeconomic institutions. The pathetic problems which constitute the social question point up the failures of modern economic life. The reasons for failure lie fundamentally in the false philosophies which govern the world of affairs. We have fluctuated between two extremes: the anarchic diffusion of power under an individualism which denied the social nature of man; and the excessive concentrations of power under finance dictatorship and statism. Individualism, socialism, fascism, National Socialism, and communism were found to be basically defective. They exaggerated either the individual or the social nature of man in such a manner as to suppress fundamental rights and duties. Being false to human nature, they could not offer a successful way of life.

On the more positive plane, the earlier chapters laid down some basic principles for a sound social order. The dignity of the individual was stressed, but also the fact that man thrives only in society. From these facts a philosophy of economic life was evolved. The great virtues of social justice and social charity were examined. In consequence, there evolves the necessity for reforming the institutions of society, through group action, so that they would tend to procure the common good. On such a foundation, it is possible to proceed to the principles which would govern an ideal social order.

A PAPAL PROGRAM FOR SOCIAL ORDER

General Principles

The working out of these principles in modern times has been primarily the achievement of Pope Pius XI. Other Catholic reformers wrote well of particular goals and special problems. They laid foundations and made beginnings suitable to their times, but they did not achieve the comprehensive grasp of society found in *Quadragesimo Anno*. Undoubtedly the great Pontiff was aided in his ideas by the writings of Heinrich Pesch, originator of the system called solidarism, and by Nell-Breuning. These profound scholars sensed that the solution of the social problem was to be found, not in individualism or statism, or in any amalgam of the two, but rather in a thoroughly new approach to socioeconomic life. Society must be reorganized in such a way that its institutions will foster individual liberty while securing the common good. The principles which would secure such a result must govern social thinking, if the world is to be restored to order and peace.

First among the needed institutional changes is the acceptance of co-operation as a basic socioeconomic principle in place of strife and enmity. This is needed particularly in two spheres: the class struggle between capital and labor, and the rule of excessive and unregulated competition as the sole governing principle in economic life.

Class Co-operation. All the modern popes have stressed the futility and immorality of the class struggle. Fortunately, we Americans have not had to contend with a strong Marxist form of this disease. But apart from the Marxist notion of the essential enmity of capital and labor there are many other types of hostility which we do have. There is the idea of the labor market itself, where worker is pitted against worker, and the class of labor against employers. This conflict has at times been modified by unionism, but often as a result of organization the struggle has simply been continued on a larger scale. The whole philosophy of power and interest groups implies struggle and dissension. Too often the idea is that what one gets, the other must lose, so that strife is inevitable.

By contrast, the social encyclicals and papal statements stress the inherent unity implied by both the productive process and the demands of the common good. The physical and technical processes of production must be carried out in team fashion, if they are to be successful. The more closely management and labor work together in a factory, the more prosperous the enterprise. Farsighted leaders in both camps have recognized this fact. Thus, both branches of the American labor movement have called for labor-management co-operation. The C.I.O. has advocated committees for this purpose. The A. F. of L. constantly stresses in its *Labor's Monthly Survey* the need for increased production as the basis of higher living standards. On the management side, the growing popularity of "human relations" programs shows an awareness of the problem. Progressive personnel literature stresses the need for recognizing the dignity of workers and of promoting teamwork and communication in the plant.

There is increasing agreement on the fact that labor and management have common interests of the highest importance. It is true that they also have divergent claims, both as to the way the product is made and the distribution of the net return. But the basic weakness of modern society is that we have abundant means for pressing special interests and claims, but we are deficient in organizing to secure common interests and mutual concerns. It is logical that we have labor unions and employers' associations to seek the distinct needs of each group. But it is equally logical that we should have organizations for promoting their common interests. Moreover, such organization is needed for the common good of society. It is not enough that each plant or each industry taken alone should function well. They should also co-operate for the good of all.

More Than Competition. It was once held that the forces of free competition alone would bring about such harmonious co-operation. Today, as was noted in Chapter V, it is evident that competition cannot be the sole governing principle in economic life. It has real merits in promoting efficiency, determining the distribution of resources and rewards, and in keeping economic life flexible and dynamic. But it is unable to protect the economy against disastrous depressions or safeguard individual businessmen from unfair and discriminating treatment. Few economists today would hold that the economic system is completely self-regulating and that no intervention is necessary to prevent business cycles. And businessmen, while proclaiming the merits of competition, have taken many steps to allay its most severe features. Price-discrimination laws, Federal Trade Commission codes of fair practices, and price-fixing laws are illustrations of this trend. Many trade associations have their rules of ethical conduct. Here again, if the premise is conceded that common interests of competitors require joint action, is it not logical that some organized institutions exist to secure such a result? Even with competition among individual firms in an industry, there are many joint problems which concern the industry as a whole. It is but common sense that methods exist for meeting such general interests, and that these too be tied in with the common good of the entire community. Co-operation in the business community is as reasonable as labor-management co-operation.

Many signs indicate that the need for greater unity has been felt. But it is not so clear that men realize the best way to achieve such unity. Unfortunately, centuries of individualism broke down the natural societies which men formed in earlier times. There were left only competing individuals and the state. This type of society proved so unworkable that individualism became self-destructive both in the economic and the political fields. In economic life, atomistic individualism gave way to consolidation and the era of trusts and mergers was with us. In political life, helpless individuals turned largely to the state for redress of grievances, and the trend toward statism was made a part of modern life. Even now we are still being asked to choose between extreme positions. Conservatives stress the evils of statism and ask for a return in the direction of individualism. Liberals note the failures of individualism and press for increased state intervention in economic life. Few seem to sense that the best answer to extreme evils is for the parties directly concerned to unite to meet directly their own common problems. This is the ideal middle way between opposing and dangerous trends.

An Organic Society. It may seem farfetched to assert that individualism and collectivism are correlative. Yet both are characterized by a mass society. Under individualism, the state is the only important social group which can give unity to millions of citizens. When individualism fails to attain social ends in the economic sphere, it is only natural that men would turn to the state, thereby enhancing its power at the expense of personal freedom. If this process is carried to its logical conclusion, we reach collectivism. Too often in the modern world such a result has been attained. The alternative is a restoration of smaller social units in both economic and political fields, with real power inhering in these groups. At the same time, their activities must be co-ordinated so as to secure essential social ends. In the economic sphere, this can be done partly by competition and the market and partly by limited state intervention. But the bulk of the co-ordinative process should be committed to the self-governing social groups which represent the diverse interests in economic life. This is the pattern which we call an organic society.

Real freedom is safeguarded only by an organic society. The analogy of an organism brings out the ideas of independence combined with interdependence, specific function co-ordinated for the good of the whole, and a hierarchy of values, with subordination in addition to co-ordination. The human body is not a mere aggregate of cells — that would be individualism. Nor is it totally and absolutely under the sway of the mind — that would be similar to statism. Rather the cells are grouped into organs, each of which has some autonomy in performing its own function, but all of which co-operate for the good of the entire body. In an organic economic society, men would be grouped according to productive function, not merely according to class. All who perform the same specific function would work together, whether they be owners, managers, technicians, or workers. They might have their own class needs, just as muscle or nerve tissues have specific needs wherever they are found, but they also have a part in the common tasks of their group. Thus men would be organized in terms of what unites them, not merely in terms of what separates them. We would have common councils of papermakers, farmers, clothing makers, and so forth, and not merely labor or employer groups in these occupations.

If real power were possessed by various intermediate social groups, the answer to many threats to freedom would be found. The present-day classes, instead of asking an outside force to intervene in their disputes and thereby surrendering freedom to this force, would get together to handle their problems directly. Such organization would be as complex and interrelated as economic functions demand. It could exist at the levels of the plant, the industry, and the national and international economic systems. Geographically, it could be local, regional, and national. It would not be arranged according to some blueprint of state economic planning. Rather it would spring naturally from common functions in the socioeconomic sphere. In such a society, the state would largely be a stimulating and co-ordinating force, safeguarding the common good at the highest level and subordinating the lesser goods of various groups to the welfare of the entire community.

While the popes seek a basic reform of society, it might be useful to digress for a moment and consider how attitudes toward organized economic life might improve present-day America. Social reform in the United States, since 1932, has not always been in the direction of an organic society. It has stimulated the organization of certain groups, especially workers and farmers. But they have tended to become pressure organs for class interests, rather than the beginnings of functional societies. Reform legislation, while badly needed, has been generally administered by the federal government. Interested parties have the right of protest, but they are not constituent members of regulatory or enforcement bodies. By contrast, in a partially organic society, the affected groups would participate in the determination and enforcement of rules necessary for the common good. Thus, for example, there would be labor leaders and employers in the National Labor Relations Board at all levels. Every economic group would be represented in the Council of Economic Advisors to the President. Where this approach has been tried, as with the War Labor Board and the Agricultural Adjustment Administration, it has proved quite satisfactory. But even such timid approximations to an organic society have not been attempted in a systematic manner. We still wait until a problem becomes explosive, fight it out on economic and political battlefields, and then call in the government to settle the dispute and police the affected parties.

Had there been more participation by the interested groups in making and enforcing social legislation, we would have had some beginnings of a society organized in the interests of the common good and protecting individual freedoms while seeking social goals. But such a partial solution would still be inadequate. Power would be concentrated in giant groups, leaving the individual submerged in the mass. By contrast, a truly organic society would honor the principle of subsidiarity, whereby higher groups left to smaller organizations powers and activities which they could handle effectively. Freedom is best protected if higher groups do not arrogate to themselves functions which could be performed well by smaller and lesser groups. The best answer to individualism and statism alike is the multiplicity of buffer societies, hierarchically arranged, with a maximum of power at the lower levels, while higher groups step in only when needed to co-ordinate and regulate in the interests of the common good.

Self-Government. Thus, modern society faces two tasks, emphasized so strongly by the present Holy Father and his predecessor. The first is the negative but important duty of protecting smaller groups from the progressive encroachment of giant power, whether it be private or governmental. The second is the positive obligation of promoting self-governing functional societies on all levels, which can share with the modern state its overwhelming burdens of seeking the common good in the socioeconomic sphere. Such societies could be formed from existing associations, provided they progressed into functional rather than mere interest or pressure groups. But they would be more than present-day labor unions, employers' associations, professional societies, or farmer organizations. Since the joint groups would be carrying out quasi-legal functions, seeking the common good in their particular areas, they should be considered as quasi-public societies, with legal status and powers. By no means should they be organs of the state. Their independence is essential for the safeguarding of freedom. But they should have many powers now assumed by the state in default of other ways of procuring the common good. Their autonomy would not involve absolute independence, as this would be but individualism on a higher scale. The state would still have the power and the duty to safeguard the common good. But it would be relieved of the crushing burden of detail and thus freed to do its main task effectively.

Such, in its main outlines, is the attitude which Pope Pius XI suggested for modern society. Others have arrived at similar ideas independently. Thus, John Maurice Clark, Professor of Economics, Columbia University, offered in 1947 an analysis of the American economy strikingly similar in its philosophy to *Quadragesimo Anno*.[1] Professor Clark noted the bankruptcy of both the individualistic and the pressure-group approaches. He stated that many of our representative groups, such as labor unions, are quasi-public institutions, whether or not they recognize this fact. Accordingly, he called for the establishment of an economic community, based on the idea of common interests and voluntary participation in mutual tasks. Such an attitude, reached by a widely respected economist, indicates that the alleged barrier to American acceptance of the papal program may be exaggerated. It may well be that difficulties arise, not from inherent objections to ideas given in the encyclicals, but rather as a result of semantics. Sound ideas, when presented in language which is strange or even emotionally disturbing, may often be rejected. Hence it is our task, not merely to evolve and apply the outlines for an ideal social order, but also to present this plan in language both intelligible to the American scholar and free from undesirable associations.

The Encyclical Program

As was noted earlier, the ideas presented here were first solemnly elaborated by Pope Pius XI. While he claimed only to

[1] See J. M. Clark, *Alternative to Serfdom* (New York: Knopf, 1948), especially pp. 121–153. C. H. Cooley, *Social Process* (New York: Scribner, 1918), and I. Polanyi, *The Great Transformation* (New York: Farrar, 1944), are cited by Clark as sources for his ideas.

be explaining and bringing up to date *Rerum Novarum,* actually he offered striking innovations in social theory. Pope Leo XIII stressed more the right of association, with emphasis upon free associations of employers and workers. Some writers read more into some of his allusions, but it is at least clear that he did not elaborate the notion of quasi-public groups established in terms of function rather than class interest.

A Problem of Terms. The language used in the encyclicals was an initial barrier to quick American understanding of the papal program. In *Quadragesimo Anno* the terms *ordines* and *collegia ordinum* were used to describe these functional associations. Elsewhere allusions were made to the medieval guilds and to a corporative society. None of these expressions conveyed an exact meaning to the average American. The term "guild" was rather accurate and descriptive, but unfortunately our history books have portrayed such an unfavorable picture of medieval life that the reference only served to distort the Pope's idea. Many Americans still use the word "medieval" as synonymous with reactionary, obscurantist, and repressive. While such usage is historically inaccurate, it is sufficiently widespread to preclude the use of the term "guild."[2] A similar emotional block prevented the use of the phrase "corporative society." This was so connected in many minds with Mussolini's corporative state that involved explanations were always in order. It is sufficiently difficult to gain acceptance of a new idea under any conditions, without taking on the added burden of unpleasant connotations.

On the other hand, great difficulty was met in translating *collegia ordinum* into a term or phrase which would be clear, accurate, and appealing. The first translations here used the phrase "vocational groups." A more accurate subsequent translation preferred "organized industries and professions." But these phrases did not seem to meet the need. As a result, the American Catholic

[2] An illustration of such historical objections is the Chicago Round Table Radio Forum, held April 7, 1940, commenting on the publication of "The Church and Social Order" under the signatures of the Administrative Board, N.C.W.C. For a further discussion of the problem of terminology, see "Let's Call It the Industry Council Plan," by Gerald J. Schnepp, in *America,* Feb. 21, 1948.

Sociological Society appointed a committee to consider the problem of terminology. By a close vote, they accepted the phrase "industry council plan" in preference to "industrial democracy," which ranked second in their list. Their choice was noted by the American Hierarchy in its November, 1948, statement, "The Christian in Action." This usage is followed in the present chapter, but two important reservations must be made. In the first place, the term "industry" narrows the concept of *ordines,* which applied to functional groups in all phases of economic life, not merely industry. Secondly, the phrase coincides with a phrase used by the Congress of Industrial Organizations in advocating its program of social reform. Thus, our approach might be tied up in many minds with the ideas of a labor organization over which we have no control. It is possible that the C.I.O. might give a connotation to the phrase which Catholic scholars might reject. In this light, any acceptance of the phrase must be tentative and provisional. It represents the considered thought of scholars and has been welcomed by our hierarchy. These same authorities can suggest changes if the need arises.

New Type of Organization. The pope calls for a new type of socioeconomic organization which would meet two needs: the common problems of the diverse groups in society and the demands of the common good. Thus, as was noted before, industrial production is in itself a unifying force. Capital and labor here cooperate for a common purpose. Their existing organizations — labor unions and employer associations — largely stress the separate and divisive interests of the groups involved. Hence, there is also needed a new type of organization which will express common interests, meet mutual problems, and seek the general good. The same principle applies to other groups, such as the trades, the professions, the farming community, and financial interests. Not only do these groups often have a capital-labor problem, but they have close relationships with each other and with industry. They also should integrate their activities in the light of the general welfare of the entire community. These facts indicate a need for welfare groups to supplement interest groups.[3]

The common-interest groups would, moreover, be quasi-public organizations with quasi-legal rights. Such an interpretation follows from the papal analogy to civil government and the allusion that such groups are at least natural, if not essential, in civil society (*Q. A.,* Nos. 83–84). Hence it is felt that, within their proper fields of activity (not defined in detail by the Pope), they would have certain public powers now adding to the burdens of the state. Many commentators envision a situation whereby a decision taken by a suitable majority in an industry would be binding on the entire industry or profession. Such a procedure would be parallel to legal or medical codes of ethics, farmers' decisions on planting or marketing quotas or industry decisions reached under Federal Trade Commission procedures, but with a stress upon self-government rather than state intervention. To indicate a possible pioneering approach unfamiliar to Americans, the formerly anarchic textile industry might achieve greater stability if some present-day practices were formalized and made universal so as to prevent unfair competition through sweatshop and stretch-out conditions of labor exploitation. Such a procedure would be to the common interest of both labor and high-minded manufacturers, and it would also promote the common good.

The functional organizations would supplement free associations which seek the special interests of the parties involved. Here is one striking contrast to the corporative or totalitarian state. Labor unions and employer associations would be free to organize and press their own demands and to engage in collective bargaining to determine conditions of work, rates of pay, and similar matters. In fact, where labor is concerned, its independent organizations might well be necessary to present its point of view intelligently and forcefully in any functional associations.

[3] See H. F. Trehey, *Foundations of a Modern Guild System* (Washington: Catholic University Press, 1940), p. 62 ff. and *passim;* and O. von Nell-Breuning, *Reorganization of Social Economy* (Milwaukee: Bruce, 1936), p. 205 and the entirety of Chaps. 10–12. See also J. Banchi, *Principi dell'Ordine Sociale Cristiano* (Rome: A.V.E., 1944), pp. 163–164.

Labor unions could, in addition to seeking special concerns, co-operate with employer groups on matters of mutual interest in the light of the common good. Indeed, a good case could be made for this approach, on the grounds that social transformations are best had by modifying existing institutions rather than starting something new and untried.

The Pope does not specify which, if any, functions of free associations might be taken over by the quasi-public groups. Thus, businessmen consider matters of prices, production, and investment as their legitimate and exclusive interests. Labor unions guard jealously their internal relations with the members against employer interference. Some commentators, especially American, favor the idea of giving industry councils broad authority in economic matters. Others feel that many such matters should be left to existing groups. This point will be discussed more in detail subsequently.[4]

Rights of Industry Councils. The quasi-public groups, like the free associations, would be substantially autonomous. This is a point of the highest importance. Since one of the major evils of the day is concentration of power and endangering of freedom, it is essential that real power reside in these minor buffer groups between individual and state. Not only should they be free from detailed government control in their proper fields, but they should take over from government excessive powers which it has been forced to assume. Of course, this autonomy should not be such as to prejudice the government's right to direct activities in the light of the common good. But such state action would be generally on a level of high policy rather than detail, directing only on broad lines and vetoing actions not consonant with public welfare.

The relationship between industry councils and the state is delicate. On the one hand, it is the duty of government to foster such self-governing groups. Moreover, it must exercise some gen-

---

[4] Trehey, *op. cit.*, p. 103, and De la Gressaye, cited in Nell-Breuning, *op. cit.*, p. 239, advocate the limited point of view. The opposite opinion is discussed later in the chapter.

eral regulatory power for the sake of the common good. But it should not dominate over them, much less absorb them as state organs. Their public-legal status would be a recognition by government of an independent group, not an absorption by the state of hitherto separate groups. Moreover, prevailing Catholic opinion seems weighted against the idea that any national economic assembly be more than an advisory legislative group to the political state. The common good is much broader in its outlines than economic welfare, with the result that the political state must represent all elements of society, not merely those connected with socioeconomic matters. As an example, the American decision to adopt the Marshall Plan was, at the time, probably contrary to our immediate economic interests. It added fuel to a dangerous inflationary situation. Yet this decision was demanded by the common good, even at the risk of economic dislocations. Such policies could be made by a political parliament, but they might not be made by an economic assembly.[5]

In the same context, Pope Pius XI discusses the need of international co-operation. The extension of these attitudes into broader spheres is logical. There is a common good of all peoples, as well of those of a particular nation. This does not mean that the Church opposes national sovereignty and advocates a world government, as will be seen in Chapter XIII. But it does indicate that even here the fact of common interests and mutual tasks should not be obscured by the seeking of immediate national advantages.

The internal structure of these functional groups should be flexible, adapted to local needs and national temperaments. The popes do not lay down a rigid blueprint which is urged for all times and peoples. On the contrary, they stress again and again the wisdom of applying general principles in the light of different conditions. Obviously, for example, a set of rules which might work well in England and Canada, with their law-abiding

[5] See Trehey, *op. cit.*, p. 147 ff. R. J. Miller, in his volume *Forty Years After*, p. 165, takes a different point of view. A. J. Osgniach, in his study *Must It Be Communism?* (New York: Wagner, 1950), p. 369, agrees with Miller. But most Catholic writers hold a contrary view.

traditions, might founder in France and the United States, noted for their individualism and impatience at legal restraint. Such diversity naturally results in different plans by Catholic social scholars, endeavoring to work out an application of sound principles to their national needs. A dozen or more such proposals have been made in the interval since the publication of *Quadragesimo Anno*.[6] Certainly scholars should feel full freedom in this regard, provided they avoid the twin extremes of dogmatism and indifferentism. No scholar or groups of scholars should arrogate the right to identify a detailed application of papal principles with *Quadragesimo Anno*. In such cases, they have added to Catholic social principles their own prudential judgments, which they must defend on their own merits, without reference to papal encyclicals. On the other hand, we should avoid the danger of giving mere lip service to proposals which the Pope considers essential for the reconstruction of the social order. Since these ideas are based on human nature and a sound understanding of society, it would be extremely rash to say that they are not applicable to any given country.

The establishment of an organic society, more than any other reform, would bring about the change of institutions which is essential to the idea of social justice. The importance of institutional change was stressed in Chapter IV. It is not enough to bring about piecemeal reforms of immediate evils, although this too must be done. Rather, it is vital that the institutions of society be such that by their very nature they tend toward the common good.

Needless to say, structural changes by themselves will not necessarily produce such a result. Institutions are important, but the spirit which pervades their members is likewise of basic moment. Pope Pius XI follows his advocacy of a functional society by a plea for a reform of morals. A case could be made for industry councils merely on the grounds of "enlightened selfishness." But, unfortunately, selfishness is rarely a cohesive bond in society. Men seek short-range interests instead of long-run wel-

6 See Trehey, *op. cit.*, Chaps. 8–11; and Nell-Breuning, *op. cit.*, pp. 233–240.

fare. They may admit the value of a program but seek to consider their own case as exceptional. Of course, there will always
be recalcitrant individuals, even in the best of societies. The
quasi-legal status of these common-interest groups would take
care of such rebels against the common good. But if the majority
of those involved are selfish and greedy, it is unlikely that any
social system will work effectively. Some altruism and concern
for the general welfare are essential.[7]

INDUSTRY COUNCILS IN AMERICAN LIFE

The treatment of industry councils thus far has been general,
with only incidental allusions to American conditions. It seems
appropriate now to attempt to reduce these principles to a workable plan for the United States. The present section will consider the ultimate goal and structure to be sought, and the following section will treat of first steps and approaches to this
goal. Needless to say, such an attempt goes beyond general encyclical principles and involves elements of personal judgment
and individual evaluation of economic life and American conditions. Of necessity, it is presented as a tentative basis for discussion
and not as a finished product.

Structure of Industry Councils

In working out the structure of an American common-interest
society, it becomes immediately evident that structure is inseparable from function. Thus, if industry councils have as their
function detailed economic planning, naturally their structure
will be more complex than if they sought more modest goals.
Consumer interests and those of related industries would then
need vigorous and effective representation in the councils. Surprisingly, there has been little discussion among American Catholic scholars of this all-important point of function. In most
commentaries on the subject, certain functions have been taken
for granted, with the bulk of discussion centered on structure.

[7] See Trehey, *op. cit.*, p. 4; and Clark, *op. cit.*, pp. 136–142. This point will be
discussed further in Chapter XIV.

In fact, the matter of function involves many highly debatable issues. The popes have given only two guiding posts for resolving this issue: the council should deal with mutual interests, and it should promote the common good. Both points are essential, with the common good the overruling consideration. Thus, if a given function, say price control, were considered a mutual interest in an industry or profession, it might still be possible that the general welfare would be impeded by the full implications involved in detailed economic planning. Such matters must be faced openly and honestly, without dogmatism or undue loyalty to past opinions.

Common Interests in Industry. At this point, accordingly, only general ideas of structure can be offered, based on noncontroversial functions. Thus, in the industrial field, certain common interests are generally acknowledged. Among these would be the need for increased productivity, if we are to maintain a progressively higher standard of living. Likewise, it is held that there must be economic expansion to keep employment at the highest possible level. Again, the prevention, or at least the mitigation, of depressions is a common interest of the highest importance.

The problem of greater productivity involves at the minimum labor-management co-operation in a given plant and industry. But its implications extend farther. While some gains can be worked out in terms of co-operation, using existing plant facilities, others call for new capital investment to increase worker productivity. This in turn brings in the question of a profit level which will stimulate investment. Profits involve both collective bargaining matters and tax policies. Thus, this one common interest demands functional organization on the plant, industry, and national levels. Labor and management would co-operate locally, on industry-wide policies, and in common national efforts to petition government for a tax policy which would stimulate economic expansion and modernization.[8] What is more, im-

---

[8] This interrelationship has been well worked out in the A. F. of L. *Labor's Monthly Survey,* in its advice to member unions. For C.I.O. viewpoints, see M. L. Cooke and

proved social organization is by itself a stimulant to production. The researches of Elton Mayo, the studies at the Hawthorne plant of Western Electric, and the results achieved where co-operation has been established all show the productive influence of social motives. Quite apart from any economic devices adopted as a result of labor-management co-operation, the fact that such social harmony exists is a direct energizing force of considerable value.

The matter of replacing class struggle with labor-capital co-operation is of prime importance. Even though we may not have the class struggle in the classical, Marxian sense, we still have barriers of hostility and misunderstanding. Labor and capital tend to stress their divided interests and pull apart instead of together. Clearly, then, one of the first functions of industry councils would be to stress and implement the common interests of capital and labor. American workers today generally understand the need for increasing efficiency through better methods or equipment. They are usually happy when their knowledge and skill are consulted through methods of communication, participation, and teamwork. Quite apart from new processes or machines, sound human relations in a factory can cut absenteeism and turnover, increase safety, raise the quality of products, reduce the number of rejected or imperfect parts, and thus increase efficiency without speeding up workers.

At the same time, workers want both job security and a fair share of the gains made in this way. Often this means giving the workers higher wages, the consumer lower prices, and the owners increased profits. If the distribution is fair, workers are usually satisfied. If gains are made without new processes or

---

P. Murray, *Organized Labor and Production* (New York: Harper, 1946), and C. S. Golden and H. J. Ruttenberg, *The Dynamics of Industrial Democracy* (New York: Harper, 1942). Progressive business opinion along these lines is contained in the writings of the Committee for Economic Development (C.E.D.), whereas more conservative views are expressed by the National Industrial Conference Board, the Chamber of Commerce of the United States, and the National Association of Manufacturers. In recent years, divergences between the positions of the several groups on this issue have narrowed considerably.

machinery, job security is frequently maintained by expanding the market through price reductions. Where new processes or machines mean technological displacement of some workers, careful planning often permits their transfer to other functions in the plant. In extreme cases, generous dismissal pay and previous offers of training for new work may be acceptable.

The matter of owner-worker co-operation is the subject of intensive study by nearly thirty American universities and many important industries. There is a growing realization that consultation and teamwork are vital for modern industries. Since many labor unions likewise emphasize common problems with the employer, it should not be difficult to achieve a form of organized co-operation which would harmonize with the industry-council plan.[9]

The other questions mentioned above, namely, full employment and the avoidance of depressions, are primarily matters of national policy. They are so involved with government monetary and fiscal policy, gathering of national statistics, general investment and income-distribution policies, and such broad issues, that local or regional measures become secondary. Some recommendations, such as those affecting inventory and construction programs or wage and price policies, would be carried out locally or on industry-wide levels. But in our present economy only a national group can see the entire picture involved in securing economic stability and call for appropriate action. The fact that the problem is national does not imply that it is exclusively governmental. On the contrary, the principle of subsidiarity would demand effective participation by the affected groups in any policy determination.

Finally, there are common interests which are basically industry-wide or regional. Such would be the case with sick industries, such as the coal and construction industries. The same would apply to regions where there are special problems, such as New England and the South. In these cases, the organization

[9] For readings on this subject, see J. F. Cronin, *Catholic Social Action*, pp. 221–223. See also List No. 9 in the Appendix of the present book.

would be appropriate to the problem, either on an industry or
regional basis. Moreover, the functions would vary in relationship
to the problems involved. A drastic overhaul might be needed in
the construction field, whereas less extensive measures might
suffice to retain industry in New England or develop it in the
South.

Manufacturing, however, is but one section of our economy,
and it is interdependent with others. We cannot have economic
health if the farming community is depressed. A program of
industrial expansion brings in financial interests. Producers of raw
materials are closely connected with industry. Transportation,
distribution, and service form important parts of national economic life. All these are matters of common concern. It is only
natural that economic society be so organized as to handle such
concerns.

Variety of Structure. Proceeding, then, from function to structure, there would be in manufacturing at least three grades of
vertical organizations: a plant labor-management council which
deals with mutual problems; an industry-wide council with quasi-
public authority to enforce standards of fair competition, decent
wages, and other matters mutually agreed upon and conformable
to the public interest; and a national council to treat such wide
problems as depressions and full employment. Parallel structures
would exist in fields similar to manufacturing, such as transportation, mining, distribution, and some service trades. Where the
capital-labor relationship is secondary, as with finance, the professions, and farming, councils would deal more with problems
of mutual interest to producers and owners, with the public
good safeguarded. Special problems, such as might be found in
the construction industry, would call for a more complete structure and more extensive function. Where the various groups
coalesce in mutual interests, they would consult and act accordingly. This would be especially true in regard to the national
council which deals with depressions and full employment.

At first glance, this approach, more modest than that offered
by many other writers, might seem to involve a cumbersome

and complex bureaucracy. This need not be so. In most cases it would involve merely broadening the functions and perspective of existing groups. In many important instances, it would involve a lessening of bureaucracy, in that it restores to lesser groups powers and functions assumed by default by the federal government. If two general principles are observed, the industry-council plan would restore greater rather than less flexibility to economic life. First, structure should be governed by function, which means that important common interests now neglected would be discussed and acted upon by all the groups involved. Secondly, there should be a systematic reappraisal of legislation on the local, state, and national levels to see what functions might be restored to autonomous, quasi-public groups affected by such legislation. The only changes in our economic life would then be for the better: diffusion of power narrowly concentrated today in government, particularly the federal government, and in financial groups; and the meeting of mutual-interest problems overlooked because of class struggle or unregulated competition.

Functions of Industry Councils

The general observations made thus far can be rendered more precise by a study of the major functions of industry councils in American life. In this way, we can see concrete objectives and plan for first steps and sound beginnings. Three guideposts furnished by the encyclicals might be helpful in picking these functions: replacement of class struggle by collaboration; supplementing competition as a regulatory principle of economic life; and the relieving of government of excess burdens by transferring many of these to smaller, quasi-public groups.

Wages. The preceding section treated certain fields of labor-management collaboration. A more difficult question arises when the subject of wages, hours, and working conditions are considered. Many commentators apparently consider these appropriate subjects for industry-council deliberations. It may be, however, that a distinction is in order here. On the plant level, such matters are not ordinarily held to be within the sphere of common interests of owners and workers. Thus, if labor asks for higher wages, the owners must either raise prices or accept less profits. Some may be driven to bankruptcy. As a result, many employers would resist such wage demands. Hence ordinary collective-bargaining matters may be divisive rather than cohesive in regard to labor and management. As such, they would be more appropriately considered by the separate free associations, namely, unions and business firms. However, on the industry level there may be a case for universalizing standards reached by collective bargaining in a large majority of the firms. An industry council on a higher level could impose conditions when they have been accepted by, say, a two-thirds majority of firms in an industry. All this does not imply that measures should not be taken to reduce class-struggle elements in collective bargaining. Some techniques in this regard will be suggested in Chapters X and XI. But collective bargaining may not be an appropriate field for the lowest levels of industry councils.

It is possible, however, that collaborative measures will ultimately have their impact upon collective bargaining. A labor group which works together with an employer on common problems can hardly forget these interests when they meet at the bargaining table. Indeed, to quote the oral views of an eminent Catholic scholar, the term "bargaining" may be replaced by a new term more descriptive of economic realities. Contract negotiations on wages might be called a "budget conference," in which both parties calculate their proper shares of a common budget. Such terminology expresses the fact that wages are tied to productivity and to the economic status of the employer. They cannot sensibly be considered apart from the conditions prevailing in a plant or industry. Such an approach would introduce the common-interest mentality into wage negotiations, even though they were not formally considered by industry councils.

Fair Competition in Industry and Agriculture. More difficult problems arise when the question of supplementing competition is considered. Among the noncontroversial fields, however, would be matters involving fair competition. At the present time, the Federal Trade Commission holds periodic meetings with industry under the title of trade-practice conferences. As a result, certain standards of fair practice are drawn up and may be given legal sanction. In other cases, trade associations for given fields determine their own standards of quality, grading, sales procedures, and the like. These latter agreements have no legal status; indeed, many are suspect as covert methods for achieving monopolistic ends. It might be an interesting experiment to reverse the present emphasis, giving quasi-legal powers to the trade associations, subject to review and veto in the public interest by either a government agency or a branch of a national economic council at the highest level of industry councils. Another consideration might be the delegating to such groups of powers now possessed by government in enforcing pure food and drug legislation, fair practices in advertising, and similar measures. The test in such cases would be the willingness of most firms to live up to good standards, with only a minority indulging in practices which savor of fraud and deception. Certainly where such good will exists, it would seem possible to give to trade groups powers now possessed by government. A similar principle might be studied in regard to regulation of banks, stock exchanges, and security issuance.

A precedent which might be studied with interest is the Federal Reserve System. Here member banks keep their own basic autonomy, subject to inspection as to the soundness of loans and also to controls on the total amount of credit. They are federated into twelve regions, thus permitting some flexibility in meeting common problems. Matters of national interest, such as credit control, are handled by a federal governmental board. This is proper, since credit regulation is of such paramount public interest that it rightly becomes a governmental matter. But the Board of Governors is advised by a committee which represents not only banking interests, but also industry, commerce, and related fields. A program of this nature safeguards the principles of organic structure, subsidiarity, and quasi-legal status.

There is fairly widespread agreement that free competition alone is not sufficient to meet the problems of the farmer. Not only are farm price fluctuations conducive of general instability, but such questions as farm ownership, credit and debt problems, and soil conservation are aggravated by unlimited competition. In this regard, the general objectives of existing American farm legislation seem sound: giving farmers some price protection and proper balance with other prices, while encouraging a level of production adequate for good national living standards. Moreover, there is considerable decentralization in the administration of our farm laws, with a high degree of participation by the parties affected. The unsound aspect of our farm program is that it has arisen largely as a result of pressure groups which may not be too concerned with the common good. A sound agricultural policy would harmonize farm prices with those of industry, so that the entire economy would function smoothly. This problem, and the question of further decentralization and transferring of governmental powers, would form a suitable field of study.

It was noted earlier that competition alone will not solve the problem of full and sustained employment. A degree of planning is required to meet this issue. Some of the actions to be taken are of necessity governmental, since they involve matters of taxes, central monetary policy, and public-works expenditures. A limited amount of planning would be possible for individual firms and industries. The important point here is that, where government decisions are necessary, all the parties concerned — business, labor, financial groups, and farm organizations — should have an integral part in the making of policy. This by itself would be adequate reason for a national economic council which would work out a common policy and recommend action by government or the individual groups comprising the council.

Finally, there are industries where drastic changes may be necessary in the interests of the common good. These are the "sick" industries, which are badly disorganized, inefficient, and subject to considerable chronic depression and unemployment. The construction industry would be a good example, and coal has found itself in such a position. Here would be proper fields for self-regulation, planning, and research, with government stimulating and supervising such activities. In practice, these fields might be very difficult subjects since, in spite of chronic depression, they have remained citadels of individualism.

Decentralization. The third major guidepost, the transferring of government powers to appropriate industry councils, has been treated incidentally in dealing with the class struggle and unregulated competition. This point, however, would be appropriate for systematic study by social scholars, determining how much of our social legislation could reasonably be administered by autonomous quasi-public groups. Certainly, if the reform of morals called for by the popes were reasonably achieved, it would be possible to secure a notable degree of decentralization. It may be, however, that even under present conditions much could be accomplished. The harnessing of existing altruism, education, and even "enlightened selfishness" might serve as stimulants to appropriate action. Only careful studies in such fields as labor legislation, social security, monetary controls, security issuance and trading, and national health care could determine accurately the appropriate areas of governmental and industry-council action.

Thus far, in discussing function, there have been only incidental allusions to structure. It would seem evident, however, that different functions will call for varying structures. Meeting the class struggle and labor-capital hostility obviously demands worker-management representation in the appropriate industry councils. The same would apply to the "sick industries," since workers are involved as well as management. Government might well be required to intervene here to protect the public interest. On the other hand, in regulating unfair competition it might be sufficient to have an autonomous industry or trade group, subject to government veto in the public interest. Finally, where the entire economy is involved, as in the case of depressions, it would be appropriate to have all economic groups represented on a national council.

The Problem of Economic Controls

The most difficult and controversial functional question has been avoided thus far. This is the problem of price fixing, with its implications, according to many, of total economic control of production, investment, and profits. Some would even include wages in the area of regulation. This attitude has been common among American commentators on the social encyclicals. Indeed, the weight of authority is predominantly on this side. A few quotations may illustrate typical attitudes.

Arguments for Total Controls. The late Monsignor John A. Ryan stated: "The occupational group would be empowered by law to fix wages, interest, dividends, and prices, to determine working conditions, to adjust industrial disputes, and to carry on whatever economic planning was thought feasible." Bishop Haas wrote in 1947: "Each such organized industry or profession would be empowered to fix wages, hours, working conditions, output, and profits." In 1949, he spoke of employers and workers meeting "to negotiate . . . the questions of wages, hours, prices, and other matters of common interest to each industry or profession." Brother Gerald J. Schnepp quoted Father Arès as giving industry councils power to achieve "stabilization of production and marketing by trade agreements on production and prices." Father Munier urges that these councils "be empowered to decide production, distribution, profits, wages, hours, conditions of work, apprenticeship, adjustment of disputes, and the like, assuming of course that they will not conflict with similar rights of other industry councils." Father Clune holds that "it can fix prices, at least to the extent of showing what costs of production are and thus indicating what a fair price would be, allowing a reasonable margin for profit."[10]

---

[10] The references in order of citation are: J. A. Ryan, *A Better Economic Order* (New York: Harper, 1935), p. 179; F. J. Haas, "The Economic Needs of the 1880's and of the 1940's," *Ecclesiastical Review*, Dec., 1947, p. 411, and address given Feb. 2, 1949, *Western Michigan Catholic*, Feb. 3, 1949, p. 11; G. J. Schnepp, "An Estimate of Quadragesimo Anno," *Catholic Mind*, Nov., 1946, p. 667, paraphrasing R. Arès, *What Is Corporative Organization?* (St. Louis: Central Bureau Press, 1939), pp. 53–54;

The authors cited do not develop in detail the implications of the functions committed by them to the industry councils. But they seem to envision a totally controlled economic system, with no price competition, and administrative allocation of profits, wages, production, and investment. They distinguish such a system from the corporative state and socialism by asserting that controls will be in the hands of the affected parties, and that government will play only a co-ordinating and supervising role. Indeed, Monsignor Ryan opposed a planned economy and "centralized control over all economic actions and processes," on the grounds that effective democracy could not long survive such a situation.[11] He did feel, however, that widespread participation in the industry councils would remove a large part of this danger.

The main argument for including prices in the field of industry-council decisions is brief but cogent. Since it is generally conceded that prices are the most important element of economic control, industry councils must regulate prices if they are to influence economic life in an important manner. Otherwise they would be reduced to fringe functions, being barred from the field which is the very heart of the economy. Inasmuch as the popes called for occupational organization as a central feature of sound economic life, how could such groups be debarred from regulating prices? Could society be reorganized if the key function were to remain autonomous? Such reasoning prompted a recent commentator, J. A. Messner, to favor price control as a function of industry councils, even though he argues elsewhere that, in a soundly organized economy, competition could be permitted to determine prices. At first sight, this appears to be an inconsistency. But the author apparently distinguishes price controls from price fixing. The former consists in appropriate institutions which will prevent unethical dealings and exploitation

---

J. Munier, *Some American Approximations to Pius XI's "Industries and Professions"* (Washington: Catholic University Press, 1943), p. 24; and G. Clune, *Christian Social Reorganization* (Dublin: Browne and Nolan, 1940).

[11] J. A. Ryan, *op. cit.*, pp. 185–186.

in the market place. Under such conditions, competition can then be trusted to bring about fair prices.[12]

Arguments for Limited Controls. It is this aspect of proposed implementation of papal ideas which has aroused the most serious opposition in the United States. Many businessmen, highly progressive in their labor relations and acceptance of social responsibility, find the idea of price fixing, with all its implications, utterly abhorrent. They feel that it would lead to paralyzing bureaucracy, stagnation of economic life, and possibly ultimate loss of freedom. Many economists and students of the social encyclicals hold the same position. They offer these arguments: the papal encyclicals do not call for such a drastic interference with economic life; once prices are controlled, all economic life must be regulated in detail; central regulation of economic life, even by representative groups, involves an intolerable bureaucracy; and detailed study of concrete problems shows that such groups would need autocratic powers to enforce their regulations. These views merit further analysis.

In regard to papal authority, two points are urged. The first is that the Pope did not call for the virtual abolition of competition, but only attacked the idea that it can be the sole regulating force in economic life. This group holds that if unfair and antisocial competition were prevented, wages determined by collective bargaining and then universalized by industry-council decisions in each industry, and depressions averted and full employment achieved by suitable planning, the useful aspects of competition could be retained. Secondly, when the Pope spoke of moderating the wage contract by some efforts to share ownership, profits, and control with workers, he used the mildest language of gentle persuasion (*Q. A.,* No. 65). Could he, then, have had in mind, when writing of industry councils, a complete surrendering of authority by businessmen to a group in which they would constitute only a minority element? Since control is the

---

[12] See J. A. Messner, *Social Ethics,* pp. 338, 342, 751–752, and 867–882. The same author attacks a planned economy on pp. 818–823 and 935–943. He defends a free market on pp. 705–710.

vital element in ownership, the proposed plan would transfer several hundreds of billions in wealth to an outside group, the only compensation being whatever profits were allocated by the councils. Certainly, if the Pope proposed such a drastic step, he would have made his thinking unmistakably clear. It would seem that the burden of proof is upon those who would change the *status quo* to such a remarkable degree. This argument is given further strength by the May 7, 1949, address of Pope Pius XII, who stated that employers should remain masters in the economic decisions of their industries.

Secondly, the price function is so central in the economy that, if prices were fixed, this would automatically involve total control. Prices not only determine profits and wages, but they indirectly set levels of investment, fix rates of production, decide the success or failure of individual firms, allocate resources, and thus govern the entirety of economic life. Moreover, the interrelationships of American economic life are such that administrative determination of prices would be a task of unbelievable complexity. Practically every producer is at the same time a consumer of scores of products of other industries. Thus, the automotive industry is one of the nation's great consumers as well as producers. If prices were determined by council action in the United States, conditions in millions of firms must be considered, as well as the interrelationships of decisions taken in one field in the light of their effect on thousands of other fields. Even a tyro in mathematics would know that group determination of prices would involve billions of variables. The magnitude of this task stuns the imagination.

Bureaucracy. Thirdly, the bureaucracy needed for the performance of this task would soon solve all unemployment problems in the United States, to say nothing of stimulating the demand for economists, statisticians, and even typists. The fact that such an organization would be nongovernmental is irrelevant. If it is central, it is of necessity highly complex in such an intricate economy as ours. And the commentators cited call for price determination, not only in each industry, but in terms of interindustry relationships and national implications. Such a group would have greater powers than the government, since control of economic life would lead to domination over the means of livelihood. Such centralization of power, even in representative groups, does not seem to be in the spirit of *Quadragesimo Anno* or consonant with the addresses of Pope Pius XII. The popes call for diffusion of authority, yet, if industry councils take over total economic control, and this is implied in price determination, it seems inevitable that centralization will ensue.[13]

The United States has made four recent attempts at price or production control, with indifferent success. The National Industrial Recovery Act led to industry planning groups during the years 1933–1935. Labor was not represented in these groups, but public officials and consumer representatives endeavored to protect the general interest. Trade associations presented codes of fair competition, which were not supposed to be monopolistic, but which regulated prices, output, nonprice competition, sales practices, and investment. The codes, as a whole, restricted output, discouraged investment and economic expansion, and raised prices. Concerted restriction of output necessarily lowers the national income and lessens employment. In the opinion of most observers, the law had already failed before the Supreme Court dealt the *coup de grâce* in 1935 by declaring it unconstitutional.[14] Some Catholic scholars held, however, that if labor and consumer groups were constituent members of the planning boards, results would have been different. This point is not self-evident, since we have had many situations where labor and employers have gotten together to maintain high prices and restricted output. Not only was this often true in the building trades, but in 1946 demands by one branch of American unionism forced a

<hr />

[13] This argument is stated by F. Hayek, *The Road to Serfdom,* and J. Jewkes, *Ordeal by Planning* (New York: Macmillan, 1948). A more moderate position is stated by B. Ward, in "Limits of Economic Planning," *Foreign Affairs,* Jan., 1949.

[14] For a dispassionate analysis, see A. R. Burns, *The Decline of Competition* (New York: McGraw-Hill, 1936), Chap. 10.

break in the existing price stabilization program and were in-fluential in starting the upward spiral of inflation.[15]

The other attempts at centralized control occurred in World War II, where we had a War Production Board, a War Labor Board, and a War Price and Rationing Board. These three measures were necessary in view of war conditions. But the complex problems of central control which they posed indicate the extreme difficulty of regulating the American economy, even under the spur of wartime patriotism. There were widespread evasions and many faulty decisions. Labor was generally satisfied to dispense with the WLB and industry with the WPB when hostilities ceased, even though both groups learned valuable lessons of collaboration from these institutions. The extent of price-control evasions led to precipitate dropping of most controls, undoubtedly contributing more than any other decision to the subsequent inflation. Yet the only alternative at the time was to make control stricter, with production allocation for industrial products and marketing controls for farm products. It is quite unlikely that public sentiment would have tolerated such strict regulation in peacetime. In this connection, it might be noted that business groups also showed little foresight, promising that removal of controls would shortly bring prices down rather than up. In fact, they soon exceeded even black-market prices. It may further be observed, as an indication of human limitations in matters of foresight, that most government economists expected an immediate postwar depression, instead of the boom which ensued. These facts make most Americans rather restive at the idea of extensive regulation of economic life.

Detailed Problems of Economic Control. Fourthly, and finally, a consideration of the detailed decisions to be made by in-

---

[15] During this period, the A. F. of L. was winning consistent wage increases averaging about 10 per cent, without price increases. But the C.I.O. initiated great national strikes which were settled at a higher figure, only when the price ceiling on steel was lifted. This does not mean that labor was necessarily to blame for the subsequent inflation — practically all authorities lay most of the blame upon an excess money supply, but it does indicate that many labor leaders consider their interests as consumers secondary to wage demands.

dustry councils in determining prices, profits, wages, and production is enough to provoke some hesitation. Thus, in the automotive industry, whose costs would determine prices? If General Motors were accepted as the price leader and only a "fair" profit allocated to this firm, then Chrysler would make no profit, Ford might go out of business, and Kaiser-Frazer would not have a chance. Most industries have their problems of high-cost and low-cost producers, new and obsolescent equipment, new investment and bankruptcies, inventions and revolutionary discoveries. On the whole, the present system is sufficiently flexible to handle such problems without undue dislocation. But it is an entirely different matter when such decisions are taken impersonally by competition and when they are made by an administrative board. Thus there would be enormous pressure by workers and owners at Ford and Kaiser-Frazer for prices which could continue these firms in business. The simplest way out would be to give a profit to all producers, which would mean prices set at the level of the highest-cost producer. This in turn would hurt consumers, restrict sales, and lessen employment. Growth and death are both necessary in an expanding economy, but it makes a vital difference whether death arises from natural causes or as a result of some decision by the persons involved. The NRA codes protected high-cost producers, at the expense of restricted production and decreased employment. It is not clear that labor participation in such decisions would have changed the result. Labor groups might also be reluctant to close down an inefficient plant which employs thousands of their members.

Of necessity, such groups would need to control new investment in an industry, since this affects prices and output. This poses a difficult problem. On the one hand, new investment is necessary if the economic system is to remain flexible and progressive. Improved methods and processes generally lower costs and thereby increase national income. Entirely new fields of activity are needed in order to keep full employment in an expanding population, and in view of technological and efficiency displacement of workers. On the other hand, the industry councils dealing with the problem would be largely constituted of workers and owners with a vested interest in stabilizing the *status quo*. Changes usually involve adjustment and some adjustments may be painful to the parties concerned. It is a valid generalization that, in deliberative assemblies, minorities with strong interests are often able to block action contrary to their wishes, when the opposing position offers only vague and indirect benefit to the majority. New investment would, in the long run, offer a higher living standard and more jobs for all. But its immediate impact may mean bankruptcy for a high-cost plant and possible loss of jobs for workers in this plant. It is probable that they would protest vehemently against the innovation. Their colleagues in industry and labor would tend to side with them. The burden of protecting public interest would then be left to government and consumer representatives.

It could be argued that in difficult administrative decisions, government and consumer groups would protect the public interest. Such an argument does not harmonize completely with the realities of pressure groups. The economic and political power of organized labor combined with organized business would be tremendous. The consumer interest has never been sufficiently cohesive and definite to lead to powerful organizations. Hence a democratic government would probably be unable to act against a coalition of capital and labor. What would happen would be a conflict of short-term, immediate common interests of powerful groups in the industry councils with the long-term general interest implied in the common good. In theory, the government should then assert the primacy of the common good. In practice, our democracy has been successful in opposing powerful pressure groups only when even stronger groups combine against them. Such issues would not arise if certain economic problems were left to competition and industry councils avoided the field of total economic control.[16]

[16] One of the most thorough studies of the problem of administrative price determination in the American economy is found in Chapters 10–12 of A. R. Burns, *The Decline of Competition*. These chapters might well serve as a basis for any discussion of the function of industry councils in determining prices.

Other technical issues of great complexity would also face the councils. Problems of determination of cost, efficiency, and the proper levels of profit and output are not simple. It would seem that the principle of minimum intervention would call for the trying of less ambitious means to secure results, before total economic control were attempted. It is questionable that the common good would be served by such a complex system of controls, in view of the difficulties outlined above. Nor can we dismiss the problem by postulating a degree of moral reform and altruism which would make all affected groups co-operate to seek the common good above individual interests. Some of the objections to complete control spring from the inherent complexity of such a process, when dealing with the gigantic American economy. In other cases, men of good will might sincerely press their evident immediate interests against what they consider a vague and theoretical ultimate good. Finally, if such moral reform is required, then all efforts should be made to secure it at once in the economic field, since the problems of modern society will not brook long delay. On the other hand, if industry councils seek less comprehensive functions, immediate changes can be sought at the same time that we are endeavoring to bring about a better moral tone in the business world.

A question naturally arises as to the argument for price controls given at the beginning of this section, alleging that without them industry councils would be relegated to minor functions. In this regard several observations might be offered. In the first place, if price control would bring the evils just noted, it would be contrary to the common good and hence opposed to the very nature of industry councils. Secondly, many of the functions assigned here to the councils are of major importance, so that the councils would hardly be reduced to an unimportant role. Thus, labor-management co-operation on the plant and industry levels, and other efforts to secure higher production and income, are indeed vital. The same applies to the prevention of depressions and the aiding of sick industries or regions.

Finally, many functions of the councils would limit competition so that it would no longer be the ruling principle in economic life. For example, antidepression measures in the fiscal and monetary fields exclude unlimited competition from an important area. Codes of fair competition and universalizing of decent wage standards in industry would regulate two obnoxious forms of competition. The whole pattern of customs and rules adopted with the common good in view would prevent the ruthlessness of an economy dominated by pitiless competition. The councils might even examine into abuses in the price field, such as monopolistic high prices or discriminatory price cutting, and regulate or abolish these evils. Social justice and the common good should be the dominant principles in economic life, as indicated by Pope Pius XI. But it is contended that the measures herein advocated would limit competition in the manner envisioned in *Quadragesimo Anno.* On the contrary, price fixing by councils would so circumscribe competition as virtually to abolish it, at the same time leading to a centralism which seems contrary to the principles of subsidiarity and organic structure and also opposed to the spirit contained in the social messages of the present Holy Father.

This point was discussed at some length at the Fribourg meeting of the International Institute of Social and Political Sciences, October, 1948. At that meeting, Father Nell-Breuning, widely considered the most authoritative commentator on *Quadragesimo Anno,* flatly stated:

> Bongras assigns control of wages and prices to the industry councils. This, however, is *not* the function of the industry councils. Price formation is in the first place a matter of the market. It is of decisive importance to organize, by way of proper institutions, a functioning *social* market economy. In a secondary place, a general price and monopoly control board, over all the industrial councils, might intervene with price regulations. The regulation of capital formation should be handled with caution; otherwise we would destroy the freedom of consumers.[17]

Later in the same meeting, this eminent author applied a similar principle to wages. His ideal is social control through permeation

[17] *Politeia,* Vol. I, fasc. 3-4, 1949, pp. 231-232.

of the market with institutions dictated by social justice. With these safeguards, competition could then be trusted to set prices and profits, determine production, and allocate resources.[18]

TABLE 1

OUTLINE OF INDUSTRY-COUNCIL PLAN

Level	Structure	Function
Plants, stores, etc.	Labor-management	Common interests of both groups, but not collective bargaining
Industry	Labor-management	Universalizing standards of fair labor practices
Industry, services, professions	Industry-government *or* industry-government-national economic council	Standards of fair competition; sound trade practices
Industry	Industry-labor-government	Stabilizing sick industries
Region	Farm-government	Applying regional regulations for crop control, soil preservation, and farm-credit programs
Region	Industry-finance-business-labor-farm government	Co-operative action on regional economic problems
National	Farmers classified by major crops produced-government-national economic council	Programs for acreage control, crop insurance, and fair average farm prices
National	Industry-finance-business-professions-services-labor-farmers-government	National economic council concerned primarily with depressions and full employment. Co-ordinates other programs for common good. Recommends necessary government policies.

[18] See also the postwar series on vocational order, by Father Nell-Breuning, appearing in *Stimmen der Zeit*. Especially pertinent to the present discussion is the article "Berufstandische Ordnung als Heilung der heutigen gesellschaftlichen Unordnung," *Stimmen der Zeit*, June, 1949, pp. 266–268.

Level	Structure	Function
International	National Economic Council-government-appropriate international organizations	Recommends actions which will stimulate sound international trade, develop backward regions, and remove economic factors leading to international strife. Weighs such programs in light of domestic effects.

APPROACHES TO INDUSTRY COUNCILS

The data given above indicate methods of approach to the papal ideal of a society based on an organic, functional attitude toward economic problems. Many of the illustrations offered suggest immediate activities which should bring worth-while results. It may be well to repeat here two broad avenues of approach which would lead to sound programs. First, as a general rule, it is better to utilize existing groups and methods than to start *de novo* on some theoretically ideal blueprint. Human advance is usually evolutionary, not revolutionary. Secondly, the criteria laid down by the Pope should guide our thinking. Sound programs would lessen class conflict, remove the evils of unregulated competition, and restore to functional groups powers unnecessarily concentrated in the state.

Steps Toward Industrial Co-operation. One of the first and most important fields for co-operation lies in the domain of labor-management relations. Obstacles to harmony should be removed and common interests stressed. One illustration of a bar to collective bargaining would be a legalistic approach to this problem, as was taken in many features of the Labor Management Relations Act, 1947 (the Taft-Hartley Act). Genuine, responsible collective bargaining is often the first step toward co-operation, even though it is in itself dealing with special rather than common interests. Then the mutual concern of both parties with higher production and job stability could serve as a bond of unity.

In this regard, Catholic scholars might well utilize the extensive literature on "human relations" and enlightened personnel policy which has appeared during the last fifteen years. Employers are being constantly told by their own experts that teamwork, communication, and participation on the factory level are vital needs today. Arguments of this nature, which are ethics reinforced by psychology and sociology, would be more persuasive than preaching down to employers in a purely negative fashion. Likewise, existing union literature on co-operation would be more telling with labor leaders than abstract arguments on the desirability of common action. Thus, our labor schools and meetings with employers would aim at definite, concrete goals which would be readily attainable. Catholic scholars might specialize in these fields so as to turn out literature for busy priests and laymen engaged in social-action work.

The next step would be the setting of industry-wide standards. This does not necessarily mean industry-wide bargaining in the sense that absolute uniformity in union contracts would be sought. One of the virtues of the industry-council approach would be its flexibility. Hence, if workers at one plant preferred an extra week of paid vacation to a pension plan, whereas the reverse obtained in another plant, the democratic approach would permit local desires to be achieved through collective bargaining. But, when the majority of an industry achieves certain standards, it should not be subject to unfair competition by a minority which does not meet these goals.

As a practical selling point to employers, proposals of this nature might be conjoined with a plan to give quasi-legal status to rules of fair competition worked out by employer groups, subject to veto when they are not in the public interest. Here again is a challenge to Catholic scholarship. Studies could be made in our universities of various trade practice conferences under the Federal Trade Commission, of NRA codes, and similar data for the 1400 classes of industries (as defined by the Wage and Hour Division, Department of Labor) in the United States.

A National Economic Council. A third step would be the advocacy of a national economic council, composed of representatives of industry, finance, business, the professions, labor, and farm groups. This council would deal primarily with the common interest of all in maintaining full and steady employment. It would not be an agency for total economic planning, but would treat problems which responsible groups acknowledge can be solved only on a national level. A persuasive argument for such a council is the fact that otherwise the problems will be handled by government alone, with the interested parties having only the right of protest.

Scholars could help by synthesizing the best available literature on depressions and full employment. Since experts differ in their approach to these problems, it is unlikely that full agreement could be reached at this time. But a great gain would be achieved if such matters could be discussed in a common forum by the groups most concerned. At the very least, it would serve an important educational purpose. But it would not be too much to expect that a gradually increasing area of agreement would be reached, from which mutually acceptable policies could be evolved and recommended, when necessary, for government action.

Finally, there could be systematic study of the field of government intervention in economic life, to determine the feasibility of returning regulatory functions to industry councils where this is advisable. If, in the nature of things, government control is still desirable, the affected parties might still be afforded at least a consultative voice in laying down broad policies and in making decisions on new issues. The effecting of policies found suitable could be achieved through normal educational and public-relations channels, and particularly by convincing business, labor, and farm groups that more effective democracy and more flexible controls can be promoted by a process of decentralization.

Studies Recommended. As a practical method of making the studies recommended here, it would be desirable that the Catholic Economic Association and the American Catholic Sociological Society have either a joint committee or two closely consulting committees to map out goals and problems. Studies could then be made either directly by scholars or by students doing graduate work under expert supervision. Scholarly material could be made available through their publications, with occasional popular summaries appearing in general periodicals or in pamphlet form. Such co-ordinated and orderly study could bring many valuable suggestions for a better social order, and this within a fairly short time.

A fruitful field of study would be the Belgian experiment along the lines of national and local industry councils. The 1948 law on this matter represents an unprecedented "reform of structure." As a considered middle way between statism and individualism, it sets up elaborate institutions for co-operation between capital and labor in the guidance of the national economy. The law is not ideal, especially since the change was introduced rather abruptly instead of springing up as a gradual and well-tested development. Nevertheless, it is worth careful observation and study.[19]

As the results of studies became available, the Department of Social Action, N.C.W.C., could work out plans for translating sound proposals into action. This could be done through its normal educational work and its contacts with national organizations of business, labor, and farmers. In working out a farm program, the experience and trained personnel of the National Catholic Rural Life Conference would be invaluable.

A further result of study on objectives for organized action would be clarification in regard to function and structure of industry councils. Where there is agreement on feasible functions, normally the question of structure would be settled automatically. Some councils would be labor-management; others might be industry-government; and still others might use suitable variants and bring in various groups which have common interests in a particular problem. Such an approach would be a major contribution to American life. Today, as a nation, we are divided

[19] See W. N. Clarke, "Industrial Democracy in Belgium," *The American Catholic Sociological Review*, December, 1949, pp. 229–257.

into two schools on matters of social reform. There are those who stress the need for reform and ask for new laws and government intervention to achieve it. On the other side, there are many who view with alarm the increasing growth of government intervention, particularly in regard to economic life. Few important groups have taken an intermediate position between these extremes.

Yet the proposals based on the papal encyclicals could well offer a middle-of-the-road program which would appeal to many high-principled persons on both sides. It would offer methods for social betterment, without the drawbacks of increased concentration of power in the hands of government. Indeed, it would reverse the recent trend and restore power to lesser groups. At the same time, it would lessen the hostility between capital and labor and mitigate the harsher aspects of competition. This could be accomplished without demanding any drastic changes in our governmental system or our ways of doing business. Moreover, much could be done without postulating a degree of moral reform which might be unrealizable in the foreseeable future.

Thus we could forge toward a society whose institutions promoted justice and charity and which organized economic life for the common good. The injustices and faulty trends in the socioeconomic field could be remedied. A middle ground could be found between the extremes of individualism and statism, between a disorganized society and an excessive concentration of power. The rights of the individual would be recognized, but also the fact that man is social and has corresponding obligations toward his fellow man. With these broad outlines of sound policy clear, a fruitful study could be made of detailed problems. The concrete rights and duties regarding capital and labor, property and government, and rural economic life and international problems could then be considered. Methods of achieving reform, particularly the reform of morals, could be treated. Such points of detail will be subject matter of the chapters to follow.

READINGS*

J. Messner, *Social Ethics*, pp. 138–143, 196–200, 332–346, 705–710, 749–752, 818–823, 867–923, 935–947.

R. Arès, *What Is Corporative Organization?*

H. F. Trehey, *Foundations of a Modern Guild System.*

J. D. Munier, *Some American Approximations to Pius XI's "Industries and Professions."*

G. Clune, *Christian Social Reorganization*, Chap. 21.

J. A. Ryan, *A Better Economic Order*, Chaps. 7–8.

Report, Commission on Vocational Organization, Government of Eire.

C. Bruehl, *The Pope's Plan for Social Reconstruction*, Chaps. 19–29.

O. von Nell-Breuning, *Reorganization of Social Economy*, Chaps. 10–12.

G. C. Rutten, *La doctrine sociale de l'Église*, Chap. 8.

J. Husslein, *Christian Social Manifesto*, Chap. 30.

R. Miller, *Forty Years After*, pp. 157–185.

J. B. Desrosiers, *Soyons Justes*, Vol. I, pp. 237–262.

J. M. Clark, *Alternative to Serfdom.*

A. R. Burns, *The Decline of Competition*, Chaps. 10–12.

M. L. Cooke and P. Murray, *Organized Labor and Production.*

C. S. Golden and H. J. Ruttenberg, *The Dynamics of Industrial Democracy.*

---

* For further readings, consult Lists Nos. 1, 4, and 8 in the Appendix.

PART II

SOCIAL PRINCIPLES IN ECONOMIC LIFE

Chapter VIII. RIGHTS AND DUTIES OF CAPITAL

THE SYSTEM OF CAPITALISM

Leo XIII, *Quod Apostolici Muneris*

9. The Church, with much greater wisdom and good sense, recognizes the inequality among men, who are born with different powers of body and mind, inequality in actual possession also, and holds that the right of property and of ownership, which springs from nature itself must not be touched and stands inviolate.

Leo XIII, *Rerum Novarum*

26. Therefore, let it be laid down in the first place that a condition of human existence must be borne with, namely, that in civil society the lowest cannot be made equal with the highest. Socialists, of course, agitate the contrary, but all struggling against nature is vain. There are truly very great and very many natural differences among men. Neither the talents, nor the skill, nor the health, nor the capacities of all are the same, and unequal fortune follows of itself upon necessary inequality in respect to these endowments. And clearly this condition of things is adapted to benefit both individuals and the community; for to carry on its affairs community life requires varied aptitudes and diverse services, and to perform these diverse services men are impelled most by differences in individual property holdings.

28. Each needs the other completely: neither capital can do without labor, nor labor without capital. Concord begets beauty and order in things.

33. But the Church, with Jesus Christ as her teacher and leader, seeks greater things than this; namely, by commanding something more perfect, she aims at joining the two social classes to each other in closest neighborliness and friendship.

37. Those who lack fortune's goods are taught by the Church that, before God as Judge, poverty is no disgrace, and that no one should be ashamed because he makes his living by toil. And Jesus Christ has con-

firmed this by fact and by deed. Who for the salvation of men, "being rich, became poor"; and although He was the Son of God and God Himself, yet He willed to seem and to be thought the son of a carpenter; nay, He even did not disdain to spend a great part of His life at the work of a carpenter. "Is not this the carpenter, the son of Mary?" Those who contemplate this divine example will more easily understand these truths: true dignity and excellence in men resides in moral living, that is, in virtue; virtue is the common inheritance of man, attainable equally by the humblest and the mightiest, by the rich and the poor; and the reward of eternal happiness will follow upon virtue and merit alone, regardless of the person in whom they may be found. Nay, rather the favor of God Himself seems to incline more toward the unfortunate as a class; for Jesus Christ calls the poor blessed, and He invites most lovingly all who are in labor or sorrow to come to Him for solace, embracing with special love the lowly and those harassed by injustice. At the realization of these things the proud spirit of the rich is easily brought down, and the downcast heart of the afflicted is lifted up; the former are moved toward kindness, the latter, toward reasonableness in their demands. Thus the distance between the classes which pride seeks is reduced, and it will easily be brought to pass that the two classes, with hands clasped in friendship, will be united in heart.

38. Yet, if they obey Christian teachings, not merely friendship but brotherly love also will bind them to each other. They will feel and understand that all men indeed have been created by God, their common Father; that all strive for the same object of good, which is God Himself, who alone can communicate to both men and angels perfect and absolute happiness; that all equally have been redeemed by the grace of Jesus Christ and restored to the dignity of the sons of God, so that they are clearly united by the bonds of brotherhood not only with one another but also with Christ the Lord, "the firstborn among many brethren," and further, that the goods of nature and the gifts of divine grace belong in common and without distinction to all humankind, and that no one, unless he is unworthy, will be deprived of the inheritance of Heaven. "But if we are sons, we are also heirs: heirs indeed of God and joint heirs with Christ."

39. Such is the economy of duties and rights according to Christian philosophy. Would it not seem that all conflict would soon cease wherever this economy were to prevail in civil society?

Pius XI, Quadragesimo Anno

101. With all his energy Leo XIII sought to adjust this economic system according to the norms of right order; hence, it is evident that this system is not to be condemned in itself. And surely it is not of its own nature

vicious. But it does violate right order when capital hires workers, that is, the nonowning working class, with a view to and under such terms that it directs business and even the whole economic system according to its own will and advantage, scorning the human dignity of the workers, the social character of economic activity, and social justice itself and the common good.

103. But, with the diffusion of modern industry throughout the whole world, the "capitalist" economic regime has spread everywhere to such a degree, particularly since the publication of Leo XIII's Encyclical, that it has invaded and pervaded the economic and social life of even those outside its orbit and is unquestioningly impressing on it its advantages, disadvantages, and vices, and, in a sense, is giving it its own shape and form.

Pius XII, On Women's Duties

On the other hand, can a woman, perhaps, hope for her real well-being from a regime dominated by capitalism? We do not need to describe to you now the economic and social results that issue from it. You know its characteristic signs, and you yourselves are bearing its burden: excessive concentration of population in cities, the constant all-absorbing increase of big industries, the difficult and precarious state of others, notably those of artisans and agricultural workers, and the disturbing increase of unemployment.

Pastoral Letter, French Cardinals, September 8, 1949

By condemning the actions of communist parties, the Church does not support the capitalist regime. It is most necessary that it be realized that in the very essence of capitalism — that is to say, in the absolute value that it gives to property without reference to the common good or to the dignity of labor — there is a materialism rejected by Christian teaching. Whatever their rank in society or their power in the economic life of the various nations, Catholics whose pride of class or attachment to worldly riches induces them to object to any change in the social structure are certainly not acting in the spirit of Jesus Christ. They are, without doubt, accomplices of the enemies of His Church and serve as the forerunners of communist revolution.

THE RIGHT TO PROFITS

Pius XI, Quadragesimo Anno

53. And in the application of natural resources to human use the law of nature, or rather God's will promulgated by it, demands that right order be observed. This order consists in this: that each thing have its

proper owner. Hence it follows that unless a man is expending labor on his own property, the labor of one person and the property of another must be associated, for neither can produce anything without the other. Leo XIII certainly had this in mind when he wrote: "Neither capital can do without labor, nor labor without capital." Wherefore it is wholly false to ascribe to property alone or to labor alone whatever has been obtained through the combined effort of both, and it is wholly unjust for either, denying the efficacy of the other, to arrogate to itself whatever has been produced.

54. Property, that is, "capital," has undoubtedly long been able to appropriate too much to itself. Whatever was produced, whatever returns accrued, capital claimed for itself, hardly leaving to the worker enough to restore and renew his strength. For the doctrine was preached that all accumulation of capital falls by an absolutely insuperable economic law to the rich, and that by the same law the workers are given over and bound to perpetual want, to the scantiest of livelihoods. It is true, indeed, that things have not always and everywhere corresponded with this sort of teaching of the so-called Manchesterian Liberals; yet it cannot be denied that economic-social institutions have moved steadily in that direction. That these false ideas, these erroneous suppositions, have been vigorously assailed, and not by those alone who through them were being deprived of their innate right to obtain better conditions, will surprise no one.

55. And therefore, to the harassed workers there have come "intellectuals," as they are called, setting up in opposition to a fictitious law the equally fictitious moral principle that all products and profits, save only enough to repair and renew capital, belong by very right to the workers.

57. Therefore, the riches that economic-social developments constantly increase ought to be so distributed among individual persons and classes that the common advantage of all, which Leo XIII had praised, will be safeguarded; in other words, that the common good of all society will be kept inviolate. By this law of social justice, one class is forbidden to exclude the other from sharing in the benefits. Hence the class of the wealthy violates this law no less, when, as if free from care on account of its wealth, it thinks it the right order of things for it to get everything and the worker nothing, than does the nonowning working class when, angered deeply at outraged justice and too ready to assert wrongly the one right it is conscious of, it demands for itself everything as if produced by its own hands, and attacks and seeks to abolish, therefore, all property and returns or incomes, of whatever kind they are or whatever the function they perform in human society, that have not been obtained by labor, and for no other reason save that they are of such a nature.

58. To each, therefore, must be given his own share of goods, and the distribution of created goods, which, as every discerning person knows, is laboring today under the gravest evils due to the huge disparity between the few exceedingly rich and the unnumbered propertyless, must be effectively called back to and brought into conformity with the norms of the common good, that is, social justice.

62. All these things, which Our Predecessor has not only suggested but clearly and openly proclaimed, We emphasize with renewed insistence in Our present Encyclical; and unless utmost efforts are made without delay to put them into effect, let no one persuade himself that public order, peace, and the tranquillity of human society can be effectively defended against agitators of revolution.

136. Those who are engaged in producing goods, therefore, are not forbidden to increase their fortune in a just and lawful manner; for it is only fair that he who renders service to the community and makes it richer should also, through the increased wealth of the community, be made richer himself according to his position, provided that all these things be sought with due respect for the laws of God and without impairing the rights of others and that they be employed in accordance with faith and right reason.

DUTIES OF OWNERS

Leo XIII, Graves de Communi

15. Certainly, the path of popular improvement is better assured and more quickly traversed, the more we have the co-operation of the well-to-do, with their wide opportunities of effectual aid. We would have them reflect upon the fact that they are not free to choose whether they will take up the cause of the poor or not; it is a matter of simple duty. Men live in a civic society not only for their own good, but also for the good of all. Some are too poor to contribute their share to the common stock; those, therefore, who can should contribute more generously. The extent of this obligation is in proportion to the amount of riches received. The larger it is, the stricter must be the account we shall have to render to God, who gave it to us. We learn the same lesson from the plague that spreads its calamity and unless a remedy be applied in time, will break out to the ruin and destruction of all classes. He who neglects to take up the cause of the poor acts without regard to his personal interest as well as that of his country.

Leo XIII, Rerum Novarum

31. The following duties, on the other hand, concern rich men and employers: workers are not to be treated as slaves; justice demands that

the dignity of human personality be respected in them, ennobled as it has been through what we call the Christian character. If we hearken to natural reason and to Christian philosophy, gainful occupations are not a mark of shame to man, but rather of respect, as they provide him with an honorable means of supporting life. It is shameful and inhuman, however, to use men as things of gain and to put no more value on them than what they are worth in muscle and energy. Likewise it is enjoined that the religious interests and the spiritual well-being of the workers receive proper consideration. Wherefore, it is the duty of employers to see that the worker is free for adequate periods to attend to his religious obligations; not to expose anyone to corrupting influences or the enticements of sin, and in no way to alienate him from care for his family and the practice of thrift. Likewise, more work is not to be imposed than strength can endure, nor that kind of work which is unsuited to a worker's age or sex.

32. Among the most important duties of employers the principal one is to give every worker what is justly due him. Assuredly, to establish a rule of pay in accord with justice, many factors must be taken into account. But, in general, the rich and employers should remember that no laws, either human or divine, permit them for their own profit to oppress the needy and the wretched or to seek gain from another's want. To defraud anyone of the wage due him is a great crime that calls down avenging wrath from Heaven. "Behold, the wages of the laborers . . . which have been kept back by you unjustly, cry out: and their cry has entered into the ears of the Lord of Hosts." Finally, the rich must religiously avoid harming in any way the savings of the workers either by coercion, or by fraud, or by the arts of usury; and the more for this reason, that the workers are not sufficiently protected against injustices and violence, and their property, being so meager, ought to be regarded as all the more sacred. Could not the observance alone of the foregoing laws remove the bitterness and the causes of conflict?

Pius XI, On Atheistic Communism

50. Therefore, We turn again in a special way to you, Christian employers and industrialists, whose problem is often so difficult for the reason that you are saddled with the heavy heritage of an unjust economic regime whose ruinous influence has been felt through many generations. We bid you be mindful of your responsibility. It is unfortunately true that the manner of action in certain Catholic circles has done much to shake the faith of the working classes in the religion of Jesus Christ. These groups have refused to understand that Christian charity demands the recognition of certain rights due to the workingman, which the Church has explicitly acknowledged. What is to be thought of the action of those Catholic

employers who in one place succeeded in preventing the reading of Our Encyclical, *Quadragesimo Anno,* in their local churches? Or of those Catholic industrialists who even to this day have shown themselves hostile to a labor movement that We Ourselves recommended? Is it not deplorable that the right of private property defended by the Church should so often have been used as a weapon to defraud the workingman of his just salary and his social rights?

Pius XI, Quadragesimo Anno

64. First of all, those who declare that a contract of hiring and being hired is unjust of its own nature, and hence a partnership contract must take its place, are certainly in error and gravely misrepresent Our Predecessor whose Encyclical not only accepts working for wages or salaries but deals at some length with its regulation in accordance with the rules of justice.

65. We consider it more advisable, however, in the present condition of human society that, so far as is possible, the work contract be somewhat modified by a partnership contract, as is already being done in various ways and with no small advantage to workers and owners. Workers and other employees thus become sharers in ownership or management or participate in some fashion in the profits received.

Pius XII, Address to Catholic Employers, May 7, 1949

The owner of the means of production, whoever he be — individual owner, workers' association, or corporation — must always — within the limits of public economic law — retain control of his economic decisions. It goes without saying that his income is higher than that of his collaborators. But it follows that the material prosperity of the entire population, which is the objective of social economy, lays upon him, more than upon the others, the obligation of contributing by savings to the increase of the nation's fund of capital. As we must not forget, on the other hand, that it is supremely advantageous to a healthy social economy when this accumulation of capital derives from the greatest possible number of sources, it is very desirable, in consequence, that the workmen also should be enabled, by the fruit of their savings, to share in the creation of the capital resources of their country.

Code of Social Principles

142. That portion of the wage which corresponds to the greater or less prosperity of the business can be settled and paid at the conclusion of the business year and in proportion to the net profits. Instead of being paid in cash it may be converted into shares in the undertaking in which the

worker has assisted. In proportion as these labor shares are created, an equal number of the capital shares may be liquidated by lot.

It is allowable for the firm not to pay the aforesaid part of the wages in the manner suggested, nor to put the amount into shares in the enterprise; but it is also allowable for the organized workers to refuse their consent to a labor agreement unless it enforces this double condition.

The replacement of capital shares by labor shares can only be made prudently by progressive stages, allowing the masses to gain the experience needed for the management of business.

THE PRESENT ECONOMIC SYSTEM

Capitalism. In discussing the details of right social living, it seems appropriate to begin with a discussion of the rights and duties of capital. We of the United States live in a capitalistic economy and our attitudes toward social life must take account of this fact. The term "capitalism" has received many definitions and there is still much discussion as to the most accurate description of the system. In general American usage, capitalism may be described as an economic system characterized by private ownership of the means of production, substantial freedom of enterprise to determine the main economic conditions of production, stress on the profit motive, and the use of funds invested in land, resources, buildings, and machines in a notable portion of enterprises. Succinctly, private ownership, free enterprise, the profit motive, and the use of invested funds are the main elements of our capitalistic system.

The definition of capitalism just given may not be accepted by many scholars, particularly those with European backgrounds. The point is not of major importance in itself, since it is mainly a matter of semantics. However, from the light of public relations and clear understanding in the United States, it does become important. Sometimes the statement is made: "Capitalism and communism are equally wrong" or "The Church condemns capitalism and communism alike." Statements of this nature are not uncommon in European Catholic literature and have occasionally been made by American writers. In 1948 considerable discussion was aroused in the United States by the report, "The Church and the Disorder of Society," given at the World Council of Churches (Protestant). The Report condemned capitalism on four grounds: subordination of human needs to economic gain, production of serious inequalities, materialism, and a tendency toward causing insecurity and unemployment. Catholic writers in turn stress the elements of individualism and social irresponsibility historically connected with capitalism. Hence some conclude that the system is as immoral as communism or socialism.

It is questionable whether the use of European terminology in discussing capitalism is appropriate here. The average American is not familiar with Weber, Sombart, Fanfani, or similar expert writers. He considers capitalism as synonymous with private property and free enterprise, and further holds that these are essential foundations of our political democracy. Most Americans, thinking in black and white terms, contrast capitalism with socialism or communism. They feel that a rejection of free enterprise means automatic preference for some system of statism. In the light of these attitudes, any condemnation of capitalism is bound to be misunderstood here. Elements which many Europeans use in the definition of the system are considered by Americans to be either abuses of capitalism or accidental features which could be corrected without impairing the essential characteristics of our present way of life. Hence, as often happens, different ideas are being discussed in relation to the same term.

If we accept general American usage in defining capitalism, then it is by no means clear that the Church condemns capitalism, particularly with the finality of its judgments on socialism and communism. Of the four items normally included by Americans in describing our economic system, two are acceptable beyond question. The Church has no objection to the use of invested funds to multiply means of production. It accepts the institution of private property, noting at the same time the social responsibility of owners and the desirability of wider diffusion of ownership. There might be more hesitation in regard to the element of free enterprise, but here much depends upon definition. The Church would not accept an unlimited freedom as demanded by individualism, but it would not reject the notion of freedom tempered by social responsibility. Indeed, it seeks to enlarge areas of freedom based on wider diffusion of productive property.

Likewise, the emphasis upon the profit motive is subject to varied interpretation. If it means, as it often did in American history, that profits are the supreme goal of business, to the exclusion of the common good and particularly to the detriment of labor's rights, then this element must be condemned. But if the seeking of profits is regulated by social responsibility, such a practice may well be legitimate. As will be noted later, the businessman has a right to a return for his services just as labor has a right to a living wage. Accordingly, there is certainly a sense in which capitalism as defined here would be acceptable in the light of Church teachings. All would depend upon the precise form which capitalism took and its embodiment of the idea of social responsibility.

It may be objected that a fifth element should be added to describe capitalism adequately, namely, the fact that the means of production are owned by a small group, with the great majority of the population in a wage-earner status. It is held that such a situation is contrary to human dignity, inasmuch as it restricts the freedom of the average individual in an important sphere of life. But the average American would not consider such a situation as intrinsic to capitalism. He would characterize a distributist society, with widespread ownership of the means of production, as essentially capitalistic. While economists might not always agree with such a broad definition of capitalism, the significant point is the reaction of public opinion here.

Since it is doubtful whether or not we have the right to condemn American capitalism in a blanket form, prudence would dictate the use of more precise terminology. The path of social reform is sufficiently difficult, without adding unnecessary obstacles in the way of language which is bound to be misunderstood. We can condemn selfish individualism. We may note the abuses which have flourished under our present system, namely, concentration of power, inequality, and insecurity. But it is arguable that such abuses can be corrected without destroying private property or placing such controls upon enterprise that it no longer remains free. It is possible to speak of the reform of capitalism, whereas the popes have given definitive condemnations of socialism and communism. Hence little is to be gained, and much to be lost, by equating all three systems in writings destined for American readers.

The Wage Contract. Historically, one of the notable features of capitalism has been the wage system, whereby one or more workers contributes skill and energy, using the property of another, to produce goods or services. The products of such activity are sold by the owner of the property, who pays the workers for their contribution and retains a part as payment for his own share in the process, namely, the use of his property. Such a system, says Pope Pius XI, "is not to be condemned." "It is not of its own nature vicious." But it is a grave abuse when capital uses its power in such a way that it scorns "the human dignity of the workers, the social character of economic activity, and social justice itself and the common good." Accordingly, the hiring of workers by an employer is an acceptable mode of economic life, provided the social aspect of the process is not ignored.

In the modern world, it would be almost impossible to have any other system. World population has expanded to such a degree that the use of machines and mass-production methods seems essential if we are to maintain even a minimum standard of living. Increases in living standards almost invariably involve an increase in invested capital. Thus, in the United States, it can be shown that real wages per worker have gone up in direct proportion to increased capital investment. Today the typical American worker has at his disposal an average of five thousand dollars' worth of tools, buildings, and resources. These multiply his skill and efficiency to such a degree that he can work only half as long as was customary fifty years ago, and yet receive three times as much real income. Such is the contribution of physical capital, which may be defined as the machines and resources bought with money capital. Even socialism and communism acknowledge the value of physical capital, although under these systems it is generally owned by the state. Socialist enterprises hire workers in much the same way as do their capitalist competitors.

An even more fundamental reason for the owner-worker distinction was noted by Pope Leo XIII, namely, human inequality. Men differ in skills, abilities, character, zeal, energy, and like qualities. Some are timid and retiring; others are forthright and resolute. There are men who are conservative and cautious, whereas their fellows may be daring and even reckless. With such major diversities in human nature, it is not surprising that men should be divided into the skilled and the unskilled and into leaders and followers. Nor is it remarkable that unequal talents are among the factors leading to inequality in wealth. In some cases individuals saved from their income, at times through several generations, to build up a great enterprise. In other instances, promoters used the money of others, obtained by borrowing or the sale of shares of ownership, to create some firm. Within an enterprise, men of exceptional ability would be given positions of responsibility. On lower levels, workers would be classified according to their skills.

Of course, not all economic inequality is traceable to differences in ability. Elements of luck, ruthlessness, favoritism, and similar factors not connected with genuine ability have been important factors in many well-known success stories. But, at least there are enough variations in human qualities that inequality is not necessarily exploitive. In general, this thesis need not be argued in America. Few in our midst accept the Marxian idea that capital is essentially predatory, stealing a surplus value which really belongs to the workers. Nor do we object to inequality of fortune or position, provided it is based on evident ability and not dishonest means. The average worker does not begrudge the manager of an enterprise his salary, nor the owner his profits provided they are "fair." But this element of fairness requires considerable definition and clarification. We must decide not only what are the proper returns for capital, but to whom they should be allocated and in what proportion. In making this decision, both commutative justice and social justice should be consulted. To the extent that what is clearly due in strict justice can be defined, we should do so. Where the situation is doubtful, the demands of the common good should prevail.

In working out this problem, several questions must be answered. We must understand clearly what capital is and what are its rights and its duties. The term "capital" is used in the United States rather loosely to designate several things. Thus, it could mean physical capital, that is, the machinery, resources, and buildings used as agents of production. More commonly the phrase "capital goods" is used to designate such physical objects. Then, capital can mean money saved and invested in capital goods. Finally, it can mean the class of owners or managers of such funds. Physical capital is unquestionably productive. It multiplies and enhances the abilities and skills of workers. Moreover, it is generally conceded that those who furnish the funds for capital goods are entitled to some share of the product, whether it be in the form of profits on investments or interest on a loan. Finally, the capitalist class, as innovators, promoters, or managers of enterprises, deserves payment for its contribution to economic life. Management of capital and enterprise is, of course, a distinct function from ownership of capital.

Management and Promotion. Since the questions of profits and interest are highly complex, it will be easier to consider first the reward to the capitalist as promoter or manager of a firm. It is possible that the promoter may contribute nothing from his own funds to a given enterprise. Yet he may have vision, daring, or experience which insures great success with the use of borrowed or invested money. A person of this nature makes a definite contribution to economic life and would be entitled in justice to a reward for this function. Organization, correct calculation of risks, and awareness of opportunities are real values and add to the wealth of the community. One could even say that the speculator, traditionally despised as a parasite, is not necessarily non-productive of economic value. Stock exchanges and commodity markets, when properly regulated, smooth out the functioning of the price system and actually lessen risk to producers.[1] The actual return imputed to the efforts of promoters is difficult to assess accurately. In a free economic system, however, the law of supply and demand tends to bring about a rough approximation of what the business community attributes to these agents. If labor is able to demand a proper wage, money capital receives its fair share, and management is suitably rewarded, the surplus remaining in a competitive enterprise is usually credited to the promoter.

Management of an enterprise is likewise a distinct function, not necessarily connected with the initial promotion of a firm or the furnishing of funds for its needs of physical capital. This distinction is clearly seen in the corporation, where day-by-day direction of the company may be in the hands of a president who is not even a stockholder. Broad policies may be laid down by a board of directors, representative of the stockholders, but the actual running of the firm is left to skilled management. In many of the largest corporations, management actually controls the appointment of directors, through the use of the proxy machinery. In small companies, the owners are usually their own managers. In such cases, their salary for management is lumped in with other "profits," but actually the directing of a firm is distinct both from its promotion and its ownership. The contribution of management is best seen when a succession of managers run the same company. It frequently happens that a firm may approach bankruptcy under poor management and make large profits under a new president, with economic conditions, market for the product, and wages remaining the same. In other cases, several competitive firms may be equally close to raw materials and market, have the same power and transportation facilities, pay the same wage rate, and yet one company may be highly success-

---

[1] For the economic value of speculation, see J. F. Cronin, *Economic Analysis and Problems*, Chap. 6.

ful and others barely survive. Obviously, such results reflect different management policies.

In view of the economic contribution made by management, it follows that salaries based on this contribution are not necessarily unjust. Some moralists are appalled at the differential between wages paid to workers and the salaries and bonuses given to corporation executives. An executive of General Motors may receive a salary of $200,000 whereas a skilled worker may receive an annual wage of $3,500. Yet, if this executive were to receive no salary and his former salary were apportioned to the workers, they would receive an annual increase of only fifty cents each. The efficient management of this company provides 400,000 jobs and makes enormous profits for the stockholders (as high as $1,500 per worker). It would seem somewhat captious, in this case, to attack the salary of a successful executive as unjust or disproportionate, at least in terms of economic contribution to the company. At the same time it would be socially desirable to emphasize incentives other than economic. Many public servants perform duties fully as complex as those of corporation executives, but receive only a minor fraction of the latters' salaries. This shows that service to the community, a sense of creative achievement, and similar nonmonetary incentives can also be attractive. If such attitudes could be created, there would be less need for disproportionate salaries which may give rise to social tensions.

The fact that many moralists examine promoter and management returns with jaundiced eyes is partially explainable by past abuses in these fields. Thus, the ethics of American promoters have not always been at a high level. Many fortunes obtained through promotion have been tainted with fraud and antisocial practices. Likewise, managers of business have been known to have retained enormous salaries and bonuses at times when their workers were underpaid and their stockholders received no dividends. But abuse of power should not obscure the principle that promotion and management can render real economic service and hence should be rewarded appropriately. As to concrete tests, particularly of management salaries, the following considerations may be useful. Where an industry is competitive, the presumption is that salaries indicate imputed contribution of the executive. If monopolistic conditions prevail, the individual situation must be studied to reach a sound conclusion. Again, when the total of executive salaries is small compared to the total wage bill and profits allocated to reserve and dividends, little is gained by comparing salaries and wages. In such cases, just wage increases must be secured by other means than lowering executive salaries. The picture would be different in a small firm where executives received large salaries while workers were underpaid.

Above all, the common good must be considered. Here we must balance many considerations and include the total picture. In favor of the present executive salary level and compensation to promoters is the need for vigorous management and economic growth in the United States. We must increase efficiency and expand our economy if we are to raise standards of living and maintain full employment. To achieve this goal, there must be incentives for promoters, business managers, and stockholders. In the past, moralists have tended too often to look upon distribution of income and wealth from a static point of view. They wrote as if the sum of national income were a fixed amount, to be distributed according to some rough equality. Actually, our national income varies tremendously. Thus, in terms of real purchasing power, it has increased 50 per cent during the last ten years. Great possibilities for further growth remain. Such growth would be unlikely if all economic incentives were taken from promoters, managers, and investors. Our economy would then be stabilized at an unsatisfactory level. Indeed, it might even run down if profits and savings were inadequate to replace worn-out equipment. This point will be elaborated again in this chapter and in Chapter X.

PROFITS AND INTEREST

The Right to Profits. The problem of business profits is not only controversial, it is also extremely complex. The term itself is by no means clear, and usage is far from consistent. Thus, the owner of a small grocery store might close his books at the end of the year and find that he has made $6,000 profits. He may be satisfied with this result. But if an economist examined the same books, he would set aside $2,000 as a return on a $40,000 investment; $4,000 for salary to the owner for managing the store; and would like to have several thousand more for reserves against future losses. If the owner had neglected to set aside a fund to match depreciation of his equipment, what seemed to be a satisfactory profit might actually be a loss. He would be living on his capital, getting a small salary for managing the store and no real return on his investment. In strict economic terms, profits constitute a residue after all wages, salaries, and other expenses have been paid; depreciation allowed on investment; funds set aside to meet loans and to insure against future losses; and interest paid on money invested or borrowed.

The papal encyclicals do not always follow this approach to profits. This is but natural, since these writings were intended for general use and hence follow common usage in denoting returns to capital. Thus, management salaries, stockholders' dividends, rent from land, and interest on loans might in certain contexts be considered as profits. This is particularly the case when abuses are denounced, such as the enormous disparity in returns to the propertied classes in contrast to the wage earners. But it is also followed at times when the right of capital to a return is justified. No neat distinction is made between types of return to the group called capitalists, especially when the argument is directed against socialists. Since socialists considered labor the only source of income, it was only natural the popes should note in very broad terms the contribution of other factors.

The present chapter follows papal usage, with some modifications. When the right to profits is considered, emphasis is given to the contribution of money capital and its consequent right to a return. This argument would justify proper dividends, interest (which is also given separate treatment later), and even rent, although the last-named item is discussed more fully in Chapter

XII. In discussing dividends, it is argued that the stockholder should get in the long run at least the current rate of interest as his return. This is based on the psychology of investors, who would not purchase stocks unless they expected this minimum return. On the other hand, payments to management are not considered profits.

When the national level of profits is treated, the stress is on corporate profits. This is done for two reasons: the current emphasis on corporate profits in discussion of appropriate levels of profit, and the ease of separating other returns from profits in a corporation balance sheet. Hence profits are considered as the sum remaining after salaries, wages, payments for materials and services, depreciation, reserves, interest, and taxes are paid. Where the element of taxes is important, profits before taxes will be called gross profits and the lesser sum, net profits. When no qualification is given, net profits are under discussion.

The right to profits must be judged both in terms of commutative and of social justice. In strict justice, capital makes a contribution to economic life by furnishing a necessary factor of production. In addition to labor, machines and raw materials contribute to the productive process. They enhance and multiply the effectiveness of human labor. Capital goods are purchased as a result of the savings of investors and lenders, who reserve a part of their current income, thus diverting some economic effort from the making of goods for consumption to the making of capital goods.[2] This contribution is made in prospect of at least two types of rewards. At the minimum, the sum contributed should be returned. The corporation does this for lenders by setting aside reserves for the retirement of its bonds. For investors, it keeps their property in good repair and makes depreciation allowances to replace equipment as it wears out or becomes obsolete.

---

[2] This assumption refers to voluntary saving. More controversial are various kinds of forced saving by consumers who pay excessive prices for products. Sometime corporations enforce such saving by their price policies. At other times bank-credit inflation or inflationary borrowing by government imposes savings on consumers. Such involuntary saving may be unjust, unless demanded by the common good.

In this connection, it is pertinent to ask whether in payment of corporation bonds, allowance should be made for price-level changes which depreciate the value of the dollar. This is indeed a knotty problem, since inflation reduces the real value of money and hence, in effect, cuts the principal of any debt. Deflation has the reverse effect. It could be argued that lenders take this risk knowingly and include it in the interest rate demanded. Such would certainly be true for the ordinary ups and downs of business. The drastic inflation following wars is more severe, but it might be contended that in time of war each citizen must sacrifice according to his ability. On the other hand, if firms set aside reserves for depressions or higher depreciation funds in inflationary times (because of higher replacement costs of equipment), such practices need not be contrary to justice. They are conserving the real value of the stockholders' investment.

The second reward to lenders and investors is a charge for the use of their money. The moral justification of this charge is treated subsequently, in connection with interest. Interest to bondholders is called such, whereas with stockholders it is a part of their dividends, together with a payment for the added risk they assume and, at times, a share of profits in the strict, scientific sense. Stockholders should receive more than the going rate of interest in view of two types of risk. They run the chance of nonpayment in poor years (corporations today tend to use reserves set aside for depressions, more to keep the firm alive than to pay out dividends) and they may lose their principal if business changes lead to bankruptcy of their company.

While strict justice looks upon profits in terms of payment for service rendered, social justice weighs them in the light of the common good. Here the overruling consideration is the health of the economy taken as a whole. This point has occasioned much recent controversy in the United States both in terms of principles and of facts. On the matter of principle, there are two main schools of thought. Followers of Keynes and Hansen generally oppose high-profit levels on the grounds that they lead to inevitable depression. They argue correctly that savings on the part of wealthy individuals and of corporations often increase quite independently of the investment need for such funds. They continue with the thesis of a "mature economy," namely, that our economic plant has so expanded that there is no continuing need for substantial investment for purposes of further expansion. Hence, they allege, such savings will remain idle, thus precipitating a depression. The only remedies are prevention of excessive savings (by union contracts or lower prices), taxation of such funds by the state, or public investment as a means of returning saved funds into circulation. By contrast, the more traditional school emphasizes both the need for economic expansion and the necessity for a profit incentive to secure needed investment. Followers of this school maintain that we need both more savings and suitable profit incentives so that these savings will be invested.

It is unfortunate that the truth in both positions has been obscured by partisan arguments and name-calling. Unquestionably the American economy is not mature in terms of human needs. We can stand improvements in food, housing, health care, education, as well as in wider distribution of comforts and some luxuries. If national income expands and more goods are produced at lower costs, the lower-income groups can raise their standards. An equal distribution of income, even at prevailing high levels, would not secure this result. Hence there is need for savings, investment, and economic expansion. Adequate profit incentives are an important factor in producing savings and turning these savings into investment. On the other hand, there is merit in the argument for a proper level of income distribution and mass purchasing power. Thus, to use an extreme example, if half the national income went to 1 per cent of the population, the saving level would be enormous, possibly 40 per cent of our income. In spite of the real needs mentioned above it is doubtful that such a large amount of savings could be absorbed by normal investment outlets. Some savings would remain idle, thus tending to produce a depression.

Much of the difficulty in resolving this controversy arises because profits and wages are considered in isolation, apart from other factors such as prices, taxes, and government monetary and fiscal policies. Mismanagement of these latter factors could cause a depression regardless of profit levels and income distribution. A change in tax policies could lead to a sharp increase in incentives to invest, without any change in present profit levels. Hence any final answer on this problem must be deferred, pending a fuller discussion of depressions, income distribution, and taxation in Chapters X and XII. It may be noted, however, that these interrelationships form a powerful argument for a national economic council, in which all factors may be weighed in the light of the common good, by a group representative of our entire economic life.

At this stage, it is fair to conclude that reasonable profits are justified in strict justice. Reasonable profits would safeguard the principal loaned or invested through sufficient reserves for depreciation, pay a fair rate of interest to bondholders and stockholders, and make adequate allowance for risks assumed. Social justice would uphold the profit incentive as a means for promoting economic expansion and higher living standards. It would call, however, for the consideration of profits in the light of the total national economic picture, so that the economic system would function for the common good of all.

Recent American Profit Levels. Normally any discussion of economic statistics for a given period would be of limited value, because the changing pattern of events would make them quickly outdated. Nevertheless, the many currents observable in recent years, particularly during the period 1946–1949, afford an opportunity to comment on several important issues. The issues and controversies of the time sharpen points which might otherwise pass unnoticed. Most important of these controversies are those dealing with the actual level of profits during the period and their impact on the general economy.

It might be assumed that in this day of abundant statistics, there would be no controversy over the actual profit level in the United States. In fact, many disputes arose in 1946–1949, mainly because various groups used different figures to bolster their arguments. It would be worth while to examine these calculations in the attempt to secure reliable attitudes for future discussions on profit levels.

Profits may be computed as a percentage of sales price or in relation to the assets of the firm. This latter method has been standard until recently, but there has been an increasing use of the sales technique of computation, partly for polemical reasons. The asset approach is generally acceptable, since it relates profits to actual investment in the firm and hence determines whether or not the investors are receiving a fair return on their contribution. Thus a firm with a huge business (say, fifty million annual turnover) but a small capital investment (e.g., two million) could make but 1 per cent on sales ($500,000) yet be receiving 25 per cent on investment. Another firm could receive 10 per cent on sales, but in view of a relatively large investment only obtain 5 per cent on its capital assets.

It should be clear that careless use of the sales approach can be highly misleading. It has some value in inflationary or boom times when business is extraordinarily good, if used as a comparison between previous years and the prosperous year. Thus, if a firm made 1 per cent on sales during the depressed period 1931–1935, and this was considered reasonable profit at the time, it is not clear that such a firm would be profiteering in securing the same margin during the inflationary years 1946–1949. Total profits would be much higher, especially in relation to assets, but the increase would be attributable to a high rate of operations. Unit profits remain the same. Another use of the sales method is for computing possible price reductions or increases. When a firm's profits amount to one cent on the sales dollar, substantial price reduction would be impossible, no matter what the total of profits in terms of assets. But if the sales approach is used on an absolute figure, as in the argument that 5 or 9 per cent on sales is not too high, such usage is meaningless and often dishonest. There is no "fair" figure for profits computed in terms of sales. Figures vary from company to company and industry to industry.

Profits may be considered before or after federal corporation taxes. Thus, the 1948 figure of thirty-four billion dollars before taxes shrinks to twenty billion dollars after taxes. For normal conditions, the second figure is satisfactory, since it represents the actual return to the firm and its investors. (There is an increasing tendency to consider even personal incomes after taxes; a practice which has some merit.) An exception might be made in the case of a labor union bargaining with a single firm, since the higher figure would be applicable to a wage increase. Assuming that the same rate of profits continued into the year covered by the union contract, and all other conditions remained unchanged, gross profits would be lowered by the full amount of the wage increase, and net profits by about 62 per cent of that amount (thus allowing for a lesser tax bill). But when some groups use profits before taxes as an argument that profits are too high, they are engaging in a dubious procedure. Tax money does not benefit the corporation.

A third point of controversy involves the use of annual as against average profit figures. Many business groups contend that high profits in prosperous times are often balanced by losses in depression periods. By taking corporation profits as a whole, a good case can be made. Thus, while all corporations might average 12 per cent on investment during the years 1946–1948, the same group would show a loss during the years 1931–1934. Hence it would be contended that a fifteen- or twenty-year average would give a more accurate picture. The merit of this argument is clear, where individual firms are concerned. They must balance bad years with good, if they are to be able to give their investors a suitable return on their money. However, when the same approach is used for all corporations lumped together, the results can be misleading. General averages may conceal the fact that some firms or even industries have made consistent profits over a long period of years, and that even a twenty-year average for these firms would be far above the going interest and risk rate for investors. Whether such profits would be excessive would be determined by considerations of monopolistic or competitive conditions, wages paid to workers, and prices charged consumers. Thus, if a firm in a competitive industry paid good wages and was fair to suppliers, above-normal profits would not indicate antisocial policies. On the other hand, if an industry consisted of two or three firms which charged uniform prices and made consistent high profits, suspicions of monopolistic practices would rightly arise.

Special profit problems come forth in times of inflation. At such times many firms receive inventory profits. They buy raw materials at a lower stage of the upward spiral and sell finished goods at a higher stage, thus making a speculative profit. Some economists would exclude such profits as unreal since they will normally be counterbalanced by inventory losses when the downward spiral begins. This argument has merit for the economy as a whole. Most firms consider inventory profits and losses as the necessary result of continued operation in uncertain times. They hope that gains will cancel out the losses. Some firms, willing to speculate in inventories, can make huge profits if they successfully ride the upswing and have low inventories when the downswing commences. Others may lack this sense of timing and go bankrupt because of inventory losses when deflation commences. Since such "profits" are speculative and likely to be canceled by subsequent losses, the argument for disregarding them in national statistics has considerable force.

Moreover, profits calculated as percentages of assets are frequently misleading for another reason during an inflationary period. Normally firms value their assets at historical cost of buildings and equipment. This does not represent their real (replacement) value when inflation has caused a permanently higher price level. Such considerations apply particularly to depreciation reserves which, according to present tax practices, must be set up on the basis of historical cost. These reserves are then inadequate to replace equipment whose price has increased sharply. Thus a multiple power lathe bought in 1938 for $100,000 may have been depreciated by annual offsets of $10,000. It wore out in 1948, but replacement cost was $200,000. This represented a capital loss of $100,000 to the firm. Present tax laws do not allow firms to meet this contingency, since they only permit depreciation based on original cost. Hence, it is contended, corporations should, under conditions of a permanently raised price level, set aside special reserves from net profits for such contingencies. By such reasoning, not excessive or forced, Professor Sumner Slitcher argued that real business profits in 1948 were closer to thirteen than twenty-one billion.[3]

Still another consideration in times of changing price levels is the ratio of profits to total national income or to income originating in corporate business. On both these scores, 1948 profits do not loom enormously high. Thus net profits in 1929 were 9.7 per cent of national income and, in 1948, they were 9.2 per cent. When other years, such as 1940, 1941, and 1947, are brought into the comparison, little significant differences are noted. If the comparison rests on shares of national income originating in corporate business, the figures given in the accompanying table lead to the same conclusion. Thus, it can be seen that the variations, while greater, are not so drastic as when profits are viewed in absolute figures. Profits in 1948 were high, but not unusually so when viewed as percentages of income flow.

TABLE 2

SHARES OF INCOME ORIGINATING IN CORPORATE BUSINESS*

Year	1929	1939	1943	1946	1948
Employee compensation (%)	74.2	80.6	72.8	80.5	74.5
Net profits (%)	18.1	13.4	11.3	14.0	16.6

* U. S. Department of Commerce

There is less tendency to charge that payments to investors have been extreme. On the contrary, some of the groups which felt that total profits were excessive in 1947–1948 were also aggrieved because investors received such a small share of net profits. In 1948, stockholders received in the form of dividends

---

[3] For a balanced discussion of opposing viewpoints, see J. W. Welcker, "Divergent Views on Corporate Profits," *Harvard Business Review,* March, 1949.

but 40 per cent of net profits, as contrasted with 75 per cent in 1939 and 69 per cent in 1929. Thus, there was little difference in money totals of dividends between 1929 and 1948, and the actual purchasing power of investment income was almost cut in half. By contrast, farmers and wage earners received sharp increases in their real income during the same period. Hence a labor spokesman before a Senate committee pleaded for a greater disbursement of corporate income to its stockholders.[4] He maintained that the reinvestment of earnings should be decided by stockholders through the buying of new stock, and not by corporate managements. Business groups argue, however, that present tax policy plus general uncertainties make stock financing almost impossible. At any rate, more and more corporate expansion is either being financed internally by withholding profits or externally through loans, with an ever decreasing amount coming from stock sales. This point will be discussed subsequently in Chapters X and XII.

The issues raised thus far indicate the complexity of the profit problem, whether considered from the viewpoint of commutative or distributive justice. In a period of the highest profits in American history, a case can be made that such profits are not excessive. Moreover, the divergence of conclusions based on the same basic situation indicates the need for a cautious and complete approach to the problem.[5] A total approach changes many conclusions based on partial data. Even more necessary is the need for studying the entire problem in the light of social justice.

If the common good requirement of social justice be invoked, then the profit level must be examined in relation to the general needs of the economy. Here the case is clear for expanded invest-

---

[4] Testimony of S. H. Ruttenberg, before a subcommittee of the Joint Committee on the Economic Report, Dec. 8, 1948.

[5] For latest statistical material, a popular source is the *United States News and World Report* or *Business Week*. Fairly objective interpretation is contained in *Labor's Monthly Survey, Fortune,* and the *Harvard Business Review*. The monthly *Letter* of the National City Bank gives selected quarterly figures. Full statistics may be found in the *Statistical Abstract of the United States*. They may be brought up to date through the *Survey of Current Business* and *The Handbook of Government Statistics*.

ment in the postwar period. Business had a long period of invest-ment drought, partly because of the depression during the 1930's and partly because of war during the early 1940's. As a result, equipment had run down and necessary replacements had been deferred for an extremely long period. Some years of sustained capital investment were required to modernize the economy, to say nothing of expanding it for the sake of greater employ-ment and higher living standards. A risk is taken when such investments are not co-ordinated and integrated with some studies as to the long-term needs of the economy. But, in the absence of an effective national economic council, it is not clear that postwar investment was excessive. J. W. Welcker concludes that "from the *facts now available* and using the *current standards* for appraising the over-all needs of our economy . . . 1948 busi-ness profits were not excessively high."[6]

A statement from a conservative labor source holds:

> In 1947, corporation profits before taxes amounted to $29.8 billion; of this $11.7 billion was paid out in income taxes to federal and state governments, $6.9 billion went to stockholders in dividends and $11.2 billion was kept in the business. The profits kept did not pay for the entire $16 billion worth of new plant and equipment purchased by busi-ness in 1947, nor furnish all of the $12 billion needed to carry larger inventories and credit to buyers. Part of these needs were provided by reserves, and part by securing more than $12 billion from loans and from sale of new capital stock.
>
> The chance to make a profit is a mainspring to efficiency and good management in a free enterprise system. To compete against other business, to pay the steady wage increases demanded by labor and still make a profit, a business firm must invent new processes and install new techniques. Labor feels that competition and the profit incentive are necessary to assure good management and productivity. Our high living standards exist because we produce more per manhour than any other nation.
>
> Profits provide business with capital needed to carry on operations, improve machinery and expand plant. Better machines produce greater value per manhour of work, the basis for higher wages; expanded plant capacity creates more jobs. Profits also furnish the tax money that pays

---

[6] *Loc. cit.,* p. 263.

a major part of government expenses. In 1948 corporation income taxes supplied more than one quarter of all money spent by the federal government. This money is providing many services to the American people which they did not have in 1926-29, such as: TVA and other flood control and electric power systems; public housing programs; help to farmers; National Labor Relations Board and Wage and Hour Administration; payments to veterans for education, medical care and pensions; old age and unemployment relief to persons outside the social security system; aid to dependent mothers and children and the blind; extension of public health service for control of disease; construction of airports; atomic energy development; aid for foreign reconstruction and membership in the United Nations as our country's contribution toward a more stable world; greatly increased defense expenditures and interest on the public debt as a result of World War II.[7]

Nevertheless, this same labor group holds that mass purchasing power is lagging behind, on the grounds that farm and labor real income is decreasing at a time when production is increasing. This involves the complex problem of a proper balance between investment and consumption, a problem which is even more difficult when complicated by postwar adjustments and an involved international situation. With inadequate data and inability to predict the future, the best that can be done is to avoid exaggerations and to allow for honest differences of opinion within the margin of unavoidable error.

In conclusion, the survey of postwar profits illustrates the many complex considerations involved in applying strict justice to the profit problem. Even more intricate is the reconciliation of any given picture with social justice, since this calls for accurate knowledge of what the common good requires at a given time. Often such demands are the subject of controversy between men of integrity and good will. This fact emphasizes the need for further joint study of problems from the viewpoint of national interest, rather than from any particular or partisan approach. At the same time, moralists should be cautious both of limiting their considerations to commutative or even distributive

---

[7] *Labor's Monthly Survey*, Sept., 1948, p. 6.

justice, to the neglect of social justice, and of passing judgments without understanding the complex needs of modern business.

The Right to Interest. The question of interest formerly loomed large in moral treatises. Pure interest was forbidden by medieval theologians because money was considered as a consumption good, which was used up in the process of spending. It was analogous to food. Thus, when a housewife borrows ten pounds of sugar, she is expected to repay the exact amount and no more. The sugar, in contrast to land, animals, or other productive property, does not produce an income which could be the title for a return. If some extrinsic consideration intervened, whereby the lending housewife incurred a loss from the loan (e.g., the lender may have been forced to go to the store to replace the stock, incurring the expense of a bus ride to and from the store) she could in justice demand repayment for her loss. Medieval writers allowed extrinsic claims, such as loss incurred, gain foregone, or a premium to cover risk. These items are often part of the modern interest charge and explain the difference in interest rates. Thus, the rate paid on a government bond could be considered pure interest (no risk), while the interest rate of a corporation bond would include the element of risk. This would be even greater for consumer financing, with high collection costs also involved. However, to medieval theologians pure interest was contrary to justice since it meant a charge for a nonproductive good. Rent or profits were not banned since these returns came from ownership of productive property.

The Church ban on usury was gradually relaxed as the complex world of business provided more and more extrinsic titles to a return. There is no need here to summarize the arguments given so brilliantly by Msgr. Ryan in his *Distributive Justice*. It may be argued that, in some cases, saving represents a sacrifice and hence a loss incurred. But often, as the learned writer noted, in modern times saving is automatic and does not represent sacrifice. At times, capital is productive, so that any loan could be considered as virtually productive (as an alternate investment would be available; hence a gain is foregone), but in depression times, such a title would not be very convincing. More weight can be attributed to the argument that legal sanction and the common good require interest to attract investment necessary for economic expansion. Thus, the state is considered to sanction interest-taking as favoring the common good, and hence uses its power of *altum dominium* to justify the necessary transfer of money. Finally, an analysis of interest used by modern economists has intriguing moral implications. Many writers today consider interest as a premium for illiquidity. This new form of the sacrifice principle notes that the tying up of funds imposes a hardship upon the lender or investor. He may need money at a time when he cannot collect the loan or sell the investment at its purchase price. He then must take a loss to get funds. This approach would supplement the virtual productivity argument, since the illiquidity principle applies in times of depressions when the other is not always applicable. At any rate, the sum of these titles, as noted by Msgr. Ryan, does create a presumptive claim in justice for the taking of interest.

As a rule, the basic factor determining interest rates is the economic productivity of capital purchased with saved funds. If such capital can produce goods, the total value of which over the lifetime of the capital instrument exceeds costs, including depreciation of the capital good, there is a net return which is the basis for interest. In the case of loans for nonproductive purposes, the lender can justify the taking of interest because of the possibility of alternative use in productive investment. Only value production gives a positive justification of interest. Sacrifice, a premium for illiquidity, and the like explain subjectively why holders of money may be unwilling to lend except at a price. Such subjective reasons might well constitute sound moral grounds for interest-taking. But the broad function of interest in economic life, and its greatest contribution to the common good, lies in its promotion and control of value-producing investment.

It is difficult to set norms in strict justice as to the proper rate of interest. Generally, the legal rate is considered fair, unless there are positive reasons for exceeding it. Negatively, it is unjust to demand higher rates merely because of the extreme need of the borrower. Thus, the not uncommon practice of charging a 10 per cent weekly rate (520 per cent annually) to workers who cannot budget their income is clearly unjust, unless extraordinary risk can be shown. The amateur bankers who lend ten dollars "until payday" and then collect eleven are definitely usurious. Finance company charges of 3 per cent monthly on unpaid balance (36 per cent annually) are probably high, even granted that collection costs are considerable and the risk fairly great.

At times grave abuses arise from interest charges connected with installment contracts. *Time* magazine (March 28, 1949) told how a woman lost her home because of the purchase of a hundred dollar radio. She defaulted on payments, a judgment was entered against her, and her home was placed on sale to meet the judgment. The only bidder was the radio-company dealer, who received the property for twenty-six dollars. After this transaction, she still owed money to the company. Of course, this scandalous but strictly legal procedure involved more than a problem of high interest rates, even though some installment charges are excessively high. On the other hand, the concern of many moralists over "usury," if used in the strict sense of unjust interest claims, seems unwarranted in present times. In recent years, interest rates have been generally low. In fact, our government has kept them artificially depressed in order to secure a low carrying rate for the enormous national debt. Individual cases of extortion constitute an injustice which should be remedied, but the net effect on the common good is negligible.

The condemnation of usury by Pope Leo XIII was directed more at general financial abuses. This point was further elaborated by Pope Pius XI, when he talked of the control of money as being a factor in economic domination. These questions may be treated more appropriately in Chapters XII and XVIII. For the present, it is safe to conclude that interest-taking promotes the public economic good and that excessive rates have not been a general problem in the United States during the last two decades.

DUTIES OF OWNERS AND MANAGERS
OF CAPITAL

Duties Toward Labor

The basic social obligation of "capital," in relation to workers, is to respect their human dignity. From this fundamental outlook, many detailed duties may be deduced. Thus, the claim of workers for a fair wage springs from their human dignity. Their right to form unions may be derived from this source. These and other considerations will be treated more at length in the chapters immediately following.

One suggestion given in *Quadragesimo Anno,* however, may be discussed at this point. This is the suggestion that the work contract be modified by a partnership contract, with the workers sharing in the profits, management, and ownership of an industry. The Pope does not advocate this move as a strict right, but he does feel that one or more of these degrees of partnership might be more consonant with the human dignity of workers. Steps in this direction would mean a cautious approach toward greater industrial democracy and the unity of economic society. At the same time, however, we must be aware of the obstacles and pitfalls surrounding these methods, at least in the light of American experience. Many, both from the side of management and from labor, oppose such moves even in theory. Others are lukewarm. Still others, while favoring the idea, are pessimistic in view of previous attempts. Only a minority of industry and labor might be considered enthusiastic proponents of anything approaching full partnership. Yet, it may be that the soundness of the Pope's proposal is not lessened by American experience and attitudes. Past failures may have arisen, not from any essential weakness in the program, but from inept approaches toward it. This analysis is borne out by a detailed study of the various approaches to partnership.

Profit-Sharing. Profit-sharing normally involves the dividing of a portion of net profits among the workers in accord with a previously developed formula. Thus, in a given company, some figure may be taken as the fair compensation of stockholders, after suitable reserves had been set aside for bad years. It may then be agreed that of the net profits remaining, 60 per cent (to use an arbitrary figure) may be divided among workers, with the remainder going to salaried employees, executives, and, possibly, stockholders. This would be in addition to a fair wage determined by normal collective bargaining. Such a procedure would emphasize the common interests of workers and employers, give labor an incentive to co-operate with management, and tend to increase workers' loyalty to the company employing them.

Some firms frankly emphasize the incentive element in profit-sharing. After a basic wage is fixed, supplementary returns depend upon increased production at lower cost. In this way, output is increased and hence workers can be paid at a higher annual rate. The Lincoln Electric Company, in Cleveland, is a strong proponent of this method. On the other hand, the incentive method of profit-sharing often causes most suspicion and even hostility on the part of organized labor. Many workers fear that this is a device to speed up production by developing a pace of operations which cannot be sustained indefinitely. To them, it is reminiscent of piece-rate methods in which unit rates were cut after employees earned a good salary by increasing output. They argue that labor shares the losses during depression times by virtue of unemployment; hence its basic wage should be independent of the ups and downs of the business cycle.

Since these objections are rather widespread and since many profit-sharing plans have failed, it is clear that caution should be used in approaching the problem. As far as any conclusion may be reached from the many plans tried in the United States, it is this: profit-sharing is not normally a good initial means to establish employee good will toward the employer; but if understanding and co-operation have been built up by other means, then profit-sharing is a sound auxiliary device for strengthening bonds already established. Where mutual trust already exists, the sharing of profits is a legitimate incentive to higher productivity, stability in employment, and greater employee loyalty.

A sound profit-incentive plan is based on the theory that there are untapped reserves in the working force which can be utilized through co-operation. Workers often have suggestions for new methods of production, devices to increase quality and cut down waste, safety programs, and the lessening of absenteeism and labor turnover. It may even happen that they could work faster without undue fatigue if the proper stimulus were applied. But the evolving of such patterns of co-operation is a complex psychological problem which will never be met by an unaided profit-sharing plan. Profit-sharing can be successful only if previously complete trust in management's integrity and competence has been developed.

Sharing Management. While the idea of profit-sharing has met with indifference on the part of business and some hostility from labor, suggestions for sharing management usually provoke violent reactions from business and indifference from a large part of labor. Business is acutely sensitive to the "prerogatives of management." It insists that responsibility must be centralized, meaning that it should rest in the hands of owners or their representatives. On the other hand, many labor unions are not interested in sharing any of management's burdens. On some specific points, such as the rate of production, they may demand a voice in what was formerly considered the exclusive field of management, but there is little general interest in any broad participation. This is even more true, as a rule, of the average worker in a factory. He has a limited conception of the broad problems of management and even less interest in assuming a share of them. Thus, at first glance, it might appear that proposals for management-sharing are unrealistic; convincing perhaps to intellectuals, but unappealing to those directly concerned.

Yet, in another sense, sharing of management not only is sound, it is one of the most important developments in recent years. Most of the adverse reaction springs from one limited interpretation of the proposal. Thus, it has been presented as involving employee representation on a board of corporate directors with (presumably) minority status. Business balks at such a notion and labor is not very interested in it. On the other hand, thousands of businessmen are becoming deeply interested in the "human-relations" literature and experience of the past fifteen years. Learned studies have been made and experiments attempted to prove that "teamwork, communication, and participation" are necessary for a smoothly functioning industrial unit. Educational programs have been developed to make workers feel an identity with company interests and a sense of common responsibility in meeting problems.

In the literature mentioned above, there is great emphasis upon treating a worker as an individual, with full recognition of his personal traits. When a worker is hired, his aptitudes and desires are ascertained and he is fitted to a suitable job. He is trained, not only for his special work, but also in the broad problems of his company. He is made to feel that the firm's problems are his own. Communication is a two-way process. His point of view is solicited; and ultimate decisions are explained to him, not merely handed down as peremptory orders. The ultimate aim is teamwork between workers on all levels and management. Such practices at the factory level are harmonized with the union contract, with the workers' representatives as definite parts of the pattern of consultation and teamwork.

There is a distinct movement in important management circles to remove worker hostility or even indifference toward the employer. The methods favored involve recognition of the dignity of the individual and an attempt to make the worker feel that he is a partner in the productive process. But, for all practical purposes, these are the very proposals which employers often reject so indignantly when proposed by moralists under the title of "management-sharing." Such is the power of semantics! Of course, some students may object that "human-relations" programs are paternalistic, whereas workers should be respected as a matter of right. But such an assumption might well be gratuitous. The literature in this field and the actual experiments attempted emphasize the need of genuine participation, not merely the setting up of forms. After all, the modern union worker is not likely to be deceived by any sham program. On the contrary, one of the serious difficulties confronting an employer with good will in this matter is the overcoming of a heritage of distrust and smoldering hostility. Nor is there any harm in the fact that these programs have been presented to employers as means for increasing production. The popes have insisted that we should pay more attention to the uniting force of production, lost sight of because of the divisive atmosphere of the class struggle.

Catholic scholars will find much of value in the growing literature on human relations. It will afford a common language with the business community for the establishing of ideas which might not be understood or accepted in the language of ethics. There is nothing wrong with promoting sound principles on the ground that they work well in practice. In fact, what is morally right should be practical, since psychology, economics, and ethics are all based immediately upon human nature and ultimately upon God. Coming from the same source, it is only to be expected that sound psychology, practical economics, and right ethics should harmonize one with the other. We Catholics might well concentrate on showing the intrinsic value of our principles, even to our own people. They can thus better promote sound policies, in circles where arguments based on papal authority would be rejected.[8]

It is also noteworthy that there is much postwar discussion of management-sharing, on the part of European Catholic groups. The terms used are (in French) *cogestion* and (in German) *Mitbestimmungsrecht.* Europeans frequently make the distinction, in discussing this problem, between social and economic questions, with the workers having a clear right to participate in the former area, but less right to enter into economic decisions. Under the heading of social questions would come various personnel matters

---

[8] A good statement of moral principles in regard to industrial relations is found in *Human Relations in Modern Business* (New York: Prentice-Hall, 1950). This book contains an extensive bibliography. See also the present author's *Catholic Social Action,* pp. 221–223, and List No. 9 in the Appendix of the present book.

and the problems of social welfare. These considerations are often included in collective bargaining and social legislation in the United States. Economic matters would include prices, output, profits, investment, and similar management decisions. American labor has not gone deeply into this field, except to the extent implied by collective bargaining over wages and other costs. Some labor leaders, however, assert that they have certain rights even in the economic sphere. Thus, the question as to the proper limits of management rights is a subject of debate in many lands.

Sharing Ownership. The normal method for sharing ownership would be employee stockholding in corporations. For unincorporated businesses, presumably some form of partnership might be worked out. The former approach was tried extensively during the 1920's in the United States and is still being practiced occasionally today. The theory behind this move was that worker-stockholders would have a greater interest in their firm and some legal right to a voice in its affairs. In practice, however, the system rarely worked out. When the stock was negotiable, some workers immediately sold it after it was given them by their company. In other plans, the workers bought the stock, only to have most of its value wiped out in the 1929–1932 fall of stock prices. Stocks are a poor medium in which to invest worker savings. They are at their lowest value at the very times when funds are normally most needed. Accordingly, the lack of broad worker interest and the disillusionment of many who bought stock led to the abandonment of most plans.

In the larger American corporations, even fairly extensive stock ownership on the part of employees would not normally give them an effective voice in running their companies. Scattered ownership of small shares is usually meaningless in terms of real power. Our larger companies are run either by management or by powerful stockholders with a large minority interest in the company. Moreover, our legal concept of trusteeship has tended to give corporate managements independent rights apart from the stockholders who employ them. Thus, an executive might refuse information to a stockholder on the grounds that

divulging it would be contrary to the best interests of the company. Hence it is unlikely that workers could legally obtain, by
stock ownership, broader powers than they already have through
their unions.

It would be a mistake so to emphasize means and devices
that the ultimate end is overlooked or slighted. The sharing of
profits, management, or ownership belong in the category of
means toward the end of further emphasizing the human dignity
of the worker. Moreover, the form they may take is in large
part a matter of experience and prudential judgment. It would
seem that the trend of American experience is in the direction
of emphasizing worker participation in management at the level
where it has concrete and daily impact on his life. If workers
are day-by-day partners in the productive process, and their unions
are included in the area of broad co-operation, participation, and
consultation, then we shall have a greater degree of partnership
than has ever previously existed in the American economy.
Moreover, such partnership would be more vital and fruitful
than was the case with earlier and less successful attempts. This
would be true because it is centered in matters which actually
are of direct and vital concern to the workers and not merely a
remote and indirect interest. Profit-sharing and, possibly, sharing
in ownership could be integrated in this program as a fully
rounded-out participation by workers in the affairs of their
company.[9]

An aspect of management-sharing which is frequently overlooked concerns the relationship of top management with lesser
executives. It frequently happens that salaried personnel on the
lower level are considered as employees, although technically

---

[9] For literature on profit-sharing and related problems, consult: *Profit Sharing
Manual* (Columbus: Council of Profit Sharing Industries, 1948); *Survey of Experiences
in Profit Sharing and Possibilities of Incentive Taxation* (Washington: Government
Printing Office, 1939, Senate Report 610); K. M. Thompson, *Profit Sharing: Democratic
Capitalism in American Industry* (New York: Harper, 1949); and J. M. Kenkel,
"Sharing Profits with Employees" (New York: Paulist Press, 1943). A balanced
appraisal is given by Robert L. Rowe, "Profit-Sharing Plans in Industry," *Harvard
Business Review*, Sept., 1949, pp. 559–584.

a part of management. They carry out orders, but do not participate in the making of decisions. Such an attitude is unfortunate, both from the viewpoint of their personal dignity and from the aspect of efficient production. The arguments for integrating lower management into policy-making operations is strong from both these aspects. Subordinate officials certainly are happier when they are consulted and not merely considered as channels for executing policy. Moreover, their experience and talent often contribute valuable suggestions. Consultation trains them for future promotion to top levels. An illustration of enlightened practice along this line is the "multiple-management plan" pioneered by McCormick & Co., Baltimore. In this firm, three boards advise the senior board of directors. The boards are drawn respectively from line executives, factory foremen, and salesmen. Unanimous recommendations from these are given to the senior board. The result has been almost invariable acceptance of the programs suggested, higher morale among the lower executive and white-collar group, and increased efficiency of operation.[10]

Duties Toward the Public

Fair Prices. One of the primary duties of business is to charge fair prices for its products. In the Middle Ages this concept went under the title of the "just price." The term "fair," being ethical in its nature, does not admit of precise mathematical definition. At the same time, it is by no means vague or meaningless. Definite and precise elements enter into its calculation. The fair or just price expresses the real value of any object, in contrast to an artificial value as determined by the abuse of a monopolistic position by seller or buyer. In such a price, there would be included as costs a decent wage to workers, enabling them to live in some comfort; a price to suppliers which permits them to pay good wages and make a reasonable profit; and, finally, a fair profit to the firm. Details concerning good wages are treated in

---

[10] For details, see C. P. McCormick, *The Power of People* (New York: Harper, 1949).

Chapter X, and some suggestions on fair profits were given earlier in this chapter. A reasonable profit would safeguard the capital investment through adequate reserves for depreciation and depressions, give the going rate of interest plus a proper premium for risk to lenders and investors, and create an atmosphere which would promote investment to expand our economy and raise our living standards.

Three elements should be sought in a sound price policy. First, prices should be reasonably elastic. Fixed prices, whether set by custom, law, or monopolistic practice, impede the free working of the economic system. New factors in supply and demand arise constantly, so the price mechanism should be allowed to adjust production to the needs of the moment. Secondly, while individual prices should be elastic, the price level should be reasonably stable. Both inflation and deflation upset long-range economic calculation and thus prevent sound progress. For this reason, competition must be subject to some orderly controls. Thirdly, subject to control in terms of the general interest, prices should generally be determined by a competitive market. Only such a device affords the necessary flexibility for a healthy economy. If the price structure is sound, in the sense that justice is assured for all concerned, the resultant competitive prices would contribute to justice and the common good more than would be possible under any system of centralized control. Thus, we favor supervised or controlled competition, in contrast to complete freedom on the one hand or monopoly on the other. But these controls would not involve price-fixing. Rather they would consist of institutions — laws, agreements, contracts, and the like — which would prevent exploitation of labor, the consumer, and other businessmen.

In the Middle Ages public authority or the common estimate of fairness determined the level of a just price. Today, such outside fixing of prices in a peacetime economy is rare, except for public utilities such as the electric power or telephone industries. We rely upon the forces of competition to bring about a reasonable price. Here again, however, we run into the fact that competition alone cannot be a sound guiding principle of economic life. This is true for two reasons: it is difficult to maintain free competition in certain fields; and, even where it does exist, it can lead to unsocial trends.

Some data on the extent of competition in the American economy were given in Chapter V. The Temporary National Economic Committee, functioning in the late 1930's, noted important areas where competition is limited, if not stifled. The number of antitrust suits and Federal Trade Commission procedures indicates that the urge toward monopolistic practices is widespread and important. Nor is it limited to large firms; the wide use of fair-price laws to maintain large profit margins shows that small business is just as anxious to escape the rigors of competition as is its larger brother. Where a monopolistic situation exists, there is the tendency to seek maximum revenue. As a rule, this means higher prices and lower output than is the case under competition, a trend which is manifestly contrary to the public interest.[11]

Monopolistic tendencies are fostered by several factors, including collusion (which is illegal), abuse of patents, sheer size (which limits the number of firms in an industry and encourages uniform prices), mergers and consolidations, and poorly drawn fair-price and antidiscrimination laws. Vigorous enforcement of current antitrust laws can do much to prevent collusion and patent abuse, but stronger laws are needed to deal with the problem of mergers. Existing laws which permit price-fixing need re-examination in the interest of the common good. Moreover, the purely negative approach of regulation and prosecution should be supplemented by a thorough study of the needs of small business, so that effective competition can be restored to many fields through the introduction of new firms. This in turn calls for a careful study of the entire field of investment opportunity, and the charges that small business cannot obtain

---

[11] For economic data on monopoly, see J. F. Cronin, *Economic Analysis and Problems,* Chaps. 10–12.

capital at reasonable costs. This point is treated subsequently in Chapter XII.

While a healthy competition can keep prices from running to extremes, it in turn must be regulated to prevent abuses at the opposite pole. Excessive competition can lead to sweatshop wages. It can also bring such pressure upon suppliers in an industry that they in turn must either pay low wages to their workers or receive less than a fair profit. The matter of wages can best be handled, at the present time, by a combination of minimum-wage laws and extensive unionization. It would be desirable, however, to have a situation whereby decent wage standards, agreed upon by a suitable majority in an industry, could be given legal sanction for all the industry. With a floor on wages, normal competitive practices should, in the long run, insure a fair profit to suppliers, since they would otherwise have little incentive to remain in business. This, however, is a distinctly long-run situation, since in the short run specialized firms with only one market have little choice but to keep going, even at a loss, rather than face the greater loss of closing down entirely. Hence this problem will be completely solved when institutional reforms are made which cut down economic instability and set up safeguards against unfair competition.

The right to a fair profit applies to business in general, not to any given firm. It is conceivable that certain firms will sustain losses because of inefficient management, obsolete equipment, changes in public taste, exhaustion of near-by raw materials, or the competition of new firms better situated in regard to materials, power, transportation, and markets. Such failures are inherent in a dynamic economy and generally lead to better quality of goods at lower prices without sacrificing good labor standards or encouraging unethical competition. This type of risk is involved in the investment process and justifies in turn some concession to investors which will induce them to take these risks. Thus, a taxation policy which virtually confiscates all gains, without adequate offset for losses, is shortsighted. It removes incentive to invest and hence stifles economic progress.

A Community Conscience. One of the great needs of the business world is the development of a sense of the common good. Decades of individualism and selfishness have imbedded in the minds of many the notion that business is a law unto itself. They feel that, if left alone, they can achieve far better results than when they are subject to public control. It is unfortunate that such dichotomy is posed, since, by giving a choice between extremes, it may lead to the very evils that business fears. If business could show self-control, plus a spirit of co-operation with labor and farmers, there would be no arguments for the necessity of public control.

It should be clear by now that solution of the great problems of full and sustained employment, balanced economic growth, and harmony among the elements of society will not come about as a matter of course. Free competition will not achieve it, much less a mixture of competition and economic oligarchies. On the other hand, businessmen will not secure this realization just by having it preached at them from the outside. The functional approach used in the preceding chapter is more likely to be persuasive. If common problems and common interests were presented to businessmen as questions for discussion, and their views asked as to means for securing objectives which they will concede to be reasonable, they may be gradually led to conclusions which all will agree are sound and in the public interest.

It is of extreme importance to note the psychology of the businessman. By the nature of his calling, he is a man of self-reliance and independence. If he is successful, he generally feels that personal energy and resourcefulness are sufficient to carry him through. His thought is that methods which worked in his case are good enough for the economy as a whole. As a rule, he is not well versed in economics or national policy. He does not realize that broad economic currents could sweep him along, like a swimmer caught in a rapids, regardless of his individual strivings. Hence he needs education, not invective. He may often have good personal standards according to a rather limited code of ethics, paying fair wages and scorning dishonest deals. He needs a broader realization of what economic life means. This is best given by the problem approach, showing him that certain vital issues cannot be met automatically. They require central action, and the only relevant choice is whether this action be taken by government alone, or whether business, labor, finance, and farmers should act jointly in presenting national economic policy.

In this connection, it is a paradoxical fact that often big business, so frequently damned as antisocial, is more advanced than the small businessman. Managers of large corporations of necessity acquire a national and even international point of view. They consult with economists and professional analysts of public policy. They even have some independence in regard to their stockholders and can often take a larger and more long-range viewpoint than is likely with small businessmen. At the same time, their prestige with smaller businessmen is so great that, as our allies in presenting a social philosophy, they would be powerful forces for good. Hence the use of publications such as the *Harvard Business Review* or *Fortune,* and of statements by organizations such as the Committee on Economic Development or the American Management Association, would be more effective than quoting material compiled by a government or labor group. In citing business leaders, it is often more compelling to use a mild but progressive assertion by acknowledged leaders than a stronger position urged by some highly publicized business- man who lacks real influence in his own community. Thus, a quotation from the Chamber of Commerce of the United States, acknowledging that central fiscal and monetary policies are important in preventing depressions, would be more useful than a powerful plea for economic planning by some businessman who is considered a maverick by his colleagues.

Above all, in dealing with business, it is essential to avoid the class warfare approach which we condemn in communism. The constant reiteration of past, but corrected, abuses is as unfair as the parallel practice of bringing up isolated labor abuses long since expiated in our penitentiaries. Even if business generally were still guilty of sins such as those of the nineteenth century and the first three decades of the twentieth, it would still be fair to pay tribute to leaders who were honest and public spirited. If reform along the lines of Catholic principles is really desired, with action taken through co-operation rather than law, then some attention must be paid to elementary psychology. Persons are won over through the discussion of problems and the acquiring of conviction that a sound middle way between individualism and statism must be found. But they are alienated by blanket indictments of their group, the more so if they are convinced that these charges are unfair and largely unfounded. Even if this is avoided, it is poor psychology to present ready-made solutions as a starting point for discussion. Better results are obtained when people are guided, through realization that alternatives will not work, to the adoption of a sound conclusion.

These points are urged in view of a cultural lag often found in the field of Catholic social action. There is a tendency to talk in the 1950's as if conditions had not changed since the 1920's. If businessmen are not given credit for reforms accepted, even if not initiated by them, they are likely to take the stand that labor and reform groups are hopelessly demanding and that every concession only leads to further abuse. If some groups in labor are slow in adapting to changed times, it is the duty of the Church, seeking justice and charity rather than any partisan advantage, to give effective leadership. There is some truth in the stand that the Church has taken the part of labor. But this means that we fought for workers' rights when labor was alone and often defenseless. It cannot mean that we are blindly on labor's side in all matters, much less that we are opposed to business as such. Labor suffered much prior to 1930 and business was guilty of grave abuses, both in regard to labor and the public welfare. This situation we rightly condemned. But today there is real hope that a spirit of co-operation can be nurtured in important circles. It is vital that we promote such trends and not live with the problems of the past.

Such an attitude was recommended by His Holiness, Pope Pius XII, on June 3, 1950, in a talk which clarified many points discussed in the present volume, especially those treated on pages 88–93, 240, 288, and 431–432.

The Pope advised social thinkers to concentrate upon such urgent problems as unemployment, development of colonial regions, and the like, rather than to devote all their energies toward vindicating impractical or even unsound ideals of equality between capital and labor. He particularly noted that the alleged right of labor to participate in management, especially in economic decisions, is not a real right. The recommendation of *Quadragesimo Anno* in this regard was repeated, but the more advanced views of certain Catholic writers were rejected.

Socially responsible private property still remains one of the major foundations of economic freedom and prosperity. As many persons as possible should become effective owners of property. Owners of productive property should collaborate for the common good, as noted in Chapter VII. Wage earners should likewise enter into this framework of co-operation, by suitable modifications of the labor contract in favor of measures of partnership. But both groups should beware of seeking their salvation by using giant collective groups — of capital, labor, or government — as the exclusive or even main source of their rights.

READINGS*

J. Messner, *Social Ethics,* pp. 262–264, 670–674, 697–861 (especially 751–753, 798–800, 811–817, 837–843, 927–930).

J. Banchi, *Principi dell' ordine sociale Cristiano,* pp. 178–179.

J. A. Ryan, *Distributive Justice.*

——— *A Better Economic Order,* Chap. 7.

O. von Nell-Bruening, *Reorganization of Social Economy,* Chap. 7.

G. Clune, *Christian Social Reconstruction,* Chap. 20.

J. Husslein, *Christian Social Manifesto,* Chaps. 18, 27.

R. Miller, *Forty Years After,* pp. 96–106.

J. B. Kenkel, "Sharing Profits with Employees."

——— "Sharing Management with Employees."

---

* For further readings, consult Lists Nos. 1, 3, 4, 5, and 9 in the Appendix.

Chapter IX. SOCIAL PROBLEMS OF LABOR

Leo XIII, Rerum Novarum

31. Workers are not to be treated as slaves; justice demands that the dignity of the human personality be respected in them, ennobled as it has been through what we call the Christian character. If we hearken to natural reason and to Christian philosophy, gainful occupations are not a mark of shame to man, but rather of respect, as they provide him with an honorable means of supporting life.

57. No one may with impunity outrage the dignity of man, which God Himself treats with great reverence, nor impede his course to that level of perfection which accords with eternal life in heaven. Nay, more, in this connection a man cannot even by his own free choice allow himself to be treated in a way inconsistent with his nature, and suffer his soul to be enslaved; for there is no question here of rights belonging to man, but of duties owed to God, which are to be religiously observed.

62. To work is to expend one's energy for the purpose of securing the things necessary for the various needs of life and especially for its preservation. "In the sweat of thy face shalt thou eat bread" (*Gen.* 3:19). . . . In fact, to preserve one's life is a duty common to all individuals, and to neglect this duty is a crime. Hence arises necessarily the right of securing things to sustain life, and only a wage earned by his labor gives a poor man the means to acquire these things.

Pius XI, Quadragesimo Anno

64. First of all, those who declare that a contract of hiring and being hired is unjust of its own nature, and hence a partnership contract must take its place, are certainly in error and gravely misrepresent Our Predecessor whose Encyclical not only accepts working for wages or salaries but deals at some length with its regulation in accordance with the rules of justice.

65. We consider it more advisable, however, in the present condition of human society that, so far as is possible, the work contract be somewhat modified by a partnership contract, as is already being done in various ways and with no small advantage to workers and owners. Workers and other employees thus become sharers in ownership or management or participate in some fashion in the profits received.

83. Labor, as Our Predecessor explained well in his Encyclical, is not a mere commodity. On the contrary, the worker's human dignity in it must be recognized. It therefore cannot be bought and sold like a commodity. Nevertheless, as the situation now stands, hiring and offering for hire in the so-called labor market separate men into two divisions, as into battle lines, and the contest between these divisions turns the labor market itself almost into a battlefield where, face to face, the opposing lines struggle bitterly. Everyone understands that this grave evil which is plunging all human society to destruction must be remedied as soon as possible.

135. And thus bodily labor, which Divine Providence decreed to be performed, even after original sin, for the good at once of man's body and soul, is being everywhere changed into an instrument of perversion; for dead matter comes forth from the factory ennobled, while men there are corrupted and degraded.

Pius XII, Address to Italian Workers, June 13, 1943

Our Predecessors and We Ourselves have not lost any opportunity of making all men understand by Our repeated instructions your personal and family needs, proclaiming as fundamental prerequisites of social concord those claims which you have so much at heart: a salary which will cover the living expenses of a family and such as to make it possible for the parents to fulfill their natural duty to rear healthily nourished and clothed children; a dwelling worthy of human persons; the possibility of securing for children sufficient instruction and a becoming education, of foreseeing and forestalling times of stress, sickness, and old age.

Pius XII, La Solennità della Pentecoste

1688. To the personal duty to labor imposed by nature corresponds and follows the natural right of each individual to make of labor the means to provide for his own life and that of his children; so profoundly is the empire of nature ordained for the preservation of man.

1689. But note that such a duty and the corresponding right to work is imposed on and conceded to the individual in the first instance by nature, and not by society, as if man were nothing more than a mere slave or official of the community.

Pius XII, Christmas Broadcast, 1942

1846. He should uphold respect for, and the practical realization of, the following fundamental personal rights: . . . the right to work, as the indispensable means toward the maintenance of family life. . . .

1850. He who would have the star of peace shine out and stand over society should give to work the place assigned to it by God in the beginning. As an indispensable means toward gaining over the world that mastery which God wishes for His glory, all work has an inherent dignity and at the same time a close association with the perfection of the person; this is the noble dignity and privilege of work which is not in any way cheapened by the fatigue and the burden, which have to be borne as the effect of original sin, in obedience and submission to the will of God.

WORK OF WOMEN AND CHILDREN

Leo XIII, Rerum Novarum

60. Finally, it is not right to demand of a woman or a child what a strong adult man is capable of doing or would be willing to do. Nay, as regards children, special care ought to be taken that the factory does not get hold of them before age has sufficiently matured their physical, intel-lectual, and moral powers. For budding strength in childhood, like green-ing verdure in spring, is crushed by premature harsh treatment; and under such circumstances all education of the child must needs be foregone. Cer-tain occupations likewise are less fitted for women, who are intended by nature for work of the home — work indeed which especially protects modesty in women and accords by nature with the education of children and the well-being of the family.

Pius XI, Quadragesimo Anno

71. That the rest of the family should also contribute to the common support, according to the capacity of each, is certainly right, as can be observed especially in the families of farmers, but also in the families of many craftsmen and small shopkeepers. But to abuse the years of child-hood and the limited strength of women is grossly wrong. Mothers, con-centrating on household duties, should work primarily in the home or in its immediate vicinity. It is an intolerable abuse, and to be abolished at all cost, for mothers, on account of the father's low wage, to be forced to engage in gainful occupations outside the home to the neglect of their proper cares and duties, especially the training of children.

Pius XII, Woman's Duties

Indeed, We have on a former occasion pointed out that for the same work output a woman is entitled to the same wages as a man.

We see a woman who, in order to augment her husband's earnings, betakes herself also to a factory, leaving her house abandoned during her absence. The house, untidy and small perhaps before, becomes even more miserable for lack of care. Members of the family work separately in four quarters of the city and with different working hours. Scarcely ever do they find themselves together for dinner or rest after work — still less for prayer in common. What is left of family life? And what attractions can it offer to children?

As to the working classes, forced to earn daily bread, a woman might, if she reflected, realize that not rarely the supplementary wage which she earns by working outside the house is easily swallowed up by other expenses or even by waste which is ruinous to the family budget. The daughter who also goes out to work in a factory or office, deafened by the excited restless world in which she lives, dazzled by the tinsel of specious luxury, developing a thirst for shallow pleasures that distract but do not give satiety or repose in those revues or dance halls which are sprouting up everywhere, often for party propaganda purposes, and which corrupt youth, becomes a fashionable lady, despises the old nineteenth-century ways of life.

HOURS OF LABOR

Leo XIII, Rerum Novarum

59. Now as concerns the protection of corporeal and physical goods, the oppressed workers, above all, ought to be liberated from the savagery of greedy men, who inordinately use human beings as things for gain. Assuredly, neither justice nor humanity can countenance the exaction of so much work that the spirit is dulled from excessive toil and that along with it the body sinks crushed from exhaustion. The working energy of a man, like his entire nature, is circumscribed by definite limits beyond which it cannot go. It is developed indeed by exercise and use, but only on condition that a man cease from work at regular intervals and rest. With respect to daily work, therefore, care ought to be taken not to extend it beyond the hours that human strength warrants. The length of rest intervals ought to be decided on the basis of the varying nature of the work, of the circumstances of time and place, and of the physical condition of the workers themselves. Since the labor of those who quarry stone from the earth, or who mine iron, copper, and other underground materials, is much more severe and harmful to health, the working

periods of such men ought to be correspondingly shortened. The seasons of the year also must be taken into account; for often a given kind of work is easy to endure in one season but cannot be endured at all in another, or not without the greatest difficulty.

60. Let it be the rule everywhere that workers be given as much leisure as will compensate for the energy consumed by toil, for rest from work is necessary to restore strength consumed by use. In every obligation which is mutually contracted between employers and workers, this condition, either written or tacit, is always present, that both kinds of rest be provided for; nor would it be equitable to make an agreement otherwise, because no one has the right to demand of, or to make an agreement with, anyone to neglect those duties which bind a man to God or to himself.

Correlative to the problems of capital are those connected with labor. Taken together, business and labor form the two most important facets of economic life. It is understandable, in this connection, that the social encyclicals concentrate so heavily upon issues pertaining to the welfare of the laboring man. In terms of both numbers and economic influence workers constitute one of the vital segments of our economy. Moreover, they are deeply involved in the social problem. In the nineteenth century, workers were victims of great injustices. While many of these have been corrected, some persist even today. But, apart from the question of injustice, the great power of labor demands that it be integrated with other elements in economic life for the common good of all. Accordingly, the many problems arising from the position of labor have been grouped under three headings: the dignity of labor, the living wage and secure employment, and labor unions. A chapter is devoted to each of these points.

The Worker Is Human. The title of this section might appear trite. Yet, inhuman and subhuman treatment of workers was a serious problem at one time or other in most industrial countries. While the crude abuses of past years have been remedied here in the United States, there is still much to be done before we can say that the full human dignity of workers has been recognized.

There is a twofold dignity of man which must be recognized in economic life. The first consideration is his worth as an individual, the intrinsic value of the human person. This means that a certain basic respect must be paid to the worker as a man, quite independently of his individual traits of character and personality. Secondly, the social nature of man must be considered. Work itself is a social function. Men naturally work in groups and their activity is normally directed toward the good of society. A factory which forces workers together in a mechanical fashion, with the employer treating them as mere numbers on a timecard, with no regard for individual differences or social groupings, violates the dignity of man. Likewise, economic institutions which place an unnecessarily heavy burden upon family life are unjust. Exhausting work, hours of labor which interfere with family life, and employment of mothers of young children would be examples of antisocial conditions of work. These problems deserve careful consideration in the light of an ideal social order. Jobs should be subordinate to man and not the reverse.

The affront to workers' dignity has come largely from two factors. The first of these is the consideration that, while work is personal and human, it is also enmeshed in economic law. The sale of labor service in a market is determined too often by the same rules which apply to inert objects such as coal, cotton, or steel. Under competitive conditions such sales are governed by the laws connected with supply and demand, as determinants of price. If the state of demand is such that a given price will not clear the market of the amount supplied, the only remedy is to lower price. If the market is not competitive, an alternative choice is to curtail supply so that it balances the amount demanded at the desired price. Prior to the rise of unions, workers were in a purely competitive market. Too often this resulted in beating down wages until they reached a level too low to support existence at even a minimum level of comfort and dignity. Thus, workers were made victims of an impersonal system. Instead of economic life serving man, the reverse was true.

It would not be possible, of course, to ignore economic law in dealing with workers. There are certain valid generalizations in economics which are as universally true as the law of gravitation. But, as was noted earlier, there is also an area of flexibility in which customs and institutions can be changed when the needs of man demand it. How this may be done to adjust economic law to the dignity of man will be considered in the two chapters which follow.

A second field where the dignity of workers suffered is found in the many conditions which surround work. Too often the employer-worker relationship degenerated into a master-slave attitude, with the worker denied the independence which should be the right of free men. In the matter of working conditions around the factory, and the special needs of women and children at work, there has often been callous disregard of elementary rights. There is no need now to rake up the worst abuses of the past; enough remains to be done today to warrant comment.

Moral Equality. Starting with a positive note, the dignity of man demands that the worker be treated as a moral equal, who happens to be in a subordinate position. There is nothing inherently wrong in the idea of one person's being in authority over another. On the contrary, authority and subordination are necessary for orderly society. Parents should be able to give commands to their children. Policemen must have the power to direct traffic and keep public peace. But authority rightly used respects the rights of the person in an inferior position. It is used for his welfare, either directly or through his participation in the common good. This principle should be used as a test of industrial relations.

Recognition of the dignity of the worker in industrial life calls for many complex adjustments. At the very beginning of the employee relationship, the element of respect should enter. Thus, when a worker is hired, this process should be in decent surroundings. Where feasible, a work history of the prospective employee should be gotten, with an effort made to fit him to a suitable job in view of his talents and interests. When he is assigned to work, his duties should be explained by a responsible officer of management and there should be initial checkups to determine how well he is adjusting to the job. It would be desirable that new employees in a large plant would meet periodically with an executive, who would explain company products, policies, and aims, with opportunities given for questions and observations. In this way, a worker is made to feel that he is a valued part of the firm, not merely another number on the timecard.

When the employee has become adjusted to his work, there should still be adequate opportunity to bring up grievances and difficulties to management representatives who have power to correct any abuses. Normally, this is now handled by unions, but in nonunion plants there should be really effective grievance machinery. This, incidentally, is also to the employer's interest, since disgruntled employees with low morale are no asset to any firm. If, by chance, a worker does not become adjusted to the job, this is no reason for summary discharge. He should be interviewed and an effort made to find the reason for failure. Possibly a transfer would be the answer. If the reason for failure is not connected with either his mechanical skill, willingness to work, or other considerations involving the factory, many enlightened firms do not write him off as hopeless. Their personnel department has psychologists, social workers, or similar counselors who give advice on personal problems not connected with factory work. Thus many men with antisocial habits caused either by personality flaws or environmental stresses are often salvaged. Quite apart from extreme cases, such help may be useful to many workers, generally reliable, but suffering from temporary strains which affect their work.

A worker should also have adequate opportunity to advance within the company. This means not only the usual seniority clauses found in union contracts, but also either in-plant training or educational programs made available to workers. Technical training, where the type of work would make it feasible, will permit a worker to prepare for a more skilled and higher paying job. Some firms either directly or through neighboring schools offer wide varieties of adult education, even in fields not connected with work. Such general education might enable an intelligent worker to acquire side knowledge which would make him fit for eventual supervisory positions. A sizable number of American industrial firms are giving such opportunities to their workers today. One very large company has even instituted some courses as training for foremen jobs.

Essential for the recognition of the workers' dignity are the programs commonly labeled communication and participation. Thus, the worker is given a form of partnership with management in a field which immediately concerns him. Communication means a two-way exchange of ideas between management and the workers. Full information is given concerning company policies and programs. What is more, the worker is consulted as an individual, through his union or both ways, in making company policies, so that he considers himself a real and worth-while part of the company. By contrast, if he is merely ordered around like a horse or a donkey, he is justifiably resentful. Participation does not of necessity involve a surrendering of management's rights to make ultimate decisions within its proper field. But these decisions will often be better because the experience and skill of workers were utilized. At the same time, the morale of the workers will be raised considerably. Of course, the more extensive partnership devices noted in the preceding chapter would be still more effective means of recognizing the workers' dignity.

All the techniques described above were taken from actual industrial practice. More and more firms are endeavoring today to devise some form of partnership and participation for their workers. These vary from the primitive suggestion box and bonus for ideas to extremely elaborate methods of consultation. While some of these programs may have been motivated by religious or ethical desires to recognize the dignity of workers, most of them arose as a result of extensive psychological studies. These investigations showed that employee morale could be an important factor in increasing production, cutting down waste and accidents, lowering absenteeism and turnover, and eliciting useful ideas and inventions. Thus, psychology confirmed what Christian morals had insisted upon, that the worker is an individual, not a number. He should be treated in accord with his individual nature and rights. If this is done, he is happy, contented, and productive. If not, he is dissatisfied and disgruntled, and thus a poor risk in any factory. In plain language, it has been found that, in employee relations, good ethics also pays profits.

Abuses and Failures. On the other hand, it would be foolish to close our eyes to the fact that such enlightened practices are by no means universal. There still exist casual hiring practices, such as the shape-up in East Coast longshore work. In such cases, workers report to be hired under conditions which guarantee no steady employment and even permit favoritism and "kickbacks" in the handing out of jobs. In other cases, little effort is made to determine employee aptitudes or to fit the man to the job. Training for advancement, where it exists, is often sporadic and unorganized. In many nonunion firms, there are no provisions for the fair handling of grievances. Some foremen are of the legendary army-sergeant type, barking out orders, cursing the workers, and considering any attempt at explanation and consultation beneath their princely dignity. There is favoritism in the assignment of work; discrimination for reasons of race, religion, or national origin; haphazard or even biased policies in making promotion; and often arbitrary and petulant discharges. Sometimes the foreman is expressing his own dissatisfaction at the anomalous position many of them occupy in modern factories, where they are in theory representatives of management, but often have less power than a union steward and less security than a union worker. Too often the foreman is the forgotten man in modern industry, and he may take out his resentment on those immediately under him.

A source of persistent complaint by workers is the "speed-up" of assembly lines. Analogous to this is the "stretch-out" in which workers are compelled to supervise several machines. In both cases, the argument is that a pace of operation is set up which burns out a worker after a few years. A younger man, working

at top speed, can meet the standard, even though he arrives home
irritable and exhausted. Older men find that they cannot keep
up with the demands of the machine or the assembly line. Before
unionization, complaints of this nature were common. Unions
normally try to include the pace of operations in their bargaining procedures. It is not uncommon today for the speed of assembly lines to be set jointly by union-management time studies.
In other and more frequent cases, management sets time standards, but the union has the right of appeal. To add to the complexity of the problem, psychological attitudes often enter the
picture. Workers disgruntled for other reasons often find the
pace of operations too severe, even though it may be faster in
competing plants where workers appear to be satisfied. Likewise, arbitrary and unexplained changes in operations are often
resisted, although the new operation may require less effort than
its predecessor. Here is an important field for labor-management
co-operation and for enlightened industrial relations.

It is true that much of the irritation which occurs in modern
factories may be the result of ignorance and poor psychology
rather than malice, but it is nonetheless rather widespread. There
are instances where top management is anxious to be fair and
reasonable, but where policies get changed and perverted along
the line of communication. In such cases, managers have failed
to implement good will by intelligent training of lesser officials
and the application of sound psychological principles. Whether
bad morale is the result of arbitrary top management or merely
ignorance at that level, it is still a disruptive force in industry. The
aspect of intelligence in the application of sound ideals must be
particularly stressed. Too often labor is blamed for ingratitude
when policies espoused by benevolent management are not appreciated. But these policies may have been vitiated by unsound
psychology. One might consider the parallel in social relations: a
person with excellent character but with an irritating personality
may be shunned, whereas another whose character is less fine, but
whose personality is appealing, may do much better, especially
in casual, everyday contacts. Sound business ideals are comparable

to good character, while psychological know-how is like personality. If both are top rate, the result is unbeatable. But either one, without the other, is seriously deficient.

In connection with human dignity, the perennial problem of man and the machine may be brought up again. Some assert that routine, repetitive, mass-production methods are injurious to human dignity. Two points may be added to previous remarks on the subject. The first is that partnership policies give a different aspect to humdrum and routine work. If each worker can see his function as a necessary part of the whole, it acquires a new meaning and importance to him. Secondly, there could be more attempts at rotating workers in semiskilled jobs, particularly in connection with assembly-line work. Thus, a certain novelty and change can be introduced even in inherently monotonous work. Some factories have used other devices, such as wiring the plant for music. The method employed is often less important than the fact that some attempt is made to consider the workers' feelings. A classic illustration of this was the famous Hawthorne experiments in industrial psychology. A select team of workers bettered its output sharply when certain improvements were made in working conditions. But, to the amazement of the psychologists, the workers maintained their gain when restored to previous conditions. The answer in this case was that the recognition given the team was a more important psychological stimulus than external conditions. Hearts may sing in slums and be broken in gilded palaces. Generally, however, external conditions, such as cleanliness, lighting, safety procedures, convenience in the placing of machinery, and little amenities are tangible indications of genuine interest in the workers.

The practical suggestion for the employer is to seek tried means to implement his Christian desire to treat the workers in accord with their human dignity. His benevolence should not take the form of paternalism, giving as a grant what workers expect as a right. Justice and fair dealing are fundamental to sound labor relations. Most workers would prefer strict treatment, if equitable and consistent, to moody outbursts of good will succeeded by manifestations of temper or despondency. Principles, not feelings, should govern industrial relations. Then the matter of seeking proper techniques is merely a question of study and observation. Personnel literature of high quality is abundant today. There are good schools for the training of top supervisory officials and excellent periodicals to report the latest experiments. This is not to imply that good human relations are a form of gadgetry, but merely that this aspect of industry has been so long neglected that many have developed a blindness to its implications. It will take study to realize possibilities and to note opportunities which have been overlooked.[1] Thus, over a period of time, the employer can replace the hostility too often smoldering beneath the surface in modern factories, first with genuine respect, and then with friendliness and good will.

Work: a Duty and a Right. If the worker's dignity is respected, then he in turn will more easily realize the basic worth of his labor. As the popes have stated, while the burden of work may be associated with God's punishment of man after the fall of Adam, it is at the same time an instrument of redemption. Man was made to work as the bird was to fly. Idleness is harmful to human character, whereas the discipline of work can develop many virtues, such as fortitude, patience, and brotherly cooperation. Work participates in the miracle of creation, since man thereby brings into being new forms and materials not found in nature. Hence there is no need for the worker to feel ashamed of his lot, no matter how humble it may seem. Some of the most difficult types of work are most necessary for the general welfare. Few persons may like such tasks as street cleaning or garbage removal, yet the community would suffer intensely if such tasks were neglected. Again, domestic and personal service is often in disrepute today. To the extent that such attitudes are the result of low wages and poor working conditions in the past, they are quite natural. But it would be wrong to feel that direct personal

---

[1] As noted in the preceding chapter, extensive reading lists are given in *Human Relations in Modern Business* and in J. F. Cronin, *Catholic Social Action*, pp. 221–223. See also List No. 9 in the Appendix to the present book.

service is inherently undignified and unworthy. Some of the most respected professions, such as medicine and teaching, embody personal service. A mother's devotion to children is one of the highest forms of this work. Hence, it would be unfortunate if any general prejudice against direct service to another were to arise.

The personal satisfaction of work often varies in accord with the skill demanded and the creative opportunities afforded. Undoubtedly skilled labor, calling for technical proficiency and craftsmanship, is more stimulating than unskilled work. There is a satisfaction in achievement, particularly when this is relatively unique. When the college professor, perhaps an internationally acknowledged genius in mathematical physics, drives up to a garage with a "queer noise" in the motor of his car, one can understand the pride of the mechanic who merely turns a knob and sends the car off with its pristine vigor. He may well boast that the professor may understand nuclear fission, but he had to come to the mechanic when the ignition timing of his car went awry.

Given man's nature, one can say that for most men, work is a duty. It is their normal means for sustaining physical existence. With many of them, it also involves support for their families. Moreover, our psychology demands work. Idleness deteriorates the character, just as an unused muscle weakens and then atrophies. Work is closely tied up with the fundamental duty of self-preservation, as well as with moral demands to use one's talents in accord with opportunities afforded. Fortunately, for many this duty is also a source of satisfaction and even pride.

At the same time, work is a right. Since it is a normal means for securing a living, the law of self-preservation, implanted by God in human nature, justifies man's ordinary claim for work. Any other method of obtaining a livelihood is, generally speaking, contrary to human dignity. If a healthy man were to remain in idleness, supported by state or private grants of relief, his character would tend to deteriorate. As a rule, such aid would be humiliating, since he would receive as a favor what he would prefer to earn as a right. Of course, the situation is different where persons are helpless because of sickness or injuries. Even here, however, it would be desirable through insurance to secure maximum aid as a matter of right.

Inasmuch as duty is correlative with right, it might be asked: who has the duty to provide work? Clearly the answer on the first level is: the owners of property. Since, in the present state of society, the ownership of productive property is relatively concentrated, the only way that most men can secure work is through the use of property belonging to the few. Hence property owners, as a class, should so use the goods of the earth that all have opportunity of securing access to work. In practice, however, this is not always possible without sound organization of society. Thus, owners have the further obligation of corresponding with sound measures of social policy. In default of such effective action, the state has the right and duty to define, within the limits of natural law, the social aspect of property rights. Likewise, as a result of default and as a lesser evil, it should provide employment for those who cannot secure work by normal means. This is but an implementation of its duty to seek the common good.

The right to work is not a right to any particular job. No man has a full vested interest in a job for which he applies or even already holds. The problem of securing employment for all willing and able to work is a matter of social justice, not commutative justice. The institutions of society must be organized in terms of the common good, so that economic life will serve its proper function and provide normal livelihood for all who want to work. No employer is bound in justice to keep men working, when there is no work for them, but this would be a great act of charity, if the firm could do this and remain solvent.

It is more difficult to assess the claim of a worker who has a job and is giving satisfactory service at a time when there is work for him to do. To lay off such a worker without cause in favor of another with no greater ability would seem to be contrary to fairness and equity. Certainly workers have a right in union contracts to insist upon seniority provisions and protection against arbitrary discharge. The contrary practice would seem to violate social justice, in that it is opposed to the common good of the plant community. It would be an affront to the human dignity of the worker, whose years of service might be summarily disregarded in favor of another whose only claim to the job might be the fact that he is a relative of an executive. But it is not clear that we can build a claim in strict justice to a job. If the worker has received a just wage, presumably the employer has discharged his obligation in commutative justice. It is doubtful that possession of a job or years of service confer a job claim which holds under obligation of restitution. But certainly it is necessary to change the institutions of society, so that the worker will be safeguarded in his job.

Undoubtedly, unemployment is one of the great evils of our time. It is tragic when millions of men seek work and cannot find it. If there is any change in social institutions which can be considered imperative, it is the removal of conditions which lead to economic instability. Fortunately, this is a common concern of all elements of the economic community, since all alike suffer from depressions. There is real hope that strong and co-operative efforts to meet this plague can be expected in our time. Some of the details involved will be treated in the following chapter.

Discrimination in Work. A question of substantial importance concerns discrimination against racial, religious, and national groups in the matter of employment. In the United States, there are considerable job disabilities affecting minority groups. They are found in the entire range of employment situations, including hiring, training, and union membership. In some cities, nearly three fourths of job specifications filed by employers with employment agencies specified religious or racial qualifications. A 50 per cent average is quite common. Newspaper advertisements often follow the same pattern.

Among the groups affected are Negroes, Jews, Mexicans, Orientals, and, to a lesser degree, Catholics. These minorities comprise a substantial segment of our population (nonwhites, fifteen million; Jews, five million; and Catholics, twenty-five million). Some national groups experience bars against them. There is not a complete acceptance of Italians, various Slavic peoples, and other recent immigrants. The degree of discrimination varies according to place and time. It is serious for Negroes, Jews, Mexicans, and Orientals, in that they are often relegated to the poorest type of jobs and given last choice when jobs are scarce. In the case of Catholics and some of the recent immigrants, the barriers are not so extensive. They are more likely to be denied certain choice jobs and advancement to executive positions than to be excluded completely from any field. Some of the discrimination is subtle in that preferment is given to members of societies to which Catholics are forbidden to belong.

With the Negro, discrimination is most extensive. He does not always have adequate opportunity to train for skilled jobs. Even if he is trained, he may not be hired. As an added difficulty, he may be denied admission to a union which may control important job openings in a field. Finally he faces the handicap of being "last hired and first fired" in many fields of work. Moreover, these obstacles have a tendency to reinforce one another. Thus, the lack of job opportunity had much to do with Negroes' failure to receive technical training. Barriers to admission in unions were such as to discourage many from getting training, even when it was available. Once a pattern was set up, there was a tendency to accept the *status quo* as normal and to oppose any measures which would interfere with it. In this way, an effective barrier was set up against full admission of Negroes to normal work opportunities. The same general program operated against Mexicans and Orientals. Many of them were originally admitted to this country to do common labor, and strong obstacles were erected against their rising in their communities.

With the Jew, there are some barriers against ready entrance into the professions. But there is also discrimination against Jews in business and in white-collar jobs, even at the relatively low level of sales clerks. There has been less evidence of any obstacles raised in manufacturing or in the skilled trades. On the other hand, Jews have not been inclined, as a group, to seek work in manufacturing, construction, transportation, and mining. Hence, it is not entirely clear what job opportunities would be available, were they to concentrate in these fields. At any rate, they do not face barriers against vocational training or entrance into unions. On the contrary, many of the nation's best-known union leaders have been Jews, whereas the few Negro top union leaders, until quite recently, have come from fields reserved for Negroes, such as railway waiters and sleeping-car porters.

With both Jews and Negroes, the pattern of economic discrimination tends to parallel local social attitudes. Because these minority groups are rejected socially in some quarters, they are often relegated to less pleasant types of work. It has been held that white, Gentile workers would not associate with them as full equals. This community attitude was then reflected in union policies. To the credit of the labor movement, it can be said that it has generally been more advanced in its racial attitudes than the nation as a whole. The C.I.O. particularly has made great strides toward full acceptance of Negroes in industry, and the A. F. of L. has improved its attitude in recent years. Union officials have often had higher standards than have prevailed among their rank-and-file members. Union officers have been leaders, not followers in the fight for racial justice.[2]

On the level of principle, it would seem that job discrimination for racial and religious reasons is clearly against the virtue of charity and very probably against justice. That any group of citizens should be relegated to an inferior position because of color or cultural background is obviously contrary to the Christian principle of brotherhood. All men are equal in the sight of God, and man has no right to set up barriers which would deny this equality. Anthropologists tell us that there is no inherent difference in intelligence and skill among various racial groups. Moreover, widespread denial of job opportunity not only is

---

[2] See H. R. Northrup, *Organized Labor and the Negro* (New York: Harper, 1944), and R. C. Weaver, *Negro Labor* (New York: Harcourt, 1946). For statistics on Negro employment, see S. Wolfbein, "Postwar Trends in Negro Employment," *Monthly Labor Review*, Dec., 1947. For further facts, see R. K. McNickle, "Discrimination in Employment," *Editorial Research Reports*, Dec. 17, 1948.

contrary to Christian brotherhood, but it seems to be definitely unjust. Men have in justice a right to a job consonant with their ability and human dignity. If a skilled Negro mechanic is forced to work as a common laborer, he is being denied his rights. Likewise, if he is paid less for the same kind of work performed by equally trained whites in his locality, he is being defrauded. It is difficult to see how such discrimination does not involve justice.

The question as to which type of justice is involved is more obscure. Earlier it was stated that a worker does not normally have a claim in strict justice to be hired for any particular job. His right to a job obtains in regard to the economic system as a whole rather than any given employer. If such is the case, then an employer does not sin against strict justice in denying a job to a properly qualified worker because of race, religion, or national origin. But social justice requires that all concerned work as circumstances permit to change the institutions which bring about the evil of discrimination. Social justice applies here, in that rights are being denied under circumstances definitely contrary to the common good. When a group is being deprived of basic rights, the common good demands that steps be taken to remedy the evil. The appropriate steps are matters of technique and prudential judgment. Such steps would include education and fair-employment practice legislation. Thus, six states and five cities currently have antidiscrimination legislation. Community pressures of various types should be used to change unjust social institutions. In this way, a pattern of justice in hiring, training, and admission into unions would be secured.[3] At the same time, we should not overlook the serious personal obligation of employers and workers, at least in charity, to avoid discrimination in employment patterns. Personal example, as well as education and legislation to change faulty social institutions, can be a means of achieving social justice in this field.

Not only is discrimination contrary to the common good because it works injustice, but it also lowers national living stand-

---

[3] For techniques, see J. F. Cronin, *Catholic Social Action,* Chap. 10.

322 SOCIAL PRINCIPLES IN ECONOMIC LIFE

ards. Untrained workers are relatively unproductive. Slum regions cost more in terms of police protection, free medical care, economic losses through vice and disease, and the like than they produce in taxes. Once again, injustice is seen to be bad economics as well as bad morals.

Unsuitable Work: Migrant Workers. Certain types of work are in themselves obstacles to the full recognition of human dignity. They impose hardships on workers and their families. Such is often the case with migratory labor. Where workers move from one job to another with some frequency, it is almost impossible to establish a decent home life, educate children, and develop proper social patterns.

One of the most important fields for migratory labor is agriculture. Many crops require little care during the ripening season, but need a large labor force for harvesting when they are ripe. Such is obviously the case with fruit, vineyards, and even truck crops. Some of these crops are highly perishable, so that the farmers must have assistance for the short period of harvesting. Much of this help is furnished by migratory workers, who move north with the ripening of crops, particularly on the East and West coasts. Usually entire families move, living in shacks or barracks for the period of employment in a region. Often the whole family, including very small children, works. As a result of this migration, children do not receive much education and have little opportunity for normal social contacts. Furthermore, employment methods are casual, so that at times families may travel to a region only to find all jobs filled. The same situation often obtains in canning industries, which are equally seasonal adjuncts to agricultural work.

There are roughly about one million migrant workers in the United States. Weekly earnings vary from a little over ten dollars in some southern states to as high as forty dollars in the state of Washington. Annual income is often under $1,000, even with husband, wife, and several children working. Nearly three quarters of the workers average less than 75 days of farm work in a year. As many as 15 per cent of the children never go to school and education for the rest is often a hit-or-miss proposition. Families often live in shacks of unbelievable squalor. They have no social security and are covered by workmen's compensation in only five states. Because hiring practices are casual, Mexican labor is imported even where there is unemployment among American migrant workers.[4]

It is easier to outline the problems of migratory workers than to offer a feasible solution for these problems. Unquestionably, many farm crops are such that temporary heavy labor demand is inevitable. These farms could not possibly support such a labor force during the entire year. Given this fact, three types of approach may be considered. First, the condition of migratory workers could be improved through public and private efforts to obtain suitable housing and a steady flow of employment. Enforcement of child labor regulations could prevent deprivation of schooling to children of migrants. Secondly, increased mechanization might lessen the labor needs for some crops and hence reduce the number of migrants. This has been done successfully for some field crops, such as wheat, where huge combines do the work of many men. It may also be found feasible for other crops, if suitable research were undertaken. Finally, it may be possible to recruit casual labor locally through the use of college students or even more mature high school students in their summer vacations. All this would assume adequate safeguards and more attractive conditions than are currently available.

Since the problem of migratory work is regional or even national, it is clear that the handling of it should be on a large scale. One possible approach is through unionization of workers to demand better wages and more regular conditions of employment. By this method, a labor union would act as a stabilizing force, just as it has been in the clothing industry. Another approach would be through action by the federal government, after a thorough study of the entire issue, including the agricultural economics involved. From the political viewpoint the union

---

[4] For further data, see *Migrant Labor, A Human Problem* (Washington: Department of Labor, 1947).

approach is preferable. If workers organized to demand better conditions, farmers would be forced to make the necessary adjustments or do without labor at a critical time. They might then welcome any help which the federal government might give. But if the government were to act first, there would be tremendous political opposition from the highly organized and effective farm lobby. A parallel case would be the condition of domestic servants. Evils in this field seemed impervious to legislative remedy, but when economic conditions gave workers more attractive alternate conditions of employment, the shortage of servants quickly led to raised standards. In many cities, this form of work is now on an organized basis, sometimes handled by teams working from a central office. Thus, necessity forced the overcoming of inertia and lethargy and led to greatly improved conditions. A similar approach may be the more feasible answer to the problem of migratory and casual labor.

It should not be assumed that farm labor is the only form of migratory labor. In addition to canneries previously mentioned, there are elements of casualness in logging, construction, shipping, and resort occupations. As a rule, however, these occupations do not pose the serious social problem associated with migratory farm labor. This latter group is close to the bottom in the economic scale. The work is so unsatisfactory that it has been done mainly by immigrants or desperate groups of unemployed workers. Mexican labor has been imported for this task, since many Americans are unwilling to accept it, save as a last resort. It is clear that this social problem should not be neglected.

Unsuitable Work: Child Labor. One of the sordid aspects of the industrial revolution, as was noted earlier, was the abuse of child labor. Today we no longer have the common spectacle of young children working fourteen hours a day in dangerous factories. But, there still remain problems connected with the labor of children. The physical, moral, and cultural dangers to child workers have not been completely removed by remedial legislation.

Work by children is physically dangerous when it taxes their strength and exposes them to sickness or, at least, to a stunting of their normal development. Such would be the case with work too difficult for their years, risky in terms of possible accidents or in unsuitable surroundings in the matter of either place or time. Factory work would be generally unhealthy for boys under eighteen. Labor in the fields would in itself be better, but often the long hours and exhausting tasks are too much for the growing boy. Even light work which carries on into the night can mean loss of sleep and hence be debilitating. Moreover, if a child works so incessantly in his free time that he has no time for recreation, he will suffer physically. Hence, it is wrong to expect full-time hard work from children still in early adolescence. Part-time work likewise should be such as not to impose too great a strain at a time when energy reserves may be low.

Child labor is morally dangerous when performed in surroundings which present unusual temptations to crime or vice. From the moral viewpoint, indiscriminate mingling of young boys with older workers in factories would be generally unwise. The tone of conversation in the average factory is hardly that of a Holy Name meeting. While adults with decent standards develop a certain protective indifference to such language, the situation is otherwise with young boys, even in this sophisticated age. A similar problem obtains with street trades, such as those of newsboys and bootblacks, especially when boys work until late in the night to catch the after-theater crowd. Night surroundings in large cities can often be corrupting.

Another drawback to certain forms of child labor is the neglect of education which they involve. This ranges from outright withdrawal from school to carelessness in regard to studies. It is generally felt in the United States that a high school education or its equivalent should be available to all children. While there may be some who lack the minimum talent or interest necessary for such training, it is still desirable that they secure a better preparation for life, perhaps in a trade school. Certainly it is unjust when a student who is willing and able to receive a standard of education considered normal in this country be deprived of this opportunity because of family poverty.

There are two moral aspects to child labor. The first is that no child should be permitted to work under conditions which are detrimental to his health, morals, or basic education. Such work would injure him and hence be contrary to his human dignity. Secondly, it is unjust when economic conditions force a child to work because total family income is insufficient to maintain decent standards. The father of a family should normally receive wages sufficient to support his family in frugal comfort. This does not mean that children should be forbidden work suitable to their age and strength. The discipline of moderate work is good training for children. They may learn habits of industry and responsibility. The income received may permit the family or the children small luxuries otherwise unobtainable. In some circumstances, it may be possible for a boy, through afterschool and summer work, to save enough to go to college. Again, in the absence of a family-allowance system, older children in large families may work to supplement a wage adequate for an average family but unsuitable in their case. Even in this situation, the family-allowance method might be better in principle.

Child labor in the United States is regulated by the Fair Labor Standards Act, which forbids the employment of minors under the age of sixteen in mining and manufacturing or at any work during school hours. Minors between the ages sixteen and eighteen may not be employed in hazardous occupations. Employment certificates may be secured by children between fourteen and sixteen, when the work will not interfere with their education or physical development. This law, however, applies only to occupations engaged in interstate commerce. Children employed by their parents in occupations other than manufacturing and mining are exempt from the act. In October, 1948, 717,000 minors aged fourteen and fifteen were at work, and 1,584,000 of the ages sixteen and seventeen. About 10 per cent of this group was employed in violation of law, mostly in agriculture. The definition of "at work" included those employed fifteen or more hours a week, and about half this group was working full time. Most significant is the fact that the number of minors working in 1948 was nearly triple the 1940 figures.

In some states, there are laws which cover the fields untouched by federal legislation. But there are still areas which are unregulated or where enforcement is difficult. This is particularly true where industrial homework is permitted. Thus, it was formerly common to farm out to contract workers at home certain types of work which did not require expensive machinery, such as stringing beads, sewing delicate work, decorating, minor assembly work for electrical devices or fountain pens, shelling nuts, cane weaving, and similar simple work. Under such conditions, it is almost impossible to regulate child labor, even though in theory the work is done only by someone confined to the home, either by sickness, injury, or home obligations. Some states, such as New York, have strict control of industrial homework, but in others it is unregulated. Wages paid are pitifully low, with average hourly earnings sometimes as low as ten cents. Often such work is competitive with work done by men in factories, with the result that there is pressure to lower wages to the starvation level. While it has some usefulness in giving work to the aged, crippled persons, or those caring for invalids, the difficulty of regulating it and the antisocial consequences often found make it a practice of doubtful value. New York State, which is trying to eliminate homework, had in 1949 nearly eleven thousand certified homeworkers, nearly all married women. How much of this is passed on to children, interfering with rest, recreation, and study, is hard to know. Sampling indicates fairly widespread abuse.

Undoubtedly federal legislation has sharply restricted abusive conditions in regard to child labor, although there are loopholes in the federal law. But there is still room for improvement in areas which can be regulated only by states or local governments. If the industry-council plan were in operation, here would be a good example of unfair competition which could be regulated

by industry-wide groups. In the meantime, there are many opportunities both for improvements, particularly in state legislation, and for better enforcement of existing laws.[5]

Women Workers. The position of women in industry has
varied considerably during modern times. With the advent of the
industrial revolution, women were employed in factories and
mines. Gradually, their place in the factory was yielded to men,
except that in both world wars the trend was reversed. In October,
1949, there were 18.6 million women in the labor force in the
United States, or nearly 30 per cent of women over fourteen years
of age. Among the occupations heavily staffed by women are:
domestic service, school teaching, secretarial and clerical work,
restaurant and laundry tasks, and sales work in stores. A sizable
group of women (over 3,000,000) work in industry, such as
textiles and clothing, paper and printing, shoe manufacturing,
glassmaking, electrical manufacturing, and metal, rubber, and
chemical industries. Women do light assembly-line work. In
some industries, such as tobacco manufacturing or women's
clothing, women comprise about 70 per cent of the working force.
A high percentage also obtains in knit goods, woolen and worsted
goods, radio manufacturing, gas and electric fixtures, boots and
shoes, and men's clothing. But even in the masculine stronghold
of heavy industry, about 12 per cent of the workers are women.
Half the women in the labor force are thirty-five years old or
older. A majority of working women are married and one fifth
are heads of families.[6]

The position of women in the business world has many social
implications. These include the question of proper wages and
working conditions, the effect on the home, and the impact on the
economy in general.

---

[5] For further information, write for material published by Child Labor Branch,
U. S. Department of Labor; Children's Bureau, Federal Security Agency; and the
National Child Labor Committee, 419 Fourth Avenue, New York 16, N. Y. See also
"State Child Labor Standards" (Washington: Government Printing Office, 1949) for
recent information on state laws in this field.

[6] For full data, see Women's Bureau (Department of Labor), Bulletin 218, *Women's
Occupation Through Seven Decades* (Washington: Government Printing Office, 1947),

Women are frequently paid lower wages than men, even for the same occupations. Thus, women schoolteachers often receive lower salaries than men doing the same task. The argument used is that men are more efficient, that they need the higher wages . to support families, and that women do not remain in an industry or occupation long enough to be considered other than learners or apprentices. On the other hand, there is no question but that women are used to supplant male workers and thus depress the wage rate. Women often accept lower wages because they enter the working force either under some pressure or with the idea that the job is temporary. Married women workers frequently seek only a supplementary income, while single girls, often living at home, will accept lower wages since their expenses are lower. When these groups take jobs which are competitive with those of men, undoubtedly they depress standards. Moreover, the elements of pressure or temporary employment make them less amenable to unionization or other steps to raise wages. The net result is competitive lowering of living standards.

Women need special consideration in the matter of working conditions. They need periodic rest intervals, a more liberal sick-leave policy, and also maternity leaves. As a rule, nightwork is considered unsuitable for women. They are less able than men to work long hours. Because of this, most states have laws regulating the employment of women. These laws may specify the maximum number of hours per day and week, rest periods, and similar considerations. Over half the states also have minimum-wage laws for women. Standards for minimum wages usually assume a self-supporting single woman, thus taking a middle ground between the single woman living at home and the married woman supporting a family. Most laws are flexible, considering both the cost of living and the economic status of an industry. Some recent (September, 1948) annual budgets for women workers in large cities varied from $2,087 (New York

---

and Bulletin 225, *Handbook of Facts on Women Workers* (Washington: Government Printing Office, 1948).

City, living in a family group) to $2,218 (San Francisco, living in a boardinghouse).[7]

The large number of married women working undoubtedly has an adverse effect upon the home. In some cases, the working period is temporary, prior to the advent of children. In other cases, either the desire or the need for work is used as a reason for refusing to have children. There are other instances where children are neglected because the mothers work. Thus, they may be sent off to school with a cold lunch and forced to play in the streets until the mother returns from work. Younger children are often left in day nurseries or even in foster homes. Such conditions are definitely antisocial. When they are caused by inadequate wages for the husband, the remedy is strong pressure for a living wage. If the mother is a widow, it would be desirable to have adequate government aid until children reach the school age, and after that partial grants so that the widow need not work full time. Fortunately, many state laws, the federal Social Security Act, and local charitable groups are helpful in these cases.

The broader question as to the desirability of women in business and industry permits no easy answer. There are strong reasons for work in the case of single girls and widows. Young girls can help out with family expenses and save in view of marriage. The fact that they had to earn a living and manage a budget might prepare them to be better wives. Undoubtedly some occupations widen the scope of a girl's social contacts and thus might contribute to a better match in marriage. Some of the professions favored by women, such as schoolteaching, nursing, and social work, give a training which is useful in both family life and women's community responsibilities.

When married women work, there is always the danger that the home may suffer. Where this is a matter of individual choice because of the desire for luxuries or a less monotonous life, this is a personal problem to be handled through education and religious motivation. But when work is a necessity to supplement

---

[7] For more details, see Women's Bureau Publication, No. 226, "Working Women's Budgets in Twelve States" (Washington: Government Printing Office, 1948).

the husband's meager earnings, it is a matter of social justice. Likewise, the lowering of standards through competition by women involves social justice.[8] Here, of course, we are faced with the fact that the modern woman is often an economic liability when she remains at home. Formerly women were able to furnish material help in meeting the economic burdens of family life. They made clothes, baked bread, canned fruits and vegetables, and even tended gardens or helped on a farm. Thus work at home was a substantial contribution to the real earnings of the family. Today the making of clothes and much of the preparation of food are done outside the home. Hence there is definite economic pressure for the wife to work, so as to assume a partial responsibility for the family budget.

To meet the social-justice problems connected with work by women, several steps might be considered. In the case of the married women, forced by economic pressure to work outside the home, the ideal would be the relief of such pressure. This could be accomplished in part by a family living wage for male workers and partially by devising methods of making women economically more productive in the home. The former approach calls for a marked enhancement of the productivity of the average worker. He would, in effect, be expected to produce as much alone as once was produced by a combined family unit. This involves a considerable strain upon our economy, although it is quite possible that it could be done. The transition would be eased, however, if modern wives were taught ways of co-operating through production at home. Definite savings could be achieved in making clothes and preparing food, without sacrificing reasonable standards of leisure or eschewing the comforts made available by modern technology.

Another step is to prevent the exploitation of women who are compelled to work. This is important, not only in justice to the women, but also so as to prevent unfair competition with male

---

[8] As an indication of the reasons why married women work, in 1940 only 15 per cent of married working women had husbands with income over $2,000, and less than 6 per cent had husbands with income over $3,000.

workers. It is necessary through unionization and minimum-wage laws to achieve equality in wages where productivity is the same. Today about 3,000,000 women are union members out of about 11,000,000 women in fields where unions operate. While this is a considerable improvement compared with conditions a few decades back, there is still important work to be done in organizing women workers for higher standards. When this is supplemented by adequate protective legislation, there will be less incentive to hire women merely because they will accept lower wages than men for the same work.

Those whose duty it is to advise young girls and married women in the matter of employment might well ponder the address on Women's Duties given by Pope Pius XII on October 21, 1945. With moving eloquence and insight, the Holy Father noted that a woman cannot be happy in a social order which does violence to her nature. Her whole being tends toward motherhood and family life. Even when by vocation, either freely chosen or in submission to Divine Providence, she may never have a family of her own, she can still choose a form of spiritual motherhood in her choice of occupation. Through such professions as teaching, nursing, or social work, she can dedicate her life to the care of others. If she is forced, on the contrary, to do work more suitable for the masculine temperament, she does violence to her nature and becomes frustrated and unhappy.

Hours of Labor. Not long ago, the eighty-four-hour week was not uncommon even in heavy industry. Men worked seven days a week, twelve hours a day. They had little family life and no opportunity to meet their religious obligations on Sunday. The average work week in industry was nearly sixty hours in 1890. It dropped to fifty by 1926, and today hovers around forty. The normal standard today in industry is an eight-hour day and a five-day work week. Since the Fair Labor Standards Act and other government laws call for time-and-one-half for hours worked in excess of forty a week (with some exceptions), the tendency for a forty-hour week has become practically universal in industry.

The federal law applies only to interstate commerce and it exempts *bona fide* union contracts which permit a more flexible distribution of hours. Some highly seasonal industries are also exempt. An example of a flexible union contract would be in the long-haul trucking industry which might accept a twelve-hour day and fifty-six-hour week before overtime applies. There are practically no legal restrictions on hours worked by men in intrastate commerce. Here the limits are usually imposed by union contracts or by competition for labor (in times of full employment) by industries enjoying better standards.

It would not be feasible to set one standard as suitable for all types of work. The demands of justice are not so rigid. Human dignity suffers when hours of work are such as to impair health and strength and to interfere with a decent family life. This sets certain absolute top limits to hours worked. If the health and strength factor were the main element, then standards would vary sharply according to conditions. Heavy work in steel mills and mines could not be compared with such occupations as watchmen or guards. But the family factor would limit work hours even in lighter occupations so that a father could have proper influence over his children and some of the relaxations as well as the duties of family life. On the other hand, there seems to be no objection in social justice to seeking standards better than the strict demands of minimum human dignity. After certain wage standards are met, workers generally prefer leisure to higher wages. The premium provisions for overtime are really penalty rather than revenue measures. They were enacted to discourage overtime, not to increase workers' wages. Hence a trend toward shorter hours, provided it did not interfere with the common good, would be a step in the right direction. It would de-emphasize the economic factor in life and provide leisure which could be used for other forms of human activity. Indeed, to the extent that work becomes more mechanical and routine, a shorter work week would lessen the strain that some might feel from monotony.

The economic effect of shorter hours is mixed. When hours of work declined, **productivity did not drop to the same degree.**

Apparently, many workers had subconsciously fixed a maximum limit on the amount of energy to be expended at work, so that they could work harder and more skillfully in a shorter week. Moreover, the trend toward shorter hours was accompanied by increasing mechanization of industry, thus adding to worker productivity. If this tendency toward higher productivity continues, then workers may well choose between ever higher standards of living and additional leisure to enjoy what they already have. It is not inconceivable that a six-hour work day and a thirty-hour week may come in the lifetime of many who are young workers today.

On the other hand, the idea that a shorter work week is a satisfactory remedy for unemployment is generally fallacious. This proposal crops up during depressions. But at these very times, sharing work might only be sharing poverty. With the total level of industrial activity down, spreading jobs would only mean a wider share of an inadequate national income. The real problem in depressions is to revive production so that the total national income would be sufficient to take care of the needs of all. This applies as well to sick industries, such as coal and, frequently, construction. The workers do not always look on things this way, since their perspective is frequently somewhat limited. They indulge in slowdowns, made-work practices, feather-bedding, and similar devices to spread employment. Often such methods are self-defeating, since they raise costs and thus reduce sales in an already depressed industry. Here again, broad institutional changes, rather than shortsighted individual or group efforts to adjust to an unsatisfactory *status quo,* are the real answer.

Summary. In modern society, the dignity of labor is better recognized than it was at the turn of the century or one or two centuries past. Gradually, by one method or other, there is greater recognition of the fact that workers are human and that conditions of work must take this into account. Today there is more of a tendency to adjust the job to the man rather than the man to the job. At the same time, there is room for considerable progress. The advanced standards of industrial relations and personnel management accepted in some progressive firms are by no means universal. Gains won in times of full employment may not be retained when production is slack. Hence, constant effort must be made even to retain the achievements of the last decade while we are pressing on to a broad acceptance of higher standards.

Satisfaction with progress should not blind us to islands of reaction still in our midst. Racial and religious discrimination is still an ugly fact. Migratory workers also belong to the status of second-class citizens. There is much exploitive child labor. Wages and working conditions for women are generally below standards set by men in similar work. The principle of equal pay for equal work is not widely acknowledged. Work by women is often a factor in lowering general wage levels in certain industries and trades. Finally, the matter of working hours is satisfactory today on the whole because full employment gives even unorganized labor some bargaining power. An increase in unemployment could change this picture, as workers compete for jobs and in desperation accept lower standards.

Those interested in promoting social justice still have many tasks in securing full recognition of labor's dignity. Most important is the educational work of bringing a sense of partnership in place of autocracy on the part of management and class hostility as labor's reaction. The spread of unionism is also necessary to buttress the dignity of workers. Until we can have self-regulation to universalize decent standards in industry, there is need of further legislation to protect child and women workers. Discrimination is a challenge both to education and legislation. The work of justice is indeed a continuing task.

READINGS*

J. Messner, *Social Ethics*, pp. 800–811.
Human Relations in Modern Business.

---

* For further readings, consult Lists Nos. 1, 4, 9, and 10 in the Appendix.

E. Mayo, *The Social Problems of an Industrial Civilization.*

B. M. Selekman, *Labor Relations and Human Relations.*

G. F. Bloom and H. R. Northrup, *Economics of Labor and Industrial Relations.*

P. Taft, *Economics and Problems of Labor.*

Chapter X. THE LIVING WAGE AND FULL EMPLOYMENT

THE LIVING WAGE

Leo XIII, Rerum Novarum

51. Nay, in this respect, their energy and effectiveness are so important that it is incontestable that the wealth of nations arises from no other source than from the labor of workers. Equity therefore commands that public authority show proper concern for the worker so that from what he contributes to the common good he may receive what will enable him, housed, clothed, and secure, to live his life without hardship. Whence it follows that all those measures ought to be favored which seem in any way capable of benefiting the condition of workers. Such solicitude is so far from injuring anyone, that it is destined rather to benefit all, because it is of absolute interest to the state that those citizens should not be miserable in every respect from whom such necessary goods proceed.

61. We shall now touch upon a matter of very great importance, and one which must be correctly understood in order to avoid falling into error on one side or the other. We are told that free consent fixes the amount of a wage; that therefore the employer, after paying the wage agreed to, would seem to have discharged his obligation and not to owe anything more; that only then would injustice be done if either the employer should refuse to pay the whole amount of the wage, or the worker should refuse to perform all the work to which he had committed himself; and that in these cases, but in no others, is it proper for the public authority to intervene to safeguard the rights of each party.

62. An impartial judge would not assent readily or without reservation to this reasoning, because it is not complete in all respects; one factor to be considered, and one of the greatest importance, is missing. To work is to expend one's energy for the purpose of securing the things necessary for the various needs of life and especially for its preservation. "In the sweat of thy face shalt thou eat bread." Accordingly, in man labor has two marks, as it were, implanted by nature, so that it is truly personal,

because work energy inheres in the person and belongs completely to him by whom it is expended and for whose use it is destined by nature; and, secondly, that it is necessary, because man has need of the fruit of his labors to preserve his life, and nature itself, which must be most strictly obeyed, commands him to preserve it. If labor should be considered only under the aspect that it is personal, there is no doubt that it would be entirely in the worker's power to set the amount of the agreed wage at too low a figure. For inasmuch as he performs work by his own free will, he can also by his own free will be satisfied with either a paltry wage for his work or even with none at all. But this matter must be judged far differently, if with the factor of personality we combine the factor of necessity, from which indeed the former is separable in thought but not in reality. In fact, to preserve one's life is a duty common to all individuals, and to neglect this duty is a crime. Hence arises necessarily the right of securing things to sustain life, and only a wage earned by his labor gives a poor man the means to acquire these things.

63. Let it be granted then that workers and employers may enter freely into agreements and, in particular, concerning the amount of the wage; yet there is always underlying such agreements an element of natural justice, and one greater and more ancient than the free consent of contracting parties, namely, that the wage shall not be less than enough to support a worker who is thrifty and upright. If, compelled by necessity or moved by fear of a worse evil, a worker accepts a harder condition, which although against his will he must accept because the employer or contractor imposes it, he certainly submits to force, against which justice cries out in protest.

Pius XI, Quadragesimo Anno

53. Far different is the nature of work that is hired out to others and expended on the property of others. To this indeed especially applies what Leo XIII says is "incontestable," namely, that "the wealth of nations originates from no other source than from the labor of workers." For is it not plain that the enormous volume of goods that makes up human wealth is produced by and issues from the hands of the workers that either toil unaided or have their efficiency marvelously increased by being equipped with tools or machines? Everyone knows, too, that no nation has ever risen out of want and poverty to a better and nobler condition save by the enormous and combined toil of all the people, both those who manage work and those who carry out directions.

61. Therefore, with all our strength and effort we must strive that at least in the future the abundant fruits of production will accrue equitably

to those who are rich and will be distributed in ample sufficiency among the workers — not that these may become remiss in work, for man is born to labor as the bird to fly — but that they may increase their property by thrift, that they may bear, by wise management of this increase in property, the burdens of family life with greater ease and security, and that, emerging from that insecure lot in life in whose uncertainties nonowning workers are cast, they may be able not only to endure the vicissitudes of earthly existence, but have also assurance that when their lives are ended they will provide in some measure for those they leave after them.

66. The just amount of pay, however, must be calculated not on a single basis but on several, as Leo XIII already wisely declared in these words: "To establish a rule of pay in accord with justice, many factors must be taken into account."

67. By this statement he plainly condemned the shallowness of those who think that this most difficult matter is easily solved by the application of a single rule or measure — and one quite false.

68. For they are greatly in error who do not hesitate to spread the principle that labor is worth and must be paid as much as its products are worth, and that conesquently the one who hires out his labor has the right to demand all that is produced through his labor. How far this is from the truth is evident from what We have already explained in treating of property and labor.

69. It is obvious that, as in the case of ownership, so in the case of work, especially work hired out to others, there is a social aspect also to be considered in addition to the personal or individual aspect. For man's productive effort cannot yield its fruit unless a truly social and organic body exists, unless a social and juridical order watches over the exercise of work, unless the various occupations, being interdependent, co-operate with and mutually complete one another, and, what is still more important, unless mind, material things, and work combine and form as it were a single whole. Therefore, where the social and individual nature of work is neglected, it will be impossible to evaluate work justly and pay it according to justice.

71. In the first place, the worker must be paid a wage sufficient to support him and his family. That the rest of the family should also contribute to the common support, according to the capacity of each, is certainly right, as can be observed especially in the families of farmers, but also in the families of many craftsmen and small shopkeepers. But to abuse the years of childhood and the limited strength of women is grossly wrong. Mothers, concentrating on household duties, should work primarily in the home or in its immediate vicinity. It is an intolerable abuse, and

to be abolished at all cost, for mothers on account of the father's low wage to be forced to engage in gainful occupations outside the home to the neglect of their proper cares and duties, especially the training of children. Every effort must therefore be made that fathers of families receive a wage large enough to meet ordinary family needs adequately. But if this cannot always be done under existing circumstances, social justice demands that changes be introduced as soon as possible whereby such a wage will be assured to every adult workingman. It will not be out of place here to render merited praise to all who, with a wise and useful purpose, have tried and tested various ways of adjusting the pay for work to family burdens in such a way that, as these increase, the former may be raised and indeed, if the contingency arises, there may be enough to meet extraordinary needs.

72. In determining the amount of the wage, the condition of a business and of the one carrying it on must also be taken into account; for it would be unjust to demand excessive wages which a business cannot stand without its ruin and consequent calamity to the workers. If, however, a business makes too little money, because of lack of energy or lack of initiative or because of indifference to technical and economic progress, that must not be regarded a just reason for reducing the compensation of the workers. But if the business in question is not making enough money to pay the workers an equitable wage because it is being crushed by unjust burdens or forced to sell its product at less than a just price, those who are thus the cause of the injury are guilty of grave wrong, for they deprive workers of their just wage and force them under the pinch of necessity to accept a wage less than fair.

73. Let, then, both workers and employers strive with united strength and counsel to overcome the difficulties and obstacles and let a wise provision on the part of public authority aid them in so salutary a work. If, however, matters come to an extreme crisis, it must be finally considered whether the business can continue or the workers are to be cared for in some other way. In such a situation, certainly most serious, a feeling of close relationship and a Christian concord of minds ought to prevail and function effectively among employers and workers.

74. Lastly, the amount of the pay must be adjusted to the public economic good. We have shown above how much it helps the common good for workers and other employees, by setting aside some part of their income which remains after necessary expenditures, to attain gradually to the possession of a moderate amount of wealth.

Pius XI, On Atheistic Communism

32. We explained clearly [in *Quadragesimo Anno*] the right and dig-

nity of labor, the relations of mutual aid and collaboration which should exist between those who possess capital and those who work, the salary due in strict justice to the worker for himself and for his family.

49. The wage earner is not to receive as alms what is his due in justice. And let no one attempt with trifling charitable donations to exempt himself from the great duties imposed by justice.

52. But social justice cannot be said to have been satisfied as long as workingmen are denied a salary that will enable them to secure proper sustenance for themselves and for their families; as long as they are denied the opportunity of acquiring a modest fortune and forestalling the plague of universal pauperism; as long as they cannot make suitable provision through public or private insurance for old age, for periods of illness and unemployment.

53. It happens all too frequently, however, under the salary system, that individual employers are helpless to ensure justice unless, with a view to its practice, they organize institutions the object of which is to prevent competition incompatible with fair treatment for the workers. Where this is true, it is the duty of contractors and employers to support and promote such necessary organizations as normal instruments enabling them to fulfill their obligations of justice. But the laborers, too, must be mindful of their duty to love and deal fairly with their employers, and persuade themselves that there is no better means of safeguarding their own interests.

Pius XI, Casti Connubii

123. And so, in the first place, every effort should be made to bring about that which Our Predecessor Leo XIII, of happy memory, has already insisted upon, namely, that in the state such economic and social methods should be adopted as will enable every head of a family to earn as much as, according to his station in life, is necessary for himself, his wife, and for the rearing of his children, for "the laborer deserves his wages" (Luke x, 7). To deny this, or to make light of what is equitable, is a grave injustice and is placed among the greatest sins by Holy Writ (Deut. xxiv, 14, 15); nor is it lawful to fix such a scanty wage as will be insufficient for the upkeep of the family in the circumstances in which it is placed.

126. If, however, for this purpose, private resources do not suffice, it is the duty of the public authority to supply for the insufficient forces of individual effort, particularly in a matter which is of such importance to the commonweal, touching as it does the maintenance of the family and married people. If families, particularly those in which there are many

children, have not suitable dwellings; if the husband cannot find employment and means of livelihood; if the necessities of life cannot be purchased except at exorbitant prices; if even the mother of the family, to the great harm of the home, is compelled to go forth and seek a living by her own labors; if she, too, in the ordinary or even extraordinary labors of childbirth, is deprived of proper food, medicine, and the assistance of a skilled physician, it is patent to all to what an extent married people may lose heart, and how home life and the observance of God's commands are rendered difficult for them. Indeed it is obvious how great a peril can arise to the public security and to the welfare and very life of civil society itself when such men are reduced to such a condition of desperation that, having nothing which they fear to lose, they are emboldened to hope for chance advantage from the upheaval of the state and of established order.

127. Wherefore, those who have the care of the state and of the public good cannot neglect the needs of married people and their families, without bringing great harm upon the state and on the common welfare. Hence, in making the laws and in disposing of public funds they must do their utmost to relieve the needs of the poor, considering such a task as one of the most important of their administrative duties.

Pius XII, Sertum Laetitiae

1465. Now if the rich and the prosperous are obliged, out of ordinary motives of pity, to act generously toward the poor, their obligation is all the greater to do them justice. The salaries of the workers, as is just, are to be such that they are sufficient to maintain them and their families.

Pius XII, Christmas Broadcast, 1942

1851. Those who are familiar with the great Encyclicals of Our Predecessors and Our Own previous messages know well that the Church does not hesitate to draw the practical conclusions which are derived from the moral nobility of work, and to give them all the support of her authority. These exigencies include . . . a just wage which covers the needs of the worker and his family. . . .

The Christian Family, American Hierarchy, 1949

The family, to exercise its good influence in full effectiveness, needs a just measure of economic security. When, in a wealthy and prospering nation, diligent and willing parents are forced to live in grinding poverty; when parents have no opportunity of owning their own home; when the aid of government is extended to those who raise crops or build machines but not to those who rear children, there exists a condition of inequity and even of injustice. Social legislation and social action must concur to improve man's economic opportunity, to enable him to marry early, to free him from the peril of unnaturally limiting his family, and to afford him some certainty of sufficiently gainful employment and some assurance that death or accident will not reduce his dependents to the status of public charges.

The Church and Social Order

27. To remedy the situation, it is necessary to adopt right principles for the distribution of the income of industry. These principles must be both economically sound and morally just. The principle that labor should be compensated to such extent only that it remains physically efficient and capable of reproducing itself in new generations of workingmen, is a vicious principle, devoid of all respect for human dignity and opposed to all sense of social responsibility. It is true that this principle was never widely held in theory, but it has been frequently applied in practice. One such application is found in the policy that labor should be compensated solely according to the principle of supply and demand. This reduces labor to the position of a commodity and makes the workingman accept the fluctuating price in a labor market irrespective of the needs of himself and family. Neither present sufficiency of income nor security for the future play a part in determining his wage standard according to this immoral theory and practice. Such theory or practice is antisocial and anti-Christian, for it denies both social responsibility and the claims of Christian ethics and in their place substitutes the principles of selfishness and force.

32. The lack of sufficient private property leads to various forms of insecurity. This insecurity not only leads to the creation of a strong social tension expressing itself in social disorder, but is also contrary to the prescriptions of Christian morality. There can be no question but that in our country we possess adequate resources, both in respect to raw materials, technical or scientific skill, and mechanical equipment, sufficient to provide both a high standard of living and also comprehensive security for all classes of society. Workingmen should be made secure against unemployment, sickness, accident, old age, and death. The first line of defense against these hazards should be the possession of sufficient private property to provide reasonable security. Industry, therefore, should provide not merely a living wage for the moment but also a saving wage for the future against sickness, old age, death, and unemployment. Individual industries alone, however, cannot in each single case achieve this objective without invoking the principle of social insurance. Some form of government subsidy, granted by the entire citizenship through legislative provision, seems to be a necessary part of such a program.

40. The first claim of labor, which takes priority over any claim of the owners to profits, respects the right to a living wage. By the term living wage we understand a wage sufficient not merely for the decent support of the workingman himself but also of his family. A wage so low, that it must be supplemented by the wage of wife and mother or by the children of the family before it can provide adequate food, clothing, and shelter together with essential spiritual and cultural needs, cannot be regarded as a living wage.

41. Furthermore, a living wage means sufficient income to meet not merely the present necessities of life but those of unemployment, sickness, death, and old age as well. In other words, a saving wage constitutes an essential part of the definition of a living wage.

42. In the effort to establish a criterion or standard of measurement of wages, it is necessary to consider not only the needs of the workingman but also the state of the business or industry in which he labors. Pope Pius XI states clearly that "it is unjust to demand wages so high that an employer cannot pay them without ruin, and without consequent distress amongst the working people themselves." Bad management, want of enterprise, or out-of-date methods do not constitute a just reason for reducing the wages of workingmen. It still remains true that a living wage constitutes the first charge on industry. If a business is prevented by unfair competition from paying a living wage, and if such competition reduces prices to such a level that decent and just wages cannot be paid, then those responsible are guilty of wrongdoing and sin grievously against moral principles as well as against the common good. The remedy lies, first, in the adequate organization of both employers and employees in their own proper associations and in their joint action; secondly, in adequate regulation and supervision by the state through proper legislative enactment.

43. No criterion or standard of wages, however, can be determined independently of price. A scale of wages too low, no less than a scale excessively high, causes unemployment. Likewise a scale of prices too low, no less than a scale of prices too high, leads to unemployment. Both create hardship and throw the economic system out of its proper equilibrium, causing unemployment for the community and hardship even for the individual who is employed, for he must pay too high a price in view of his wages or he receives too low a wage in view of prices. What is needed is a reasonable relationship and a harmonious proportion. Pope Pius XI states:

"Where this harmonious proportion is kept, man's various economic activities combine and unite into one single organism and become members of a common body, lending each other mutual help and service. For then only will the economic and social organism be soundly established and attain its end, when it secures for all and each those goods which the wealth and resources of nature, technical achievement and the social organization of economic affairs can give. These goods should be sufficient to supply all needs and an honest livelihood, and to uplift men to that high level of prosperity and culture which, provided it be used with prudence, is not only no hindrance but is of singular help to virtue."

44. Wages are an essential element in the determination of prices. In the final analysis the cost of raw materials cannot be segregated from wage costs, for the production cost of raw materials presupposes a multiplicity of wage costs as a component element. If wages continuously change, then there must be a continuous change in prices, unless it is assumed that all wage changes will affect only the profits of owners. As a matter of fact they do not. The economic organization might function just as easily on one price level as another, but it cannot function well if the price level is frequently changing. Rapid or frequent fluctuations disturb the harmonious proportions between income and prices, not only for owners and employers, but also for the workingmen themselves.

45. This consideration is no argument against a necessary increase of wages whenever and wherever the wages are inadequate to provide a decent living. But it is an argument in favor of attaining a relative degree of stability in the price level as soon as commutative justice and social justice permit. A cogent reason for aspiring to such a condition of stability is the higher interest of the family as against the single or unmarried workingman or employee. The single man benefits more from a wage increase than does the family man if the end result is an increase in prices. The family man is penalized in multiple fashion with every increase in prices. Stability in the price level, therefore, and even a reduction in prices as a secular trend, is desirable as one means of distributing our national income more widely and more effectively for the common good. Such a long-range policy will supplement the benefits of an increased family wage in view of increased family burdens, as recommended by Pius XI.

46. We do not wish to imply that a universal increase of wages will automatically solve our problem of unemployment and idle factories. Some wage increases come not out of the profits of the wealthy but out of the increased prices for the poor. The first requirement, therefore, is that the lowest-paid workingmen be the first to receive an increase of wages, and simultaneously that prices be not raised but excessive profits be reduced. The ultimate aim, therefore, must be a reasonable relationship between different wages and a reasonable relationship between the prices obtained for the products of the various economic groups.

47. Because economic society has not followed the moral laws of justice and charity, the principles of interdependence have been violated, and we have precipitated unemployment with all its consequent hardships and

misery. To withhold just and reasonable wages from the workingman has injured him directly and immediately, but it has also injured the common good and the interests of the very owners of property. Their factories, their commercial establishments, and their equipment have frequently stood idle as a result. Unless workingmen as a class have sufficient income to purchase their share of the goods which our economic system is capable of producing, the markets will automatically be closed to the sale of goods, and idle factories and unemployment are the disastrous results.

Social Reconstruction

Since our industrial resources and instrumentalities are sufficient to provide more than a living wage for a very large proportion of the workers, why should we acquiesce in a theory which denies them this measure of the comforts of life? Such a policy is not only of very questionable morality, but is unsound economically. The large demand for goods which is created and maintained by high rates of wages and high purchasing power by the masses is the surest guarantee of a continuous and general operation of industrial establishments.

The several states should enact laws providing for the establishment of wage rates that will be at least sufficient for the decent maintenance of a family, in the case of all male adults, and adequate to the decent individual support of female workers. In the beginning, the minimum wages for male workers should suffice only for the present needs of the family, but they should be gradually raised until they are adequate to future needs as well. That is, they should be ultimately high enough to make possible that amount of saving which is necessary to protect the worker and his family against sickness, accidents, invalidity, and old age.

Until this level of legal minimum wages is reached, the worker stands in need of the device of insurance. The state should make comprehensive provision for insurance against illness, invalidity, unemployment, and old age. So far as possible the insurance fund should be raised by a levy on industry, as is now done in the case of accident compensation. The industry in which a man is employed should provide him with all that is necessary to meet all the needs of his entire life. Therefore, any contribution to the insurance fund from the general revenues of the state should be only slight and temporary. For the same reason, no contribution should be exacted from any worker who is not getting a higher wage than is required to meet the present needs of himself and family.

Municipal clinics where the poorer classes could obtain the advantage of medical treatment by specialists at a reasonable cost would likewise seem to have become a necessity. A vast amount of unnecessary sickness and suffering exists among the poor and the lower middle classes because they cannot afford the advantages of any other treatment except that provided by the general practitioner. Every effort should be made to supply wage earners and their families with specialized medical care through development of group medicine.

Pastoral Letter, Hierarchy of Quebec, February, 1950

131. In the present state of labor relations, a collective bargaining agreement negotiated with a labor union may be considered as the normal means for determining a just wage. It ceases to be such a norm, however, if imposed by undue pressure from any source.

Code of Social Principles

135. To estimate justly the value of labor and to give it its exact remuneration, both the individual and social character of labor must be taken into account. A just wage, then, is determined not by one but by many considerations.

136. The first point to consider is the sustenance of the worker and his family. A living wage, providing for the maintenance of the worker and his family, and insurance against risk of accident, illness, old age, and unemployment, is the least wage due in justice from the employer.

137. Two consequences follow from the foregoing idea of the living wage:

a) The family allowance system has in recent years shown a satisfactory development. It is fitting that the payment of such allowances should form a part of all agreements, whether individual or collective, between masters and men.

b) There is also a tendency for social insurance to become legalized. It must necessarily be made general, and is preferably carried on by industrial assurance societies, i.e., societies supported and directed jointly by the masters and men in each industry, under the control and with the support of the public authority.

When the state requires membership in family-allowance or social-insurance societies, or when it subsidizes them, it ought at the same time to discriminate between families where the mother remains at home and those in which the mother works outside the home, and provide a more favorable scale for the former.

138. The second point to consider is the condition of the business. It would be unjust to demand wages from it which it cannot pay without ruin.

On the other hand the minimum wage does not always satisfy the requirements of justice. Various important reasons may require, either in justice or equity, the payment of something further, e.g.:

a) More abundant, more perfect, or more economical production than usual;

b) The greater or less prosperity of the business to which the worker is attached.

139. The third point to consider is the common good and its requirements. The common good requires that the worker can not only live on his wage but also save and build up a modest fortune.

On the other hand a wage level that is too low or excessively high gives rise to that lamentable evil — unemployment. Social justice demands a wage policy which offers employment to the largest possible number of workers and through it the means of providing for their maintenance.

140. It is important that by harmonious co-ordination of the various branches of economic activity — agriculture, industry, and the rest — a reasonable relationship be established between wages and the price of goods as well as between the various prices of goods themselves.

141. Under the present system, the organization within an industry of parallel and distinct groups of employers and employed, establishing mutual collective labor agreements, and setting up permanent organizations of contact by joint committees with equal representation, provides the best probability that justice will be observed in regard to wage rates.

The organization of relations between industries along regional, national, and even international lines, can contribute largely toward a balance between wages and prices which would produce a sufficient abundance of goods to satisfy the needs of a decent subsistence and raise men to a level of comfort and culture which would facilitate the exercise of virtue.

FULL EMPLOYMENT

Pius XI, Quadragesimo Anno

74. But another point, scarcely less important, and especially vital in our times, must not be overlooked: namely, that the opportunity to work be provided for those who are able and willing to work. This opportunity depends largely on the wage and salary rate, which can help as long as it is kept within proper limits, but which on the other hand can be an obstacle if it exceeds these limits. For everyone knows that an excessive lowering of wages, or their increase beyond due measure, causes unemployment. This evil, indeed, especially as we see it prolonged and injuring so many during the years of Our Pontificate, has plunged workers into misery and temptations, ruined the prosperity of nations, and put in jeopardy the public order, peace, and tranquillity of the whole world. Hence it is contrary to social justice when, for the sake of personal gain and without regard for the common good, wages and salaries are ex-

cessively lowered or raised; and this same social justice demands that wages and salaries be so managed, through agreement of plans and wills, insofar as can be done, as to offer to the greatest possible number the opportunity of getting work and obtaining suitable means of livelihood.

75. A right proportion among wages and salaries also contributes directly to the same result; and with this is closely connected a right proportion in the prices at which the goods are sold that are produced by the various occupations, such as agriculture, manufacturing, and others. If all these relations are properly maintained, the various occupations will combine and coalesce into, as it were, a single body and like members of the body mutually aid and complete one another. For then only will the social economy be rightly established and attain its purposes when all and each are supplied with all the goods that the wealth and resources of nature, technical achievement, and the social organization of economic life can furnish. And these goods ought indeed to be enough both to meet the demands of necessity and decent comfort and to advance people to that happier and fuller condition of life which, when it is wisely cared for, is not only no hindrance to virtue but helps it greatly.

Pius XI, On Atheistic Communism

52. But social justice cannot be said to have been satisfied as long as workingmen are denied a salary that will enable them to secure proper sustenance for themselves and for their families; as long as they are denied the opportunity of acquiring a modest fortune and forestalling the plague of universal pauperism; as long as they cannot make suitable provision through public or private insurance for old age, for periods of illness and unemployment.

Pius XII, Sertum Laetitiae

1466. May it also be brought about that each and every able-bodied man may receive an equal opportunity for work in order to earn the daily bread for himself and his own. We deeply lament the lot of those — and their number in the United States is large indeed — who, though robust, capable, and willing, cannot have the work for which they are anxiously searching. May the wisdom of the governing powers, a farseeing generosity on the part of employers, together with the speedy re-establishment of more favorable conditions, effect the realization of these reasonable hopes to the advantage of all.

The Church and Social Order

35. We do not wish to imply that individual employers as a class are willfully responsible for this present state of insecurity, but we do claim

that a system which tolerates such insecurity is both economically unsound and also inconsistent with the demands of social justice and social charity. Security of the workingmen, therefore, as against unemployment, old age, sickness, accident, and death, must be frankly accepted as a social responsibility of industry jointly with society. The distribution of the burden justly between the various groups must be determined, first, through mutual council and honest agreement between the employers and the employees, and, secondly, through the regulation of government acting in its sovereign capacity as promoter of the common good.

36. Not all responsibility rests upon government. In truth, a large measure of responsibility rests upon the proper collaboration of employers and employees or of property owners and wage earners. The economic system itself and the principles which guide its executives must help to achieve security by establishing a fair distribution of income between capital and labor. It must strive to establish an equilibrium between farm income and city income. If the rate of wages (not the annual income) of the industrial worker in the city is out of balance with the rate of returns of the farmer in the country, then there is bound to be unemployment and insecurity. Hence the duty of both groups is to work for a just balance between themselves, instead of encouraging selfishness and greed which defeat the interest of both and violate the principles of morality.

37. The same can be said of the various classes of industrial labor. Here also there must be a balance between various groups, both organized and unorganized. Unless this be true, the economic system cannot function smoothly and there will inevitably be unemployment, because the one class of workingmen cannot buy the high-priced products of the other class of workingmen with their limited income. If skilled laborers, who, through rigid organization, have a monopoly control of their craft, raise their rate of hourly wages too high, they do not gain their advantage exclusively from the wealthy, but from the poor also, in terms of excessive prices. Higher wages as a rule should come out of excessive profits and not out of increased prices.

38. Heartening, indeed, are the beginnings toward the greater security of the people that have already been made through legislative enactment and public policy. The immediate benefits of these laws to working people may be small and some modifications perhaps desirable, but it is highly gratifying that the principle upon which they rest has become a part of our national policy.

One of the consequences of man's dignity is his right to work as the normal means for sustaining life. In modern times, this usually means a right to a job. But not every job will meet the test of ministering to the basic needs of man. Only if the rate of pay is adequate to support really human existence, and the stability of employment is such that man can have reasonable assurance about the future, can we say that a job meets the essential demands springing from a worker's rights. A living wage for the worker and a condition of full employment which bolsters job security are both needed if economic life is to meet human needs.

THE LIVING WAGE

Moral Concept of a Living Wage. The introduction of the concept of a living wage was a great moral achievement for the Church in the nineteenth century. Prior to that time, other and harsher doctrines were accepted both in theory and in practice. Both classical economic theory and the realities of the day left the wages of labor to the price-fixing mechanism of a free market. Labor was treated as a commodity, with its wage governed exclusively by conditions of supply and demand. Furthermore, it was widely held that the wage fund available for the payment of workers was a relatively stable amount, so that the pressure of increased population would only lead to misery and starvation. The Iron Law of Wages was a shackle binding labor to unending wretchedness.

At the time, some moralists justified this condition, at least in terms of the virtue of strict justice, in that the labor contract was freely entered upon. A worker agreed to accept a given rate of pay by the fact that he willingly accepted the job. Perhaps in charity, or even in distributive justice, there might be a claim for more. But contractual justice was satisfied when the wage agreed upon was paid. Moreover, the equality of justice was met when the worker received the market value of his services. Value was appraised as a result of the interaction of supply and demand schedules in a free market and expressed in terms of the price of labor (wages). Hence the going rate for labor was considered the just rate.

Karl Marx and the socialists reacted strongly to this trend, swinging to the other extreme. They held that all value arose through labor, so that the worker was entitled to the full amount of the value of the product. Socialism denied to capital any right to a return from gains achieved through the labor of workers. The appropriation of such surplus value was considered theft.

Popes Leo XIII and Pius XI opposed both extreme views. While Pope Leo stated that through the labor of workers states grow rich, his successor clarified his thought by noting that labor's contribution is wonderfully enhanced by machinery and other physical capital. Both upheld the right of management and investors to their just share from the joint product. But, at the same time, they denied the theory that labor was a commodity whose value was to be determined exclusively by the market. In ringing words, Pope Leo stated that over and above the wage contract there is natural justice, the imperious demand that the wage be sufficient to support the worker who is thrifty and upright. Here again, his illustrious successor added clarity, by specifying that this wage be sufficient to support not only the worker, but his family as well.

The argument given to justify the claim in justice for a living wage derives basically from the dignity of man. In the labor market, a worker is selling more than an economic service. He is offering his work as the only normal means he has for human existence. The wage he receives affords him the wherewith to live as befits a man. This means, not only food, clothing, and shelter for himself, but also the requirements for family living, since family life is normal for most men. He must receive enough to live in decency at any given time and to make provisions for sickness, old age, and like contingencies of existence.

Accordingly, there is an *intrinsic value* in human labor which serves as a basis for a claim in strict justice. The market value of such work might, from the moral point of view, be considered as almost irrelevant in terms of the basic right to live. When medieval moralists wrote of a just price, they noted that the need of the seller did not justify a buyer in driving down a price below its fair level (unless, perchance, the buyer did not want the article at its fair price and was buying merely to accommodate the seller). Since the worker is selling something of intrinsic worth: services which are both personal (and hence affected with human dignity) and necessary for his existence, there is necessarily a floor upon wages. Above the minimum amount needed for decent living, it would be allowable and just to establish differentials based on skill, zeal, initiative, resourcefulness, and similar qualities. The market value of such contributions might legitimately be considered.

The reasoning used above is not based on individual needs, but upon the basic requirement for all men to live as befits normal human beings. This is what moralists term the *absolute* family living wage, in contrast to a relative wage based on special situations. Hence male workers should be paid enough to support a normal family in decent comfort. It would not be unjust, necessarily, for a lower wage level to exist in classes of work usually reserved for single women or minors. If, however, such work were competitive with that of family men, so that their wages were being driven down through such competition, social justice would be violated. It would then be a duty for all concerned to change the institutions of society so that this evil would be remedied. Such methods as unionization, universalizing collective-bargaining contracts in an industry, prohibiting industrial homework, or insisting upon equal pay for women doing the same work as men would bring about this result. On the other hand, where family needs are above normal, either because of a large number of children or excessive sickness, the individual employer is not bound in justice to meet this need. This situation can be met through a family-allotment system, medical insurance, and suitable employment for older children.

There may be individuals in the working force who are subnormal in terms of their contribution to production. Such might be the case with the very old, learners, and handicapped persons. While their claim in terms of human dignity is equal to that of a robust and able worker, the individual employer would not usually hire them if he had to pay a wage equal to that of a worker who contributed a normal share to the output. In such cases, there would be an analogy to the buyer who offered less than the intrinsic worth of a product simply as an accommodation to the seller. He would not, in the circumstances, hire their labor at a rate determined by their basic needs. This argument applies especially to handicapped persons since, as a rule, learners and the very old do not have the same needs (as a class) as do fathers of young children. Accordingly, an employer would not necessarily act unjustly in paying a lower rate to inefficient workers, especially when he hired them as a service to the workers themselves.

The standard of a decent living wage varies according to time and place. It is relevant to the resources and economic organization of a given country. Of course, there is a basic minimum of food, clothing, and shelter necessary to sustain life itself. But the higher standard of decent comfort is relative to economic conditions. An American housewife and her teen-age daughters would feel a sense of real deprivation today if they did not have some nylon or rayon stockings. Such might not be the case with a Central European peasant woman. Hence, there is no absolute, world-wide living wage. The requirement in strict justice is that an employer pay a wage suitable for an adult male to support an average family in decent comfort. Above this, social justice requires that the institutions of national and international society be such that economic life function smoothly and prosperously. Every effort should be made to see that the earth's resources be exploited to the full extent made possible by technical progress and sound organization of economic life. Then wages paid can mean a maximum standard of living, in view of the resources and knowledge of the time and place.

It may be objected that, in American social life, there is excessive emphasis upon conventional standards of living which are far more costly than such absolute needs as adequate food, clothing, housing, medical care, and education. Thus, it is held that as incomes rise needs also rise. What is a luxury today may be a conventional necessity tomorrow. We are like squirrels in a cage, very active but going nowhere. There is some merit in this objection, but it could be carried too far. In the United States today some families lack the minimum in the field of absolute needs. Here the productive ability and the earnings of the husband must be enhanced so that he can provide adequate food, clothing, housing, and medical care for his dependents. The first need in social justice is a proper structure of economic society, so that all able and willing men can earn a living wage for the care of their families. When such a stage is reached, we can then face the problem of conventional necessities, adjusting our standards to the productive capacities of our economy.

An Obligation in Justice. One of the most difficult problems in connection with the right to a living wage has been its definition in terms of justice. Older writers often held that the contractual obligation of wages held in justice, but that a living wage (apart from contract) was binding only under the virtue of charity. The definite expression of the papal encyclicals served to clear up this difficulty, but some controversy remained. With moralists agreed that payment of a living wage was a matter of justice, it was still argued whether this obligation was in commutative, distributive, or social justice. The importance of this discussion is great. If the payment of a living wage is due in commutative justice, then problems of restitution arise when the obligation has been willfully evaded. If the denial of a living wage is excusable at the time (because of inability to pay), what would be the obligation subsequently if the employer made a fortune? Would he be obligated to make up the difference between actual wages and the living wage over the years when he was unable to pay? These questions indicate the difficulties which surround the application of strict justice to this question. In terms of personal fault, a sin against charity or social justice may be as serious in God's eyes as a violation of strict justice. But the added problem of restitution makes repentance more difficult in the latter case.

Many writers quote papal authority, teaching on a clear question of morals, to favor the thesis of an obligation in strict justice. Pope Pius XI spoke of the "salary due in strict justice to the worker and his family" (*A.C.,* No. 32). In summarizing his treatment of capital and labor in *Quadragesimo Anno,* he says: "Relations of one to the other must be made to conform to the laws of strictest justice — commutative justice, as it is called — with the support, however, of Christian charity" (No. 110). An examination of the Latin texts of these encyclicals reinforces these opinions, since the term *aequalitas* is frequently used, a term which applies properly only to strict justice. Again, the discussion in *Quadragesimo Anno* (No. 73) of the possibility of dissolving a business unable to pay a living wage indicates the extreme gravity of the obligation. It is true that such a drastic measure could also be required by social justice. But the context — a Christian discussion between workers and the employer on the matter — seems rather to imply strict justice. It might be compared to a proceeding in bankruptcy, where creditors discuss with a debtor the advisability of continuing a business, with the possibility of further loss, or of dissolving it at once to salvage the assets which remain.

Moralists generally have been reluctant to accept this thesis. Only the weight of papal authority served to sway many of them to change their views in more recent editions. Much of their difficulty arose from the apparent lack of *aequalitas* between the wage demanded for the worker and the market value of his services. While these writers recognized that moral impossibility to pay (because of competition and the like) would often excuse the individual employer from this obligation, yet they hesitated to promulgate an obligation which must be so frequently ignored in practice. Some may have been affected by the special problems in the case of substandard workers. Finally, there was the lack of the clear definition which one usually expects in duties holding in strict justice. Even if one holds to the absolute, as contrasted with the relative family living wage, it still varies according to time and place, even within a given country. Thus, in the United States, costs of living are generally less in small towns and rural villages than they are in large cities. One would then have a strict obligation, but with prudent and informed men possibly disagreeing as to the exact terms involved.

These difficulties are not insurmountable. The equality of justice is furnished by the intrinsic value of human labor, in that it is both personal and necessary for man's normal existence. Where a worker is a substandard producer, an employer may pay less than the just price (in terms of intrinsic value) as a favor to the worker.[1] Nor is the problem of widespread exemption from this obligation, because of impossibility to pay, necessarily serious. As the Pope clearly states, such a condition brings into play a new obligation, in social justice, to join in group action to change the institutions of economic society, so that the causes of injustice will be removed. Finally, the lack of precision in determining an obligation does not excuse employers from a fair and reasonable effort to pay a living wage. In the United States, particularly, there are sufficient cost-of-living studies to permit a rough approximation of a family living wage in any locality. One might compare this problem to the obligation arising from an automobile accident, in which a car was demolished and the passengers seriously injured. It is difficult to assess the exact value of an automobile, unless it is new, and even more of a problem to evaluate the loss suffered through injuries, temporary or permanent. Here is a case where the obligation in justice is often clear, but not necessarily exact.

In terms of individual conscience, an employer is bound to pay a living wage to adult male workers, where the general class of work is such as normally to attract heads of families. Even if the worker is unmarried, he must receive a salary which permits him to look forward to marriage. If the class of workers be normally unmarried, such as young girls acting as stenographers or sales clerks, he may then pay an individual living wage rather than a family wage. But if the employer is paying women lower wages for the same amount and quality of work as is done by

---

[1] See St. Thomas Aquinas, *Summa Theologica*, II, II, 77, 1.

men, he certainly offends against social justice and the common good. He is acting unjustly toward such of his competitors as may be employing men to do the same work. He is also acting contrary to the demands of the common good.

When the employer cannot pay a living wage, because of unfair competition or the unhealthy state of the industry (not the firm) he is then excused from his duty in strict justice, but bound in social justice to seek better economic conditions so that he may be able to pay a living wage. If, however, the reason for inability to pay is inefficient management, obsolete methods or equipment, and like conditions in the firm, he is not of necessity excused from his obligation. Rather he should seek to modernize his production methods and, if necessary, write off obsolete equipment through a loss of capital or a petition in bankruptcy. If such an approach is not feasible, he must consider whether the welfare of his workers and the common good might be better served if he went out of business. Here it must be noted that the Pope did not command dissolution of business in all cases. There are many instances in American labor history where temporary wage sacrifices by unions tided a firm over a bad period and enabled it subsequently to prosper and pay union wages.

Some writers have discussed the question of the relative priority of wages to profits and interest when a question of paying a living wage arises. Here would be a conflict of rights, since the right to profits and interest is also in justice. It has been held that in such cases, the claim of a living wage would have priority, since it is the worker's only method of decent livelihood, whereas the employer may have other resources, such as savings or, in extreme cases, the possibility of becoming a laborer himself. Discussions of this nature, while theoretically attractive, are often unrealistic. In many cases, an equal distribution of all profits among workers would not raise their wage level appreciably. Interest claims are legal debts, and default on them would put a firm into bankruptcy. Even more important is the problem of social justice, involving the common good. If the profit incentive were removed, industry would stagnate because of the lack of new investment or even replacement of deteriorating capital.

The crux of the problem is not normally a matter of distribution of the product of an individual firm, as Pope Pius XII noted in his letter to *Semaines Sociales* in 1947, but rather that of increasing production so that there will be a larger product to be distributed. The discussion just summarized considers the economy in static terms, whereas its dynamic aspects are more important. This does not preclude the possibility that in individual cases abnormally large profits or salaries for management have been paid at the expense of the worker. Such situations should be treated as they arise, but, in general, the payment of a living wage will be made possible only through the reform of the institutions of society, rather than through a wider distribution of an inadequate total product. Of course, proper distribution of income may be one of the institutional reforms to be achieved. But, in this case, it will be sought in terms of its dynamic effect on economic expansion, rather than as an egalitarian measure of distributive justice.

Undoubtedly moralists will define the problem of restitution in terms of the reasonable and flexible norms already found in books of theology. Thus, if an employer were excused, through moral impossibility, from the obligation to pay a living wage, it would hardly seem likely that moralists would hold him to subsequent restitution when his conditions changed. Rather a current obligation would commence at the time he became able to pay. In this respect, he would be judged by moral principles analogous to those used in cases of bankruptcy. By contrast, if an employer were able to pay and fully aware of his obligation when he refused to pay, he would be held in strict justice to restore the difference between the actual salary and a reasonable living wage. Even this requirement would be subject to the normal conditions laid down by theologians for restitution, with certain excusing circumstances qualifying the duty of restitution. These points are noted, not to explain away any obligation, but rather to remove the objection that commutative justice could hardly apply to a living wage, since it would create intolerable burdens utterly impossible to enforce.

Problems connected with a living wage and the dignity of labor should be a special concern of priests and religious who are in the position of employers. In the past, our record in this regard has not always been good. Church institutions have at times been notorious both for low wages and arbitrary practices, such as the discharge of workers who have given most of their lives to an institution, and who are let out either because of old age or a change of administration. Cynics have remarked that some in our midst apply vows of poverty to workers, even though Canon Law makes no provision for vicarious acceptance of religious vows. Undoubtedly, such situations occur with the best of motives. Church institutions rarely have adequate funds, so that their administrators understandably try to economize in the attempt to have the most money for the primary purpose of the venture. This would be especially true for schools, institutions of charity, and even some parishes. Yet charity should not be served at the expense of justice. We should give good example in regard to the social teaching of the Church as well as in matters of piety.

Many bishops now require that wages and working conditions be considered in letting construction contracts. It would be most desirable that when bids are let, the award go, not to the lowest bidder absolutely, but to the lowest bid from a reputable firm which pays decent wages and treats its workers fairly. Likewise, the Church as employer cannot afford to lag behind in other phases of industrial relations, such as proper hours, working conditions, grievance machinery, seniority provisions, protection from arbitrary discharge, security for old age, and such normal features of reasonable employment. These are usually matters of justice, not works of supererogation. We should be more reluctant than lay employers to seek excuse from such obligations on the grounds that we cannot afford to meet them.

The emphasis upon commutative justice in the matter of living wages should not obscure the fact that the primary problem here is a matter of social justice. Only when the institutions of society are reformed to eliminate unfair competition, disorder in economic life, unemployment, and depressions, can we hope to have a fair standard of living for all. Some of these adjustments will be noted in detail when the economic implications of a living wage are treated subsequently. So vital are these requirements in social justice that one of the best-known commentators on *Quadragesimo Anno* holds that the obligation in strict justice to pay a living wage does not come into effect until society is so reorganized (through social justice) that the economic value of a workers' contribution equals a living wage. He would make the obligation absolute in social justice, but only conditional in commutative justice. "If, however, the economic structure is disturbed, or if it proves to be impossible to give labor its proper place in the system, then the value of work done will more or less fall short of family requirements. Then the employer cannot be required, either on the basis of commutative justice or for some other reason, to pay family wages. On the contrary, in this instance he is unable to pay them. The attempt to pay them in spite of it would merely result in further dislocation of the economic structure, and would endanger the employer himself."[2] On this reasoning, the employer would be bound in strict justice only to pay a going wage, but in social justice he should cooperate to make a living wage possible. While this reasoning was not followed in the discussion above, it is nonetheless a carefully thought out interpretation of the encyclical. Certainly its paramount emphasis on social justice as making the payment of a living wage possible is beyond exception.

Standards for a Living Wage. While it is difficult to define with precision a money figure for a living wage, the task is not insuperable. There are variants in costs of living according to time and place. The determination of what is a typical family involves some arbitrary decisions. Nevertheless, there exist sufficient data for estimates of living costs and means for adjusting

---

[2] O. von Nell-Breuning, *Reorganization of Social Economy*, p. 177.

these figures as costs increase or decline. The basic tool available at this writing is the city worker's family budget, as determined by the Bureau of Labor Statistics for June, 1947. It was based on studies in thirty-four cities, with a four-person family as the base. The father was thirty-eight years old, the mother thirty-six and not gainfully employed, and the children included a thirteen-year-old boy in high school and an eight-year-old girl in grade school. It estimated costs in terms of a moderate budget, above the subsistence level and below the luxury level. The figure given would of necessity be adjusted for families of different sizes. The Bureau considers that a two-person family would need 65 per cent of the budget; a three-person family, 84 per cent; and a five-person family, 114 per cent. The budget includes actual costs of food, clothing, housing, medical care, taxes and contributions, and moderate comforts, such as cigarettes and motion pictures.

The family lives in a five-room dwelling where the wife does all the cooking, cleaning, and laundry without paid assistance. They have a mechanical refrigerator and a washing machine. Meat is served several times a week, with cheaper cuts on week-days and a more expensive meat dinner for Sunday. Turkey is served on Thanksgiving. Little is allowed for luxury goods purchases: the children get an ice-cream cone and a bottle of soft drink per week, and the father one bottle of beer a week. He buys one heavy suit every two years and a light suit every three years. His wife gets a new heavy wool coat every four years and four dresses a year. In largest cities, transportation is public, but in smaller places, the family owns a cheap, used car. They have a small radio and attend a movie about once every three weeks. They do not have a telephone, but make three paid calls a week. A small amount of life insurance is carried. Modest contributions are made to religious and charitable groups.

For the family given, the cost of living in June, 1947, ranged from a high of $3,458 in Washington, D. C., to a low of $3,004 in New Orleans, La. About 34 per cent of such families in Washington in 1947 received less than this amount. Surprisingly, single-person spending units were below their budget ($1,769) in the same ratio. On the other hand, about half the six-person families were below the estimated budget ($4,512) for their group.[3]

While Washington living costs are among the highest in the country, the differential between large cities is not too great. In 1947, the median cities surveyed, Richmond and Cleveland, had four-person budgets of $3,223 and $3,200, or about enough to permit a five-dollar a week wage differential between these cities and Washington. Smaller cities may have lower rents and food costs, but the differences are not substantial. Land cost and local taxes

TABLE 3

HELLER COMMITTEE BUDGET FOR FAMILY OF FOUR

San Francisco

BUDGET FOR WAGE EARNER

Item	Annual cost including sales taxes with controlled rent	
	September, 1948	September, 1949
Total cost	$4,111.22	$4,040.54
Income and payroll taxes	275.82	263.00
Federal income tax	215.82	203.00
Unemployment compensation disability benefits tax	30.00	30.00
Old Age insurance tax	30.00	30.00
Total consumption items	3,835.40	3,777.54
Food	1,408.51	1,321.27
Clothing	428.05	407.78
Housing	450.00	456.00
House operation	131.65	132.06
Furnishings	137.29	135.44
Miscellaneous	1,279.90	1,324.99
Automobile	439.06	467.09
Medical and dental care	282.16	290.73
Life Insurance	115.27	115.27
Recreation	119.50	120.48
Other items	323.91	331.42

[3] *Monthly Labor Review*, Dec., 1948, p. 623. See also "City Worker's Family Budget" (Washington: Bureau of Labor Statistics, 1947), and the Heller Committee budget given in Table 3.

are lower and hence business rents and needed price markups can be adjusted downward. But a lower rate of turnover may often cancel this advantage. With national chain stores and mail-order houses available to nearly everyone, it is difficult to see where important differences could arise in the cost of goods. Services are generally cheaper in small towns, rents are lower, and some families can obtain supplementary income through growing some of their own food. But a very large percentage of our population lives in large cities and must meet these costs. When the 1947 figures are adjusted to 1950 costs, the weighted average cost for a four-person family in the cities studied for January, 1950, is $3,370.

In face of these costs, average weekly earnings in all manufac-turing industries were about fifty-six dollars in early 1950. Some heavy industries paid nearly seventy dollars, many paid sixty, but textile (employing many women) paid from forty-five to thirty-five. Soft-coal mining reached a high of seventy-five, but retail trade averaged about forty. No statistics are available to permit an accurate breakdown in terms of men and women workers, but a rough estimate would give the average male worker a weekly wage of sixty dollars, whereas a woman would receive slightly less than forty.

The most recent income figures for families apply to the year 1948. Census Bureau studies indicate that, during that year, 17.5 million families (out of a total of 38.5 million) received less than $3,000 a year total income. An additional 8 million were in the $3,000–$4,000 range. Since 4 of the 17.5 million below $3,000 were farm families, an allowance can be made for lower living costs and for nonmonetary income in their cases. Of the 13.5 mil-lion remaining, 3.5 million may be deducted to allow for the very old or the very young. But a hard core of 10 million urban fam-ilies remains, composed of family heads who might be expected to have children. About 1.7 million urban families of four or more persons received less than $2,000 in 1948. The exclusion of farm families does not imply that there are no cases of extreme poverty in rural areas. Even with every allowance for lower costs and nonmonetary income, the fact that 1.7 million farm families had less than $1,000 income in 1948 indicates economic distress. The impact of poverty may be lessened in many cases because there are so many two- and three-person families in the United States. About 60 per cent of our families have less than four persons, and only 20 per cent have more than four persons. It is probable that economic conditions, however, are themselves an important factor in bringing about family limitation.[4]

While we do not have enough statistics to paint a picture of absolute accuracy, the general trend of the situation is clear. The Church upholds the right to a family living wage. And Catholic teaching certainly does not favor the average of two children as an ideal family. We preach against artificial birth control and consider at least three or four children as normal in a family. If we consider the six-person family as reasonable, then living costs in large cities would range from about $4,500 to $5,000 for this family in 1950. On the basis of the 1950 average wage for manufacturing, we might conclude that male workers would generally receive about $3,200 annually, or about enough to support a wife and one child in decent circumstances. Since the Church emphasizes the wage paid to the father of the family, so that the wife might be able to bear and bring up children, this figure seems to be the most pertinent. Clearly, then, in this prosperous country, the average worker faces extreme difficulties in raising a family according to Catholic ideals.

It may be objected that the statistics quoted are deficient, in that they fail to include nonmonetary income in the family. Thus, a wife who is adept at sewing and cooking can contribute importantly to family income. She can sew clothes, draperies, and the like. She can also bake bread, make jams, and can various fruits and vegetables when they can be bought cheaply. The husband can learn to do elementary carpentry, plumbing, and electrical work around the house. If land is available, a vegetable

---

[4] The Census Bureau studies are contained in *Low-Income Families and Economic Stability* (Washington: Government Printing Office, 1949). See also the 1948 Survey of Consumer Finances in the *Federal Reserve Bulletin,* June, 1949.

garden can be cultivated. Growing children can share in these tasks as their strength and skills permit. Undoubtedly such methods have been used by many families to supplement an inadequate income. They are also useful in training children to habits of work and responsibility. But there are two difficulties to be faced, before we may feel that large families can become more self-supporting. The first is a problem of education. Our society tends more and more toward a tradition of seeking leisure time in ever greater quantities. The family which followed the pattern outlined above would be, to some degree, fighting a growing trend in the opposite direction. Secondly, many of these activities require more space than is available in city apartments. They presuppose home ownership. But the figures given above show how difficult it would be for the average couple to take the risk of purchasing a home.

In the light of these cold statistics, Catholics in the United States might well indulge in prolonged and serious thought. While we preach against artificial birth control, impartial studies show that the size of the average family is shrinking in both Catholic and non-Catholic areas. Yet, we have done little more than exhort and plead against this evil. We have placed a heavy burden on the consciences of individual Catholic parents, stressing the encyclical *Casti Connubii*. But in that very encyclical, and in *Quadragesimo Anno*, Pope Pius XI emphasized the need to change the institutions of society, so that the economic system will be able to sustain the charge of a living wage for all workers. The duty of the individual in marriage is clear, but so likewise is the duty of society and all its members to practice social justice. So long as present conditions remain, we must ask our Catholic parents to bear the painful sacrifices involved in rearing children in large cities today. But the voice of the late Pontiff seems to thunder forth our parallel duty to devote our utmost energies toward achieving the social reforms needed to make family life normal rather than a heroic martyrdom.

In view of these facts, it would be expected that our colleges and universities would be making detailed studies of the problem. We would be in the forefront of those fighting for adequate housing, good medical care at reasonable costs, better wages, and, above all, a comprehensive program of social reform which would so increase our national income that these burdens would be lightened. One would expect hundreds of priests and laymen to be thoroughly trained in Catholic social principles, trying to evolve solutions suitable for the American economy. Working with them would be thousands devoted to the cause of social education and social action. Such would be a logical conclusion from the cold facts about the cost of living and average incomes in America today. But, in all fairness, we must confess that we have not risen to the challenge nor appreciated the full implications of family problems in modern life.

It may be that part of the blame lies with certain families, in the sense that they have yielded too easily to a prevailing philosophy of materialism. Some may be unwilling to sacrifice luxuries or even to embrace the inherent hardships of family life. Perhaps our standard of sacrifice must be raised, as well as standards of living. But this goal likewise calls for more than conventional effort. A certain heroism may be required for the Catholic family to swim against the current. But if we call our people to lives of austerity and sacrifice, we must train them through education, personal spiritual formation, and special services to families, such as Cana Conferences and thorough preparation for marriage. Moreover, where sacrifice is asked, we must not overlook the potent educational force found in personal example.

Economics of a Living Wage. The payment of a living wage is more than a moral problem; it also involves intricate questions of economics. The Pope noted this point, when he asserted that the state of the business and the effect on the common good must be considered in wage determination. It has already been stated that for many businessmen, in the present condition of economic life, the granting of a family wage might be difficult, if not impossible. The answer given then stressed the need for social changes, so that total production would be adequate for such a wage. This point deserves further study.

First, it might be asked whether our physical resources are sufficient to afford the present-day population enough to satisfy minimum reasonable needs. Do we have the raw materials and industrial plant to give a good living standard to 150,000,000 people? This standard means enough food of the proper quality, adequate housing, clothing, medical care, education, and minimum comforts. In this regard, a fairly recent study may be of service.[5] The Twentieth Century Fund estimated in 1946 that an adequate standard of living for Americans is possible in terms of our resources, but that changes must be made and productive capacity expanded. It is obvious from our war production that we can produce enough food. But for a high-quality diet, there should be more emphasis upon meat, dairy products, fruits, and protective vegetables. These are more expensive than starches, cereals, and low-grade proteins, but they are nutritionally more valuable. In this regard, the study noted that education as well as higher incomes would be a factor in raising nutrition levels, since some high-income families were found undernourished as a result of insufficient dietary knowledge.

The housing problem is more difficult. Until 1947, there had been little building of houses since 1929. In the meantime, population expanded and existing housing deteriorated. The result was an acute postwar housing shortage. Construction at high prices served to meet part of this demand, but there was little housing built for low-income groups. Moreover, much of the relatively low-cost housing would be suitable for families with one or two children at most. Here again the economic pressure toward family limitation has been felt. Not only are city apartments strong incentives for the childless or small family, but the typical one- or two-bedroom postwar home in the suburbs follows the same pattern. Hence, if couples who desire large families are going to find suitable housing, steps must be taken either to raise

---

[5] J. F. Dewhurst (ed.), *America's Needs and Resources* (New York: Twentieth Century Fund, 1946). A simplified version of this study was produced in 1949 under the title *U. S. A., Measure of a Nation* (New York: Macmillan).

their incomes or to make such houses available for workers getting present wage rates.

The production of adequate clothing, household furniture, automobiles, and similar items which rate as necessities or comforts would not require any physical changes in our economic system. If they are lacking, the explanation must be found in terms of prices and incomes. To make them available, in many cases, either prices must come down or wages rise. On the other hand, medical care and, to a lesser degree, education can be adequate only if the supply of doctors, nurses, hospitals, clinics, and teachers be increased. This is particularly true for rural areas and depressed regions of the economy such as the South.

Thus, if the demands for a universal family wage be translated into such terms as resources, equipment, and trained man power to produce goods and services, the goal is far from unattainable. On the contrary, time and certain minor adjustments would enable us by 1960 (the date used in the Twentieth Century Fund study) to achieve this result. But the economic problems involved are not so simple. Unquestionably goods and services can be had, but in many cases prices form a formidable obstacle. Here we meet the delicate problem of a proper balance between wages and prices, and among various prices, mentioned in *Quadragesimo Anno*.

There is no one simple solution to this problem. The obvious answer of raising wages without regard to productivity or economic organization is not enough. If wages were raised in certain sections of our economy today, the result would be higher prices and further distortion of price relationships. In other fields, the effect might be declining employment. This might be true for the services, such as domestic help, barbering, waiting on table, serving in hotels, and the like. The only permanent method for raising standards is to lower the cost of goods and services, without lowering wages. Labor cost must go down, but not labor income. With lower prices, real wages (the purchasing value of money wages) will go up. Stating the same idea in a different way, standards of living will rise as productivity increases. There

may be cases where higher standards can be had simply by paying higher wages at the expense of lower profits, but such would
not be true of the economy as a whole. Thus, if the high profits
of 1948 were cut in half and this half distributed among the
nearly fifty million spending units in the United States, average
annual income would be increased from $170 to $250, depending
on the norms used in calculating profits. This would hardly
close the gap between many incomes and the family wage.

Over a long range, increased productivity (or lower costs) can
be achieved by two methods: better economic organization, and
the use of more capital per worker by means of mechanization.
Where an industry or profession is disorganized, too many
workers turn out too few goods or services. The occupation in
question is inefficient. Its products are bound to be relatively
high priced. From the viewpoint of the economy as a whole,
there is a waste of labor. Effort which might be used to turn out
needed goods or services is wasted in unproductive tasks. The
housing field is a good illustration of this problem. High hourly
wages, often coupled with restrictive labor practices; hand-pro-
duction methods; multiple handling charges for materials; obsolete building codes; and other similar factors all contribute to
low productivity in this field. If the industry were well organized,
with some degree of mechanization and mass production, it
would be possible to lower costs without cutting the annual
wages of construction labor or reducing the profits of contractors.
The same observation applies to the problem of medical care.
There is duplication of expensive equipment, haphazard methods of payment for services, uneven utilization of specialized
skills, and maldistribution of available facilities. With better organization, through prepayment plans, voluntary clinics, industrial medical plans, and similar devices, it would be possible to
give doctors incomes equal or better than those currently received
and yet give better and cheaper medical care. Some detailed
suggestions on housing and medical care will be given later in
this chapter.

Within our industrial system there is still room for better organization. In spite of constant efforts to improve efficiency, many firms still have a relatively low level of productivity. One field for improvement lies in personnel policies and industrial relations. Good organization and especially good industrial relations can cut costs in many ways. Thus, strikes are costly to a business. Without assuming that all strikes are the fault of employers, it is nonetheless true that some firms go for years without labor trouble, whereas their competitors have had many stoppages. Again, annual labor turnover for American industry averages between 50 and 60 per cent. One firm estimates the cost of each separation at $500, mostly because of the inefficiency of new workers. Absenteeism is also costly. This expense has been cut by good industrial relations. Moreover, there is the problem of partial efficiency of workers. Some engineers hold that the average worker produces about half of an optimum compatible with good health and morale. Here likewise costs can be cut through intelligent policies. Finally, occupational injuries cost American business over two billion dollars annually. Good safety policies not only pay off in employee welfare, but save production expenses and cut the rates of workmen's compensation insurance. Some firms have lowered such insurance rates as much as 25 per cent by a vigorous safety program.

An important example of faulty economic organization is the postwar situation in government. The 1949 federal budget took about 20 per cent of the national income. This means roughly that 20 per cent of our economic energies were being used for services which often are nonproductive in terms of raising national living standards. This is particularly true of the heavy military expenditures which contribute so prominently to the total budget. It happens that under existing world political conditions, such diversion of energy is unavoidable. We must pay for past wars, contain Soviet aggression through foreign aid, and maintain military supremacy. Nevertheless, such diversion of energies and resources, necessary as they may be, will prevent living standards from rising as high as they otherwise might. Further damage is done by waste and inefficiency in government administration. It is equally true that waste and duplication in private business dissipates energies and resources. Competition normally prevents waste, whereas monopoly and monopolistic competition tend to foster it. Only when the maximum of effort is used for the production of desired goods and services, and this in a well-organized manner, can the economic system function at its best and afford the highest standard of living. Needless to say, such a high standard of living does not necessarily mean a maximum of physical output. Leisure, cultural activity, and similar gains are legitimate goals, even at the expense of lower production of goods.

In other phases of economic life, costs can be reduced through mechanization. The better term is "rationalization," as used by Europeans to cover all methods for increasing efficiency. Thus, the cost of food can be reduced through the use of machinery, fertilizer, improved seeds discovered through research, better insect sprays, and irrigation. Spoilage and wastage can be lessened for some foods by means of canning or quick freezing near the farms. (This would also serve the social advantage of decentralizing industry.) New and better fibers, whether natural or synthetic, and improved production processes can lower the cost of clothing. Mass distribution methods also lower costs, but with the social loss involved in bringing big business into a field now occupied by small stores. But mass distributors do not necessarily need to own their retail outlets (large meat producers do not).

If the costs of the necessities of life were to decline, without lowering wages paid to their producers, wage earners would have more money for moderate comforts and services. This would increase employment in the various services, professions, and trades. Here we see both the virtues and the limitations of competition. Competition brings constant pressure to reduce costs, and hence conduces to higher living standards. But at the same time it contributes to the disorganization of economic life (as in the construction industry) and thus raises costs. The ideal, as noted in Chapter VII, would be better organization of society, but with a competitive spur toward bringing new and improved products at lower costs. It is assumed, of course, the lowering costs would not be achieved either by decreasing wages or raising production standards to levels which workers would find oppressive. If legitimate competition were removed, it is to be feared that production would tend to stagnate through inefficiency and bureaucracy. This would mean a declining standard of living, as increased population pressed its needs upon a static or regressing productive mechanism.

How a Living Wage Is Achieved. A universal family wage in the United States will be had only through increased production. This was seen, in part, to involve lower costs achieved by organization and "rationalization." In the light of this general principle, we might examine various concrete methods used to bring about higher living standards.

The commonest device for achieving higher standards of living is the obtaining of wage increases, usually through union negotiations. If higher pay is obtained without causing prices to rise, the worker's standard of living is thereby increased. Should prices be forced up proportionately, normally no real gain is achieved. Possibly the workers directly involved might gain at the expense of other consumers, but ordinarily inflationary wage demands are imitated elsewhere and no one benefits. Hence, it is a good general rule that wage gains should be sought only when they do not involve higher prices. This is possible when profits are sustained for a few years at a level above normal, indicating an increase in productivity in the firm or industry. In the past, unions have generally followed this rule of the thumb, getting occasional raises as profits increased.

The above rule does not mean that there should be a strict correlation between productivity in a given industry or company and its wages. Some industries advance technically much more rapidly than others. If wages followed suit, great inequalities would result. Where technological progress is dramatic, it is better that prices drop thereby benefiting the entire community. Likewise, when a firm secures exceptional profits through good management, whereas its competitors' profits are low, workers should not base their claims on the exceptional firm. This would lead either to unequal wage rates in the industry or disruption of the industry through excessive demands upon less efficient employers.

Some exceptions might be noted to the principle just explained. Thus, when an inflationary situation exists, workers may usually demand increases so as to maintain a previous standard of living, even though this may bring the risk of further price rises. This exception might not hold in great emergencies, such as war, when it might be expected that standards of living would decline. The same is true when there are at a given time irremediable shortages. Thus, if for some reason the supply of meat animals was quite low, it would be foolish to demand higher wages so that the workers could buy more meat. It usually takes about two years to bring up the levels of herds and flocks, and no wage increases can change this fact. Wage changes cannot bring about improvement when shortages are physical and not easily remedied. They may help when low supply is due to economic reasons and the prospect of a better market will bring about necessary adjustments.

A second case for wage increases, even at the expense of higher prices, would occur in industries or occupations where existing wages are badly substandard. In such cases, the higher prices would be acceptable, since the community should not receive cheap goods or services when this involves sweatshop work. At times, however, such advances might cause the market for the product to contract and thereby lead to unemployment in the industry. This is not necessarily bad, since it would bring about a better allocation of labor resources, directing these workers into fields where their labor produces more economic value and hence gives them higher wages. Timing is important in these situations. If advances are sought at a time of prosperity and full employment, adjustments can be made more easily. When they are forced as business declines, workers may be laid off with no alternative employment available. But gradual changes will bring about a better balance between various prices and lead more workers into industries which can pay good wages.

While it is a general rule that wage increases should be noninflationary, it is well that labor exerts a gradual but consistent pressure for higher standards. This forces business to increase efficiency and thereby justify the higher wages. In theory, higher wages should follow productivity increases. But moderate demands (averaging about 2 to 3 per cent increase in standards per year, the long-term American average gain in productivity) need not necessarily await proved cost declines, since experience shows that they will usually bring about the condition they presuppose. Gradualness of change is vital, since this permits adjustments without undue disruption of existing price relations. In all this, it is assumed that labor is doing its share and not indulging in limitation of output, feather-bedding, or similar restrictive practices. The economy loses when production is curtailed, whether this be done by business or labor monopoly.

This same reasoning applies to legal minimum wages. Certain economists argue that the setting of legal minimum wages is harmful. They conclude that it will lead to lowered employment in the industry, because higher prices will generally cause contracting markets. It is held that, in a competitive economy, workers receive the economic value of their contribution.[6] Hence, instead of raising the real wage of workers, such laws would only exclude less efficient workers and thus drive them into further competition with low-paid workers in noncovered fields.

From a *static* viewpoint there is partial merit in this reasoning. It is only partial, since it overlooks the possibility that an employer may be exploiting a worker, paying him less than the economic value of his contribution. Under perfect competition such ex-

---

[6] This argument was presented cogently in a pamphlet entitled "The Economics of Minimum Wage Legislation" (Washington: Chamber of Commerce of the United States, 1947). For a contrary view, see R. A. Lester and J. Shister (edd.), *Insights into Labor Issues* (New York: Macmillan, 1948), Part II. See also A. M. Ross, *Trade Union Wage Policy* (Berkeley: Univ. of Calif. Press, 1948).

ploitation is, in theory, impossible. The worker would find another employer who would bid higher for his services. But competition in the labor market is quite imperfect. The barriers of custom, immobility of labor, and lack of knowledge of job opportunities prevent many workers from securing the best price for their labor. In such cases it is possible that a worker is being paid less than he earns, so that a minimum wage might raise his income without affecting prices or employment.

Moreover, when the *dynamics* of the situation are considered, wages may be raised even in situations where the worker is currently paid his full economic value. Higher labor costs will generally force employers to seek means for lowering costs. New machines will be used and more efficient methods adopted. As a result, workers will earn the higher wages which they now receive. Such adjustments take time, so that higher minimum-wage standards should be introduced slowly and with much flexibility. While some industries or firms may founder in the process, the economy as a whole should benefit.

What is sought, above all, is a gradual reorganization of production, so that our labor force will earn a family wage. The actual achieving of this reorganization is a matter of "rationalization," but sensible pressures by organized labor and minimum-wage laws will stimulate business in this direction. At the same time, labor-management co-operation should be promoted as a method of increasing efficiency in plants and industries. Workers must become cost-conscious in matters of waste, absenteeism, slowdowns, and indifference. Furthermore, labor must realize that business needs the profit incentive if it is to attract needed capital for mechanization and expansion. Labor unions should support such tax revisions as are necessary to bring about economic growth. Only if the economy is growing, particularly in the form of new industries with highly productive machinery, can we shift workers gradually from low-paying, marginal occupations to jobs which can sustain a decent wage level.

It must be further recognized that in some cases more drastic measures must be taken. Where an industry is thoroughly sick and disorganized, wage pressures may only add to the problem. Such is certainly the case with the construction industry, where high hourly wages did not bring about a decent annual wage during the 1930's. Labor added to its own difficulties by restricting production through quotas, rejection of mechanized help, and other practices which lowered productivity. Yet union practice, while suicidal in the long run, was intelligible as a short-range program. Workers were trying to spread work and stretch out jobs. Little would be gained if labor were to accept lower wages and increase production, while the industry was disorganized. Only when unions, organized business, and possibly government get together on a long-range plan to bring planning and efficiency into this industry, can we hope to have it sound and prosperous.[7]

As practical wage hints, the suggestions found in the A. F. of L. *Labor's Monthly Survey* have been most helpful. The older labor organization is more aware of cost and profit problems than has always been the case with its younger rival, the C.I.O., whose programs emphasize over-all purchasing power, without going into the economics of particular industries as carefully as does the A. F. of L. A few summary points drawn from various sources may be listed here:

1. Gradual wage increases without price increases (about 2 to 3 per cent annually) are normally sound.

2. Wage standards may be maintained in times of inflation (unless absolute shortages demand a lower standard of living), even though prices may rise.

3. Wage levels may be improved by union action or minimum wages in substandard industries, even at the expense of higher prices and economic adjustments in the industry.

---

[7] A release issued by a San Francisco union showed that in 1948, with union workers getting from $12 to $22.50 a day, total on-site labor costs for three houses selling for $12,000 each was $1,829.15 per house, or about 15 per cent (*The Labor Leader*, March 28, 1949, p. 2). National averages are higher, with one third the cost of building attributable to labor on the site. See *Monthly Labor Review*, May, 1949, "Labor Share in Construction Cost of New Houses." Nevertheless, building-trade unions have been notoriously conservative and have taken little initiative toward bringing about better economic conditions in their industry.

4. Equalization of wages for the same work in the same industry is a sound short-range objective. Equalization of wages in different industries and occupations requiring comparable skill is a suitable long-range objective. It is long range because the state of economic organization (*Q.A.*, "the state of the business") differs and adjustments are necessarily slow.

5. Since a universal family wage presupposes countless changes in economic life, labor should co-operate with management in increasing productivity, facilitating investment and expansion, and reorganizing sick industries.

6. The seeking of higher wages merely because of a monopoly power held by labor, beyond the needs for a decent wage and without accompanying productivity increases, would be morally wrong and contrary to the common good. It might conceivably violate strict justice by forcing conscientious employers, who were paying good wages, out of business.

7. Sharp lowering of costs through increased productivity should be passed on to the consumer after labor, management, and investors receive their proper shares. Since many sections of the economy can be "rationalized" only with difficulty, workers in these fields will be more likely to gain through lower general prices than through higher wages.

8. In theory, a good argument can be made for keeping money wages stable, with all gains passed on in the form of lower prices, thereby raising real wages. This would enable persons with fixed incomes, such as government and other salaried employees, to share the gains of higher productivity without periodic pressures for increased salaries. On the other hand, some economists favor gently rising price and income levels on the grounds that they stimulate business enterprise and prevent debts from becoming increasingly burdensome. It is difficult to resolve this question on a theoretical level, since there are sound arguments for both points of view. Accordingly, no strong objection can be raised to the union practice of seeking higher money wages, where productivity has increased, rather than passing on all gains in the form of lower prices. Of course, when the gain in productivity

is exceptional, as a result of some revolutionary saving, it is expected that prices would be lowered.

In the light of all these points, the much-criticized 1948 General Motors agreement would appear to have more merit than has been conceded by businessmen and labor leaders. This agreement adjusted wages upward or downward (with a limitation on the downward movement) as cost of living changed, and provided for an annual 3 per cent increase on the grounds that greater productivity should lead to higher standards of living. The cost-of-living clause maintains standards when prices fluctuate, and the annual standard-of-living increase is desirable. Contracts of this nature would remove wage negotiations from union agreements and thus get rid of a major source of friction and uncertainty. Nor should it be objected that union politics demand dramatic gains, so that the workers will appreciate the value of the union. A sound union security clause, good grievance machinery, and extensive labor-management co-operation will entrench a union, without the necessity of dramatic but upsetting wage demands. This, of course, presupposes employer willingness to support measures which will strengthen union security. Such a presupposition is not generally too much to expect in these days, except where unreconstructed individualism obtains with employers or union leaders.

Housing and Medical Care. The ideal solution for the economic problems of family life would be the payment of a family living wage, achieved by the methods outlined above. These changes will not be made overnight. In the meantime there are many pressing problems to be met. Until they are solved, there is a need for more immediate measures in the fields of housing and medical care.

The long-range problem of housing involves steps to reorganize the industry so as to achieve greater efficiency and lower costs. For present-day needs, however, certain steps can be taken, usually with government help. Many efforts can be made on both federal and local levels. Thus, the federal government could finance research into methods for securing low-cost housing. There are devices for achieving a greater degree of standardization in building, without condemning people to live in houses which lack variety and originality. Local pressures could be used to change obsolete building codes, so that new and cheaper materials can be used. In general, building codes should be drawn in terms of function rather than in terms of specified materials (e.g., a wall should be required to support a certain weight, rather than to have a given thickness of concrete, brick, and so forth). State governments might strive for uniform codes throughout the nation, thus avoiding present wasteful practices whereby manufacturers must meet hundreds of varying codes.

The need for government subsidy for low-cost housing is widely recognized today. Under present laws, local communities have considerable discretion as to the use of such funds. Community interest should see that a sufficient proportion of these dwellings contains three or more bedrooms, so that larger families can be accommodated in such houses. Moreover, aid could be given to middle-income families in the form of long-term loans at low interest rates. It is to the public interest that such families be given every incentive to own homes in surroundings suitable for family life. Activities of this nature form an important duty of Catholic social action, blessed by the Holy Father as recently as July, 1949.

Government housing experts estimate that population increase alone during the decade commencing with 1950 would call for six million new dwelling units. In addition, there will be need for replacement or major rehabilitation for about sixteen million dwellings. It can be seen that even the high construction rates of 1948 and 1949 of about a million units a year must be maintained or exceeded if adequate housing is to be secured for the American family. Actually, it is quite unlikely that this will be done unless some effective method is found to reduce costs.

The problem of medical care is currently surrounded by considerable controversy, much of it unnecessary in that it involves avoidable misunderstandings. In this discussion, three points will be treated: the physical availability of medical care, the costs of medical care, and general health insurance.

In the United States, at this writing, there are important shortages of medical facilities, particularly for rural regions and low-income states. In these cases, there are not enough doctors, nurses, clinics, technicians, and hospitals. It is unlikely that these needs can be met by private initiative, particularly in the low-income states. An argument can be made for federal subsidy both for the construction and equipping of buildings and for the training of necessary personnel. A further problem exists in cities where adequate facilities and trained personnel are available, but where their cost is excessive for low- and middle-income families. The most successful method for meeting this problem is the formation of clinics, whereby a number of specialists work in the same building under some type of common direction. This avoids unnecessary duplication of expensive equipment and makes thorough medical care available at the same price as is currently paid for less adequate treatment. At the same time, it does not lower doctors' incomes or interfere with their full freedom of practice. The promotion of such clinics would be a form of social justice especially suitable for Catholic doctors.

A valuable technique for handling medical costs for some moderate-income families is the institution of industrial or union group health plans. Since it has been estimated that the cost of sickness, in terms of lost industrial production, is about eight billion dollars a year, or a productivity decline of 5 to 7 per cent, management often calculates that such assistance saves money in the long run. Some firms feel that a direct money profit is made by such programs, while others consider the gain indirect, through better morale and industrial relations. One careful study made by the Industrial Hygiene Foundation showed that a chemical industry spent $21,335 in medical care and estimated its return at $87,032, or $4.08 for each dollar spent. There was less sickness, fewer accidents, and lower insurance costs. Labor turnover also declined. In addition to industry, some labor unions have secured medical care for their members. Thus, the Union Health Center of the International Ladies Garment Workers Union occupies six floors of a New York skyscraper. It has a staff of 148 doctors, 35 nurses, 5 pharmacists, and 27 technicians. This center handled 68,000 persons in 1948, with 410,000 visits by these patients. Patients pay one dollar a visit, as a rule, with the remainder (up to $300 a year) paid by employers through union contracts. Other unions participate in health-insurance devices, without having their own medical centers.

In regard to the costs of medical care, a distinction must be made between ordinary medical care and extraordinary problems. The cost of ordinary medical care is not unreasonable. The total amount spent for medical care in the United States is low, when compared with national expenditure for luxuries. Moreover, the rapid growth of prepayment plans indicates that the economic problems connected with certain types of illness are being met. Nevertheless, there is room for further improvement along these lines. Present-day coverage is more adequate for hospital care than for payment of doctors' bills and the cost of expensive medicines. Hence there is need both for extension of coverage in regard to existing plans and for rapid growth of plans which deal with fees and high-cost medicines. But sound social policy would dictate progress along lines which have proved their worth rather than radical experimentation with new devices.

One problem remains, however, which is not being met adequately today, namely, the cost of extraordinary medical care. In this category one would include chronic illnesses, such as arthritis and certain forms of heart disease; crippling sickness, like poliomyelitis or mental illness; operations which are unusually costly; and disease which requires the constant use of high-cost drugs. Sickness of this type usually wrecks the finances of a family. If it strikes the main wage earner, income is cut off at the same time that needs are greatest. Moreover, such illness is not ordinarily met by present-day prepayment plans. Indeed, the prepayment method is not intrinsically suitable for these cases, since their incidence is scattered and unpredictable. The insurance method is the only logical device for such a situation, just as it is the only sound way of meeting the costs incidental to a fire. Unfortunately, this problem is too often overlooked in the heated discussions surrounding the general argument on health insurance.

The question of extraordinary medical costs might well be considered as a challenge to social action. Possibly the problem might be met by private insurance, analogous to automobile collision insurance. An insurance company might fix a total annual amount to be paid by the patient, either directly or through prepayment plans, and cover all costs above this amount. It is likely that such insurance could meet the requirements of actuarial soundness and yet be relatively inexpensive to the holder. If such needs could not be met through private insurance, however, here would be a case where a limited form of public-health insurance would be justified.

The analysis just given does much to answer the question as to the advisability of national-health insurance. If the approach advocated here is sound, there is no need for a detailed study of the arguments for or against such a plan. Clearly it would be contrary to the principle of subsidiarity for the government to intervene in matters already being handled by private initiative. Even granting the present inadequacy of private approaches through prepayment plans and similar devices, it would be better to aid methods which are basically sound rather than to replace them with a new and cumbersome approach. At the same time, the medical profession would be doing itself a great disservice were it to remain contented with a merely negative approach to the problem of the economics of medical care. It is not enough to fight proposals which it fears might lead to socialized medicine. The real problems which occasioned these proposals must be met adequately and within reasonable time. The state does have the moral right and duty to intervene in matters concerning the common good, when individual initiative fails to meet serious needs. It is primarily the duty of the medical profession to see that sound organization and adequate private payment plans answer the needs of the American public, so that in the future extensive government intervention will not even be seriously considered.

The economic problems of medicine afford an excellent opportunity for social action by thousands of Catholic doctors. They are well aware of our teaching in regard to family life and also know the medical costs of bringing children into this world and rearing them to maturity. Such doctors are within their rights in opposing programs for medical care which they consider unsound and dangerous. But they should at the same time be in the forefront in proposing practical plans for making medical care available, through prepayment, to all families and individuals. They, better than laymen, can suggest methods for lowering the costs of such care without decreasing quality or denying to doctors their proper incomes. Finally, they can endorse the insurance method, whether private or public, for the field where it is really needed, namely, for extraordinary and almost catastrophic expenses from chronic or crippling illness. Such a positive approach would meet the needs of our time, without risking the real values of private initiative and local autonomy.

Social Insurance. The availability of various forms of social insurance constitutes an addition to the worker's wage. One of the elements in a family wage is the ability to make provision for sickness, accidents, and old age. This could be handled in either of two ways: the payment of a wage sufficient to enable an earner to set aside funds for such contingencies, or the establishment of public or private insurance to meet these needs. The former method may be considered theoretically superior, since it leaves more initiative in the hands of individuals. However, the special conditions of modern life offer an argument for social insurance. With instability and uncertainty so prevalent, it is difficult for individuals to save for hard times or old age. The most that the average wage earner can be sure of saving over the years is the amount paid on a life-insurance policy. He may accumulate property, particularly by buying a house, but it is not desirable that a worker be forced to mortgage his house to meet unforeseen needs. In regard to accidents at work and occupational diseases, most states have fairly adequate workmen's compensation laws. The accident coverage is generally good, and there is an increasing tendency toward including diseases incidental to an occupation.

The United States already has other forms of social insurance, including unemployment compensation, old-age and survivors' insurance, and limited aid to states caring for the indigent aged, dependent children, and the blind. These likewise may be considered efforts to meet legitimate needs. Unemployment is a hazard which works the greatest hardships. In modern times, it is difficult even for the most thrifty worker to build up adequate personal reserves for such an emergency. Hence it is much better that funds be gathered to meet this need, rather than force such workers onto relief and public or private charity. Likewise, the conditions of present-day life make it unlikely that most workers will be able to provide fully for old age. The social-insurance principle meets this contingency. Moreover, much can be said for the idea of supplementary pensions paid directly by industry to its employees. The economic system should support a worker throughout his entire life, so that an employer who hires a worker through most of his working life would have an obligation to help support him in his old age. This is but an application of the principle of a family living wage and would, in fact, justify lower take-home pay in view of the amounts set aside for pensions. Social services provided through public or private insurance are real income for the worker and should be added to his cash income in assessing the adequacy of a wage. In addition, industry pension plans tend to lower turnover, increase morale, and thus cut down the cost of production.

At the same time, the current demand for industrial pensions poses serious economic questions. If the pension is based merely on a company promise to pay, without the setting aside of reserves, its value is lessened. Not only is there danger of nonpayment, but the employee who leaves the company has no equity to collect. On the other hand, if the pension is funded, a tremendous investment problem would be faced. Some actuarial sources calculate that widespread, fully funded pensions would ultimately demand private investments of nearly 200 billion dollars, a staggering figure. It would seem that the soundest solution is the enlarging of social security benefits, with private industry pensions supplementing them on a nonfunded basis. While this would leave private pensions less secure, it would avoid the almost impossible investment problem posed by widespread, fully funded pensions. There is no investment issue connected with federal social security, which is basically a bookkeeping system for determining individual credits. Actual payment of old-age and survivors' benefits is made by the current working force to the retired force.

Notice might well be taken of the Family Allowances Act, passed by the Dominion of Canada in 1944. This act gives graded allowances, ranging upward from the first to the fourth child, and downward thereafter. Payments are tax free and made directly to the mothers. This is one of thirty-four schemes existing in various countries, varying from state subsidies to pooled contributions by employers to a common fund for supplementary allowances. In one sense the United States has a family-allowance plan, in that income-tax exemptions of $600 per child mean a current subsidy of at least $120 for each child. This compensates only in part for the average cost of $500 for each additional dependent in a family.

Many Catholic students of the family have advocated the family-allowance procedure as a means of meeting family needs in the United States. These proposals would call for a living wage for the average family as the basic ideal. Above this level there would be grants for children over a given average. The financing of such a project might be arranged through a fund or funds established by various types of contributions. Money could come from employers, employers and workers, or from general tax revenues. Administration could be decentralized, either through state or local governments or through industrial and similar commissions. Certain precedents are available for such a plan, including differential pay for servicemen and for some teachers according to need, and the several social-security grants which depend on need. The arguments in its favor largely stem from the Christian ideal of family life. It is further argued that many services for the family, now obtained through government grants, could be purchased directly by the persons involved, were a family-allowance procedure in effect. Accordingly, the principle of subsidiarity would be better served by this method. On the other hand, the absence of any sustained and organized effort to secure family allowances would make their advent here improbable in the near future. The current American trend, unfortunately, is often in the direction of family limitation rather than family aid as a means of raising living standards.

The economics of social security parallels to a considerable degree the economics of a living wage. To the extent that increased social security means a raising in standards of living, its feasibility depends upon gradual changes in productivity so that the total national income will be able to support these charges. Some of the methods for handling certain contingencies are self-supporting. Such would be the case with industrial medicine or group medical practices which provide total care at a cost no higher than previous haphazard methods. In other cases social insurance payments will, in the long run, mean a lower wage bill for industry. Unemployment insurance, old-age pensions, and even health insurance need not, of necessity, increase the long-run wage bill of industry. There could be different forms for paying workers a wage adequate to meet the hazards of modern life. Most of the costs would need to be met anyway through taxes or charity contributions.

From an ethical point of view, social insurance is an integral part of a family living wage. It could be argued that, with an adequate wage, social insurance would be unnecessary. Such might be the case for predictable burdens, such as old age and death. But even an adequate wage would not provide all workers with means to meet unemployment, sickness, and accidents. These hazards do not fall evenly upon all families. Only the insurance principle, spreading the risk widely, is able to provide protection for everyone. It may be debated whether or not private insurance is preferable to state insurance. In principle, decentralization is desirable. But unemployment can hardly be insured against privately. Nor can the pressing needs of old age await the universal payment of a living wage. Industrial health and pension plans are good, but they cover only a small percentage of the population. A possible answer is government insurance, with full allowance in the form of tax exemption for private plans which meet minimum standards. Thus, if health insurance were universal, but limited to chronic or serious illnesses and to operations, employers might be given full credit for any adequate method they may have adopted, whether it be industrial medicine or union-management health and welfare funds. In this way the advantages of both full coverage and local initiative would be retained. We would have provision for the general welfare, without the welfare state.[8] All this must be qualified by the data to be given in Chapter XII, on the desirability of property distribution as a basic safeguard for liberty. In seeking to protect people in respect to the contingencies of life, we must also be sure that the methods used will not force them to accept security at the price of freedom.

FULL EMPLOYMENT

Even more critical than the question of a living wage is the problem of employment security. Most men, if compelled to make a choice, would prefer a secure job with lower pay to a well-paying job whose future is uncertain. This is especially true of those who suffered during the great depression of the 1930's. Many, although able and willing to work, lost their life savings, their homes, and their other property. Their families suffered from anxiety, malnutrition, and even despair. It was a bleak tragedy to millions and they are not anxious to repeat it.

---

[8] On social insurance, see F. Baerwald, *Fundamentals of Labor Economics* (New York: D. X. McMullen, 1947), Chaps. 11–16; and L. F. Buckley, "Ethical Aspects of Social Insurance" (New York: Paulist Press, 1948). The Ewing Report, *The Nation's Health* (Washington: Government Printing Office, 1948), contains much excellent material on the economics of medical care.

From a technical viewpoint, we may distinguish four types of unemployment: frictional, seasonal, chronic, and cyclical. Frictional unemployment occurs where workers are shifting from one job to another. In many cases immediate changes cannot be made. Hence there are always some workers who are temporarily unemployed. Moreover, some seasonal unemployment is considered normal in industries affected by weather or styles, although today there is much less willingness to accept this as inevitable. Chronic unemployment might also be called underemployment. It denotes a state of balance in economic life, in which production is stable but resources are not being used fully. Thus, we might have a situation where business is prosperous in some ways, but about eight million workers are consistently out of work, as was the case during the years 1938–1940. Finally, there is cyclical unemployment, or the periodic joblessness caused by depressions. Presumably, the depression is followed by a wave of prosperity with full employment again. But with economic imbalance and disequilibrium, another depression will surely follow.

In studying the causes and remedies of unemployment, emphasis will be placed on depressions, since there is considerable overlapping in regard to both causes and cures between chronic and cyclical unemployment. The treatment given here will be brief and almost impressionistic, inasmuch as an adequate discussion of the subject would require at least several chapters and preferably a large volume. Only condensed views on the main issues will be offered.[9]

Causes of Unemployment. One of the major fluctuating elements in our economy is the production of heavy, durable goods such as steel, lumber, automobiles, furniture, refrigerators, and similar items. Durable goods may be divided into two classes: producer goods, such as machines or factories; and consumer products, such as automobiles. The important point about these

[9] For a more lengthy treatment, see J. F. Cronin, *Economic Analysis and Problems,* Chaps. 17–19; F. Baerwald, *op. cit.,* Chaps. 8–10; and S. H. Slichter, *The American Economy* (New York: Knopf, 1948).

goods is that, being lasting, their use may be prolonged indefinitely when conditions preclude their replacement. Construction may be postponed; machines may be repaired rather than replaced; and the family automobile, refrigerator, and radio may be made to serve a little longer. Hence any serious business uncertainty, threatening profit prospects for firms or employment for individuals, can be quickly turned into a depression if fear psychology causes widespread postponed buying of durable goods.

Some instability is inherent in these industries for two reasons. First, in an investment boom there is a tendency to expand capacity beyond the ability of the market to absorb output at current prices. Thus, even with postwar housing shortages, some builders overproduced in certain price classes and were left with unsold houses. Again, many "war baby" producers got into the radio and frozen food industries, so that output clogged the market and some went bankrupt. Secondly, there is a tendency to bunch production in heavy industries. After a war or depression, there is usually a quick rush to modernize plant, replace obsolescent equipment, and embark in new industries. A number of expansion plans mature simultaneously, with the result that heavy industry booms for a few years and then subsides. If no counterbalancing orders are available, such as public works, a Marshall Plan, or an Atlantic Pact, we are likely to lapse into a depression.

A second element of instability is found in our monetary and fiscal system. To the extent that any boom is founded on credit, it has self-limiting factors. Short-term debts are particularly troublesome, since they may not be renewed if future business prospects look doubtful. A wave of forced liquidation of debt brings distress selling of inventories, cancellation of orders, and serious, depression-producing unemployment. Consumer debt can also be a cyclical factor. When consumers go into debt, either through installment purchases or mortgages on homes, they usually refrain from further commitments to buy durable goods. If this happens to a large number simultaneously, the slump in buying of heavy products would be depressing. Unfortunately, there is some tendency for a majority of consumers to buy large amounts of durable goods simultaneously as the nation emerges from a war or a depression. This could mean a self-limiting boom, unless the orders are spread more evenly through government regulation of installment buying and pressure on banks to hold down short-term debt. Even long-term debt is an aggravating factor in depressions, in that it means heavy fixed payments when income is low. This adds to the incentive to cut wages or employment.

Tax policies affect employment levels also. Taxes redistribute income and influence business prospects. A budget surplus, used to retire debt, normally cuts spending and consumption. The reverse applies to a deficit, especially when financed by bank credit rather than through personal savings. Recent tax policies have adversely affected investment, both in bonds and stocks. The Treasury has kept interest rates at an artificially low level, so as to reduce carrying charges on the immense public debt. Since the Treasury rate influences private bond rates, investors do not receive enough to warrant the risk they would take.

This situation is further aggravated by the high surtaxes on personal incomes. A wealthy investor faces several hazards. First, his return is lowered by a 38 per cent corporation income tax. Then, the portion of the net income paid as dividends may be cut in half by surtaxes. Thus, if Mr. Smith, a wealthy man, were to invest $100,000 in a new enterprise, it might make no money for several years. When profits come, they may not be used to offset previous losses beyond two years. If, after five years, the firm earned $20,000 (a very generous estimate) annually on the investment, the net income after corporation taxes would be about $12,000. With present dividend policies, Mr. Smith would receive about $5,000, half of which the government would take in surtaxes. Hence his annual rate of return, when profits were available, would be 2½ per cent, or what he could get from tax-exempt government bonds without any risk.

An unsound fiscal policy stifles investment and hence leads to underemployment. It also makes recovery from a depression more difficult, since there is less stimulus to new investment which would make jobs. Finally, it aggravates excessive concentration of power in two ways. First, corporations tend to expand internally by withholding profits from dividend payments, hence expanding existing units rather than promoting new enterprise. Secondly, government makes up the slack in private investment through public works, thereby increasing the number of persons dependent upon the central government.

A third major element of instability is lack of balance between prices. Prices may get too high or too low for several reasons. Business monopoly, excessive rigidities, or grasping policies by other organized groups, such as farmers or labor unions, can force prices up. When prices are too high, demand for the product normally decreases, causing unemployment. If the product is necessary, such as food, consumers will buy it, but curtail elsewhere. Likewise, when prices are too low, as happened with farmers during the 1920's, large numbers of producers are unable to buy and hence markets are unstable. Faulty organization of economic life, as well as greed, can be a cause of high prices. Such is the case with the construction industry and medical care today. This is a further argument for various devices to cut costs, make goods and services available more cheaply, and hence expand production and employment, thereby leading to higher standards of living.

Finally, there is the factor of income distribution as an influence on economic stability. The use of income varies according to the income levels of the recipients. Thus, low-income groups tend to spend most of their incomes, with very little net savings (apart from insurance) over the years. Higher-income groups do not ordinarily use their entire incomes for consumption. They form the main source of private (as distinguished from corporate and institutional) savings. It is definitely conceivable that a faulty ratio of distribution could lead to an excess of savings beyond the capacity of the investment market to absorb. This is the more true since investment is largely for a mass market, so that if the great mass of low-income consumers were to receive an inadequate share, the general consumption level would not encourage investment. Saved funds would remain idle and cause a depression. The exact ratio of income distribution which would be desirable is difficult to assess, since other factors influence the situation. Thus, today, the bars to private investment in industry are so great that only a small sum of private savings could be absorbed. If the incentive to invest were restored, it is likely that our economy could absorb between 10 and 20 per cent of the national income in the form of total savings, including retained corporate earnings. The lower figure would be used by business, with the remainder going to such forms of investment as houses.

In the light of the complexity surrounding the problem of depressions, it is an oversimplification to consider inadequate purchasing power as the sole reason for a business slump. Our present tax system has produced a greater equalization of incomes than has ever before obtained in American life. In spite of this, the fear of depressions is ever present. Thus, the 1949 recession occurred at a time when both incomes and savings were high. Certainly there is no comparison between income distribution after taxes today and the conditions obtaining in 1929. Nor can mass purchasing power be raised by any simple device, such as raising of wages through union contracts. What may happen is simply the inducing of higher prices and further distortions in our economic structure. Wages are both purchasing power to consumers and costs to business. Assuming that profits are normal, any effort to raise wages (unless labor costs are cut through higher efficiency or mechanization) would be only self-defeating, since prices would rise and cancel the gains. Indeed, unwise wage increases may decrease total labor income, to the extent that higher costs may induce layoffs of workers. Many firms may find that increased prices, caused by such wage concessions, lead to slackening demand and hence curtailed production and employment. Higher wages do not always produce higher purchasing power.

Total purchasing power can be raised if funds are injected from a source outside the productive system, such as a government bonus to veterans or the Marshall Plan, provided this is not financed out of current taxes. The value of such a stimulus depends upon general economic conditions. If there were serious distortion in prices, debt, and investment patterns, such assistance would be only temporary. It would postpone rather than avert a crash. On the other hand, if basic conditions were good, a tonic of this nature might start an economic revival.

The important point is that economic conditions are closely interdependent. As a rule, no one cause is sufficient to bring on a depression, so that no one remedy is usually adequate. Thus, to use an extreme example, if we were to concentrate on purchasing power as the sole cause of depressions, barbers might charge five dollars for a haircut, taxis fix their rates at a dollar a mile, and farmers band together to get fifty cents a quart for milk. Presumably, such actions might raise the income and purchasing power of the recipients, but a widespread following of their example might wreck the national economy. The same is true in reverse, as when businessmen consider wages only as costs, and seek to cut wages when conditions look doubtful. Such a policy not only cuts purchasing power, it also intensifies fear psychology and causes workers to postpone buying durable goods.

The very complexity of the problem raises political difficulties in obtaining a solution. At any given time, there may be several conditions favorable to a business slump or boom. When the event occurs, partisans of a particular solution point with triumph to the "vindication" of their viewpoint. Thus, if a depression were to occur in the years 1950–1952, it could be attributed to any or all of the four major causes noted above, since it can be argued that each of them is upsetting business at this writing. Undoubtedly zealots for one "sovereign" remedy will then argue that business failed because their suggestions were not followed. Thus, a common tragedy, which should be subject to dispassionate and patriotic analysis of the highest kind, becomes a subject of political and pressure-group debate.

Another type of unemployment which has significance today is technological displacement, or machine and efficiency induced unemployment. This belongs under the category of chronic rather than cyclical joblessness, but it deserves mention here. The process of increasing efficiency, whether through machines or better organization, will in some cases cause worker displacement. This would happen whenever the demand for the product or service is not sufficiently elastic to be stimulated by lower prices and thus keep the demand for labor constant. Of course, there are other situations where a cheaper product may be so heavily in demand as to increase employment, even with labor-saving machinery. But it is clear that, in many instances, workers will lose their previous jobs. In the long run, this is not bad, since productivity per worker must be increased if the economy is to produce enough for a living wage for all. But the short-run adjustments create problems which must also be considered in the discussion of unemployment.

Remedies for Unemployment. The matter of remedies for depressions and other causes of joblessness naturally parallels the study of causes. Thus, for the instability in the production of durable goods, two types of cure are offered. The first consists of efforts to iron out the cycles through better forecasting and planning. It is suggested that firms or industries employ economists and statisticians in the effort to predict business trends and future markets. They would be aided by more comprehensive surveys by national groups, both business and governmental. When a boom in construction or machine replacement is in the offing, firms which could postpone capital commitments would be advised to do so. This would be to their own interest, since shortages and competition for available labor and resources tend to raise prices at such times. Hence, if funds could be set aside for later capital use, the firm would get a better bargain. This might apply even when the new plant or equipment would give a minor competitive advantage, since higher costs might cancel out the gains. Government agencies would likewise be encouraged to postpone such public building programs as are not urgently needed. This would save public funds and put more balance into economic life.[10]

As a second remedy for instability in durable-goods purchases, there are several steps available in the form of governmental action. Thus, the regulation of consumer installment buying, as adopted during World War II and the period following, tends to prevent precipitate purchases of durables, especially when these are financed by short-term debt. General government monetary policies also can discourage banks from unwise lending, although currently the money inflation caused by government fiscal policies (financing government deficits with bank credit and depressing the interest rate) negates the powers possessed by our monetary authorities. The Federal Reserve System can put brakes on a boom mainly by curtailing the amount of bank credit available for business loans. It does this by raising the reserves required of banks or by increasing its own lending rate to banks (the rediscount rate). It can also sell government bonds on the open market, retaining the funds and thereby reducing bank reserves. But the Treasury has stifled all these programs by encouraging banks to buy huge sums of government bonds with bank credit. This gives the banks so much reserve that the Federal Reserve System is unable to tighten credit control. Moreover, since the Treasury is supporting the price of government bonds, it is impossible for the Reserve System to sell them freely lest it break the market. Thus, the war between the Federal Reserve System and the Treasury leaves the country almost helpless to control monetary causes of booms. By contrast, the Employment Act of 1946 authorizes in principle the use of public works to balance the economy in times when durable-goods demand is off. War spending in the 1940's quickly liquidated the depression of the preceding decade. Likewise, Marshall Plan aid after the war was an important factor in stimulating business, when certain conditions seemed to presage a recession in private spending.

There is no question but that the postponing of public works

---

[10] For a business plan along these lines, see "Business Management Action Against Depression" (Washington: Chamber of Commerce of the United States, 1948).

so as to level off durable-goods spending is a sound policy. Likewise, when a depression occurs, heavy government spending can afford employment and stimulate business revival, if other conditions have been corrected. But the notion of a permanent government investment program to provide jobs, on the grounds that there is not enough private demand to secure full employment, seems a counsel of despair. It would inflate the already enormous government debt and increase the dependence of the economy upon government. Every effort should be made to remove causes of depressions, so that private business can go ahead, before we increase the area of public control over economic life.

Some suggestions have already been given in regard to monetary and fiscal policies for preventing depressions. There is no space for technical details, but our central monetary system, the Federal Reserve Bank, should have full power to influence bank credit policies and also consumer short-term debt, particularly through installment buying. Here, if anywhere, is a clear case where the common good outweighs particular short-term interests. Indeed, it would be desirable that all commercial banks be under Federal Reserve Control, since unchecked credit inflation can lead to a severe depression.[11] It is most unfortunate that a shortsighted program for cutting the cost of carrying the public debt has acted to deprive monetary authorities of most controls over inflation.

Even more serious are the haphazard tax policies which afflict America today. Revenue is sought with little regard to the economic effect of taxes. Thus, a wartime tax on transportation, enacted expressly to discourage unnecessary travel, was carried over into peace years. If this impedes travel in postwar years, the gains to government may be more than offset by the economic loss of crippling a major industry. Undoubtedly, the serious problems caused by world events call for a higher level of taxation than ever before in history. Yet scientific taxation would remove

---

[11] The Federal Reserve system does not pass on individual loans, but bank inspectors can be severe in appraising loans in times of inflation. Reserve Board policies affect total credit, interest rates, and the like. See J. F. Cronin, *op. cit.*, Chap. 18.

direct burdens which interfere with economic expansion, and collect from the higher incomes and profits made possible by such growth. This observation would surely apply to practical prohibition of private investment as embodied in present corporation taxes and personal income surtaxes. The principle of taxation according to ability to pay could be kept, but with special treatment accorded to income derived from new, job-creating investment.

There would be many technical problems involved in incentive taxation, but the goal of expanding production warrants our experimentation with such devices. As an illustration, new stock issues (not refunding) could be afforded special treatment. Dividends paid on such stock might be subject to ordinary taxes, but not surtaxes, during the first fifteen years after issuance. A new firm, which is not merely a new name for existing firms, could be allowed a fifteen-year period to balance losses against profits. Such proposals might cost the Treasury a minor amount of taxes, but the gain in economic expansion would be worth the sacrifice. Actually, if business continued to expand, total taxes would be higher. Furthermore, the impetus toward stock financing, in contrast to debt, would add to economic stability. The incentive toward new ventures would tend to bring greater competition and reverse the trend toward excessive centralization of power in existing corporations. Nor would this be discriminatory against existing corporations, since their cost of doing business would not be affected. Such a device would restore the incentive to invest, without removing the principle of income taxes graduated according to ability to pay. Undoubtedly the technical difficulties faced in tax reform are enormous. The proposals given above are more easily stated than achieved. But the American people and their Congress must grapple with these problems and work out solutions which meet essential needs.

The question of price rigidity is important in regard to depressions. When costs and prices get out of line in a serious way, they are bound to affect economic life. Higher costs generally squeeze profit margins and cause businessmen to defer expansion and to tighten inventory policies. They contract orders and thus subject the boom to a severe test. If the contraction is not offset elsewhere and becomes rather widespread, it can lead to a depression. On the other hand, price adjustments are healthy in economic life. They tend to promote efficiency and increase productivity. The problem is to secure adjustments without causing a depression. This is best done if the economic system is kept flexible at all times. Then price changes can be going on all the time without reaching a cumulative climax at any given period.

In the business world two factors can keep prices flexible. The first is a policy of encouraging investment, which keeps competition alive and thus promotes efficiency. The second method is a strong antitrust policy intelligently adapted to the needs of our times. A competitive economic system does not so easily develop unbalanced prices. At the same time, monetary and fiscal policy should avoid excessive or deficient money supply, so that price distortions will not be introduced because of faulty monetary functioning. For the farm scene, a wise price policy would insure adequate income for farmers, but at the same time encourage lower costs to consumers. This can be done soundly, as in business, only through greater efficiency. Low farm prices caused by overplanting and glutted markets are not healthy. If lower prices are secured by government subsidy alone, they add to an already oversized federal budget. Finally, in regard to labor, the best objective would be decreasing labor cost but increasing labor incomes. Again, this involves co-operation and efficiency. Here two extremes must be avoided: lowering labor cost merely by reducing wages; and increasing worker income as a result of the economic power of organized labor, without any increase in efficiency. This last observation is, of course, subject to the earlier qualification in regard to thoroughly substandard wages. By these methods, the balance between prices, as noted in *Quadragesimo Anno,* would be achieved.

The matter of income distribution, at least through taxation, hardly needs adjustment today in favor of the lower-income groups. While taxes for everyone are high, the heavy burden of surtaxes on higher incomes tends to equalize the economic status of all groups in the population. It is difficult to make a fortune today, except through capital gains which are taxed at a maximum of 25 per cent. To become wealthy one needs to discover oil or to happen upon some type of business which expands rapidly, so that income may be realized in the form of capital gains rather than salaries or profits. Of course, inequality exists even now, but the tremendous disparity of even twenty years ago no longer obtains. While this equalization is a move in the right direction, it would be dangerous to carry it to the point where economic incentive were removed. We must have savings to provide for expansion of business, and a sufficient profit prospect to warrant the risk involved in starting new enterprises. Otherwise, the economy stagnates, thereby throwing on government the burden of giving jobs to an expanding population. Nor is it socially healthy that most private expansion be financed by corporations, banks, and insurance companies, which today furnish the bulk of the nation's savings.

The artificial injection of purchasing power by the government, either through deficit spending or through bank credit or other forms of inflation, is essentially a palliative. It does not attack the causes of the problem. This is not to imply that the theory of compensatory spending is in itself unsound. On the contrary, even conservative writers today often advocate a budget surplus in good times, used to retire debt, and government deficits in poor times for the purpose of a mild inflationary stimulus to the economy. But the national budget is so high today that surpluses are unlikely, unless economic activity can be spurred to such a level that it could readily carry even present-day government costs. Furthermore, with the national debt at astronomical levels, even deficit financing might be a problem in a future depression. Hence unorthodox monetary methods may be considered necessary. Thus, in a time of crisis, the Federal Reserve System might be empowered to purchase government bonds in huge quantities in the open market. These bonds would be retired, not merely set aside for subsequent resale. If such an injection of credit did not stimulate the economy, more customary methods of deficit financing could then be tried. Since the previous Board action would have liquidated a portion of the national debt, the new financing would not raise the debt above the level which obtained prior to Federal Reserve action.[12]

For a time, labor unions made much of the guaranteed annual wage as a means for attaining security. Publicity was given to the successful plans operating in the United States. It was noted that even industries previously considered seasonal had succeeded in stabilizing production and giving the workers a secured wage. Many said that this policy could be a buffer against depressions. In this regard, realism compels us to keep matters in perspective. The most drastic and disturbing fluctuations in employment are not results of seasonal production or changes in styles. Rather, it is the sharp drop in the durable-goods segment of the economy which is so upsetting. Here is where there is both the greatest need for annual wages and yet the severest problems in achieving stability in production. One might note the paradox: the granting of guaranteed wages is easily done where it is least needed, and it is extremely difficult where the need is greatest.

There are two possible methods for guaranteeing annual wages: stabilizing production so as to give steady employment (guaranteeing hours of work); or setting aside reserve funds by industry, with the possible aid of government subsidy, to pay normal wages for a stated number of hours a year (guaranteeing pay). The first procedure is hardest to achieve in the durable-goods field. The production of heavy goods is usually in response to derived demand. Steel, lumber, cement, and like products rarely have a direct market. They are component parts of some other object, and the need for them depends on the sale of automobiles,

---

[12] The technical problems involved are not considered here because of space limitations. Any action which involves monetizing the public debt would raise ethical problems, to the extent that inflation might dilute the value of government bonds. But, in a depression, all values suffer, so that even bondholders would be better off to have a business slump offset than to endure the disastrous effects of a major depression.

refrigerators, buildings, and other durables. Hence it is practically impossible for such firms to plan production or to store products for future use. To achieve planned production, it would be first necessary to iron out the cycle in heavy goods. If this were achieved, guaranteed wages would then be superfluous. On the other hand, if the fund method were used, great caution would be needed. The setting aside of huge reserves would constitute a serious economic problem. Prices would need to be raised, so as to permit the accumulating of a reserve fund. Furthermore, the amount guaranteed would of necessity need limitation, since it would be quite impractical to gather reserves adequate for a prolonged depression. When these difficulties are considered, one is inclined to a cautious attitude in regard to widespread wage guarantees. Generally speaking, it would be better to concentrate upon removing causes of fluctuations rather than doctoring the symptoms. If the discussion of the problem, and union pressure for wage guarantees, were to stimulate common action against depressions, the result would be worth while. In the meantime, improvement of unemployment insurance might be more practical as an immediate step for industries subject to severe fluctuations. Concerns more immune to the business cycle might well formalize their status by guarantees of work and wages, as a stimulant to employee morale.[13]

Finally, in regard to technological unemployment, the only lasting remedy is an investment climate which stimulates industrial expansion and the growth of new industries and services. Growth in efficiency is in itself good, since it increases productivity and lays the basis for higher wages. But to absorb workers possibly displaced in this manner, the economic system must grow. Population increases also call for the same result. In this

---

[13] For literature on guaranteed wages, see M. Latimer, *Guaranteed Wages* (Washington: Government Printing Office, 1947); J. L. Snider, *The Guarantee of Work and Wages* (Cambridge: Graduate School of Business Administration, Harvard University, 1947); A. D. H. Kaplan, *The Guarantee of Annual Wages* (Washington: Brookings Institution, 1947); W. A. Berridge and C. Wolfe, *Guaranteed Employment and Wage Plans* (Washington: American Enterprise Association, 1948); and M. T. Waggaman, "The Case for the Guaranteed Annual Wage" (New York: Paulist Press, 1948).

way, we will gradually approach a total of goods and services which, when properly distributed, would mean a universal family living wage.

It is indeed unfortunate that an objective of such vital common interest should be obscured in partisan squabbles. The distrust which grew up in the years of conflict between business and labor carries through even to problems which are really deep concerns of both parties. The difficulty is aggravated by the remnants of individualism in both groups, with each seeking short-term and immediate interests, not realizing that the problem of economic stability cannot be solved by single firms or labor unions, or even by labor and industry together, to the exclusion of farmers, finance, and government. It would be most desirable that a major conference of the affected parties be held, to reconvene periodically, merely to discuss methods of meeting depressions and underemployment. Such a group would not, of course, add to economic theory, but it might educate practical men in the consequences of matters fairly widely agreed upon by economists. A council of this nature could be set up in connection with the Employment Act of 1946. Instead of an exclusively governmental Council of Economic Advisers to the President and the Congressional Joint Committee on the Economic Report, there would be representatives of the parties most directly concerned. Such a group could ultimately lead to a full-fledged National Economic Council, which could advise all affected groups on policies leading both to economic stability, full employment, and a constantly increasing standards of living.

READINGS*

J. Messner, *Social Ethics*, pp. 599–600, 759–769, 800–811, 901–908.
J. A. Ryan, *A Living Wage*.
——— *Distributive Justice*, Section 4.
O. von Nell-Breuning, *Reorganization of Social Economy*, Chap. 9.
R. J. Miller, *Forty Years After*, pp. 119–149.
F. Baerwald, *Fundamentals of Labor Economics*, Chaps. 3–16.
S. H. Slichter, *The American Economy*.

* For further readings, see List No. 10 in the Appendix.

Chapter XI. LABOR UNIONS

THE RIGHT TO ORGANIZE

Leo XIII, Rerum Novarum

72. For man is permitted by a right of nature to form private societies; the state, on the other hand, has been instituted to protect and not to destroy natural right, and if it should forbid its citizens to enter into associations, it would clearly do something contradictory to itself, because both the state itself and private associations are begotten of one and the same principle, namely, that men are by nature inclined to associate.

76. Furthermore, if citizens have free right to associate, as in fact they do, they also must have the right freely to adopt the organization and the rules which they judge most appropriate to achieve their purpose. We do not feel that the precise character in all details which the aforementioned direction and organization of associations ought to have can be determined by fast and fixed rules, since this is a matter to be decided rather in the light of the temperament of each people, of experiment and practice, of the nature and character of the work, of the extent of trade and commerce, and of other circumstances of a material and temporal kind, all of which must be carefully considered. In summary, let this be laid down as a general and constant law: workers' associations ought to be so constituted and so governed as to furnish the most suitable and most fitting means to attain the object proposed, which consists in this, that the individual members of the association secure, so far as possible, an increase in the goods of body, of soul, and of property.

Leo XIII, Longinque Oceani

We wish to be understood as referring in a special manner to the working classes, who assuredly have the right to unite into associations for the promotion of their interests, a right acknowledged by the Church and unopposed by nature.

Pius XI, Quadragesimo Anno

30. They were with criminal injustice denying the natural right to form associations to those who needed it most to defend themselves from ill-treatment at the hands of the powerful. There were even some Catholics who looked askance at the efforts of workers to form associations of this type as if they smacked of a socialistic or revolutionary spirit.

35. Under these conditions, Catholics seem almost forced to join secular unions. These units, however, should always profess justice and equity and give Catholic members full freedom to care for their own conscience and obey the laws of the Church. It is clearly the office of bishops, when they know that these associations are on account of circumstances necessary and are not dangerous to religion, to approve of Catholic workers joining them, keeping before their eyes, however, the principles and precautions laid down by Our Predecessor, Pius X, of holy memory. Among these precautions the first and chief is this: side by side with these unions there should always be associations zealously engaged in imbuing and forming their members in the teaching of religion and morality, so that they in turn may be able to permeate the unions with that good spirit which should direct them in all their activity. As a result, the religious associations will bear good fruit even beyond the circle of their own membership.

Sacred Congregation of the Council, to the Bishop of Lille, June 5, 1929

(*Summarized.*) On the occasion of a severe industrial dispute, referred by Catholic employers to Rome for judgment, the Sacred Congregation issued a lengthy decree, based largely on preceding papal documents. The more pertinent points in the light of the present context are: "The Church recognizes and affirms the right of employers and employed to form industrial associations, either separately or jointly, and sees in such organizations an efficacious means toward the solution of the social question. . . . The Church under existing circumstances considers the formation of these industrial associations morally necessary. . . . It is the desire of the Church that industrial associations should be instruments of peace and concord, and with this object in view she suggests the institution of joint commissions as a bond of union between them."

Pius XII, Allocution to Belgian Workers, September 11, 1949

Unions have arisen as a spontaneous and necessary consequence of capitalism embodied in an economic system. As such, the Church gives her approval to them, always with the condition that, depending on the laws

of Christ as their unshakable foundation, they endeavor to promote a
Christian order in the world of workers.

Pius XII, Broadcast to German People, September 4, 1949

May it please God that the day be not distant that those organizations
of self-defense, that the defects of the economic system hitherto existing
and above all the lack of Christian mentality have made necessary, could
cease to function.

The Church and Social Order

26. Labor can have no effective voice as long as it is unorganized. To
protect its rights it must be free to bargain collectively through its own
chosen representatives. If labor when unorganized is dissatisfied, the only
alternative is to cease work and thus undergo the great hardships which
follow unemployment.

Pastoral Letter, Hierarchy of Quebec, February, 1950

100. Present circumstances render more pressing and more imperious
the *obligation* for workers . . . to exercise this right [to join unions].

101. Every man has an obligation to seek to protect the security of
his professional [economic] interests. He has the duty to seek to obtain
for himself and his family all that is necessary in order to live a truly
human life and to safeguard them against future hazards. He has the
duty to contribute to the welfare of his fellows, especially those united
to him in common interests. He has the duty to collaborate in restoring
a social order which would be more balanced in favoring respect for
justice in all the activities of labor, industry, and commerce. The isolated
worker cannot do this. But union with his fellow workers will permit
him to fulfill this imperious social duty. In the present state of things,
accordingly, there exists a moral obligation to participate actively in one's
economic organization.

COLLECTIVE BARGAINING
Strikes

Leo XIII, Rerum Novarum

56. Labor which is too long and too hard and the belief that pay is
inadequate not infrequently give workers cause to strike and become voluntarily idle. This evil, which is frequent and serious, ought to be remedied
by public authority, because such interruption of work inflicts damage not
only upon employers and upon the workers themselves, but also injures
trade and commerce and the general interests of the State; and, since it is

usually not far removed from violence and rioting, it very frequently jeopardizes public peace. In this matter it is more effective and salutary that the authority of the law anticipate and completely prevent the evil from which it would seem that conflict between employers and workers is bound to arise.

Pastoral Letter, 1919

A dispute that cannot be adjusted by direct negotiation between the parties concerned should always be submitted to arbitration. Neither employer nor employee may reasonably reject this method on the ground that it does not bring about perfect justice. No human institution is perfect or infallible; even our courts of law are sometimes in error. Like the law court, the tribunal of industrial arbitration provides the nearest approach to justice that is practically attainable; for the only alternative is economic force, and its decisions have no necessary relation to the decrees of justice. They show which party is economically stronger, not which is in the right.

Australian Hierarchy, Peace in Industry

Under modern conditions, the right to organize in trade unions and the right to strike, under certain defined conditions, are inseparable.

It would be futile to urge the formation of trade unions if the Church did not realize that this involves recognition of the right to strike, as a last resort, and when other measures of achieving social justice have failed.

The Church recognizes the right of individuals to withhold their labor collectively because it regards the prevailing system of industrial capitalism as a diseased growth, born of man's rebellion against Christian principles of social life, and bearing within itself the seeds of social anarchy and chaos.

The Catholic regards as futile the protests of those who proclaim their indignation on every occasion on which a union employs the strike weapon, but who nevertheless wish to perpetuate the very system which makes strikes inevitable. With the rise of industrial capitalism, the strike has been the only weapon which a propertyless proletariat has possessed against the injustices so often perpetrated by employers.

Too often did workers find that the concessions which they had won had not been gained as the result of some spontaneous act of justice by their employers, but as the result of strikes, after appeals for justice had been refused. Slowly but surely individual employers found that they could no longer ride roughshod over the rights of their employees, for the strike, backed by union funds, hit their pockets and might even threaten the existence of their firms.

As the individual employer gave way to the large company, the dependence of the worker on his union became more and more complete.

Against these powerful bodies, which often assumed the position of a state within a state, the power of the individual worker to secure justice for himself and his family was negligible. Where reason and persuasion failed and just concessions were not forthcoming, it was only economic pressure placed on the company by a collective withdrawal from work which was effective in securing social justice.

Nevertheless, even where the cause of the workers is just, the Church has maintained that the strike should not be used unless all other methods of settling a dispute have failed.

Four conditions of a just strike have been laid down commonly by theologians: (1) The cause of a threatened strike must itself be just and rightful. (2) There must be sufficient hope of success. It is morally wrong to plunge workers into a strike in which they have no hope of success and from which they will emerge in a worse condition than before. Nevertheless it does not always follow that because a strike is lost it is in vain. (3) The benefit to be gained must not be out of proportion to the harm inflicted. In the case of strikes which seriously affect the entire community, the onus thus placed on those who decide to strike is therefore very great. (4) Before a strike is declared, every effort must first be made to settle the dispute peacefully through conciliation, arbitration, and other more peaceful methods.

The strike is a weapon of industrial war, arising from an unjust and disordered system of society. The rules which regulate it must therefore be carefully observed.

Pastoral Letter, Hierarchy of Quebec, February, 1950

179. There are certain categories of workers who would seriously imperil the common good, were they to strike. In this not too frequent situation, the law may suppress or suspend the right to strike, but not without at the same time giving such workers some compensating methods which are adequate to obtain justice. The law should, for example, provide for compulsory arbitration, adequately safeguarded in regard to impartiality, effectiveness, and promptness of decision.

180. Since strikes always involve serious consequences and are justifiable only after normal means for securing a just agreement have been exhausted, the law may limit the exercise of the right to strike, for all workers, by imposing on the parties the obligation to submit to certain procedures such as negotiation, conciliation, and arbitration, before recourse to a work stoppage.

181. (*Summarized.*) Since laws which suspend or delay the right to strike have the effect of maintaining the status quo, such laws should be carefully drawn to prevent any appearance of partiality. When workers

feel that delay is both unnecessary and prejudicial to their interests, they become extremely restless under the law. The state should improve existing laws so as to avoid such dangers.

Code of Social Principles

117. The public interest is the first criterion for estimating the lawfulness or otherwise of any concerted cessation of work. To this criterion must be added regard for justice and charity.

118. This public interest is more immediately at stake when it is a question of services directly established for the good of the country, and of undertakings — even private ones — that supply the most essential common needs. Certain services are even so indispensable to the community that it is difficult to put forward any supposition that would justify a strike.

119. The danger of such strikes justifies the legislative measures that in many countries forbid the use of this dangerous arm by those employed in the public services. But it is also the duty of the legislator to seek by study, and supply by law, such guarantees as will in a less costly fashion assure, especially to those who are forbidden to strike, the gain or the advantages which might be the outcome of a strike that is justifiable both in its aim and methods.

120. There is a preventive remedy for strikes, as for every conflict, whether in private undertakings or in public services — arbitration. The joint action of organized industry and of public authorities should tend toward the organizing of conciliation and arbitration by means of permanent bodies supported by effective sanction.

LABOR-MANAGEMENT CO-OPERATION
Leo XIII, Rerum Novarum

25. Manifestly, it is the Church which draws from the Gospel the teachings through which the struggle can be composed entirely or, after its bitterness is removed, can certainly become more tempered. It is the Church, again, that strives not only to instruct the mind but to regulate by her precepts the life and morals of individuals, that ameliorates the condition of the workers through her numerous and beneficent institutions, and that wishes and aims to have the thought and energy of all classes of society united to this end, that the interests of the workers be protected as fully as possible.

28. Each needs the other completely: neither capital can do without labor, nor labor without capital. Concord begets beauty and order in things.

33. But the Church, with Jesus Christ as her teacher and leader, seeks greater things than this; namely, by commanding something more perfect,

she aims at joining the two social classes to each other in closest neighborliness and friendship.

37. Those who lack fortune's goods are taught by the Church that, before God as Judge, poverty is no disgrace, and that no one should be ashamed because he makes his living by toil. And Jesus Christ has confirmed this by fact and by deed, who for the salvation of men, "being rich, became poor"; and although He was the Son of God and God Himself, yet He willed to seem and to be thought the son of a carpenter; nay, He even did not disdain to spend a great part of his life at the work of a carpenter. "Is not this the carpenter, the Son of Mary?" Those who contemplate this divine example will more easily understand these truths: true dignity and excellence in men resides in moral living; that is, in virtue; virtue is the common inheritance of man, attainable equally by the humblest and the mightiest, by the rich and the poor; and the reward of eternal happiness will follow upon virtue and merit alone, regardless of the person in whom they may be found. Nay rather, the favor of God Himself seems to incline more toward the unfortunate as a class; for Jesus Christ calls the poor blessed, and He invites most lovingly all who are in labor or sorrow to come to Him for solace, embracing with special love the lowly and those harassed by injustice. At the realization of these things the proud spirit of the rich is easily brought down, and the downcast heart of the afflicted is lifted up; the former are moved toward kindness, the latter, toward reasonableness in their demands. Thus the distance between the classes which pride seeks is reduced, and it will easily be brought to pass that the two classes, with hands clasped in friendship, will be united in heart.

38. Yet, if they obey Christian teachings, not merely friendship but brotherly love also will bind them to each other. They will feel and understand that all men indeed have been created by God, their common Father; that all strive for the same object of good, which is God Himself, who alone can communicate to both men and angels perfect and absolute happiness; that all equally have been redeemed by the grace of Jesus Christ and restored to the dignity of the sons of God, so that they are clearly united by the bonds of brotherhood not only with one another but also with Christ the Lord, "the firstborn among many brethren"; and further, that the goods of nature and the gifts of divine grace belong in common and without distinction to all humankind; and that no one, unless he is unworthy, will be deprived of the inheritance of Heaven. "But if we are sons, we are also heirs: heirs indeed of God and joint heirs with Christ."

39. Such is the economy of duties and rights according to Christian philosophy. Would it not seem that all conflict would soon cease wherever this economy were to prevail in civil society?

Pius XII, Letter to Semaines Sociales, 1947

Touching this third section, We should like for Our part to emphasize a point on which sensible people today are generally agreed, namely, that the highly important question of dividing up the so-called "social product" has by this time received sufficient treatment. A more urgent problem requires our immediate attention. We must make sure that goods are made available for the use of men, and in increasing quantities. In a word, production is the problem of the hour.

Pius XII, Address to Catholic Employers, May 7, 1949

We have just made reference to the preoccupations of those who are engaged in industrial production. Mistaken and disastrous in its consequences is the prejudice, alas! too widely held, which sees in these problems an irreducible clash of rival interests. The opposition is only apparent. In the economic domain management and labor are linked in a community of action and interest. To disregard this mutual bond, to strive to break it, can only betray a pretention to blind and preposterous despotism. Employers and workers are not implacable adversaries. They are co-operators in a common task. They eat, so to speak, at the same table, seeing that they must live, in the last analysis, from the gross or net profits of the national economy. Each receives his income, and in this regard their mutual relations do not in any way imply that one is at the service of the other.

To receive one's wage is a prerogative of the personal dignity of anyone who makes his productive contribution in one form or another, as employer or laborer, toward the output of the nation's economy. In the accounting of private industry salary totals may be listed under costs to the employer. But in the national economy there is only one type of costs, which consists in the national resources utilized with a view to national production, and which must, in consequence, be constantly replenished.

From this it follows that both parties are interested in seeing to it that the costs of national production are in proportion to its output. But since the interest is common, why should it not manifest itself in a common outward expression? Why should it not be allowable to assign to the workers a just share of responsibility in the establishment and development of the national economy? Especially today when the scarcity of capital and the difficulty of international exchange are paralyzing the free flow of expenditure on national production?

Pastoral Letter, 1919

Religion teaches the laboring man and the artisan to carry out honestly and fairly all equitable agreements freely arranged, to refrain from injuring person or property, from using violence and creating disorder. It teaches the owner and employer that the laborer is not their bondsman; that in every man they must respect his dignity and worth as a man and as a Christian; that labor is not a thing to be ashamed of, if we listen to right reason and to Christian philosophy, but is an honorable calling, enabling a man to sustain his life in a way upright and creditable; and that it is shameful and inhuman to treat men like chattels, as means for making money, or as machines for grinding out work. The moral value of man and the dignity of human labor are cardinal points in this whole question. Let them be the directive principles in industry, and they will go far toward preventing disputes. By treating the laborer first of all as a man, the employer will make him a better workingman; by respecting his own moral dignity as a man, the laborer will compel the respect of his employer and of the community.

The settlement of our industrial problems would offer less difficulty, if, while upholding its rights, each party were disposed to meet the other in a friendly spirit. The strict requirements of justice can be fulfilled without creating animosity; in fact, where this arises, it is apt to obscure the whole issue. On the contrary, a manifest desire to win over, rather than drive, the opponent to the acceptance of equitable terms, would facilitate the recognition of claims which are founded in justice. The evidence of such a disposition would break down the barriers of mistrust and set up in their stead the bond of good will. Not an armistice but a concilation would result; and this would establish all parties in the exercise of their rights and the cheerful performance of their duties.

Social Reconstruction

The establishment of shop committees, working wherever possible with the trade union, is the method suggested by this group of employers for giving the employees the proper share of industrial management. There can be no doubt that a frank adoption of these means and ends by employers would not only promote the welfare of the workers, but vastly improve the relations between them and their employers, and increase the efficiency and productiveness of such establishments.

DUTIES OF WORKERS

Leo XIII, Rerum Novarum

30. Among these duties the following concern the poor and the workers: To perform entirely and conscientiously whatever work has been voluntarily and equitably agreed upon; not in any way to injure the property or to harm the person of employers; in protecting their own interests, to

refrain from violence and never to engage in rioting; not to associate with vicious men who craftily hold out exaggerated hopes and make huge promises, a course usually ending in vain regrets and in the destruction of wealth.

78. Offices in the associations are to be distributed properly in accordance with the common interest, and in such a way, moreover, that wide difference in these offices may not create discord. It is of special importance that obligations be apportioned wisely and be clearly defined, to the end that no one is done an injustice. Let the funds be disbursed equitably in such a way that the amount of benefit to be paid out to members is fixed beforehand in accordance with individual needs, and let the rights and duties of employers be properly adjusted to the rights and duties of workers. If anyone in these two groups feels that he has been injured in any way, nothing is more to be desired than that prudent and upright men of the same body be available, and that the association regulations themselves prescribe that the dispute be settled according to the decision of these men.

79. It must also be specially provided that the worker at no time be without sufficient work, and that the monies paid into the treasury of the association furnish the means of assisting individual members in need, not only during sudden and unforeseen changes in industry, but also whenever anyone is stricken by sickness, by old age, or by misfortune.

Pius XI, Quadragesimo Anno

33. Thus associations of this kind have molded truly Christian workers who, in combining harmoniously the diligent practice of their occupation with the salutary precepts of religion, protect effectively and resolutely their own temporal interests and rights, keeping a due respect for justice and a genuine desire to work together with other classes of society for the Christian renewal of all social life.

140. No less praise must be accorded to the leaders of workers' organizations who, disregarding their own personal advantage and concerned solely about the good of their fellow members, are striving prudently to harmonize the just demands of their members with the prosperity of their whole occupation and also to promote these demands, and who do not let themselves be deterred from so noble a service by any obstacle or suspicion.

Pius XII, Discourse to Members of Italian Electrical Industry, January 25, 1946

To obtain the desired concord between labor and capital, recourse is had to the professional organization and the labor union, understood not as weapons destined exclusively for a defensive or offensive war which would provoke reactions and reprisals, not as a flowing river which submerges and separates, but rather as a bridge to unite these groups.

Pius XII, Address to Christian Association of Italian Workers, June 29, 1948

But if you are not to grow faint along the road, if you are to keep alive the flame that burns in your hearts, if especially you are to win over the young to your cause, you must keep always before your eyes the noble objective toward which your movement is on the march. Your ultimate purpose is the formation of authentic Christian workingmen, equally distinguished for skill in the practice of their profession and for fidelity in the practice of their religion; men who are capable of reconciling harmoniously the stubborn defense of their economic interests with the strictest sense of justice, and with the sincere disposition to collaborate with the other classes of society toward Christian reconstruction in every walk of social life.

Such is the high aim of the movement of Christian workers, even if it is divided into particular and separate associations, some of which attend to the defense of their legitimate interests in the matter of labor contracts — which is the specific office of the trade union — others to activities of mutual assistance in economic matters, such as the consumer co-operatives, and others to the moral and religious welfare of the workers, like the associations of Catholic workingwomen.

Do not let yourselves deviate from this goal, which is more important than any purely transitory form of union organization. The future of the unions themselves depends on the faithfulness with which you pursue this goal. In fact, if ever they should aim at exclusive domination in the state and society, if they should seek to exercise absolute power over the worker, if they should reject the strict sense of justice and sincere good will to collaborate with the other social classes, they would betray the expectations and the hopes which every honest and conscientious worker places in them. What must be thought when a worker is kept from his labor because he is not *persona grata* to the union, when workers are forced to abstain from labor for political purposes, when they are led astray down not a few other mistaken paths that lead very far away indeed from the true good and often invoked unity of the working class?

Pius XII, Allocution to Belgian Workers, September 11, 1949

The temptation to abuse the force of organization [is] a temptation as strong and as dangerous as that of abusing the power of private capital. . . .

The force of organization, however powerful one may wish to suppose it, is not of itself and considered in itself an element of order.

Church and Social Order

28. New developments in the organization of labor, under the great impetus which has been given by recent legislation and governmental policy, make it opportune to point out that the principle of force and domination is equally wrong if exercised by labor under certain conditions by means of a monopoly control. To defend in principle or to adopt in practice the theory that the net result belongs to labor and that capital shall receive only sufficient to replace itself is an invasion of the rights of property. This is only a more subtle form of the contention that all means of production should be socialized. Clearly all such proposals disregard the contribution which the owner of property makes in the process of production and are palpably unjust.

It is not, however, the excessive claims of labor on the income from industry which constitute the most immediate problem in labor relations today, but rather the abuse of power which not infrequently results in violence, riot, and disorder. Employers at times abuse their economic power by discriminating unfairly against unions, by establishing lockouts, by importing from outside the community strikebreakers who are furnished with arms, and by provoking in other ways ill feeling which precipitates violent disorder. Employees on their part allow themselves at times to be misled by men of evil principles so as to engage in the criminal use of violence against both persons and property. Leo XIII in his Encyclical *Rerum Novarum* spares neither group in his denunciation of such immoral conduct. He calls upon the public authority to protect and defend vigorously the rights of all, forestalling preferably the rise of disorder by eliminating the economic abuse from which this disorder springs.

There have been frequent allusions in the preceding chapters to the place of labor unions in modern industrial life. It would be pertinent at this point to treat more at length the subjects of labor's right to organize, collective bargaining, and the duties of workers. These are perennial questions, but the emphasis on various phases naturally shifts as circumstances change. Thus, in the 1930's, there was great stress upon labor's rights. In the 1940's, the focus was more upon the duties of labor and the rights of the public. One might indulge the hope that the 1950's might concentrate upon labor's opportunity, together with other economic groups, to work out a common pattern for the general welfare.

THE SOCIAL FUNCTION OF
ORGANIZED LABOR

The Right to Organize. When Pope Leo XIII spoke out for the right of labor to organize into freely chosen unions, he took a courageous and pioneering step. At the time, the old guilds of workers had been abolished, in some countries for several centuries. Scattered labor unions were formed to counter the evils associated with the Industrial Revolution, but the place of organized labor was far from secure. All too often unions were considered, either in law or in fact, as organized criminal conspiracies. Against such a background, the position of the Pontiff seemed almost revolutionary. Today most democratic countries accept the labor union as a legitimate part of industrial society. Nevertheless, it would be useful to review briefly the reasons why labor has the right to organize.

In regard to unions, papal documents stress man's natural right to form societies consonant with the proper aims of his existence. As noted in Chapter III, there are many forms of human society, of which the civil state is only one, even though pre-eminent in its sphere. Public society exists to serve the needs of man and to foster his legitimate private groups, such as the family. It may regulate lesser social groups in the interest of the common welfare, but it may not abolish or even unduly hamper societies which are natural to man. Certainly the common concerns of workers to protect their interests would justify their organizing for such a purpose. Moreover, in modern life the structure of society is such that the individual must ordinarily act through groups to secure his rights. So great is the power of the civil state, and the size and might of industry, that the unorganized worker is left without an effective voice in matters of vital concern. Only through the existence of buffer groups, close enough to the individual to hear his pleas, but powerful enough to be recognized by government and economic societies, can we hope

-to safeguard the common man from the tyranny of entrenched power.

The right of labor to organize may also be derived from other and more basic rights. We have noted the human dignity of labor and the consequences which follow from this fact. The worker has the right to decent treatment, just wages, and some security from the vagaries of economic life. He cannot normally achieve these rights, acting merely as an individual. He lacks the ability, experience, and knowledge necessary to present his case effectively to his employer. He could not marshal economic statistics to buttress his plea for higher wages, nor could he quote such laws as may have been enacted to protect him. Even were he able to present his views cogently, there would still be employers who might be indifferent to his rights or so bogged down in inertia that they fail to see the possibility of change. Unfortunately, the threat of economic force may be needed at times to secure rights. But the isolated individual has no real power. He needs the job more than the job needs him. Even where employers are conscientious and anxious to be fair, the sheer size of much modern industry makes individual dealings impossible. With the utmost of good will on both sides, it is still necessary to have formalized and organized methods for handling grievances, rights, and claims. Such a procedure is effective only when the machinery of appeal is distinct from the employer and his representatives. It is a sound principle that no one is a judge in his own case, so that, even with the best of employers, one could hardly secure full justice through an appeals' system under the control of the employer.

In these times, it is particularly important to stress the representative and co-ordinating function of unionism. Historically, most unions were born as a result of injustice. They were weapons to be used against exploiting employers. In the light of their origin, it is understandable that a class-struggle mentality still pervades many of them. As a result, many instinctively associate them with situations of hostility and aggression. Such an attitude, while natural in the perspective of history, expresses only a minor phase of unionism. Even if most injustice and exploitation were removed, unions would still have a legitimate place. They are the normal voice of labor, necessary to organize social life for the common good. There is a positive need for such organization today, quite independently of any social evils which may prevail. Order and harmony do not happen; they are the fruit of conscious and organized effort. While we may well hope that the abuses which occasioned the rise of unions may disappear, it does not thereby follow that unions will have lost their function. On the contrary, they will be freed from unpleasant, even though temporarily necessary, tasks and able to devote all their time and efforts to a better organization of social life.

The Duty to Organize. In view of the broader functions of unions, many moralists now hold that workers have a duty to join unions. The soundest basis for such an opinion is the obligation of all to participate in group action aimed to infuse a proper order in economic life, so that the institutions of society will be directed toward the common good. This institutional reform cannot be achieved by individual effort alone. It is essentially social. In industrial life, it transcends the boundaries of the single plant or industry. Even where an employer pays good wages and has excellent working conditions, there are common problems of economic society in the solution of which labor has both an interest and a duty to participate.

If the reason for labor organization were merely the achievement of individual rights, undoubtedly it could be argued that where such rights are adequately protected, unions would be unnecessary, much less obligatory. But in the wider pattern of modern life, there are two arguments for unions, even with workers whose employers are imbued with both good will and skill in human relations. The first is the need for positive organization of economic life for the common good. Even unselfish individualism will not achieve such positive order. It may seek good goals, but not in a formal and orderly pattern. Secondly, in view of the power concentration in modern life, there is need for buffer groups to safeguard individual rights. Although a given em-

ployer is anxious to protect the rights of his workers, these rights
may be invaded as a result of actions taken outside of his sphere
of competence. There may be arbitrary action by government or
selfish moves by other economic groups. Hence workers in this
well-regulated concern would need to act with other workers to
protect interests common to all.

Not all moralists would accept the argument given above. They
argue that it is based on an ideal union situation which is not in
existence in the United States today. They hold that present-day
unions are selfish pressure groups, not necessarily dedicated to
seeking the common good of society or the social order envisioned in Chapter VII. Moreover, they would contend that
many modern unions are so large that they constitute giant power
groups, in which the rights of workers are secondary to the interests of the union organization. Against this point of view is
the fact that unions today constitute the only group directly
seeking the workers' rights. It would seem better to join such
organizations and try to improve them where they are deficient,
rather than wait for an ideal situation to eventuate. Social change
normally is based on modification of existing institutions, rather
than upon creation of entirely new groups.

The argument for labor's duty to organize is even stronger
where the worker is a victim of injustice. When wages are unfair, working conditions poor, and the dignity of workers inadequately acknowledged, there is a more immediate reason for
organized action. It is true that the state might intervene through
legislation to remedy conditions, but this would only add to an
already excessive concentration of power. Nor can it be said that
a worker need not press his rights. If he were merely an isolated
individual, such abstention might be legitimate. But he has
duties toward his family and his fellow workers. His family
suffers when his wage is inadequate. Even if the worker is single,
he or she may not ignore the rights of fellow workers. Social
justice obliges such workers to unite for common action to secure
the rights of all.

The question then arises: does a worker sin if he refuses to join a union? No simple answer to this question may be given. A parallel may be found in the duty to vote. One's obligations toward civil society are comparable to those obtaining with economic societies. A citizen may not evade essential duties such as the payment of taxes, aid in time of war or disaster, and like necessities. But where abstention from civic duty would not necessarily impede the common good, as might be the case when one did not vote in a minor election where both candidates were worthy, a citizen would not be blameworthy. On the other hand, in times of crisis, such as the Italian elections in 1948, one might be obligated under pain of grave sin to exercise one's right to vote. Likewise, the obligations of social justice would seem to depend upon the circumstances. Consistent refusal to accept one's duties in social justice, where nonparticipation could seriously impede the common good in a vital matter, would be a grave sin. Failure in an individual instance, where the issues were not clearly important or where individual participation would not affect the result, might be excused. But even a single abstention could be seriously wrong in a given situation. Such might be the case in a close Labor Board election where a choice lay between a sound Christian-minded union and one inspired by communism or infected with racketeering. Likewise, where a union is the only means to remedy serious injustices, a worker might not abstain from voting in a Labor Board election merely because of indifference to the welfare of his fellow workers.

In practice, much social education is necessary before we can approach the problem of unionization in terms of personal obligation under pain of sin. To the ordinary Catholic today, the connection between individual action and the obtaining of the common good is not sufficiently clear to make this a problem for the confessional. This is particularly true in the United States, where religious education has hitherto largely ignored the social obligations of the individual in modern life. Our immediate problem is to cast aside the individualism and casuistry which has too often crept into our moral teachings and to instruct our people in social justice and civic morality. Workers should be taught that the union is normally necessary for their protection and that they have a duty to work together for the good of all. It is more important now to give workers a trained conscience than to try to impose moral burdens before they are educated to see their necessity. Such a general attitude does not preclude the strongest kind of urging in emergency situations. But the main present problem is to wipe out the heritage of individualism. This is especially needed for the young and women workers, who may not feel the personal needs which obtain for fathers of families.

The Duty to Recognize Unions. If workers have a right and even a duty to join unions, it follows that employers must recognize such organizations and deal with them in their spheres of competence. This obligation is currently recognized in our federal laws, which protect labor's right to organize and impose upon employers the duty of collective bargaining. Today, most employers are at least reconciled to the status of organized labor. They may not like to deal with unions or they may object to certain tactics of these unions, but few are aggressively antagonistic to the extent of trying to crush an existing union. Some of the largest corporations have found that unions are a necessity in big industry. Their representatives admit that if their unions were to founder, some similar device would be needed to handle grievances. Experiments with company-dominated unions have not been satisfactory, even from the viewpoint of the most reactionary firm. It was found that, where workers do not have a really independent grievance machinery, abuses thrive and morale suffers. From a purely selfish viewpoint, these larger firms would concede at least a limited function to organized labor. By contrast, many smaller employers, even those with excellent labor-relations policies, still think that unions are a reflection upon their integrity. Such employers are unaware of the broader aspects of unionism, quite apart from aggressive tactics to remedy injustices.

While the employer's duty to recognize a union chosen by his workers is clear, the precise implications of this obligation are not always so evident. Federal laws prevent his interference with the workers' free choice in the selection of a union. In general, this would also seem to be a sound moral principle. But difficult problems arise where the union chosen may be Communist-dominated or racketeering. In such a situation, the employer faces a complex choice. He is asked to recognize not merely a legitimate labor union, but rather one which might reasonably be presumed to be contemplating unjust actions. A union dominated by Communists is dedicated to class hostility. It may call strikes for purely political purposes. A racketeering union may bedevil both the employer and the workers. In such cases, the employer might rightly argue that he is relieved of his obligation to recognize the union, since its corrupt overtones pervert it from its legitimate function. This attitude was embodied in the Labor Management Relations Act, 1947, which denied government protection to unions whose officers would not sign non-Communist affidavits and to unions which failed to furnish suitable financial accounting to their members.

The principle that recognition may be denied in certain cases assumes both good faith and definite knowledge of the facts. No employer could salve his conscience on the grounds that all unions are communistic or racketeering. He must be certain that the union in question is actually under the control of the Communist Party, as proved by open Party membership of its top officers or their consistent adherence to the Party Line, as expressed in communist publications. It is not enough for an employer to label unions as Communist-led merely because he disapproves of their economic philosophy. Nor should they be called racketeering because they bargain hard for the rights of their members. It is not difficult today to get accurate information on the political leanings of unions or the legitimacy of their conduct. Fortunately, the grip of both Communists and racketeers upon organized labor is rapidly becoming negligible at this writing.

Certain economic groups have taken the stand that unions are unsuitable for their members, since in their activity the right to strike may not be recognized. This would hold for policemen, firemen, nurses, and similar essential public servants, whether or not they are actually employed by government. Such a position is thoroughly untenable. The right of workers to organize is quite distinct from the right to strike. Unions have important functions other than economic pressure through the strike. Moreover, they can use other weapons, such as publicity or appeal to higher authorities, to secure justice for their members. In view of this, it is morally wrong for civic or other authorities to refuse recognition to freely chosen unions of public servants. Like private employers, they might withhold recognition from Communist-dominated groups, especially where espionage or sabotage might be feared.

The problem of union recognition and collective bargaining has, in recent years, directly involved the Church acting as an employer. Unions have been established in our schools, newspapers and printing establishments, cemeteries, and hospitals. In such cases, Church authorities have been confronted with difficulties similar to those faced by secular employers. Their management authority has been curtailed by collective bargaining in regard to wages, hours, grievances, seniority, hiring and discharge practices, and other features relating to working conditions. Like other employers, many Church authorities may have felt piqued when first confronted with the fact of unionization, considering it as a possible reflection on their treatment of the workers. Such a reaction, however, is not of necessity well founded. Workers for religious groups, because of their reverence for the spiritual functions of their employers, may be especially diffident in bringing up problems connected with their work. The fact that they form a union may not indicate that abuses exist, but merely that they want an outside spokesman in their special situation.

When churchmen act as employers, they naturally have the same obligations toward workers as have other employers. Indeed, in the light of papal teaching, their conduct should be exemplary in regard to union recognition and collective bargaining. They would be expected to negotiate freely and willingly, invoke conciliation where differences have not been resolved, and even use arbitration in matters where its value is generally recognized. At the same time, it must be remembered that the Church as an employer has the same moral rights as other employers. Its negotiators could argue inability to pay, the need for safeguarding a going business, the case for considering ability above seniority in regard to promotions, and similar pleas. These representatives may fight union claims, even to the point of provoking a strike, when they are considered unjust. It would be legitimate to refuse recognition to a Communist-dominated or racketeering union. Good example does not involve automatic concession of every union claim. It simply means that Church employers practice the principles of social justice with fidelity and generosity.

Catholic Unions. The popes have consistently favored in principle the idea of separate unions for Catholic workers. This was desirable on the grounds that members of Catholic unions would be given adequate instruction in social and moral principles governing their activities. Moreover, it was historically necessary in many countries where the only alternative was a union dominated by Marxism. At the same time, the pontiffs gave permission to bishops to sanction membership in nonreligious unions, where conditions of time and place made this necessary. Such would obviously be the case in lands where Catholic workers were in a minority, so that a separate labor organization would be ineffectual. Even where Catholics were in a majority in a region or a trade, there would still be the necessity of national action, best handled by a union which represented all the workers in a given country. In 1945, Pope Pius XII permitted the Christian Association of Italian Workers to join with a general, noncommunist federation of labor, for the purpose of more effective action for labor's rights. Moreover, in addressing this group, the Pontiff stressed the opportunities and duties inherent in this situation, where Catholic workers can be Christian apostles in their environment. At the present writing, about 2,500,000 workers are affiliated with Christian trade unions in ten countries. Most of these workers are Catholics, although there are sizable Protestant groups in the Netherlands and Switzerland.

Where Catholics join nonreligious unions, the Church has a duty to provide some parallel associations for the religious training of Catholic workers. This has been done in the United States through our labor schools, the Young Christian Workers, and the Association of Catholic Trade Unionists. The spread of the labor-school movement has been particularly remarkable, with scores of schools in all parts of the country. On the other hand, some among the clergy have taken the position that general Catholic associations, such as the Holy Name Society, adequately meet the needs of Catholic workers. Such a position does not seem consonant with the directions of the popes or the needs of modern times. The instruction of *Quadragesimo Anno,* and the earlier position of Pope Pius X in *Singulari Quadam,* seem definitely to envision a separate organization which would consider exclusively the religious and moral problems connected with work today. Moreover, the nature of the problems themselves call for specialized treatment. The general principles of justice and charity, as preached in our pulpits, need more exact application for the concrete situations of industrial life. Just as we have distinct courses in ethics for student doctors and lawyers, and might well have broader Catholic professional groups for a continuing application of principles to current problems, so we should have some steady and consistent medium for applying social principles to the day-by-day problems of workers.

Access to Unions. If labor organization is considered a virtual necessity today, it would seem to follow that in justice every worker should have the opportunity to join a union of his own choosing. Federal law compels employers to grant such freedom to workers. But restrictions on unions are much milder. In general, they may adopt such laws as they choose in regard to admission of members. As a result, there have been questions in regard to standards set by some unions, particularly in the matters of racial discrimination and limitation of membership by high initiation fees or other devices. Conversely, there is also the problem of compulsory membership through the union shop or like methods.

Discrimination against prospective union members for reasons of race is contrary to justice. This is particularly the case when such rules bar a man from an entire field of skilled employment. While it was stated earlier that no worker has a strict right to obtain a given job, it is something different when a trained worker is excluded from the exercise of his skill in any job, and this because of color. As a result of such action, he may well be reduced to a lower standard of living, probably beneath the minimum of justice. Moreover, the motive for exclusion is contemptible. Hence those who set up such rules establish a social institution which is acting contrary to the common welfare. They are denying fellow workers a chance to develop their skills and abilities at suitable work. This would be a definite violation of social justice.

The situation whereby union membership is restricted through high initiation fees, quotas, apprenticeship limitation, or nepotism would seem to parallel the case of racial discrimination. Yet, there are significant differences which may change the moral aspect of this problem. In the first case, it was assumed that there were job opportunities available and that minorities were excluded from access to such jobs. By contrast, the theory behind restriction in total union membership assumes a shortage of work opportunities. It is primarily a device for adjusting the supply of skilled labor to the demand. Its purpose is to prevent chronic unemployment caused by a surplus of trained workers in a limited field. Here it would seem that nondiscriminatory quotas or other barriers to apprenticeship or union membership would not in themselves be unjust. Where long experience showed a consistent need (as for pressmen in a two-newspaper city), it would be foolish to train more workers than could possibly be used. Exclusion would not be denying a worker a right to a job, since there are no jobs available. The experience and seniority of existing union members would assure them of first claim upon any openings. At the same time, it must be recognized that abuses are possible under this system. It is not unheard-of for unions to issue "temporary" work permits for long periods or to restrict training to such a degree that shortages exist in the field. Such a practice could be the basis for an abusive labor monopoly. Abuses of this nature would be adverse to the common good and hence contrary to social justice.

A somewhat related problem involves various forms of compulsory union membership, such as maintenance-of-membership clauses, the union shop, and the closed shop. Maintenance-of-membership clauses compel a union member to retain his membership for the duration of the contract. The union shop forces all workers in such a plant to become union members. Under the closed shop, an employer may hire and employ only union members. In some cases, he may hire such workers directly, while in others he may agree to apply to the union for competent workers. Each of these devices has been attacked as restricting the worker's freedom to get a job under conditions of his own choosing. As a result, the Labor Management Relations Act, 1947, outlawed the closed shop and permitted unions to ask for other forms of security only after a majority of the employees eligible to vote had indicated their approval in a secret Labor Board election.

On the other hand, there is a strong case for union security. It is held to be equitable on the grounds that workers who receive the benefits of union protection should pay for its costs. Moreover, it is normally a stabilizing influence in industrial relations. Union security generally improves union relations with the employer, insofar as it frees the union from the need of constantly fighting to maintain its existence. Insecure unions must of necessity dramatize to members the gains that they are winning, in order to hold their allegiance. As a result they become belligerent and aggressive. They are normally suspicious of the employers, interpreting every doubtful move as a union-busting tactic. By contrast, when the union has security, it can make concessions which appear just, even though it may have trouble convincing the membership of its wisdom in so doing. Experienced union leaders are generally more conservative than the members. They have a broader knowledge and hence can more readily understand the difficulties confronting an employer.

This was shown during World War II, when Congress adopted the opposite theory and permitted strikes after a poll of union members. The results proved conclusively that the workers were more restive and anxious to strike than was the case with their leaders. Strike votes are almost invariably in favor of a strike, even when conducted by secret governmental ballot.

Another reason why union security contributes to labor-management stability derives from the disciplinary powers of a union. If the union's powers of discipline are removed, it has no weapons against unauthorized strikes, slowdowns, and similar irresponsibility. It is true that the employer can punish such workers, but often only at the price of seriously lowered morale in the plant. Discipline from the union is better received and more effective. Because of these facts, many employers as well as union leaders were unhappy over the limitation of union security in the Taft-Hartley Act. Privately many will admit the folly of governing collective bargaining by statute, especially when the law showed evidence of such a naïveté in regard to the realities of industrial life. When labor legislation is necessary, it should be primarily the work of industrial-relations experts, not lawyers.

From an ethical aspect, the arguments against union security, even in its extreme form of the closed shop, are not conclusive. The right to work is not an unconditional right. The worker has social responsibilities as well as individual rights. He may not exercise his right to work in such a manner as to be contrary to the common good. Thus, to use a noncontroversial example, a worker with a contagious disease may rightly be excluded from work which involves the handling of food. Even in general industry, many employers insist upon health examinations for prospective employees. Protective labor legislation for women and children circumscribes their right to work, in the interest of the general welfare. Thus, it can be said that the theory of social limitations upon the right to work is unassailable. In practice, it would seem that the arguments given above would indicate that, in principle, union security can contribute to the common good.

It is true that the closed shop can occasion serious abuses, such as union autocracy and corruption, but these evils can be attacked directly without abolishing an institution which serves such useful functions.[1]

COLLECTIVE BARGAINING

The most common purpose of union organization is collective bargaining over wages, hours, and working conditions. Unions represent their members in agreeing upon a contract which governs their employment. This fact implies many rights and duties both in regard to unions and employers.

Aims of Collective Bargaining. Union-management negotiations in collective bargaining should seek to give both workers and employers their rights and their equitable claims in matters of wages, hours, and working conditions. Workers have a right to a just wage and hours and working conditions consonant with their human dignity. The employer has a right to a fair profit and responsible performance of work by his employees. Moreover, the public has a right to expect conscientious dealings on both sides, so that unnecessary strikes or lockouts will not cause serious inconvenience or even hardship. In addition to rights there are equitable claims. The worker is seeking higher standards of living than the minimum of strict justice. The employer desires wholehearted co-operation from his workers. And the public wishes to share in the gains achieved through increased productivity.

The principles governing negotiations on wages and hours were noted in the preceding chapters. The workers ask for a living wage and reasonable hours as matters of justice. They may press for higher wages on the basis of skill and experience. Where gains are made through increased capital investment, investors also have a right to a fair share. Workers may, in strict justice, claim such a share as will bring them up to a living wage. Be-

---

[1] The best treatment of the closed shop is by J. L. Toner, *The Closed Shop* (Washington: American Council on Public Affairs, 1942). This was originally a doctoral dissertation at the Catholic University of America.

yond this level, social justice would require that the distribution be such as to meet the requirements of the common good. In our present economy, this would involve adequate incentives to investors and a broad income distribution, either through lower prices or higher wages, needed to raise living standards, increase employment levels, and maintain economic stability. Thus, workers' claims to a living wage are in strict justice, at least on a par with investors' right to interest and profit. Above this level, social justice would warrant further claims, provided that labor did not seek to appropriate to itself exclusively gains made through increased capital investment.

In regard to working conditions, the claims most strongly pressed include those for grievance procedures and job security. The right to grievance machinery, assuring the worker of a system of appeals against conditions which he finds oppressive, would be a matter of justice. It is a recognition of human dignity. Social justice would likewise favor provisions regulating job security. Protection against arbitrary discharge would be equitable. More controversial are seniority provisions regulating lay-offs and promotions. In view of the fact that older workers are generally family men, it would be consonant with human dignity to afford them job protection. The employer is benefited through the retention of a stable and contented working force. Likewise, it is equitable to invoke seniority in promotion where abilities are equal. The principle of absolute seniority in promotion, disregarding ability, is less acceptable. It might be legitimate where the nature of work is such that skills do not vary appreciably. But it would not be suitable in regard to promotion to executive positions where abilities are usually the controlling factor.

Other items in union contracts, such as paid vacations and holidays, are more in the nature of claims than rights. They raise the worker's standard of living and may legitimately be sought when the condition of business permits. But an employer who might give two week's vacation with pay would be in his rights in turning down a request for a third week. The same reasoning would apply to claims such as pensions, a guarantee of work or wages, and medical insurance. If the employer is not paying a living wage, the workers might in justice demand either a living wage or its equivalent through pensions and medical plans. But where these are claims above the minimum standard, it would be equally legitimate for workers to ask them and for employers to deny them. The controlling principle would be the common good — social justice rather than commutative.

The most controversial element in current collective bargaining concerns the so-called union invasion of management rights. In recent years, unions have concerned themselves with questions formerly considered the exclusive prerogative of management. Grievance machinery, regulation of discharge, and seniority provisions are widespread today, whereas they once were considered sole functions of management. More recently, unions have questioned the speed of assembly lines, the use of materials considered harmful, and even prices and profits of the firm. They are interested in new techniques, labor-saving machinery, and transfer of functions from one plant to another. At times, unions have opposed technological progress and have insisted upon made work and feather-bedding. Management, in turn, has rebelled strongly against these invasions, holding that its responsibility for running the firm is essentially indivisible. Corporation executives claim that they are legally responsible to their investors and must guard the solvency and prosperity of their company.

This controversy cannot readily be solved in terms of rights. Union penetration is not socialism; it is but a more intelligent expression of the need for security and the workers' desire for responsibility and creative expression. Progressive union leaders realize that broad policies of a firm affect the workers' welfare. More than this, they are aware that national economic patterns condition employment levels and general prosperity. They rightly claim that they cannot be indifferent to such matters and still effectively represent the interests of their members. Questions such as the speed of the assembly line affect employers' costs, but they also impinge upon the health and welfare of the workers. Broader economic policies relate to job security. Hence there is something more than the employer's alleged right in strict justice to use his property as he desires. Property rights are social as well as individual. The common good and social justice must also be considered. The employer's right to manage property is conditioned by the transcendent claims of social justice. Hence unions would be within their rights in asking a *consultative* voice on all matters deeply affecting the welfare of their members. Beyond this point, the unions could not say that justice *requires* them to be given the right to participate as equals with employers in making the economic decisions in an industry. Justice might *permit* them to press such issues as claims rather than rights, but an employer would likewise be within his rights in refusing to accede to such claims. The employer controls the economic decisions in his firm (Pope Pius XII, May 7, 1949), subject, of course, to the demands of social justice. But the unions may not normally unilaterally determine and enforce the claims of social justice in this field. In disputed points, this is the duty of the state.

There is a better solution to this dispute than either the pressing of claims or state intervention to determine the demands of the common good. Recent management literature has stressed the virtues of teamwork and partnership in production. It is held that consultation of workers improves morale markedly, increases output, and lowers costs. In effect, industrial-relations experts are advocating as a policy what unions are claiming as a right. But union claims are not based on abstract ideological dogmas. They are seeking the welfare of their members. If the employer, through labor-management co-operation, adopts a policy of consulting his workers through their unions, the issue of management rights will not arise. It is to the interest of management as well as workers to end the feeling of insecurity and to obtain a stable and co-operative working force. Thus costs can be lowered and technological progress assured, without creating fear and insecurity among workers.[2]

---

[2] There are two excellent studies of this problem: N. W. Chamberlain, *The Union Challenge to Management Control* (New York: Harper, 1948), and S. H. Slichter,

While certain areas of collective bargaining must be clearly defined, when rights are concerned, the ideal would call for emphasis upon interests and problems. Although the union protects the rights of the workers, surely it is also to the employer's interest that they be treated fairly. Likewise, while management may insist upon its prerogatives, the problems which confront the company are at the same time labor's problems. Hence constructive collective bargaining actually mitigates the divisive elements separating capital and labor. It can be a prelude to a broad spirit of co-operation which is indispensable for soundly organized economic life. Mutuality of interest is a product of good will and trust, born of day-by-day efforts to iron out differences, until an attitude of general understanding and confidence is reached. There is no simple formula for attaining this result. It is forged through long experience, not bought ready made at a nostrum counter.[3]

Justice in Strikes. Strikes are to collective bargaining what quarrels are to married life. They are temporary breakdowns of unity, leading to widely varying results. They can clear the air and bring a new and better understanding. Or they may create lasting bitterness, smoldering beneath a surface truce. Finally, they could cause a complete break in relationships between the affected parties. Furthermore, like quarrels between spouses, they are often the source of serious suffering to innocent third parties. They may go beyond the quarrel stage and degenerate into industrial warfare. Or they may be sudden flare-ups which bring to the surface concealed tensions, and actually relieve difficulties through open discussion. Anger often produces the speaking of suppressed truth so that both parties are better off for the exchange of views. Nevertheless, while strikes may pro-

---

Union Policies and Industrial Management (Washington: Brookings, 1941). Chamberlain's conclusions fit in remarkably with the industry-council plan as explained in Chapter VII.

[3] See E. T. Cheyfitz, Constructive Collective Bargaining (New York: McGraw-Hill, 1947); H. Lazarus and J. P. Goldberg, "Collective Bargaining" (Washington: The Public Affairs Institute, 1949); and Causes of Industrial Peace Under Collective Bargaining (Washington: National Planning Association, 1948–).

duce good *per accidens,* they are dangerous weapons. Sound social principles circumscribe the right to strike with many qualifications.

That workers in general have the right to strike is usually conceded. Some authors are so concerned with possible evils that they consider the strike a weapon of extreme desperation, to be used only when its necessity is clear and overwhelming.[4] Others are not so rigorous in demanding justification for work stoppages. The American public justifies strikes on the grounds that workers cannot be compelled to remain at the job. Moralists are more likely to emphasize the justice of workers' claims as the excusing circumstance. They permit a strike for a just cause when other means of securing a fair treatment fail. Many writers compare a strike to war and pose similar conditions for its justification. The strike must be (1) for a just cause; (2) necessary because other means have failed; (3) such that the gains sought will outweigh the evils occasioned, with a reasonable hope for success in the strike; and (4) carried on by lawful and morally sanctioned means. These conditions imply many complex decisions.

A just cause involves at least some claim which is fair and equitable. Father Clune goes further and says: "The workers may strike only for something to which they have a strict right in justice."[5] Such a view appears unnecessarily rigorous. Between the minimum due in strict justice and the maximum which is clearly unjust, there is a wide range. It would certainly seem acceptable for workers to press rights which are matters of equity rather than strict justice. Moreover, social justice itself would seem to sanction strikes for equitable claims of the type discussed earlier in this chapter. These are interests to which the workers do not have a strict right but to which they have some title in fairness. Yet their title is not sufficiently clear that the employer would necessarily be acting wrongly in denying it. Such, for instance, are claims to a higher standard of living above the

---

[4] Cf. G. Clune, *Christian Social Reorganization* (Dublin: Browne and Nolan, 1940), Chap. 19.

[5] *Op. cit.,* p. 406.

minimum of justice. Higher productivity makes such an increase possible, but it is disputed as to who should share the fruits of this gain. Workers may claim something (above the living wage); stockholders may consider this a reason for additional profits (above a fair minimum); and the public may wish to share in the form of lower prices.

Strict justice gives no answer to this problem, and the dictates of social justice would not be completely clear. Yet the workers' share in the productive process would give them a claim in equity, without prejudice to equal claims by stockholders and consumers. In such cases, a strike may conceivably be the only method for workers to press their claims. The alternative would be for them to resign themselves to a denial of their interests or to seek some outside source to award this to them. The second method, as will be noted subsequently, would probably be contrary to social justice. Hence, the limitation laid down by Father Clune would leave workers' claims to the benevolence of employers, after the clear minimum demands of strict justice had been met. This does not seem to harmonize with the dignity of man and the partnership status for labor which we seek. Accordingly, we conclude that workers may strike for claims as well as rights, but that a greater justification would be required for the former than the latter, since equity is less compelling than strict justice.

The concrete determination of the justice or equity of a strike issue is not easy. The critic must understand the realities of industrial relations to be able to appraise correctly the issues involved. Thus, a strike for noneconomic reasons, such as for union recognition, may be vitally important for the workers. Only when the union is recognized may they be sure that their rights can be enforced. Again, workers may strike over an unjustified discharge of a fellow worker. Here they feel that precedent is essential, in that if the principle of unjustified discharge is allowed, no worker may be safe. On the other hand, there have been strikes motivated by considerations of union or civic politics. It would be unjust for a union leader to provoke a strike merely for the sake of his own personal pique or ambition. Political strikes, especially general strikes, are usually wrong, since there are better alternative methods in a democracy for securing political ends. They may not always be wrong, since sometimes they are a dramatic form of the right of petition, calling public attention to the inadequacy or injustice of administrative decisions. As an illustration, it sometimes happens that a legal means exists for settling a dispute without recourse to a strike, but that the use of this means involves intolerable delays, often for years. Direct efforts to secure a settlement would seem justified here.

Even more difficult are problems connected with secondary, sympathy, and jurisdictional disputes. In these cases, the employer is often an innocent victim caught in the crossfire between warring parties. There is little difficulty when the employer of primary and secondary strikers is the same person. Thus, if Corporation A had a strike in its New York plant called for a just cause, workers in its Detroit plant could strike to enforce the just claim of their fellow employees. Again, if one employer in an industry had a strike, and workers for other employers in the same industry had reason to feel that conditions obtained through the strike would become general, they might reasonably go out for their own protection. Otherwise, they would be victims of the divide-and-conquer strategy. Father Clune goes further and justifies, on the principle of indirect voluntary, a strike against the main supplier of a mill which is trying to break a just strike through the use of strikebreakers.[6] But he would not concede the justice of a sympathy strike merely because what hurts labor in one place hurts all workers. In other words, where workers have a real and tangible, even though indirect and secondary, interest in a just strike, this may be an excusing reason for them to go on strike. But if the interest is remote and fanciful, they would not be justified in striking.

---

[6] *Op. cit.*, pp. 416–417. The moral principle of the indirect voluntary permits a person to perform an action which is in itself morally good or indifferent, but from which an evil result may follow. This is permitted provided that the agent acts from correct motives, that the good result does not follow as a result of the evil, and that the reason for acting is sufficiently serious to outweigh the unintended but foreseen evil. Thus, a woman might, to save her life, permit radium treatments for cancer of the cervix, even though this might result in sterility.

Jurisdictional disputes are strikes over the allocation of work. They may be sanctioned where the employer has clearly violated a contract or the unwritten customs of the trade. But where he is merely an innocent party, a victim to the conflict of claims between two unions, such a strike does not seem just. In such cases social justice would call for resort to other methods, such as an impartial board to arbitrate the claims. If the affected parties cannot agree to disinterested judgment, then the state has the right and duty to enforce such an agreement.

Likewise, there are industries and occupations where the public interest is so paramount that strikes may not be tolerated or, at best, permitted as a last resort. Here the clear demands of the common good transcend the interest of the parties. In such cases alternate methods for solving the dispute must be set up, even though they involve techniques (such as compulsory arbitration) which would otherwise be unacceptable. One might here distinguish between an absolute and a relative public interest. In the first case, even one day's strike would be intolerable. This would be true of police, the army, firemen, emergency nurses in a hospital, electric power workers (if no service at all were maintained), or a total paralysis of all means of public transportation on a broad scale. In the second case, grave public inconvenience would be caused, but no disaster provided the strike were not prolonged unduly. This would be true of telephones, a major form of transportation, garbage collection, atomic energy production in time of international tension, war strikes in major industries, coal mining, oil transportation or production, milk and food delivery, or a limited strike in electric power production. In the first instance, strikes should be prohibited by law, with compulsory settlement of disputes. In the second category, strikes should be delayed by law, with public hearings and other pressures for an equitable settlement and an emergency power to stop the strike when disaster threatened. It does not follow from this that all strikes by public workers are unjustified. Many public servants are not performing emergency duties. Often a strike is the only means for publicizing the conditions of underpaid or mistreated government workers. Federal or state laws to prohibit such strikes by public workers are unjust if they do not provide effective alternative means for meeting rights and equitable claims.

Thus, in normal disputes between employers and their workers, a just cause for a strike may be found either in a right which has been denied or an equitable claim which is being pressed. This principle may be applied with limitations to secondary and sympathy strikes where the workers are striving for valid claims which otherwise might be lost. Even greater limitations should be imposed on jurisdictional strikes since satisfactory alternate methods for handling such disputes can be set up. Finally, in industries or occupations vitally affecting the public interest, the public good demands other means than a strike for deciding the justice of the case.

Other Conditions for a Strike. A strike for a just cause would not be legitimate if other means of settlement were not exhausted. The normal means of settlement are negotiation, conciliation, and arbitration. Thus, it would be unjust to call a "quickie" strike to settle a dispute, if no efforts had been made to negotiate the point. Damage would be caused to the employer and the public, without reasonable attempts to forestall this evil. There may be cases where solid grounds exist to believe that negotiations would be useless and that the employer would use the time to prepare strikebreaking methods. In such a situation, a sudden strike might be justified. Normally, however, both parties should attempt to bargain in good faith until it is clear that no settlement can be reached. Genuine collective bargaining involves efforts by both sides to present reasonable offers and to discuss the merits of the issues in question. A take-it-or-leave-it attitude would be permissible only after a complete breakdown of fair discussions. A certain amount of "padding" of claims or the use of poker-playing methods would not be unfair, since such tactics are usually expected and discounted in advance.

When negotiations break down, federal or state conciliation machinery is usually available. At times, private parties may serve as mediators. Here again both groups would be bound in justice to use such services, unless there are solid reasons to believe that conciliation is invoked merely to waste time and weaken the economic power of one party. Since there are profound psychological elements involved in the negotiation of contracts, it is often helpful to gain the aid of friendly or disinterested third persons.

If conciliation fails, it is possible to submit the dispute to judicial arbitration. Many industries have permanent arbitrators who handle contract disputes as well as grievances. In other cases, *ad hoc* arbitration is invoked when a situation reaches an impasse. On the other hand, most industries and labor unions are violently opposed to arbitration of issues, claims, and even rights in the *negotiation* of contracts. Employers claim that this would mean the abdication of basic managerial rights to an outsider who rarely can be as familiar with the industry as the parties directly concerned. Unions likewise are reluctant to entrust their rights or even claims to a third party. If disputes were only over rights, there would be less difficulty. But interests and claims are not easily subject to judicial decision. Even where economic rights are involved, such as a fair wage, an employer may be understandably reluctant to entrust to another a decision which may mean life or death to the company. History bears out these attitudes. Thus, decisions by the War Labor Board were often unsatisfactory to both parties. Both sides complained that they were denied just claims and awarded demands that were put in merely for the sake of padding. Labor courts in democratic countries have not been successful in adjudicating interests.[7] Compulsory arbitration, enforced by law, would amount to complete government control over industry and labor, since the economics of collective bargaining are far-reaching in their implications. Moreover, the existence of an outside court often tends to break down normal collective bargaining. One party or other merely goes through the motions, hoping to gain more from the outside

---

[7] See *Labour Courts* (Geneva: International Labor Organization, 1938).

agency than it could get directly. All these results are seriously contrary to the common good and hence involve a violation of social justice.

Compulsory arbitration might more easily be justified in the *administration* of a contract previously reached by collective bargaining. The contract settles clearly defined and limited rights and claims, so that its carrying out is a matter of justice. Actually, most modern agreements do have an arbitration clause. It is less satisfactory to subject to arbitration all disputes arising after a contract has been signed. Unforeseen issues, not covered by the contract, may arise. If they are important they should be handled by negotiation rather than by an outsider. Compulsory arbitration, with all its limitations, is likewise acceptable for jurisdictional disputes and absolute public interest disputes. In these cases, the evils caused by a strike outweigh the disadvantages attendant upon compulsory settlement of claims. Decisions in jurisdictional disputes are more akin to the interpretation of contracts and customs than they are to the awarding of claims. There is usually a body of precedent or analogy to similar situations which permits equitable decisions in such matters. Then, for absolute public-interest disputes, such industries or occupations are usually under a fair degree of government control already. Thus, compulsory arbitration would not here be extending appreciably the area of state penetration into private life.

The third major condition, that a strike should promise more good than the evil it occasions and that it have some chance of success, likewise must be judged in the light of industrial realities. Often workers remain on strike for a single cent an hour more than has been offered by the employer. It might take them years to gain what they seem to have lost in wages. Yet, there are intangibles involved in such situations which preclude an oversimplified treatment. Unions may feel that concessions made one year would be a precedent for further pressures later. There may be a principle of discrimination involved, with one union getting less than another. This could lead to the playing off of one against the other until both were rendered impotent. Most union leaders

— there are unfortunate exceptions — like most employers realize that a strike is a serious weapon, to be used only as a last resort. Even if they could flaunt public opinion, and only a few think they may today, they know that a strike is a terrific internal strain upon a union. Many a union has been broken as a result of strikes. Hence when either an employer or a union risks a strike because of seemingly trivial issues, it may often be necessary as a matter of principle or vital psychology. The surface cause of a dispute may be but a last straw in a long history of irritations, just as quarrels between individuals may erupt violently for apparently slight reasons. Thus, it is almost impossible to generalize as to which causes of strikes outweigh the attendant evils. This has to be done in each individual case by persons experienced in the ways of industrial life.

In any strike, the public might well remember that the workers are not necessarily the real cause of the inconvenience it may suffer. If the strike is just, then the employer is morally wrong and hence to blame for public distress. The public is not always well informed as to the issues involved, particularly where local newspapers may take a partisan attitude. Again, even where the facts have been presented fairly, outsiders not experienced in industrial relations may be unable to interpret the issues correctly. At times, both employers and unions have been unjustly blamed for occasioning a strike on trivial issues, when in the circumstances they were of great importance. Thus, strikes have been condemned from pulpits because they were not over wages, whereas in fact working conditions and union-management relations are normally more vital to workers than wages. Apart from inflationary times, wage disputes are usually a secondary cause of strikes. Hence to pass moral judgment on strikes, it is necessary to have both general background knowledge of industrial relations and full information on the particular dispute.

Finally, as a condition of a just strike, it should be waged by morally acceptable means. It is not legitimate to engage in sabotage or other destruction of the employer's property. Nor is violence permissible, save in self-defense against clearly threatened violence from groups supporting the employer. If the employer uses strikebreakers against a just strike, the strikers would be permitted to boycott and attempt to persuade others to boycott goods so produced. This is merely inducing people not to cooperate in an unjust action by buying products made under unethical conditions. Picketing is lawful for the same reasons. Of course, there are forms of mass picketing which are conducive of violence. But mass picketing is not in itself wrong, since it has a legitimate purpose which may be intended. It is a more effective manner of advertising the strike and also it conduces to striker morale and solidarity, when they see their fellows on the picket line. Not all strike violence is induced by strikers. In the past, and in some industrially backward parts of the country today, it was a standard employer tactic to provoke violence so as to discredit the strikers in the eyes of the public. One notorious employer ordered strikebreakers to jostle and insult pickets while he paraded up an down thumbing his nose at them. Nor was he a small employer in an uncultured region. He was president of an important corporation, located near a city noted for its high degree of musical culture.

It is often questioned whether strikers may use any means short of violence to prevent strikebreakers from defeating a just strike. This would involve forcible exclusion of strikebreakers (without harming them) through mass picketing, blocking of plant entrances, and the like. It also brings up the sit-down strikes of the 1930's. This question is not so simple as it might seem on the surface. American opinion condemned the sit-down strikes as violation of property rights. But property rights are not absolute. They are conditioned by the public interest and social responsibility. Legitimate authority may force an employer not to use his property in an unsocial manner. The fault with mass picketing or sit-downs to exclude strikebreakers was not in what was done, but in the absence of authority to do it. It is the duty of the state to enforce social obligations upon property owners, at least when this involves the use of force. Such actions by strikers were vitiated in two ways: they were judges in their own cause, and they usurped civil authority. They sought justice, but it was lynch justice. It may be that extraordinary situations might justify such summary action, as when public authority has so broken down or been so corrupted in favor of the owners that it would be unable or unwilling to do justice. Direct action then would be in the nature of a limited revolt for strictly defined ends. And revolt is justifiable in extreme situations when normal political means will not secure a just government. Such an exception is isolated and rare. The normal method is to appeal to civil authority and, if justice is not done, to use democratic means to change the personnel of government.

If all the four conditions laid down are fulfilled, a strike may be just. Of course, it would be impossible to make any generalization as to run-of-the-mill American strikes and to say whether or not they have often been just. Two points do have validity: with some exceptions, most union leaders do not call strikes without serious reason, since the risk they run is too great; secondly, many newspapers do not give fair reports of the strikers' case, either through bias or through the necessary brevity found in tabloids or provincial papers largely interested in local news. Hence it is necessary to find the facts before judging.

When a strike is considered justified, social justice would warn us not to cross picket lines or buy "hot goods." If the need to patronize the employer is extreme (he might be the only supplier of necessities), one might cross a picket line, but social justice would indicate that the evil be compensated for by appropriate measures, such as indicating to the strikebreakers one's opinion of the situation. This action is judged in terms of social justice, since the principles of co-operation in evil would not ordinarily be too useful in appraising such a situation. Individual, highly indirect co-operation by the purchase of "hot goods" or any goods or services in a picketed store, theater, restaurant, or hotel probably would not affect matters sufficiently to make an appreciable difference. This may not be true if a community leader, such as a prominent public official, professional man, or clergyman, were to cross a picket line. His influence would often be such as to make his action substantial co-operation in an unjust action.

In conclusion, it might be said that the prevalence and importance of strikes is frequently overstressed. Strikes are dramatic, whereas industrial peace seems prosaic. Lincoln Steffens observed that any newspaper can "break" a police chief simply by reporting and headlining routine crime news. Similarly, a bad public opinion can be created in regard to unions by overemphasis upon exceptional strikes, to the neglect of continuing examples of labor-management co-operation. The percentage of total working time lost by strikes in the period 1935–1939 was 0.27. Even the dramatic strikes of 1946 totaled only 1.43 per cent. The year 1947 had a percentage of 0.41 and 1948 had 0.37. These figures are somewhat low, since they measure only direct stoppages, not indirect effects. Nor do they allow for the unusual impact of highly critical strikes. But they do serve as a useful antidote to exaggeration.[8]

THE DUTIES OF LABOR

The duties of labor might be considered from three aspects, insofar as workers are dealing with employers, unions, and the public. With employers, they are engaged in joint operations for production. In regard to unions, they are forging a new force which should be highly influential in social policy. Finally, the rights of the public should not be overlooked in any actions taken in respect to either employers or unions.

Duties Toward Employers. A worker is bound in justice to work diligently and fairly in return for a decent wage. "An honest day's work for an honest day's pay" is the old maxim. Conscientious work means more than avoidance of loafing. It also involves care of property, concern with the quality of work, and a proper interest in the welfare of the employer. Concern

---

[8] Figures on strikes, like other labor statistics, are reported in the *Monthly Labor Review*. For a good, up-to-date, ethical study of strikes, see G. Clune, *op. cit.*, Chap. 19. The author studies the subject in greater detail than is usual, although he is more severe in some conclusions than is the case with the present text. The classic American study is D. A. McLean, *The Morality of the Strike* (New York: Kenedy, 1921).

for work should be especially great when the rate of pay is high, since the laborer is expected to earn this high wage. All this does not imply that a worker should be constantly employed at top speed. This would wear him out prematurely and injure his health. But he should adopt a pace suitable for maximum performance over a number of years. Furthermore, proper interest in the employer's welfare would call for the pointing out of defects in material, passing along suggestions for improved processes, and the like.

Difficult problems arise when questions about "soldiering," "feather-bedding," and "made work" come up. At first glance, such practices seem a clear violation of justice. They involve the demanding of pay for inadequate work or no work at all. But in the concrete setting of economic life, matters are not so simple. The worker who stretches out the job to make it last is thinking in terms of annual income rather than hourly wages. He expects the job to provide a year-around living for him, so he regulates his pace of operations so as to secure continual employment. Economically this is bad, since it adds to costs and thus hinders production. But from the viewpoint of strict justice, the worker might offer the justification that his labor should provide a living and that he is slowing down to ensure this. Since his contract does not specify a particular rate of production, he might interpret his implied obligation to do his best by saying that in the circumstances this is the most which could be expected. This problem can really be solved only through social justice, by so organizing the industry that secure annual employment can be had.

The same observation applies to feather-bedding and made work. These are employment measures rather than monetary exactions for work not done. They are devices used to force an industry or occupation to give employment to all members of a craft. Regrettable as they are from an economic and even moral point of view, the practical remedy is not the negative approach of decrying abuses. The real answer is to provide a solution for the unemployment problem. This means rationalization of a chronically depressed industry, so that steady and full employment can be had for trained craftsmen in that field. If the issue arises because of job displacement through technological progress, the remedy is a gradual introduction of improvements, so that the existing working force, particularly skilled workers, can be provided for. On the other hand, if labor groups resist technological advance, they are acting contrary to social justice. It was noted in the preceding chapter that a disorganized economy is the major obstacle to the payment of a universal family living wage. Only through increased productivity can we lower costs without decreasing wages. We need to turn out more goods and services with our existing labor force so that, when they are properly distributed, all will have enough.

At the same time, organized labor should recognize the evils of restrictive practices, whatever their subjective justification. More than any other practice, they give unions a bad name in the public mind. The public expects fair value when it pays a worker. It is understandably resentful when necessities are high priced because of work limitation. This is particularly the case in times of full employment. Here soldiering and feather-bedding may well be contrary to strict justice. At any time, the unions concerned would be wise to prepare a constructive, long-range program for remedying the conditions which have occasioned these practices.

In this light a special duty of workers, in social justice, is their willingness to co-operate with management to secure more efficient production. Labor-management co-operation is one of the main techniques for raising living standards. Moreover, it is desirable for its own sake since class hostility is contrary to the nature of industrial life. As was observed before, the uniting force of production is as important as the divisive force of distribution. This duty of co-operation implies a corresponding willingness of employers to do their share in meeting the legitimate demands of labor. Workers must be assured that generous efforts on their part will not mean that they will work themselves out of their jobs. The resulting increase must be distributed fairly among the workers, as well as among stockholders and consumers.

Co-operation will be achieved in practice only through long-range educational methods and by patient adjustments on both sides. The Church can help by its teachings in labor schools and employer forums. In some cases, there must be a new type of union leadership and employer attitudes. Where unions are new, particularly when they won their place by prolonged struggle against strong employer resistance, the pattern of aggressiveness is almost inevitable. It takes time to work out harmony between groups hitherto bitterly hostile. Aggression may also be a product of ideology, as when unions are Communist-led or employers are strongly individualistic. Unsocial attitudes on either side lead to conflict.

With all the faults of some unions, employers must bear a large share of the blame for an aggressive situation. As a rule, they get the type of union which their own conduct calls for. When they are "hard boiled" and try to break the union, it will become a fighting organization. If they are coldly impersonal, the union normally takes a strictly business attitude. Here one has an armed peace rather than either co-operation or conflict. Occasionally one finds collusion rather than real co-operation, the difference being that both sides unite in policies contrary to the public interest. More frequently there is a situation which might be called accommodation, where common interests are recognized but only in a limited fashion. Conflict and hostility are avoided, but positive friendliness and complete mutuality are absent. The test of full co-operation is progression beyond normal collective bargaining to joint efforts to increase productivity and to lower costs. The needle trades in the United States have progressed further along these lines than most industries. It is this final stage which is the goal of Catholic social teaching.[9]

---

[9] The analysis given here is adapted from the article "Varieties of Labor Relations" by B. M. Selekman, *Harvard Business Review*, March, 1949. The author concludes that the ideal of co-operation is unattainable here on a broad scale within the near future, but that accommodation is a realizable goal. He considers the fifteen case studies of the National Planning Association (*The Causes of Industrial Peace*) as mixtures of

We Catholics can do more than we have in the past to promote co-operation. At times we have been so preoccupied with labor's rights that we have appeared almost hostile to employers as a class. Sometimes we have been slow in recognizing new trends toward accommodation and even co-operation on the part of employers. From a purely psychological aspect, it is better to praise the good where we find it and to try to extend its application, than to concentrate upon denunciation of the bad. When one compares employer attitudes in the 1940's to those prevailing in the 1930's, it must be recognized that important progress has been made. Increasing emphasis is laid upon good industrial relations, personnel policies, and human relations. These trends are good starting points for the broader aims which we seek.

Duties in Regard to Unions. Workers have many duties as union members. Among these one of the most important is that they make the effort to see that their union follows sound principles. This involves attendance at meetings, conscientious voting in union elections, and even running for union office. Where unions have gone bad, either through communism or racketeering, there is nearly always a history of poorly attended union meetings. Workers are often content to let small cliques or factions run their unions, provided they get results. At times, this produces an entrenched bureaucracy which consolidates its power either through a political machine or by changing the union constitution. In this light, the obligation to take interest in union matters might well be compared to one's civic obligations, the more so since unions today are quasi-public institutions. Union members should not emulate corporation stockholders in the doubtful practice of evading responsibility behind the anonymity of a large organization.

At the same time, workers should avoid the opposite extreme of undue pressure on union officers. Holding union office is a

---

accommodation and co-operation. See also C. S. Golden and H. J. Ruttenberg, *The Dynamics of Industrial Democracy*, and S. H. Slichter, *Union Policies and Industrial Management*, Chap. 15 ff.

task beset with many trials and rewarded with ingratitude and abuse. It is almost a vocation rather than an attractive profession. While some union leaders may live well, a majority works long hours, particularly at night, under extreme tension. For one overpaid union racketeer, there are hundreds of underpaid and overworked servants of workers. So true is this that there exists at times a problem of social justice in relation to union employees. Unions, like Church and similar groups, occasionally expect their workers to toil long hours at inadequate pay for the sake of the cause.

The picture of unionism gained from the columns of Westbrook Pegler is often a travesty on the reality. He normally cites facts when speaking of persons — the libel laws insure that — but these facts are frequently exceptional rather than typical. Union members should be as fair to the officers as they should be to their employers. It is wrong to pressure them to solve unfounded grievances or to seek impossible contract demands. A good union servant should have some security in his office, consistent with the normal risks involved in democratic elections. Prolonged tenure in the case of union executives is not in itself different from the same tenure for corporation officials. Experience and competence should be rewarded by the confidence of the members.

Union officers in turn have duties toward their members. They owe them faithful and honest service, representing them with integrity and courage. They should consider themselves as servants of the workers. Any trend in the direction of autocracy and dictatorship violates the human dignity of the members. This does not mean that some discipline and leadership are not useful in unions. On the contrary, they are essential if the union is to function smoothly. Since public interest demands that labor organizations act as responsible and trustworthy groups, their leaders must have some power to enforce continuity of policy. It would be intolerable if any agreement were subject to repudiation by a small but vocal minority of members.

Union officials should insist that orderly methods be followed in handling grievances, with no wildcat and unauthorized strikes. They should have the courage to stand for sound policy. When their experience tells them that membership wishes are unwise, they should use all their ability to persuade the members to follow a wiser course. Of course, at this writing union discipline is harder to enforce than formerly. The Labor Management Relations Act, 1947, in the attempt to prevent union autocracy, went too far and deprived unions of the powers needed to make them responsible organizations. Thus, under a union shop, a member may be expelled only for nonpayment of dues. He might be a communist agitator, a thief, or a chronic trouble-maker for the union and the employer, yet he may not be deprived of union membership if he pays his dues.

Union officials should serve the interest of their members in relation to the employer. While they should explore all forms of labor-management co-operation, such activities must be open and upright. Collusive, underhand dealing with employers to the detriment of the workers is thoroughly dishonest. A union official who accepts secret payments from company officials to "go light" in his demands upon them is like a grafting public official. He betrays trust and is guilty of dishonesty. If the betrayal is serious, one might say that he has no right in justice to the salary which he takes from the union. He is receiving it only through fraud and deception.

On the other hand, there is no objection to personal friendliness between union officials and corporation executives. A private chat at the dinner table might solve problems in an hour which would take weeks in a grievance committee. Often there are matters of saving face which must be met and which can be discussed quietly. It sometimes happens that a union membership still distrusts an employer and is suspicious of every move he makes, whereas the union officials are convinced that his views have genuinely improved. Until the membership acquires trust, union officers must be aggressive and hard hitting in all public relations with the company. They must win through hard fighting victories which the employer was actually willing to concede without an argument. Thus, union officials temporarily may be compelled to show toward an employer hostility which they do not actually feel. These are interim problems, preliminary to the establishment of trust, not only felt, but openly expressed. In such a situation, private meetings with employer representatives would be legitimate, provided they were aimed at the genuine welfare of the members and that the latter had an opportunity to discuss and approve any agreements reached.

Union officials naturally should be honest in handling the funds of the membership. It would be desirable to have preliminary financial reports of a local on a quarterly basis, at least, with an annual detailed audit of funds both of the local and of the parent union. Members likewise should have fair opportunity to vote for their leaders in an honest election. In view of past abuses, there is a case for government regulation of such matters, in the attempt to preserve genuine democracy in unions. Labor groups today are no longer private associations; they are quasi-public bodies and hence have public responsibility. Present legal methods of handling such problems are inadequate, going too far in some instances and not far enough in others. Thus, efforts to strip union officials of certain powers because they have been abused are unwise. As noted before, unions must have disciplinary powers if they are to remain responsible organizations.

On the other hand, safeguards for the civil rights of union members are still inadequate. A union member unjustly expelled (where there is a union shop) often can secure justice only in the civil court. This is an expensive process, and many courts still will not assume jurisdiction in such cases on the grounds that unions are private societies. A more direct and adequate approach would be state or federal courts of labor civil rights which would, upon request, supervise elections, examine financial statements, and hear appeals from union disciplinary actions. These latter appeals could be handled in two ways. Normally, the court would act only after all recourse within the union constitution had been exhausted. Where grave harm was threatened, however (as when expulsion would deprive a worker of his livelihood), the court could intervene at once and stay execution of the order, if a *prima facie* case were made for the plaintiff in the appeal. Then the normal union appeals procedure would go on and a final judgment would be made by the court if a ruling adverse to the member were sustained by the union appeal machinery. Such direct methods would be more effective and sounder than the cumbersome, legalistic, and indirect approaches of the Taft-Hartley Act.

Other aspects of union duties have been treated in relation to various problems discussed in these chapters. The union should be equitable in its wage demands. It should be willing to work toward labor-management co-operation. It should not engage in collusion with employers to foster monopoly or restraint of trade. While the closed shop is morally legitimate, there is a correlative responsibility to admit all qualified members which the labor market can sustain without discrimination as to race, religion, or national origin. Above all, unions must recognize the primary claim of the common good. Individualism is as bad in labor as it is in industry, farming, or finance. Labor must accept social responsibility. From the individual union member to the great national federation, there should be a recognition of the public interest. If labor rightly decries excessive government intervention in its internal affairs, it must accept the correlative responsibility of keeping its own house in order. Such abuses as communism, racketeering, and autocracy have no place in organized labor. It is better that they be rooted out from within. But if unions default in this duty, government has the right to safeguard the common good in this field.[10]

Duties Toward the Public. Labor owes to the public a sense of responsibility in collective bargaining. This is manifested above all by the avoidance of crippling strikes called for trivial reasons.

---

[10] The classic treatment on this subject is J. Seidman, *Union Rights and Union Duties* (New York: Harcourt, 1943). An older book which is still highly valuable for its insight into organized labor is R. R. Brooks, *When Labor Organizes* (New Haven: Yale, 1937). For a sprightly series of essays from the Catholic viewpoint see W. J. Smith, *Spotlight on Labor Unions* (New York: Duell, Sloan & Pearce, 1946).

Strikes are more than a test of strength by the parties directly affected; they also can be a cause of much suffering to innocent groups not involved in the struggle. When a strike is just, and called for a serious reason, the public is less dissatisfied with the dislocation of its life. If it is well informed about the facts, it can bring pressure to bear on the employer to give justice to the workers. It is a different matter, however, when personalities, union politics, pique, and like extraneous reasons bring on strikes. Unfortunately, there has been in recent years sufficient surface evidence of irresponsibility to provoke a strong public reaction against organized labor. Even with due allowance for propaganda and bias in reporting labor disputes, there is a certain residue of cases which cause justifiable public resentment.

There is also a public interest in the internal conduct of labor unions. Given the tremendous power of organized labor, it is essential that this power be used in a restrained and reasonable manner. Hence much importance attaches to the presence or absence of labor education, the quality of the training afforded union members, and the tone of the labor press. Labor should have the maturity commensurate with power. It has attained its manhood and must now take its part in common community burdens. Most labor leaders are eager to assume such duties. They take their part in community-chest programs, Red Cross drives, and bond sales. But the labor movement could acquire more finesse in public relations. It could drop the class-hostility approach in its press and speeches, particularly where employers are prepared for co-operation or, at least, accommodation. Of course, labor's limitations in realizing the full implications of its quasi-public status are paralleled in other sections of the community. Many businessmen and farm leaders are victims of the same cultural lag, and their press often reflects narrow class interests rather than community concerns. Unreconstructed individualists remain in all groups. Nevertheless, business as a whole has shown more awareness of the need for good public relations than has the labor movement. Fine words may not always be backed up by deeds in the business community. But labor too often has concealed fine deeds behind the smoke screen of careless public utterances.

More is needed than protestations of public interest. There must be a detailed working out of common programs on all levels. From the single small factory, through giant industries, to the great national federations of business and labor, there should be a realization of common concerns and general responsibilities. Collective bargaining should move in the direction of co-operation for the welfare of all. It should never degenerate into collusion to exploit the consumer. Co-operation in turn should be carried into ever higher levels through frequent conferences of the various local and national organizations. It would be desirable that friendly relations and informal meetings be a normal thing between top labor and business leaders. Even more valuable would be close relations between the expert advisers, such as lawyers and economists, and the leaders in these fields. While economics is not an exact science comparable to mathematics or physics, there are nevertheless broad areas of agreement among experts. Certainly there is little justification today for juggling statistics or distorting trends in the attempt to prove a position taken merely for partisan reasons. Thus, all trained economists realize that living standards will rise only through increased productivity. This in turn can be achieved through capital investment and through labor-management co-operation. Gains obtainable through redistribution of present income are, on the whole, negligible, especially when considered in terms of their effect upon capital formation. Except where prices and profits are badly out of line, there need be little difference in the economic attitudes of capital and labor.

Actual public stands and collective-bargaining positions by labor in recent years have at times varied from the ideal stated above. On the credit side, both major labor federations have stressed the need for increased productivity. They have favored labor-management co-operation. The A. F. of L., in its *Labor's Monthly Survey*, has constantly reiterated this theme in its advice to locals engaged in collective bargaining. But its crafts have resisted many cost-cutting devices in the housing field, whereas C.I.O.'s Walter Reuther has stressed the advantages of rationalization in this disorganized industry. Both groups have been laggard in facing the economics of increased capital formation, especially in terms of tax and profit implications. In this respect, *Labor's Monthly Survey* has been more realistic than C.I.O.'s *Economic Outlook*. The C.I.O. has been more impressed with the Keynes-Hansen thesis of economic maturity, with emphasis upon public rather than private investment. It has also stressed purchasing power economics to the comparative neglect of cost economics. Again, many liberal but independent economists criticized certain labor groups regarding their use of statistics in the inflationary period of 1946–1948. By using a 1945 base, some labor economists argued that labor had suffered a great loss in real income after the war. They also became alarmed at drastic declines in savings in 1948. These points are sufficiently important to warrant an extensive quotation of the contrary viewpoint.

> Surely, allowance should be made for the inaccuracy of the cost-of-living index under conditions of a war economy. If the 1945 index number is raised 10 points to take care of such factors as black markets, deterioration of quality of goods, and the like, it is found that the "real" national income in 1948 was equal to that in 1945 and "real" weekly earnings of factory workers in 1948 were roughly the same as in 1945.
>
> At first sight, this seems disappointing. Actually a tremendous success has been achieved since 1945. At that time we worked 48 hours a week; our schools were half-empty; many children were left without material care. Now, we work 40 hours a week, enrollment in schools and colleges is at an all-time peak, millions of women who worked in factories during the war are back in their homes. In terms of overall output per man-hour, this country has made, since 1945, considerable progress.
>
> This is not all, however. In 1945, goods and services worth $67.2 billion were diverted to war. In 1948 we did not spend more than $20 billion for defense. Personal consumption expenditures totalled $121.7 billion in 1945 and $178.5 billion in 1948. With correction for changes in prices, the real purchasing power of the population has increased by approximately 17 per cent. Since the share of labor in this aggregate did not change much in these three years, the advance in economic welfare of the working population was of the same order of magnitude.

> . . . There can be no objection to the efforts of labor unions to raise
> real wages to the level of the standard budget of the Department of
> Labor, or higher. But this goal implies a substantial increase in the
> amount of goods and services available for the working population —
> more houses, more choice food, better facilities for recreation, better
> education of children, more health protection, and so forth. These prob-
> lems cannot be solved by changes in wages, profits, and prices, but
> require constructive efforts in the direction of a better utilization of
> national resources, increased productivity of labor, and the like.[11]

Elsewhere the author notes that much of the decline of savings
is explained by the purchase of automobiles and other durables,
not available during the war. On the basis of this analysis, it
would seem that certain labor economists were not giving their
chiefs completely sound advice in regard to collective bargaining.
While this particular problem is a closed book at the present
writing, it does point a lesson which has more than transitory
value. Sound economic analysis could do much to bridge the gap
between capital and labor and to emphasize common interests
rather than divisive claims.

The failure of many labor unions to consider the economic
implications of their wage demands has caused concern to
several American economists. They feel that if recent trends
persist, union demands will cause dislocations which will wreck
the present economic system. Nor is this view based merely on
isolated instances, such as the coal industry, whose product is
being priced out of the market. Rather it is felt that the need
for dramatic gains may lead to continuing wage demands upon
many industries, far above the amount warranted by increased
productivity. These fears further point up the need for statesmanship on both sides of the labor-management situation.[12]

If both labor and business can deepen their realization that
they have all to gain by working together, we can well hope for
continuing advances in our standard of living. Better organization

---

[11] W. S. Woytinsky, "Economic Outlook, 1949," *The New Leader*, April 23, 1949.
The New Leader is a liberal, Social-Democratic publication.
[12] See C. E. Lindblom, *Unions and Capitalism* (New Haven: Yale, 1949), and N. W.
Chamberlain, *The Union Challenge to Management Control*.

will be achieved, costs will be cut, efficiency increased, and social harmony promoted. The attainment of this goal would be a suitable objective for all educational and opinion-molding forces in the nation.

READINGS[*]

J. Shister, *Economics of the Labor Market.*
S. H. Slichter, *Union Policies and Industrial Management.*
R. A. Lester, *Economics of Labor.*
F. Baerwald, *Fundamentals of Labor Economics.*
P. Taft, *Economics and Problems of Labor.*
G. Clune, *Christian Social Reconstruction*, Chaps. 15–20.
E. Cahill, *Framework of a Christian State*, Chap. 21.
N. C. McKenna, "The Catholic and His Union."

---

[*] For further readings, see List No. 10 in the Appendix.

Chapter XII. PROPERTY

Leo XIII, Rerum Novarum

10–17. (*Summarized.*) Man differs from beast in that he has the right of ownership. His ability to foresee the future and meet its needs is an added reason for this right. This is a natural right, anterior to the formation of the state and independent of it. But the broad right of ownership does not preclude the institution of private property,. "However the earth may be apportioned among private owners, it does not cease to serve the common interest of all, inasmuch as no living being is sustained except by what the fields bring forth. Those who lack resources supply labor, so that it can truly be affirmed that the entire scheme of securing a livelihood consists in the labor which a person expends either on his own land or in some working occupation, the compensation for which is drawn ultimately from no other source than the varied products of the earth and is exchanged for them" (No. 14). Private possessions are clearly in accord with nature, since only by man's labor can nature be truly productive. Theories which permit use of land, but deny ownership [single tax], overlook the improvement of land through cultivation. "Rightly, therefore, the human race as a whole, moved in nowise by the dissenting opinions of a few, and observing nature carefully, has found in the law of nature itself the basis of the distribution of goods, and, by the practice of all ages, has consecrated private possessions as something best adapted to man's nature and to peaceful and tranquil living together" (No. 17). Civil and divine law [against theft] sanction such an institution.

18–23. (*Summarized.*) Property also fits in aptly with family obligations. A father protects his children through saving and the right of inheritance. The family is certainly prior to the state, even though subject to just laws. Moreover, the equality envisioned by socialism would in reality lead to turmoil and dissension. "Let it be regarded, therefore, as established that in seeking help for the masses this principle before all is to be considered basic, namely, that private ownership must be preserved inviolate" (No. 23).

55. But it will be well to touch here expressly on certain matters of special importance. The capital point is this, that private property ought

to be safeguarded by the sovereign power of the state and through the bulwark of its laws. And especially, in view of such a great flaming up of passion at the present time, the masses ought to be kept within the bounds of their moral obligations. For while justice does not oppose our striving for better things, on the other hand, it does forbid anyone to take from another what is his and, in the name of a certain absurd equality, to seize forcibly the property of others; nor does the interest of the common good itself permit this. Certainly, the great majority of working people prefer to secure better conditions by honest toil, without doing wrong to anyone. Nevertheless, not a few individuals are found who, imbued with evil ideas and eager for revolution, use every means to stir up disorder and incite to violence. The authority of the state, therefore, should intervene and, by putting restraint upon such disturbers, protect the morals of workers from their corrupting arts and lawful owners from the danger of spoliation.

Pius XII, Discourse, May 20, 1948

The recognition of this right [of property] harmonizes with the dignity of the human personality, with the recognition of inviolable rights and duties inseparably inherent in the free personality received from God.

Only those who deny to men the dignity of free persons can admit the possibility of substituting for the right of private property (and consequently the very institution of private property) some system of insurance or legal protection by public law. May we never see the day when, on this point, a chasm will be formed to separate peoples.

Pius XII, Radio Address, September 1, 1944

Private property is in a special manner the natural fruit of labor, the product of an intense activity on the part of the man who acquires it through his energetic will to ensure and improve, by his own forces, his own living conditions and those of his family, to create for himself and those dear to him a field in which they may rightly enjoy, not only economic freedom, but political, cultural, and religious freedom as well.

Pius XII, Discourse to Italian Workers, June 13, 1943

. . . not to abolish private property, the foundation of family stability, but to work for its extension as the reward of the conscientious toil of every working man and woman, so that little by little may be diminished that mass of uneasy and rash people who, sometimes from taciturn despair, at others through broad instinct, allow themselves to be carried off by false doctrine or by the clever tricks of agitators who are bereft of all moral sense.

The Church and Social Order

20. The Church has always defended the right to own private property and also to bequeath and to inherit it. We have vindicated this right even to the point of being falsely accused of favoring the rich against the poor. The Church teaches that the right to own property is based on the natural law of which God Himself is the author. By the law of nature man must provide for himself and his family and he can fully discharge this obligation only if there exists an established system of private ownership.

PROPERTY RIGHTS: SOCIAL AND INDIVIDUAL

Pius XI, Quadragesimo Anno

45. First, then, let it be considered as certain and established that neither Leo nor those theologians who have taught under the guidance and authority of the Church have ever denied or questioned the twofold character of ownership, usually called individual and social according as it regards either separate persons or the common good. For they have always unanimously maintained that nature, rather the Creator Himself, has given man the right of private ownership, not only that individuals may be able to provide for themselves and their families, but also that the goods which the Creator destined for the entire family of mankind may through this institution truly serve this purpose. All this can be achieved in nowise except through the maintenance of a certain and definite order.

46. Accordingly, twin rocks of shipwreck must be carefully avoided. For, as one is wrecked upon, or comes close to, what is known as "individualism" by denying or minimizing the social and public character of the right of property, so by rejecting or minimizing the private and individual character of this same right, one inevitably runs into "collectivism" or at least closely approaches its tenets.

49. It follows from what We have termed the individual and at the same time social character of ownership, that men must consider in this matter not only their own advantage but also the common good. To define these duties in detail when necessity requires and the natural law has not done so, is the function of those in charge of the state. Therefore, public authority, under the guiding light always of the natural and divine law, can determine more accurately upon consideration of the true requirements of the common good, what is permitted and what is not permitted to owners in the use of their property. Moreover, Leo XIII wisely taught "that God has left the limits of private possessions to be fixed by the industry of men and institutions of peoples."

Code of Social Principles

94. Men have received from nature, and consequently from the Creator, the right of private property, both to enable each to provide for the sustenance of himself and of those dependent on him, and to secure at the same time, by this institution, that the natural resources of the world may effectively fulfill the purpose assigned them by Providence, which is to provide for the essential needs of the entire human race. The right of property, then, has a twofold character: the one individual and private, the other social and public.

95. Appropriation of land and of the instruments of production is therefore legitimate. But the right of private property is neither identified with nor dependent on its use. Commutative justice only forbids the owner to injure the rights of others. In such a case only does it oblige to restitution. As to the rest, the use of the right of private property depends on all the other virtues, especially social justice, individual and social charity, and munificence.

The owner's use of his superfluous wealth, that is of the revenue not necessary for the maintenance of a standard of living in keeping with and befitting his position, depends, just as in the case of the use of the capital itself, on all virtues other than commutative justice. Consequently, almsgiving on the one hand, and, on the other, the financing of an industry, which gives rise to both remunerative work and useful products, must be considered as praiseworthy uses of superfluous wealth.

96. As far as necessity demands, public authority, taking into consideration the common good, has the right to determine in the light of natural and divine law, what use owners may or may not make of their possessions.

97. Under the influence of various factors such as geographical position, the nature of the soil and subsoil, industrial technology, customs, laws, and so on, private ownership may take on different forms and have a wider or narrower application.

Though the system of private ownership, which the public authority may determine, cannot be looked upon as absolutely unchangeable, still the natural right of private property and of transmitting one's goods by inheritance must always be safeguarded. These are rights which the public authority may not abolish. Nor has it the right to extinguish private property by excessive burdens and taxation.

TAXATION

Leo XIII, Rerum Novarum

67. But these advantages can be attained only if private wealth is not drained away by crushing taxes of every kind. For since the right of pos-

sessing goods privately has been conferred not by man's law, but by nature, public authority cannot abolish it, but can only control its exercise and bring it into conformity with the commonweal. Public authority, therefore, would act unjustly and inhumanly, if in the name of taxes it should appropriate from the property of private individuals more than is equitable.

Pius XI, Quadragesimo Anno

49. That the state is not permitted to discharge its duty arbitrarily is, however, clear. The natural right itself both of owning goods privately and of passing them on by inheritance ought always to remain intact and inviolate, since this indeed is a right that the state cannot take away: "For man is older than the state," and also "domestic living together is prior both in thought and in fact to uniting into a polity." Wherefore the wise Pontiff declared that it is grossly unjust for a state to exhaust private wealth through the weight of imposts and taxes. "For since the right of possessing goods privately has been conferred not by man's law, but by nature, public authority cannot abolish it, but can only control its exercise and bring it into conformity with the commonweal." Yet when the state brings private ownership into harmony with the needs of the common good, it does not commit a hostile act against private owners but rather does them a friendly service; for it thereby effectively prevents the private possession of goods, which the Author of nature in His most wise providence ordained for the support of human life, from causing intolerable evils and thus rushing to its own destruction; it does not destroy private possessions, but safeguards them; and it does not weaken private property rights, but strengthens them.

Pius XI, On Atheistic Communism

75. The state must take every measure necessary to supply employment particularly for the heads of families and for the young. To achieve this end demanded by the pressing needs of the common welfare, the wealthy classes must be induced to assume those burdens without which human society cannot be saved nor they themselves remain secure. However, measures taken by the state with this end in view ought to be of such a nature that they will really affect those who possess more than their share of capital resources, and who continue to accumulate them to the grievous detriment of others.

Pius XII, Discourse on Public Finance, October 2, 1948

The Church . . . addressing herself to those who have some share of responsibility in the treatment of public finance questions . . . beseeches them: In the name of human conscience, do not destroy morals from the top. Forego those measures which, despite their technical virtuosity, shock and wound the people's sense of the just and unjust, or which relegate to the background their vital urge, their legitimate ambition to harvest the fruits of their own labor, and their anxiety over family security, all considerations which merit first place in the mind of the legislator and not the last.

The financial system of the state should aim at reorganizing the economic situation in a manner that would assure the people the material conditions of life indispensable for following the supreme end assigned by the Creator: the development of intellectual, spiritual, and religious life.

Bishops' Statement, 1933

Our Catholic scholars, economists, and moralists should study our crushing burden of taxation which is, in itself, an indictment of government and of our economic system. Legislators have a serious responsibility whenever they impose taxes. The general welfare of the people should always be kept in mind in performing this duty. To impose taxes unjustly or in a reckless manner or in the interest of special groups or according to the immoral practice of trading votes, too common among legislators, must be regarded as a violation of the oath of office and the betrayal of a sacred trust. Taxation is unjust that favors the strong rather than the weak, the rich rather than the poor. Legislators and men in political life, who in imposing taxes sacrifice the general welfare of the people in order to advance their own interests and to continue in office, deserve the severest censure.

Excessive taxation has been a serious hindrance to the revival of business. Patriotic citizens should fearlessly condemn the extravagant expenditure of the people's money by government agencies and bureaucracies. In recent years the cost of government has mounted to staggering proportions, even though the average income of our citizens has been greatly reduced or practically wiped out. This tremendous increase in government expenditures has not brought any corresponding gain to our people.

In our country, where the responsibility of selecting honest and competent officials and of forming opinion devolves upon the citizens, it is all the more important that thoughtful and informed men become tax-conscious, that they realize that there will be a day of accounting for endless bond issues, and that they exercise their influence to the utmost to arouse and to sustain in the people at large an intelligent interest in public expenditures.

In the simplest language possible taxation, which ultimately is passed on in great measure to the laboring and trades classes, should be explained to the people. Citizens should be interested in knowing how their money is being spent. They should be informed to what an extent taxation increases the price of the very necessaries of life. Studies on this vital subject should be put out in the most popular form. Public opinion should continue to demand that expenditures by the government for nonessentials be eliminated; that our educational system be simplified; that bureaucracies be limited; that the injustice of favoring special groups at public expense should cease; also, that a clear and simple statement of the cost of government be made available to all our citizens.

Code of Social Principles

143. Taxation laws which are just, and justly applied, are binding in conscience. Catholic sociologists should endeavor to correct wrong opinions on this matter, and in the name of social justice to lead good people to participate loyally in the expenses of the state.

144. Taxation, i.e., contributing to public funds without immediate gain to the contributor, is not a real, but a personal obligation upon citizens, in the sense that it does not bear immediately upon property, but on its owner.

145. So far as the common good allows, distributive justice requires that taxes should not be directly proportionate to incomes, nor levied on a scale increasing at a constant rate, but on a scale whose rate of increase gradually diminishes until at the upper limit it approximates to a proportional tax. Such a tax may be called "progressive."

146. In theory, the ideal would be a single progressive tax on income. But in practice a part of the public revenue must be obtained through indirect taxes, which are more willingly accepted and do not so easily become oppressive.

147. Direct taxation has, however, the advantage of asking from the citizens a conscious sacrifice which gives them an interest in public affairs.

148. In the choice of taxation, the legislator should have regard to these three rules:

a) To avoid taxes which bring manifestly harmful results and those which admit of fraud, since the latter encourage habits of evasion.

b) When imposing new taxes, to tap sources of revenue rather than funds which are economically sterile and otherwise reasonable. In any case, established forms of taxation are generally adjusted by their methods of application, or by reactions that bring about by degrees an equitable distribution of these public charges.

c) Sumptuary taxes, on luxuries or undue extravagance, deserve to be encouraged. Even if their result is not great, the moral lesson they teach enlightens and strengthens the public conscience, and serves the common good at least to that extent.

149. Very high taxes on legacies, though justifiable in exceptional cir-

cumstances, undermine the principle of property. They scarcely differ
from confiscation, and hinder the building up of national reserves.

DUTIES OF PROPERTY OWNERS

Leo XIII, Rerum Novarum

35. On the use of wealth we have the excellent and extremely weighty
teaching which, although found in a rudimentary stage in pagan philosophy, the Church has handed down in a completely developed form and
causes to be observed not only in theory but in everyday life. The foundation of this teaching rests on this, that the just ownership of money is
distinct from the just use of money.

36. To own goods privately, as We saw above, is a right natural to
man, and to exercise this right, especially in life in society, is not only
lawful, but clearly necessary. "It is lawful for man to own his own things.
It is even necessary for human life." But if the question be asked:
How ought man use his possessions, the Church replies without hesitation:
"As to this point, man ought not regard external goods as his own, but as
common so that, in fact, a person should readily share them when he sees
others in need. Wherefore the Apostle says: 'Charge the rich of this
world . . . to give readily, to share with others'" (*Summa*, II, II, 66, 2).
No one, certainly, is obliged to assist others out of what is required for
his own necessary use or for that of his family, or even to give to others
what he himself needs to maintain his station in life becomingly and decently: "No one is obliged to live unbecomingly." But when the demands of
necessity and propriety have been sufficiently met, it is a duty to give to the
poor out of that which remains. "Give that which remains as alms." These
are duties not of justice, except in cases of extreme need, but of Christian
charity, which obviously cannot be enforced by legal action. But the laws
and judgments of men yield precedence to the law and judgment of Christ
the Lord, who in many ways urges the practice of almsgiving: "It is more
blessed to give than to receive," and who will judge a kindness done or
denied to the poor as done or denied to Himself. "As long as you did it
for one of these, the least of My brethren, you did it for Me." The substance of all this is the following: whoever has received from the bounty
of God a greater share of goods, whether corporal and external, or of the
soul, has received them for this purpose, namely, that he employ them for
his own perfection and, likewise, as a servant of Divine Providence, for
the benefit of others. "Therefore, he that hath talent, let him constantly
see to it that he be not silent; he that hath an abundance of goods, let
him be on the watch that he grow not slothful in the generosity of mercy;
he that hath a trade whereby he supports himself, let him be especially
eager to share with his neighbor the use and benefit thereof."

Pius XI, Quadragesimo Anno

47. In order to place definite limits on the controversies that have arisen over ownership and its inherent duties there must be first laid down as a foundation a principle established by Leo XIII: the right of property is distinct from its use. That justice called commutative commands sacred respect for the division of possessions and forbids invasion of others' rights through the exceeding of the limits of one's own property; but the duty of owners to use their property only in a right way does not come under this type of justice, but under other virtues, obligations of which "cannot be enforced by legal action." Therefore, they are in error who assert that ownership and its right use are limited by the same boundaries; and it is much farther still from the truth to hold that a right to property is destroyed or lost by reason of abuse or nonuse.

48. Those, therefore, are doing a work that is truly salutary and worthy of all praise who, while preserving harmony among themselves and the integrity of the traditional teaching of the Church, seek to define the inner nature of these duties and their limits whereby either the right of property itself or its use, that is, the exercise of ownership, is circumscribed by the necessities of social living. On the other hand, those who seek to restrict the individual character of ownership to such a degree that in fact they destroy it are mistaken and in error.

50. Furthermore, a person's superfluous income, that is, income which he does not need to sustain life fittingly and with dignity, is not left wholly to his own free determination. Rather the Sacred Scriptures and the Fathers of the Church constantly declare in the most explicit language that the rich are bound by a very grave precept to practice almsgiving, beneficence, and munificence.

51. Expending larger incomes so that opportunity for gainful work may be abundant, provided, however, that this work is applied to producing really useful goods, ought to be considered, as We deduce from the principles of the Angelic Doctor, an outstanding exemplification of the virtue of munificence and one particularly suited to the needs of the times.

56. Unquestionably, so as not to close against themselves the road to justice and peace through these false tenets, both parties ought to have been forewarned by the wise words of Our Predecessor: "However the earth may be apportioned among private owners, it does not cease to serve the common interests of all." This same doctrine We ourselves also taught above in declaring that the division of goods which results from private ownership was established by nature itself in order that created things may serve the needs of mankind in fixed and stable order. Lest one wander

from the straight path of truth, this is something that must be continually kept in mind.

Pius XI, On Atheistic Communism

48. To be sure of eternal life, therefore, and to be able to help the poor effectively, it is imperative to return to a more moderate way of life, to renounce the joys, often sinful, which the world today holds out in such abundance; to forget self for love of the neighbor.

A JUST DISTRIBUTION OF PROPERTY

Leo XIII, Rerum Novarum

65. We have seen, in fact, that the whole question under consideration cannot be settled effectually unless it is assumed and established as a principle, that the right of private property must be regarded as sacred. Wherefore, the law ought to favor this right and, so far as it can, see that the largest possible number among the masses of the population prefer to own property.

66. But if the productive activity of the multitude can be stimulated by the hope of acquiring some property in land, it will gradually come to pass that, with the difference between extreme wealth and extreme penury removed, one class will become neighbor to the other. Moreover, there will surely be a greater abundance of the things which the earth produces. For when men know they are working on what belongs to them, they work with far greater eagerness and diligence. Nay, in a word, they learn to love the land cultivated by their own hands, whence they look not only for food but for some measure of abundance for themselves and their dependents. All can see how much this willing eagerness contributes to an abundance of produce and the wealth of a nation.

Pius XI, Quadragesimo Anno

57. Therefore, the riches that the economic-social developments constantly increase ought to be so distributed among individual persons and classes that the common advantage of all, which Leo XIII had praised, will be safeguarded; in other words, that the common good of all society will be kept inviolate.

58. To each, therefore, must be given his own share of goods, and the distribution of goods which, as every discerning person knows, is laboring today under the gravest evils due to the huge disparity between the few exceedingly rich and the unnumbered propertyless, must be effectively called back to and brought into conformity with the norms of the common good, that is, social justice.

60. The immense multitude of the nonowning workers on the one hand, and the enormous riches of certain very wealthy men on the other, establish an unanswerable argument that the riches which are so abundantly produced in our age of "industrialism," as it is called, are not rightly distributed and equitably made available to the various classes of people.

61. Therefore, with all our strength and effort we must strive that at least in the future the abundant fruits of production will accrue equitably to those who are rich and will be distributed in ample sufficiency among the workers . . . that they may increase their property by thrift, that they may bear, by wise management of this increase in property, the burdens of family life with greater ease and security, and that, emerging from that insecure lot in life in whose uncertainties nonowning workers are cast, they may be able not only to endure the vicissitudes of earthly existence, but also have assurance that when their lives are ended they will provide in some measure for those they leave after them.

63. . . . It will be impossible to put these principles into practice unless the nonowning workers through industry and thrift advance to the state of possessing some little property.

Pius XI, On Atheistic Communism

50. Is it not deplorable that the right of private property defended by the Church should so often have been used as a weapon to defraud the workingman of his just salary and his social rights?

Pius XI, Caritate Christi Compulsi

15. We advocated so energetically a more equitable distribution of the goods of the earth and indicated the most efficacious means of restoring health and strength to the ailing social body and tranquillity and peace to its suffering members.

Pius XII, Sertum Laetitiae

1464. The fundamental point of the social question is this, that the goods created by God for all men should in the same way reach all, justice and charity helping.

Pius XII, Christmas Broadcast, 1942

1840. The dignity of the human person, then, requires normally, as a natural foundation of life, the right to the use of the goods of the earth. To this right corresponds the fundamental obligation to grant private ownership of property, if possible, to all. Positive legislation regulating private ownership may change and more or less restrict its use. But if legislation is to play its part in the pacification of the community, it must prevent the worker, who is or will be a father of a family, from being condemned to an economic dependence and slavery which is irreconcilable with his rights as a person. Whether this slavery rises from the exploitation of private capital or from the power of the state which dominates all and controls the whole field of public and private life, even going into the realm of ideas and beliefs and of conscience, this lack of liberty can have more serious consequences, as experience shows and proves. . . .

1851. These exigencies include, besides a just wage which covers the needs of the worker and his family, the conservation and perfection of a social order which will make possible an assured, even if modest, private property for all classes of society. . . .

Pius XII, La Solennità della Pentecoste

1683. Every man, as a living being gifted with reason, has in fact from nature the fundamental right to make use of the material goods of the earth, while it is left to the will of man and to the juridical statutes of nations to regulate in greater detail the actuation of this right. This individual right cannot in any way be suppressed, even by other clear and undisputed rights over material goods. Undoubtedly the natural order, deriving from God, demands also private property and the free reciprocal commerce of goods by interchange and gift, as well as by the functioning of the state as a control over both these institutions. But all this remains subordinated to the natural scope of material goods and cannot emancipate itself from the first and fundamental right which concedes their use to all men; but it should rather serve to make possible the actuation of this right in conformity with its scope. Only thus can we and must we secure that private property and the use of material goods bring to society peace and prosperity and long life, that they no longer set up precarious conditions, which will give rise to struggles and jealousies, and which are left to the mercy of the blind interplay of force and weakness.

1684. The native right to the use of material goods, intimately linked as it is to the dignity and other rights of the human person together with the statutes mentioned above, provides man with a secure material basis of the highest import, on which to rise to the fulfillment, with reasonable liberty, of his moral duties. The safe guardianship of this right will ensure the personal dignity of man, and will facilitate for him the attention to and fulfillment of that sum of stable duties and decisions for which he is directly responsible to his Creator.

Pius XII, Discourse to Italian Workers, June 13, 1943

Not to abolish private property, the foundation of family stability, but to work for its extension as the reward of the conscientious toil of every working man and woman. . . .

Pius XII, Discourse to Catholic Action Men, September 7, 1947

What you can and ought to strive for is a more just distribution of wealth. This is and this remains a central point in Catholic social doctrine. The natural course of affairs, no doubt, brings with it — this is neither economically nor socially abnormal — an unequal distribution, within certain limits, of the goods of the earth. But the Church is opposed to the accumulation of these goods in the hands of a relatively small and exceedingly rich group, while vast masses of people are condemned to a pauperism and an economic condition unworthy of human beings.

A more just distribution of wealth is, then, a high social aim worthy of your efforts. Its successful realization presupposes that individuals as well as groups show the same comprehension of the rights and needs of others as they have of their own rights and their own needs. To cultivate this instinct in your own lives and to awaken it in others is one of the noblest tasks of the Men of Catholic Action.

Pius XII, Radio Broadcast, September 1, 1944

In defending, therefore, the principle of private property, the Church pursues a high ethicosocial purpose. She does not intend to defend absolutely and simply the present state of affairs, as if she saw in it the expression of God's will, nor to defend as a matter of principle the rich and the plutocrat against the poor and the indigent. Far from it! Right from the beginning she has been the defender of the oppressed against the tyranny of the powerful, and has always sponsored the just claims of all classes of workers against every injustice. But the Church aims rather at securing that the institution of private property be such as it should be according to the designs of God's wisdom and the dispositions of nature: an element of social order, a necessary presupposition to human initiative, an incentive to work to the advantage of life's purpose here and hereafter, and hence of the liberty and the dignity of man, created in the likeness of God, who, from the beginning, assigned him for his benefit domination over material things.

Take away from the worker the hope of acquiring some goods as personal property, and what other natural incentive can you offer him to make him work hard, to save, to live soberly, when not a few men and peoples today have lost all and have nothing left but their capacity to work? Or perhaps men want to perpetuate the economic conditions of wartime by which, in some countries, the public authority has control of all means of production and provides for everybody and everything, but with the lash of a severe discipline? Or perhaps they want to lie down before the dictatorship of a political group which will, as the ruling class, dispose of the means of production, and at the same time of the daily bread and hence of the will to work of individuals?

The social and economic policy of the future, the controlling power of the state, of local bodies, of professional institutions cannot permanently secure their end, which is the genuine productivity of social life and the normal returns on national economy, except by respecting and safeguarding the vital function of private property in its personal and social values. When the distribution of property is an obstacle to this end — which is not necessarily nor always an outcome of the extension of private inheritance — the state may, in the public interest, intervene by regulating its use or even, if it cannot equitably meet the situation in any other way, by decreeing the expropriation of property, giving a suitable indemnity.

For the same purpose small and medium holdings in agriculture, in the arts and trades, in commerce and industry should be guaranteed and promoted; co-operative unions should ensure for them the advantages of big business; where big business even today shows itself more productive, there should be given the possibility of tempering the labor contract with a contract of co-ownership.

Pius XII, Address to Small Craftsmen, October, 1947

For the Church wishes to impose a definite limit on the subordination of man to the machine. Small craftsmen as a class may be regarded as a militia chosen to defend the personal dignity and character of the worker. But, for more than a century, they have had to fight for their existence against great industrial enterprises.

Socialization, Australian Hierarchy, 1948

(Summarized.) "In the economic sphere, it is therefore a most important task of government to encourage that type of economic organization in which the family and the home may prosper. The normal economic order — that order which is best adapted to the real needs of mankind — is one in which the majority of men are working proprietors; that is to say, where they earn a living for themselves and their families by working their own property, whether that property is a farm, a shop, a workshop, or a factory. This is the best economic order precisely because the institution of the family is strongest where this system prevails. This type of economic order may be adapted to enterprises which require more capital than one family can contribute. Where the amount of capital actually needed for the conduct of the business is greater than one man can supply, the necessary capital is best made up in the form of a partnership in which each of the partners has an effective share of control." For still larger enterprises, producers' co-operatives can raise the needed funds. There must, of course,

be some wage earners, but they should not be too numerous nor should
the door to effective ownership be closed.

Some property may be owned by the state, but private ownership should
be the prevailing pattern, since it safeguards the family and is a bastion of
freedom. Agriculture particularly should be encouraged by the state, as
this field is especially suitable for private ownership. But in industry, we
must recognize the law of natural dimensions, and realize that bigness is
not a goal to be sought for its own sake. Public policy should encourage
small and medium-size enterprise in suitable fields. Most of the work
now done today by large corporations could just as well be done by small
firms and co-operatives. The state should encourage decentralization and
organize research bureaus for small producers. This, generally speaking, is
far better than nationalization in the attempt to better the workers' status.

The Church and Social Order

22. The two great dangers which society faces in the present state of
economic organization are, first, the concentration of ownership and
control of wealth, and, secondly, its anonymous character, which results
from some of the existing business and corporation laws, whereby responsibility toward society is greatly impaired if not completely ignored. The
civil authority, in view of these dangers, must so regulate the responsibility of property that the burden of providing for the common good be
equitably distributed. It must furthermore establish such conditions through
legal enactment and administrative policy that wealth itself can be distributed so each individual member of society may surely and justly come
into possession of the material goods necessary for his own livelihood.
It is not the government alone which has this responsibility, as will become
clear from the further considerations to be noted.

25. It is freely admitted that modern industry requires considerable
concentration of capital, but it is not admitted that concentration of ownership and control is consequently necessary or beneficial to the common
good. The concentration of capital, however, with mass employment does
create a new and more impersonal relationship between capital and labor.
The problem is one of providing equitably for the distribution of income
between those who supply capital and those who supply labor.

26. In too many instances an undue portion of the income has been
claimed by those who have ownership or control of capital, whilst those
on the other hand who have only their labor to invest have been forced
to accept working conditions which are unreasonable and wages which
are unfair. This condition arises from the fact that labor policies have
been dictated by false principles in the interests of the owners or capitalists.
Secondly, it arises from the fact that labor frequently has had no voice

in the regulation or the adjustment of these problems. Labor can have no effective voice as long as it is unorganized. To protect its rights it must be free to bargain collectively through its own chosen representatives. If labor when unorganized is dissatisfied, the only alternative is to cease work and thus undergo the great hardships which follow unemployment.

31. Our present economic order rests upon the sanctity of private property. Private property, however, is not well distributed at present among the members of human society. Whilst it is dangerous to exaggerate the disproportion between those who possess adequate property and those who constitute the proletariat or the propertyless, nevertheless, it is certainly within the bounds of truth to state that the existing situation constitutes a grave social evil. Private property in the judgment of many thoughtful men tends to become less and less the characteristic note of our present society. If the majority of our citizens possess insufficient private property to be independent of a wage income for even a short period of time, then there is grave danger to the entire social fabric. Social stability rests upon this basis of individual ownership of property. There should be more of it and not less of it, if our existing economic system is to remain secure.

32. The lack of sufficient private property leads to various forms of insecurity. This insecurity not only leads to the creation of a strong social tension expressing itself in social disorder, but is also contrary to the prescriptions of Christian morality. There can be no question but that in our country we possess adequate resources both in respect to raw materials, technical or scientific skill, and mechanical equipment sufficient to provide both a high standard of living and also comprehensive security for all classes of society. Workingmen should be made secure against unemployment, sickness, accident, old age, and death. The first line of defense against these hazards should be the possession of sufficient private property to provide reasonable security. Industry therefore should provide not merely a living wage for the moment but also a saving wage for the future against sickness, old age, death, and unemployment. Individual industries alone, however, cannot in each single case achieve this objective without invoking the principle of social insurance. Some form of government subsidy granted by the entire citizenship through legislative provision seems to be a necessary part of such a program.

PROPERTY IN FARM LAND

Pius XI, Quadragesimo Anno

59. . . . the huge army of rural wage workers, pushed to the lowest level of existence and deprived of all hope of ever acquiring some property in

land, and therefore permanently bound to the status of nonowning worker unless suitable and effective remedies are applied.

75. A right proportion among wages and salaries also contributes directly to the same result; and with this is closely connected a right proportion in the prices at which the goods are sold that are produced by the various occupations, such as agriculture, manufacturing, and others.

102. Even today this is not, it is true, the only economic system in force everywhere; for there is another system also, which still embraces a huge mass of humanity, significant in numbers and importance, as for example, agriculture, wherein the greater portion of mankind honorably and honestly procures its livelihood. This group, too, is being crushed with hardships and with difficulties, to which Our Predecessor devotes attention in several places in his Encyclical, and which We Ourselves have touched upon more than once in Our present Letter.

Pius XII, La Solennità della Pentecoste

1692. Of all the goods that can be the object of private property, none is more conformable to nature, according to the teaching of *Rerum Novarum,* than the land, the holding on which the family lives, and from the products of which it draws all or part of its subsistence. And it is in the spirit of *Rerum Novarum* to state that, as a rule, only that stability which is rooted in one's own holdings, makes of the family the vital and most perfect and fecund cell of society, joining up in a brilliant manner in its progressive cohesion the present and future generations. If today the concept and the creation of vital spaces is at the center of social and political aims, should not one, before all else, think of the vital space of the family and free it of the fetters of conditions which do not permit one even to formulate the idea of a homestead of one's own?

1693. Our planet, with all its event of oceans and seas and lakes, with mountains and plains covered with eternal snows and ice, with great deserts and tractless lands, is not, all the same, without habitable regions and vital spaces, now abandoned to wild natural vegetation, and well suited to be cultivated by man to satisfy his needs and civil activities; and more than once it is inevitable that some families, migrating from one spot or another, should go elsewhere in search of a new homeland.

Pius XII, Discourse to Italian Farmers, November 15, 1946

(*Summarized.*) Labor on farms "still reflects the natural order willed by God, namely, that man, with his own labor, ought to rule material things, and not that material things rule man." Farmers are rooted in nature. They are producers as well as consumers. This gives them economic force and power of resistance in critical times. They gain simple virtues, which they should conserve at all costs.

Farmers have a right to a decent reward for their work, but they should not be lured into seeking quick profits at the expense of human need. "Show yourselves to be honest sellers, not greedy calculators to the damage of the people. . . ." They should beware of the vices so often found in city economic life. ". . . it happens too often that human needs no longer regulate, according to their natural and objective importance, economic life and the employment of capital, but, on the contrary, capital and its desire for gain determine those needs and in what measure they ought to be satisfied. In this way, it is not human labor destined for the common good that attracts to itself capital and places it at its service, but, instead, it is capital that moves the work, and man himself, here and there like balls in a game. If now the city dweller suffers from this unnatural state, how much more is it contrary to the intimate essence of the farmer's life."

Farmers should seek principal help from their own co-operative effort. They should also unite with laboring groups into a great community of workers. Thus we would have an organic society, instead of one ruled by great powers groups.

Bishops' Statement, 1933

One hope for relief in the universal misery of the present lies in the reversal of the policy which produced the factory and the factory system. This reversal, without depriving men of the benefits of industrial progress, would reinstate them as independent homeowners in rural communities. Such a change in the living conditions of millions of people would be a revolution, but some radical adjustment in restoring the balance between rural and urban population is imperative if our country is to survive and if our civilization is not to disappear.

Code of Social Principles

98. In certain countries in particular there has arisen a rural problem, under circumstances detailed below: (1) the existence of estates, untilled or undertilled, whose use and improvement are indispensable to the common good; (2) cultivation which, though technically satisfactory, has by its mass production led to the use and growth of a rural proletariat in great poverty, who are forced to leave the land, to emigration, or to some other alternative hurtful to the common good.

In all such cases the state has the right, when less radical means have failed, to decree the division of cultivation and, if need be, of properties. The exercise of the right is always subject to the granting of a just and well-considered indemnity to all those whose legitimate rights would be injured by the measures taken toward division.

THE RIGHT TO PRIVATE PROPERTY

Historically, the attitude toward property is central in a social philosophy. As the embodiment of tangible wealth, property is of necessity one of the foundations of economic life. Its accumulation makes men of wealth. Its widespread distribution normally brings about a stable society. Men risk their lives to acquire or to conserve it, while others, fearing the passion for wealth, take solemn vows relinquishing the right of ownership. To many, it is a bastion of security and a guarantee of freedom. It is no wonder, then, that the concept of property rights normally determines the entirety of a social philosophy. The rights of man and of the state are so closely correlated with those of property that often the one can be deduced from the others.

Disputes over the rights of property were among the major factors occasioning the social encyclicals. The Socialists reacted to the abuse of property by calling for state ownership of all productive wealth. Proudhon said: "Property is theft." To which Bishop von Ketteler replied: "The notorious dictum, 'property is theft,' is something more than a mere lie; besides a great lie, it contains a terrible truth. Scorn and derision will not dispose of it. . . . As deep calleth unto deep, so one sin against nature calls forth another. Out of the distorted right of ownership, the false doctrine of communism was begotten."[1] Then came *Rerum Novarum*, which vindicated the right of property against socialism, but also denounced the abuses of property owners. Even within the Church, controversy continued, with some holding that the right of property was contingent upon its proper use. But, when *Quadragesimo Anno* was issued, it clearly upheld the right of property, defined its individual and social character, noted the powers of the state in regard to it, and even more strongly denounced abuses connected with it. Finally, the repeated discourses and encyclicals of Pope Pius XII stressed both

---

[1] Sermon on "The Christian Idea of the Rights of Property," cited in J. J. Laux, *Ketteler's Social Reform* (Philadelphia: Dolphin Press, 1912), pp. 38–39.

the need for more widespread distribution of property and the ideal that most men become owners of property.

The Right to Ownership. The classical treatment of property, the *Summa Theologica* of St. Thomas Aquinas, distinguishes between man's right to ownership and the institution of private property. The former is a right derived from natural law. Man, by virtue of reason and free will, is lord over nature. The grossly imperfect exists to serve the more nearly perfect. Hence the things of the earth are for the use of man. He has dominion over the beasts of the field and even more so over inanimate nature.[2] By contrast, the institution of private property, whereby men have the right to own and use as their private possessions material things (acquired lawfully), is not a direct right of nature in the same sense as dominion over the material world. Each individual man does not have in his nature the right to private ownership, in the sense that strict justice would be violated if he were not an owner. Rather mankind as a whole has found that the institution of private property fits so closely with human nature that without it the peace and order of society and the prosperity of the economic order would be gravely injured.

Institutions of this order come under the form of law called *jus gentium* (taken from the natural equity of the Roman praetors, applying justice to nations not under Roman statutory law). *Jus gentium* is a justice and equity toward which peoples tend in accord with human nature. It is more solemn and immutable than positive law, since it is dictated by the deep needs of man's nature. Yet it is subject to modification and improvement as the customs of men change through the years. In this light, we might hold that Suarez and St. Thomas considered the right of private property as dictated by man's nature and natural to human society, but not technically under natural law.[3] Modern writers consider the institution of private property as so closely tied up with the well-being of human nature that it is akin to

[2] II, II, 66, 1.
[3] See Suarez, *De Legibus*, II, 17–19; St. Thomas, *Summa*, I, II, 95, 2 and 4; I, II, 94, 5, *ad* 3; II, II, 57, 3; I, 98, 1, *ad* 3; *In Polit.*, II, 4.

natural law. As population increases and the society become more complex, the case for private property becomes stronger.

The arguments of St. Thomas for private property have lost none of their luster through the centuries. His position may be quoted in full:

> Two things are competent to man in respect to exterior things. One is the power to procure and dispense them, and in this regard it is lawful for man to possess property. Moreover, this is necessary for human life for three reasons. First, because every man is more careful to procure what is for himself alone than that which is common to many or to all; since each one would shirk the labor and leave to another that which concerns the community, as happens when there are a great number of servants. Secondly, because human affairs are conducted in a more orderly fashion if each man is charged with taking care of some particular thing himself, whereas there would be confusion if everyone had to look after any one thing indeterminately. Thirdly, because a more peaceful state is ensured to man if each is contented with his own. Hence it is to be observed that quarrels arise more frequently where there is no division of things possessed.
>
> The second thing that is competent to man with regard to external things is their use. In this respect man ought to possess external things, not as his own, but as common, so that, to wit, he is ready to communicate them to others in their need.[4]

These arguments are based on such enduring qualities of human nature that they possess the virtue of timelessness.

The first argument is that private property fosters initiative, whereas common ownership leads to slovenly neglect. This element of human interest in one's own is so obvious that proof is unnecessary. Even children tend to treasure their own toys. A businessman will slave to make his firm a success, whereas the hired manager (unless a personal incentive is present) tends to be careless and timeserving. In colleges and like communities, common property is often neglected. The community car often lacks gas, gets infrequent oil changes, and generally receives much more abuse than would usually happen when an auto is privately owned. People generally take care of their own lawns

---

[4] *Summa*, II, II, 66, 2; cf. W. J. McDonald, *The Social Value of Property according to St. Thomas Aquinas* (Washington: Catholic University, 1939).

and yet are careless in littering public parks. Government-owned business is often unimaginative and routine, whereas private business tends to be enterprising and resourceful. There are exceptions to these statements, but usually only where some equivalent motive substitutes for pride of ownership. A manager may be ambitious for success, feeling that his record will bring promotion. He may fear the penalties of failure. The instinct of self-seeking is deep. It may be modified by Christian altruism, but only in a few persons is altruism so dominant that they take care of common goods as if they were their own. So long as human nature remains in this pattern, and fallen nature is prone to evil, private ownership will be more successful than common possessions.

Secondly, private ownership leads to an orderly handling of human affairs. The distinction of ownership leads to a division of duties. The man who owns a farm will cultivate it. The proprietor of a store will order goods and sell them. If ownership were indeterminate, men would follow their impulses and instincts in a most haphazard fashion. In pleasant weather, there would be an inordinate number taking care of the fishing needs of the community. If snow blocked the streets, most men would prefer to meet their indoor duties, rather than clear off the snow. The alternative to this chaos would be central organization of life by the state. But if all economic power were centered in the state, freedom would be lost. In the absence of universal altruism, the normal method of getting men to work would be the use of fear and compulsion. Experiences in the Soviet Union bear this out. The Communists first tried the ideal of "from each according to his ability, to each according to his needs." But the system soon degenerated into a cruel incentive system for labor, with a reign of absolute terror superimposed.

· Finally, private possessions tend to promote a peaceful society. If goods were held in common, there would be frequent quarrels over the most desirable things. Farmers would fight to cultivate the best land. Workers would want the most pleasant jobs. Each would seek a share of distribution more favorable to himself. The

result would be mob rule, with the strongest or the most cunning
holding the best positions. Even in religious communities, under
a vow of proverty and practicing the virtue of charity, there are
strains and tensions because of common possessions. With only
one morning newspaper in the common room, some may be
unhappy because a colleague persists in reading every word. Not
all will agree on the programs to be heard on the community
radio. These sacrifices are endured and sublimated through religious ideals, but they would be occasions of quarrels outside the
monastery walls. Hence, common ownership does not readily
accord with fallen nature, except in cases where people voluntarily embrace a life involving the counsels of perfection.

Such is the authentic teaching of St. Thomas on the right to
property. It is against this background that one must judge statements that the Church Fathers taught communism. Writers have
cited out of context oratorical passages denouncing avarice
and misuse of property, or exhorting the practice of Christian
poverty, to show that great Church writers have denounced the
institution of private ownership. Yet, a careful study of the entire
teaching of these authors leads to a different conclusion.[5]
Some of the Fathers, as also St. Thomas, emphasized the view
that private property is necessary because of original sin. Man in
the state of innocence would have had the altruism necessary for
common ownership. Yet it is not necessary to stress only the
sordid aspects of human nature to justify private property. There
is a certain element of creative achievement, which partakes of
the divine, in the possession and ennobling of material things.
Pope Leo XIII emphasized the function of private property in
aiding family life and giving security and stability to this fundamental social unit. Pope Pius XII has repeatedly noted the connection of property with the assurance of human dignity. As will
be developed later, only through widespread ownership can we
have full assurance of man's freedom.

---

[5] See G. O'Brien, *An Essay on Mediaeval Economic Teaching* (New York: Longmans,
1920), pp. 41–62; J. A. Ryan, *Alleged Socialism of the Church Fathers* (St. Louis:
Herder, 1913).

Hence we conclude that man's nature calls for private property as a basic social institution. Ownership confers certain rights in strict justice. While these rights are qualified by definite duties, failure to live up to duties does not take away the right. Pope Pius XI is clear on the point that neither abuse nor nonuse destroys the title to property. This is a reply to the views of certain theologians who defined property rights in terms of social function, so that if the function is not performed, the right is abrogated. The popes do not elaborate on the means for acquiring property rights, mentioning only original occupation of natural property (discovery of land, hunting of wild animals, fishing) and labor. Labor gives a full title to the product if it is expended on one's own property, and only a partial claim if lawfully expended on the property of another. In addition, property may be justly acquired through exchange or purchase, by gift, and under certain conditions by unquestioned possession (right of prescription).

Return From Property: Rent. If the right of property is upheld, then it follows logically that the property owner must receive the normal return from his possessions. Where these possessions consist of capital goods, this return is called profits. Money, considered as the equivalent of capital, is productive of interest. Both these types of return were treated in Chapter VIII. There remains one further method of realizing upon property, namely, rent.

Rent is a differential return based on the value of land, whether this value derives from fertility or from location. In regard to fertility, it is obvious that not all land is equally productive. It is possible to have two farms of equal size, given the same amount of labor and sown to the same crop, receiving the same benefits of climate and weather, yet producing strikingly different yields. Since the product of one farm may be consistently greater than that of another, it is obvious that the better land will be valued at a higher rate. The differential is called economic rent. It is normally capitalized in the form of a higher price for good land.

The same observation holds true when value conferred by

location is considered. Sites near good forms of transportation are generally more desirable for industrial use. Business usually pre-fers locations close to population centers. A central point in a metropolis might be the ideal place for a department store. Such a situation might yield many times the revenue of the same amount of land in a small town remote from large population groupings.

Economic rent must be distinguished from rent in normal usage, since this often includes elements other than the differential value of land. Thus, rent for a house usually includes interest on capital investment, depreciation, and maintenance expenses, in addition to the charge for the use of the land. Again, when the value of farm land has been improved through extensive irriga-tion, use of fertilizers, and similar capital expenses, there is a yield upon capital as well as the native fertility value of the land itself.

The right to such returns has been questioned by two groups: the socialists and the single taxers. It was only normal that socialists should attack private land ownership, since this is one of the most valuable forms of property. If property is considered as the source of all exploitation, land should be a prime target for the socialists. By contrast, the single-tax group did not object to private land ownership. Their difficulty arose from the fact that economic rent was an unearned increment. In the case of farm land, it was based upon the accidental fact that some land is more fertile than other land. For city property, rent was consid-ered as appropriation of values conferred by community improve-ments. The entire metropolis pays for street paving, transporta-tion, fire and police protection, and the like. Yet the landowner appropriates the value arising from population concentration, at the same time paying only a part of the civic improve-ments which confer this value. Accordingly, it was suggested that this entire increment be taxed away. The landowner would maintain title to his land (in contrast to socialism) and enjoy the fruit of any improvements made through his own investment, but he would not profit from fertility or location.

Against socialism, the case is clear. Regardless of the abuses which have existed in regard to property rights, the remedy is not abolition of property. Property is a source of freedom. If its concentration imperils freedom, the answer is diffusion of ownership, not absolute concentration through state ownership of all property. The nature of man, as well as the needs of the family, demand the institution of private property.

When the question of the single tax is considered, it is not easy to give a sweeping answer. A reply to their views might be along two lines. First, in the existing state of society any such tax would confiscate the legitimate investment of millions of persons. Whatever merit there may be in the unearned-increment argument, at this time such values have already been capitalized. In general, the persons who originally profited from land speculation have long since sold their holdings. Current possessors paid a price which includes the imputed value of economic rent. Accordingly, if this item were to be taxed at the present time, the result would be virtual confiscation of property. Thus, a farmer whose land is valued at $100 an acre bought this land with the expectation that it would yield an average value of $10 more than marginal land would yield. He must receive this return or he would be getting nothing on his investment. Moreover, he could never recover the original cost, since all unimproved land would be valueless under a single-tax system.

Secondly, it is not entirely clear that the single-tax theory would be sound even in a country which was being settled for the first time. A tax which would remove the entire value accruing to land might in effect attack the institution of land ownership. Apart from permanency of tenure, there would be no incentive to own rather than rent land. Indeed, ownership might well be a liability, since any accident which would prevent the owner from realizing the value of land would leave him liable to taxation, with no income to meet these taxes. He would then be compelled to give up his land. Thus, in effect, nonuse would be considered a reason for denial of property rights. It would be sounder policy to attack abuses directly through appropriate legislation than to rely upon a tax program which might undermine such a basic human institution. Moreover, in practice this theory would amount to socialism. If all the value of land, as such, were taxed away, there would be no value to land and no incentive to own any given piece of land rather than another. Under such conditions, it is likely that the state would then assume the function of allocating property in land, since individual owners would lack the incentive to hold any given piece of land.

Individual and Social Aspects of Property. St. Thomas stated that while ownership may be private, use should be common, so that an owner is ready to communicate his goods to others in their need. Pope Pius XI made this point more exact by distinguishing between the individual and the social aspects of property. While individual ownership is a right, social obligations also attach to property. These social duties may be evident from the nature of the common good or they may be specified by positive law, whether divine or human. The state normally determines, in the absence of natural or divine law, what should be the duties of owners. Thus, it directs property into its proper place in the universal pattern of the common good. In so acting, government should be careful not to destroy the right of ownership in the guise of regulation or taxation.

That property has a social aspect is evident from even casual consideration. When a man buys an automobile, he acquires a personal possession. It is his to use or to leave idle, to sell or to give. But the ownership and use of a car involves clear social responsibilities as well. The owner, in most states, must register his title and acquire license tags. Before he is allowed to drive, he normally must have a permit and this usually involves an examination on his ability to drive and his knowledge of traffic laws. In using the car, he is bound by traffic regulations. He must drive on the right side of the street, at proper speed, and observe signal lights and signs. His brakes and headlights must be in order. In some states, he must secure periodic inspections of the car. All these requirements exist because the common good demands such regulation of private property in automobiles. If people drove haphazardly, lives would be endangered and traffic hopelessly entangled. Social obligations here are clear and binding.

As a general rule, it might be stated that the social aspect of property increases insofar as an object affects other persons deeply. Things which are close to the individual and do not normally affect others do not have important social connotations. Ordinarily such items as personal clothing, furniture in the home, or a tractor on the farm would have little social import. But improper clothing might offend public decency. A radio in the home should not blare loudly at night. If a tractor is driven on the public highways, it must observe traffic rules.

There are types of property which necessarily involve social obligations. Thus, a large factory may employ thousands of workers. It can be a major influence in the community. Its products may be used throughout the nation or even the world. Even if this factory were owned by a single individual, he could not be blind to the many duties implied by the type of ownership he enjoys. This is all the more true where a corporation owns such property, since corporation law gives shareholders the rights of ownership, but exempts them from many of its duties. Stockholders are not legally liable for the debts of the company (except that its property, their equity, may be sold to pay debts) nor are they legally responsible for the actions of their officers (unless they explicitly ordered criminal actions). Thus, we have ownership shorn of much of the right of control and property without clear-cut personal responsibility. Here, above all, would be an instance where the state would have the right and duty to specify and enforce social obligations.

Father Miller, in his excellent treatment of property, lists six fields in which state determination of social responsibility is common. These include building ordinances and zoning laws, requirements that idle land be used (England and Italy), regulation of banking, laws on security issuance and exchange, the right of eminent domain, and the issuance of money.[6] One could go

---

[6] R. J. Miller, *Forty Years After*, pp. 87–88.

further and state that practically all social legislation involves regulation of property rights in the interest of the common good. Here the emphasis must rest upon the true concept of the common good and God's purpose in economic life.

Regulation must not be carried to such an extreme that it degenerates into collectivism. This would be a denial of the individual aspect of property rights, a threat to human liberty, and hence a false interpretation of the common good. The community exists to serve its members, not to dominate over them or absorb them. But this in turn does not mean a passive, *laissez-faire* attitude by the state, since this would be an abdication to individualism and a denial of the common good. A careful balance between the extremes of individualism and collectivism must be kept at all times. Naturally the emphasis on state intervention will vary according to circumstances of time and place. A small, self-sufficient country with a good balance between agriculture and industry might need less public emphasis on social duties than would be the case for a larger nation with difficult social problems. Again, the impact of social obligations is normally greater in times of war or emergency than in periods of peace and normalcy. In a period of war, both the social aspect of property and the right of the state to direct its use for the common good are naturally intensified.

It would be wrong to emphasize the function of the state in specifying the social aspects of property to the neglect of obligations springing from natural and divine law. Thus, certain natural rights which are possessed by individuals involve limitations on the use of property. Labor's right to organize and to seek a living wage is bound to affect the employer's use of his productive property. Even in the absence of law, an owner is obligated to consider the social implications of property use. A farmer who would cultivate his land in such a way as to cause erosion on other farms would be acting unsocially. A mining firm which would endanger lives or property by its methods of extraction would be doing wrong. Owners would likewise have a duty to avoid unnecessary work on Sunday, so that their employees could

attend divine worship. While the state may enforce such obligations in the light of the common good, they also oblige individual
consciences under social justice even in the absence of public
law.

One of the more intriguing moral problems of our day concerns the changing aspects of property rights under American
corporation law. Normally there is associated with the idea of
ownership the assumption that the owner has control over his
property. But in many large corporations ownership is separated
from control in a rather definitive manner. This situation arises
from both factual situations and legal decisions. Factually, the
large number of stockholders makes any joint action to control
their company a virtual impossibility. Most big corporations are
controlled either by management (through use of the proxy
machinery) or by large minority stockholders. Moreover, the
courts have often so interpreted the powers of a corporate board
of directors as to give it independent authority. Many corporations have refused information to stockholders on the ground that
such divulging of facts would be contrary to the interests of the
company. Courts have upheld them in these decisions. Because
of this, it is not too much to say that a share of stock is not
so much a title of real ownership as a contingent claim upon
profits.

In the light of this analysis, it is questionable whether stockholders always share the moral responsibilities which go with the
properties they "own." If they do not have the full rights of
ownership, they may well be exempt from many of its duties.
Thus, if a stockholder could have no effective voice in determining a corporation's labor policies, he could hardly be held
accountable for them. It would seem that the major share of
responsibility would rest on those who exercise actual control,
namely, the board of directors and the management of the firm.
Futhermore, in most cases the stockholder could not even be
charged with indirect co-operation because of his purchase of
corporate stock. If such purchases were made when the company
was organized, the buyer would have no advance knowledge of

the future policies of the corporation. If, on the other hand, the stock were bought subsequently, such purchases would normally neither help nor hinder the corporation. It has already received its money and is not usually affected by resales of stock in the securities markets. Hence the stockholder could not reasonably be charged responsibility for immoral decisions made by a firm whose stock he owns.

An ethical problem would arise, however, in regard to the receipt of dividends from a corporation whose policies were contrary to justice. Even though the stockholder could not be blamed for the decisions in question, he may profit by them. Thus if a corporation makes high profits through fraud, excessively high prices bolstered by a monopolistic situation, or through exploitation of labor, it would seem that part of these profits would be tainted. The stockholder would be in a position similar to the receiver of stolen goods. On these grounds, he would be obliged to sell the stock and, in the absence of more direct methods of restitution, to give to charity such portion of his returns as might reasonably be imputed to profits obtained unjustly.

This problem might well be given further study by moral theologians. The masterly analysis of Berle and Means, *The Modern Corporation and Private Property,* has not lost its value since it was published in 1933. These authors outline in detail the various devices used to separate ownership from control and the resultant change in the nature of property ownership. Pope Pius XI also alluded to this problem in *Quadragesimo Anno* (Nos. 105, 132). Undoubtedly this situation enhances the social aspect of property so affected, if for no other reason than the obscurity surrounding individual rights and duties under the circumstances.

There are other types of intangible ownership which also might be studied. Among these are patents, trademarks, and similar restrictive devices. Clearly such important types of property rights must be made to serve the common good and not merely the interests of owners. In the past, they have often been abused and made to bolster monopolistic practices in industry. Again, the power of banks in the aggregate to create credit money involves the power to appropriate goods. The government uses the same device for inflationary financing to meet budget deficits. Such tremendous powers must be carefully regulated in the light of the common good. They should be used only in accord with the principles of commutative and social justice.

Taxation. Papal treatment of taxation is not extensive. Pope Leo XIII warns against confiscatory taxes which would destroy property rights in the guise of collecting public funds. Pope Pius XI notes that this warning does not preclude progressive taxation, bearing heavily on the wealthy. Sharing the common burdens in accord with ability to pay, far from destroying property, might well safeguard it against the possibility of violent revolution. Finally, Pope Pius XII emphasizes the need for preserving economic incentive and directing taxes in terms of an efficient economic organization which would provide the material basis for cultural and spiritual values.

The complexity of modern life and the heavy cost of war and preparation against war necessarily involve a high cost of government. Thus, in the United States today about 20 per cent of the national income goes for taxation and in other countries the amount is even higher. Most of these costs are necessary, although savings would be possible through greater efficiency in some phases of government. Accordingly, a high level of taxation seems inevitable. The only method of relieving the relative burden would be a continuing increase in the general national income. A forty-billion-dollar federal budget would be less troublesome if the national income were three hundred billion instead of two hundred.

It happens that taxation is in turn one of the important determinants of the level of national income. If taxes were so directed as to absorb practically all the savings of the community, there would be no investment and no economic expansion. The economy would be stagnant and unemployment would rise, since industry could not provide for a growing working population. Hence two factors must be balanced in working out a just system of taxation. The tests of equality of sacrifice and payment according to ability would dictate progressive income taxes, which naturally bear most heavily upon the wealthier classes. Yet the need for retaining the profit incentive and of stimulating investment is also vital, if the economic system is to expand and provide more jobs. Hence taxation should not preclude all saving in the group which is prone to invest, nor should it make investment impossible by so taxing gains that the risk becomes prohibitive. As was noted in Chapter X, it would be possible to retain the principle of progressive taxation, but to allow special treatment of funds used to provide new jobs through capital investment.

Practically all taxes have social aspects. Thus, sales taxes bear most heavily on low-income groups and so discourage consumption and bring about lower living standards. Taxes on a commodity or service tend to lessen the use of the goods or services. Sometimes this restriction may be deliberate, as with liquor or tobacco. At other times, imposts of this kind may have been enacted for emergency reasons (as with wartime "luxury taxes") and retained merely because of revenue needs. The entire pattern of an industry could be changed by taxation. When some states adopted chain-store taxes which rose progressively with the number of stores owned by a single firm, they practically broke up chain ownership. The relative positions of butter and oleomargarine are largely determined by tax laws. Tariffs and export taxes have great economic effects. Unfortunately, it often happens that such laws are enacted without full consideration of their effect upon the common good.

Since taxation is of far-reaching importance, the United States should re-examine its entire fiscal policy. Even if there were not known abuses, the sheer size of federal, state, and local budgets would make this imperative. Methods which worked well when government costs were less than 10 per cent of national income might not be feasible today. We rightly had a Hoover Commission to study the most efficient way of reorganizing the federal government. An equally distinguished and representative group could well consider our entire fiscal program. Present taxes discourage equity financing and small business, channel

economic expansion into the form of enlarging existing corporations, reward debt financing in preference to the more socially
desirable equity financing, and place heavy burdens on industries
which already find survival difficult. There are conflicts between
fiscal policy and monetary policy. The tremendous impact of
government cash collections on the ups and downs of business
has received inadequate study. Under any system, the burden
of present-day government is bound to be great. But wise tax
laws can so distribute and regulate this burden that business
incentive will be retained and unnecessary shocks avoided.[7]

Duties of Owners. In addition to the general responsibility for
using property in accord with the common good, owners have
certain specific obligations in respect to their wealth. Pope Pius
XI notes that the wealthy are bound to use their superfluous
income in the practice of almsgiving, beneficence, and munificence. His language in this passage is strong: *gravissimo teneantur
divites praecepto.* The Latin terms *praeceptum* and *grave* are
both normally used only for the most serious obligations, although
the Latin superlative is sometimes weaker than the positive.
Thus, all moralists use the phrase *praeceptum sub gravi* as connoting a duty obliging under pain of mortal sin. This obligation
is not in justice but under other virtues, such as charity.

Superfluous income has been defined as the excess over an
amount needed to live becomingly in accord with one's state in
life. At the same time, moralists have not refined this definition
by precise rules as to what is "becoming" in various states. Nor
have they clarified the moral conditions involved in advancing to
a state of great wealth. Venturing into an inadequately explored
field, certain conclusions might be offered. A man with ability and
enterprise might, through the use of morally acceptable means,
advance to a state of wealth. As he progresses, it would be

---

[7] Moral principles of taxation are treated in J. A. Ryan, *Distributive Justice,* Chap.
20; and E. Cahill, *Framework of a Christian State,* p. 520 ff. For economic implications,
see "Monetary and Fiscal Policy for Greater Economic Stability" (New York: Committee for Economic Development, 1948); H. M. Groves, *Postwar Taxation and
Economic Progress* (New York: McGraw-Hill, 1947); and J. F. Cronin, *Economic
Analysis and Problems,* Chap. 20.

legitimate to reinvest his savings in the business so as to promote its expansion, at the same time meeting the normal demands of charity appropriate to his income level.

His personal motivation should not be evil. Thus, he should avoid disordered pride, ambition, or avarice. He might be inspired by satisfaction in achievement, desire to help his family, and interest in the community. The building of an enterprise which produces useful goods or services and furnishes needed employment is morally sound. If this process brings great wealth, the owner might then live in accord with healthy community standards for persons in his position. While lavish display, motivated by pride or vanity, would be wrong, yet such luxuries as a large house, servants, two cars, and a winter trip to a warm climate would not necessarily be inappropriate. He might give his children the best of education and protect his family by large insurance policies.

At all times, however, such a wealthy man should be concerned over the needs of charity in his community and nation. Superfluous wealth, above the sound customary needs of his station, should be considered as money held in trust, to be used in accord with the social virtues. Thus, in time of war or national hardship, the luxuries noted above might not be permissible, even to the very rich. Again, there would be a greater obligation to help in local community needs than to meet conditions elsewhere.

The notion of beneficence implies the Christian virtue of charity, giving help not merely because it is a duty, but rather in terms of love of neighbor. St. Thomas and the popes insist that the helping of the needy out of one's superfluous income is a strict obligation, which could oblige under pain of mortal sin if the need were great and the wealthy man the only source of relief. But it is much more desirable to have a spirit of generous giving, springing from a compassionate heart. This is the true Christian ideal.

Munificence applies to great gifts, such as foundations or research grants. This is a form of liberality which is especially fitting for the very wealthy. They can thus endow universities or hospitals, found great libraries or research projects, open new fields of medical inquiry, and otherwise aid mankind in a notable way. Pope Pius XI goes further and applies this virtue to the investment of superfluous income in job-producing industries and occupations. Indeed, he considers such ventures as a form especially suited to the needs of these times. It was this same notion which moved the great Jewish philosopher, Moses Maimonides, to note that the best form of almsgiving is to give a man an opportunity to support himself.

It might appear that insufficient attention is given to the old-fashioned virtue of thrift. Yet, even this virtue can be carried to extremes. Saving, like wealth itself, has a twofold aspect, the individual and the social. From an individual viewpoint, it is desirable as a means for providing against sickness, old age, and unforeseen contingencies. It can enable a family to own a home, see to the education of children, and even give financial aid to the children in getting a start in business or a profession. Such measures are also socially desirable, in that they foster family stability. But from a socioeconomic viewpoint, savings are part of the income flow in the community. For technical reasons, money must circulate constantly or a depression results. Hence savings should go back into circulation in the form of investments. Wealthy persons often make such decisions directly. The lower-income groups keep their funds in banks or buy insurance, so that the banks or insurance companies make the investments. For savings to be socially useful, there should always be offsetting investment outlets.

The securing of such outlets is a vital, but often neglected, aspect of public fiscal and monetary policy. Thus, individual thrift is good. But it is much more useful when it is integrated into a consistent social policy, which aims to promote sufficient economic expansion to provide new jobs and constantly improving standards of living. If, by chance, savings were excessive in relation to investment outlets, the resultant deflation would eat up excess savings. Oversaving beyond available total capital opportunities is self-defeating and injurious to economic stability.

These remarks on the duties of property owners should be integrated with the study of justice and charity in Chapter IV. As noted there, a broad field of Christian social action exists beyond the strict demands of justice. There are many opportunities for community service which could not be determined in the language of justice, whether this be commutative, distributive, or social. Here is the opportunity for the enlightened conscience, motivated by charity, directing the use of wealth as a bond which unites various social groups in the community.

A WIDER DIFFUSION OF OWNERSHIP

The Ideal of Distributed Ownership. While the popes have defended the institution of private property, they have not supported past and present practices of distribution of both income and wealth. Each of the three great social popes has solemnly pronounced the need for a better diffusion of ownership. Pope Leo XIII made the advantages of actual ownership the major arguments for private property. Pope Pius XI reiterated the need for more equitable distribution of wealth and income and attacked existing abuses in this regard. It remained for Pope Pius XII to carry this argument further and to apply it to small business and other forms of distributed productive property. He likewise attacked directly the concentration of economic life into giant cities and huge industrial enterprises. The Australian hierarchy applied these principles in a comprehensive and astute manner. American bishops went further in the 1919 pronouncement than they have in more recent statements on the matter of wider distribution of productive ownership.

The central argument for property diffusion is freedom. Long ago, St. Thomas Aquinas noted that the difference between freedom and slavery lies in property ownership. He said that the despot rules over slaves, who cannot resist his rule, since they own nothing. But government over free men is different, since, "although they are subjected to the rule of their president, nevertheless they have something of their own, whereby they are able to resist the power of the ruler."[8] When the state owns all productive wealth, as under communism, the subject is of necessity a slave. Likewise, when the most important kind of wealth in a community is owned by a few, the many suffer a real limitation of their freedom. Thus, in the United States, to apply the words of *Quadragesimo Anno,* immense power and despotic economic domination have been concentrated in the hands of a few, and these few are not the owners, but the managers of invested wealth.

There have been adequate studies to prove that less than a thousand large corporations own most of the corporate business wealth in the United States. Their strategic control of vital raw materials and essential industries gives them great power over the hundreds of thousands of smaller corporations and the millions of unincorporated businesses and farms. While ownership of corporations is technically vested in the hands of their stockholders (about six million), actual control in large firms rests with self-perpetuating boards of directors, powerful minority stockholders, large investment banking houses, and giant insurance companies. By way of reaction, there have arisen giant labor unions, farmers organizations, and government regulatory agencies. Thus, the individual is lost sight of in battles between mammoths.

The fact that the great abuses of the 1920's are now past does not alter the fundamental situation. Business has a far greater sense of public responsibility. Government regulation has been salutary and effective. Labor and the farmers have made great gains. Even the small businessman has been able to hold his own in many fields. But we must consider how many workers are employed by large corporations where of necessity it is difficult to treat them as individuals. Many executives, drawing large salaries, are essentially employees of great chains or sprawling industries. Even the top management of billion-dollar corporations may be subject to the control of absentee financial ownership, more interested in assured profits than in the welfare of its workers or even executives. We cannot honestly say that these men have

[8] *Summa,* I, 81, 3, *ad* 2.

lost their freedom, but it has been minimized to an unhealthy degree.

Moreover, giantism has aggravated concentration into large cities, in which the obstacles to a normal family life are greater. It is difficult for many to own or rent homes suitable for several growing children, where they would have wholesome opportunities for play and association with other children. On the farms, there are the migrants and the sharecroppers who often live in poverty with little hope of owning the land they till. All this is not to deny the real advantages of mechanization and mass production. But we have grown far beyond the optimum size needed for economic efficiency and have ended up with unsocial power concentrations. More recently, both economic reasons and the fear of atomic war have prompted some decentralization and diffusion of industry. But a complex and far-reaching problem remains.

Distribution of Wealth and Income in America. It is difficult to obtain figures on the actual distribution of wealth in the United States. It is even more of a problem to interpret facts and to put them in proper perspective. Thus, certain studies of probated wills have been used to prove a high degree of concentrated ownership of wealth. In rebuttal, other studies have emphasized the wide distribution of physical assets in the United States. Authors have surveyed such facts as stock ownership, possession of automobiles, radios, refrigerators, and insurance policies, and like types of ownership to reach the conclusion that wealth was widely diffused in the United States. Unfortunately, errors in interpretation vitiated many of the facts adduced in these studies. It is true that consumer goods, even of an expensive variety, are widely owned in this country. About twenty-five million families own their own homes. There are probably six million owners of stocks and bonds. In addition, persons with bank accounts and insurance policies have an indirect interest in the business assets financed with their funds. The possession of savings accounts and government bonds gives many persons some form of security.

From these facts, many persons conclude that no real problem of wealth diffusion exists. But such pleaders miss two important distinctions. In the first place, wealth in the form of durable consumer goods, while it affords personal satisfaction, is no real safeguard of freedom. The wage earner or the corporation executive who owns an automobile, a radio, or even a home is still economically dependent upon a giant corporation for his job. If he lost the job, all these forms of wealth could be quickly swept away. He does not have the relative independence which comes from ownership of productive property. Then, in the second place, statistics on widely diffused holdings of corporate property are meaningless in terms of control. The average stockholder makes no attempt to direct the policies of his corporation, nor could he have an effective voice even if he tried. Thus, he has the form of ownership without one of the most important substantial attributes of property, namely, the power of control.

Control of large corporate wealth is highly concentrated, not diffused. The 75 million citizens who have entrusted over 52 billion dollars to life-insurance companies have no real control over the use of such funds. This type of wealth in turn involves tremendous economic power. Thus, the thesis of effective wealth diffusion is invalidated, to the extent that a large number of individuals do not have direct control over productive property which would serve as a basis for independence. Today such persons exercise economic power only as members of giant groups, such as political or labor organizations.[9]

Available information indicates that the trend toward economic concentration is increasing, especially through corporate mergers. While various federal laws prohibit monopoly through collusion or even stock ownership in competing companies, a Supreme Court policy has thus far prevented the government from interfering with mergers of assets. Thus, relatively mild and transitory forms of monopoly are interdicted, whereas the permanent variety is quite legal. The Federal Trade Commission has issued

---

[9] As noted earlier, the basic study on this problem is A. A. Berle and G. Means, *The Modern Corporation and Private Property* (New York: MacMillan, 1933). For a briefer treatment, see J. F. Cronin, *Economic Analysis and Problems,* Chaps. 2, 5, and 11.

several warnings about the danger of monopoly through mergers and has requested tightening of antitrust laws to meet this need. Certainly the merger problem should be an integral part of any study of monopoly control. At the same time, impartial students have found exaggerations and misinterpretation in the FTC studies.[10]

To avoid exaggerations, it must be noted that, in 1939, 92.5 per cent of business establishments could be classified as small. Small business, thus defined, includes manufacturers with less than 100 employees, wholesalers with less than $500,000 annual sales (1950 prices), and retailers and service groups with less than $100,000 annual sales. Such firms employed nearly 45 per cent of all persons engaged in business (including proprietors as employees) and did about 34 per cent of the dollar output of all business. Moreover, the percentage of such firms in relation to the total population is growing. Unfortunately, however, they operate almost exclusively in areas in which their economic power is negligible. This is the crux of the argument against concentration.

In fairness to large enterprise, we may repeat here that present tax laws favor industrial concentration. They put a premium on retention of earnings for business expansion, rather than the obtaining of funds through stock issuance. Many firms secure funds from banks or insurance companies, thereby adding to the power of financial groups. Likewise, small firms tend to plow back earnings instead of receiving them as personal income for the proprietor. Later the firm can be sold with the profit received

---

[10] A *Report of the Federal Trade Commission on the Merger Movement. A Summary Report* (Washington: Government Printing Office, 1948). See also the *Report of the Federal Trade Commission on the Concentration of Productive Facilities, 1947* (Washington: Government Printing Office, 1949). An excellent study of the problems of small business is contained in the brochure by the Joint Committee on the Economic Report, "Factors Affecting Volume and Stability of Private Investment" (Washington: Government Printing Office, 1949). Earlier studies by the Temporary National Economic Committee further document the facts on concentration. For references and summaries, see J. F. Cronin, *Economic Analysis and Problems,* Chaps. 2, 5, and 11. For a critical review of FTC studies, see the article by J. Lintner and J. K. Butters in the February, 1950, issue of the *Review of Economic Statistics.*

as capital gains rather than normal income, thus resulting in a lower tax bill but also contributing to the merger movement. All these considerations reinforce the argument given earlier for a radical reconsideration of American tax laws.

There is equal confusion in regard to income distribution. This subject has been the topic of debate between conservative and liberal groups, with both sides often misusing statistics. Hence, before any presentation of current income figures, it might be useful to clarify some common misconceptions based on tendentious arguments by pressure groups.

In the conservative camp, many publicists emphasize current trends toward greater equality in incomes, especially after taxes. They rightly note that the share attributable to nonlabor income (dividends, interest, rents, and profits) has definitely declined since 1929, in terms of percentage of national income received by individuals. They assert that no important social gains could be achieved by a further redistribution of current incomes. The need is for more production rather than for equalizing shares in present-day production. This essentially sound position has been vitiated at times by careless language in presenting income statistics. Economists would object particularly to the use of the term "labor payments" for all "earned" income, that is, all income except that derived from rents, interest, and dividends. While it may be argued that salaries and the income of the self-employed are payments for labor, yet the average reader associates the term "labor" with wage earners. Hence an assertion that "90 per cent of the national income is in the form of labor payments" would be misunderstood by an overwhelming majority of readers. The arguments against further equalizing of incomes do not need such doubtful support as that afforded by ambiguous language.[11]

---

[11] No specific sources need be cited for the material summarized here. In general, the conservative position has been given in newspaper advertisements, editorials, writings of columnists and broadcasts by commentators, articles in popular magazines, and direct-mail literature. The liberal position is often found in trade-union literature and in newspaper articles, editorials, columns, radio broadcasts, and similar sources. In presenting both viewpoints, allowance has been made for popular misconceptions

Literature from liberal sources, in turn, often either exaggerates disparities in income or fails to allow for a bias inherent in some statistics. Thus, national income figures, broken down into classifications, almost necessarily involve some distortions. In general, certain groups receive nonmoney income which is not usually computed in national averages. Such would be the case for farmers and domestic servants. These groups would have a higher standard of living than that suggested by their income totals. Again, some persons in the lowest-income groups (below $1,000) may not be so destitute as might be presumed from their cash receipts. They may be elderly persons living with relatives or supporting themselves from their capital. Distortions of this nature are inherent in country-wide figures. On the other hand, there is the possibility that statistics might be misinterpreted. An illustration of this would be the decline in liquid savings during 1947 and 1948. This could mean that families were forced as a result of high prices to dip into savings. But it could also mean that many families were buying automobiles, refrigerators, houses, and similar durable goods, using savings accumulated for this purpose.

Even where figures are not selected for partisan arguments, they must be used with care, if their full significance is to be realized. As an illustration, perfectly accurate studies of family incomes may not go into possible unsocial sources of such funds. A family may achieve a high living standard because the wife works and decides against having children. In other cases children may be neglected because the mother is forced to work to supplement an inadequate income received by the husband. Again, data on compensation of employees include salaries, often running into six figures, together with wage incomes. Reports on income received in the higher brackets, to be complete, should include capital gains along with salaries, dividends, interest, and rent. Gains from the sale of property are an important source of income for wealthy groups. With these qualifications, certain recent

---

arising from careless or misleading statements, even where the original assertion may have been technically correct.

statistics on income distribution are presented here, with remarks on their social significance.

The total national income for selected years is given in Table 4 below. The years 1929, 1933, 1939, 1948, and 1949 were chosen to give highest, lowest, and normal prewar figures as well as recent postwar incomes. The breakdown is in terms of shares going to major economic groups. This is not the same as personal incomes, since compensation paid to some groups may not be received by the individuals concerned. Not all corporation profits are paid out as dividends, nor do employees normally receive in the current year money paid out for social-security benefits. Figures are given in billions of dollars, with percentage of the total income given in italics under each figure.[12]

TABLE 4

NATIONAL INCOME BY DISTRIBUTIVE SHARES

	1929	1933	1939	1948	1949*
Total national income	87.4	39.6	72.5	226.2	222.5
Compensation of employees	50.8	29.3	47.8	140.3	142.2
	58.1	*74.0*	*65.9*	*62.1*	*63.9*
Business and professional	8.3	2.9	6.8	24.5	24.1
	9.5	*7.3*	*9.4*	*10.8*	*10.8*
Farm	5.7	2.3	4.5	18.4	15.0
	6.5	*5.8*	*6.2*	*8.1*	*6.7*
Rental income of persons	5.8	2.0	3.5	6.6	6.6
	6.6	*5.1*	*4.8*	*2.9*	*3.0*
Corporate profits (before taxes; inventory gains or losses excluded)	10.3	−2.0**	5.8	32.6	30.3
	11.8	*−5.1*	*8.0*	*14.4*	*13.7*
Net interest	6.5	5.0	4.2	3.8	4.3
	7.4	*12.6*	*5.8*	*1.7*	*1.9*

* Estimated.
** Deficit.

[12] Basic sources for income statistics are the United States Department of Commerce, particularly the National Income Number of the *Survey of Current Business;* the Federal Reserve Board, annual report on consumer spending, in the *Federal Reserve Bulletin;* the United States Treasury, Bureau of Internal Revenue, in *Statistics of Income;* the Securities and Exchange Commission, *Statistical Bulletin;* and various reports of the Census Bureau. Most of the figures are available in the *Economic Reports* of the Council of Economic Advisers and in the *Statistical Abstract of the United States.* Further comments are given in List No. 2 in the appendix to the present volume.

Another useful study is the breakdown on family income, 1946–1948, in terms of income levels and percentages of families in each level. The figures given in Table 5 were obtained from the Federal Reserve Board study on consumer finances. Since these figures do not include nonmoney income, they tend to exaggerate somewhat the incidence of poverty. Thus, a city family with a total income under $1,000 would face starvation, whereas a farm family with the same cash income would not be completely destitute.

TABLE 5
FAMILY INCOME 1946–1948

Annual money income before taxes	Per cent of families in each income bracket			Per cent of total income received		
	1946	1947	1948	1946	1947	1948
Under $1,000	15	13	11	2	2	2
$1,000–$1,999	20	18	15	9	7	6
$2,000–$2,999	22	20	20	17	13	12
$3,000–$3,999	18	17	20	19	15	18
$4,000–$4,999	10	11	12	14	13	14
$5,000–$7,499	9	13	14	16	20	21
$7,500 and over	6	8	8	23	30	27

The figures given in Table 5 could be used to determine adequacy of family incomes in terms of the requirements for a living wage. A more useful tool for this purpose, however, is the 1949 Census Bureau study of family and personal incomes in 1947. The year used permits direct comparison with the Labor Department cost-of-living studies. Breakdowns in terms of city and rural income and of families of various sizes eliminate the bias inherent in national surveys which combine farm cash incomes with those of city dwellers and individual incomes with those of families. Conservatively assuming that $3,000 would be the 1947 minimum for decent living for a four-person family in a city, we find that one third of the four-person urban families received less than $3,000. About 44 per cent of six-person urban families received less than $4,000. And 54 per cent of urban

families with seven or more persons received total incomes under
$4,500. Thus, from one third to over one half of the city families
with children received total incomes under the minimum budget
for moderately comfortable living. Since 1947, incomes have
increased somewhat more rapidly than the cost of living, with
more of a trend toward equalization.[13]

Of the two subjects studied in this section, the matter of wealth
distribution is currently more important than that of income
distribution. Concentration of control over vital productive wealth
means enormous centralization of power and diminution of
effective freedom. By contrast, the degree of income concentration under present tax laws is not clearly excessive. Social problems derived from low incomes exist, but the remedy is not generally redistribution of the present income total. As noted in
Chapter X, higher incomes ultimately come from increased production, achieved through better economic organization, higher
investment levels, and labor-management co-operation. Accordingly, emphasis in the section to follow will be on better distribution of productive wealth, not income.

Remedies for Concentration of Productive Wealth. A glance
through the quotations from the writings and addresses of Pope
Pius XII indicates the preoccupation of this great Pontiff with
the problem of diffusion of ownership. Indeed, this emphasis
on widespread ownership of productive wealth is the special
contribution of the present Holy Father. This problem has also
been considered in great detail by the Australian hierarchy, which
worked out concrete suggestions for achieving greater decentralization in the ownership of productive wealth.

Facing this problem in terms of American conditions, a social
scientist usually comes up with two broad lines of solution. The
first consists of preventing further concentration and of endeavoring to break up existing giants. The second is the more
positive and constructive approach of trying to foster small business and individual ownership, without necessarily attacking

---

[13] "Consumer Income," *Current Population Reports* (Washington: Census Bureau,
1949), p. 17. See also the income studies cited in Chapter X.

SOCIAL PRINCIPLES IN ECONOMIC LIFE
504   SOCIAL PRINCIPLES IN ECONOMIC LIFE

present-day giants. Both techniques have their merits and difficulties. Indeed, this is one of the most thorny and most neglected
of American social problems.

Before any attempts are made to break up giant corporate
groups, there must be an immediate policy of containment so as
to prevent further concentration. In the United States, the most
effective weapon would be a vigorous antitrust policy. This involves not merely the enforcement of existing laws, but their
extension to remove loopholes. Here the recommendation of the
Federal Trade Commission that the Sherman and Clayton Acts
be strengthened through FTC power to review mergers seems
essential. Any method or situation which has the effect of producing either monopoly or substantial restraint of trade should be
subject to government review and effective court orders directed
toward remedying the situation. Corrective power must not be
limited merely to conspiracies in restraint of trade. It must also
embrace factual situations which effect such restraint, even
though conspiracy is not evident.[14] The government has acted
before to break up monopolies, although this is a difficult and
prolonged task. But such action is an essential weapon in the
struggle against excessive economic concentration.

Government purchasing policies could be an effective device
for aiding small business. In some fields, the government is one
of the greatest buyers in the country. A broad policy of favoring
small business could be laid down to all departments, with a
certain area of discretion permitted on bids. Thus, instead of
rigidly adhering to the policy of awarding contracts to the lowest
bidder, it might be possible to purchase supplies by prorating
orders among the lowest third of the bidders, with a certain
priority to small industries and suppliers. Long-range military
programs could fit into this pattern, the more so since modern
bombing methods make dispersal advisable. Moreover, government research and advisory services for business could give special

[14] This subject is discussed in more detail in J. F. Cronin, *Economic Analysis and Problems*, Chaps. 10–12.

emphasis to the needs of small business, since such firms do not usually have the funds for research.

The present tendency toward giving smaller firms tax advantages is generally healthy, although it is sometimes unfair. Thus, in certain fields (where the industry is small by nature) a small firm might actually be dominant, whereas in others a very large corporation might be fiercely competitive with other large companies. Some states have experimented with taxes which are strongly discriminatory against chain stores, by imposing license fees which increase progressively with the size of the chain. Methods of this type are likewise crude, in that they do not discriminate against desirable and undesirable multiple units. More direct approaches, such as attacks on monopoly or positive aid to small groups, are usually more satisfactory.

In some fields, bigness is essential. Until recent technological developments made small firms possible, steel was basically a large industry. The capital investment and equipment needed was such that only large corporations could enter the field. Mass production of automobiles is likewise, by its very nature, a large industry. But even in the mass-production fields, there is often greater centralization than is required by the economics of the situation. The technical nature of production usually involves an optimum size. When a firm expands beyond that size, it is merely duplicating efficient producing units. Often the same output could be produced by a number of smaller firms at optimum size. This is the evil of the merger movement, which absorbs such efficient companies. But they may have no choice, currently, since they are presented with attractive offers of purchase on the one hand and the threat of destructive and unfair competition on the other. This happens even when profit ratios are better for small firms. Given a fair chance to get started, and protected against ruthless competition, such companies can survive and prosper in our economy. But they can rarely survive an all-out attack by a giant competitor.

The greatest problem today, in addition to giving protection and encouragement to existing small business, involves the initial financing of such firms. There are many serious and almost prohibitive obstacles to their birth. These include shortage of equity funds, lack of incentive to invest, and high cost of small investment. The first two problems were discussed in Chapter X. There it was noted that present policies dry up the source of savings and place a heavy penalty upon investment. It was recommended that, without first changing existing surtax rates, special exemptions be given to investors who place their savings in new firms or new equipment for the expansion of existing firms. Thus, an incentive would be given to high-income groups to use their savings in a socially desirable manner without changing present high surtax rates.

If, as a result of this step, there is still found to be a shortage of funds for equity capital, cautious experiments might be made in tapping such institutional sources of savings as savings banks and insurance companies. Today they are forced by law to confine most of their security investments to the less socially desirable forms of bonds or loans. Possibly such firms would be permitted to form venture capital foundations which would invest in promising enterprises and exercise suitable supervision so as to protect their equity. Some communities have had success with foundations for raising capital to attract new firms to their midst. The American Research and Development Corporation has pioneered in nationwide promotion of new firms, raising its funds in Wall Street.[15] Developments of this type could indicate a pattern which might be used by institutional investors after state laws had been appropriately amended. If these two sources of savings prove inadequate, consideration might be given to more direct changes in income-tax laws.

The cost of security flotation is likewise a major obstacle to small business. Thus, the latest Securities and Exchange Commission report notes that the flotation costs of common stocks

---

[15] See *Business Week*, April 9, 1949, p. 30 ff; and *The New York Times* (Sunday), Financial Section, May 1, 1949, p. 1. Equity or venture capital is a type of investment in which the investor becomes part owner of the enterprise, in contrast to loan capital where the investment is a debt carried by the owners.

were eight times those of bonds. Preferred stock costs three times as much as bonds. The cost for all common stocks averaged about 10 per cent, but small issues (under $500,000) cost nearly 28 per cent, in contrast to an average of slightly over 8 per cent for issues in the twenty–fifty million dollar range. The largest element of costs in all groups involved commissions and discounts, which reflected both the risk involved in the sale and the difficulty of disposing of common stocks.[16] From this it can be seen that existing machinery for promoting equity investment is currently extremely expensive for small firms.

With tax policies inhibiting individual investors and state laws excluding institutional investors, the trend toward concentration is increased. Large firms can expand through retained earnings and can even enter the capital market without excessive cost, although even these firms find bonds cheaper. But the man with the invention or plan which could be the basis for a new small business faces tremendous obstacles. He might, with great difficulty, get a loan, but the threat of foreclosure would hang over him during the period of initial losses due to problems of development and market exploitation. If he can convince an investment banking house of the value of his project, he must pay nearly one third of the funds raised merely for the cost of flotation. So he normally sells his invention to a large corporation or lets his plan go the way of all dreams.

The need for a framework which will foster and protect small business is one of the great social problems of today. Unfortunately, it has tended to be more a slogan than a stimulus to effective action. Fostering of small business demands combined action on the three fronts noted above: making savings available, restoring incentive to invest, and establishing institutions for the promoting of small firms. If, in addition, a sound antitrust and tax policy affords government protection to such companies, we can gradually reverse the trend toward giantism and restore

---

[16] See *Cost of Flotation, 1945–1947* (Washington: Securities and Exchange Commission, 1949).

economic freedom based on widespread actual ownership.[17] These methods would be in the traditional American pattern and would not involve great changes in our economic methods.

The more drastic proposals of the distributists will be discussed in Chapter XVI. The emphasis on producer co-operatives, found in the pastoral letter of the Australian bishops, would likewise involve a radically new departure from our tradition. The American co-operative movement has had only limited success in the producer field. Moreover, when co-operatives get large, they tend to develop many of the evils of large corporations. Members lose active interest in running the co-operative, with the result that self-perpetuating managements keep control. Methods which may be highly successful in Australia may not be suited to a nation of our size or to the temperament of our people. Hence the recommendations given here are within the framework of our traditions in the small business field. It is to be hoped that real and effective action will be taken to extend the material basis for man's freedom.

THE RURAL PHILOSOPHY OF THE PAPAL ENCYCLICALS

Problems of rural life have not received a treatment in papal writings and discourses comparable to problems of urban labor. The reason for this is obvious. There are more volumes on sickness than on health. The city proletariat — the nonowning workers of the encyclicals — was in a state of acute crisis. Poverty, exploitation, and unemployment had reduced them to wretchedness and bitterness. Many were toying with the program of socialism when Pope Leo XIII wrote. In later times, workers were still more obsessed with problems of insecurity. The philosophy of communism was spreading rapidly in their midst. With such tensions prevailing, it is understandable that the wisdom of papal teaching was directed primarily to the problems of industry.

---

[17] See A. D. H. Kaplan, *Problems of Small Business* (New York: McGraw-Hill, 1949), a study sponsored by the Committee for Economic Development. This excellent treatment offers many valuable analyses and suggestions.

It was not that social problems were absent from the farm. But some of the most difficult questions facing the farmer arose from the general economic system, with its main roots in industry and finance, and also from war-caused expansion of output. The farmers were victims of depressions, but the cause was often national monetary and income policies. Thus, one of the references to farming in *Quadragesimo Anno* concerns the right proportion of prices needed to secure full employment. Even with such crises, the owner of rural land had more resources than the city dweller. If he were not in debt, he could at least normally have his food and lodging, with a minimum cash income for other needs of life. An exception to this statement would be the "huge army of rural wage workers, pushed to the lowest level of existence and deprived of all hope of ever acquiring some property in land . . ." (*Q. A.*, No. 59). Here the reference is probably directed to the millions in China and India, although it applies to a lesser degree to Occidental nations, including our own sharecroppers and migrant farm workers. Indeed, the rural proletariat is often more depressed than nonowning city workers. Hence an important objective of social policy would be the spread of actual land ownership among farmers as well as city dwellers.

The popes give agriculture a place of special honor among the occupations of mankind. In *Rerum Novarum* the arguments for private property seem to envision the workers' buying of small plots of land for their homes and modest food needs. *Quadragesimo Anno* refers to agriculture as the occupation "wherein the greater portion of mankind honorably and honestly procures its livelihood" (No. 102). Finally, Pope Pius XII has repeatedly referred to the ideal of widespread ownership of productive property, both in industry and in land. He sees in farming a unique example of the natural order of things, willed by God. There man is the producer, not the speculator. He is master of material things, not servant. Farming is directed to meet the real needs of mankind, not the artificial demands of a complex economic system. Hence, among all the forms of private property, and uses of the goods of the earth, farm land

and agriculture must be rated in a position of unique importance.

The American rural economy has its share of problems. Many of our farmers have become deeply enmeshed in the more speculative phases of our economic system. There have been periods of deep indebtedness, speculation in farm land, widespread concentration on hazardous single crops, and long years of distress and crisis. The farmer over many decades felt that he was a second-class citizen, a victim of urban exploitation. He sold in a free world market, but bought in a market dominated by tariffs and monopolies. He paid discriminatory freight rates and usurious sums for loans. His distress communicated itself to the tenants and farm laborers who aided in the production of crops. Often they led lives of poverty and insecurity. In recent years, however, the lot of the American farmer has improved. There have been many efforts to give him economic stability. Farm prices have been supported, credit has been made available, and many types of production aids have been supplied. The farmers have accomplished much through their own organizations, especially the co-operatives. Nor has the Catholic Church in the United States been idle. The splendid work of the National Catholic Rural Life Conference has been outstanding in American Catholic social action. Its members have evolved a many-sided program. These efforts receive more extensive treatment in Chapter XVII.

CONCLUSION

It is evident from the foregoing that the problems connected with property are intricate and involved. While the Church stanchly defends the right of ownership, it is not satisfied with many current aspects of property. There is too great concentration in both ownership and control. This is in itself a problem insofar as great abuses are possible. Furthermore, it connotes the absence of diffused ownership of productive wealth and thus involves the impairment of an important foundation of freedom and security. The popes have called for more actual owners as well as the use of property in the interests of the common good. So long as the institution of private property is abused, there will be insistent demands for increased state control over economic life. This in turn forces the state to assume such powers that it becomes an object of concern.

READINGS *

J. Messner, *Social Ethics*, pp. 202–206, 634–637, 785–800, 823–843.
R. J. Miller, *Forty Years After*, pp. 74–94, 111–116.
J. A. Ryan, *Distributive Justice*, Chaps. 1–8, 20–21.
O. von Nell-Breuning, *Reorganization of Social Economy*, Chap. 6.
C. Bruehl, *The Pope's Plan*, Chaps. 5–9.
G. C. Rutten, *La Doctrine sociale de l'Église*, Chap. 5.

---

* For further readings, consult Lists Nos. 1, 4, 11, and 14 in the Appendix.

Chapter XIII. THE STATE IN ECONOMIC LIFE

Leo XIII, Diuturnum Illud

3. Indeed, very many men of more recent times, walking in the footsteps of those who in a former age assumed to themselves the name of philosophers, say that all power comes from the people: so that those who exercise it in the state do so not as their own, but as delegated to them by the people, and that, by this rule, it can be revoked by the will of the very people by whom it was delegated. But from these, Catholics dissent, who affirm that the right to rule is from God, as from a natural and necessary principle.

4. It is of importance, however, to remark in this place that those who may be placed over the state may in certain cases be chosen by the will and decision of the multitude, without opposition to or impugning of the Catholic doctrine. And by this choice, in truth, the ruler is designated, but the rights of ruling are not thereby conferred. Nor is the authority delegated to him, but the person by whom it is to be exercised is determined upon.

There is no question here respecting forms of government, for there is no reason why the Church should not approve of the chief power being held by one man or by more, provided only it be just, and that it tend to the common advantage. Wherefore, so long as justice be respected, the people are not hindered from choosing for themselves that form of government which suits best either their own disposition, or the institutions and customs of their ancestors.

5. But as regards political power, the Church rightly teaches that it comes from God, for it finds this clearly testified in the Sacred Scriptures and in the monuments of antiquity; besides, no other doctrine can be conceived which is more agreeable to reason, or more in accord with the safety of both princes and peoples.

12. But in order that justice may be retained in government it is of the highest importance that those who rule states should understand that

political power was not created for the advantage of any private individual; and that the administration of the state must be carried on to the profit of those who have been committed to their care, not to the profit of those to whom it has been committed.

Leo XIII, In the Midst of Solicitudes

[Civil power] by its nature is constituted to seek after the common good, the supreme goal which is the source of human society. . . . This good is, after God, the first and last law of society.

In this order of speculative ideas, Catholics, like all other citizens, are free to prefer one form of government to another precisely because no one of these social forms is, in itself, opposed to the principles of sound reason or to the maxims of Christian doctrine.

Leo XIII, Immortale Dei

2. Furthermore, the civil power must not be subservient to the advantage of any one individual, or of some few persons, inasmuch as it was established for the common good of all.

Leo XIII, Rerum Novarum

48. Therefore, those governing the state ought primarily to devote themselves to the service of individual groups and of the whole commonwealth, and through the entire scheme of laws and institutions to cause both public and individual well-being to develop spontaneously out of the very structure and administration of the state. For this is the duty of wise statesmanship and the essential office of those in charge of the state. Now, states are made prosperous especially by wholesome morality, properly ordered family life, protection of religion and justice, moderate imposition and equitable distribution of public burdens, progressive development of industry and trade, thriving agriculture, and by all other things of this nature, which the more actively they are promoted, the better and happier the life of the citizens is destined to be. Therefore, by virtue of these things, it is within the competence of the rulers of the state that, as they benefit other groups, they also improve in particular the condition of the workers. Furthermore, they do this with full right and without laying themselves open to any charge of unwarranted interference. For the state is bound by the very law of its office to serve the common interest. And the richer the benefits which come from this general providence on the part of the state, the less necessary it will be to experiment with other measures for the well-being of workers.

52. Nevertheless, those who govern must see to it that they protect the

community and its constituent parts: the community, because nature has entrusted its safeguarding to the sovereign power in the state to such an extent that the protection of the public welfare is not only the supreme law, but is the entire cause and reason for sovereignty; and the constituent parts, because philosophy and Christian faith agree that the administration of the state has from nature as its purpose, not the benefit of those to whom it has been entrusted, but the benefit of those who have been entrusted to it. If, therefore, any injury has been done to or threatens either the common good or the interests of individual groups, which injury cannot in any other way be repaired or prevented, it is necessary for public authority to intervene.

75. Let the state protect these lawfully associated bodies of citizens; let it not, however, interfere with their private concerns and order of life; for vital activity is set in motion by an inner principle, and it is very easily destroyed, as We know, by intrusion from without.

Pius XI, Quadragesimo Anno

25. With regard to civil authority, Leo XIII, boldly breaking through the confines imposed by Liberalism, fearlessly taught that government must not be thought a mere guardian of law and of good order, but rather must put forth every effort so that "through the entire scheme of laws and institutions . . . both public and individual well-being may develop spontaneously out of the very structure and administration of the state." Just freedom of action must, of course, be left both to individual citizens and to families, yet only on condition that the common good be preserved and wrong to any individual be abolished. The function of the rulers of the state, moreover, is to watch over the community and its parts; but in protecting private individuals in their rights, chief consideration ought to be given to the weak and the poor.

49. To define these duties in detail, when necessity requires and the natural law has not done so, is the function of those in charge of the state. Therefore, public authority, under the guiding light always of the natural and the divine law, can determine more accurately upon consideration of the true requirements of the common good what is permitted and what is not permitted to owners in the use of their property.

78. When we speak of the reform of institutions, the state comes chiefly to mind, not as if universal well-being were to be expected from its activity, but because things have come to such a pass through the evil of what we have termed "individualism," that, following upon the overthrow and near extinction of that rich social life which was once highly developed

through associations of various kinds, there remain virtually only individuals and the state. This is to the great harm of the state itself; for, with a structure of social governance lost, and with the taking over of all the burdens which the wrecked associations once bore, the state has been overwhelmed and crushed by almost infinite tasks and duties.

80. The supreme authority of the state ought, therefore, to let subordinate groups handle matters and concerns of lesser importance, which would otherwise dissipate its efforts greatly. Thereby the state will more freely, powerfully, and effectively do all those things that belong to it alone because it alone can do them; directing, watching, urging, restraining, as occasion requires and necessity demands. Therefore, those in power should be sure that the more perfectly a graduated order is kept among the various associations, in observance of the principle of "subsidiary function," the stronger social authority and effectiveness will be and the happier and more prosperous the condition of the state.

110. The public institutions themselves, of peoples, moreover, ought to make all human society conform to the needs of the common good, that is, to the norm of social justice. If this is done, that most important division of social life, namely, economic activity, cannot fail likewise to return to right and sound order.

Pius XI, On Atheistic Communism

30. Man cannot be excepted from his divinely imposed obligations toward civil society, and the representatives of authority have the right to coerce him when he refuses without reason to do his duty. Society, on the other hand, cannot defraud man of his God-granted rights. . . . Nor can society systematically void these rights by making their use impossible.

32. The genuine and chief function of public and civil authority consists precisely in the efficacious furthering of this harmony and co-ordination of all social forces.

75. It must likewise be the special care of the state to create those material conditions of life without which an orderly society cannot exist. The state must take every measure necessary to supply employment, particularly for the heads of families and for the young. To achieve this end demanded by the pressing needs of the common welfare the wealthy classes must be induced to assume those burdens without which human society cannot be saved nor they themselves remain secure. However, measures taken by the state with this end in view ought to be of such a nature that they will really affect those who actually possess more than their share of capital resources, and who continue to accumulate them to the grievous detriment of others.

76. The state itself, mindful of its responsibility before God and society, should be a model of prudence and sobriety in the administration of the commonwealth. Today more than ever the acute world crisis demands that those who dispose of immense funds, built upon the sweat and toil of millions, keep constantly and singly in mind the common good. State functionaries and all employees are obliged in conscience to perform their duties faithfully and unselfishly, imitating the brilliant example of distinguished men of the past and of our own day, who with unremitting labor sacrificed their all for the good of their country.

Pius XII, Summi Pontificatus

1418. Indeed, as Our great Predecessor, Leo XIII, wisely taught in the Encyclical *Immortale Dei,* it was the Creator's will that civil sovereignty should regulate social life after the dictates of an order changeless in its universal principles; should facilitate the attainment in the temporal order, by individuals, of physical, intellectual, and moral perfection. . . .

1419. Hence, it is the noble prerogative and function of the state to control, aid, and direct the private and individual activities of national life that they converge harmoniously toward the common good.

1420. To consider the state as something ultimate, to which everything else should be subordinated and directed, cannot fail to harm the true and lasting prosperity of nations. This can happen, either when unrestricted dominion comes to be conferred on the state as having a mandate from the nation, people, or even a social class, or when the state arrogates such dominion to itself as absolute master, despotically, without any mandate whatsoever. If, in fact, the state lays claim to and directs private enterprises, these, ruled as they are by delicate and complicated internal principles which guarantee and assure the realization of their special aims, may be damaged to the detriment of the public good, by being wrenched from their natural surroundings, that is, from responsible private action.

1429. The idea which credits the state with unlimited authority is not simply an error harmful to the internal life of nations, to their prosperity, and to the larger and well-ordered increase in their well-being, but likewise it injures the relations between peoples, for it breaks the unity of supranational society, robs the law of nations of its foundation and vigor, leads to violation of others' rights, and impedes agreement and peaceful intercourse.

Pius XII, La Solennità della Pentecoste

1675. In the general framework of labor, to stimulate the sane and responsible development of all the energies, physical and spiritual, of individuals and their free organization, there opens up a wide field of action where the public authority comes in with its integrating and co-ordinating activity exercised first through the local and professional corporations, and finally in the activity of the state itself, whose higher moderating social authority has the important duty of forestalling the dislocations of economic balance arising from plurality and divergence of clashing interests, individual and collective.

1685. To safeguard the inviolable sphere of the rights of the human person and to facilitate the fulfillment of his duties should be the essential office of every public authority. Does not this follow from the genuine concept of the common good which the state is called upon to promote?

1689. From that it follows that the duty and the right to organize the labor of the people belongs above all to the people immediately interested: the employers and the workers. If they do not fulfill their functions, or cannot because of special extraordinary contingencies fulfill them, then it falls back on the state to intervene in the field of labor and in the division and distribution of work according to the form and measure that the common good properly understood demands.

1690. In any case, every legitimate and beneficial interference of the state in the field of labor should be such as to safeguard and respect its personal character, both in the broad outlines and, as far as possible, in what concerns its execution.

Pius XII, Women's Duties

The state and politics have, in fact, precisely the office of securing for the family of every social class conditions necessary for them to exist and to evolve as economic, juridical, and moral entities.

Pius XII, Christmas Broadcast, 1942

1833. The whole political and economic activity of the state is directed to the permanent realization of the common good, that is to say, those external conditions necessary for the bulk of citizens for the development of their qualities, their functions, and their material, intellectual, and religious life. . . .

1834. That social life, as God willed it, may attain its scope, it needs a juridical order to support it from without, to defend it and protect it. The function of this juridical order is not to dominate, but to serve, to help the development and the increase of society's vitality in the rich multiplicity of ends, leading all individual energies to their perfection in peaceful competition, and defending them with appropriate and honest means against all that may militate against their full evolution. Such an order, that it may safeguard the equilibrium, the safety, and the harmony of society, has also the power of coercion against those, who only by this means can be held within the noble discipline of social life.

Code of Social Principles

150. The state, the guardian of justice and of the common good, should take positive action in economic life.

151. Nevertheless, to withdraw from lesser authorities duties which they can fulfill themselves in order to hand them over to the state would be both an injustice and an injury to social order.

152. It is wise to entrust the direction of less important business to groups of lesser importance, because the state will then be in a position to fulfill more perfectly the functions which belong to it alone: to direct, watch, stimulate, or restrain according as circumstances or necessity may demand.

153. This action relates in the first place to the protection of human life. With this higher purpose is connected protective legislation for labor, limiting the length of the working day, forbidding nightwork, providing for Sunday rest, hygiene, and security of employment.

The state can also rightly take the means which are in its power to ensure justice and good faith in business. It has the full right to combat unjust speculation and every kind of usury by both preventive and repressive means. It should not fail to protect consumers, especially against fraud in connection with essential commodities.

154. That form of company in which the partners limit their risk and may relinquish their share is not of its nature illicit. Still, under cover of anonymity, very serious evils are perpetrated to the harm of both shareholders and public. It is important, then, that the public authority should keep strict control over these companies and eventually revise their legal status.

155. The state, while in principle leaving to individuals the ownership and management of enterprises, lawfully interferes, either to protect these enterprises against foreign competition (by customs duties of a compensatory but not prohibitive kind), or to help it to enter foreign markets (through consular services and commercial agents).

156. It belongs to the state to give a general direction to the national economy, and for that purpose to set up a national economic council, representative of the corporative organization, which will enable the public authorities to keep in close touch with qualified and competent representatives of every branch of production.

157. Special reasons may urge the state to take over the entire manage-

ment as a state monopoly, of certain industrial, commercial, or agricultural undertakings. But in general it should avoid absorbing the country's economic life in this way. If the nature of a service requires that the undertaking shall not be wholly in private hands, the state should endeavor, preferably to conducting it as a state concern, to retain a partial interest through some form of leasing out or granting concessions. In such cases private initiative may take a suitable share with the public authority, and under its supervision, in the management of service or undertakings of public interest, such, for instance, as railways.

It is particularly desirable that the bank which has the responsibility of issuing fiduciary money should be distinguishable from the state, though acting under state control and with its assistance.

158. In any case, the central authority should not act as though it were itself alone the state, for the state is the organized nation with all the living forces that compose it. A co-ordination of all these forces is particularly necessary in great undertakings of public importance which tend to develop the national resources, such as the control of rivers, canals, harbors, oil wells, mines, and forests.

159. The different states are mutually dependent in the economic order and so should pool their experience and efforts by means of suitable institutions, in order to bring about, along with occupational and interoccupational organization, international economic co-ordination.

PUBLIC OWNERSHIP AND NATIONALIZATION

Pius XI, Quadragesimo Anno

79. Just as it is gravely wrong to take from individuals what they can accomplish by their own initiative and industry and give it to the community, so it is also an injustice and at the same time a grave evil and a disturbance of right order to assign to a greater and higher association what lesser and subordinate organizations can do. For every social activity ought of its very nature to furnish help to members of the body social, and never destroy and absorb them.

114. For certain kinds of property, it is rightly contended, ought to be reserved to the state, since they carry with them a dominating power so great that cannot without danger to the general welfare be entrusted to private individuals.

115. Such just demands and desires have nothing in them now which is inconsistent with Christian truth, and much less are they special to socialism. Those who work solely toward such ends have, therefore, no reason to become Socialists.

Pius XI, Divini Illius Magistri

41. These rights have been conferred upon civil society by the Author of nature Himself . . . in virtue of the authority it possesses to promote the common welfare, which is precisely the purpose of its existence. . . .

42. Now this end and object, the common welfare in the temporal order, consists in that peace and security in which families and individual citizens have the free exercise of their rights, and at the same time enjoy the greatest spiritual and temporal prosperity possible in this life, by the mutual union and co-ordination of the work of all. The function, therefore, of the civil authority residing in the state is twofold, to protect and foster, but by no means to absorb, the family and the individual, or to substitute itself for them.

Pius XII, Summi Pontificatus

1424. No one of good will and vision will think of refusing the state, in the exceptional conditions of the world today [1939], correspondingly wider and exceptional rights to meet the public needs. But even in such emergencies, the moral law, established by God, demands that the lawfulness of each measure and its real necessity be scrutinized with the greatest rigor according to the standards of the common good.

Pius XII, Discourse to Members of Italian Electrical Industry, January 25, 1946

One cannot imagine that, with collective organizations, competition will be really removed, for with the elements of the struggle being changed, the conflict between labor and private capital will reappear as a conflict between labor and state capitalism. In effect, whatever manner collectivism may be organized for the distribution of returns, whether in equal or unequal parts, whether in proportion to the hours of work or in accord with the needs of individuals, one cannot avoid the rise of struggles and differences in regard to the share received, the conditions of work, and the conduct, not always without blame, of the governing powers, so that the working class is faced with the danger of being a slave to public authority.

Pius XII, Address to Italian Workers, March 11, 1945

The Catholic Associations support socialization only in cases where it appears really necessary for the common welfare; in other words, when it is the only means to remedy an injustice and to ensure the co-ordinated use of the same forces to the benefit of the economic life of the nation, so that the normal and peaceful development of that economic life may open the gates to material prosperity for all, a prosperity which may become a sound foundation for the development of cultural and religious life. In any case, the Associations recognize that socialization carries with it the obligation of fitting compensation, such as in concrete circumstances is just and fair to those concerned.

Pius XII, Letter to Semaines Sociales, July 10, 1946

This remark applies, for example, to the particular problem which interests you at this moment: the nationalization of enterprises. Our Predecessors, and We Ourselves, have more than once touched upon the moral aspect of this measure. Now it is evident that, instead of making life and work in common less mechanical, this nationalization, even when it is licit, risks rather to make them more so, and that, consequently, the profit accruing from nationalization to a true community, such as you understand it, is highly questionable.

Pius XII, Letter to Semaines Sociales, July 18, 1947

In this report you recall the fact, of which We were already aware, that Our letter of last year to the *Semaine Sociale* of Strasbourg had provoked some controversy, some of it even political in character. This would seem to make it plain that certain circles are inveterately prone to discover in the directives of the Popes just so many attempts to meddle in the purely political questions of the day.

For a case in point, Our remarks on "nationalization" were so interpreted. As a matter of fact, We were treating the subject here on a much higher plane. There was no question of the moral liceity of nationalization insofar as it furthers the material welfare of the nation. Under the aspect of a requirement of the common good, its liceity had already been treated in the Encyclical *Quadragesimo Anno,* as well as by Ourselves in Our address to the Italian Catholic Workers' Associations on March 11, 1945.

Contrariwise, the question as it bore directly on the objective of the *Semaine Sociale* of Strasbourg was to find out whether nationalization afforded an appropriate instrument of national unity and community spirit. The problem with which We were faced called for the most energetic possible development of "unitary or co-operative associations" — for there was question of these, as the context clearly indicated. In addressing Ourselves to this subject, We had at heart the promotion of little and medium business; and We repeated simply what We had enlarged upon in greater detail under other circumstances. There was consequently no need of further elucidation, even aside from the fact that Our conclusion derives quite naturally from the principles of the Church in matters social, as they have been expounded from time immemorial, independently of any special contingencies of party politics or vocabulary.

Pius XII, Address to Catholic Employers, May 7, 1949

Meanwhile feverish attempts are under way to work out other juridical types of organization for the social economy, and at the moment preference favors state enterprise and the nationalization of industry. There can be no question that the Church also admits — within certain just limits — state ownership and management, judging that "certain forms of property may legitimately be reserved to the public authority: those which represent a dominating power so great that it cannot without danger to the general welfare be entrusted to private individuals" (*Quadragesimo Anno*). But to make of this state enterprise the normal rule for public economic organization would mean reversing the order of things. Actually it is the mission of public law to serve private rights, not to absorb them. The economy is not of its nature — not more, for that matter, than any other human activity — a state institution. It is, on the contrary, the living product of the free initiative of individuals and of their freely established associations.

Socialization, The Australian Hierarchy, 1948

(*Summarized.*) 3. Socialization can be used in two senses, as identical with socialism or as connoting public ownership of utilities, monopolies, and basic industries. "In the latter use of the term, 'socialization,' as such, is not offensive to Christian principles."

17. Even when some form of property must be controlled by the state, it does not necessarily follow that the central government should be the controlling force. Lesser civil units should do this when they can.

63. "By nationalization, we mean the specific act whereby the government compulsorily substitutes public ownership for private ownership in a particular industry."

66. "While nationalization of certain industries may be justified under certain conditions, it is quite clear that the nationalization of *all* the means or production is absolutely wrong in principle and cannot be held by Catholics. It is equally wrong whether its achievement is proposed by peaceful or by violent means, whether it is achieved piecemeal or at one stage."

67-68. Such nationalization would destroy the economic basis of family life and human freedom as well.

69. "A system which, while avoiding complete nationalization, extends public ownership far beyond what is required by the common good, is opposed to Christian teaching."

73. "The nationalization of industries which are capable of being conducted in small units cannot be reconciled with Christian thought." [In

Nos. 71, 72, and 75, the document makes allusions which apparently condemn the extreme nationalization program of the British Labor Party.]

76. "The Church recognizes that, under present conditions, there are certain forms of enterprises and industry which are of quite extraordinary importance to the community, and which may legitimately come under public control in one form or another, although not necessarily by means of nationalization."

77. "Among these are banking and insurance; the manufacture of steel and heavy chemicals; rail, sea, and air transport; public utility services (electricity, gas, tramways); armaments."

78. In such cases, the question of efficient operation is secondary to that of economic power exercized through their control.

84. "Among the industries which should be publicly controlled, there are some which may legitimately be nationalized."

85. ". . . recourse should be had to it only if and insofar as other less drastic measures have been shown by experience to be insufficient." Frequently state control may be more effective than public ownership.

89. "Even if in a particular case nationalization proves to be justifiable, it is an expedient which may have dangerous results. 'Instead of diminishing the mechanical character of life and work . . . ' writes the present Holy Father, 'nationalization, even when morally legitimate, is more likely to increase it.' "

90–91. This happens both from the increase in bigness and the vested interest government has in preserving its monopoly.

94–97. It is proposed that co-operatives, rather than government, take over industries and occupations deemed suitable for nationalization.

98. "In the case of the nationalization of a particular enterprise, it is obvious that a just compensation should be paid."

100. To summarize, communism, socialism, and socialization which is the equivalent of socialism, should be rejected. Limited nationalization is not rejected in principle, but the real goal of public policy should be extension of private ownership of productive property. This is the main test for judging the wisdom of proposed policies.

Code of Social Principles

103. By nationalization is meant that an undertaking belongs to the national community, represented by the political power. It may be limited to ownership, or extend to management and profits. It cannot be condemned in principle on grounds of Christian ethics.

104. Where undertakings already worked by private persons are concerned, their taking over is subject to just compensation.

105. Nationalization, taken in its widest sense and applied to all industries or the majority of them, amounts by force of circumstances to collectivism, which was condemned by the Encyclical, *Rerum Novarum*.

106. Nationalization, if applied generally, still runs the risk of arriving at the same result, even when limited to mere ownership or management.

107. Not even a system of more or less self-governing public undertakings would seem to be acceptable, if it includes the majority of undertakings.

Private initiative of individuals or groups can only be limited to the extent that the common good manifestly requires. It is very needful to preserve the two great stimulants to production, *viz.:* the prospect of acquiring property and lawful competition.

108. Considerations of public interest may in particular cases demand or suggest public management, either national, provincial, or municipal. In that case the setting up of autonomous bodies, carrying on industrially under the control of public authorities and for the benefit of the community, can be recommended in preference to wholly official administration.

109. It is understood that the right of supervision by the state is to be exercizable when private organizations are entrusted with the maintenance of public services, and whenever the public interest calls for it.

110. In undertakings which are subject to concessions placed with private organizations, it is desirable that the agreements shall contain clauses securing liberty of contract and fair wages to the workpeople, and providing for family allowances.

111. In case of war, famine, or serious and manifest abuse, the state has not only the right, but the duty, to set up a special organization for checking monopoly and usurious speculation in necessary articles of consumption.

SOCIAL LEGISLATION

Leo XIII, Rerum Novarum

51. Equity, therefore, commands that public authority show proper concern for the worker, so that from what he contributes to the common good he may receive what will enable him, housed, clothed, and secure, to live his life without hardship. Whence, it follows that all those measures ought to be favored which seem in any way capable of benefiting the condition of workers. Such solicitude is so far from injuring anyone, that it is destined rather to benefit all, because it is of absolute interest to the state that those citizens should not be miserable in every respect from whom such necessary goods proceed.

53. Wherefore, if at any time disorder should threaten because of strikes or concerted stoppages of work, if the natural bonds of family life should be relaxed among the poor, if religion among the workers should be outraged by failure to provide sufficient opportunity for performing religious duties, if in factories danger should assail the integrity of morals through the mixing of the sexes or other pernicious incitements to sin, or if the employer class should oppress the working class with unjust burdens or should degrade them with conditions inimical to human personality or to human dignity, if health should be injured by immoderate work and such as is not suited to sex or age — in all these cases, the power and authority of the law, but of course within certain limits, manifestly ought to be employed. And these limits are determined by the same reason which demands the aid of the law, that is, the law ought not undertake more, nor should it go farther, than the remedy of evils or the removal of danger requires.

54. Rights indeed, by whomsoever possessed, must be religiously protected; and public authority, in warding off injuries and punishing wrongs, ought to see to it that individuals may have and hold what belongs to them. In protecting the rights of private individuals, however, special consideration must be given to the weak and the poor. For the nation, as it were, of the rich, is guarded by its own defenses and is in less need of governmental protection, whereas the suffering multitude, without the means to protect itself, relies especially on the protection of the state. Wherefore, since wage workers are numbered among the great mass of the needy, the state must include them under its special care and foresight.

Pius XI, Quadragesimo Anno

28. A new branch of law, wholly unknown to the earlier time, has arisen from the continuous and unwearied labor to protect vigorously the sacred rights of the workers that flow from their dignity as men and as Christians. These laws undertake the protection of life, health, strength, family, homes, workshops, wages, and labor hazards, in fine, everything which pertains to the condition of wage workers, with special concern for women and children. Even though these laws do not conform exactly everywhere and in all respects to Leo's recommendations, still it is undeniable that much in them savors of the Encyclical, *On the Condition of Workers,* to which great credit must be given for whatever improvement has been achieved in the workers' conditions.

Pius XI, Casti Connubii

126. If, however, for this purpose [family needs], private resources do not suffice, it is the duty of the public authority to supply for the insufficient forces of individual effort, particularly in a matter which is of such

importance to the commonweal, touching as it does the maintenance of the family and married people. If families, particularly those in which there are many children, have not suitable dwellings; if the husband cannot find employment and means of livelihood; if the necessities of life cannot be purchased except at exorbitant prices; if even the mother of the family, to the great harm of the home, is compelled to go forth and seek a living by her own labors; if she too, in the ordinary or even extraordinary labors of childbirth, is deprived of proper food, medicine, and the assistance of a skilled physician, it is patent to all to what extent married couples may lose heart, and how home life and the observance of God's commands are rendered difficult for them. Indeed, it is obvious how great peril can arise to the public security and the welfare and very life of civil society itself when such men are reduced to such a condition of desperation that, having nothing which they fear to lose, they are emboldened to hope for chance advantage from the upheaval of the state and of established order.

127. Wherefore, those who have the care of the state and of the public good cannot neglect the needs of married people and their families, without bringing great harm upon the state and the common welfare. Hence, in making laws and disposing of public funds, they must do their utmost to relieve the needs of the poor, considering such a task as one of the most important of their administrative duties.

Pius XII, Address to Italian Workers, June 13, 1943

It is not only the social status of workers, men and women, which calls for reconditioning and reform. The whole complex structure of society is in need of adjustment and improvement, thoroughly shaken as it is in all its foundations.

Not to aim at making the lives of individuals depend entirely on the whims of the state, but to procure rather that the state, whose duty it is to promote the common good, may through social institutions, such as insurance and social-security societies, supply support and complete all that helps to strengthen workers' associations and especially the fathers and mothers of families who are earning a decent livelihood for themselves and their dependents through work.

Woe to him who forgets that a true national society incorporates social justice and demands a just and fitting sharing by all in the goods of the country.

INTERNATIONAL ECONOMIC LIFE

Pius XI, Quadragesimo Anno

89. Furthermore, since the various nations largely depend on one another in economic matters and need one another's help, they should strive with a

united purpose and effort to promote by wisely conceived pacts and institutions a prosperous and happy international co-operation in economic life.

Pius XI, On Atheistic Communism

76. In international trade relations let all means be sedulously employed for the removal of those artificial barriers to economic life which are the effects of distrust and hatred. All must remember that the peoples of the earth form but one family in God.

Pius XI, Ubi Arcano Dei

20. For the love of country and of race, though a spur to many deeds of virtue and of heroism when guided by Christianity, may become also the seed of widespread injustice and iniquity when it transgresses the bounds of right and justice, developing into a spirit of excessive nationalism. They who fall into this error surely forget that all peoples, as members of the universal Christian family, are linked together by the common ties of brotherhood; that other nations also have a right to live and seek prosperity. . . .

Pius XI, Caritate Christi Compulsi

4. Right order of Christian charity does not disapprove of lawful love of country and a sentiment of justifiable nationalism. . . . If however, egoism, abusing this love of country and exaggerating this sentiment of nationalism, insinuates itself into the relations between people and people, there is no excess that will not seem justified.

Pius XII, La Solennità della Pentecoste

1693. When this happens, emigration attains its natural scope, as experience often shows; We mean the more favorable distribution of men on the earth's surface suitable to colonies of agricultural workers; that surface which God created and prepared for the use of all. If the two parties, those who agree to leave their native land, and those who agree to admit the newcomers, remain anxious to eliminate as far as possible all obstacles to the birth and growth of real confidence between the country of emigration and that of immigration, all those affected by such a transference of people and places will profit by the transaction: the families will receive a plot of ground which will be native land for them in the true sense of the word; the thickly inhabited countries will be relieved, and their peoples will acquire new friends in foreign countries; and the states which receive the emigrants will acquire industrious citizens. In this way the nations which give and those which receive will both contribute to the increased welfare of man and the progress of human culture.

Pius XII, Nell' Alba

1758. First: within the limits of a new order founded on moral principles there is no room for violation of the freedom, integrity, and security of other states, no matter what may be their territorial extension or their capacity for defense. If it is inevitable that the powerful states should, by reason of their greater potentialities and their power, play leading roles in the formation of economic groups, comprising not only themselves but smaller and weaker states as well, it is nevertheless indispensable that in the interests of the common good they, and all others, respect the rights of those smaller states to political freedom, to economic development, and to the adequate protection, in the case of conflicts between nations, of that neutrality which is theirs according to the natural as well as international law. In this way, and in this way only, shall they be able to obtain a fitting share of the common good and assure the material and spiritual welfare of the peoples concerned.

1760. Thirdly: within the limits of a new order founded on moral principles there is no place for that cold and calculating egoism which tends to hoard economic resources and materials destined for the use of all, to such an extent that the nations less favored by nature are not permitted access to them. In this regard, it is a source of great consolation to see admitted the necessity of a participation of all in the natural riches of the earth even on the part of those nations which, in the fulfillment of this principle, belong to the category of givers and not to that of receivers. It is, however, in conformity with the principles of equity that a solution to a question so vital to the world economy should be arrived at methodically, and in easy stages with a necessary guarantee, always drawing useful lessons from the omissions and mistakes of the past. If, in the future peace, this point were not to be courageously dealt with, there would remain in the relations between people a deep and far-reaching root blossoming forth into bitter dissensions and burning jealousies, which would lead eventually to new conflicts.

Pius XII, Christmas Broadcast, 1942

1852. The progress and the extent of urgent social reforms depend on the economic possibilities of single nations. It is only through an intelligent and generous sharing of forces between the strong and the weak that it will be possible to effect a universal pacification in suchwise as not to leave behind centers of conflagration and infection from which new disasters may come.

Pius XII, Summi Pontificatus

1429. A disposition, in fact, of the divinely sanctioned natural order divides the human race into social groups, nations or states, which are mutually independent in organization and in the direction of their internal life. But for all that, the human race is bound together by reciprocal ties, moral and juridical, into a great commonwealth directed to the good of all nations and ruled by special laws which protect its unity and promote its prosperity. Now no one can fail to see how the claim to absolute autonomy for the state stands in open opposition to this natural law that is inherent in man — nay, denies it utterly — and, therefore, leaves the stability of international relations at the mercy of the will of rulers, while it destroys the possibility of true union and fruitful collaboration directed to the general good.

Pius XII, Address to Sacred College of Cardinals, June 2, 1945

It is essential that the hate, the diffidence, the stimuli of an extreme nationalism should give way to the growth of wise counsels, to the flowering of peaceful designs, to serenity in the exchange of views, and to mutual brotherly comprehension.

Pius XII, Address to Congress of International Exchange, March 7, 1948

(*Summarized.*) International exchange, instead of fostering economic balance among nations, has often degenerated into political maneuvering and even a source of exploitation. Men are confused as to the remedies. Some favor nineteenth-century internationalism, with others supporting regional trade pacts. Some want the mechanism of free markets to rule, while others demand central direction of all economic life. Christian principles offer four lines of solution.

1. Economic life means social life. To seek the material basis of cultural and spiritual life, there must be an external order and social norms. "An appeal to an automatic and magic law is a mirage, no less vain in the economic order than in any other sphere of human activity."

2. Economic life means social life — the life of human beings. It cannot be conceived without liberty. This will come neither from *laissez faire* nor from submission to mighty organizations. Men should rather demand that their economics be so directed toward social ends that liberty is guaranteed and protected.

3. National economy is itself a natural unity. "Accordingly, international economic relations have a function which, although positive and necessary, is only subsidiary. . . . At this juncture, it would perhaps be

opportune to examine whether or not a regional union of national economies would render possible a more efficacious development of the forces
of production."

4. There must be victory over the principles that egoism and utility
should be the main basis of economic life. Rather there must be solidarity
and co-operation among free and autonomous nations.

Some inconsistent nations demand free trade for their own goods, but
deny it to other peoples. Likewise, certain champions of the rights of
private property "so interpret and use the relationships of private property
that they succeed — even better than their adversaries — in overturning
this very institution, so natural and indispensable to human life, and
especially to the family."

Pius XII, Christmas Message, 1948

The Catholic doctrine on the state and civil society has always been
based on the principle that, in keeping with the will of God, the nations
form together a community with a common aim and common duties.
Even when the proclamation of this principle gave rise to violent reactions,
the Church denied her assent to the erroneous concept of an absolutely
autonomous sovereignty divested of all social obligations.

The Catholic Christian, persuaded that every man is his neighbor and
that every nation is a member, with equal rights, of the family of nations,
co-operates wholeheartedly in those generous efforts whose beginnings
might be meager and which frequently encounter strong opposition and
obstacles, but which aim at saving individual states from the narrowness
of a self-centered mentality.

The function of the state in economic life has been the subject
of frequent allusions throughout the course of this book. From
the beginning of the discussion, man's social nature has been
stressed, with political action noted as one of the major manifestations of social life. The virtues of social and distributive
justice involve the state. Again, the unsound philosophies of
economic life, condemned earlier, showed their major symptoms
in their attitudes toward the state. By contrast, the Catholic ideal
of economic life assigned an important though limited function
to civil authority. Moreover, when the concrete problems of
capital, labor, and property were treated, questions of public

policy and social legislation arose frequently. Accordingly, it is quite appropriate at this point to offer an explicit and orderly treatment of civil power in economic affairs.

Civil Authority. The Church has steadily affirmed the divine origin and the pre-eminent authority, in its sphere, of the civil state. This must seem remarkable to those not familiar with Catholic dogma, since it would appear that throughout history the Church has been more in conflict with various governments than their ally. From the persecutions of early Rome, through the uneasy struggles of the Middle Ages and the sharp conflicts with nascent nationalism at the time of the Protestant Revolt, to the decisive opposition to modern statism, the Church, one, holy, Catholic, and apostolic, has found occasion to fulminate against civil powers. Yet it has stood equally firm against those who would deny or unduly limit the authority of civil rulers. Anarchism and nihilism were rejected by Pius IX in the same Syllabus which condemned communism. The social contract of Rousseau, and the doctrine that the ultimate and only source of civil power is the people, have been rejected with the same firmness as that displayed toward the nazi and communist teaching that the state is absolute in its powers, with the individual merely a creature of the state.

Man is by nature both a social and a political animal. And, since God made human nature, it can be stated that societies deeply rooted in that nature, such as the family and the state, have their origin in God. The concept of society is broader than that of the state. National society includes the organized people of a region, with their government, their families, and their various social groups in diverse spheres of life. In this society, civil government is supreme in its sphere. Its main function is to promote the common good in the material and cultural orders. While it is supreme, it is not to be all-absorbing. It must foster and stimulate lesser social groups, not swallow them up. It may govern and direct their activities in the light of the general welfare, but control should not be usurpation. Its august authority in matters within its competence does not give it the power to invade fields reserved to lesser or equal social groups. There are sacred individual rights which the state must respect. It must be even more reserved in dealing with the family. In purely religious matters, the Church is an independent society not subject to civil control.

Even external religious ceremonies have stressed the sacred character of public power. The ancient kings of Israel were anointed by the high priest, a custom which still prevails with modifications in many Christian states. Our liturgy carries prayers for kings, emperors, and rulers. They are permitted within the sanctuary at solemn services and accorded special honors. Theologians have taught that just laws, enacted for the common good, are binding in conscience. By contrast, the unfortunate casuistry which has grown up in recent years about the *lex poenalis,* a purely penal law obliging not in conscience but only in terms of civil penalty, has extended a valid concept to the point where many lose respect for all law. True, some may understandably find it difficult to discern the aura of sacredness about civil power in a day when political machines choose rulers, where graft and corruption are not uncommon, and where many laws are passed for private advantage rather than the common good and hence may not be just laws. But the Church, in defending civil power, has not thereby sanctioned the personal character of rulers. Moreover, in a democracy there is little excuse for a purely negative attitude toward government. If it is not good, it is within our power and among our duties to make it good. At any rate, the presumption is always in favor of government and law, with the burden of proof on him who decides to disregard authority.

As noted earlier, the doctrine of the divine origin of civil authority does not preclude the democratic selection of rulers. Indeed, the great Christian writers, Aquinas, Suarez, and Bellarmine, have stressed the importance of the consent of the governed in making laws and choosing rulers. The widespread American impression that the Middle Ages were times of autocracy does not allow for the immense power of customary law, based on the will of the people, in that period. If the popes in

the nineteenth century appeared fearful of the democratic trends
of the time, it must be remembered that modern democracy was
too often born amidst blood and rapine. While De Lammenais
had a vision of great reforms ensuing from popular rule, others
were more impressed with the irreligious philosophy of violence
and destruction held by some of the actual promoters of revolt
in nineteenth-century Europe and in the French Revolution. Pope
Leo XIII, whose teaching in *Immortale Dei* and *Libertas Praestantissimum* has been quoted against the Church by many
American Protestants, is the same pope who acted decisively
against antidemocratic Catholic movements in France. The present Holy Father, while holding firmly to the traditional teaching
that the Church is neutral in regard to the form of government,
provided it rules justly, has more than once suggested that, under
modern conditions, a democracy is the best safeguard of individual freedom. Finally, it must be noted that the 1949 revision of
the Baltimore Catechism stresses the duty of citizens to vote and
to see that government is wholesome.

Government in Economic Life. When *Rerum Novarum* was
written, the philosophy of individualism and *laissez faire* was
still strong in the world. It was only natural that in this document the Pope should stress the duty of government to intervene
in the interests of the common good. The Pope insisted upon
the power and obligation of the state to protect poor and defenseless workers. This teaching was reiterated in *Quadragesimo
Anno,* with words of praise for the social legislation enacted in
the intervening years, some of it inspired by Leonine doctrine.
In the meantime, however, the ugly specter of statism had appeared, so that Pope Pius XI considered it opportune to give
more detailed treatment to the economic function of government.
Further clarification in important matters has been added by
the present Holy Father.

The power of the state to intervene in economic life springs
directly from its supreme concern over the common good and
is controlled and regulated by that principle. This authority
might be considered under both negative and positive aspects.

Negatively, the state has the right and duty to intervene when any situation threatens the common good. Among the illustrations given in *Rerum Novarum* are the limitations of the hours of work, protection of working women and children, safeguarding the health of workers when it is threatened by bad working conditions, and the prevention of disorders due to strikes. In *Casti Connubii,* Pope Pius XI mentions problems connected with family life, such as housing, medical care, adequate food, and decent wages. Pope Pius XII, in his 1945 address to Italian workers, gives social insurance as an illustration of proper state action. In all these cases, "the law ought not to undertake more, nor should it go farther, than the remedy of evils or the removal of danger requires" (*R.N.,* No. 53).

The controlling principle is the common good, or the welfare of society as a whole and of its constituent parts as members of the social group. When the rights of any group are threatened or the human dignity of persons violated, the state should intervene. In the light of history, it was only natural that the emphasis should have been on protecting the rights of workers. They were the victims of abuses in the economic society which developed after the industrial revolution. Now that labor has acquired considerable power, however, it in turn may need regulation. The state may be required to protect small or large business. In principle, apart from the wisdom of its provisions or the timeliness of its enactment, the Taft-Hartley Act is as justifiable as the Social Security Act or the Employment Act of 1946.

In acting to prevent abuses the state should follow the principles of subsidiarity and minimum intervention. It is not the function of government to procure all good or prevent all evil, but only to deal with matters affecting the general welfare. Hence, a higher authority should not step in where a lesser group is able and willing to meet the needs of the moment. The federal government should not act where the states are doing an efficient job in handling a given situation. Nor should it impose a pattern upon private activities such as labor-management relations, when collective bargaining or like private arrangements are securing results consonant with the common good. Furthermore, when intervention is necessary, it should be at the minimum level required by conditions. An abuse which could be remedied by public control measures would not justify nationalization of an industry. The misuse of a power would not normally justify its abolition, unless this was the only possible method of preventing serious harm.

Changing conditions naturally affect the scope of state authority. In times of peace and stable prosperity, government would have less occasion to exercise its power than it would in a period of war or a major depression. The concept of reserve and emergency powers, so deeply imbedded in our laws, is basically sound. But government intervention is not a normal or desirable condition. One might go further and assert that many of the negative state functions should be considered in the light of a lesser evil. It would be more desirable that various social groups, under the supreme co-ordinating power of the state, would themselves establish conditions which make remedial legislation unnecessary. This is the positive function of public authority.

As noted in Chapter VII, the primary and positive duty of government is to promote an organic social order which by its nature tends to procure the public economic good. The modern state is the victim of centuries of individualism. Society has been atomized into millions of conflicting groups, each seeking its own interest, with few concerned with the general welfare. As a result, the state has been forced to step into countless situations and remedy conditions which were hurting society. This burdening of modern government has injured the state itself, through loading it down with innumerable tasks, and has hindered it from exercising its primary mission of aiding lesser groups to govern themselves. Furthermore, it has contributed to the giantism of modern life, which is endangering the freedom of individuals. The fact that such actions have been necessary in the circumstances does not make them more desirable in the light of Christian ideals. Until organic reform is achieved, we may legitimately continue to promote suitable social legislation, but our first emphasis should be upon a fundamental change in our social structure in favor of smaller, self-governing societies.

The direction taken by many modern governments, particularly the Socialist regimes in Europe, should be reversed. Instead of taking powers from lesser groups, they should be seeking to restore, as prudence dictates, authority previously assumed. "Thereby the state will more freely, powerfully, and effectively do those things that belong to it alone because it alone can do them: directing, watching, urging, restraining, as occasion requires and necessity demands" (*Q.A.,* No. 80). Society should be organic, based on interrelationship of subordinate and co-ordinate groups working for the common good, and not mechanical, based on power forcing together scattered and hostile groups. This is why Pope Pius XII, in his letter to the *Semaines Sociales* of 1946, warned against the trend toward nationalization, which was making society more rather than less mechanical.

Facing the situation in the United States, we find two rough trends, neither of which is completely satisfactory in the light of Christian principles. The liberals and reformers are so obsessed by the negative function of the state, the power to remedy abuses, that they are calling for more and more laws and increasing use by the federal government of its reserve authority. Conservatives see the evil in this trend and decry it, but their approach is likewise negative. They would return to a condition of *laissez faire* without taking positive action to remedy abuses which occasion state intervention. We need badly a middle-of-the-road position which will frankly recognize social problems and work out methods for their removal by means of self-governing economic groups. And not the least of these social problems is the very absence of such groups working together organically for the common good.

In this light, the primary duty of our federal government, in the years to come, is to promote co-operation in economic life and to decentralize powers to such collaborative groups. Such a statement should not prejudice us against needed social reforms which call for legislation in the interval. But the main emphasis should be upon such ideals as fostering labor-management co-operation; establishing a consultative council, representing all economic groups, to deal with depressions and full employment; the increase of consultation and self-regulation in administering existing laws; and the gradual promotion of self-regulation, un-der federal direction for the common good, by organized groups of labor, business, industry, finance, farmers, and the professions. Thus, the state would be restored to its true and rightful posi-tion as the supreme guardian of the common good, aiding and stimulating lesser groups in this direction, fostering their growth rather than absorbing them, and contributing to a maximum of individual freedom and national well-being.

Nationalization. The problem of nationalization is currently of considerable importance in working out a theory of state in-tervention in economic life. Since World War II ended in Europe, there has been a wave of socialization in many countries. This was justified by the emergency conditions, by special problems (such as the ownership of certain large industries by collaborators with the enemy and the subsequent seizure of such property), by the alleged bankruptcy of capitalism, or, finally, by doctrinaire reasons connected with theoretical socialism. The result has been nationalization of many industries in England, France, and Italy. The trend in England is especially interesting, since common ties of language and customs make its problems nearer to us. More-over, England is going further in the way of doctrinaire socialism (nationalization for the sake of public ownership, even when an industry is functioning well in private hands) than other Euro-pean nations in the noncommunist sphere. Such movements natu-rally raise moral questions, both as to the licitness of the trend and its prudence.

At this writing, the Catholic stand on nationalization is so clear as to leave little room for discussion. The broadest principles on this question were laid down in *Rerum Novarum*, in which socialism (total nationalization) was condemned. The issue was further refined in *Quadragesimo Anno*, which held that certain forms of property might be reserved to the state. These would be cases where private control would involve such a concentration of economic power that the general welfare would be imperiled (*Q.A.,* No. 114). Here, however, a certain element of prudential judgment is required, if this principle is to be applied correctly. Clearly, nationalization as such is allowable in certain instances. The problem is to decide whether the general welfare is endangered by a given situation where private ownership involved excessive concentration of economic power. In postwar Europe, many Catholics applied this principle too freely, taking it in isolation from other parts of the Church's social teaching. They neglected particularly the principle of subsidiarity and the stress on diffusion rather than concentration (either in private or state hands) of productive property. Hence Pope Pius XII was impelled on numerous occasions to warn against excessive zeal for nationalization. His teaching on the subject was elaborated in masterful fashion by the Australian bishops. In the light of these developments, there should be little uncertainty as to the Church's position on the matter.

In the first place, it is clear that nationalization, with fitting compensation to the owners, is not in itself unlawful. It is a permissible exercise of the sovereign power of the state to protect the common welfare. Such a device may be considered when a private group has such economic power as to be a virtual superstate. A good example would be the central banking system of a nation in its function of controlling the general supply of money (not the piecemeal lending by individual banks). Since broad monetary controls virtually direct the entire economic course of a nation, such power is too great to be left in private hands.

Our Constitution left to the federal government the right to coin and print money. But, in the meantime, the modern banking system acquired an even greater power to issue money, namely, the all-important form of money known as bank credit. Bank deposits, subject to check, are the really basic form of money today and such deposits can be created by the lending activities of banks.[1] Hence, it would be essential that such sovereign power be returned to state control. This was done in the United States when the Federal Reserve System was created and particularly when our banking laws were strengthened in 1933 and 1935. Thus, a government authority, the Board of Governors of the Federal Reserve System, determines broad policies in the field of bank credit. This has been done here without interfering with private ownership of individual banks and private initiative in making loans. Likewise, the government of the United States has reserved to itself supreme authority in the field of atomic energy, rightly concluding that such a decisive industry should not be left in private hands exclusively. Here, however, military and national security considerations were more important than the economic.

The fact that nationalization or government ownership is at times legitimate does not justify its adoption as a broad policy. It must be justified in each individual case and not sought for its own sake. Nationalization is clearly wrong when it is adopted as a step toward progressive socialization of the economy. This is merely socialism by degrees. It is likewise wrong when it is the result of a doctrinaire policy of seeking public ownership of major industries, regardless of their social efficiency. Thus, England may well have been justified in nationalizing its coal mines on the grounds that their misuse in private hands had been hurting the public interest. But the proposed seizure of the iron and steel industry would be highly questionable, since this industry is both efficient and hardly capable of exercising economic domination under a Labor government. In fact, we in the United States would not go so far as the Australian bishops in their listing of industries subject to direct public control (No. 77 in their statement), although our broad economic controls do affect these industries.

Thirdly, when a problem arises where nationalization is con-

---

[1] For technical details, see J. F. Cronin, *Economic Analysis and Problems*, Chap. 18, and the references given there.

sidered, every effort should be made to find less drastic measures for meeting the situation. Thus, various forms of public control, leaving ownership and most operating policies in private hands, would in most instances be preferable. Regulatory law would be preferable to government ownership, if the former has any chance of succeeding. Limited ownership through the use of yardstick plants (such as the Tennessee Valley Authority in the electric industry) would be preferable to total ownership. In the rare cases where public ownership might be justified, there might be private operation (as with the atomic-energy plants). Finally, if the industry is to be publicly owned and operated, it is normally preferable that government corporations, separate from the political machinery of the state, carry out such operations.

Fourthly, even where nationalization might be indicated by the conditions of a particular industry, the final judgment must be made in the light of the total public good. It must be remembered that nationalization does not attack one of the cardinal evils of the modern day, namely, the centralization of economic power in the hands of a few. On the contrary, it increases this evil, since it gives to the state power which might have been scattered in a hundred private corporations. Nor is the fact that the workers, as citizens, are owners of nationalized industry in any way decisive. Ownership so thinly diffused allows of little possibility of effective control. It is more likely that political authorities, with absolute economic power in their hands, will control the citizen. The whole trend of nationalization is pointing in the wrong direction. Social policy should seek to extend rather than restrict effective ownership of productive wealth.

In view of these arguments, it should be clear that the Church is not happy over the trend toward nationalization. Such facile solutions postpone even further the establishing of a truly organic society, in which private groups co-operate for the public good. The present Holy Father, in his address to Catholic employers, speaks almost despairingly of a "ripe opportunity being missed, because it was not grasped at the right time." He is referring to the section of *Quadragesimo Anno,* treated in Chapter VII, as the right mean between the extremes of statism and individualism. We in the United States are more fortunate, in that the opportunity still remains here. But the result will not come automatically. To quote further from the same address:

> Undoubtedly, the putting into practice of this doctrine cannot be done in a day. Its realization requires of all wisdom, perspicacity, and foresight, together with a large amount of common sense and good will. It requires of them, above all, a deep-rooted resistance to the temptation of each working for his own advantage at the expense of others . . . or at the expense of the common good. It requires that altruism which only true Christian virtue, strengthened by the help and grace of God, can inspire.[2]

This is a challenge which our generation must meet, if it is to restore economic life to its true place in the divine plan of the universe.

Social Legislation. The main principles dealing with social legislation have already been considered. They were grouped under two headings: the negative, or state intervention where the common good is threatened; and the positive, in which the state endeavors to promote conditions which lead to maximum prosperity, through organic collaboration of various groups to secure the general welfare. In this sphere, comments by Church authorities are much more favorable than is the case with nationalization. Both *Rerum Novarum* and *Quadragesimo Anno* advocated social legislation, with the latter document praising developments occurring in the forty-year interval. But even here, some caution is necessary. It is to be hoped that future trends will emphasize the positive more than the negative aspects of state intervention, so that the institutions of society will by their own nature, rather than through public control, tend toward the common good.

Social legislation in the United States has, on the whole, been more in the direction of controlling abuses than of promoting an organic society. Moreover, if a generalization may be hazarded,

---

[2] Pope Pius XII, Address to the International Union of Catholic Employers Associations, May 7, 1949.

it has normally been within the bounds of sound social principles. Usually the government has intervened only when the public interest had been threatened and lesser means were either unsatisfactory or unlikely to be tried. As a general rule, the federal government has not stepped in where the state governments were able and willing to meet the need. The exercise of power has in most instances met the test of minimum intervention, not exceeding the needs of the situation. There has been some failure in the matter of decentralizing controls and attempting to foster self-regulation rather than federal control. But the value of our social legislation is evident from a cursory examination of the main types of control.

An important phase of American social legislation has been in the realm of finance. Thus, the Federal Reserve Act established the foundations of a central banking system, while the Banking Acts of 1933 and 1935 perfected the framework of the structure. There is still more to be done before the task is completed. Many state banks remain outside the federal system, thereby impeding the task of over-all credit control. Then, the division of powers between the Federal Reserve and the Treasury weakens the power of the central bank. Since a sound and effective credit policy is essential for sustained national prosperity, both these defects should be remedied. It might be politically difficult to force state-chartered banks into the federal group, but this is surely a case where the public economic good should prevail.

Likewise in the sphere of finance, we have had fairly extensive control over all phases of security issuance and trading, as well as speculation in commodities. The Securities Act and the Securities Exchange Act have both protected the public against the abuses so rampant before 1930. Other laws regulate over-the-counter trading and investment trusts. Thus, our financial system is probably in the best condition in the nation's history. The main problem today is the lack of adequate equity capital for business, particularly small business. But this results from our tax laws and other conditions, rather than any obstacles raised by security regulation.

The main laws for controlling business are the antitrust laws, notably the Sherman Act, the Clayton Act, and the Federal Trade Commission Act. These laws have not been so effective as was originally hoped, partly because of loopholes in the laws themselves and partly because of Supreme Court decisions. The laws do not contain the explicit power to prevent mergers through purchase of corporate assets, even though such mergers may tend to restrain free trade. Moreover, the Supreme Court has, until recently, construed the laws so narrowly as to limit their effectiveness. Administrative enforcement has not always been good. Again, price-fixing has been legalized under certain conditions. Finally, there has not been sufficient effective action to stimulate the growth of small business as competitors to corporate giants. The time is ripe for a thorough reconsideration of our legislative hodgepodge in this field and the adoption of a uniform and consistent national policy which will aid small business and prevent monopoly.

We have not relied merely on fair competition to safeguard the rights of consumers. The Food, Drug, and Cosmetic Act gives a considerable measure of protection to the consumer in regard to spoiled, adulterated, and misrepresented products. There is also some control over unfair advertising. On the negative side, the price-fixing laws noted earlier tend to lead to higher prices than would otherwise be the case. Likewise, it is not clear that our farm policies are entirely fair to the consumer. The ideal of reasonable income to the farmer is sound, but it should not be based on prices rigidly and arbitrarily supported on the basis of past conditions which may not be entirely relevant today. Again, our tariff policies have often been based on an excessive desire for protection, stifling international trade and competition beneficial to consumers. This has been remedied somewhat since the Reciprocal Trade Acts were passed.

Natural monopolies have been regulated by both the federal and the state governments. The federal government controls railroad rates through the Interstate Commerce Act. It likewise regulates the airlines, the waterways, and interstate trucking and bus transportation. State and local governments normally regulate electric-power rates and those for gas, local buses and street railways, and telephones. Past abuses in these fields have largely been remedied.

While many of the laws affecting business were in response to misuse of power, those affecting the farmer have been efforts to meet his distressed condition. The farmer has been aided in securing both short-term and long-term credit, in the orderly marketing of his product, in the development of co-operatives, in securing more production and preventing soil erosion, and in obtaining better prices for his products. Farm prices have generally been supported by efforts to plan production in line with probable demand, by devices to store surpluses, and by direct federal price supports. Price supports usually mean federal purchasing of crops when prices drop below a predetermined parity level, which is calculated to give a right balance between farm and industrial prices. It was recently proposed to guarantee farm income instead of prices, letting the price fall in a free market (thereby benefiting consumers) but supplementing the income of farmers when those lower prices did not bring in an adequate return. This proposal has occasioned much controversy in the United States. Yet, in principle, it is sounder than present legislation. Under present laws the consumer pays twice for farm stability, first in the form of higher prices and then for government purchases of surpluses which would threaten the price structure. The subsidy proposal would actually lessen the cost to the consumer, if it were accompanied by suitable measures to limit crop production to the expected market at reasonable prices. Apart from the controversial price-support measures, American farm policy has generally been socially constructive. Moreover, its administration has been more decentralized than has been customary in Washington.

Recent laws affecting labor have been on the whole favorable to the needs of the workers. The four central laws have been the National Labor Relations Act, the Fair Labor Standards Act, the Social Security Act, and the Employment Act of 1946. The first-named gave federal support to labor's right to organize. This fostering of labor unions could be a basis for a better organized society. The second law dealt largely with minimum wages, although it also controlled some abuses in the child-labor field. The protection afforded by a 75 cent minimum wage level, while not generous, does represent an improvement. This same condition obtains for the old-age benefits and unemployment-insurance benefits set up in the Social Security Act, although benefits have not yet been adjusted, at the present writing, to meet the higher postwar price levels. Finally, the Employment Act accepted the principle of federal concern over the problem of full employment and the business cycle. One great weakness in this act is the fact that the Council of Economic Advisers to the President is a purely governmental agency. It would be strengthened if all economic groups could be united in a permanent advisory council which would face these critical problems.

By contrast to the legislation just noted, the Labor Management Relations Act, 1947, was an extreme measure regulating abuses in the labor movement. It amended the National Labor Relations Act so as to establish strong controls over organized labor. Federal intervention in this case was probably justified, particularly in regard to national emergency strikes and jurisdictional strikes. However, many writers have questioned the wisdom of the law as enacted. The main complaints are that it tended to substitute government control for collective bargaining between the parties, that it weakened the internal discipline of unions in the effort to prevent abuses, and that its detailed approach was legalistic in a field where psychology and human relations were paramount. As stated earlier, labor-relations law, where necessary, should be written by industrial-relations experts, with lawyers in a decidedly secondary place.

Many of the social problems of labor have been met by legislation on the level of the state governments. Unemployment insurance is currently administered by the states. Many of them have laws dealing with labor relations. They usually handle problems connected with health and hygiene in factories and also workmen's compensation for accidents and industrial disease. Many states also have laws regulating working conditions where women are employed and determining the type of work suitable for children eligible to work. The only generalization feasible for such diverse laws is that this is a field suitable for social legislation.

There have been several attempts by the federal government and some state governments to meet the problem of housing. The national authorities have given loans to individuals and groups for the purpose of building approved types of dwellings. In addition, there have been direct programs of slum clearance and low-cost public housing. Measures of this nature have not yet been adequate to meet the need. Nor has anything substantial been done to remedy the essentially disorganized state of the construction industry, with its high-cost, inefficient approach to this vital problem.

Finally, national measures in the field of health are still limited. Two major problems exist in this sphere: a shortage of medical facilities and personnel, particularly in small towns and rural areas; and the high cost of hospitalization, operations, and chronic illness. Most experts agree that government aid on all levels will be required to meet the shortage problem. But there is serious disagreement as to meeting the costs of medical care. Ordinary medical costs are within the province of most persons. But hospitalization, operations, and chronic illnesses are unpredictable and uneven in their impact. Only an insurance principle can readily meet such needs. Present private insurance (prepayment) plans cover a considerable portion of the population in regard to hospital expenses. But only a few are currently insured in regard to surgeons' fees, complex diagnostic expenses, and doctors' bills for chronic illness. If private initiative fails to meet this need, this is unquestionably an appropriate field for social legislation. If American health insurance, whether private or governmental, were limited to unpredictable and uneven costs, leaving aside routine medical practice, most of the objections currently leveled by the medical fraternity would not apply.

We might then conclude that the general pattern of social legislation in the United States has been soundly conceived. It has been largely negative, in that it sought to remedy abuses. Probably there has been a tendency toward overcentralization in its administration, a particularly irritating fault in a land as large and as diverse as ours. But there remains before us a new and mainly unexplored field of positive social legislation, which would aim at promoting labor-management co-operation, reasonable self-government in industry and the professions to avoid unfair and destructive competition, and national co-operation to meet the problems of full employment and periodic depressions.

The Welfare State. There has been much controversy in postwar years about the welfare state. It has even become a political issue in the United States. Because of these discussions, some explicit mention should be given to the problem, even though the principles offered in this chapter implicity deal with it.

Since the phrase "welfare state" has been a slogan rather than a precise classification, it is impossible to pass judgment upon it without first offering a definition. Those who condemn the welfare state consider it as a government which places security above individual initiative, gradually absorbing to the state the function of being the primary, if not the exclusive, source of individual welfare. Thus, defined, the welfare state might be considered as the first step toward socialism. A classic example would be postwar England, where the objective is mass welfare and the means selected includes equalization of incomes and socialization of business.

The distinction between objective and means permits us to pass judgment upon the welfare state. The objective, as such and properly understood, is not unlawful. On the contrary, it is the duty of government to seek the common welfare. But it does this by supplementing and aiding private initiative, not by replacing it. As noted earlier, this involves both negative and positive aspects. Negatively, the government should intervene when social conditions threaten serious harm to the welfare of its citizens or any substantial group within the community. Positively, it is preferable that public social policy foster conditions which, through private initiative properly co-ordinated, will bring about maximum well-being for the public.

Hence the controversy really should be a discussion of means rather than ends. Is public policy supplementing private ownership and individual initiative or is it rather tending to supplant them? Is the government arrogating to itself powers which could readily be performed by private groups? Are we using socialist techniques in preference to those discussed in Chapter VII? Are the principles of subsidiarity and minimum intervention observed? When these questions are answered, we can rightly pass judgment upon the welfare state. Clearly government should not take over functions which are being performed satisfactorily by private groups. Even where private initiative has failed to produce suitable results, the first efforts by government should be positive rather than negative. It should attempt to stimulate private activity, not to absorb it. Only when these measures fail would the state be justified in adopting direct welfare measures.

Applying these principles to the American scene in early 1950 is not easy. Trends are confused and conflicting rather than clear cut. Different schools of thought and various philosophies prevail at different times and in different fields. Because of this diversity and uncertainty, it is clear that federal welfare policies are by no means uniformly inspired by a socialist or statist philosophy. It may be argued that certain policies and certain objectives of pressure groups may logically lead in the direction of socialism. But the total picture is one of confusion and uncertainty, rather than doctrinaire tendencies in any direction. No consistent policy can readily be discerned. Rather there is improvisation for particular needs. It may be argued that the balance of programs involves unnecessary federal intervention and hence leads toward socialism. This point is debatable and much too complex to be discussed here.

What is clear, however, is the point noted earlier that we tend to discuss the problem in terms of extremes. The debate centers about the right of government to intervene in economic life. But this right should not be questioned. The real issue involves the proper method of intervention, a problem discussed in detail in Chapter VII. Where government finds it necessary to take action in the interests of the general welfare, this should normally be in terms of stimulating and fostering private initiative rather than replacing it. Unfortunately this vital point is often obscured in the heat of political controversy. One side tends toward a *laissez-faire* philosophy. Its opponents correctly defend the right of the state to seek the general welfare. In the confusion the real issue is too often forgotten, namely, the question of a proper and positive philosophy in government action upon economic matters. Only in the light of the genuine middle-of-the-road policy advocated in the papal encyclicals can we work out a sound attitude toward the welfare state.

International Economic Life. A difficult, yet important, problem facing the state in relation to economic action is its international policy. Trade between nations is normal. Varieties of climate, resources, aptitudes, and skills make some exchange among different peoples essential. Even great and richly endowed nations and empires have not achieved economic self-sufficiency. From the broader viewpoint of the common good of peoples, there is a still stronger case for reasonable freedom of trade relations. Some nations lack resources, so that their only hope for a decent standard of living is the exchange of products made with their labor for the goods of more fortunate peoples. Richer nations have an obligation in charity and social justice to consider the needs of poorer countries. Not only should there be adequate trade, but barriers to immigration and emigration should not be insuperable. In this way, the great riches of the world will accrue fairly to all.

From an ethical viewpoint, it is necessary to adopt a middle ground between extreme nationalism and excessive internationalism. The love of one's country is normal and laudable. But this should not be carried to the point where it becomes a worship of the nation, to the derogation of the rights and claims of other sovereign peoples. At the other extreme, those who deride national independence as outmoded are unrealistic. Culture, tradition, race, customs, and language often form a strong bond uniting people into a single nation. It would be expecting the unusual from human nature to think that these bonds can be ignored. Nor is complete internationalism likely to be feasible from an administrative standpoint. Many large nations find it difficult to handle fairly all their internal problems. Regional differences and special needs bring serious difficulties. These would be multiplied many times over if one were to seek a world government which would replace national sovereignty. The problems experienced by the United Nations today spring from real conflicts of interest. They would not be resolved merely by declaring world citizenship. It seems more feasible to seek a limited transfer of sovereignty and the gradual building up of the ideal of an international common good, to which all should and would contribute.

A similar approach to the economic aspect of international life is needed. Here the extremes are complete free trade and autarky. As noted in the address of Pope Pius XII, the nineteenth-century ideal was absolute freedom of trade. This followed from the philosophy of individualism and the teachings of the classical school of economics. The mechanism for such trade was the international gold standard, which was used to settle balances not covered by equal exchange of goods. If a nation were buying more than it sold, it would lose gold. This would cause internal credit contraction, unemployment, and lower prices. At the lower prices, its goods would be more attractive and balance would be achieved. Conversely, the nation selling more than it bought would receive gold. This would cause credit expansion, higher prices, and thus make its goods less attractive in comparison with other countries. Balance again would be had. Such was the simple, automatic mechanism of international trade. But, in practice, this device had serious drawbacks. It left the internal economy of a nation subject to influences not under the control of a people. Any international crisis or upset in foreign exchange markets would mean domestic depression or inflation. Thus, the already difficult problem of achieving economic security and full employment was further intensified. It was only natural, as a result, that nations tended more in the direction of nationalism.

The move toward nationalism often degenerated into a race for autarky or a selfish and excessive policy of protectionism. Before World War II, international trade was often bogged down in a welter of quotas, blocked currency, bilateral negotiations, barter agreements, and similar efforts to build one nation's economy at the expense of others. Germany was the great offender in the race for autarky. The United States was notorious for unreasonable tariff barriers. Undoubtedly the economic tension generated in this struggle contributed to international unrest and was a factor in developing warlike attitudes.

Sound international economic relations must respect two major principles: first, it must be acknowledged that each nation has a right to internal security and stability; and, secondly, each nation must be ready to co-operate with others for the common good of all. The first principle rejects nineteenth-century automatism, while the second is contrary to twentieth-century autarky. If these principles are applied to economic life, a sound program can be developed.

National security demands that international trade, although necessary, should take a subsidiary position. Insofar as this is possible, the internal economy of a nation should not be subject to the vagaries of world trade. Certainly, the domestic monetary and price systems should be immunized from serious shocks resulting from short-range and random fluctuations in foreign exchange or trade. In principle, the present arrangements under the International Monetary Fund are sound. They provide for reasonable controls over currency fluctuations, instead of a purely automatic system. A further degree of immunity obtains in the United States, where we have a managed currency, quite independent of gold. An additional factor in giving us stability is the relatively small proportion of our trade consisting in imports and exports. Other nations, more dependent on foreign trade, must calculate more carefully the relative value of their currencies in comparison with those of customers, suppliers, or competitors. But, at least, we have a mechanism today for careful consultation on foreign exchange matters instead of either automatism or irresponsible nationalism.

It is also legitimate to seek some measure of protection for domestic industries through tariffs and quotas. But these must not be abused to the extent of stifling all trade. If nations wish to sell abroad, they must also buy. It is economic folly to be pushing sales in other nations and yet erecting barriers so that they will be unable to sell to us so as to pay for what they bought. Protection of domestic industry should be reasonable. It should conserve heavy capital investment and safeguard against unfair foreign competition. But it should not foster domestic monopoly or penalize the consumers of a nation in the interests of a favored few producers.

As a general rule, when a domestic industry is efficient and capable of meeting most national needs, it should receive protection. When it is small and inefficient, it is unwise to try to remove competition and thus subsidize high-cost production. Should this latter course be necessary for military reasons, in the light of national security, it is better to subsidize the domestic industry directly instead of making all consumers pay more because of tariffs. This is simple arithmetic. If we can produce 130,000 long tons of manganese ore at a cost of forty dollars a ton and can import a million tons at thirty dollars a ton, it would be cheaper to pay a ten-dollar subsidy on the smaller amount than to make the steel industry pay forty dollars for the entire amount. Of course, subsidies raise taxes, whereas tariffs bring income. But it is better to have lower prices, with slightly higher taxes, than higher prices brought on by tariffs.

In working out measures to increase freedom of trade, it is often better to start with regional pacts than to attempt to remove all barriers throughout the world. The less ambitious program is more likely to succeed. It is more easily modified and adapted in the light of experience. As an illustration, Europe would undoubtedly be more prosperous if it could experiment with a customs union. If a united free Europe found itself deficient in food and raw materials, and unable to penetrate the Iron Curtain with reasonable trade agreements, it might well turn to India, parts of Africa and South America, and similar regions for a more balanced trade. It could export machinery and finished goods, receiving food and raw materials. The United States, with its resources so seriously depleted by the recent war, might in turn foster trade and its own internal security by more extensive foreign purchases of iron ore, lead, copper, oil, and like basic materials. Thus, its domestic resources would be conserved against the threat of Soviet expansion or even war. By such regional controls and measures, a certain balance could be restored, with greater freedom of trade than has existed since the 1920's.

An ambitious proposal to normalize international trade is the projected International Trade Organization, sponsored by the United Nations and submitted to the member nations in 1948. The I.T.O. would have five main objectives: (1) maintaining full employment and economic growth within each member nation; (2) encouraging economic development and reconstruction throughout the world; (3) modification of trade barriers and commercial restrictions; (4) prevention of restrictive business practices; and (5) the control of intergovernment commodity agreements through mutual understandings, consultation, and co-operation. These principles can all be accepted as sound and in harmony with the ideals of international common good. Such an organization, together with the International Monetary Fund and the International Bank for Reconstruction and Development, would promote the welfare of peoples and lay an economic foundation for world peace.[3]

---

[3] An excellent study of these proposals is found in the pamphlet by Sister Thomasine, O.P., "The International Trade Organization" (Washington: Catholic Association for International Peace, 1948). See also Clair Wilcox, *A Charter for World Trade* (New York: Macmillan, 1949). For the economics of international trade, see the brief treatment and references in J. F. Cronin, *Economic Analysis and Problems*, Chap. 13. A superior ethical treatment is found in J. Messner, *Social Ethics*, Sections 191–201. See also *A Code of International Ethics* (Oxford: Catholic Social Guild, 1940) for the views of Catholic scholars throughout the world.

CONCLUSION

The modern state is overwhelmed by a multiplicity of burdens and duties. We have moved from the extreme of *laissez-faire* to a situation which is uncomfortably close to statism. Paradoxically, this move has been made in the interests of the common good. The many evils consequent upon social disorganization have forced upon government the task of bringing justice and security to many oppressed by the existing social order. The real reform of the state can only be subsequent to other reforms called for in the preceding chapters. Wider diffusion of ownership, labor-management co-operation, and the establishment of common-interest organizations would of themselves relieve government of many powers and responsibilities currently assumed. Such is the great problem of our age. To it we must bring the rich resources inherent in the teachings of the Church. We must face courageously and intelligently the basic spiritual evils of the day and seek through the Church remedies appropriate for our generation.

READINGS*

J. Messner, *Social Ethics*, pp. 140–212, 373–669, 674–678, 922–927, 951–980 (see especially pp. 196–200, 207–212, 573–579, 593–601, 922–927).

E. Cahill, *The Framework of a Christian State*, Chap. 23.

C. Bruehl, *The Pope's Plan for Social Reconstruction*, Chap. 8.

H. R. Rommen, *The State in Catholic Thought*.

J. Messner, *Social Ethics*, Book III.

J. A. Ryan and F. L. Boland, *Catholic Principles of Politics*.

G. Clune, *Christian Social Reorganization*, Chap. 12.

G. Gonella, *A World to Reconstruct*.

---

* For further readings, consult Lists Nos. 1, 4, 5, 6, 7, and 12 in the Appendix.

Chapter XIV. THE CHURCH AND SOCIAL REFORM

❧

SPIRITUAL NATURE OF MODERN CRISIS

Leo XIII, *Graves de Communi*

10. For it is the opinion of some, which is caught up by the masses, that the social question, as they call it, is merely economic. The precise opposite is the truth. It is first of all moral and religious, and for that reason its solution is to be expected mainly from the moral law and the pronouncements of religion.

Leo XIII, *Sapientiae Christianae*

2. When Christian faith and life fail, the solid foundation of human society must fail together with them. Force only is then left for the maintenance of public peace and order. But force without the aid of religion is weak; and, being apt to beget a slavish submission rather than obedience, it bears with it the seeds of great disturbance.

Leo XIII, *Rerum Novarum*

40. Finally, the Church does not consider it enough to point out the way of finding the cure, but she administers the remedy herself. For she occupies herself fully in training and forming men according to discipline and doctrine; and through the agency of bishops and clergy, she causes the health-giving streams of this doctrine to be diffused as widely as possible. Furthermore, she strives to enter into men's minds and to bend their wills so that they may suffer themselves to be ruled and governed by the discipline of the divine precepts. And in this field, which is of first and greatest importance because in it the whole substance and matter of benefits consists, the Church indeed has a power that is especially unique. For the instruments which she uses to move souls were given her for this very purpose by Jesus Christ, and they have an efficacy implanted in them by God. Such instruments alone can properly penetrate the inner recesses of the heart and lead man to obedience to duty, to govern the activities of his

self-seeking mind, to love God and his neighbors with a special and sovereign love, and to overcome courageously all things that impede the path of virtue.

42. For when Christian morals are completely observed, they yield of themselves a certain measure of prosperity to material existence, because they win the favor of God, the source and fountain of all goods; because they restrain the twin plagues of life — excessive desire for wealth and thirst for pleasure — which too often make man wretched amidst the very abundance of riches; and because finally, Christian morals make men content with a moderate livelihood and make them supplement income by thrift, removing them far from the vices which swallow up both modest sums and huge fortunes, and dissipate splendid inheritances.

Pius XI, Mens Nostra

23. Now, even as temporal goods and the various advantages flowing from them, together with a certain measure of wealth, have, in this age of ours, been extended somewhat more freely to workmen and others hiring out their labor, thereby raising them to a happier condition of life, we may regard as a bounty of the provident and merciful God that the treasure of the Spiritual Exercises also has been scattered abroad among the common mass of the faithful thus serving as a counterpoise to hold men back, lest borne down by the weight of fleeting things and immersed in pleasures and delights of life, they fall into the tenets and morals of materialism. For this reason We cordially commend the works for the Exercises, which have sprung up already in certain regions, and the exceedingly fruitful and opportune "Retreats for Workmen," together with the associated sodalities of perseverance; all of which, Venerable Brethren, We commend to your care and solicitude.

Pius XI, Quadragesimo Anno

98. The first and most necessary remedy is a reform of morals.

127. Yet, if we look into the matter more carefully and more thoroughly, we shall clearly perceive that, preceding this ardently desired social restoration, there must be a renewal of the Christian spirit, from which so many immersed in economic life have, far and wide, unhappily fallen away, lest all our efforts be wasted and our house be built not on a rock but on shifting sand.

129. "Wherefore," to use the words of Our Predecessor, "if human society is to be healed, only a return to Christian life and institutions will heal it." For this alone can provide effective remedy for that excessive care

for passing things that is the origin of all vices; and this alone can draw away men's eyes, fascinated by and wholly fixed on the changing things of the world, and raise them toward Heaven. Who would deny that human society is in most urgent need of this cure now?

131. For what will it profit men to become expert in more wisely using their wealth, even to gaining the whole world, if thereby they suffer the loss of their souls? What will it profit to teach them sound principles of economic life if in unbridled and sordid greed they let themselves be swept away by their passion for property, so that "hearing the commandments of the Lord they do all things contrary"?

132. The root and font of this defection in economic and social life from the Christian law, and of the consequent apostasy of great numbers of workers from the Catholic faith, are the disordered passions of the soul, the sad result of original sin which has so destroyed the wonderful harmony of man's faculties that, easily led astray by his evil desires, he is strongly incited to prefer the passing goods of this world to the lasting goods of Heaven. Hence arises that unquenchable thirst for riches and temporal goods, which has at all times impelled men to break God's laws and trample upon the right of their neighbors, but which, on account of the present system of economic life, is laying far more numerous snares for human frailty. Since the instability of economic life, and especially of its structure, exacts of those engaged in it most intense and unceasing effort, some have become so hardened to the stings of conscience as to hold that they are allowed, in any manner whatsoever, to increase their profits and use means, fair or foul, to protect their hard-won wealth against sudden changes of fortune. The easy gains that a market unrestricted by any law opens to everybody attracts large numbers to buying and selling goods, and they, their one aim being to make quick profits with the least expenditure of work, raise or lower prices by their uncontrolled business dealings so rapidly according to their own caprice and greed that they nullify the wisest forecasts of producers.

136. No genuine cure can be furnished for this lamentable ruin of souls, which, so long as it continues, will frustrate all efforts to regenerate society, unless men return openly and sincerely to the teaching of the Gospel, to the precepts of Him who alone has the words of everlasting life, words which will never pass away, even if Heaven and earth will pass away. All experts in social problems are seeking eagerly a structure so fashioned in accordance with the norms of reason that it can lead economic life back to sound and right order. But this order, which We Ourselves ardently long for and with all Our efforts promote, will be wholly defective and incomplete unless all the activities of men harmoniously unite to imi-

tate and attain, insofar as it lies within human strength, the marvelous unity of the divine plan. We mean that perfect order which the Church with great force and power preaches and which right human reason itself demands, that all things be directed to God as the first and supreme end of all created activity, and that all created goods under God be considered as mere instruments to be used only insofar as they conduce to the attainment of the supreme end. Nor is it to be thought that gainful occupations are thereby belittled or judged less consonant with human dignity; on the contrary, we are taught to recognize in them with reverence the manifest will of the divine Creator who placed man upon the earth to work it and use it in a multitude of ways for his needs. If these principles are observed by everyone, everywhere, and always, not only the production and acquisition of goods but also the use of wealth, which now is seen to be so often contrary to right order, will be brought back soon within the bounds of equity and just distribution. The sordid love of wealth, which is the shame and great sin of our age, will be opposed in actual fact by the gentle yet effective law of Christian moderation which commands man to seek first the Kingdom of God and His Justice, with the assurance that by virtue of God's kindness and unfailing promise, temporal goods also, insofar as he has need of them, shall be given him besides.

143. But above all, let them hold in high esteem and assiduously employ for the good of their disciples that most valuable means of both personal and social restoration which, as We taught in Our Encyclical, *Mens Nostra,* is to be found in the Spiritual Exercises for all the laity, but also the highly beneficial Workers' Retreats. For in that school of the spirit, not only are the best of Christians developed, but true apostles also are trained for every condition of life and are enkindled with the fire of the heart of Christ. From this school they will go forth as did the Apostles from the Upper Room of Jerusalem, strong in faith, endowed with an invincible steadfastness in persecution, burning with zeal, interested solely in spreading everywhere the Kingdom of Christ.

Pius XI, On Atheistic Communism

41. As in all the stormy periods of the history of the Church, the fundamental remedy today lies in a sincere renewal of private and public life according to the principles of the Gospel by all those who belong to the Fold of Christ, that they may be in truth the salt of the earth to preserve human society from total corruption.

44. And here We wish, Venerable Brethren, to insist more particularly on two teachings of our Lord which have special bearing on the present

condition of the human race: detachment from earthly goods and the precept of charity. "Blessed are the poor in spirit" were the first words that fell from the lips of the divine Master in His sermon on the mount. This lesson is more than ever necessary in these days of materialism athirst for the goods and pleasures of this earth. All Christians, rich or poor, must keep their eye fixed on heaven, remembering that "we have not here a lasting city, but we seek one that is to come." The rich should not place their happiness in things of earth nor spend their best efforts in the acquisition of them. Rather, considering themselves only as stewards of their earthly goods, let them be mindful of the account they must render of them to their Lord and Master, and value them as precious means that God has put into their hands for doing good; let them not fail, besides, to distribute of their abundance to the poor, according to the evangelical precept. Otherwise there shall be verified of them and their riches the harsh condemnation of St. James the Apostle: "Go to now, ye rich men; weep and howl in your miseries which shall come upon you. Your riches are corrupted, and your garments are moth-eaten; your gold and silver is cankered; and the rust of them shall be for a testimony against you and shall eat your flesh like fire. You have stored up to yourselves wrath against the last days. . . ."

45. But the poor, too, in their turn, while engaged, according to the laws of charity and justice, in acquiring the necessities of life and also in bettering their condition, should always remain "poor in spirit," and hold spiritual goods in higher esteem than earthly property and pleasures. Let them remember that the world will never be able to rid itself of misery, sorrow, and tribulation, which are the portion even of those who seem most prosperous. Patience, therefore, is the need of all, that Christian patience which comforts the heart with the divine assurance of eternal happiness. "Be patient, therefore, brethren," We repeat with St. James, "until the coming of the Lord. Behold the husbandman waiteth for the precious fruit of the earth, patiently bearing until he receive the early and the later rain. Be you therefore also patient and strengthen your hearts, for the coming of the Lord is at hand." Only thus will be fulfilled the consoling promise of the Lord: "Blessed are the poor!" These words are no vain consolation, a promise as empty as those of the Communists. They are the words of life, pregnant with a sovereign reality. They are fully verified here on earth, as well as in eternity. Indeed, how many of the poor, in anticipation of the Kingdom of Heaven already proclaimed their own: "for yours is the Kingdom of Heaven," find in these words a happiness which so many of the wealthy, uneasy with their riches and ever thirsting for more, look for in vain!

59. But "unless the Lord keep the city, he watcheth in vain that keepeth

it." And so, as a final and most efficacious remedy, We recommend, Venerable Brethren, that in your dioceses you use the most practical means to foster and intensify the spirit of prayer joined with Christian penance. When the Apostles asked the Saviour why they had been unable to drive the evil spirit from a demoniac, our Lord answered: "This kind is not cast out but by prayer and fasting." So, too, the evil which today torments humanity can be conquered only by a world-wide holy crusade of prayer and penance. We ask especially the contemplative orders, men and women, to redouble their prayers and sacrifices to obtain from Heaven efficacious aid for the Church in the present struggle. Let them implore also the powerful intercession of the Immaculate Virgin who, having crushed the head of the serpent of old, remains the sure protectress and invincible "Help of Christians."

77. Everywhere today there is an anxious appeal to moral and spiritual forces; and rightly so, for the evil we must combat is at its origin primarily an evil of the spiritual order.

Pius XI, Ubi Arcano

17. Characteristic it is of this immoderate desire after temporal goods to engender evils of every kind, especially moral corruption and strife. For since in themselves such goods are but mean and of no account, they fail to satisfy the soul of man. Coming from the hand of God, this is destined for no less than the Beatific Vision, and so must ever remain ill at ease and restless until it finds its home in God.

30. Nor is he who desires this peace called upon to abjure the goods of this life; rather shall he, as Christ Himself has promised, receive them in abundance: "Seek first the kingdom of God and his justice, and all these things shall be given you besides." We have "the peace of God which surpasses all understanding," and it is precisely for this reason that it restrains our blind appetites and prevents that strife and discord which the love of gain necessarily begets.

55. Great, without question, is the number of those who profess Catholic teaching concerning social authority and the due regard for it, concerning the right and duties of laborers on land or in industry . . . and finally the rights of the Creator, Redeemer, and Lord, Jesus Christ Himself, over men and nations — and yet by their spoken and written word, and the whole tenor of their lives, act as if the teaching and oft-repeated precepts of the Sovereign Pontiffs . . . had lost their efficacy or were completely out of date.

56. In all this we recognize a kind of moral, juridical, and social modernism, and We condemn it as strongly as We do dogmatic modernism.

Pius XI, Caritate Christi Compulsi

13. For God or against God — this once more is the alternative that shall decide the destinies of all mankind, in politics, in finance, in morals, in the sciences and arts, in the state, in civil and domestic society.

16. "This kind can only be cast out by prayer and fasting." These divine words, it appears to us, find a peculiar application in the evils of our own times that can be averted only by means of prayer and penance.

19. Thus, prayer of itself assures the presence of God among men, according to the promise of the divine Redeemer: "Where two or three are gathered together for my sake, there am I in the midst of them."

20. In addition, prayer will remove the fundamental cause of present-day difficulties which We have mentioned above — that is, the insatiable greed for earthly goods.

25. But to prayer we must also join penance, the spirit of penance and the practice of Christian penance.

27. Penance is of its very nature a recognition and re-establishment of the moral order in the world that is founded on the eternal law, that is, on the living God. He who makes satisfaction to God for sin recognizes thereby the sanctity of the highest principles of morality, their internal binding power, the need of a sanction against their violation.

29. It is a weapon that strikes right at the root of all evil, that is, at the lust for material wealth and the wanton pleasures of life. By means of voluntary sacrifices, by means of practical and even painful acts of self-denial, by means of various works of penance, the noblehearted Christian subdues the base passions that tend to make him violate the moral order.

30. No leader in public economy, no power of organization will ever be able to bring social conditions to a peaceful solution, unless first in the very field of economics there triumphs moral law based on God and conscience.

Pius XII, Summi Pontificatus

1398. The radical and ultimate cause of the evils which We deplore in modern society is the denial and rejection of a universal norm of morality as well for individual and social life as for international relations; We mean that disregard, so common nowadays, and the forgetfulness of the natural law itself, which has its foundation in God. . . . When God is denied, every basis of morality is undermined; the voice of conscience is stilled or, at any rate, grows very faint. . . .

1400. The consequence is that the moral values by which, in other times, public and private conduct was gauged have fallen into disuse; and the much vaunted laicization of society, which had made ever more rapid progress, withdrawing man, the family, and the state from the beneficent and regenerating effects of the idea of God and the teaching of the Church, has caused to reappear . . . the signs of a corrupt paganism.

1402. With the weakening of faith in God and in Jesus Christ, and the darkening in men's minds of the light of moral principles, there disappeared the indispensable foundation of the stability and quiet of that internal, and external, private and public order which alone can support and safeguard the stability of states. . . . Dissensions come not only from the surge of rebellious passion, but also from a deep spiritual crisis which has overthrown the sound principles of private and public morality.

1437. For true though it is that the evils from which mankind suffers today come in part from economic instability and from the struggle of interests regarding a more equal distribution of the goods which God has given man as a means of sustenance and progress, it is not less true that their root is deeper and more intrinsic, belonging to the sphere of religious belief and moral convictions. . . . The re-education of mankind if it is to have any effect, must be, above all things, spiritual and religious. Hence it must proceed from Christ as from its indispensable foundation; must be actuated by justice and crowned by charity.

1444. There is no opposition between the laws that govern the life of faithful Christians and the postulates of a genuine brotherly humanitarianism, but rather unity and mutual support.

Pius XII, Christmas Message, 1948

Fidelity to the divine patrimony of truth confided to the Church does not in any way condemn the Catholic Christian — as not a few believe or seem to believe — to an attitude of diffident reserve or cold indifference in the face of the grave and urgent duties of the present hour. On the contrary: the spirit and example of our Lord, who came to seek and save what was lost; the commandments of love and, generally speaking, the special significance that radiates from the Gospel; the history of the Church, which proves how she has always been the stanch and constant support of every force for good and peace; the teachings and exhortations of the Roman Pontiffs, especially in the course of recent decades, dealing with the conduct of Christians toward the neighbor, society, and the state — all this serves to proclaim the believer's duty to take his share, generously, courageously, and according to his station and capacity, in questions that a tormented and agitated world has to solve in the field of social justice, no less than on the international plane of law and peace.

A convinced Christian cannot confine himself within an easy and egotistical isolationism when he witnesses the needs and miseries of his brothers; when pleas for help come to him from those in economic distress; when he knows the aspirations of the working classes for more normal and just conditions of life; when he is aware of the abuses of an economic system which puts money above social obligations; when he is not ignorant of the aberrations of an intransigeant nationalism which denies or spurs the common bonds linking the separate nations together, and imposing on each one of them many and varied duties toward the great family of nations.

Bishops' Program of Social Reconstruction, 1919

Changes in our economic system will have only partial and feeble efficacy if they are not reinforced by the Christian view of work and wealth. Neither the moderate reforms advocated in this paper, nor any other program of betterment or reconstruction, will prove reasonably effective without a reform in the spirit of both labor and capital. The laborer must come to realize that he owes his employer and society an honest day's work in return for a fair wage and that conditions cannot be substantially improved until he roots out the desire to get a maximum of return for a minimum of service. The capitalist must likewise get a new viewpoint. He needs to learn the long-forgotten truth that wealth is stewardship, that profit making is not the basic justification of business enterprise, and that there are such things as fair profits, fair interest, and fair prices. Above and before all, he must cultivate and strengthen within his mind the truth which many of his class have begun to grasp for the first time during the present war, namely, that the laborer is a human being, not merely an instrument of production; and that the laborer's right to a decent livelihood is the first charge upon industry. The employer has a right to get a reasonable living out of his business, but he has no right to interest on his investment until his employees have obtained at least living wages. This is the human and Christian, in contrast to the purely commercial and pagan, ethics of industry.

Secularism, Statement of American Hierarchy, November, 1947

This, in essence, is what we mean by secularism. It is a view of life which limits itself not to the material in exclusion of the spiritual, but to the human here and now in exclusion of man's relation to God here and hereafter. Secularism, or the practical exclusion of God from human thinking and living, is at the root of the world's travail today. It was the fertile soil in which such social monstrosities as fascism, nazism, and communism could germinate and grow. It is doing more than anything else to blight our heritage of Christian culture, which integrates the various aspects of human life and renders to God the things that are God's.

Secularism takes God out of economic thinking and thereby minimizes the dignity of the human person endowed by God with inalienable rights and made responsible to Him for corresponding individual and social duties. Thus, to the detriment of man and society, the divinely established balance in economic relations is lost.

When disregard of his responsibility to God makes the owner forget his stewardship and the social function of private property, there comes that irrational economic individualism which brings misery to millions. Helpless workers are exploited; cutthroat competition and antisocial marketing practices follow. When men in labor organizations lose the right social perspective, which a sense of responsibility to God gives, they are prone to seek merely the victory of their own group, in disregard of personal and property rights.

THE WORK OF THE CLERGY

Leo XIII, Letter to Italian Bishops, December 8, 1902

For this purpose We desire that the aspirants to the priesthood, while abstaining . . . from all participation in actual movements outside, should, toward the end of their seminary course, be duly instructed in the papal documents which have to do with the social question and Christian democracy. Later on, when advanced to the priesthood, let them employ themselves with the people who at every period have been the special object of the Church's most affectionate care. . . . To defend the principles of justice and Christian charity in which all the rights and duties of civil society find a fair and equitable balance, such in its outstanding characteristics is the grand duty and object of social activities.

Pius X, Il Fermo Proposito

The priest, raised higher than other men to fulfill the mission he has received from God, ought to keep himself equally above all human interest, all classes of society. His proper field of action is the Church where, as ambassador of God, he preaches the truth, and inculcates along with respect for the rights of God, respect also for the rights of every creature. Acting thus, he does not expose himself to opposition; he does not appear as a party man, supporting one side and going against another; nor for the sake of avoiding collision with certain tendencies, and of not irritating by argument minds already embittered, does he put himself in danger of disguising the truth, or of suppressing it, which in both cases would be to fail in his duty; nor is it necessary to remark that having very often to treat of material things, he might find himself involved in responsible liabilities, hurtful alike to his person and to the dignity of his ministry. He ought not, therefore, to join an association of this kind except after mature consideration, with the approval of his bishop, and in those cases only where his assistance is safe from all danger and is evidently useful.

Nor does this in any way diminish his zeal. The true apostle ought to become all things to all men, to save all: like our divine Redeemer, he ought to be moved with compassion, seeing the multitudes distressed, lying like sheep that have no shepherd.

Let them each one strive by the efficacious propaganda of the press, by the living exhortation of speech, by direct help in the above-mentioned cases, to ameliorate, within the limits of justice and charity, the economic condition of the people, supporting and promoting those institutions which conduce to this end, and those especially which aim at fortifying the multitude against the invasion of socialism; thus to save them at once from economic ruin and from moral and religious destruction. In this way the co-operation of the clergy in the works of Catholic action has a deeply religious end; it will never become a hindrance, but will be a help to their spiritual ministry by enlarging its sphere and multiplying its fruits.

Benedict XV, Letter to Bishop of Bergamo, March 11, 1920

Let no member of the clergy suppose that activity of this kind is something foreign to his priestly ministry because the field in which it is exercised is economic. *It is precisely in this field that the salvation of souls is imperiled. Therefore it is Our will that priests consider it as one of their duties to give as much of their life as possible to social science and social action,* by study, observation, and work, and to support in all ways those who, in this sphere, exercise a wholesome influence for the good of Catholics.*

Pius XI, Ad Catholici Sacerdotii

8. The priest contributes most effectively to the solution, or at least the mitigation, of social conflicts, since he preaches Christian brotherhood, declares to all their mutual obligations of justice and charity, brings peace to hearts embittered by moral and economic hardship, and alike to rich and poor points out the only true riches to which all men both can and should aspire.

---

* In this and the following sections of the quotations, many passages are italicized by the author. The purpose of this is to emphasize teachings which form the doctrinal basis of the companion volume to this work, *Catholic Social Action.*

Pius XI, Quadragesimo Anno

19–23. (*Summarized.*) Since *Rerum Novarum* many scholars, both priests and laymen, "have zealously undertaken to develop, with the Church as their guide and teacher, a social and economic science in accord with the conditions of our time" (No. 19). Lay auxiliaries, through college and university courses, social congresses, study clubs, and sound publications have brought this science into the full light and stress of life. Even those who do not recognize the authority of the Church have accepted its teaching on social matters. Furthermore these teachings have been put into practice. The clergy have devoted themselves to the welfare of the workers and have trained them for leadership.

24. There have also been established everywhere new and continuously expanding organizations in which workers, craftsmen, farmers, and employers of every kind, with the counsel of the Church and frequently under the leadership of her priests, give and receive mutual help and support.

27. *Sacred ministers of the Church, thoroughly imbued with Leo's teaching, have, in fact, often proposed to the votes of the peoples' representatives the very social legislation that has been enacted in recent years and have resolutely demanded and promoted its enforcement.*

142. A difficult task, certainly, is thus imposed on priests, and to meet it, all who are growing up as the hope of the Church, must be duly prepared by an intensive study of the social question. Especially is it necessary that those whom you intend to assign in particular to this work should demonstrate that they are men possessed of the keenest sense of justice, who will resist with true manly courage the dishonest demands or the unjust acts of anyone, who will excel in the prudence and judgment which avoids every extreme, and, above all, who will be deeply permeated by the charity of Christ, which alone has the power to subdue firmly but gently the hearts and wills of men to the laws of justice and equity. Upon this road so often tried by happy experience, there is no reason why we should hesitate to go forward with all speed.

143. These Our Beloved Sons who are chosen for so great a work, We earnestly exhort in the Lord to *give themselves wholly to the training of the men committed to their care, and in the discharge of this eminently priestly and apostolic duty to make proper use of the resources of Christian education by teaching youth, forming Christian organizations, and founding study groups guided by principles in harmony with the Faith.*

Pius XI, On Atheistic Communism

61. To priests in a special way We recommend anew the old-repeated counsel of Our Predecessor, Leo XIII, to go to the workingman. We make this advice Our own, and faithful to the teaching of Jesus Christ and His Church, We thus complete it: "Go to the workingman, especially where he is poor; and in general, go to the poor." The poor are obviously more exposed than others to the wiles of agitators who, taking advantage of their extreme need, kindle their hearts to envy of the rich and urge them to seize by force what fortune seems to have denied them unjustly. If the priest will not go to the workingman and to the poor, to warn them or to disabuse them of prejudice and false theory, they will become an easy prey for the apostles of communism.

62. Indisputably much has been done in this direction, especially after the publication of the Encyclicals *Rerum Novarum* and *Quadragesimo Anno*. We are happy to voice Our paternal approval of the zealous pastoral activity manifested by so many bishops and priests who have with due prudence and caution been planning and applying new methods of apostolate more adapted to modern needs. But for the solution of our present problem all this effort is still inadequate. *When our country is in danger, everything not strictly necessary, everything not bearing directly on the urgent matter of unified defense, takes second place. So we must act in today's crisis. Every other enterprise, however attractive and helpful, must yield before the vital need of protecting the very foundation of the Faith and of Christian civilization. Let our parish priests, therefore, while providing of course for the normal needs of the Faithful, dedicate the better part of their endeavors and their zeal to winning back the laboring masses to Christ and to His Church.* Let them work to infuse the Christian spirit into quarters where it is least at home. The willing response of the masses, and results far exceeding their expectations, will not fail to reward them for their strenuous pioneer labor.

63. But the most efficacious means of apostolate among the poor and lowly is the priest's example, the practice of all those sacerdotal virtues which We have described in Our Encyclical *Ad Catholici Sacerdoti*. Especially needful, however, for the present situation is the shining example of a life which is humble, poor, and disinterested, in imitation of a divine Master who could say to the world with divine simplicity: "The foxes have holes and the birds of the air nests, but the Son of Man hath not where to lay His head." A priest who is really poor and disinterested in the Gospel sense may work among his flock marvels recalling a St. Vincent de Paul, a Curé of Ars, a Cottolengo, a Don Bosco, and so many others; while an avaricious and selfish priest, as We have noted in the above-

mentioned Encyclical, even though he should not plunge with Judas to the abyss of treason, will never be more than empty "sounding brass" and useless "tinkling cymbal." Too often, indeed, he will be a hindrance rather than an instrument of grace in the midst of his people. *Furthermore, where a secular priest or religious is obliged by his office to administer temporal property, let him remember that he is not only to observe scrupulously all that charity and justice prescribe, but that he has a special obligation to conduct himself in every truth as a father of the poor.*

Pius XI, Firmissimam Constantiam

23. If you truly love the laborer (and you must love him because his conditions of life approach nearer to those of the divine Master), you must assist him materially and religiously. Materially, bringing about in his favor the practice not only of commutative justice but also of social justice, that is, all those provisions which aim at relieving the condition of the proletarian; and then religiously, giving him again the religious comforts without which he will struggle in a materialism that brutalizes him and degrades him.

Pius XII, Discourse to Members of Italian Electric Industry, January 23, 1946

We bless with the fullness of our heart the work of the chaplains of labor, who, raised above all partisanship and excluding material interest, bring together with God the light of truth and the flame of love which can bring souls together.

Pius XII, Letter to French Episcopate, January 6, 1945

[The clergy], encouraged by your work and example, will seek to meet the needs of the hour by deepening their study of social problems, from which depend, when they are solved in the light of the Gospel and the repeated teachings of the Holy See, the raising of workers to a level of life which is more fitting and more in conformity with the eminent dignity of the human person.

Pius XII, Radio Address to German Catholics, September 4, 1949

Since Our Predecessor, Pope Leo XIII, almost sixty years ago issued the encyclical *Rerum Novarum,* few problems have engaged the interest and solicitude of the Supreme Pastors of the Church more than the social question. All that they could do to collaborate, with doctrine and counsel, for a solution or at least a mitigation of social inequalities, has been done. *What is necessary is that the social doctrine of the Church should become the patrimony of all Christian consciences and that this doctrine be put into practice.* Social activity, however, requires sacrifice on the part of all concerned. These sacrifices must be made, and today, more than at any other time, do not admit of any further delay.

APOSTOLATE OF THE LAITY

Leo XIII, Letter to Bishop of Grenoble, June 22, 1892

We wish to say that it is the part of Christian prudence, while holding firm in the profession of dogma and remaining free from compromise with error, not to repulse — rather let us say — to know how to promote the collaboration of all men of good will in the pursuit of good, both individual and above all social.

Pius X, Il Fermo Proposito

Our Predecessor Leo XIII, of holy memory, fully perceived this, and pointed out, notably in the famous Encyclical *Rerum Novarum,* and in later documents, the object to which Catholic Action should be specially devoted, namely, the practical solution of the social question according to Christian principles.

Further, in order that Catholic Action may be effectual on all points, it is not enough that it be adapted to actual social needs only; it ought *also to be invigorated by all the practical methods furnished at the present day by progress in social and economic studies,* by experience already gained elsewhere, by the condition of civil society, and even by the public life of states. Otherwise there will be a risk of groping for a long time for new and hazardous things, while good and safe ones are ready to hand, and have been already well tried; or again, there will be the danger of proposing institutions and methods suitable, perhaps, in former times, but not understood by people of the present day; or finally, there will be the danger of stopping halfway by not using, in the measure in which they are granted, those rights of citizenship which modern constitutions offer to all, and therefore also to Catholics.

You see how anxious We have been to explain and inculcate the manner in which Catholic Action . . . is to be supported and promoted. It is not sufficient to point out what is good; it must be put into practice.

Pius XI, Firmissimam Constantiam

19. Catholic Action should never take responsibility in matters that are purely technical, financial, or economic because such matters lie outside the scope and purpose of Catholic Action.

Pius XI, Quadragesimo Anno

19. It is not surprising, therefore, that many scholars, both priests and laymen, led especially by the desire that the unchanged and unchangeable teaching of the Church should meet new demands and needs more effectively, have zealously undertaken to develop, with the Church as their guide and teacher, a social and economic science in accord with the conditions of our time.

20. And so, with Leo's Encyclical pointing the way and furnishing the light, a true Catholic social science has arisen, which is daily fostered and enriched by the tireless efforts of those chosen men whom We have termed auxiliaries of the Church. They do not, indeed, allow their science to lie hidden behind learned walls. As the useful and well-attended courses instituted in Catholic universities, colleges, and seminaries, the social congresses and "weeks" that are held at frequent intervals with most successful results, the study groups that are promoted, and finally the timely and sound publications that are disseminated everywhere and in every possible way, clearly show, these men bring their science out into the full light and stress of life.

96. . . . the contribution made thereto of Catholic Action principles and their application, not indeed by Catholic Action (which excludes syndical or political activities from its scope), but by those sons of Ours whom Catholic Action imbues with Catholic principles and trains for carrying on an apostolate under the leadership and teaching guidance of the Church....

138. Let well-merited acclamations of praise be bestowed upon you and at the same time upon all those, both clergy and laity, who, We rejoice to see, are daily participating and valiantly helping in this same great work, Our beloved sons engaged in Catholic Action, who with a singular zeal are undertaking with Us the solution of the social problems insofar as by virtue of her divine institution this is proper to and devolves upon the Church. All these We urge in the Lord, again and again, to spare no labors and let no difficulties conquer them, but rather to become day by day more courageous and more valiant. Arduous indeed is the task which We propose to them, for We know well that on both sides, both among the upper and the lower classes of society, there are many obstacles and barriers to be overcome. Let them not, however, lose heart; to face bitter combats is a mark of Christians; and to endure grave labors to the end is a mark of them who, as good soldiers of Christ, follow Him closely.

141. For We are now confronted, as more than once before in the history of the Church, with a world that in large part has almost fallen back into paganism. That these whole classes of men may be brought back

to Christ whom they have denied, we must recruit and train from among them, themselves, auxiliary soldiers of the Church who know them well and their minds and wishes, and can reach their hearts with a tender brotherly love. *The first and immediate apostle to the workers ought to be workers; the apostles to those who follow industry and trade ought to be from among them themselves.*

142. *It is chiefly your duty, Venerable Brethren, and of your clergy, to search diligently for these lay apostles both of workers and of employers, to select them with prudence, and to train and instruct them properly.*

146. Venerable Brethren and Beloved Sons, let us not permit the children of this world to appear wiser in their generation than we who by the divine Goodness are the children of the light. We find them, indeed, selecting and training with the greatest shrewdness alert and resolute devotees who spread their errors ever wider day by day through all classes of men and in every part of the world. And whenever they undertake to attack the Church of Christ more violently, We see them put aside their internal quarrels, assembling in full harmony in a single battle line with a completely united effort, and work to achieve their common purpose.

147. Surely there is not one that does not know how many and how great are the works that the tireless zeal of Catholics is striving everywhere to carry out, both for social and economic welfare as well as in the fields of education and religion. But this admirable and unremitting activity not infrequently shows less effectiveness because of the dispersion of its energies in too many different directions. Therefore, let all men of good will stand united, all who under the Shepherds of the Church wish to fight this good and peaceful battle of Christ; and under the leadership and teaching guidance of the Church let all strive according to the talent, powers, and position of each to contribute something to the Christian reconstruction of human society which Leo XIII inaugurated through his immortal Encyclical *On the Condition of Workers,* seeking not themselves and their own interests, but those of Jesus Christ, not trying to press at all costs their own counsels, but ready to sacrifice them, however excellent, if the greater common good should seem to require it, so that in all and above all Christ may reign, Christ may command, to whom be "honor and glory and dominion forever and ever."

Pius XI, On Atheistic Communism

39. The most urgent need of the present day is therefore the energetic and timely application of remedies which will effectively ward off the catastrophe that daily grows more threatening. We cherish the firm hope that the fanaticism with which the sons of darkness work day and night

at their materialistic and atheistic propaganda will at least serve the holy purpose of stimulating the sons of light to a like and even greater zeal for the honor of the divine majesty.

55. To give to this social activity a greater efficacy, it is necessary to promote a wider study of social problems in the light of the doctrine of the Church and under the aegis of her constituted authority. If the manner of acting of some Catholics in the social-economic field has left much to be desired, this has often come about because they have not known and pondered sufficiently the teachings of the Sovereign Pontiffs on these questions. *Therefore, it is of the utmost importance to foster in all classes of society an intensive program of social education adapted to the varying degrees of intellectual culture.* It is necessary with all care and diligence to procure the widest possible diffusion of the teachings of the Church, even among the working classes. The minds of men must be illuminated with the sure light of Catholic teaching, and their wills must be drawn to follow and apply it as the norm of right living in the conscientious fulfillment of their manifold social duties. Thus they will oppose that incoherence and discontinuity in Christian life which We have many times lamented. *For there are some who, while exteriorly faithful to the practice of their religion, yet in the field of labor and industry, in the professions, trade, and business, permit a deplorable cleavage in their conscience, and live a life too little in conformity with the clear principles of justice and Christian charity.* Such lives are a scandal to the weak, and to the malicious a pretext to discredit the Church.

56. *In this renewal the Catholic press can play a prominent part.* Its foremost duty is to foster in various attractive ways an ever better understanding of social doctrine. It should, too, supply accurate and complete information on the activity of the enemy and the means of resistance which have been found most effective in various quarters. It should offer useful suggestions and warn against the insidious deceits with which Communists endeavor, all too successfully, to attract even men of good faith.

64. *Catholic Action is in effect a social apostolate also,* inasmuch as its object is to spread the Kingdom of Jesus Christ not only among individuals, but also in families and in society. It must, therefore, make it a chief aim to train its members with special care and to prepare them to fight the battles of the Lord. This task of formation now more urgent and indispensable than ever, which must always precede direct action in the field, will assuredly be served by *study circles, conferences, lecture courses, and the various other activities undertaken with a view to making known the Christian solution of the social problem.*

65. The militant leaders of Catholic Action, thus properly prepared and armed, will be the first and immediate apostles of their fellow workmen. They will be an invaluable aid to the priest in carrying the torch of truth, and in relieving grave spiritual and material suffering, in many sectors where inveterate anticlerical prejudice or deplorable religious indifference has proved a constant obstacle to the pastoral activity of God's ministers. In this way they will collaborate, *under the direction of especially qualified priests,* in that work of spiritual aid to the laboring classes on which We set so much store, because it is the means best calculated to save these Our beloved children, from the snares of communism.

66. In addition to this individual apostolate which, however useful and efficacious, often goes unheralded, *Catholic Action must organize propaganda, on a large scale, to disseminate knowledge of the fundamental principles on which, according to the pontifical documents, a Christian Social Order must build.*

68. We are thinking likewise of those associations of workmen, farmers, technicians, doctors, employers, students, and others of like character, groups of men and women who live in the same cultural atmosphere and share the same way of life. *Precisely these groups and organizations are destined to introduce into society that order which We have envisaged in our Encyclical* Quadragesimo Anno, *and thus to spread in the vast and various fields of culture and labor the recognition of the Kingdom of Christ.*

69. Even where the state, because of changed social and economic conditions, has felt obliged to intervene directly in order to aid and regulate such organizations by special legislative enactments, supposing always the necessary respect for liberty and private initiative, Catholic Action may not urge the circumstance as an excuse for abandoning the field. Its members should contribute prudently and intelligently to the study of the problems of the hour in the light of Catholic doctrine. They should loyally and generously participate in the formation of the new institutions, bringing to them the Christian spirit which is the basic principle of order wherever men work together in fraternal harmony.

72. But in this battle joined by the powers of darkness against the very idea of Divinity, *it is Our fond hope that, besides the host which glories in the name of Christ, all those — and they comprise the overwhelming majority of mankind — who still believe in God and pay Him homage may take a decisive part.* We therefore renew the invitation extended to them five years ago in Our Encyclical *Caritate Christi,* invoking their loyal and hearty collaboration "in order to ward off from mankind the great danger that threatens all alike." Since, as We then said, "belief in God is

the unshakable foundation of all social order and of all responsibility on earth, it follows that all those who do not want anarchy and terrorism ought to take energetic steps to prevent the enemies of religion from attaining the goal they have so brazenly proclaimed to the world."

Pius XI, Caritate Christi Compulsi

14. In such a union of minds and forces they ought to be first who are proud of the Christian name. . . . *But let all those also loyally and heartily concur who still believe in God and adore Him, in order to ward off from mankind the great danger that threatens all alike.* For, in truth, belief in God is the unshaken foundation of all social order and of all responsibility on earth; so it follows that all those who do not want anarchy and terrorism ought to take energetic steps to prevent the enemies of religion from attaining the goal they have so brazenly proclaimed to the world.

Pius XII, La Solennità della Pentecoste

1694. What remains for Us but, in the spirit of Leo XIII and in accordance with his advice and purpose, to exhort you to continue to promote the work which the last generation of your brothers and sisters has begun with such stanch courage? Do not let die in your midst and fade away the insistent call of the two Pontiffs of the social Encyclicals, that voice which indicates to the faithful in the supernatural regeneration of mankind the *moral obligation to co-operate in the arrangement of society, and especially of economic life, exhorting those who share in this life to action no less than the state itself. Is not this a sacred duty for every Christian?*

Pius XII, Letter to Semaines Sociales, 1947

The present hour, from whatever standpoint it is viewed, summons the faithful to exert their every energy to render to the social teaching of the Church its maximum of efficiency and of practical results. It is an illusion to imagine, as some people do, that anticlericalism and anti-Catholic fanaticism can be disarmed by confining the principles of Catholicism within the domain of private life. This "minimalist" attitude would, on the contrary, merely afford new pretexts to the enemies of the Church. Catholics will maintain and approve their positions in proportion to the courage they display in converting their intimate convictions into action over the entire range of life, public as well as private.

Pius XII, Christmas Broadcast, 1947

In the day of battle your place is in the vanguard, fighting at the front. The timid and those afraid to come out in the open are very close to becoming deserters and traitors [context: struggle against world communism].

Pius XII, Allocution to Sacred College of Cardinals, June 2, 1948

Only on the principles of Christianity and in accord with its spirit can social reforms, called for imperatively by the necessities and aspirations of our times, be carried out. They demand from some the spirit of renunciation and sacrifice, from others the sense of responsibility and endurance, from everybody hard and strenuous work.

Wherefore we turn to the Catholics of the whole world, exhorting them not to be satisfied with good intentions and fine projects, but to proceed courageously to put them into practice. *Neither should they hesitate to join forces with those who, remaining outside their ranks, are nonetheless in agreement with the social teaching of the Catholic Church and are disposed to follow the road she has marked out,* which is not the road of violent revolution but of experience that has stood the test and of energetic resolution.

Pius XII, Allocution to International Union of Leagues of Catholic Women, September 12, 1947

Consequently, heavy is the responsibility of anyone, man or woman, who has the right to voting, especially when religious interests are at stake. As they well know, abstention in such case would of itself be a grave and deadly sin of omission. On the contrary, to use, and to make good use of, this right is to work effectively for the true good of the people and to act as loyal defenders of the cause of God and of the Church.

Pius XII, Address to Women of Italian Catholic Action, July, 1949

First of all, We say that everything that can contribute to a sound social policy for the good of the family and Christian youth can always count on the efficacious support of the Church.

We repeat now to you what We said to the men of Catholic Action some two years ago. The Catholic Church strongly supports the requirements of social justice. These requirements include provision for the people of the necessary houses, and above all for those who desire to found a family or are already doing so. Can there be conceived a social need of greater urgency? How sad it is to see young people, at the age when nature is more inclined to marriage, forced to wait years and years, merely because of the lack of a place to live, and always with the danger that in this nerve-wracking waiting their morals may deteriorate. Encourage, then, as much as you can, with your propaganda and your labors, the provision of houses so that the dignity of marriage and the Christian education of children may not suffer from this need.

Bishops' Statement, 1933

The change of thought, of temper, and the militant spirit manifested against the very basic things for which Christianity stands call for Catholic lay leaders in great numbers. They must be informed, thoroughly Catholic-minded, fearless, and capable of stating simply and clearly the position of the Church on every vital question of today which has a moral aspect.

Given such leaders, Catholic Action cannot but profoundly influence public opinion.

PAST ACHIEVEMENTS

Leo XIII, Rerum Novarum

75. Many of our Faith are indeed to be highly commended, who, having rightly perceived what the times require of them are experimenting and striving to discover how by honest means they can raise the nonowning working class to higher living levels. They have championed their cause and are endeavoring to increase the prosperity of both families and individuals, and at the same time to regulate justly the mutual obligations which rest upon workers and employers and to foster and strengthen in both consciousness of duty and observance of the precepts of the Gospel — precepts, in truth, which hold man back from excess and prevent him from overstepping the bounds of moderation, and, in the midst of the widest divergences among persons and things, maintain harmony in the state. For this reason, we see eminent men meeting together frequently to exchange ideas, to combine their forces, and to deliberate on the most expedient program of action. Others are endeavoring to unite the various kinds of workers in suitable associations, are assisting them with advice and money, and making plans to prevent a lack of honest and profitable work. The bishops are giving encouragement and bestowing support; and under their authority and auspices many from the ranks of the clergy, both regular and diocesan, are showing zealous care for all that pertains to the spiritual improvement of the members of these associations. Finally, there are not wanting Catholics of great wealth, yet voluntary sharers, as it were, in the lot of the wage workers, who by their own generous contributions are striving to found and extend associations through which the worker is readily enabled to obtain from his toil not only immediate benefits, but also assurance of honorable retirement in the future. How much good such manifold and enthusiastic activity has contributed to the benefit of all is too well known to make discussion necessary. From all this, We have taken auguries of good hope for the future, provided that societies of this kind continually grow and that they are founded with wise organization.

Pius XI, Quadragesimo Anno

22. Furthermore, after the terrible war, when the statesmen of the leading nations were attempting to restore peace on the basis of a thorough reform of social conditions, did not they, among the norms agreed upon to regulate in accordance with justice and equity the labor of the workers, give sanction to many points that so remarkably coincide with Leo's principles and instructions as to seem consciously taken therefrom? The Encyclical *On the Condition of Workers,* without question, has become a memorable document and rightly to it may be applied the words of Isaiah: "He shall set up a standard to the nations."

23–39, 125, 140. *(Summarized.)* The teachings of *Rerum Novarum* were made the subject of intensive study and then put into practice. Efforts were undertaken to better the lot of the workers. New organizations were formed. Governments broke away from the principles of *laissez faire* in order to protect the poor, with Catholics assisting in the legislatures. "A new branch of law, wholly unknown to the earlier time, has arisen from the continuous and unwearied labor to protect vigorously the sacred rights of the workers that flow from their dignity as men and Christians. These laws undertake the protection of life, health, strength, family, homes, workshops, wages, and labor hazards; in fine, everything which pertains to the condition of wage workers, with special concern for women and children" (No. 28). Workers' associations were formed, as well as groups uniting other classes. Unfortunately, there has been less success in forming associations of employers and managers of industry. Clearly, however, the fruits of *Rerum Novarum* were many and of vital importance.

It is lamentable, however, that some Catholics do not hesitate out of greed for gain to exploit the workers. "Even more there are men who abuse religion itself, and under its name try to hide their unjust exactions in order to protect themselves from the manifestly just demands of the workers" (No. 125). This conduct gives a pretext to those who charge that the Church favors the rich and is unconcerned with the poor. The history of the Church and *Rerum Novarum* itself shows that this charge is a calumny.

It is happy to note signs of social reconstruction within the ranks of the workers. Many of their leaders, imbued by Christian principles, "are striving prudently to harmonize the just demands of their members with the prosperity of their whole occupation" (No. 140). Also many young men, destined by talent or wealth to be leaders of society, are studying social problems deeply, and one may hope that they will dedicate themselves wholly to the restoration of society.

Pius XI, On Atheistic Communism

35. With good reason outstanding statesmen have asserted that, after a study of various social systems, they have found nothing sounder than the principles expounded in the encyclicals *Rerum Novarum* and *Quadragesimo Anno*. In non-Catholic, even in non-Christian countries, men recognize the great value to society of the social doctrine of the Church. Thus, scarcely a month ago, an eminent political figure of the East, a non-Christian, did not hesitate to affirm publicly that the Church, with her doctrine of peace and Christian brotherhood, is rendering a signal contribution to the difficult task of establishing and maintaining peace among the nations. Finally, we know from reliable information that flows into this Center of Christendom from all parts of the world, that the Communists themselves, where they are not utterly depraved, recognize the superiority of the social doctrine of the Church, when once explained to them, over the doctrines of their leaders and their teachers.

37. Faithful to these principles, the Church has given new life to human society. Under her influence arose prodigious charitable organizations, great guilds of artisans and workingmen of every type. These guilds, ridiculed as "medieval" by the liberalism of the last century, are today claiming the admiration of our contemporaries in many countries who are endeavoring to revive them in some modern form. And when other systems hindered her work and raised obstacles to the salutary influence of the Church, she was never done warning them of their error. We need but recall with what constant firmness and energy Our Predecessor, Leo XIII, *vindicated for the workingman the right to organize,* which the dominant liberalism of the more powerful states relentlessly denied him. Even today the authority of this Church doctrine is greater than it seems; *for the influence of ideas in the realm of facts, though invisible and not easily measured, is surely of predominant importance.*

Pius XII, Sertum Laetitiae

1468. It is a source of joy to Us to know that the above-cited Encyclical, *Quadragesimo Anno,* as well as that of the Sovereign Pontiff, Leo XIII, *Rerum Novarum,* in which is indicated the solution of the social question in accordance with the postulates of the Gospel and of the eternal philosophy, are the object, in the United States, of careful and prolonged consideration on the part of some men of keener intellect whose generous wish pushes them on toward social restoration and the restrengthening of the bonds of love amongst men, and that some employers themselves have desired to settle the ever recurring controversies with the workingman in accordance with the norms of these encyclicals, respecting always the common good and the dignity of the human person. What a proud vaunt it will be for the American people, by nature inclined to grandiose undertakings and to liberality, if they untie the knotty and difficult social question by following the sure paths illuminated by the light of the Gospel, and thus lay the basis of a happier age. . . .

In an earlier chapter, reasons were given why the Church was interested in the social problem. It was there noted that the Church's concern was both direct and indirect: direct, insofar as social problems are also moral problems; and indirect, because social evils often impose great burdens on individuals, to the detriment of their religious and moral life. The social question has often led to other evils, such as statism, which are reactions to the tensions caused by economic life. For all these reasons, the Church has felt it her right and duty to pronounce on the moral aspect of the social problem. But the contribution offered by religion is more than the negative, though highly useful, function of passing judgment on moral evil. It can offer positive help through its encouragement of Christian virtue and through its ministry of prayer and sacrament. Since the root causes of the social problem are moral and religious, it follows that truly basic remedies must be in the same sphere.

Moral Basis of the Social Problem. The statement that the basis of modern problems is moral and religious, though profoundly true, is often misinterpreted. Some writers go so far as to assert that the only source of modern evils is moral and consequently the only remedies to be used are purely religious. Such theorists would discard such "purely temporal" measures as social legislation, organization of economic life, work with labor and business, and other such forms of activity in the material world. At least they would say that such reforms are useless, unless moral reform is first achieved. Accordingly, they would have us emphasize first things first, seeking first the Kingdom of God, knowing that all other things would then be added to us.

Actually, the dichotomy between moral and social reform is artificial and unnecessary. As one author puts it, it is like arguing whether food or breath is more necessary for human existence.[1] Both are necessary for life, and both social and moral reforms are needed in modern society. Such certainly is the mind of the popes, as can be gathered by even casual reading of the encyclical and other references throughout this book. Moreover, the two are often interrelated. Not only is moral renovation needed for basic social reform, but it could well be argued that conditions which dehumanize men are serious obstacles to religious life. If economic abuses deprive men of freedom, immerse them in material concerns, and stir up bitterness and resentment in their hearts, it is quite difficult to make such men fully Christian. Faulty economic life can be a strong force acting against virtuous living. Hence the statement that modern problems are primarily moral and religious should not be interpreted to mean that they are exclusively so and that the only remedies are prayer and Christian living. There is a strong moral and even religious element in much social reform, since this actuates the virtues of social justice and social charity. We are not confronted with a choice of "either or" but rather our policy should be both religious and social reform. In the language of *Summi Pontificatus* (No. 1444), there need be no conflict between religious reformers and humanitarian programs.

Some social problems are primarily technical. Thus, it is possible to have such evils as depressions, underemployment, and insecurity in a Christian society which lacks proper organization and technical competence. Indeed, the very virtue of thrift, under certain circumstances, could for economic reasons bring on a depression. Again, such problems as soil erosion and depletion of natural resources could arise from ignorance of physical law rather than lack of good will. In such cases, more than good will is needed. Economic science and proper organization are also necessary. One might go further and state that some advocates of purely spiritual reform have fallen into a subtle and pernicious form of individualism. They write as if society would be sound if all individual members were good men. This overlooks the

---

[1] O. von Nell-Breuning, *Reorganization of Social Economy*, p. 198.

inner laws which govern society as such, apart from its constituent members. It must be organized so as to promote the common good. Undoubtedly good will would contribute powerfully
to such organization, but it is a preliminary to it, not identical
with it.

In other cases, human motivation (and hence moral and religious attitudes) is a vital element in social reform. Negatively,
the moral evils to be described subsequently are obstacles to
sound economic life. Postively, the virtues also treated in this
chapter are essential to deep and lasting reform. It is unthinkable
that any purely technical program of thorough social renovation
could succeed if most men were selfish, greedy, and materialistic.
Society cannot be organized for the common good if its members
are selfishly individualistic. A mere collection of competing individuals is not a society. A mass must be held together by force,
since it lacks an internal basis for cohesion. Thus, the alternative
to sound organization based on social justice and social charity
is either disorder or a form of order imposed by force. Neither
of these situations accords with the dignity of man and the
ultimate purpose of economic life.

Furthermore, proper moral motivation is, generally speaking,
unobtainable without a religious renewal in society. This does
not mean that some men without formal religious beliefs cannot
live good lives. God has so deeply implanted his law in the minds
of men that, even where men see Him obscurely and in a distorted fashion, they nevertheless often follow His commands.
But in the case of very many persons, it is almost impossible to
live morally without religious belief. If this world is considered
the ultimate reality, then materialism and selfishness are natural
consequences to millions. Might becomes right, and force the
ultimate determinant in society. Life is a bitter struggle for survival, with no mercy to the loser. It is true that the powerful
influence of the Christian tradition prevents the logical unfolding of the consequences of unbelief. But if society continues to
move away from God, it will scarcely be able for long to believe
in the dignity of man. The utter denial of man's rights, as prac-

ticed under communism, is but an unfolding of the ultimate implications of a secular society. It seems that man can remain man only by aspiring upward to love of God. If he ceases to climb, he descends to the level of brute creation.

Yet, so interrelated is human existence, there must often be social reform as a prelude to full religious life for millions. The harshness of economic life has so dehumanized many that they have lost interest in the divine. We must first be men if we are to be Christians. Men who are ground down by despair and oppression may seek solace in spiritual consolation, but often they are brutalized and debased. It is difficult for both love and hatred to rule the human heart, and when men are filled with hatred as a result of mistreatment, they do not easily rise to love of God. It follows then that, as we urge men to live closer to God, we must concurrently be eager to remove the social and economic obstacles to religious life.

We might well quote in this connection the 1947 Lenten pastoral of Emmanuel Cardinal Suhard, the late Archbishop of Paris:

> To convert the world, it is not enough to be saints and preach the Gospel. Rather it is impossible to be a saint and live the Gospel we preach without spending ourselves in a common effort to provide everyone with housing, employment, food, leisure, and education necessary for a decent human life. . . . The group is saved only by the group, which alone has grace of state for the purpose. . . . In practice, this will mean that Catholics agree, not to abandon their normal sphere of activity, but to establish fruitful and brotherly contacts with all those around them . . . rendering service without regard to beliefs or opinions.[2]

In these striking words, the Cardinal summarized the apostolate of today. We are called, not exclusively to personal sanctification, but to the ministry of bringing Christ to others. In doing this, we cannot overlook the material conditions of life which so powerfully influence, for good or evil, the lives of all men.

Spiritual Evils in Modern Life. Papal documents cited in connection with this chapter emphasize problems in the spiritual

---

[2] *Growth or Decline* (South Bend: Fides Publishers, 1948), pp. 86–87.

order as sources of present-day ills. One of the most important texts was not included in the excerpts, however, since a brief background exposition is needed to explain its meaning. On August 25, 1910, Pope Pius X condemned in strong language a movement in France known as *Le Sillon*. This organization was a powerful force at the time, advocating many programs of social and political reform which would be considered admirable today. But, although Catholic in membership, it was largely secularistic in ideology. Its program was based on a naïve optimism, holding that a vague good will in economic life plus the political form of democracy would solve the problems of the world.

The condemnation of this movement emphasized two main points: any view of human nature which prescinds from original sin and concentrates exclusively upon man's natural goodness is radically defective; and a reform program which neglects spiritual weapons contained in the teaching of the Church is bound to be inadequate. A Catholic should use the totality of resources at his disposal in the field of social reform and not confine himself to the minimum which would be the least-common denominator in a secularist world. But the Holy Father warned against the notion that holiness alone would be sufficient to solve the social problem. Speaking to the clergy, he said:

> As, moreover, in the conflict of interests and, especially in the struggle with dishonest forces, a man's virtue or sanctity even may not be sufficient to ensure him daily bread, and as social machinery ought to be so organized that by its natural play it should paralyze the efforts of the vicious and put their legitimate share of temporal happiness within the reach of all men of good will, it is our earnest wish that you take an active part in the organization of society for this purpose.[3]

Pope Pius X then advocated the training in social sciences of carefully prepared members of the clergy so that they could give guidance to a Catholic social movement.

In more recent times, the growth of spiritual ills has intensified.

---

[3] Cited in *The Church and Labor*, by J. A. Ryan and J. Husslein (New York: Macmillan, 1924), p. 120. Only a brief excerpt is given in the book cited. The full text (in French) is available in the *Acta Apostolicae Sedis*, II, p. 607.

Greatest among these are the denial of God (under communism) and the ignoring of God (under secularism). It could even be argued that secularism has features which are worse than communism, in that hatred of God at least involves an acknowledgment of His power, whereas ignoring of God is a supreme insult. Certainly, if we were to judge the matter by purely human standards, most men find it harder to be ignored than to be hated. The latter at least implies that the subject is capable of doing something, whereas when a person is ignored, he is considered to be beneath notice.

Secularism is the same as the moral, juridicial, and social modernism condemned in *Ubi Arcano*. It is the building of life upon purely material and natural foundations. A secular society is concerned only with temporal goals. Expediency and not principle is its ruling guide. It is only natural that such a society should be materialistic, selfish, and greedy. Class hatred, exploitation, and the use of force are again normal under these conditions. Moral life decays. Pleasure is the supreme goal. Sensuality is enthroned. Internal dissension and war between nations are not unlikely. Thus, all the specific evils enumerated in the excerpts given in this chapter can be classed as fruits of secularism.

A secular and materialistic society lacks moral weapons to fight communism since its philosophy is too similar to that of its opponent. It is no accident that many enemies of communism in the United States argue that our system is superior since it provides more material satisfactions. On that basis, as was noted earlier, it would be logical to embrace the slavery of communism if, perchance, Soviet production began to surpass ours. It is no wonder that many Catholic writers in Europe, who consider present-day capitalism essentially materialistic, argue that it is no better than communism. Such a view is not advocated in these pages, since it is felt that the force of Christian tradition has in practice modified the extremes of materialism and selfishness. Moreover, Americans today pay increasing attention to the denial of human freedom under communism. This is a happy contrast to the all too common attitude during the 1930's, when liberals were so enamored of the possibilities inherent in economic planning that they often overlooked the cruelties perpetrated upon the Russian people.

The evil offspring of materialism, namely, greed, selfishness, and thirst for pleasure at all costs, are strong enemies of a sound social order. If economic life is to be merely a mad pursuit of wealth, without regard to the welfare of others, it must remain a battleground for conflicting interests. Nor can society be safely built upon a foundation of selfishness, since this is essentially divisive. It tears men asunder. And, since stable production of needed goods requires some unity and co-operation, the tendency is to use force to unite men who will not get together as a result of good will. Thus, we have the statism and giantism of modern life.

Some of the results of unhealthy moral conditions are enumerated in *Quadragesimo Anno*. First among these is the economic instability which plagues present-day life and makes prudent planning by individuals practically impossible. This in turn is fostered by financial manipulation which subordinates production of real wealth to the vagaries of stock, commodity, and foreign exchange markets. A further separation of production from its real purpose is found in the abuse of corporate privileges, whereby directors of corporations misuse the funds committed to their trust and perpetrate fraud and deception under the mantle of corporate anonymity. If manipulation and corporate fraud have been greatly lessened here by the 1933–1935 reform laws, the final abuse listed by the Pope still obtains. This is the stimulation of baser human desires for the sake of profit. Modern advertising often appeals to men's vices, ranging from relatively harmless incitements to vanity to none-too-subtle efforts to trade upon sex. Thus, many obstacles are raised to sound moral life. "Dead matter comes forth from the factory ennobled, while men there are corrupted and degraded" (*Q.A.*, No. 135).[4]

---

[4] For further illustrations, see R. J. Miller, *Forty Years After*, pp. 267–284.

Unless some success is had in the effort to remove or mitigate these vices, it will be impossible to bring about the restoration of a sound social order. For a good society it is not necessary that all men be good, but rather that the moral level be adequate to support sound institutions and wholesome conditions. Then, it would be possible to contain and, if necessary, coerce the anti-social minority which might obstruct sound economic life. Such certainly was the situation in the best period of the Middle Ages, where many men were greedy, avaricious, and selfish, but where the social order imposed upon them a pattern which conduced to the general welfare.

Virtues Needed in Modern Life. To secularism we must oppose the Christianization of society. This is something more than revival of religious life in individuals, although such also is necessary. A Christianized society is one whose institutions are so permeated by sound principles that of their very nature they tend to produce wholesome results. Thus, Christian family life would involve an economic basis which aids in virtuous living, such as a home in suitable surroundings and a living wage for the father, and the practice of piety, charity, and similar virtues by the family unit. A Christian order in labor-management relations would envision the replacing of strife by co-operation, with both groups working together to achieve sustained high production and employment, in an atmosphere of mutual respect and recognition of rights and of human dignity. Christian economic society would carry further this pattern of co-operation, with great emphasis upon protecting and extending individual freedom, not only through economic security, but through the principle of subsidiarity (protecting the autonomy of lesser groups) and widespread diffusion of ownership of productive wealth.

We might well apply here the Jocist techniques, with their emphasis upon the total Christianization of one's environment. Personal virtue is good, but it is not enough. Salvation is not merely a matter of protecting one's own interests. The Christian is apostolic. He seeks to determine the influences in daily life which are adverse to Christian living and strives to work, both individually and in an organized manner, to replace them with sound institutions. The Jocist ideal is opposed to "spiritual selfishness," if we may use this phrase to describe those who advocate withdrawal from this evil world and concentration upon personal perfection. Rather we must obey the law of Christian love and bring to others the good tidings which we have had the happiness to receive.

The virtues of social justice and social charity, discussed in Chapter IV, certainly call for the attempt to infuse Christian ideals into the institutions of social life. As individuals we must be just and kindly, but we must also make the guiding principles of labor unions, employer associations, farmer groups, professions, and the government itself reflect these great virtues. Spiritual isolationism was condemned by the present Holy Father, as well as the philosophy of minimism, which holds that Catholics should concentrate on personal virtue and not try to bring sound influences into public affairs. Catholic Action is an *apostolate* of the laity whereby each social group tries to bring Christian principles into its own environment. Workers should influence other workers, employers raise the standards of their fellows, and farmers bring life-giving ideals to other farmers.

This does not mean that the work of the apostolate would sanction a neglect of personal virtue. On the contrary, the apostle finds that his influence upon others is dependent upon his own perfection. First, there is the need for prayer. Unless God builds a house, they labor in vain who work at it. Its foundation is on sand. The Christian apostle must ask the aid of God's grace in his work. But even prayer can be social. Not only is our worship corporate as well as individual, but Pope Pius endorses retreats for special economic groups, such as workers. It would indeed be a sound policy to have Catholic organizations among diverse social groups, not merely for the purpose of studying Christian principles in their fields, but also for common prayer and worship.

The Christian apostle should not neglect the virtue of penance. The sins of the world are a grave derogation of God's majesty. Penance, sacrifice, and austerity are commanded as reparation for sin both in the Old and New Testaments. The cardinal doctrine of the Redemption emphasizes the worth of vicarious atonement. Accordingly, we should do penance for personal sin, but also for those who do not repent of their evil. If some in the modern world have forgotten the fact that God is a supreme judge, as well as a loving father, then it is our duty to make reparation for the wrongs done and the ingratitude manifested by others.

Finally, the popes emphasize the virtue of detachment from earthly things. This is the opposite of greed and avarice. Christian detachment is a freedom from the strong ties to wealth and worldly goods. It is a matter of proper perspective, whereby these things are considered, not as goods to be sought for their own sake, but in relation to spiritual and cultural goals in life. Accordingly, Christian detachment does not preclude a reasonable concern for earning one's living. It could even permit the seeking of wealth — although this would be a lesser ideal than voluntary poverty. In such cases, wealth should be sought as a means to some nobler end, not as an all-sufficient goal in itself. It is clear that if men had a detached attitude toward worldly goods, there would be less selfishness, fewer quarrels and dissensions, and more harmony and co-operation in economic life. On the other hand, present-day insecurity is in itself an enemy to the spirit of detachment, since it forces men to worry over earthly things. Hence detachment would not only aid in improving economic life, but a sounder organization of economic affairs would promote detachment in the case of many persons.

In all these matters the Church can aid by her purely religious functions, as compared with her teaching on the moral law. By prayer, sacrament, and organized religious life, she can bring to many the inspiration to lead better lives. It is only natural then that the Church can rightly be considered a powerful force leading toward a better social order. The results of such leadership will be achieved more fruitfully as clergy and laity alike, in their respective positions, devote their energies to bringing about a better world.

The Work of the Clergy. In the task of spiritual and social reform, it is only natural that the clergy should have an important part. As priests consecrated to lifelong service of God as their exclusive master, they are ministers of the sacraments, teachers both by example and precept of the law of God, and shepherds of the flock of Christ's faithful. There is little need here to elaborate upon the spiritual mission of the priesthood. For this, priests are trained for long years in the seminary. In the austere ritual of the Pontifical, as they received Holy Orders, they have been given grave admonitions to offer themselves to a life of unremitting service, both of God and of the people committed to their care. Each year, in their annual retreat, they renew the spirit of dedication. Daily, at the altar, in offering up the sacrifice of the Mass, they revive their own spirit of sacrifice. Likewise, each day they devote an hour or more to prayer, especially in the recitation of the Divine Office. For this they are prepared both by formal training and the generous instincts of their heart.

They are also prepared to teach the faithful and the world in matters spiritual. Over the years they have studied the life-giving truths of Holy Writ. They know in detail the dogmatic and moral teachings of the Church and its Canon Law. But when it comes to teaching refined moral principles in regard to the social problem, the situation is extremely uneven. On the one hand, we in the United States can be proud of the progress made since Monsignor Ryan, Bishop Haas, and Father McGowan, with a few associates, entered upon their lonely task of pioneering. The list of labor-school directors, given at the end of *Catholic Social Action,* is in itself impressive. A distinguished and large number of priests have received formal university training in the social field. Nearly a thousand have gotten concentrated instruction in priests' schools and the Institute of Catholic Social Studies. Many seminaries give courses on social problems and others have informal study groups and clubs.

But on the other hand, there are important omissions. Most seminaries do not have the intensive training in social problems called for in *Quadragesimo Anno* and other papal instructions. There are large industrial dioceses where practically no work is done on socioeconomic problems. The bulk of the clergy has done only casual reading on the subject. There are too few authorities in the field apart from schools and universities. Because many priests are not too familiar with the subject, they naturally hesitate to face such difficult problems. In a few unfortunate cases, there are priests who do speak freely on social questions, but form their attitudes from the secular press, and often in its most biased aspects, thus giving forth opinions which are not only uninspired by Catholic social principles, but at times contrary to these teachings.

The really tragic fact, however, is the lack of a sense of urgency and imperativeness in regard to the social problem. No conscientious reader could read all the papal messages collected in this volume and fail to realize that the Holy See has stressed these questions as being of the highest importance. For sixty unbroken years the Voice of Peter has instructed, urged, pleaded, and encouraged Catholics to dedicate themselves to the work of social reform. To deal only with recent statements, Pope Pius XI, in 1937, urged that the social question be considered the *first and most important* of parochial duties in addition to meeting the normal needs of the faithful (*A.C.,* No. 62). The present Holy Father has repeatedly inveighed against the timorous, the indifferent, the "isolationists," those who are "minimists," and all who abstain from their duties in this hour of world crisis. In other fields, where Christian ideals are threatened, it is heartening to see the organization and discipline which produces remarkable results. American Catholics have done well in encouraging public decency in motion pictures, radio, and magazines; in maintaining a magnificent school system; in protecting the home and the family from divorce and birth control; in making special collections for relief in Europe; and in developing highly complex and efficient social welfare services.

The record of Catholic response to recognized need would lead to optimism in regard to the social problem. In other fields, such

as education, charities, and Canon Law, progress has been substantial. From a slow beginning we moved rapidly to a situation
in which most dioceses have well-trained staffs to meet the problems connected with schools, welfare activities, and the canonical
aspects of marriage. Social action may well be in the preliminary
stage today. A few full-time social action directors are doing
splendid pioneer work. Many more priests and laymen are connected with labor schools, with the Jesuits outstanding among
the religious orders. Diocesan activities and seminary training
vary sharply in both quality and quantity. While few of our
best-known preachers have concentrated on the social question,
yet it has been discussed in various pulpits and on the radio.
General Catholic periodicals, such as *America, Commonweal,* the
Sign, and the *Catholic Mind,* treat social problems with considerable insight. Our schools, universities, and learned societies are
giving increasing attention to the question of economic life. At
the same time, much remains to be done before social action here
corresponds to the urgent pleadings of the popes.

The reasons for this condition are obvious and understandable.
It goes without saying that we are not in the slightest way in-
different to the solemn teachings and urgings of the Holy See.
On the contrary, our religious devotion is exemplary. While
Americans, as a nation, are too prone to boasting, the Church
in the United States might be permitted, in the spirit of St.
Paul, to proclaim its faithfulness to the Vicar of Christ, successor
to St. Peter, the rock upon which the Saviour built His Church.
The difficulty, rather, is inherent both in the complexity of the
social problem and our timidity as a minority group, often but
a few generations removed from the immigrant status. Thus,
we have the spectacle of many non-Catholics praising the wisdom
of Catholic social teaching, while we ourselves keep our light
under a bushel. Moreover, even the ethical aspects of the social
problem are difficult and involved, and their concrete application
requires care and study. Many priests are not trained in these
problems because they did not learn them in the seminary and
did not have the time and opportunity for later study. Some

seminaries, in turn, have failed because their professors of moral and pastoral theology have not had the training to speak on the subjects with assurance and conviction. The result is that thousands of priests, who have both interest and good will, are reluctant to venture into so difficult a field.

Hence the immediate task before us is a program of education, as has been outlined in more detail in *Catholic Social Action*. Where seminaries are not offering "an intensive study of the social question" (*Q.A.*, No. 142), it is imperative that these courses be given, even if it means further training for their professors. It would not be beneath the dignity of a Doctor of Sacred Theology to spend a summer at the Institute of Catholic Social Studies. Priests, both diocesan and religious, who have not received social training could profit by intensive courses or by study clubs. The excellent practice of having for priests diocesan or regional schools, of a few weeks' duration, might well be extended. Moreover, it would be desirable for industrial dioceses to have a university trained specialist in the social field, as many already have in the fields of education, social welfare, and Canon Law.

Once the clergy is trained, it will be possible to proceed faster with the work of Catholic Action as outlined in papal documents. The popes envision the primary duty of the clergy in the social field as one of teaching. They are to teach the laity in all walks of life and inspire them to be apostles to their fellows in their respective occupations and professions. Workers could be taught in labor schools. Employers can be reached in study clubs and forums. The use of lectures, forums, radio and television programs, Confraternity study clubs, the secular and Catholic press, and like adult education devices has already been explained in *Catholic Social Action*. The ambitious and laudable program for formal education in the schools, so brilliantly developed by the Commission on American Citizenship, can be further put into practice so that it will bear abundant fruit. Then we can effectively preach our message of social justice and social charity, co-operation in place of division and hostility, and efficient organization of economic life to promote the common good.

All this does not imply that the work of the clergy need of necessity stop with a program of education. Priests who specialize in the social field will naturally gravitate to other activities, such as mediation and arbitration in labor disputes. They might, with due caution, advocate views on social legislation. Pope Pius XI mentioned with approval this latter activity (*Q.A.*, No. 27), although special conditions here make it less advisable as a general practice than would be the case in Europe. American priests have served on state labor boards and one, who is presently a bishop, headed the federal Fair Employment Practices Commission. The precautions needed for such specialized work, and the virtues emphasized in *Quadragesimo Anno* for priests working in this field, are explained at more length in *Catholic Social Action* and need not be repeated here.

A final way of teaching is through example and close contact with the faithful, especially the workers (*A.C.*, No. 63). The virtues discussed earlier are best taught by the example of our own lives. This example is particularly important, as noted by Pope Pius XI in the passage cited, when the priest by his office administers temporal property. In such activities we should be outstanding in our practice of social justice and social charity.

The Work of the Laity. The work of the laity is commonly expressed in the social encyclicals by the phrase "Catholic Action." This phrase is frequently used in the United States, but it often deviates from the technical meaning used by the popes. One might well distinguish between action by Catholics, Catholic action, and Catholic Action. The first might refer to any kind of activity by Catholics acting as such. It could range from mass meetings or parades to fund-raising drives for churches and charities. The second could include more specifically religious and apostolic work by Catholics, whether organized or unorganized. The Christopher movement might well be placed in this category along with the Legion of Decency. Catholic Action, in turn, has been defined as "the participation of the laity in the apostolate of the Church's hierarchy."[5] It is usually an organized body of the laity, mandated by the bishop to do apostolic work under the guidance of the hierarchy. One of the primary forms of this apostolate, as noted in the excerpts given at the head of this chapter, is in the field of Christian social reconstruction. Furthermore, these same documents envision specialized forms of Catholic Action, in accord with diverse social needs. Workers, employers, farmers, professional men, and young people should be imbued with the spirit of Christ, so that they may work in their own environment in spreading the message of justice and charity.

Catholic Action for the social apostolate, officially and formally organized, is rare in the United States. We have a strong Catholic labor school movement. The Association of Catholic Trade Unionists is doing good work in several dioceses. There is some activity with employers and professional groups. With doctors, lawyers, and nurses, however, most of the emphasis is upon the special ethical problems proper to their fields rather than upon their participation in socioeconomic reconstruction. In many parts of the country, there are small but vigorous organizations of Young Christian Workers and like groups influencing students and adult workers. It is particularly encouraging to note the widespread interest among seminarians in these movements and their national study weeks held each summer. Of course, the National Catholic Rural Life Conference and the Department of Social Action, National Catholic Welfare Conference, have promoted social action in their respective fields. The former group has been successful in organizing diocesan branches, but such activity is not part of the function of the Department of Social Action.

Perhaps the best way to evaluate American efforts for a Catholic lay social apostolate would be to compare our activities with the program given in the excerpts from papal writings. The popes envision organized groups of laity in every walk of

<hr>

[5] Pope Pius XI, *Discourse to the Catholic Associations of Rome*, April 19, 1931. A reading list on this subject is given in *Catholic Social Action*, pp. 215–216.

life, intensely prepared in the social teaching of the Church, zealously spreading these ideals by the use of every modern device for disseminating information, influencing others through personal contact and the power of example, and thus contributing strongly to the restoration of all things in Christ. By contrast, if we are honest in evaluating our own efforts, we must admit that the bulk of the Catholic laity hardly knows that the Church has a social teaching. Most of our organizations, with a few heroic exceptions, have not entered into these problems to any appreciable degree. An immense task of study, formation, and inspiration lies before us.

One of the more recent attempts at inspiring a lay apostolate, the Christopher movement, has included social questions in its field of endeavor. Undoubtedly it is accomplishing much good through individuals who begin to realize their mission of bringing Christ to others. But such activities are at best but a partial solution to the problem before us. What is needed above all is *organized* activity. As Pope Pius XI noted in his encyclical *On Atheistic Communism,* "in addition to this individual apostolate which, however useful and efficacious, often goes unheralded, Catholic Action must organize propaganda on a large scale to disseminate knowledge of the fundamental principles on which, according to the pontifical documents, a Christian social order must build" (No. 66). It is precisely in this field of organized social education and social action that we have done least. This is not to disparage the excellent work now done in many dioceses, but merely to note the fact that achievements vary sharply from place to place and, in their totality, fall short of our needs.

Undoubtedly the uneven work of lay organization in the social apostolate reflects the spotty nature of the training received by the clergy. Where priests have become proficient in this field, whether by formal training or self-education, they have been able to accomplish much in the way of social education and social action. The progress in obtaining curricula and textbooks for social teaching in the schools has meant much in the case of our youth. Unquestionably the Catholic laity of tomorrow will be far better informed in regard to Catholic social teaching than is the case at present. With equal advances in the formal training of the clergy, one can reasonably expect a flowering of the social apostolate. This will be of inestimable benefit to our nation, insofar as it promotes peace and co-operation in the fields of social life.

A concluding word might be said of the spreading of Catholic ideals among non-Catholics. This point was discussed in several parts of *Catholic Social Action,* along with other aspects of the social apostolate of the laity. Here we might note the repeated pleas by recent pontiffs for co-operation on the part of those who do not accept our religious belief. They ask believers in God, and even men of good will who may not have formally expressed their faith, to join hands in saving Christian civilization. Certainly, the field of social action is eminently suitable for such joint endeavor. In the first place, the problems are common to all. We all suffer equally from the threats of world communism and domestic economic crises. Secondly, the principles of solution are universally acceptable. While we receive our social teaching from nearly two thousand years of Catholic tradition and accept the authoritative interpretation of moral principles by the Supreme Pontiff, nevertheless the actual content of our social ethic should be acceptable to any believer in God, or even to men who accept the dignity of man, without consciously basing it upon faith in the Almighty.

In the main, the problem of securing co-operation involves questions of language and technique. The average American, even though he is a Catholic, is not always able to understand fully the language of the social encyclicals and papal addresses. They are often expressed in the terminology of ethics or moral theology. It is not enough to translate official documents into English. There must be a second effort, in popular writings, to embody these ideas in language which is currently used by businessmen, labor leaders, and scholars in the field of social science. A theologian might understand the concept of man's solidarity based on the nature, origin, and destiny of all men.

But to the average worker, it would be better to say that we are all brothers under God.

If the ideas contained in Catholic social teaching were expressed in words commonly used by various occupational and professional groups, they would be widely accepted for their evident truth. Men have found by experience that extreme solutions are dangerous. They have seen the bankruptcy of both individualism and all forms of statism and are ready for a social order based on the dignity of man and the proper organization of society. This is not to imply, in blind optimism, that the truth has but to be explained properly to be accepted and put into practice. Selfishness, greed, pride, and cruelty still reign in many hearts. But there are enough men, like Nicodemus, who are seeking the truth, perhaps even timorously and furtively, but nonetheless looking for the light. It is our duty to make strong efforts to bring to them the treasures conferred upon us by the divine teaching of our Saviour.

Hence the challenge to the laity engaged in Catholic Action is both to study and to act. Programs of study were noted at length in *Catholic Social Action,* as well as methods for carrying these principles into the world of business. It is not enough to have Catholic groups for the personal sanctification of the faithful. This is good, but it is incomplete. The Catholic today is called to be an apostle, especially in the social field. The faithful have an integral and important part in the task of restoring all things in Christ.

Past Achievements. A considerable portion of *Quadragesimo Anno* is devoted to achievements since *Rerum Novarum.* This latter document in turn refers to the excellent work of the social Catholics of the nineteenth century. Here indeed is a glorious story of thought and action whose history is still to be written in definitive form. The industrial revolution had scarcely begun to manifest the sordid abuses which constituted the social question when scholars in the Church commenced a program of countering these evils. At the very beginning of the nineteenth century, two German scholars, Adam Mueller and Franz von

Baader, opposed individualism and came out for a more organic conception of social life. A few decades later, in France, there was strong agitation for social and political reform, with the names of Vicomte de Villeneuve-Bargement and Vicomte de Melun outstanding. Their ideas of social legislation and social security were remarkably advanced since much of their program was not realized widely until the twentieth century. When the socialist program became a subject of broad discussion after the middle of the nineteenth century, Bishop Wilhelm Emmanuel von Ketteler filled brilliantly the dual role of antagonist of socialism and protagonist of the rights of workers. Many of his ideas were put into practice through the Catholic Center Party and the programs of Canon Moufang, of Mainz. Later, Father Heinrich Pesch developed a sound and coherent social philosophy based on Christian principles.

In France, after 1871, the cause was taken up by two noblemen who were army officers in the war with Germany. Count Albert de Mun and Count René de La Tour du Pin were so impressed by the horrors of the Paris Commune that they began a crusade of social counterrevolution. De Mun ran for parliament and introduced legislation calling for extensive social reform. Among French employers, Jacques Joseph Harmel and his son Léon put religious principles into practice in their textile mills. It was widely held that *Rerum Novarum* was the crowning point and vindication of a century of social Catholicism.

French social Catholicism continued into the twentieth century, with the *Action Populaire* and the *Semaines Sociales* promoting progress in thought and application of principles. The work likewise continued in Germany until the time of Hitler, and strong movements grew in Belgium, Switzerland, and Holland. Progress in the English-speaking world was slower, with such names as Cardinal Gibbons and Cardinal Manning noted for the defense of labor. Later English leaders included Monsignor Henry Parkinson and Father Charles Plater. The Catholic Social Guild of Oxford produced much notable literature. Outstanding in twentieth-century America were Monsignor John A. Ryan and his many followers. Nevertheless, generally speaking, the growth of social Catholicism was slower in English-speaking lands than on the continent of Europe.

The publication of *Quadragesimo Anno* gave a considerable stimulus to Catholic social thought in the United States. This document coincided with our greatest depression and appeared shortly before the most extensive program of social reform ever undertaken in this country. Instead of a small group centered about Monsignor Ryan and the Department of Social Action, National Catholic Welfare Conference, more and more Catholic scholars and social action leaders entered the field. Great strides were made in the matter of labor education. An ambitious program of general social education was initiated by the Commission on American Citizenship at the Catholic University. Many universities and colleges developed strong staffs in the field of social studies and such training in seminaries became more common.[6]

In the light of these rich developments, it is understandable that Pope Pius XI should have devoted such an important part of *Quadragesimo Anno* to a summary of achievements in the intervening forty years since *Rerum Novarum*. It is rare that one can say precisely that secular courses of action were influenced by religious ideas, although several modern governments have acted explicitly upon the social principles of the popes. Generally speaking, the influence of ideas is often intangible but great.[7] Ideas affect men and movements and thus are embodied into concrete programs of action. The parallel between the teaching and the subsequent action strongly suggests influence. In Catholic countries, such as France, it is easier to trace connections, but even there, many crosscurrents exist. The govern-

---

[6] The work of social Catholicism is described in P. T. Moon, *The Labor Problem and the Social Catholic Movement in France* (New York: Macmillan, 1926); G. T. McEntee, *The Social Catholic Movement in Great Britain* (New York: Macmillan, 1927); H. Somerville, *The Catholic Social Movement* (London: Burns, Oates, 1933); and R. Kothen, *La Pensée et l'action sociales de Catholiques, 1789–1944* (Louvain: Warny, 1945). Further references are given in J. F. Cronin, *Catholic Social Action*, pp. 214–215.

[7] See R. M. Weaver, *Ideas Have Consequences* (Chicago: Univ. of Chicago Press, 1948).

ments of Ireland, Portugal, and Belgium have openly borrowed from the encyclicals. But even international documents, such as the formulation of rights proclaimed in the treaty of Versailles and the Universal Declaration of Human Rights, often follow closely ideas proposed by the popes. "The influence of ideas in the realm of facts, though invisible and not easily measured, is surely of predominant importance" (*A.C.*, No. 37). This progress in man's thinking should be an encouragement, when the task ahead seems great, and a stimulus to stronger efforts in the field of social education and action.[8]

READINGS*

J. Messner, *Social Ethics*, pp. 262–280.
J. F. Cronin, *Catholic Social Action*.
R. J. Miller, *Forty Years After*, pp. 267–299.
E. Cahill, *The Framework of a Christian State*, Chap. 15.
J. A. Ryan, *Social Doctrine in Action*.
J. Husslein, *The Christian Social Manifesto*, Chaps. 20, 31–33.
O. von Nell-Breuning, *Christian Social Reorganization*, Chap. 18.
G. C. Rutten, *La doctrine social de l'Église*, Chap. 4.

---

[8] For developments in Catholic social thought, see the valuable work by Dr. M. J. Williams, *Catholic Social Thought* (New York: Ronald, 1950), Chapter 9. The author is not a Catholic.

* For further readings, consult Lists Nos. 1 and 13 in the Appendix.

PART III

AMERICAN CATHOLIC SOCIAL THOUGHT

Chapter XV. AUTHORITATIVE AND INFLUENTIAL INTERPRETATIONS

The preceding two parts were based primarily upon papal teaching in the fields of social ethics and morality, as interpreted and applied to American conditions by the present author. Every effort was made to present both a faithful interpretation of papal encyclicals and addresses and a clear distinction between moral truth and an author's views on the application of such truth to certain conditions of time and place. In this section, the emphasis will shift from direct interpretation of papal teaching to a presentation and, where this is fitting, an evaluation of schools of social thought among American Catholics.

Trends in social thinking among American Catholics vary considerably in importance and influence. On the one hand, we have the formal teaching of the bishops, who share with the pope the divine mission of teaching the faith. At the other extreme, there are views which represent the economic or social predilections of certain authors, particularly the monetary faddists, with only a remote connection with Catholic religious and ethical teaching. Between these extremes are schools which represent conscientious efforts to apply the social teaching of the Church to conditions here. Such schools deserve separate mention and treatment, insofar as they may emphasize as primary certain aspects of our social ethic or stress some type of economic reform as of predominating importance.

The present chapter treats of interpretations which are called authoritative and influential. Here the use of the term "authoritative" is, to use the language of philosophy, at least analogous if not equivocal. On the one hand, the official teaching of the bishops is authoritative in the strict sense of the term. They speak for the Church, under the supreme authority of the Holy See. By contrast, the inclusion of selected Catholic University dissertations involves a different kind of authority: the authority of scholarship rather than the power given to the bishops by divine commission to go forth and teach all nations. Statements by the bishops' representatives in the National Catholic Welfare Conference embody varying degrees of authority. These may range from official statements of the Department of Social Action, approved by one or more of the bishops, to personal views of the staff members. As a general rule, any book or article by a staff member of the Department represents the personal view of the author rather than an official stand by the N.C.W.C. or any of the bishops. It is quite possible that the several staff members may have different opinions on the application of Catholic social principles to American life, and that these opinions do not of necessity have the support of the bishops. Accordingly, this chapter summarizes views in order of decreasing authority, considered from the viewpoint of official Church teaching.

STATEMENTS BY THE AMERICAN HIERARCHY

From the beginnings of the Catholic Church in America, various bishops have set forth their views in sermons, pastoral letters, and other media. It would be beyond the scope of this book to attempt to summarize such positions. What is given here is a brief digest of major documents issued since 1919 and signed by a group of representative bishops. These views are authoritative, not in the formal sense of a Church council which can under the proper conditions enact binding legislation, but in the sense that they represent a careful exercise of the teaching mission committed to the bishops.

Social Reconstruction. On February 12, 1919, Bishops Muldoon, Schrembs, Hayes, and Russell, acting as the Administrative Committee of the National Catholic War Council, issued a statement on Social Reconstruction. This document charted a program for social reconstruction in the wake of World War I. It noted several other plans for a better social order, issued by the American Federation of Labor, a group of British Quaker employers, the National Chamber of Commerce in the United States, and the British Interdenominational Conference of Social Service Unions. After analyzing these proposals, the bishops announced their own objective. They did not attempt a comprehensive scheme for national reconstruction, since they judged that such an effort would be premature in the light of current American attitudes. Rather they drew attention to reforms considered desirable at the time, with a few general principles which would serve as guides to more distant developments.

The first and most immediate problem considered was the rehabilitation of those affected by the war, particularly men in the armed services and women in industry. The document advocated the retention of the United States Employment Service to alleviate problems connected with re-employment and unemployment. It further suggested that women be replaced by men in operations considered unsuitable for the weaker sex, although necessarily filled by them during the war. Strong tribute was paid to the National War Labor Board and its continuance in a suitable peacetime form was advocated. It was held that wage rates paid during the war should be continued in the peace period, in the effort to raise all workers to the level of a living wage or higher. "The large demand for goods which is created and maintained by high rates of wages and high purchasing power by the masses is the surest guarantee of a continuous and general operation of industrial establishments." This passage, as is evident, foreshadowed an attitude which was to become common during the 1930's and thereafter.

The war efforts to remedy unsuitable housing conditions should stimulate peacetime private endeavors along the same line. Moreover, attempts should be made to reduce the cost of living. One device for achieving this would be the promotion of co-operative stores, thereby reducing the uneconomic toll paid to a large group of middlemen. Co-operatives would, moreover, train their members to economic self-government and relieve the political state of excessive responsibility. In addition, minimum-wage laws should be enacted by the several states, at rates suitable for the decent maintenance of a family, in the case of male adults, and adequate for the proper support of women workers. Until this level is reached, the worker should be protected by comprehensive social insurance, dealing with illness, invalidity, unemployment, and old age. These funds should generally be paid by industry, on the grounds that industry should give complete support to those who work for it. Low-cost municipal medical clinics and the practice of group medicine should make such care available to low- and middle-income groups. Beyond this, it is desirable that shop committees be established to give labor some share in industrial management. This would improve labor-management relations and increase productivity. Furthermore, universal vocational training would be a great service to workers. Finally, state laws and such federal measures as are constitutional should be enacted to abolish the continuous employment of children in industry before the age of sixteen years. Such are the immediate and practicable reforms advocated for the years of reconstruction.

For the long range, three major problems remain to be faced: inefficiency and waste in production and distribution, insufficient incomes for most wage earners, and excessive incomes for the privileged few. The reforms outlined above would meet many of these evils, but more is needed. Workers must rise from the level of mere wage earners and become owners, at least in part, of the instruments of production. Co-operative productive societies and copartnership arrangements can do much in this regard. Moreover, workers must receive greater income. In addition, the government should prevent or regulate monopolies and provide graduated income, excess profits, and inheritance taxes. Finally, a new spirit of justice and charity must replace the attitudes of greed and self-serving.[1]

---

[1] *Bishops' Program of Social Reconstruction* (Washington: National Catholic Welfare Conference).

This far-reaching and prophetic program, as is evident, was largely put into practice in the intervening years. Some of the basic problems remain, however, as has been noted throughout the present text. In particular, concentration of productive wealth and economic power has grown, while more and more obstacles have been raised to diffused ownership of productive wealth. Some gains are to be recorded in the granting of labor a greater say in economic matters affecting the worker's interests, but a spirit of complete co-operation and partnership is not yet attained.

Bishops' Pastoral Letter. In the same year, on September 26, a pastoral letter was issued by the entire American hierarchy and signed in their name by James Cardinal Gibbons. The letter notes men's obligations in justice and charity and applies these principles to industrial relations. Justice has been violated in this field, as evinced by the many postwar strikes. But more than the rights of capital and labor are involved in such disputes; there is a public interest as well, which is of pre-eminent nature. In this public interest, it is necessary to cure industrial strife by removing its causes. Co-operation must replace class conflict, a co-operation based on recognition of the moral value and the basic dignity of man. Friendliness should temper the application of justice. Among the rights of labor is the right to form unions, but there is a correlative duty of observing contracts and agreements. Where disputes cannot be settled by direct negotiation, they should be submitted to arbitration. Even though this may not bring about perfect justice, it is better than deciding issues by the test of economic force.

Labor's right to a living wage should be implemented in practice. Capital in turn has the right to expect a fair day's work for a fair day's pay "and the right to returns which will be sufficient to stimulate thrift, initiative, enterprise, and all those directive and productive energies which promote social welfare." An especial need is for associations which will draw capital and labor more closely together. Special interest groups, such as labor unions or trade associations, should be supplemented by joint-interest groups. Workers would then have a sense of participation

in their industry, employers would enjoy the fruits of co-operation, and consumers would be benefited by larger and steadier
production. In addition, there should be efforts to make as many
wage earners as possible property owners, particularly as regards
productive property.[2]

An interesting point in this document is the foreshadowing
of ideas so strongly stressed by Pope Pius XI and the present
Holy Father. This is particularly true of the proposals noted in
Chapter VII of this book. The Pastoral Letter emphasizes the
need for common-interest groups, whereas the Bishops' Program
lays more stress upon productive societies. The latter suggestion
reflects back to the ideas of Bishop von Ketteler, whereas the
former anticipates *Quadragesimo Anno* and the many statements of Pope Pius XII. The insistence upon wider ownership of
productive property, while expressing the ideas of Pope Leo XIII,
is likewise anticipatory of the great stress laid upon this point in
recent papal pronouncements. On the other hand, the suggestion
for compulsory arbitration of labor disputes is more advanced than
recent statements by American bishops. Many authorities today
are reluctant to support such a method of solving industrial
disputes, in spite of its obvious attractiveness. It is feared that,
granted the superiority of justice to economic force in settling
issues, arbitration of interests would involve far-reaching outside
interference with industry and labor. Hence, more recent statements have stressed fact-finding and the influence of public
opinion as the more general method for seeing that justice is
done.

Statement on Present Crisis. The next major statement was
issued on April 26, 1933, in the midst of our greatest depression.
It was signed by the archbishops and bishops of the Administrative Committee, National Catholic Welfare Conference. This
document quotes freely from the encyclicals *Quadragesimo Anno*
and *Caritate Christi Compulsi,* noting that materialism, greed, and
selfish individualism led to the existing crisis. Great stress is laid

---

[2] *Pastoral Letter, September, 1919* (Washington: National Catholic Welfare Conference,
1920), pp. 57–63.

upon the concentration of economic power and the denial of basic human rights, leading to great disparity in wealth and income. Both individualism and communism are condemned. Economic nationalism, carried to extremes, may be profoundly immoral. Our farm policy has been unsound, with agriculture crushed under heavy burdens. But the great curse of the day is unemployment, caused to a large degree by concentration of economic power and the seeking of excessive profits.

The remedies for these evils are both spiritual and economic. Christian principles should be restored in economic life. Studies are needed to apply moral truths in the field of everyday action. Workers have a right to organize and to secure a living wage. The worker's right to an equitable share in the profits should be given due consideration. Workers should rise to a real share of ownership, and their attitude toward employers should be one of co-operation and friendliness. An especial need is the application of moral principles to large corporations and the prevention of abuses in such cases. But we should not depend upon government to bring about all reforms. Rather we should organize self-governing economic groups to share the burden of social control. Taxation should be just and not excessively burdensome to industry or individuals. Excessive costs of government are draining national wealth without securing corresponding benefits.

In bringing about social reform, Catholic Action and the training of Catholic lay leadership should have an important part. One important reform movement is the promoting of a trend back to the land. Without losing the benefits of technical progress, we should give men the greater independence which comes from land ownership. But our greatest contribution is our Christian heritage, which should appeal to those suffering under the great hardships of the day. Prayer should be our first source of strength in meeting this unique crisis.[3]

A special feature of this statement is the emphasis upon a greater interest in the land as contrasted to city living. While rural

[3] *A Statement on the Present Crisis* (Washington: National Catholic Welfare Conference, 1933).

America is not usually Catholic, yet it is held that our culture can contribute much to those who live on farms. Indeed, living on the land is especially helpful to the family, since it gives children a wholesome environment.

The phrase in the statement concerning a worker's right to an equitable share in the profits might not be universally accepted today. The phrase is not elaborated or explained, to indicate the precise nature of the right asserted. We might hold that, where profits are excessive and a living wage is not paid, the worker could assert in strict justice his right to a wage. But this is not a right to profits as such. Pope Pius XII, in his address of May 7, 1949, noted that the virtue of distributive justice does not apply to private concerns in this matter. Hence it cannot be argued that this claim holds in distributive justice. It might, however, be held that in social justice, such a distribution might, under certain conditions, promote the common good. But this would not give the worker any general and unqualified right to participate in profits. It would apply only in such cases where an institution of this nature would promote the general welfare. Of course, Pope Pius XI urged profit-sharing as a suitable modification of the wage contract, but he did not characterize such an institution as a right.

The Church and Social Order. In 1940, on February 7, the Administrative Board of the National Catholic Welfare Conference issued the statement "The Church and Social Order." This was an ambitious and detailed restating of Catholic social principles, with some general applications to American conditions. The document notes the right and duty of the Church to pronounce on moral problems in the economic sphere, while avoiding such questions as are purely technical. In this connection, the study applies the doctrine of stewardship to property and asserts the dignity of human labor. Because human beings are involved in economic matters, and their actions are morally right or wrong, the Church can properly pass judgment upon such conduct.

In a more detailed treatment of ownership, the outlines of *Quadragesimo Anno* are followed. The social as well as the individual aspect of property rights is to be stressed. In this regard, two great dangers should be faced: the concentration of the ownership and control of wealth, and the fact that control is diluted through the anonymity of the corporation. Civil government should act, in view of these dangers, to see that property truly serves the common good.

When property is used to employ the labor of others, new issues arise. There is the danger of forgetting the personal nature of labor, and also the possibility of undue concentration of income in the hands of property owners. A fairer distribution of income would consider the claims of labor, but labor should not seek an excessive amount, nor should it indulge in violence in pressing its claims. Here again, the common good must be considered above all.

The lack of fair distribution of wealth and income has led to insecurity in modern society. Industry should pay, not merely a living wage, but a saving wage, supplemented when necessary by social insurance. It should take its proper part in efforts designed to foster security. Most important of these is the achievement of economic balance in wages and prices, so that depressions may be cut off at their source. If this can be done with the aid of labor, by modifying the wage contract with some form of partnership or profit-sharing, so much the better. But, at any rate, labor's right to a living wage is the first claim upon industry, prior to any claim by the owners to profits. A saving wage constitutes an essential part of the definition of a living wage, so that the wage earner can make provision for the future.

The securing of decent wages is a matter of economic organization and of proper legislation. Wages and prices must keep their proper balance, since an excess in either direction can cause unemployment. Price levels should be kept reasonably stable. It does little good to raise wages, if prices go up also. Where possible, wage increases should come from excessive profits. But, whatever means be used, it must be remembered that workers should have sufficient income for mass consumption, or our economic system will founder.

The really basic change needed, however, is the establishment of a sound social order, which would be a middle way between individualism and collectivism. This is the system described earlier in Chapter VII. Such a co-operative approach, however, presupposes a reform of morals and a profound renewal of the Christian spirit. Instead of selfishness, there must be concern for the common good. In such a society, the civil state would be neither the disinterested bystander of *laissez faire* nor the absolute power of a collectivist society, but a sovereign promoting the general welfare without being bound to interfere minutely in matters which could be handled by lesser groups. This can be achieved if the ideas of class conflict and inherent hostility between workers and owners, and between various competitors, are replaced by the concept of common interests and mutual concerns. This would be carrying out the Gospel idea of brotherhood. It would be a concrete manifestation of the spiritual reform which must be at the heart of social reform.[4]

POSITION OF THE SOCIAL ACTION DEPARTMENT

The position taken by the American bishops in the several statements outlined above naturally was the guiding rule used by the Department of Social Action, in the National Catholic Welfare Conference. Since this agency is under the direct control of the bishops, it is only to be expected that its statements and programs would follow closely the official pronouncements of the hierarchy. Nevertheless, there are several reasons for a separate consideration of the Department's position. One derives from its title: Social Action. It is the work of the Department to assist in putting principles into practice. Its action programs, while inspired by the teachings of the popes and bishops, are nonetheless

---

[4] *The Church and Social Order* (Washington: National Catholic Welfare Conference, 1940).

distinct from general statements. Again, the Department or its members pass judgment in current socioeconomic issues. Such a task involves the application of principles and naturally is not so authoritative as the general truths enunciated by competent authorities. Since, however, such application is often influential, it deserves mention in a study of Catholic social principles.

Social Education. One of the characteristic functions of the Department has been social education in the broadest sense. This includes attempts to influence public opinion, its works of adult education, writings and publications, and assistance in formal school education. What is sought is the ambitious objective of changing the social climate in the United States, so that men will be more receptive to the ideals of the papal encyclicals.

One type of influence achieved by the Department involved the use of conferences, investigations, and joint statements together with various secular and religious groups. Thus, during the 1920's, the Department collaborated with Protestant and Jewish representatives to investigate strikes and to issue statements applying moral principles to these issues. More recently, a "Pattern of Economic Justice" was worked out in conference with such groups and issued by the several participating bodies. In this way, the principles of natural law and social ethics have been applied to the problems current at any given time.

Conferences have also been held, both separately and jointly, with groups representing economic interests. One of the most important series of meetings was held in 1941 and 1942 with all the major business, labor, farm, and religious groups in the country. These meetings were private and did not seek or receive any publicity. But a considerable amount of good will and mutual understanding was engendered. It seems likely that these private meetings paved the way for much of the co-operation among economic groups which was so manifest during World War II.

Department members participated in hundreds of meetings and conferences held in Washington and elsewhere to discuss social problems during the turbulent years 1920–1949. As a result, the staff members were able to meet and influence groups from every walk of life, with practically every economic philosophy, and seeking the most diverse aims. The ultimate results of this type of work are difficult to assess. But the force of ideas should not be underestimated. It would seem that the publicity given during the years 1948–1949 to the social teaching of the Church and the social action work of Catholic priests would indicate that the influence has been real and substantial. Certainly statements by various economic and religious groups, and even the pattern of social legislation, are closer to the Catholic ideal today than was the case in 1920.

An important part of the program of social education was directed toward Catholics. As an illustration, two major national Social Action Congresses were called in 1938 and 1939. These conferences gathered together representatives from the entire nation and explored the full field of Catholic social teaching as applied to American conditions. Undoubtedly they did much to stimulate and encourage work in this vital field. Moreover, they revealed the great growth in social studies and social action which had occurred during the 1930's.

A continuing program of adult education is handled by the Catholic Conference on Industrial Problems. This conference was organized in 1922 for the purpose of diffusing Catholic social teaching and applying it to American industrial conditions. The main technique used is a series of public meetings, normally lasting two days, in which important problems are discussed by government officials, employers, and labor leaders. In each meeting, there is usually a concluding talk applying the principles of the social encyclicals to the issue under discussion. These meetings are well publicized, so that the influence of the talks is usually much greater than would be evinced by the crowded meeting rooms. Since practically every major city in the United States has been the scene of several meetings, the Conference has undoubtedly performed a major task of social education.

A special type of social education has been schools for the clergy. There is usually a priests' meeting on the day following each Industrial Conference. In addition, formal schools lasting from one to six weeks have been held intermittently since 1938. One of the most extensive of these schools is the Institute of Catholic Social Studies, conducted at the Catholic University each summer. While this activity is not technically a function of the Department, the founder and current director of the Institute is at present a staff member of the Department. As a result of these activities, several thousand priests have been given some instruction in Catholic social principles and techniques of social action. Moreover, a monthly mimeographed publication "Social Action Notes for Priests," keeps this education current with news, quotations from notable talks, and book reviews.

Staff members have given thousands of talks, radio addresses, and lectures during the years 1920–1949. At the beginning, Dr. Ryan and Dr. Lapp covered the nation with lectures to schools, organizations, and public meetings in the attempt to acquaint American Catholics with the work of the Department. Staff members have frequently appeared on national radio programs. Several of them speak on regular lecture forums in addition to giving talks on special occasions.

The volume of writings attributed to Department members is extensive. A dozen or more books and hundreds of articles in newspapers and periodicals have appeared under their names. The Department has continuously put out pamphlets in the fields of social principles, industrial relations, and international life. One of its members writes a weekly column which is syndicated in the Catholic press. Earlier, the Department issued a weekly "News Sheet" released to the Catholic press, labor journals, and Catholic organizations in foreign countries. This service interpreted current economic events in the light of social principles.

The Department has also assisted in the work of bringing social principles into our Catholic school system. Its services and facilities were always available to the Commission on American Citizenship, at the Catholic University, which is performing the monumental task of integrating social principles into the school curriculum. Staff members have taught at the Catholic University and have assisted students doing graduate work there.

They have also participated in meetings of Catholic learned societies, particularly those engaged in social and economic studies. In these many ways, a widespread and successful program of social education has been carried out.

Applied Social Principles. The task of applying social principles to American conditions has been carried out on several levels, ranging from occasional statements on issues of the day to careful studies of a broad scope. A good example of the first type would be the comments in the earlier "News Sheet" and the more recent column, the "Yardstick." Views expressed in this manner are normally personal to the staff member enunciating them. They are not usually submitted to the bishops for study and approval. It would be difficult to catalogue stands taken in these informal statements, since this would require summarizing the history of the period. They reflect the major controversies of the hour. In the 1920's, there was much emphasis upon labor's right to organize. In the 1930's, the New Deal program was naturally discussed, with a generally favorable attitude taken. Staff members were particularly sympathetic, in a qualified manner, with the National Industrial Recovery Program, since they considered it a step in the direction of organized co-operation in economic life. During this period also the problem of unemployment was frequently treated, with emphasis upon pump-priming public works and a spreading of purchasing power. In the 1940's, such questions as price control, inflation, and labor legislation were under consideration. The staff generally favored price control measures, advocated the Employment Act of 1946, opposed compulsory arbitration of strikes, and opposed many provisions of the Labor Management Relations Act, 1946.

At times, the Department is asked by government agencies to give testimony on proposed legislation. Positions given in these circumstances are somewhat more official, since statements are usually cleared with the episcopal chairman of the Department. In general, the Department has favored the social legislation program enacted since 1933. Indeed, many of the major laws merely carry out suggestions given in the Bishops' Program of

Social Reconstruction in 1919. Such measures as those protecting labor's right to organize, establishing minimum wages, and granting social security were naturally approved as first steps toward social justice.

Many influential studies and statements were issued by the Department or its staff members. Putting aside temporarily the writings of Msgr. John A. Ryan, we might note the study issued by Father McGowan in 1933 under the title "Towards Social Justice." This brochure was an extensive commentary on *Quadragesimo Anno* and was widely used for labor schools, study groups, and similar meetings. A central theme in this study is the plan for economic life organized on a basis of co-operation rather than strife. This thought was carried over into a 1935 statement "Organized Social Justice," signed by 131 leaders of Catholic social thought. This same program has been reiterated in annual Labor Day statements put out by the Department and signed by its director.

A study of Department literature during its thirty years of existence shows a preoccupation with the problems of labor and the underprivileged. This concern was so consistent as to give some persons an impression of undue stress upon the rights of labor and underemphasis upon its duties. But attitudes must be studied in the light of contemporary history. The extent of rugged individualism and social callousness in the United States during the period 1920–1940 was so great as to call for strong countermeasures. In the 1920's, there was strongly organized opposition to labor unions. Later, many persons advocated a "hands off" policy by government in face of our greatest depression. The social reform measures of the 1930's, taken for granted today, were enacted in the face of bitter and sustained opposition. Dire consequences were predicted and often the laws themselves were flouted. Thus, the National Labor Relations Act, which merely protected labor's right to organize, was a dead letter during the period 1935–1937, until the Supreme Court upheld its constitutionality. Even then bitter strikes were necessary to force major corporations to accept labor unionism. With such powerful groups arrayed against the workers and their elementary rights, it was only natural that those preoccupied with social justice should concentrate upon defending these rights.

During this period, the papal principles of co-operation were stressed by the Department, but it was felt that one side refused to attempt a program of friendliness. Happily, today there are signs that conditions have improved. Labor's right to organize is not generally questioned. It is usually agreed that unemployment is a national problem, not an inevitable plague which must be endured but not remedied. Instances of labor-management co-operation are being highly publicized. Personnel policies emphasize the human element in production, and the American Management Association is constantly stressing the fact that workers and owners have important interests in common. It may be that the 1950's will see a new emphasis, with the Department encouraging and fostering these important trends which approximate closely the ideals of social justice and social charity.[5]

SOCIAL THEORIES OF MONSIGNOR RYAN

The one single name most frequently and justly associated with Catholic social thought in the United States is that of Msgr. John A. Ryan. Msgr. Ryan was more than a pioneer in the usual sense of the term. He not only laid foundations upon which others might build, but he erected an imposing and complete structure of doctrine which was profoundly influential in all circles, Catholic and non-Catholic alike. To many, "Father Ryan," as he was often called even after he was made a prelate, was the personal embodiment of Catholic social ethics applied to American economic life.

The distinguished career of Msgr. Ryan reflected both his gifts of mind and his integrity of character. Not only was his mind

---

[5] The work of the Department has been studied in two unpublished Catholic University masters' dissertations: Sylvia M. Batdorf, "The Work of the Social Action Department of the National Catholic Welfare Conference in All Phases of Industrial Relations" (Washington, D. C., 1933), and Rev. William J. Lee, S.S., "The Work of Industrial Relations of the Social Action Department of the National Catholic Welfare Conference, 1933–1945" (Washington, D. C., 1946).

keen and intuitive, but he had the unique advantage of being expert both in moral science and in economics. In the former field, he was for years professor of moral theology and industrial ethics at the Catholic University. His competence in economics was intensive and extensive. At times, he would modestly deprecate this knowledge, as when he disclaimed expert views in the field of monetary theory, but the soundness of his principles guided him to correct conclusions even in fields where he had not the time to engage in specialized study. But, with all credit to keenness of intellect, the outstanding quality of Msgr. Ryan was strength of character. His fairness, objectivity, and courage made him an ideal leader in troubled times. He was neither dogmatic nor doctrinaire. Although he was rarely in error in important matters, he did not hesitate to change views outmoded by new or unusual conditions. He was an independent thinker in the best sense of the phrase: guided not by party or blind attachment to schools, but only by the truth.

Ethical Views. The publications of Msgr. Ryan are too numerous to summarize here. Only a few high lights of major opinions can be offered in this limited space. In the ethical field, the best single source is the book, *Distributive Justice,* which he characterized in his autobiography, *Social Doctrine in Action,* as his outstanding work. The volume deals with distribution, in the economic sense, and follows the customary divisions in regard to sharing the national product: rent, interest, profits, and wages. Under each heading, he discusses five main points: the actual economics of distribution, injustices in current distribution, principles of fair and just distribution, unsound systems, and remedies and reforms.

He upheld the right of the landowner to economic rent, which may be defined as the differential return accruing from the scarcity value of good land (either from the viewpoint of productivity in agriculture or location for business) as contrasted with valueless land. It excludes returns for capital improvements, and thus is distinguished from rent in ordinary usage. He held this position against the socialists, who would nationalize land,

and the single taxers, who would take away economic rent. But he maintained that the right to economic rent was subsidiary to the rights of tenants and employees to a decent livelihood and the right of the state to levy reasonable and nonconfiscatory taxes.

He also upheld the right of the capitalist to pure interest, which is a charge for the use of money as such. Ordinary interest is a complex charge, including insurance for risk and often collection costs. The classic arguments for interest taking were examined and each was found to lack universal validity. Nevertheless, he held that the presumption is in favor of interest taking, since it is a socially sanctioned institution which is not clearly unjust. But he would also modify this right by subordinating it to the worker's claim for a living wage.

"The businessman in competitive conditions has a right to all the profits he can obtain, but corporations possessing a monopoly have no right to unusual gains except those due to unusual efficiency."[6] This fits in with classical theory on profits, which considers them a residual return after all expenses are paid under competitive conditions, except that most economists would classify gains due to exceptional efficiency as salaries to management. The important point, however, is that the author did not quarrel with returns commonly labeled profits, provided they were obtained under conditions of fair competition. It goes without saying that the payment of decent wages is one element in fair competition.

Finally, the worker has a right to a living wage, and any additional amount he can secure in competition with his fellow workers and the other agents of production. The living wage would be an ethical minimum, and premium wages would be paid for the scarcity value of unusual skill or productivity. The arguments for a living wage were first formulated by Msgr. Ryan in his doctoral dissertation, *A Living Wage,* which was published in 1906. The argument for a living wage is based

---

[6] *Op. cit.,* 1926 edition, p. 396. An excellent summary of Msgr. Ryan's ethical views is contained in Chapter 24 of the 1942 edition of this work. This is reprinted here as Appendix II.

fundamentally on the dignity of the human person and the subordination of the economic order to the needs of man. Man
needs some material goods which he can get only by access to
private property. The owners who give him access, through
employment, must offer him enough to enable him to live as
befits a man. Other economic groups share this obligation in a
secondary manner. This would apply to the landowner, the loan
capitalist, the consumer, and men of wealth. Moreover, the state
is bound to use its power to see that this obligation is met.

Msgr. Ryan consistently held that the obligation to pay a living
wage was the first charge on industry, prior to the right to rent,
interest, and profits. He argued that to wage earners, their wages
were the only means they had to secure access to necessary goods,
whereas the other groups had alternative means, such as living
on capital or even becoming wage earners if necessary. At the
same time, in other writings, he stressed the need of better
economic organization, so that the system would be able to
produce enough goods which, properly distributed, would constitute living wages for all. It was for this reason that this present
book modified somewhat Msgr. Ryan's thesis that profits or interest might not morally be taken if a living wage were not being
paid. It was held in Chapter X that, in a conflict between the
right of the worker in strict justice to a living wage and the just
rights of owners to interest and profits, the common good might
at times allow the payment of interest and profits. The reason
given was the need of such incentives to stimulate job-giving
investment and economic expansion.

Economic Theories. The economic views of Msgr. Ryan are
contained throughout his prolific writings. The best single
source is his book, *A Better Economic Order,* published in 1935.
Since heroic selection is necessary, three main points might be
stressed: income distribution, prices, and economic organization.

The author's theories on income distribution were traced in his
autobiography to the writings of the English economist, John A.
Hobson. The works were mostly concerned with the problem of
depressions, which Hobson attributed to oversaving and under-

consumption. Subsequently these views were popularized in the United States by Alvin Hansen and especially by the late Lord Keynes, although Keynes's theories differed somewhat from those of Hobson. There is a twofold emphasis in the various income theories, inasmuch as they stress both over-all income flows and savings-investment problems. Classical economics tended to center upon the cost problems of the individual firm, with wages considered primarily as costs. Early classical writers were inclined to ignore the problem of overproduction or underconsumption on a general scale, since they felt that the price mechanism would prevent such happenings. If any productive factor, including labor, were overpriced, the law of supply and demand would bring down its price until it found a buyer. Hence no goods could be in a permanent oversupply. As a practical application of this theory, wages were cut during depressions in order to bring down the price of labor and hence increase demand for workers until it equated the supply. Apart from the inhumanity of such practices, many economists suspected that there was a fault in the economic theory which defended such crises as inevitable.

In carrying out this view, these writers stressed the fact that wages were purchasing power as well as costs. They attributed depressions to the fact that consumers do not receive enough to buy the goods which have been produced. Accordingly, they suggested as remedies for depressions such measures as wage increases, price cuts, and progressive taxation aimed at a more equitable income distribution. This analysis was accepted in full by Msgr. Ryan, with the result that practical programs advocated by him fell within the categories just listed. He further advocated, with Lord Keynes and Hansen, compensatory spending by government to make up for gaps in private capital spending and to stimulate economic recovery.

Economists today are approaching a synthesis between the classical and the underconsumption approaches, as might be noted in Chapter X of the present book. Most reputable authors give more attention to general income flows than was formerly the case, and compensatory government spending is quite respectable at the moment in academic circles and even among some business groups. On the other hand, there is a tendency to believe that there are other causes of business crises in addition to income distribution. Inherent cyclical behavior is found in the durable-goods industries, both in regard to capital expenditures and consumer purchases of heavy goods. Furthermore, cost and price relationships can get out of line in a serious manner. Monetary policies, particularly in regard to short-term debt, also must be considered. Finally, government fiscal policies are becoming more and more influential in affecting economic life.

The savings-investment problem likewise is given more attention today than was once the case. It is no longer held that savings will automatically flow into investments through the working of supply and demand affecting interest rates. Yet not all authors would hold with Hobson and Hansen that there is an absolute excess of savings beyond the capacity of the economic system to absorb. This is particularly the case since Msgr. Ryan's books were written, inasmuch as a heavy taxation burden imposed in the meantime has tended to equalize income distribution much more than was the case before 1940. Hence the emphasis in the present book is rather upon removing obstacles to investment, particularly in the case of small business. It was held that the economic system must expand, if jobs are to be provided for all and a progressively higher standard of living secured. Redistribution of income alone was considered insufficient, mainly because the total product is not yet adequate to provide suitable standards for all, but also because present taxes have largely removed the possibility of enormous incomes. Accordingly, the stress here is upon higher production, achieved both by investment in productive capital and by labor-management co-operation. This would bring about higher living standards but it would not of itself abolish depressions. This latter step involves complex monetary and fiscal management by government, and greater co-operation among economic groups, preferably through a national economic council.

The second major element in Msgr. Ryan's economic theories concerned prices and free competition. He was an inveterate foe of monopoly, with its tendency to secure maximum revenue above the level of competitive prices. The author felt that the enormous profits of the 1920's and the inequitable distribution of income prevailing then were in large part caused by monopolistic conditions in business. He advocated strict control of corporations and tightening and enforcing of antitrust laws. As noted earlier, he would not quarrel with profits obtained under conditions of fair competition, but he felt that the American economy was mixed, with areas of freedom and areas of restraint, ranging from monopolistic competition (monopoly by brands or trademarks) and oligopoly (control by a few firms in an industry) to strict monopoly. As immediate remedies for these and other abuses in business, he felt that federal government action was the only feasible way in the United States at the time. It was in this light that he enthusiastically endorsed the New Deal and considered it the best approximation to social justice thus far obtained here. He advocated and defended practically all the social legislation enacted during the years 1933–1940. It was his opinion that the growth of organized labor and the increased social consciousness of government would be first steps toward realizing the ethical and economic programs summarized here.

At the same time, Msgr. Ryan realized the inadequacy of any approach based on group conflict, excessive reliance upon legislation, and dependence upon the existing economic order. Hence he enthusiastically embraced the teaching of *Quadragesimo Anno* in regard to organized economic life. This encyclical had as its central point a doctrine which was foreshadowed in the 1919 Bishops' Pastoral Letter, a document which undoubtedly reflects his advice and counsel. He fought hard for the ideal of economic life organized in terms of co-operation rather than conflict. He felt that the National Industrial Recovery Act of 1933 might well have been the steppingstone to such a goal, had it really included all economic groups in the making of decisions. His expression of this philosophy is given in his final major work, *Social Doctrine in Action:*

The occupational groups would seek to modify competition by maintaining standards of fairness with regard to wages, hours, prices, and business practices; to avoid private industrial dictatorship by enabling labor to share in all industrial policies and decisions, and to exclude political or bureaucratic industrial dictatorship by keeping the immediate and day-to-day control in the hands of agents of production. They would be prevented from injuring the consumer or the common good by governmental action, "directing, watching, stimulating and restraining, as circumstances suggest or necessity demands." This form of government control is different from and much less than that contemplated by collectivism. Moreover, the consumers could protect themselves through some form of representation in relation to the governing bodies of the occupational groups.

In a word, the occupational group system would aim to bring into industry sufficient self-government to reduce to a minimum the conflicting interests of the various industrial classes, to place industrial direction in the hands of those most competent to exercise it, and to permit only that amount of centralized political control which is necessary to safeguard the common good.[7]

A year later, the final revision of *Distributive Justice* carried these remarks on the industry council plan:

The occupational group might be empowered by law to fix wages, interest, dividends, and prices, to determine working conditions, to adjust industrial disputes, and to carry on whatever economic planning was thought feasible. All the groups in the several concerns of an industry could be federated into a national council for the whole industry. There could also be a federation of all the industries of the nation. The occupational groups, whether local or national, would enjoy power and authority over industrial matters coming within their competence. This would be genuine self-government in industry.

Of course, the occupational groups would not be entirely independent of the government. No economic group, whether of capitalists or laborers, or of both in combination, can be trusted with unlimited power to fix their own profits and remuneration. While allowing to the occupational groups the largest measure of reasonable freedom in the management of their own affairs, the state, says Pius XI, should perform the

---

[7] *Social Doctrine in Action* (New York: Harper, 1941), p. 244.

tasks which belong to it and which it alone can effectively accomplish, namely, those of "directing, watching, stimulating, and restraining, as circumstances suggest or necessity demands."[8]

Here it will be noted that in both texts the author envisioned the possibility of price-fixing as a function of the common-interest groups, although in each case he used "might" rather than "should." It would seem clear, however, from his earlier interest in the National Industrial Recovery Act that he did favor administrative determination of prices by all groups concerned, in contrast to the position taken in Chapter VII of the present volume.

The breadth and sanity of the views summarized here explain why Msgr. Ryan has consistently been considered as "the" authority in Catholic social circles. His scholarship and good sense secured for him pre-eminence in his own right. With no intention of disrespect to Church authorities who honored him with high office, it can fairly be said that the man enhanced the office rather than the reverse. His position was prominent as director of the Department of Social Action, N.C.W.C., and professor of Industrial Ethics, Catholic University. But such offices were but opportunities to exercise his talents and enlarge his contacts. Had he remained at St. Paul Seminary, undoubtedly the world would have beaten tracks to his door.

SELECTED WORKS OF CATHOLIC SCHOLARSHIP

Monsignor Ryan was literally a pioneer. For a long period, he was practically alone in the field of Catholic scholarship in regard to socioeconomic problems. He gradually acquired a few followers, many of them prominent today in their own right. But it was only after the publication of *Quadragesimo Anno,* coinciding with an aroused national awareness of the social problem, an awareness which stemmed largely from the 1929 depression and the subsequent New Deal reform movement, that American

---

[8] *Distributive Justice* (1942 edition), pp. 340–341; copyright 1916, 1917, 1942 by the Macmillan Company and used with their permission.

Catholics began to take a scholarly interest in the social question. After 1931, an increasing number of Catholics, including priests and nuns, received their doctorates in economics. Many were trained in Catholic universities, but a sizable number studied in such secular universities as Harvard, Columbia, California, and London, England. A growing number of such economists have acquired the status required for contributions to some of our best scholarly periodicals, such as the *Harvard Business Review* and the *Quarterly Journal of Economics,* both of which in 1949 carried articles signed by priest-economists.

In 1944 a Catholic Economic Association was formed, as a means of bringing Catholic economists together for consultation and self-help. After a slow beginning, this organization has shown increasing signs of promise. Its meetings are more frequent. More and more articles appearing in its journal can be considered as substantial contributions to Catholic socioeconomic thought. Likewise, many articles in the *American Catholic Sociological Review* deal with subjects treated in these pages. Promising as are these developments, it would be unfair to all concerned to conclude that we have arrived at maturity in this field. Our literature cannot yet compare in richness and variety with that of countries possessing an older culture, such as France and Germany. Yet, the trends are worth noting, particularly because they are toward sound objectives. As further illustration of recent developments, three Catholic University dissertations are summarized here. The selection of these studies was somewhat arbitrary. They were chosen mainly because they dealt with subjects given major stress in the present book. In such an arbitrary selection, other excellent theses by Catholic scholars in many universities were passed over. Space does not permit even a listing of these superior works.[9]

---

[9] A lengthy list of publications by Catholics in the field of economics is given in P. J. Fitzpatrick and C. Dirksen, *Bibliography of Economic Books and Pamphlets by Catholic Authors, 1891–1941* (Washington: Catholic University Press, 1941). The annual catalogue of the Catholic University Press lists doctoral theses which are still in print. For a full list of Catholic University theses, the most convenient source is a recent doctoral study in each of the various schools which deal with social problems

Social Justice. In 1942, the Rev. William Ferree, S.M., wrote his dissertation on *The Act of Social Justice*. The main purpose of this study was to inquire whether social justice was a fully distinct virtue, with its own proper act, or whether it was merely the directing of actions, commanded by other virtues, to the common good which is the universally accepted formal aspect of social justice. The author concluded that social justice is substantially the same as legal justice, in the Thomistic sense. Its characteristic action is *organization* for the purpose of securing the common good. It could be called the virtue which organizes external human acts according to the social necessities of human nature. As a result, the emphasis it places is upon institutions or social habits, rather than isolated good deeds commanded by other virtues. Putting this conclusion in the technical language of philosophy, the author designates four causes in relation to social justice: (1) *Efficient Cause:* only members of a group are capable of an act of social justice. (2) *Material Cause:* the proper matter of social justice is the organization of human actions into the social media and institutions of which society is composed. Other virtues performed under the aspect of social justice take on this new material aspect. (3) *Final Cause:* social justice seeks the common good, which is the perfection of the hierarchy of human institutions. (4) *Formal Cause:* the precise form of social justice is the ordering of actions to the common good.

This dissertation contributed materially to the clarification of Catholic social thinking in the United States. It gave a formal and powerful impetus to the concept of group action and institutional reform. Previously, some writers tended to emphasize almost exclusively the element of individual responsibility and personal obligations, without giving adequate consideration to the influence of environment and the need for changing the character of economic society.

Organized Economic Life. A second notable dissertation was written by Rev. Harold Francis Trehey, M.A., and entitled

(Theology, Philosophy, Social Science). Such dissertations often list on their rear covers the full series in their respective fields.

Foundations of a Modern Guild System. This study was written in 1940. It dealt with the basic principles underlying a common-interest society, studying these in the light of the medieval guild system and some modern attempts at group co-operation. Several of these principles have been studied explicitly in Chapter IV of the present text, whereas others were treated implicitly or combined with those given formal mention. Among the principles studied were: Liberty, Organic Structure, Subsidiarity, Self-Government, Graded Structure, Public-Legal Status, General Welfare, and State Intervention. These basic rules enable men to judge whether or not a society is truly organic and to evaluate proposals for reform in terms of sound ethics. They derive fundamentally from the dignity of the human person and the requirement that society seek the common good and the welfare of its members. As such, they offer a middle ground between individualism and statism.

These principles were studied in relation to the medieval guilds. Then an effort was made to work out the basic elements of a modern guild system which would seek the common good. An elaborate study of a proposed structure was offered as part of the treatise. This was examined in the light of some approximations in France, Switzerland, and Canada. An analysis was given of the relations of the guilds to the civil state. Finally, the question of how such a structure could be built up was given, with emphasis upon gradual building from below rather than imposition by state fiat.

Dr. Trehey's study was likewise influential in elaborating for Catholics the implications of *Quadragesimo Anno.* It was particularly valuable for its study of principles, since these have more enduring value than any effort at a concrete blueprint, no matter how cleverly it is contrived. Of special interest was the stress upon subsidiarity, since Americans too often tend to seek immediate government action to remedy evils, instead of devising means for self-reform and self-government.

The third study in the general field of social principles was *Some American Approximations to Pius XI's "Industries and*

Professions." It was written in 1943 by Rev. Joseph David Munier. This study dealt with the same general subject as the one preceding, but emphasized American institutions which might be considered as close to the encyclical idea. The topics studied were the railroad industry, the bituminous coal industry, industry committees under the Fair Labor Standards Act, and the National War Labor Board. It was felt that actions taken under railroad and coal legislation were for the good of the industries concerned rather than for the common good. By contrast, the industry committees and the WLB actions were directed toward the general welfare of the nation as a whole.

The test of organization and representation was then applied, with varying results. In most cases there was adequate if not complete organization of the groups studied. They were not merely government agencies. Members of the boards were generally representative. But the scope of action was severely limited to specific problems, rather than to the full range of common interests of the parties concerned. In this way, they fell short of the ideal of genuine mutual-interest organic groups. Cooperation and collaboration were too limited. The same limitations were noted in relation to another requirement, the principle of subsidiarity. All the social institutions studied were initiated by government, which is not necessarily contrary to the ideal of industry self-government. But the boards and committees established did not, as a whole, enjoy the relative autonomy which would be desirable if we are to decentralize power and enhance the authority of lesser groups. From this it follows that the groups did not enjoy real, independent public-legal status, as advocated by Catholic authorities. Their functions were limited and rather strongly dependent upon government. Hence the conclusion is reached that the legislation studied was only a limited approximation of the encyclical ideal, and that it often tended in the contrary direction.

This study likewise rendered a distinct service, showing that the main social efforts in the direction of collaborative action had in fact major inadequacies and even at times tended in wrong directions. There is still a prolonged task of education ahead before this nation will accept a pattern of action which will really be a middle way between individualism and statism. Undoubtedly scholarly works such as those examined here will aid materially in clarifying thinking and thus lead to sound programs of conduct.[10]

The material analyzed in this chapter demonstrates a trend of consistent and serious effort to apply social principles to American conditions. The various statements by the bishops adapt papal encyclicals to domestic problems. As a rule, but not invariably, they are general in nature. More specific programs have been evolved by the Department of Social Action, N.C.W.C. Finally, the several authors discussed come directly to grips with the economic problems of the day where they impinge upon moral issues.

As applications come closer to the concrete, they cease to be authoritative statements of Church doctrine and involve a mixture of universally accepted principles with the prudential judgment of individuals or groups in regard to the implementation of these norms. Such diminution of authority does not imply that applications are of inferior value. On the contrary, principles would remain sterile unless they were put into practice. But the value of any given effort to apply rules must be judged on its own merits. Its correctness may be debatable, even among those who accept the principles as universally true. Some disagreements and even changes of policy in regard to practical programs are inevitable. What is suitable for one age may be less adapted to the needs of a later generation. In practical fields, in contrast to principles, neither change nor stability are of necessity desirable for their own sakes. So long as men have sound moral rules for guiding their conduct, and discuss the application of these rules with intelligence, good will, and good faith, one can fairly expect the working out of a harmonious social order.

---

[10] Unfortunately, the three dissertations studied here are all out of print. They are normally available, however, in many major libraries throughout the country.

READINGS

A Program for Social Reconstruction.
Bishops' Pastoral Letter, 1919.
A Statement on the Present Crisis, 1933.
The Church and Social Order.
J. A. Ryan, *Distributive Justice.*
——— *The Church and Labor.*
——— *Social Reconstruction.*
——— *A Better Economic Order.*
——— *Seven Troubled Years.*
——— *Social Doctrine in Action.*
W. Ferree, *The Act of Social Justice.*
H. F. Trehey, *Foundations of a Modern Guild System.*
J. D. Munier, *Some American Approximations to Pius XI's "Industries and Professions."*

Chapter XVI. DISTRIBUTISM AND THE CO-OPERATIVE MOVEMENT

The subjects studied in this chapter cannot in any strict sense be called Catholic schools of thought. Distributism has found favor among Catholics, and several of the most famous names associated with it, such as Belloc and Chesterton, are Catholics. But in this country, the torch has been carried mainly by non-Catholics, with Agar, Borsodi, and O. E. Baker among the most publicized advocates. The same observation is even more true in regard to the co-operative movement. Here it has been primarily Protestant in origin and acceptance. It has found favor largely with rural Catholics in the United States, although there are notable exceptions to this statement even among farming Catholics. In Canada, the great movement in Antigonish is mainly Catholic in inspiration. But it would be chauvinistic to claim any large measure of credit for the Church in either the origin or the American dissemination of these ideas.

At the same time, however, there is much in these movements which admirably conforms with the social pattern based on Catholic principles. They emphasize so strongly the dignity of the human person, and the need for ownership of actual productive property as a bulwark of man's rights, that they fit naturally into the framework outlined in these pages. Hence it would not be incorrect to label them as schools of thought among Catholics, even though they are not exclusively Catholic social systems.

DISTRIBUTISM

Person and Property. There are two interrelated central ideas which characterize the philosophy of distributism. They comprise an emphasis upon human dignity and freedom, and the view that only by widespread ownership of productive property can man safeguard these fundamental qualities. Distributism is anthropocentric, not in contrast to a theocentric movement, but rather in protest against statism and other forms of concentration of power. It advocates diffusion of power as the only way to secure man's freedom. The alternative is the servile state, whether it take the form of socialism, communism, or monopoly capitalism.

Freedom can be possessed in varying degrees. It is almost nonexistent under communism. In such a society, the individual can have a limited personal liberty only by strict subservience to the Party Line and the agility needed to change his views when the line shifts with drastic suddenness. In socialism and various approximations thereto, economic freedom is exercised primarily as a member of the state. To the extent that the socialist state remains democratic, the individual can rule his life through political action. But he is free only as a member of an inordinately large group, with little direct and immediate control over the economic phase of his life. Yet economic life is of the highest importance, since it provides the means for sustaining physical life. He who rules access to food, rules men who need this food to live. It is for this reason that monopoly capitalism also restricts man's freedom. If the bulk of the means of production is controlled by the few, the majority enjoy only a limited degree of liberty. Powerful industrial combinations can often dominate over the political state, thus attaining a close approximation to autarchy.

By contrast, when a man owns productive property, he achieves considerable independence. This is greatest when the property is agricultural land, since this normally provides food, shelter, and clothing. It is still substantial when property is in the form of a store, factory, or service establishment. Certainly in a small, well-integrated economy, trade among such firms and with the farming community gives everyone an opportunity to live in freedom and security. This is not so true in a large economy, since the incidence of depressions affects independent owners as well as wage earners. But the former often have more security than the latter, even in an economy subject to economic crises. They usually have savings and some resources to fall back upon until conditions improve.

The isolated wage earner suffers most from inequality and insecurity. He loses most in freedom and human dignity when he is one of thousands working in a large plant or industry. In a smaller plant, the wage earner does enjoy the advantage of closer contact with the owner and the possibility of a personal relationship more consonant with human dignity. In both cases, he suffers from insecurity, in that he often has no resources when a depression forces him out of work. At times this insecurity is less in the small firm, since employers who know him personally are often reluctant to let him go unless as a last resort. It is true that the union movement has attacked both these evils in the United States, but only at the cost of adding another element of bigness to our society. The union worker has greater freedom and security, although he often obtains this as a member of a very large organization which may be as remote from him, in its higher branches, as the executives of a large corporation. We might also add the qualification that working conditions in small plants, under the pressure of remorseless competition, are often inferior to those enjoyed in larger firms.

Hence the distributist ideal would involve industrial decentralization and widely diffused ownership of productive wealth. It is recognized that in modern times specialized production is often a necessity. Only extremists in this movement would advocate complete self-sufficiency. Nor is it felt that the system of wage earnership should be abolished. Realists recognize that not all men have the desire or the ability to conduct their own business, trade, or profession. Certain forms of production require factory methods and even occasionally assembly-line techniques. But the distributist would advocate that, with rare exceptions, such factories be smaller than the giants existing today. They would regulate size to an optimum for efficient production, with due regard to the human factors involved. The present situation, by contrast, is one where size is increased for the sake of financial power and monopolistic control.

The question naturally arises as to how standards of living would be affected by such programs. Here the distributists interpose their own definition of such standards. They do not accept the ideal that the goal of man's life is the possession of a constantly increasing stock of gadgets and luxuries. Rather they consider many such items as anodynes to deaden the pain felt from the loss of more substantial values. They envision the function of consumption in modern society as being quite contrary to its rational position in relation to man's needs. Through advertising and promotion we are constantly forcing men to consume more and more, so that they can support an ever growing industrial system. Man's greatest needs are freedom, independence, and security. The possession of assured access to sufficient food, clothing, housing, education, and medical care safeguard these values. It may be pleasant to have additional luxuries, such as an automobile for pleasure, radio, television, motion pictures, a wide variety of clothes, and professional amusements and games. But if the price for securing such luxuries is a system which endangers basic freedoms, by all means we should accept a lower standard of living. It is better to be a free man with sufficient possessions than a well-fed and pampered slave.

The Curse of Bigness. The central evil in modern society is concentration of power and a bigness which dwarfs the individual. In economic life, this manifests itself in the giant corporation and the centralization of financial power. Small business faces increasingly great obstacles, as was noted in Chapter XII. Many small factories must sell to giant firms in such a way that they are practically subsidiaries. In the distribution field, competition by the chain store, the department store, and the mail-order companies is frequently too difficult to meet. Even successful small firms are often absorbed by mergers. Thus, a small ice-cream company, serving a local market and buying milk from neighborhood farmers, is swallowed up by a giant. Often production conditions are left unchanged. The same market is served; the same machinery is used; and milk is bought from the same farmers. But another independent owner is gone, with all policies directed from a remote central office. In such diverse fields as theaters, wineries and distilleries, and machine tool shops, colossi have supplanted small firms. Even in the farming field there are trends toward centralization.

In the large factory, machines have often been diverted from their purpose as tools to serve man and have become masters which rule him. There is nothing creative or stimulating in assembly-line production. The man who spends the entire day in a monotonous, repetitive task derives no pleasure or stimulus from his work. All his actions must keep the pace of the machine. At the worst, he may be the victim of an inhuman speed-up which wears him out before his time. Even at the very best, he does nothing inspiring or creative. It is true that there is monotony in farming or small craftsmanship. But here at least there is the creative sense and the feeling that one is one's own master.

The curse of bigness is best seen in the large city. In the metropolis, millions of people live in the same area. Noise and congestion are the normal features of such life. Paradoxically, this is a lonely and impersonal way of living. In apartment houses, people often do not know their own neighbors. Shopping in the stores or eating in restaurants is often impersonal. The automat and the vending machine or the self-service store are the ultimate apotheoses of the machine ideal. In such an environment the family grows only with the greatest difficulty. It is often impossible to find suitable accommodations for children. Play spaces are lacking. The feverish pace and tensions of such life accentuate neurotic or antisocial tendencies in children and adults alike. It is no accident that city slums are breeding grounds for crime, vice, and disease. When men cannot live fully human lives, they are not likely to live moral or spiritual lives.

Society itself becomes infected with the virus of bigness. Things are considered desirable merely because they are large. The biggest social club is thought by many to be the best. Men boast of size instead of quality. They look down upon other civilizations which still prefer cultural values to material achievement. Even more dangerous evils may result. The centralization of economic power is soon paralleled by concentration of political power. We have the giant, all-encroaching state. Men seek from political grants the freedom which they do not gain by economic independence. The result is the servile state, the welfare state, or whatever epithet one may use. National governments absorb more and more of the functions of lesser political units. Government becomes a vast, sprawling bureaucracy, absorbing ever greater amounts of national wealth. It becomes more independent of the average citizen, supplying him with many benefits which he could secure himself, if he had economic freedom. Society ceases to be the servant of the individual and becomes his master, even if a generous and benevolent master.

Decentralization. In the face of such problems, distributists call for decentralization of ownership and power. First, they would sponsor a return to the land by many who now live in cities. While realizing that small farms could not support our entire population, and that many would be unwilling to seek rural life or are unfitted for its burdens, distributists would nevertheless advocate policies which would promote wider ownership of land. They would make available to farmers such necessities as good education and medical care. Public policy in such matters as taxes and social programs would be oriented in favor of small farmers and diffused ownership of land. By educational and training devices, they would inculcate in city dwellers an appreciation for the virtues of rural living. Thus many who are virtual proletarians today would be given real stability and independence.

As a second step, social policy should favor small factories and stores in contrast to present-day giants. The method most frequently advocated is discriminatory taxation. Thus, a chain of stores or theaters would be taxed at an increasing rate for each unit owned. If the first unit had to pay a license tax of $100, the tenth might be charged $1,000. The present progressive tax levied on corporations profits would be even more steep in its ascent. It might range from 20 per cent on amounts under $50,000 to 60 or 70 per cent on firms whose profits were in the millions. Other devices, such as enforcement of antitrust laws, prohibition of unsocial mergers, and positive aids in financing, management, and research for small business would likewise be favored. Some writers do not feel that small firms need any special help, other than a chance to compete fairly, since they consider many modern giants as too big to be efficient. They survive only by virtue of financial power and monopoly influence rather than through real economies achieved by supersize.

Most distributists advocate programs which call for strong initial exercise of state power. While the ultimate aim is the diffusion of authority, their immediate goals can be achieved only by giving to government powers which would be considered drastic even in this age of centralization. Thus, the state would break up existing enterprises by taxation, and this with considerable loss to investors and owners. It would remake the pattern of economic life. In this respect, distributism is reminiscent of the early theory of communism, whereby the state assumed dictatorship with the goal of its own ultimate abolition. In the case of communism, the goal of theory was not achieved in practice.[1]

Critique of Distributism. In discussing distributism, it is necessary to distinguish between the ideals professed and the means suggested for attaining these ideals. Few thoughtful students of social problems would quarrel today with the objectives of distributism. The notion that freedom must be safeguarded and that

---

[1] One of the most recent distributists' programs for America is *Decentralize for Liberty,* by Thomas Hewes (New York: Dutton, 1947).

widespread diffusion of productive property is a bulwark of liberty is rather generally conceded. It is likewise evident that many modern trends are in the wrong direction. The individual is being submerged in struggles between power groups. Stated in such broad terms, distributism would command approval from many diverse schools of thought.

Disagreement would set in when details are studied, and particularly in regard to methods for achieving the goals which most men would accept. The most serious difficulty arises when one discusses such things as bigness, machine production, and city life. That these are currently surrounded with abuses is evident. But it is not so clear that they are so inherently bad in all their phases that the remedy is their virtual abolition. Even if this latter remedy were considered necessary, doubts may arise as to the wisdom and practicality of the methods advocated by various distributist writers.

In the first place, the matter of bigness is relative, not absolute. A ten million dollar automobile plant or steel factory would be puny. But a food store with such an investment would be mammoth. The optimum size, considered in terms of efficient production, varies considerably from industry to industry. Hence any proposals for penalizing bigness through taxation might touch lightly the largest firm in a small industry and punish severely a small firm in a field where bigness is essential. If it is held that small or medium-sized business is often more efficient than giant firms, there would be no inherent need to discriminate against the large companies. It would be better to take action to secure fair competition. This means, of course, enforcement of antitrust laws and supervision of mergers. More than that, it would involve some standards of fair competition, possibly enforced through Federal Trade Commission agreements. Finally, it would call for steps to remove the more serious disabilities affecting small business, namely, lack of capital, inability to do research, and inadequate training in management.[2]

---

[2] The best available conclusions, with further references, on the profitability of small business are given by A. D. H. Kaplan, in *Small Business: Its Place and Problems* (New

There are many advantages to the positive approach of stimulating small business in contrast to the negative method of trying to break up large firms. The direct approach is more feasible both economically and politically. It does not involve any break with our traditions or virtual confiscation of wealth through punitive taxation. It is evolutionary rather than revolutionary, an important point for any program which must command wide acceptance. Hence the methods proposed in Chapter XII are considered perferable to those advocated by Belloc, Hewes, and such distributists.

Likewise, there may be more direct methods for meeting the problems inherent in large factories and large cities. For the factory, personnel experts have worked out programs for bettering human relations, decentralizing authority, and otherwise bringing in a personal relationship between the worker and management. These techniques, coupled with union policies, can restore to labor an effective voice in economic matters. Sound education in turn can give workers more substantial control over their unions. Thus, they would achieve economic freedom through group action which they initiated and directed. This in turn would release creative energies in ways not feasible in routine work. As was noted in Chapter III, routine and monotony are not limited to modern assembly-line work. They exist as well in professional tasks, housekeeping, and farming, to mention a few occupations which might be approved by distributists. Above all, if the type of society called organic, directed toward common interests and featured by subsidiarity and self-government, were achieved, there would be definite assurance of liberty and creative outlets.

The problem of the large city is serious, but here again the recommended approach is positive. Methods which would stimulate small business would generally tend to decentralize industry. Small business normally shuns the large city, because costs of

York: McGraw-Hill, 1948), p. 80. The author concludes that medium-sized business is generally the most efficient, but that small business *can* often compete profitably with large firms. Apparently supersize is a bar to efficiency.

rent, transportation, and taxes are too high for firms with a small turnover. Even larger firms are tending to decentralize as a matter of economics. Many large cities are now breaking up into self-sufficient suburban communities, with complete shopping centers and educational and cultural facilities. If in addition vigorous steps were taken to cut down the cost of housing, one of the major difficulties in the way of family life today would be removed. Education could do much to bring about a better sense of cultural values and to destroy the myth that bigness is in itself a quality. All these approaches would stimulate or modify existing institutions, rather than call for a revolutionary change which is rarely practicable in society.

One might conclude that the distributists have done a notable service to modern life by calling attention to serious evils and dangerous trends. In this sense, it might be correct to note a distributist tendency in the addresses of Pope Pius XII. But when the remedial program of many distributists is examined, one does not find the moderation and care which are characteristic of the papal programs. The Church likewise seeks a revolutionary change in society, but its methods are gradual and evolutionary. It is better to transform an existing order than to seek to impose by government action some detailed plan, no matter how appealing the blueprint may seem.

THE CO-OPERATIVE MOVEMENT

The Philosophy of Co-operation. The co-operative movement has a philosophy which is quite similar in many respects to that of the distributists. It holds to the fundamental idea that freedom is achieved through ownership of productive wealth. The techniques it advocates are somewhat different, although many distributists also favor co-operatives. To the ideal of economic freedom, it also adds another, that of social solidarity. It would be possible to conceive of an element of individualism in many distributist writings. They emphasize independence, without either excluding or including the notion of social living. But the co-operative philosophy is basically social. It embodies the joint action of consumers and producers for the welfare of all concerned.

There is no need here to enter into the details of co-operative techniques. They have been treated adequately in scores of books and pamphlets. A summary presentation of these works, with references, is available in other texts by the present author.[3] Fundamentally, in co-operatives the parties concerned, consumers or producers, unite to eliminate the middleman. Thus, a group of farmers may sell directly to city markets or canneries. As consumers, they may buy fertilizer from the factory instead of paying the cost of several intermediate handlings. In this way, it is hoped to secure the savings obtainable by cutting out unnecessary distribution costs. But more than this, the ideal co-operative affords a training in democracy and solidarity. In the typical store, there is but one vote per member, regardless of the number of shares he purchased. Policies are determined in meetings attended by the members. The advantages of ownership and group action are thus combined.

Co-operators consider their movement as an ideal answer to both individualism and statism. Against the one, they feature group action and a social spirit. In contrast to the other, they would decentralize ownership and power. It is true that many co-operators envision a completely co-operative society, with giant federations owning factories, mines, and like means of production. But they maintain that in such a society, ownership would be held at the bottom, not the top. Likewise, policies would be determined by individual members and their own groups rather than by giant corporations. Hence the co-operative ideal would give true decentralization of authority and power.

Most co-operators attack the profit motive itself as undesirable. They consider it too often synonymous with greed. Thus, they oppose a service society to one motivated by profit considerations. This aspect gives to their writers a touch of idealism which has appealed to many religious persons. Clergy of all faiths

---

[3] See *Catholic Social Action*, Chap. 9 and Appendix; and *Economic Analysis and Problems*, Chaps. 14 and 15.

have studied the movement and some have become its enthusiastic advocates. With the Catholic clergy, extreme interest is found more among those concerned with rural life. By contrast, many Protestant ministers in city parishes were keen students of the program during the 1930's. More recently, some labor groups have evinced an interest in the co-operative movement. They are concerned, not merely with the money savings promised, but also with the opportunity it gives for union members to achieve a higher degree of solidarity.

In one of the most successful examples of religious sponsorship of co-operation, namely, the movement in Antigonish, Nova Scotia, the element of social education and building of self-reliance predominates. It could even be said that co-operation is a technique which spontaneously flows from efforts at self-education and self-help. The basic story here is well known. A group of mining and fishing communities found themselves seriously impoverished, at times to the point of destitution. With the aid of St. Francis Xavier University, the people were taught to understand their problems and what could be done to meet them. By co-operative purchasing and selling, they were able to rise from the slough and achieve stability and modest prosperity.

The co-operative ideal, then, is nothing less than a new society different from both capitalism and socialism. It would enhance human freedom and strengthen the social ties among men. By removing greed from the social structure, the great evils which weaken modern society would be eliminated. The classless state would be achieved, not by the dictatorship of Marxist communism, but by the common action of free men. Stated this way, it is understandable why the movement has aroused such enthusiasm among its supporters. Yet it is not entirely clear that it could produce the results it promises.

Evaluation of the Co-operative Movement. It will not be necessary to repeat here the economic difficulties faced by co-operatives. Their success has been uneven. It is most striking when there is a large and uneconomic spread in the cost of distribution. Less success has been achieved, in most instances, in meeting the challenge of efficient, large-scale distributors, such as chain stores or mail-order houses. Some of these difficulties may be attributed to lack of resources, but in other cases it is doubtful that the cumbersome structure envisioned in the democratic co-operative would have the flexibility and freedom needed to match such able competitors. Certainly, it is a fact that the economic results of consumer co-operation in the United States have not been sufficiently attractive to date to insure its wide growth. But advocates of the movement would state that any emphasis upon this fact would be mistaken. The economics are secondary to the idealism in the system. Hence it is important to evaluate its ideals.

In discussing the philosophy of co-operation, one might validly distinguish between existing co-operative movements and the completely co-operative society. There can be little quarrel with, and much approbation of, the movement as it has manifested itself in the United States and Canada. In general, it has operated on a small scale. It has promoted effective ownership and social solidarity among its members. The educational value of such efforts has been considerable and salutary. Moreover, any extension which appears feasible at this moment would be to the good. It is a useful corrective of extreme individualism, and often with an economic group which has been traditionally quite individualistic, namely, the farming community. The ideal of self-help is valuable today, when too many run to government to correct all evils.

But there are aspects to the co-operative movement which require more careful scrutiny before it is accepted without reservations. On example would be the elimination of the independently owned store and the middleman. They are certainly more vulnerable to co-operative attacks than would be the case with chain stores or large distributors. It is highly questionable whether freedom and independence would be promoted by such a move. A comparison between the salaried manager of a chain store and the salaried manager of a co-operative shows some similarities. The independent store owner has more freedom than either.

Technically, the co-operative replaces one owner by a hundred or more. But some corporations have hundreds of thousands of stockholder-owners. In these cases, it has been found that the further this type of ownership is diffused, the more ethereal it becomes. There is a difference with co-operative shareholders, in that each has the same vote regardless of the number of shares owned, and each must cast his vote personally, not by proxy. Yet, even with such differences, there is a qualitative distinction between personal ownership and control and group ownership.

This point would be accentuated if co-operatives grew to the size envisioned by their most enthusiastic supporters. A completely co-operative economy would involve mammoths comparable to the largest of modern corporations. It is inconceivable that real democracy could flourish under such conditions. Of necessity, the governing boards of such groups would be generally independent and self-perpetuating, like a corporate board of directors. Thus, actual power would be centralized to a degree even more extreme than exists today. A co-operative bureaucracy would be no more tolerable than other forms of concentrated control. Moreover, experience with the movement shows that such fears are more than mere speculation. Where co-operatives have grown to huge size, as in England, they have become supercorporations. Their intentions may be good, but this comment applies to socialism as well. What modern society needs is a diffusion of real ownership and power. A universal co-operative movement would, in all likelihood, work in the opposite direction.

Caution should also be used in equating the profit motive with greed. The total income of many small store owners is often less than that of unionized truck drivers. Profits, as the term is used in co-operative literature, generally comprise the entire net income of a proprietor. Economists would break this down into his salary for managing the store, interest on his capital, and net profits where they exist. Most proprietors are fortunate to earn the first two items, both of which are entirely legitimate. The co-operatives themselves pay salaries to their managers and limited dividends, when earned, as interest upon money invested by shareholders. It is unfair to treat the profit motive as something essentially sordid, in contrast to the service ideal. Proprietors seek profits as payment for their services and as a means for earning a living. Co-operative employees likewise expect to be paid for their services as their method of securing their livelihood. Of course, monopolistic or speculative profits may be reprehensible, but this is no reason to reject the entire profit system. Papal statements have condemned excessive profits, but they did not deny the owner a right to a fair share on his capital or to a reasonable salary for his efforts. On the contrary, they upheld such returns against the socialist claim that only labor should receive returns from the national product. While it is legitimate for customers to own stores and receive rebates in place of profits, it is equally acceptable in principle for proprietors to own stores and receive a profit for their services and investment.

We face a paradox, accordingly, in regard to co-operatives. On the one hand, the existing movement had done considerable good. It deserves to be promoted. But, on the other hand, if co-operatives grew to the extent hoped for by their proponents, they would probably be an unhealthy development in the economy. In all likelihood, the system would be bureaucratic and undemocratic. Hence we are placed in a position of wishing them success, but not too much success. We hope that they accomplish limited objectives, but we would oppose the blueprint of a completely co-operative economy just as much as we would object to socialism or monopoly capitalism. Diffusion of power must be real, not merely nominal, if society is to remain healthy.

American Conditions. In the United States, there is no visible indication that co-operatives will become dangerously overgrown. The movement is not new here. It has had some successes, but also definite failures. On the whole, the consumer co-operative movement has not penetrated our large cities. Credit unions have had more urban success and apparently meet a continuing need. The most financially successful co-operatives are of the producer and marketing variety, specializing primarily in the sale of farm products. Yet these latter often deviate most from the spirit of democratic control. Many of them are more akin to the business partnership than to the true co-operative, with its numerous members, regular meetings, and voting power restricted to one vote per member, regardless of holdings. All in all, there is little likelihood that the co-operative approach will supplant the profit system here.

At the same time, some of the reasons why co-operatives fail to grow are not admirable qualities in the American public. The biggest noneconomic obstacle to the movement springs from our individualism and lack of social solidarity. Co-operation both presupposes and promotes some spirit of community homogeneity. It needs this spirit to get a start and then it intensifies the sense of oneness and common interests. But such an attitude is also desirable for other social ends as well. Hence those striving to promote co-operatives are encouraging other ventures in the social field by these same efforts.

The economic obstacles to consumer co-operatives are many, but among the most important is the entrenched power of big producers and distributors. The chain store and like mass-distributing and selling agencies are increasing their holds in the general field of distribution. Their influence is formidable, and it is difficult for both co-operatives and independent proprietors to compete with them. The very factors which have helped to stunt the growth of co-operatives also increase the general problem of bigness in our economy. Accordingly, even those who do not feel that a universal pattern of co-operatives is the answer to our needs might well join with its proponents in achieving the immediate objective of preventing giantism in economic life.

Even granting the need for more community spirit and a diffusion of economic power, it is not necessarily true that our common interests as consumers would be the primary means for achieving social collaboration. Another method, not necessarily antithetical, is stress upon our common interests as producers. This latter approach appears to fit better with current American psychology. It seems that our interests as consumers are often too scattered and diffused to serve as an easy focal point for organization. True, we can become consumer-conscious in special situations, as during a time of inflation. Consumers in limited fields can often group together, such as tenants trying to hold rental charges down in an inflationary period. But, as a rule, our purchasing choices are too scattered and individualistic to offer any internal impetus to organization.

Production, particularly of the industrial type, by its very nature organizes those connected with it. Even when production is individualistic, as with farming, the problem of marketing serves to provide central contacts and interests and hence can stimulate common action. This point has been stressed in Catholic social teaching. It is one of the anomalies of modern times that we have permitted divisive forces, arising from conflict over distribution of the product, to blot out our common concerns in working together for production. Certainly it seems more natural to devote our primary attention to restoring a common-interest mentality in the producer field. Such an approach is easier and more in accord with the nature of our society.

Papal Statements. It is probable that this point explains the relative silence of the popes in regard to the consumer co-operative movement. None of the major documents cited in these pages goes into the problem explicitly or at length. In enumerating sound social projects, there are occasional allusions to co-operative ventures, such as credit unions. But, even the major address of Pope Pius XII on agriculture, given on November 15, 1946, makes but an incidental reference to the subject. The Pope tells the farmers that "your principal help must come from yourselves, from your co-operative unions, especially from your credit unions."[4] More recently, the Holy Father had strong words of praise for Belgian co-operatives. He eulogized the *Fédération nationale des coopératives chrétiennes*, as: "Magnificent fruit

---

[4] See "The Pope Speaks on Rural Life" (Des Moines: The National Catholic Rural Life Conference, 1947), p. 11. An earlier compilation, issued in 1944, entitled "Catholic Churchmen and Co-operatives" (Des Moines: National Catholic Rural Life Conference) illustrates the remarkable contrast between enthusiastic support by bishops and clergy and the practical silence of the popes.

from the tree of the Church's social teaching! What a contribution these co-operatives have brought both to the bettering and
the securing of the economic situation of the worker and his
family! This certainly is a work of authentic solidarity. . . . We
bless it!"[5] But the context in both cases clearly refers to such
types as producer, marketing, and credit co-operatives. Certainly
the Catholic Belgian movement has not developed any strong
consumer co-operatives. Much less is there such a condition as the
completely co-operative society envisioned by some authors.

It would seem correct to say that individual projects have received letters of approval, but that there is no extended moral
treatment of the philosophy of the movement, such as has
been accorded to capitalism, socialism, communism, and like
systems. If the analysis given here is correct, that a completely
co-operative society would be bureaucratic and top heavy in its
centralization of economic power, then such a result would be
clearly contrary to the social teaching of the Church. Even a substantial invasion of the field of small business might not be a
change for the better. Here much depends upon the actual diffusion of economic power and the reality of the control exercised
by consumer-owners. If co-operatives replaced giant chains, there
might be a social gain, but this is not so clear where small independent owners are involved.

The social teaching of the popes is more akin to the distributist idea than it is to the philosophy of some co-operators.
Structurally, the popes have advocated diffusion of power through
increase of responsible ownership. This means as much ownership of productive wealth by individuals or partners as is feasible
in modern life. Functionally, these free owners should co-operate
with others in their industry or profession in organizations designed to seek the common good of all as well as the mutual
interests of producers. Producer and marketing co-operatives
would be more akin to this ideal than consumer co-operatives.
The latter group would be structurally unsound, were they to

[5] Allocution of September 11, 1949, to Belgian workers.

achieve their goal of an integral co-operative society. In such a society, the individual would have no economic power save as a member of a gigantic group. This seems to be socialism from the bottom up instead of the more traditional form of socialism from the top down.

It is distressing to reach such conclusions about a movement which has so many virtues. Possibly such judgments would have been unnecessary, had not some writers been so sweeping in their claims and hopes for a co-operative society. Certainly the men connected with the movement are almost universally men of high ideals, dedicated to the service of their fellow men. They can rightly take pride in such achievements as those of Antigonish and many here in the United States. Often they can assert, with truth, that they have remedied conditions of exploitation which had obtained under existing conditions. But when they set up a total philosophy of economic life, they must be judged, not in terms of past achievements under special conditions, but rather in the light of the probable operation of such a society.

We have successful cases of isolated socialism in the United States, such as the Tennessee Valley Authority development of water power and regional resources. But we do not take this as a pattern for our whole economic life. Likewise, we must conclude that the total plan found in some co-operative literature would be as adverse to the Catholic ideal as socialism or monopoly capitalism. This conclusion is offered only as the considered and reluctant judgment of the present author, based on his own interpretation of the more enthusiastic writings of some authors favoring a co-operative society and also his own interpretation of papal writings. Needless to say, there are Catholics who disagree with this conclusion and who feel that a co-operative society would embody the ideal of service and social solidarity. Literature embodying this position is cited in the reading lists and the appendix.

As a practical point, one might distinguish between the co-operative movement and a co-operative social order based on complete ownership of the economy by federations of consumer co-operatives. The former is a reality, whereas the latter is but a project of certain writers. The one has achieved solid results and deserves careful study and, in proper circumstances, enthusiastic support. The other is not likely to become a reality in this country and may be freely debated in the realm of ideas. The two are not so interconnected that by supporting the movement one is leading to the realization of the plan. One might well applaud the achievements of the Tennessee Valley Authority and still feel that he is not thereby aiding the cause of state socialism. Likewise the achievements of social solidarity and aid to those in economic distress, arrived at through consumer co-operation, can be welcomed without endorsing group ownership of all means of production. Even more so, one can approve the approach to an organic society achieved by producer and marketing co-operatives. What they have done, they have done well. And, since it is highly unlikely that they will expand beyond their proper field, we may wish them success and aid them in their endeavors to grow and prosper.

READINGS*

On Distributism:

J. Messner, *Social Ethics,* pp. 920–922.
H. Belloc, *The Restoration of Property.*
———— *The Servile State.*
G. K. Chesterton, *What's Wrong With the World?*
H. Agar and A. Tate (edd.), *Who Owns America?*
A. J. Penty, *Post-Industrialism.*
R. Borsodi, *Flight from the City.*
———— *Prosperity and Security.*
W. Marx, *Mechanization and Culture.*
E. T. Peterson (ed.), *Cities Are Abnormal.*
A. D. H. Kaplan, *Small Business: Its Place and Problems.*
W. D. Nutting, *Reclamation of Independence.*
T. Hewes, *Decentralize for Liberty.*

On Co-operatives:

J. R. Ward (ed.), *United for Freedom.*
———— *Ourselves, Inc.*
J. K. Bolles, *The People's Business.*

* For further readings, consult List No. 14 in the Appendix.

J. Baker, *Co-operative Enterprise*.

G. Boyle, *Democracy's Second Chance*.

A. M. Carr-Saunders, *et al.*, *Consumers' Co-operation in Great Britain*.

M. W. Childs, *Sweden, The Middle Way*.

M. M. Coady, *Masters of Their Own Destiny*.

E. Cowling, *Co-operatives in America*.

J. Daniels, *Co-operation, An American Way*.

B. B. Fowler, *The Lord Helps Those*.

F. Hall and W. P. Watkins, *Co-operation*.

J. E. Ross, *Co-operative Plenty*.

E. Schmiedeler, *Co-operation, A Christian Mode of Industry*.

U. S. Inquiry on Co-operative Enterprise.

J. P. Warbasse, *Co-operative Democracy*.

Chapter XVII. CATHOLIC RURAL PHILOSOPHY

The Church has shown an abiding interest in problems connected with the land. Numerous popes have testified to their special affection for the farmer. Moreover, in many countries, Catholic rural organizations are among the most flourishing forms of Catholic life. The United States is no exception in this regard. While the Church is not generally strong in rural areas, it is nonetheless disproportionately active in these regions. The National Catholic Rural Life Conference has shown a vigor and comprehensiveness in its programs unexcelled by any urban Catholic group. It has also worked out a thorough philosophy of rural life, as well as varied methods for putting this into practice.

The literature put out by the NCRLC is extensive, but the basic document is the *Manifesto on Rural Life,* a composite work embodying the thought of practically all the members of the Conference. This document was approved in 1938 and published in 1939. It was given warm approval by the Holy Father and is strikingly similar to many points in his 1946 address to the Italian farmers. These two sources will be used as the primary references in this chapter.[1]

MORAL VALUES IN RURAL LIFE

One of the main reasons for extensive Catholic interest in rural problems derives from the moral values inherent in farm life.

---

[1] The *Manifesto* is published by The Bruce Publishing Company, Milwaukee. The papal address has been reprinted by the NCRLC under the title "The Pope Speaks on Rural Life." These editions will be used in the citations given here.

Many phases of country living contribute to Christian culture. It fosters family life. It contributes to the character of those living on farms. There is a stability and sound conservatism about rural life which is favorable to religious ideals. For all these reasons, we can truly say that the farm is the cradle of many of the best elements in a nation's culture.

The Family. Farm life is family life. Practically every phase of rural activity tends to strengthen family bonds, whereas city living imposes many obstacles and difficulties in the way of the family. This can be seen from the nature of work on the farm. The whole family participates in the common task. As soon as children are old enough to work, they have their share of the chores. They may be given charge of some particular animal or allowed to cultivate their own plot of land. This gives them a sense of independence and self-reliance. But they also have a portion of common duties. They may milk the cows or turn them out to graze. They help bring in firewood or assist in the kitchen. Thus, their independence is tempered by a sense of social solidarity. This social sense is closely tied up with the family, thereby deepening and reinforcing the ties which bind all together. By contrast, city labor is often divisive. The family does not often have a natural interest in the work done by its various members, except insofar as it contributes to total family income. Children in the city are not normally integrated into a family productive unit. They may aid in small duties around the home, but most of their activity and recreation is done outside the home. Thus, one form of life is cohesive and centripetal, whereas the other is divisive and centrifugal.

The farm family is particularly well adapted for children's needs. They have space to live, to play, and to work. From the economic viewpoint, they are assets to the family, instead of liabilities as often happens in city life. Today they have practically all the advantages of city children — education, companionship, and recreation — without the disadvantages of crowded conditions, immoral influences, and excessive strain and tension. The country child faces more constructive challenges than is often the case with his city cousin. He must be resourceful and quick thinking, but he learns this constructively from meeting farm economic problems. The city child is also usually resourceful, but he often gains these qualities in contests with his fellows or by surmounting the hazards of the streets. It is this ingenuity which has so often distinguished Americans: both the positive and useful form of achieving marvels of production, and the less desirable form of mere cleverness sometimes associated with antisocial practices. The former quality is more likely to be derived from the farm, whereas the latter is more a product of urban living.

Studies on family life reflect the stability imparted to the family by the farm. Thus, divorce rates are much higher in the cities than in the country. By contrast, birth rates are higher on the farm. City populations are dying out. Their rate of reproduction is not high enough to make them self-perpetuating. Only through their constant draining of the surplus farm population can modern cities keep their numbers. These results are natural in view of the differences in environment: the one favoring and fostering the family, the other placing numberless obstacles in its way. In the light of Church interest in the family, it is not surprising that the Pope said that "the tiller of the soil still reflects the natural order of things willed by God."[2] The Pontiff goes on to say:

> This, then, is the deep-seated cause of the modern conflict between city and country: each viewpoint produces altogether different men. The difference of viewpoints becomes all the more pronounced the more capital, having abdicated its noble mission to promote the good of all groups in society, penetrates the farmer's world or otherwise involves it in its evils. It glitters its gold and a life of pleasure before the dazzled eyes of the farm-worker to lure him from his land to the city where he may squander his hard-won savings. The city usually holds nothing for him but disillusionment; often he loses his health, his strength, his happiness, his honor, and his very soul there.[3]

At the same time, there are disadvantages in rural living. They are not inherent or inevitable; indeed, they should be removed

---

[2] *Op. cit.*, p. 10.   [3] *Ibid.*, pp. 10–11.

if families are to remain on farms. Farm families still suffer at times from isolation, scarcity of social and cultural contacts, and lack of educational and religious facilities. Their health and hospital care is often inadequate. Sometimes, there is a cultural barrenness in the country, caused by overconservatism and excessive individualism. Too many farmers are blind traditionalists, unwilling to adapt new methods and processes. All this makes rural life less attractive, particularly for children who learn from motion pictures and radio some of the surface glamour and excitement of the city. This makes them less content with their way of living. Poor economic practices tend to lower living standards, thereby further accentuating the contrasts between farm and factory. Unless family farms adopt better methods, they will remain unable to support the large families they encourage.

Farmers too often fail to realize the values inherent in education and cultural development. It is true that low per-capita incomes have frequently stifled the growth of rural schools, but even when income is available it is not always willingly used for such aims. The same is true in regard to beautifying the home and the use of laborsaving machinery. Thus, farm children today want electric lighting and inside plumbing. The lack of such comforts is sometimes caused by conservatism as much as by economic stringency. Church and other groups should take an interest in these matters, since they influence the choice of young farmers as to their future way of life. There is no inherent reason why the farm should not offer all the real advantages of city life, together with its own special attractions.[4]

Family Farms. Because the farm is the natural cradle of the family, it is understandable that the NCRLC should favor family farms instead of large commercial farms. The ideal is a relatively small farm owned by its operator. In contrast to this ideal are large commercial farms, often absentee owned and operated. Likewise, farm tenancy is less desirable than outright ownership of the land.

---

[4] *Manifesto*, Chap. 1.

The size of the family farm naturally varies with the type of farming involved. A plot of land suitable for truck farming would be wholly unsatisfactory for cattle grazing or wheat cultivation. Moreover, with modern machinery a farm family can cultivate more land today than would be possible with hand methods. The farm becomes too large when it is permanently dependent upon a supply of farm laborers who have no hope of ownership. These giant farms are often more efficient from the strictly economic point of view. But economic efficiency is not the sole consideration in life. Just as in city life we favor small business in contrast to giant corporations and chains, so for the country we prefer the less efficient but more humanly satisfying form of farm ownership. Pope Pius XII is very clear on this point. "During the last century and even at the present time, there have been discouraging examples of attempts to sacrifice farming to other ends. If one is looking for the highest and most rapidly increasing national economy, or for the cheapest possible provisioning of the nation with farm products, there will be in either case a temptation to sacrifice the farming enterprise."[5] In another section of the address, he attacks speculative ownership or unwise proposals for nationalization or collective farming. He concludes: "The Church teaches that the whole economy of a people is organic and that the productive capacities of a national territory should be developed in healthy proportion. The conflict between country and city would never have become so great if this fundamental truth had been observed."[6] Any program which subordinates agriculture, with its family values, to considerations of productive efficiency alone would be contrary to the common good and to the organic nature of economic life.

Quite apart from the explicit statements of the present Holy Father, the traditional Catholic position on private property is based on the assumption that real ownership of productive wealth should be widespread. Any contrary condition is an abuse of

[5] *Op. cit.*, p. 4.
[6] *Op. cit.*, pp. 10–11.

this right. Large industrial farms, and even more so collective or state farming, diminish the incidence of real ownership. The same is true of an abnormal or an increasing rate of farm tenancy. As has been stated before, it is difficult to secure real freedom in a personal or political sense, when large numbers of individuals are not economically free. And full economic freedom presupposes actual ownership of productive wealth.[7]

Accordingly, the *Manifesto* viewed with serious concern the increase of farm tenancy in the United States. It quoted figures to the effect that the ratio of farm tenants had increased from 25.6 per cent in 1880 to 42.1 per cent in 1935. Fortunately, since 1935 the trend has reversed, so that a government report could state that "fewer of the nation's farms were operated by tenants in 1945 than in any census year since 1890" and "farms operated by full owners were more numerous in 1945 than in any census year since 1925."[8] War prosperity undoubtedly explained much of the change, as well as the activities of the Farmers' Home Administration (formerly the Farm Security Administration).

To facilitate family ownership of farms, the NCRLC favors private and governmental measures which definitely foster small farms. They would have tax and aid programs graduated in such a way that a differential exists in favor of the smaller group. Furthermore, they favor resettlement programs for suitable city families, which would reverse the trend from the farm to the city. There is still land available in the United States for such families, if only they are carefully prepared for the change. Likewise, land should be made available for young farmers who wish to establish their own families. In this regard, European systems of inheritance are often socially more desirable than our own, since there the farm passes intact to the eldest son. Here, if title to the farm is divided among the children, the one cultivating it

---

[7] See W. D. Nutting, *Reclamation of Independence* (Nevada City, Calif.: Berliner and Lanigan, 1947). Rev. George H. Speltz wrote a Catholic University doctoral thesis on the subject, *The Importance of Rural Life According to the Philosophy of St. Thomas Aquinas* (Washington: 1945).

[8] *Graphic Summary of Farm Tenure in the United States* (Washington: Government Printing Office, 1948), p. 2.

must buy out his brothers and sisters and hence start with a burden of debt. If it is necessary to go into debt to secure a farm, there should be provisions for long-term credit and low interest rates. Where necessary, advice and aid should be given to new operators so that they can make a success of their venture on the land.

The family farm program should not be confused with either the completely self-sufficient farm, as advocated by some enthusiasts, or the few acres in the country owned by an industrial worker. Some writers have advocated a self-contained farm, supplying practically all of its own food and clothing, with practically no dependence upon cash crops. Such a program seems unnecessarily onerous on the farmers. It is good to have diversified crops and to be self-supporting in regard to food. But it is straining matters too far to go back to the hand loom for clothing or the hand mill for flour. The NCRLC does not advocate such self-sufficiency, although it does favor somewhat diversified farming in contrast to the single cash crop which makes farm life an economic gamble.

The second program, of a combined rural-industrial economy, is desirable in itself, but not to be confused with the family whose first business is farming. The factory worker who owns and tills an acre or two of land is raising his family in a more wholesome environment. He has added security in that his food needs are not dependent upon his factory job. He may even get some additional income from the sale of surplus farm products. But he is primarily an industrial worker living on the land, not a farmer.

The family farm would be commercial, in the sense that it would produce cash crops for sale in city markets. It would be mainly self-sufficient for food, but it would buy clothing and some food from stores. It would use machinery (which would be anathema to some theorists who would return to primitive farming conditions) and all the other conveniences and comforts which it could afford. The farmer would own an automobile so that the family could enjoy the social life of the village or city. Since he depends upon cash markets to supply his money income, he is naturally concerned with economic devices which minister to farm security. These range from marketing and purchasing co-operatives and other forms of self-help or group action, to participation in state and national programs for general agricultural stability and economic balance between farm and city.

There is no conflict between family farms and homestead projects where families become self-sufficient in the matter of food, while earning cash income by occupations outside the farm. Both have a place in a well-integrated economy. Commercial farming, of a family type, is essential for the food needs of the industrial population. It is almost impossible to support the population of a modern nation on the land, even were such an eventuality desirable. There is a definite sacrifice in efficiency as farms become smaller. Machinery cannot be used to its full advantage and energy is wasted in doing many tasks instead of one primary job. Some people do not have the desire or the temperament to operate a farm. But, with modern machinery and techniques, it would be possible to support a large population with family-sized commercial farms. At the same time, efforts should be made to facilitate rural living for industrial workers who desire a little land. Decentralization of industry would aid this trend.[9]

Rural Culture. In addition to family values, rural life affects individual character. Indeed, it has produced its own definite psychological traits in farm dwellers. Thus, Emerson Hynes, in the June, 1948, issue of the *American Catholic Sociological Review,* enumerates seven quantitative and five qualitative differences between farm and city life. Rural occupations are more diversified; they are influenced more directly by nature; population density is less; mobility is also less; fertility is higher; costs are lower; and social statistics vary sharply, sometimes in favor of the country (as with crime, divorce) and sometimes in favor of the city (standards of living, medical care). Qualitative differ-

---

[9] *Manifesto,* Chaps. 2 and 3. For a good description of the Granger Homestead project and the fundamental philosophy of the family farm, see L. G. Ligutti and John C. Rawe, *Rural Roads to Security* (Milwaukee: Bruce, 1940), Chaps. 6–11.

ences include a different philosophy of life; distinct psychological traits, such as conservatism; self-contained family life; deeper but more limited social contacts; and varying types of arts and skills.

Rural attitudes differ clearly, although often intangibly, from those of most city dwellers. There is definite meaning to the phrase: close to nature. The farmer is constantly engrossed in such deep realities as birth, growth, and death. He lives in a world of biology. His environment is organic in the original sense of the term. By contrast, the city dweller often lives in a mechanical world. His work concerns machines and inanimate products, and often such abstractions as buying and selling, finance, statistics and calculations, and other impersonal things. Of course, urban residents deal with other human beings. They have their families, with the basic human problems and contacts implied in this. But this is often a different world from that in which they work. By contrast, the farmer is close to life in all his work. He is engrossed with elemental nature and hence may find it easier to think of nature's God. It may be more than a coincidence that the religious literature of the Old and New Testaments is full of references to various forms of living things and to nature in its elemental form of sea and sky. It is at least possible that the preoccupation with the mechanical and the works of man leads city people more easily into a humanistic and secularistic mentality, forgetting God and His works. At any rate, religion and religious values are held with greater tenacity by farm families than is often the case with urban families.

The versatile nature of farm life tends to develop a well-rounded human being. A farmer's life is varied. Today he must have skills ranging from making simple repairs in a tractor to some knowledge of soil chemistry. He nurses injured animals and builds houses and barns. He must adapt his plans to the varied pattern of weather and season. Since he sells for a market, he must know something of business and economics. Thus, he has a chance to develop many aspects of his nature, much more than is the case with the assembly-line worker. This in turn affects personality and character. There is a stability and self-assurance which goes with the known possession of skill and the conquest of obstacles and difficulties. This is evident in the skilled city craftsman, and it is even more true with the versatile and competent farmer.

These qualities are further accentuated when the farmer owns his land. He then has the added stability which goes with ownership and relative independence. He has more control than is normally the case with urban workers of such essentials as food, clothing, and housing. For the essentials of life, at least, he is not so subject to the vagaries of an economic system. Moreover, he is his own boss. He does not get detailed orders in regard to every phase of his activity. This is why he becomes restive under government controls. It is noticeable that the tremendous extension of federal power in recent years softened its impact considerably when it reached farm areas. The administration of farm legislation is normally less bureaucratic and more decentralized than has been the case for most social legislation. In the past, rural independence had been carried too far. The farmer was too conservative in the matter of adapting new techniques, particularly in such matters as soil conservation and increasing soil fertility. But at least, this was an antidote to the pragmatism and experimentalism which too often prevailed among urban groups.

The self-reliance of the farmer has now extended into useful forms of social co-operation. Thus, in the United States there are over ten thousand organizations for co-operative marketing or purchasing. About one fifth of the farm products sold commercially are marketed through such groups. Farmers often buy such items as fertilizer, seed, cattle feed, and gasoline through their own purchasing groups. In addition, they have credit organizations, co-operative insurance, and irrigation, telephone, and electrification projects achieved through common action. As an illustration, two out of three farms are now electrified, whereas the use of electricity on farms was relatively rare two decades ago.

Thus, the principle of self-help, stressed by the present Holy Father, has been vital and fruitful in our farm life. The isolation fostered by scattered homesteads, in contrast to the village community where farmers live and drive to their outlying holdings, has been largely broken down both by new forms of transportation and by community projects. Today farm life is in many ways more social and more effectively organized than is the case with city life. The cities are intensively organized from one aspect, but the individual participates less in actual community work. He delegates such actions to civic or union officials and remains content to pay taxes or dues. Thus city dwellers are generally farther removed from an organic social life, whereas our rural population is now participating richly in such organic activities.

Many of the social problems connected with rural life exist where the family-type farm is not the norm. Farm workers, for example, are often underpaid and insecure. This is particularly the case with migratory workers, although it also obtains for stable workers on large commercialized farms. The institutions of tenancy and share cropping are likewise fraught with social evils which could be removed by long-term plans for fostering ownership. In other cases, social ills can be traced to a long history of low income for farmers. This is especially true for educational and medical facilities. Since it happens that whole states are affected by low-average incomes this becomes a national rather than a local problem. As a result, there is considerable pressure for federal aid both in the educational and the medical fields.

Position of the NCRLC. The position of the National Catholic Rural Life Conference has generally been followed in presenting the material in the present chapter. It has issued a wealth of literature, in addition to the documents cited here.[10] Through its frequent meetings and many subdivisions, its program has been widely disseminated and put into practice. While the Conference concentrates on the philosophy and social objectives of

---

10 Some of the most important material includes: *Agricultural Handbook for Rural Pastors and Laymen*, by Thomas E. Howard (Des Moines: NCRLC, 1946); *The Family, The Church, and Environment*, a study-discussion outline with excellent bibliography (Des Moines: NCRLC, 1947), and the four volumes thus far issued under the general title of *Catholic Rural Life Objectives* (Des Moines: NCRLC, 1935–1944). These last-named volumes reprint papers from annual meetings and constitute a mine of information on the philosophy and problems of rural life.

rural life, it also deals with economic problems and encourages its members to work with existing farm organizations which seek better economic conditions for the farmer.

The central point stressed by the Conference is the desirability of the family-type farm. It advocates the preserving and the extension of such farms, both by methods of education and self-help and by government legislation. It also recognizes the inter-dependence of farm and city and maintains that a high level of industrial employment would aid the farmer through providing him with steady markets. It has deplored the artificial cleavage between urban and farm workers. This latter point, incidentally, was strongly stressed by Pope Pius XII. "You tillers of the soil form within your families a community of labor. You and your fellow-members and associates also form another community of labor. Finally you desire to form with all the other occupational groups a great community of labor. This is in keeping with what has been ordained by God and nature. This is the true Catholic concept of labor. Work unites all men in common serv-ice to the needs of the people and in a unified effort toward perfection of self in honor of the Creator and Redeemer."[11] Thus, a truly organic economic society could be founded, with common action by owners and workers in both city and country.

The Conference further advocates public and private efforts to enable those with the desire and ability to cultivate the land to become farm owners. It has consistently supported the Farm Security Administration and its successor, the Farmers' Home Administration. It has advocated measures which would enable tenants to become owners. Until such a goal is reached, it favors long-term tenure, which would give the tenant incentives to improve the land and his home. Moreover, the Conference fos-ters attempts to encourage industrial workers to own a home and a few acres of land. Part-time farming and decentralization of industry are considered valuable assets to family life. Some mem-bers of the Conference have sponsored successful homestead proj-

---

[11] *Op. cit.*, pp. 11–12.

ects in which city dwellers achieved the additional security of life on the land, while retaining work in factories or mines.

The Conference has called for the stimulation of a genuine rural religious and cultural life. It holds that the parish should take the initiative, not only in providing strictly religious services, but also in fostering the social and cultural lives of its members. This would involve recreational aids, study groups, training in the arts and crafts, and, where necessary, training in farm skills. Above all, the parish should give a pride in rural living and a realization of the values it confers upon the farmer. Particularly needed, in some cases, is a stress on the worth of general education and the need for keeping children in school as long as possible.

Various meetings have dealt with the economic problems of the farmer. In these discussions, the plight of farm laborers and migrant workers has been noted. Members have favored the extension of social security to farm labor and various devices for aiding migrants. Particular stress has been laid upon farm co-operatives.

> Farm co-operatives are necessary. Were it not for co-operative enterprise, the family-type farmer would be at the mercy of the economically powerful in society. Unorganized, he would find himself pitted as an individual against the organized forces of concentrated wealth. The farmer cannot allow himself to become a slave either of a domineering state or of the economic dictatorship of the mighty of the earth. The farmer will be free only insofar as he is organized.[12]

But the *Manifesto* is also concerned with the rural community merchant, and feels that his interests should be consulted and safeguarded when the question of a consumers' co-operative is considered. Moreover, co-operatives are not proposed as a panacea for all conceivable economic and social ills.[13] Finally, they should be infused with a Christian spirit of idealism, and not degenerate into selfish or exploitive groups.

---

[12] *Manifesto*, p. 56.
[13] *Op. cit.*, pp. 31, 58.

An important statement was issued by the NCRLC in 1949, dealing with the question of industrialism and agrarianism. This statement favored in principle the use of technology on the farm. "It is neither economically nor philosophically correct to regard industrial method and mass production as intrinsically wrong or incapable of reformation. Such an attitude seems hard to reconcile with the Christian duty of redeeming the temporal and of promoting social reconstruction." The machine has conferred genuine benefits upon mankind. It has increased standards of living, provided jobs, and often relieved man of onerous and exhausting labor. These advantages should not be overlooked because the machine has at times been abused and man made the servant of the machine instead of the reverse. Particularly disturbing is the fact that ownership is more difficult under our present industrial economy. But these abuses are not inherent in technological advance. They can be corrected by progressive humanizing of the industrial process, suitable government action, and sincere co-operation between the various segments of society.

While the Conference favors reasonable decentralization, it does not hold that corporate enterprise, the division of labor, or the factory system are wrong in themselves or responsible for all the ills of contemporary economic life. It does not subscribe to the view that mass production is essentially secular, in contrast to individual craftsmanship which would be the only desirable method of economic production. Such an acceptance of modern methods is held to be in harmony with the papal encyclicals, which lay down methods of economic reform. "One does not reform what is wholly corrupt." While broad ownership of productive property is socially desirable, it is not essential that each worker individually own his tools of production. The economic needs of society must be considered in judging the division of labor, so that the total effects on the individual, the family, and society are weighed in appraising its legitimacy. Even the distribution of land is not an end in itself, especially if it only leads to poverty or abuse of natural resources. But the family farm should be favored in contrast to concentration of land ownership.

Moreover, garden homes and rural living can be reconciled with an enlightened industrialism.

The full restoration of economic life will come about only through co-operation within and between various economic groups, joined together according to their occupations and professions. But this form of organization will vary from group to group. Agriculture requires somewhat different treatment than industry. In this regard, while self-help should be encouraged, government has a role to play in supervising and regulating planning by the economic groups. Its aid is particularly important in fostering international trade and the best world-wide distribution of agricultural products. All groups should work together for the improvement of the economic order. "In a technological society, agriculture cannot dispense with industry, nor industry with agriculture. Both should join forces in working for individual and institutional reform according to the norms of social justice and social charity."[14]

ECONOMIC PROBLEMS OF THE FARMER

There are many serious economic problems connected with agriculture. For a way of life which affords so many social values, it is especially beset with difficulties and pitfalls. It offers security and independence, yet no major occupation is so uncertain and insecure as agriculture. This paradox arises from many factors, ranging from the vagaries of weather to fluctuations in demand and prices. Three primary problems may be noted here: production uncertainties, shifts in demand and prices, and credit difficulties.

Causes of Distress

Uncertain Production. While agricultural output in the United States, taken as a whole, is remarkably constant from year to year and even within a given year, these averages conceal tragic problems for certain regions or for individual farmers. So great is the size of our country that drought in one region may be offset by

---

[14] The complete text is given in *The Christian Farmer*, Feb., 1949.

abundant production in another. Total farm income may be high, but at the same time a given segment may be badly depressed. One crop may be successful and another a failure. The biggest factor in these fluctuations is weather and conditions induced by weather, such as blights or insect plagues. There can be excessive rainfall or too little rain. An early spring may induce planting, only to be followed by a sudden frost. Citrus fruits may have a good season in California and a poor one in Florida. The next year conditions may be reversed. In the winter of 1948–1949, abnormally heavy snows isolated herds of cattle and flocks of lambs, so that dramatic efforts were needed to save the situation in part. Cycles of rainfall have particularly affected our wheat and corn production. Insect pests have been a constant problem. Accordingly, a farmer has no assurance in a given year that he will have an abundant crop, a poor one, or none at all.

The uncertainties in production have made many farmers reluctant to make capital expenditures which would, in the long run, increase output and lower costs. Such measures as the use of more machinery, irrigation and soil conservation, purchase of additional land so that labor resources may be used fully, change of crops and entrance into new forms of production — all these involve risks which the farmer often hesitates to add to the existing uncertainty of output. This is particularly true when, as is often the case, such changes involve going into debt. Few farmers have forgotten the debt problem of the 1920's which, added to low prices, made agriculture the most seriously depressed section of our economy.

Fluctuations in Demand and Prices. In addition to the problems inherent in uncertain supply, farming has had to cope with wide variations in demand and consequent price changes. Leaving aside war problems, there are two main types of demand change. The first is a long-term shift in total demand at going prices. This can come from domestic events or from changes in other countries. Thus, in the case of cotton, there has been tremendous domestic competition from synthetic fibres. At the same time, cotton prices here have been too high to compete in the world market. Again, the use of wheat for human consumption has been affected by dietary shifts among consumers. The opening of new land abroad and trends toward autarky have hurt the permanent foreign market. As a result, the probable future supply of both cotton and wheat could be sold in a free market only at prices which would ruin the farmer.

A second major cause of demand and price fluctuation is the general instability in economic life. When a depression prevails in the nation, general purchasing power is cut and consumption restricted. City consumers buy less, particularly of the more expensive varieties of foods, such as meat. The result is an excessive supply as related to effective demand. Under such conditions, prices of farm products drop sharply in a free market. In the technical language of economists, such demand is inelastic: a very sharp price drop is needed to bring about a notable increase in the amount demanded. The unemployed or those with curtailed incomes cut back food expenditures to the minimum and sacrifice many other things besides. Even when food prices drop, consumers are more likely at first to make other expenditures with the savings thereby acquired. Nor can the farmer, in a free market, adjust production so as to hold up prices. On the contrary, the lower prices drop, the more he is likely to produce so as to maximize his total income. This, of course, further gluts the market and depresses prices. The only way out, short of bankruptcy, is government aid to control production or stimulate consumption.

Credit Problems. The elements of instability thus far cited naturally add to the credit problems of the farmer. Private lending institutions are reluctant to invest in what seems to be such a poor risk. Even his own co-operative groups are unable to help when it is most needed, since the demand for aid would be too great. As a result, the farmer is unable to make adjustments which might help him to secure greater stability. Thus, for example, storage of livestock feed might be a sensible procedure for leveling out production variations in wheat and corn. But the individual farmer is hesitant to borrow for the purpose of constructing storage bins. Even if he were willing, lending institutions are often hesitant about such risks.

Another credit difficulty is that private lending groups are so conservative and tradition-minded that they do not always appreciate long-term needs. As an illustration, the best thing for many Southern farmers would be to get out of cotton production and into dairy, meat, or vegetable production. In other cases, they should expand and mechanize in order to cut down costs. In the first situation, land depleted by one-crop farming should be restored by fertilizer and other methods. But all this involves costs and some risks. The risks are reasonable, in that continued cotton farming by present methods is bound to be a losing proposition. Cotton produced under these conditions could not compete either with synthetic fibers or with cotton marketed by other countries. Yet, the education of farmers, banks, and others to make this change is a tremendous task. The result is a continued decline in living standards or political pressure to secure government subsidy for uneconomic production.[15]

Remedies for Distress

Production Problems. Some of the problems outlined above cannot be handled directly. It would be expecting too much of a government or private agency to ask it to improve weather conditions, even in this day when airplanes "seed" clouds to produce rain. But, for crops which can be stored, it is definitely possible to retain a surplus from good years for the sake of making up a deficit in poor years. For example, corn and wheat might be stored for purposes of livestock feeding or future sale. Such storage should not normally be made a duty of the individual farmer for several reasons. The first is the cost of keeping this type of inventory. The second, and most important, is the fact that such needs are uneven and unpredictable in incidence. In

---

[15] Two of the best recent texts on farm problems are *Agriculture in an Unstable Economy*, by Theodore W. Schultz (New York: McGraw-Hill, 1945), and *Future Food and Agriculture Policy*, by John D. Black and Maxine E. Kiefer (New York: McGraw-Hill, 1948). Professor Schultz's most recent work, *Production and Welfare of Agriculture* (New York: Macmillan, 1949), discusses the Brannan plan.

cases of this nature, the accepted business methods of meeting risks is through insurance. Here a program of crop insurance could turn the trick. This method must not be confused with government price support or commodity purchasing programs. It is designed only to meet the hazards of uneven production, not to take care of the economics of deficient demand. Since weather conditions vary so widely in this country, sound actuarial principles would call for a national organization to handle such insurance. In default of private enterprise, it would be the function of government to offer a crop-insurance program.

Where crops cannot easily be stored, it might be possible to work out cash insurance methods. Farmers in good years might pay premiums and receive payments when a crop fails. The only difficulty with this approach is that, with perishable goods, a fairly widespread good crop drives down prices, so that farm income would not necessarily be high even though production is high. However, it may be possible for the government to lend money to canneries and quick-freeze companies enabling them to carry heavy inventories over several years, provided they in turn worked out some reasonable guarantee with the farmer. This would have the effect, in practice, of stabilizing production where weather is the main factor of instability.

Stable Income for Farmers. In discussing farm prices and income, two elements of uncertainty were noted: long-term shifts in demand, and depression-caused decline of demand. The only remedy for the former is a change in the pattern of supply. Some farmers, preferably those with high costs, should get out of the contracting crop and into another type of food or fiber production. Normally, the price mechanism should handle such a shift in an automatic manner. When prices get too low, the high-cost farmer cannot make a living turning out the particular commodity and hence has an incentive to change over into some line which is more in demand. The concrete difficulty here is lack of knowledge as to the real cause of low prices and as to suitable alternative lines. Possibly the difficulty may be in high costs which might be lowered through better fertilizer or mechanization. It may be that research would discover new uses for the product, such as in industry. Cotton has been used on roads, and grains could, in the event of an oil shortage, turn out alcohol for synthetic rubber and use in internal combustion engines. All this is too bewildering for the average farmer. It points up the need for co-operative, state, and national action to equate supply and demand at prices which will mean reasonable prosperity for the farmer. This may mean lowering supply, increasing demand, or cutting costs.

When the problem of declining demand arises because of inadequate income on the part of consumers, there are various methods, in addition to direct attacks on depressions, for meeting the problem. Three are most likely to be considered today: adjusting supply to demand at reasonable prices by production control, guaranteeing prices through government storage loans or purchases at "parity," or a federal program to stabilize farm income even though prices are free and production normally free from control. Each of these merits appraisal.

The method of production control to keep prices at fair levels was used here extensively in the 1930's. By one device or other, whether acreage limitation or marketing penalties, farmers were enabled to keep the level of output so adjusted that surpluses would not drive prices down. Although the laws did not specify what was to be done with idle land, their administrators tried to encourage production of foods needed to raise the dietary standards of the American people. At the present time, a program of production control is not generally favored as the sole measure of farm relief. The farmers do not like it, both because of the red tape involved and their natural reluctance to cut down production. Independent experts oppose it because it lowers output even though the food and fiber needs of the population may be great. People may need much more than they can afford, in depression times, to buy at prices which bring a fair return to the farmer. Hence sentiment today opposes a program of exclusive production controls.

The second method, currently in use, consists of price guaran-

tees to the farmer. The producer is assured of a minimum price
for his output, regardless of the amount produced and the normal
trends of the markets. This is done either by nonrecourse storage
loans or by government purchases of perishable products. The
government today disposes of the latter items through school-
lunch or foreign-relief grants. In the 1930's, it often gave these
goods to poor consumers by a stamp plan. Stamps were issued
to poor clients which enabled them, upon the purchase of specified commodities, to secure without cost a certain amount of
surplus goods. When goods are stored, it is assumed that they
might be sold in a poor crop year. Production controls are an
integral part of any price-support program. Otherwise the government would be forced to carry ever-increasing surpluses. Nevertheless, effective administration of such controls has been difficult
to achieve.

There are two major objections to the parity-price program.
The first is that it likewise keeps prices high for the consumer,
regardless of dietary needs. Thus, the consumer-taxpayer actually
pays twice for his food and fibers. First, he pays the high parity
price. Then he pays in taxes the cost of government subsidies in
the form of purchases or loans. These latter costs will probably
mount, now that European reconstruction has removed the artificial markets of the past nine years. The second major objection
arises from the mechanics of the parity formula. It is based on
an historical record of the purchasing power of farm products,
in terms of industrial goods, in a period (1909–1914 for many
crops) which was considered a time of reasonable farm prosperity. Thus, if five bushels of wheat bought a pair of shoes in the
base period, the fair price of wheat today would be such that
the same exchange could be consummated. This example, while
greatly oversimplified, brings out the fundamental difficulty with
present parity formulas. It may have happened during the interval that great changes have occurred, such as declines either
in the cost of producing a farm commodity or in the long-term
demand for such a product. In the former situation, a ratio lower
than parity will bring a fair return. In the latter, it is necessary

to lower production or decrease costs and prices in order to clear the market and prevent continuing surpluses. It is true that support programs do not always involve the payment of full parity prices, but they do hinder the beneficent workings of the price mechanism in meeting long-term changes. This interference with the price mechanism is not necessarily inherent in the parity program. It would be possible by adjusting parities to favor one crop rather than another. Thus, if more corn and less wheat were needed, the former crop may be given a 90 per cent parity price whereas the latter would receive only 60 per cent. Unfortunately, political considerations have often interfered with such a use of parities. As a result, they have often led to very high prices to the consumer, excessive costs to government, and the encouragement of unmanageable surpluses.

A third approach, much discussed at this writing, would guarantee farm income but leave prices to be adjusted in a free market. Here a farmer would be promised a certain assured unit price (possibly with a differential favoring family-type farms), but would sell his output in a free market. His sale receipts would then be presented to the appropriate government agency and he would receive a check for the difference between actual price and the guaranteed price. Where long-term shifts demand production control, this could be accomplished either by lower assured prices or by direct methods of controlling production or marketing. Prices would be announced well in advance of the crop year, so that farmers could reasonably plan production. If a long-term shift were necessary, it might even be possible to announce prices for several years in advance to make long-range planning feasible.

The advantage of this method is that it gives assured income to the farmer and at the same time meets the dietary and fiber needs of the consumer. Production could be kept at a level approximating needs rather than effective demand at parity prices. The consumer would benefit from lower food and clothing costs. The farmer would receive a stable income. And the general economy would be better off for both these reasons and also for the contracyclical effects of such payments. They would be highest in depression times and lowest in times of prosperity. Farm incomes would remain high at a time when industry is depressed and prices generally are falling. This would stimulate consumption and help lead to industrial revival.[16]

When a bill to implement this third approach was proposed in late 1948, it received strenuous objections from business sources and commentators both in newspapers and radio. The main difficulty was its probable cost. Yet this objection does not have the merit which it seems to have on the surface, as a little arithmetic will show. Thus, if the parity price for wheat is two dollars a bushel and half of it was actually sold at this price in a depression year and the other half stored under government loans at the same price, the total cost to the economy for a billion bushels produced would be two billion dollars. Under the plan presently considered, the entire amount would be sold, clearing possibly only a billion dollars in the market. The government would pay another billion in support prices. The total cost to the economy would be the same, but this time consumers would be able to have the entire amount produced. In other words, it is politically probable that the government will guarantee farm income either directly or through parity prices and loans. Since farmers will get the same amount anyway, it is better to let them produce than to pile up unmanageable surpluses or invoke production controls below the level of human needs.

The question naturally arises as to how such complex government programs fit into Catholic social philosophy in general and the rural philosophy in particular. The answer may be given in two stages. First, under present conditions, it is impossible for the farmer to meet his major economic problems by self-help alone, even with the aid of his local or national associations. At

---

[16] For a thorough study of the Brannan Plan, see Chapter 15 of T. W. Schultz, *Production and Welfare of Agriculture*. The author lists in detail the merits and demerits of current and proposed remedies for the ills of agriculture and offers his own lines of solution. A study of this type should be consulted to supplement the broad and necessarily superficial treatment given in the present chapter.

the same time, the public economic good demands that such an important class in our economy be prevented from lapsing into destitution. Unless farm life is made more secure and attractive, there will be even greater migration from the farms than has occurred in recent years. Nor can we invoke the law of supply and demand to meet the situation, since this works very poorly in the case of farm products. Individual farmers cannot adjust production to demand at reasonable prices except over the very long run. This can mean years of desperate poverty and wide-spread bankruptcy, a social cost which the nation cannot tolerate. Hence this is clearly a case for government action.

Secondly, under the ideal we are seeking, the determination and much of the administration of such programs would be shared with self-governing occupational groups. Detailed proposals would be worked out by farm organizations and reviewed by a national economic council in the light of the general welfare. The resulting program would be offered to the government for legislative action when this is necessary. If the political arm accepts the program, and this would be likely under the circumstances, administration would be as decentralized as possible, with much of it falling to organized economic councils of farmers and their representatives. Such councils would be distinct from present organizations, such as the Farm Bureau, the Grange, and the Farmers' Union. None of these presently qualifies as a common-interest group for all farmers nor has their history been one of unquestioning concern for the common good of the nation, as contrasted with farmers' special interests. The Farmers' Union has been most in sympathy with NCRLC programs, but the political affiliations of some present officers are doubtful.

Another method, based on the principle of using existing groups rather than seeking new ones, might involve the combined representation of all organizations in occupational councils, just as trade unions and trade associations might staff common-interest groups in industry. In either method, some difference in personnel or objectives must be secured if the object of co-operative action for the common good is to be secured. A combination of pressure groups or special-interest organizations, even though extremes may neutralize one another, does not ordinarily lead to co-operation. They may achieve compromise or accommodation, but not full collaboration.

Miscellaneous Farm Aids. If the third proposal discussed above were adopted, it would fit in well with the NCRLC program. Family farms would have an assured cash income, in addition to their relative self-subsistence achieved by a minimum planting of food crops for home use and the possession of a few cattle, hogs, and chickens for home consumption. With a basic economic foundation assured, it would be easier to secure private, co-operative, or government credit for long-term needs, such as the purchase of land or machinery, or the improvement of presently owned land. Other long-range programs, such as soil conservation, research, and shifts in production to goods more useful to the community, could proceed more surely with such fundamental security assured. The farmer today is more willing than formerly to experiment and adopt new methods. But, since these normally involve either costs or risks, the community should give him some assurance that he will not lose in the process. Then we can have production adapted to community needs, with this vital segment of the national economy kept at a level of reasonable security and prosperity.[17]

In conclusion, we may note the objection that the unbelievably complex government aids to agriculture, both federal and state, are leading toward socialism or the welfare state. This charge may seem paradoxical, in that farmers are traditionally independent and individualistic. But it is levied, along with the companion observation that if farmers are guaranteed security, the same government support will be asked for industrialists, storekeepers, and the like. These charges may be answered in two ways. First, agriculture differs from most industries in that pro-

---

[17] Details of miscellaneous aids may be found in Chapter 14 of the present author's *Economic Analysis and Problems*. The treatment given there does not apply, however, to the problems analyzed in the preceding section, since farm legislation in the matter of price supports has changed in the interval.

duction cannot readily be adjusted by farmers to meet declines in demand at reasonable prices. Nor can costs be pared so easily. The farm-production cycle is determined by nature. For crops, it is usually one year in duration. For some animals, it may be a two- or three-year cycle. Hence farmers cannot meet demand changes in the same way as steel or automobile manufacturers. The latter also lose during depressions, but not so heavily as if they were forced, either by nature's cycle or the inherent difficulty of combining to adjust production, to continue at full production and get what the free market would bring for their goods. Farmers must organize to protect themselves, as industry and labor do, and this means self-help, co-operative groups, and government aid in a proportion determined by conditions.

Secondly, it is legitimate for the state to give appropriate help to industry and trade for the purpose of aggregate security against depressions. (Individual security is not afforded by farm plans, nor would it be a suitable objective for government aid to business.) This would consist of monetary, fiscal, and other policies designed to prevent or to counteract swings of the business cycle. Such aid would likewise be called for by the public economic good. It would supplement self-help and measures secured by organizations, such as labor unions and trade associations. Preferably it would be formulated by a national economic council, representative of all economic groups. In industry, as in agriculture, neither individual action nor collective self-help is adequate to meet the major economic problem of depressions and unemployment. The automatic workings of the market, while helpful in adjusting costs which are unbalanced, do not offer a solution of the problem either. Hence the state must intervene as the supreme custodian of the general welfare.

The problems of agriculture form a special situation, both from the social and the economic points of view. They are not unrelated to those of business and industry. On the contrary, all economic groups should co-operate and co-ordinate their activities with a view to the common good of the nation. But the differences in the case of agriculture call for a modification of general approaches to meet those particular needs. Such consideration would be a normal reaction of a sound economy to the needs of an important group. But it is the more vital in this case, since the social and spiritual benefits of agriculture must be preserved in our economy. The farm family is one of the great foundations of national strength. We weaken or neglect it at our peril.

A sound family-farm policy in many ways involves a paradox. On the one hand, one of the reasons for deep rural poverty is the relative overpopulation of many farms, in relation to their productive capacities. The remedy for this situation involves measures which will increase efficiency of production. This in turn may displace many persons from marginal farms. Yet, at the same time, we desire to resettle more families on the farm. Only the most careful and intelligent planning will reconcile these apparently contradictory aims. We must resettle surplus farm population on other farms, where able and willing workers can earn an adequate living.

The challenge implied in these goals calls for constructive statesmanship on the part of all interested in the farm problem. It is indeed unfortunate that such a vital economic problem has become enmeshed in political considerations, often of the most partisan type. Here is indeed a field for fruitful Christian social action.

READINGS *

The Pope Speaks on Rural Life.
Manifesto on Rural Life.
J. Messner, *Social Ethics*, pp. 914–917.
Catholic Rural Life Objectives.
L. G. Ligutti and John C. Rawe, *Rural Roads to Security.*
T. W. Schultz, *Agriculture in an Unstable Economy.*
—— *Production and Welfare of Agriculture.*
J. D. Black and M. E. Kiefer, *Future Food and Agriculture Policy.*
T. E. Howard, *Agricultural Handbook for Rural Pastors and Laymen.*
The Family, Church, and Environment.
P. A. Waring and C. S. Golden, *Soil and Steel.*

* For further readings, see List No. 15 in the Appendix.

O. E. Baker, *et al., Agriculture in Modern Life.*
W. Gee, *The Social Economics of Agriculture.*
H. Schwartz, *Seasonable Farm Labor in the United States.*
Farmers in a Changing World (1940 Agricultural Yearbook).
D. E. Lindstrom, *American Rural Life.*

Also the various publications of the United States Department of Agriculture.

Chapter XVIII. SPECIALIZED APPROACHES BY CATHOLICS

The preceding chapters of this section dealt with groups or schools which professedly covered the entire range of socio-economic problems in their selected fields. They offered a general philosophy for the attaining of designated ends. In addition to these groups, however, there are certain Catholic schools which are more specialized in their approach. The present chapter treats of three diverse schools of thought which have influenced Catholic social thinkers. These schools differ markedly in content, but they are quite similar in approach. In content, they treat of such distinct topics as emphasis on spiritual reform, stress on monetary reform, and defense of our present business system. But each school tends to consider its field as uniquely important, inasmuch as it has been neglected by other writers dealing with socioeconomic problems. These writers are similar to physicians who feel that the medical fraternity has overlooked some remedy and in doing so has rendered a disservice to the public. Father Furfey holds that the need for spiritual reform has been insufficiently stressed. The monetary school thinks that no remedial action which excludes its program is adequate. And Father Keller emphasizes merits of our present economic system which he feels have been passed over in Catholic social writings.

The approaches to be studied have in common certain merits and demerits. In their favor, of course, is the correction of faulty and limited presentations of Catholic social teaching. To the extent that these writers are correct in their analyses, they render a definite service by completing a structure hitherto deficient.

But such stresses also embody possible dangers. The uninitiated, not familiar with the entirety of Catholic thought, might be misled by these writings. They might consider the specialized approach as the only sound path to social reform. Hence they would fall into an error as serious as that which these authors endeavored to correct.

This danger is real. In spite of careful qualifications by the original authors, there is a definite likelihood that many readers will be moved by strong pleadings for a position and overlook the cautions inserted by the writer. When an author marshals powerful arguments for a position which he considered to be neglected, his treatment is almost of necessity one-sided and unbalanced. Hence, in studying these schools, two points of criticism will frequently be offered, even though they may seem unfair to the authors discussed. In the first place, note will be taken of what the writers did *not* say, as well as what they actually said. Such criticism does not mean that the authors should necessarily have given a different treatment from that actually offered. Rather it is an effort to introduce perspective which might otherwise be overlooked. Reverting to the medical analogy, a doctor might recommend to an intern a certain book on diet, at the same time warning him not to be carried away by the author's enthusiasm for the subject. He would note that the author treats diet in a superior fashion, but that exercise, sleep, and other factors are also important in preventive medicine.

A second point of criticism involves the mention of certain extremist positions which illustrate the potential dangers involved in a specialized approach. Thus, in contrast to Father Furfey's carefully worded statements, there may be some schools which hold that spiritual reform is the *only* way to social reform. The author is not to be blamed for this result, any more than one could blame a physician who is an enthusiast on diet for the vagaries of the dietary faddists. The noting of possible abuses of a sound position should not be considered as an attack on the original views which have been distorted. But, when the danger is real, it would be imprudent not to advert to it.

One further point may be noted in introducing these schools of thought. With the possible exception of Father Furfey's views, these positions are not Catholic in the sense that they are held exclusively by Catholics. Thus, the monetary reform movement is by no means confined to Catholic circles. It is studied here because many Catholic writers have taken it up, and some of them have cited encyclical sources as justification for their views. Likewise, the defense of American business is not a Catholic monopoly. Even the citation of papal encyclicals to this effect is not confined to Catholics. Thus, in 1949, a large corporation which suffered a prolonged strike called by Canadian Catholic unions used *Quadragesimo Anno* to buttress its arguments against the strikers. Nevertheless, the positions discussed here have sufficient influence among Catholic social thinkers to warrant the treatment given in these pages.

THE ECONOMICS OF THE SPIRIT

The Personalist Approach. The best American presentation of an emphatically spiritual approach to the social problem is found in the writings of Father Furfey, especially *Fire on the Earth* (1936); *Three Theories of Society* (1937), and *The Mystery of Iniquity* (1944). The author adopted this specialized approach because he felt that certain Catholic schools were overemphasizing natural means and neglecting the supernatural. At the same time, he warned against an exclusively spiritual attack on social evils. He would not undo what was currently being done, but he would complete it and restore it to balance by adding vital elements which he considered to be lacking at the time.

The central doctrine of the Furfey school is the idea of a supernatural sociology, based on the Scriptures and the lives of the saints. He contrasts a social science built merely on reason to one which also includes the teachings of Revelation. There is, of course, no conflict between the one and the other, since reason and Faith are both sources of truth. But reason by itself is badly incomplete, since it prescinds from vital truths known from Holy Writ and the religious teaching of the Church. Thus, the doctrine of the Mystical Body of Christ, wherein all believers are members of the same body, is a better foundation for social solidarity than arguments based on reason alone. Nor should we adopt a minimum position for the sake of winning over, in concrete programs, those who do not accept our religious faith. This is both wrong and unnecessary. It is wrong to the extent that we pick and choose among Church doctrines, publicizing only those which are convenient for our immediate purposes. It is unnecessary because people with diverse beliefs can nevertheless co-operate on concrete matters without suppressing their views. Catholic and Protestant firemen work side by side in putting out fires. Moreover, the total view harmonizes with the position of the popes, who constantly state that the social problem is first of all moral and religious, and that true social reform can only be had when preceded by religious reform.[1]

In the light of this analysis, the preferred technique of reform is personalist rather than political. Our actions should be performed primarily as members of the Mystical Body rather than as members of the civil state. Personalist action is defined as that external action which has charity as its motive. This could range from almsgiving to common liturgical prayer, since both are social functions. Even secret actions performed for this motive can be called social. A person may give alms anonymously and yet be social since his action was motivated by love and strengthens the Mystical Body. This motivation excludes individualism, for charity is by nature unselfish. Personalist action is not incompatible with political action, but complements it by supplying a higher motive. Moreover, failure in the field of legislative measures for social reform will not discourage the believer, since his personal practice of the social virtues is incomparably more important. Laws will not work anyway unless people are prepared to obey them, and this preparation must be spiritual.

One might go even further and adopt the technique of non-

---

[1] See references to papal writings in Chapters II and XIV. The ideas given here are developed in the three books by Fr. Furfey noted above. The first two were published by Macmillan (New York) and the last-named by Bruce (Milwaukee).

participation in an evil world. The Scriptures speak of the world as evil. True, in this context "world" has a technical meaning, being confined to things and persons detracting from God. It refers to the pagan secularist society of Christ's day, but our present society is also both secularist and materialist. Hence, if the world is evil, one should not co-operate in such evil or risk its occasions of sin. Moreover, withdrawal is a dramatic form of protest, a witness-bearing that we have no part in this sinful life. Separatism, not conformism, should be our approach. One method of achieving lay withdrawal (the religious life, particularly the contemplative, is already a form of separatism) would be the establishment of Catholic village communities, as economically and politically independent as circumstances permit. These laymen would have no vows and live normal married or single lives. But they would endeavor to seek religious fervor away from the scandals of the world. If this is not feasible, one might try to practice the counsels of perfection, such as voluntary poverty, in the midst of the world. This would involve loss and suffering. We would be looked upon as eccentric, if not worse. But so were the saints considered. We could choose worse company.[2]

A Critique of Personalism. The publication of Father Furfey's works aroused considerable discussion in the United States, since they were in effect a criticism of existing Catholic approaches to the social problem. Many readers felt that the author considered contemporary social action programs as partial solutions at best, often tainted with conformism and even naturalism. Some scholars were also of the impression that they were being charged with major inadequacies, inasmuch as they took a purely scientific approach to sociology. On the other hand, many Catholics received these works with great enthusiasm. They felt that

---

[2] The basic ideas outlined here were developed in *Fire on the Earth*, pp. 119–136, and amplified in the other works of Father Furfey. See also Elizabeth Walsh, *The Saints and Social Work* (Silver Spring, Md.: Preservation of the Faith Press, 1937). The analysis of nonparticipation through withdrawal is not an integral part of Father Furfey's teaching. His treatment of this program in *Fire on the Earth* was more in the nature of reporting than endorsement.

Father Furfey rendered a notable service by indicating what we could do *as Catholics,* in contrast to the minimum which we could accomplish jointly with unbelievers. He was given particular credit for emphasizing aspects of papal encyclicals which too often were understressed. Such were the diverse receptions given to his works. It might be useful, now that the fires of controversy have died down, to attempt a balanced appraisal of these ideas.

Certainly, as was noted in Chapter XIV, it is evident that the roots of modern social problems are moral and religious. Any program of social reform which denies this truth is wrong. An approach which prescinds from it is radically incomplete. We would be tragically neglecting our resources if our concrete programs were always identical with those of a political party or social-reform movement not motivated by religious ideals. What must be feared, however, in the school under discussion is the danger of exclusive emphasis upon the spiritual.

The social problem is highly complex in nature, and no one type of remedy would be adequate to meet it. Thus, some social problems are primarily technical. The Church, as such, does not enter into this field, but churchmen as social scientists and lay apostles may and should know economics and sociology as means of putting into practice a social order conformable to God's purpose in putting man on earth. Examples here would be the technical aspects of the business cycle and depressions, labor relations, and agriculture. Again, some problems are mixed. Good will and sound motives are necessary, but also adequate scientific knowledge. Most social problems fall into this category, in which neither good will nor sound economic principles would be adequate taken alone, but where both must be conjoined. A saint might be a poor farmer or personnel director if he neglected to study the technical problems involved, whereas a university-trained expert may fail in practicing human relations if he has no love for his fellow man. Finally, many of the organizations fostered by social-action leaders are but institutional embodiments of such virtues as social justice and social charity.

Another danger which may arise from this school is that of individualism or spiritual isolationism. Thus, Pope Pius XII, on January 22, 1947, stated that they are "simply unwitting deserters or dupes who, in deference to a misguided supernaturalism, would confine the Church to the 'strictly religious field' as they say, whereas by so doing they are but playing into the hands of their enemies."[3] It is true that this statement does not apply directly to the point in question, since it deals with another issue, but it does indicate a danger to be avoided. Father Furfey warns against such individualism, but it does not seem adequate to say that any action taken through charity as a member of the Mystical Body is thereby social. It may indeed be social, but it may not be the form of social action necessary to meet a given concrete problem. Giving of alms secretly is laudable, but it does not deal directly, for example, with a problem of communist infiltration into a labor union. It is not enough to make people holy, even by example. The institutions of present-day society must be reformed and permeated with sound principles. This is a task for organization, not merely individual action.

There are possibilities of serious misunderstanding in the technique of nonparticipation. If taken in the sense of detachment and unworldliness, then it fits in with our age-old Christian tradition. It leads to personal virtue and is by no means incompatible with dedication to the cause of social reform. On the contrary, the reformer who gives up worldly goods, when they could be secured, is better able to criticize greed and avarice in the world. He cannot be accused of envy of the rich, since he has given up what wealth he might have had.

But, if nonparticipation is understood in the sense of withdrawal from the world and its evils, and involves lack of interest in the struggle for social reform, it becomes seriously inadequate. It may have its merits, in terms of individual sanctification. It may also have some value in bearing witness. But if it were to be the preferred technique, then the approach of the Catholic

---

[3] Address to members of *Renascita Cristiana*, cited in *Catholic Mind*, July, 1947.

Church through the centuries has been badly deficient. We rightly have our monastic orders and contemplatives giving their lives exclusively to religious perfection and worship of God. But we also have our bishops and diocesan priests who live in the world and are apostles to the world. Recent popes have further emphasized the need for lay apostles, who will permeate their environment with the leaven of Christ's teaching. The idea of separate Catholic communities may not be condemned as wrong, but, as Father Furfey notes in *The Mystery of Iniquity,* the greater need today is for movements like that of Jocism, which sends Catholic apostles into the factories and mines. We honor and revere our martyrs, but the list of canonized saints also includes confessors and apostles. It is not for everyone to withdraw and concentrate upon saving his own soul; some must be in the active ministry. Of course, there is no inherent conflict between the two approaches, provided neither is considered as the *exclusive* way to heaven. One may rightly choose either approach, as God's grace inclines the individual. But, to the extent that some persons have misread Father Furfey's books and missed his careful qualifications, it is necessary to point out the danger of exclusivism.

The statements of the popes on the primary need for spiritual and moral reform must not be taken out of context. Even the excerpts from papal writings given in connection with Chapter XIV indicate clearly the complexity of the social problem and the means needed to solve it. In all candor, it must be stated that the heavy emphasis upon personalism and nonparticipation, in the books under study, does not accord with apportionment of subjects in the social encyclicals, as can be seen from the excerpts given throughout the present book. This does not involve any misreading of papal documents on the part of Father Furfey, who is professedly emphasizing an aspect which he felt had been neglected. But readers who have not consulted the original documents may well gain a misleading impression from the selected texts given in these books.

The social problem is primarily moral and spiritual. But the most badly needed method of reform *in situ* is the permeation of social institutions with social justice and social charity. To do this, every step must be taken to free men from avarice, greed, and worldliness. A sense of spiritual values and submission to the transcendent authority of the Creator and Redeemer is likewise necessary. Individual apostles, both lay and clerical, must use all available means to secure grace and the help of the Holy Spirit. Personal formation is a prelude to sound action. But with motivation and help, their concrete actions will often be in the world of business and labor, seeking a better organization of society in terms of the common good.

Some Catholics may prefer the safer, more consoling, and at times easier path of seeking personal sanctity and offering their prayer and penance for the world. But they should help, not look down upon, those who face the arduous task of being in the world, but not of it; of bringing Christ to a hostile environment, not merely welcoming him in Church or cloister; of working in season and out of season, in toils and tribulations, spending and being spent, worn down by the solicitude of the churches, going to the Acropolis to preach Christ to a skeptical and agnostic crowd; and ending their lives weary and broken in the service of the Master. Ministering angels hover over the deathbeds of such men, as well as over the bare boards of a monastic cell where a holy sister or monk is preparing to go to an eternal reward.

In fairness to the personalist school, it should be noted that many of its devotees live heroic lives in bringing Christ to the least fortunate of their brethren. They work in slums, among the very poor, living in conditions which involve great personal sacrifice. Such work is indeed beyond criticism. But it is no derogation of heroic sanctity to note that these activities are but partial solutions of the problem. Work must also be done to root out the socioeconomic causes of destitution, racial discrimination, and like evils. While some minister to the victims of injustice, others must strive to change institutions which lead to oppressive conditions. These approaches are complementary. In stressing either one, we should not overlook the other.

Extremist Schools. The stress in the writings of Father Furfey has been, on the whole, a welcome addition to Catholic social literature. It has inspired many to imitate the saints in working among the poor and the neglected. Thus, the deeds of Christian charity found in Friendship House groups and among the votaries of *The Catholic Worker* belong in the tradition of a St. Vincent de Paul. But among Catholics who emphasize the spiritual approach, not all show the care and exactness of expression found in the books by Father Furfey. This comment applies particularly to the *Integrity* group. While it has made real contributions, its leaders appear to concentrate upon a rather narrow array of spiritual weapons as their main armament in the fight against present-day evils.

The zealous followers of *The Catholic Worker* have many achievements to their credit. They have been exemplary in helping the unfortunate. Many have made remarkable personal sacrifices in devoting their lives to individuals who might really be classed as "forgotten men." In addition, they have often protested and demonstrated against injustice, whether it be in a labor dispute or in terms of racial discrimination. On the other hand, the publication advocated pacifism and conscientious objection to the recent war, with members refusing military service. There is a strong emphasis upon back-to-the-farm programs as the main solution to economic problems. Because of attitudes like those indicated, many friends of the movement feel that a certain dogmatism and narrowness has at times pervaded its approach. This strain may limit its usefulness and even partially offset the good done through heroic charity.

The sponsors of *Integrity* act as a gadfly upon the American Catholic conscience. Their barbs make fascinating reading. Their concern is with integral Catholicism. They will have no compromise with the world and, apparently, no avoidable dealings with it. The present social order is seen by this group as so hopelessly corrupt that it should be scrapped and replaced rather than reformed. As an economic system, they have embraced distributism. The city, the factory, the machine are not merely ugly, they are evil. Social reform which is other than revolutionary involves reprehensible compromise. At times they seem to be fighting, at least in the social field, not merely what is wrong, but also what is naturally (in contrast to supernaturally) good. Occasionally they have been less than kind in their judgment of fellow Catholics, tarring them too readily with the brush of conformism. In their writings, they imitate the faith of the saints, but not always their humility.

Their faith in God and the power of His grace is admirable. It might be even better if, keeping this spirit of trust and prayer, they were willing also to use fully those gifts of nature, particularly intelligence and natural virtue, which also spring from the bountiful hands of the same God. They might note, with the popes and the late Cardinal Suhard, that material conditions often offer a formidable obstacle to virtue, so that in making man more human, we prepare him to be made more Godlike. In the words of Pope Pius XII, we must "take cognizance of social conditions which, whether one wills it or not, make difficult or practically impossible a Christian life."[4] Or, to quote his predecessor, "If you truly love the laborer . . . you must assist him materially and religiously. Materially, bringing about in his favor the practice not only of commutative justice but also of social justice, that is, all those provisions which aim at relieving the conditions of the proletarian; and then, religiously, giving him again the religious comforts without which he will struggle in a materialism that brutalizes him and degrades him."[5] We must sanctify and transform this world, not flee from it. We need apostles as well as martyrs.

SCHOOLS OF MONETARY REFORM

In contrast to the preceding schools, monetary reformers are by no means exclusively Catholic. Agitation for reform of the money system has appeared in most industrial countries in times of depression. It has been a periodic phenomenon in the United

---

[4] *Solennità della Pentecoste*, No. 1676.

[5] *Firmissimam Constantiam*, No. 23.

States from the very beginnings of the Republic. Accordingly, its vogue among certain Catholics is only normal. What is more pertinent here is the fact that such writers often quote papal encyclicals as additional authority for their views. The references in *Rerum Novarum* to "rapacious usury" and "the arts of usury" are cited together with the well-known passage of *Quadragesimo Anno,* where speaking of economic dictatorship, it is said:

> This dictatorship is being most forcibly exercised by those who, since they hold the money and completely control it, control credit also and rule the lending of money. Hence they regulate the flow, so to speak, of the life-blood whereby the entire economic system lives, and have so firmly in their grasp the soul, as it were, of economic life that no one can breathe against their will (No. 106).

Thus, it is held that the popes have also condemned the financial abuses which are castigated in the books cited below.

Catholic writers have gone to various lengths in discussing the problem. They range from the fairly moderate presentations of Hollis and Benvenisti to extremes in Drinkwater and Fahey.[6]

Some of the Catholic social reformers in the nineteenth century, particularly in Austria, adopted similar positions, often with obnoxious overtones of anti-Semitism. The positions discussed here might be called extreme, not only because of their economic unorthodoxy, but also because of certain psychological elements contained in their presentations. In most cases, the authors are not trained economists. They usually offer a very simple solution for what has been considered a most complex problem. To explain why such an obvious approach escaped the experts in the field, the authors usually have recourse to the conspiracy hypothesis. They allege that bankers have invented a mumbo jumbo to cover up their machinations, taking in not merely their victims, but so-called experts as well. It remained for these honest

---

[6] C. Hollis, *The Breakdown of Money* (New York: Sheed & Ward, 1934); J. L. Benvenisti, *The Iniquitous Contract* (London: Burns, Oates, 1937); F. H. Drinkwater, *Money and Social Justice* (London: Burns, Oates, 1934); and D. Fahey, *Money Manipulation and Social Order* (Dublin: Browne and Nolan, 1944).

writers, in the simplicity of their hearts, to detect what scholars have overlooked.

> The only difficulty is an artificial one, arising from an almost complete boycott of the truth on the part of the ordinary press, the cinema, and the wireless, as well as (of course) the professional exponents of "economics." But anybody of ordinary intelligence, who cares to look over the invisible hedge of boycott, can easily look into the matter now and see the truth for himself.[7]

Arguments of the Reformers. As a rule, the central point which creates frenzied excitement in the schools under discussion is the admission (by incautious economists!) that banks can create credit money in the course of their operations. This fountain-pen money is made out of thin air, but brings enormous profits to the banks. What is even worse, in times of war or depression, the government goes to the banks to borrow a credit which could just as easily be created by its own fiscal mechanism, without leaving an enormous debt for posterity to pay. Thus, the central banking system is considered an octopus, preying upon the more productive parts of the economic system. Other authors, such as Benvenisti, attack the phenomenon of compound interest as the one means of growing enormously rich on the toil of others.

A certain plausibility is given to the monetary reform school by the fact of depressions and violent price-level changes. It is obvious that in a time of depression people are short of money. Goods remain unsold and inventories accumulate, not because of satiety on the part of consumers, but simply because they cannot afford to buy. It is easy to conclude from this fact that there is a shortage of money. With certain writers this becomes a bloodsucking conspiracy. Banking groups drive down prices so that they can the more easily buy in the wealth of a nation.

Of course, most reputable economists also envision monetary causes of depressions. Their analyses and proposed remedies vary, but few of any prominence would hold that monetary factors are exclusive sources of business slumps. Of those who stress

---

[7] F. H. Drinkwater, *op. cit.*, pp. ix–x.

money and credit, some hold that there are inherent weaknesses in the present system, but most feel that a basically sound mechanism has been mismanaged. No economist of stature holds for the conspiracy theory.[8]

Objections to Monetary Proposals. It is obviously impossible in the space herein available to offer a thorough discussion of this school of thought. Such a treatment would call for a two-volume study, one to explain money and banking, and the other to describe and answer the various reform systems. Careful and patient study is necessary to master such an intricate field and there are no short cuts. Accordingly, the most that can be given here are some popular arguments against the conspiracy theory. If men of sound judgment can be convinced that there are no deep plots being concealed, and that the complexity of monetary problems is inherent in the subject rather than a camouflage to conceal dishonesty, they may be willing to undertake the studies needed to acquire some competence in this field.

In the first place, the few quotations culled from the popes do not support the superstructure usually built upon them. Usury, in the sense of excessive interest rates, is not a major problem today. It exists in the small-loan field, but it does not affect in any important way the workings of the economic system. Nor need we worry today about anyone getting fabulously rich through the workings of compound interest. The United States is the wealthiest nation in the world, but no American fortunes have been made merely by reinvesting interest received on loans. With present income-tax rates and living expenses, a person not engaged actively in business, or at least in more lucrative investments than loans, would necessarily be living out of capital rather than accumulating more funds.

The indictment by Pope Pius XI would apply more to the

---

[8] For literature on the subject, see G. D. H. Cole (ed.), *What Everybody Wants to Know About Money* (New York: Knopf, 1933); J. E. Reeve, *Monetary Reform Movements* (Washington: American Council on Public Affairs, 1943); M. G. Myers, *Monetary Proposals for Social Reform* (New York: Columbia Univ. Press, 1940); P. Einzig, *Monetary Reform in Theory and Practice* (New York: Macmillan, 1936); and L. V. Chandler, *The Economics of Money and Banking* (New York: Harper, 1948).

investment-banking system than the commercial banks attacked by the reformers. Ordinary banks are not usually permitted here to make capital loans to business. The credit which leads to economic dictatorship is exercised through the flotation of stocks and bonds, not through loans. American writers have treated of "financial empires" which dominate over our economic system, but they normally refer to insurance companies and investment houses, rather than to ordinary banks. Credit creation, in the sense used by Father Drinkwater and others, is not involved. Stocks and bonds are sold to individuals and institutions either in open markets or through private sales, much the same way as any other commodity is sold. It is only because few firms have the experience and resources to market securities that such firms exercise considerable power in the industrial and business world. Naturally, the fifty billions or more controlled by the life-insurance companies give them enormous economic power. But they do not even have the name "bankers." Of course, since 1933, investment and commerical banking have been completely divorced by law in the United States.

It would seem the part of common sense to discount the conspiracy hypothesis. After all, economists are not fools, nor have they been corrupted by secret subsidies from the banking fraternity. A gigantic conspiracy of this nature could hardly remain hidden from the general public. Some person of integrity would break down and tell all. This is the more true since banks appear to suffer in depressions as much as others. About four thousand banks failed during the 1929 depression, and seven thousand more went under in the decade preceding. Must one then assume a supermonopoly which controlled the fountain pens used to create money?

No bank would fail if it could create funds at will. Actually, bank profits are not unusually high. They are required by law to withhold profits until a reserve is accumulated which is equal to the amount of their capital stock. On this combined equity, it is rare that a bank earns more than 8 per cent. During depressions their losses often exceeded that amount. On individual loans, bank profits average 1 per cent, which is less than the sales profit of most industries. No individual bank can create credit indefinitely and at will. Rather, it may loan only a major fraction of the funds given to it by depositors, keeping a minor fraction as a legal reserve. These deposits must be repaid in full to their owners. The myth of "fountain-pen money" arose from the ability of the banking system *as a whole* to expand credit. The mechanism which makes this possible is explained in reputable textbooks.

The American banking system is thoroughly regulated in the public interest. Its loans are checked for soundness by bank examiners. Credit policies are controlled by our central banking system through the Federal Reserve Board of Governors. The Board is an agency of the United States government, appointed by the President and approved by the Senate. Individual banks contribute to the capital of the twelve Federal Reserve banks, but they receive practically no profit from the funds subscribed, nor do they control Federal Reserve policies. Hence, it may be legitimate to recommend reforms in our money system, but it is false to consider the American banking system as a superstate controlling both government and business.

Excessive reliance upon monetary reforms as means for curbing depressions is a dangerous delusion. Money is not real wealth. In itself, it is useless as food, clothing, or housing. Its main value is that it is an extremely convenient embodiment of real wealth and a marvelous means for exchanging such wealth. It maintains this conventional value so long as the normal rules of sound finance are followed. But, if we were to follow the advice of the monetary reformers and create money haphazardly as a business stimulant, we would be courting disaster. Those who control real wealth — goods and services — would refuse to surrender this for money now considered worthless. The result would be skyrocketing inflation, as happened in Germany in the 1920's and in China in the 1940's. The economic system would be paralyzed, as primitive barter replaced the complex exchange media so necessary today. Monetary tinkering may be compared to a dangerous drug. In an emergency and in the hands of competent experts it may prove successful. But uncontrolled and amateur use would be fatal.

A sounder approach would be to consider the monetary problem as one of many phases involved in the public economic welfare. Credit control and measures to curb inflation and deflation are vitally needed. They are too important to rest in private hands, so they are rightly under public control in most countries today. But steps taken to meet proper credit needs should be part of a harmonious over-all pattern of sound economic action. They should be correlated with suitable means to stimulate investment, to secure a sound distribution of income, to provide a tax system which meets the needs of the common good, to insure a right relationship in matters of wages and prices, to even out the peaks and troughs in the purchase of durable goods, and generally to co-ordinate the activities of many economic groups for the welfare of all. A national economic council, broadly representative of all parties concerned, might achieve this. It will not be secured by monetary reform alone.

The remarks just made do not imply, of course, that there are no monetary problems or that mismanagement of money could not lead to grave economic harm. What is criticized here is the extremist view that some secret fault in our monetary system, existing as a result of a conspiracy among bankers, is the basis for our economic evils. The faults existing in present-day monetary management are well known and have been discussed openly in the press and in learned journals. These faults are not laid at the doors of commercial bankers. Our problem, rather, is the immense monetary power of the federal government and the uncertain and haphazard way in which it is frequently used. The centralization of monetary controls in government is not in itself wrong. Indeed, we would be better off if there were more centralization. At present this important power is exercised by two major government agencies which do not always work in harmony, namely, the Federal Reserve System and the Treasury. If full centralization could be achieved in monetary policy, and this power exercized jointly with a national economic council, conditions would be greatly improved.

In our present situation, the Federal Reserve Board seems to follow more closely the ideals of the common good. It is concerned with policies which promote general economic stability. Treasury programs, on the other hand, emphasize only a limited aspect of the common good, namely, the stability of government bond prices and the ease of government financing. Political considerations, in a partisan sense, are more likely to intrude into Treasury decisions. The Treasury, in turn, is influenced by Congress in terms of tax and spending programs. Thus, banking controls to stem an inflationary movement could be nullified by excessive spending and timorous tax policies. Thorough coordination of fiscal and monetary policies, for the common good, has yet to be achieved.

A DEFENSE OF AMERICAN BUSINESS

The final school to be considered here is likewise a specialized Catholic interpretation of the Church's social teaching. The writings of Father Edward A. Keller, C.S.C., fall into two broad categories, one dealing with papal encyclicals and the other presenting selected facts about American economic life. Both analyses are motivated by the purpose of correcting exaggerations by liberal groups. The author felt that this latter element was presenting a false view of the social problem in America and a distorted, overselective picture of the papal encyclicals. In making these corrections, however, the author faced the danger that his views in turn might be misinterpreted. Thus, in presenting what might be called the conservative aspect of the social encyclicals, there is the possibility that uncritical readers might consider the pope a defender of the *status quo*. Likewise, a correction of errors in regard to current distribution of wealth and income might lead to insufficient attention to the problems which exist in this area. It is true that the author qualified his studies by indicating their limited scope. Nevertheless, in the interest of a completely balanced presentation of both the fields discussed, it might be useful to spell out in more detail the full picture in each field.

The studies to be analyzed here include the pamphlet, "The Church and Our Economic System"; a book, *A Study of the Physical Assets, Sometimes Called Wealth, of the United States, 1922–1933;* a brochure, "The National Income and Its Distribution"; and a small book, *Who Gets How Much for Doing What in America?*[9] The teaching contained in these studies merits more study than is feasible here, but some clarifications are in order.

Encyclicals and American Life. The study entitled "The Church and Our Economic System" begins with the statement that it "makes no attempt to give a full exposition of the social justice program of the Church. It seeks to point out that the encyclicals do not condemn our economic system of free enterprise but instead give a strong moral foundation for such a system." The author notes that papal statements enunciate moral principles which must be applied to local conditions by experts in the various nations of the world. He objects, however, to the practice too common here of applying such principles to supposed facts and preconceived conclusions and thus sanctioning with Church authority what is really the social bias of an individual or a group.

As proof that the encyclicals give a moral foundation to free enterprise, the author cites the popes' defense of private property and their qualified endorsement of free competition. He then asserts that unlimited competition, in the *laissez-faire* sense, was never the dominant ruling principle of the American economic system. Common law and (after 1890) various regulatory statutes prevented both excessive competition and monopoly. The author then shows that large incomes are not of necessity antisocial, provided that they are employed in useful investment. He further notes that our federal government never restricted the right of

---

[9] The pamphlet is a reprint from *Ave Maria,* March 1–15, 1947; the book on physical assets was printed at Notre Dame in 1939; the income pamphlet was published by the same press in 1947; and the second book was published, in 1948, by the American Economic Foundation, New York, with F. G. Clark and R. S. Rimanoczy as coauthors.

SPECIALIZED APPROACHES BY CATHOLICS701

labor to organize, nor did we have the abuses of child labor which existed in England.

The study next cites encyclical pages condemning socialism, stating that the Church has taken a middle position between the extremes of nineteenth-century individualism and socialism. In regard to the economic function of government, the popes likewise adopt a middle-of-the-road view between communist absolutism and *laissez-faire* noninterference. In discussing taxation and returns to capital, the popes are quoted in opposition to crushing taxes and excessive wages. While the Church favors unions, it opposes the class struggle.

It is extremely difficult to criticize the views summarized above, since they are admittedly selective and one-sided. Taken out of their historical context, they undoubtedly distort the social teaching of the Church. But they appeared originally as magazine articles intended to correct equally distorted and one-sided selections by liberal Catholic groups. Possibly such a polemical approach was necessary in the circumstances, to the extent that papal teaching was being presented as an unqualified condemnation of American business in all its aspects. Unfortunately many readers may not know the controversies which gave rise to these articles and may overlook the author's qualifications in regard to their selective nature. In that light, certain suggestions may be offered in order to complete the picture.

While the Church defends private property, it does not thereby sanction existing distribution of ownership, particularly in regard to productive wealth. The popes have been clear on this point and the present Holy Father has emphasized it. The same statement applies to the distribution of income. The popes do not condemn large incomes *per se*, but they have repeatedly stated that past practices in regard to income distribution were highly unjust. Whether this condemnation applies to present-day America is a matter of economic analysis which the author treats elsewhere. Likewise, the citing of passages against excessive taxation would be more clear were they supplemented by qualifying remarks. Pope Pius XI has made clear that these warnings

are not to be interpreted as opposing a form of progressive taxation, which demands of the wealthy a relatively large share of
contributions to the public treasury.

It was unfortunate that Father Keller, in defending American
business, chose the pre-New Deal period as an illustration. While
it may be technically correct to state that this period was not completely *laissez faire,* in the sense that we had some government
regulation of industry, certainly the dominant mentality was
individualistic, particularly in the 1920's. Since the author wrote
in 1947, his position would have been stronger had he chosen
to portray advances in business thinking during the preceding
decade. There is little point in defending a period which few
business writers today attempt to justify. Thus, while we may
not have gone to the extremes in the matter of child labor, the
exploitation of children was a serious problem in American
history.

The discussion of socialism and government intervention in
business likewise needs completion. While *Quadragesimo Anno*
condemned the philosophy and methods of socialism, it did not
exclude its program of immediate social reform or even reject
limited nationalization. Again, in treating the socioeconomic
function of the state, an opportunity was missed when the analysis
was confined merely to selected teachings of Pope Leo XIII.
Pope Pius XI gave a masterly treatment of the proper economic
function of government, in his discussion of organized economic life. Among the first duties of the state is the promotion
of self-governing economic groups actuated by social justice. This
is the true middle way between statism and individualism.

A complete picture of American business in the light of the
Church's social teaching would probably differ both from Father
Keller's study and the views he criticizes. It would note substantial progress in the nineteen years since *Quadragesimo Anno*
was written. Business would be given credit for growth in a
sense of public responsibility, particularly in regard to industrial
relations. The increased power of labor would be recognized,
but also some serious abuses of this power. At the same time,

there would be unpleasant features in the picture. The growth of giantism in all fields — business, labor, farming, and government — would be deplored. The enhancement of social tensions, especially as a result of pressure-group government, would be noted adversely. Perhaps the greatest lack in present-day America is the absence of a coherent philosophy to replace statist and individualist trends. We need above all the ideal of an organic society, in which self-governing social groups would work together for the common good. In a word, America needs a ruling philosophy similar to that of the papal encyclicals.

Distribution of Wealth and Income. The study analyzed above, and others by Father Keller, present certain economic facts about the United States in regard to distribution of wealth and income. Here likewise the author is selective, endeavoring to correct common misapprehensions in regard to both subjects. He argues that extremes of fabulous wealth contrasted with bitter poverty are not characteristic of present-day America. He correctly cites our wide distribution of consumer wealth in the form of homes, automobiles, and similar durable goods. In the matter of productive wealth, stock ownership of corporate property is well distributed. In addition, farms, small businesses, and service establishments are widespread in the United States. Hence there is no significant concentration of wealth here.

To complete the story, however, two points must be added, namely, the disproportionate economic power of large corporations and the narrow concentration of control in such groups. The essential point here is that corporations are predominant in the most vital fields of economic activity. They do over 90 per cent of the business in such spheres as mining, electric light and power, manufactured gas, manufacturing, transportation, and communications. Finance might also be included in this list, although it is slightly under the figure given. At the other extreme, only agriculture and the service trades were strongly noncorporate, with less than one third of the business done by corporations. General trade and contract construction were in between these extremes. While there are 500,000 corporations in this country, the six hundred largest own over half the corporate wealth. Technically, six to ten million stockholders control our corporate business, but well-documented studies show that ownership and control are normally separated in the larger corporations. Stock ownership in America today is not the ownership of productive property as envisioned by the popes. Too much economic power is concentrated in big business, big labor, and big government, and too little power remains for individuals whose freedom is buttressed by the ownership of productive wealth.

In discussing income distribution, Father Keller analyzes 1944 Treasury income-tax statistics and the national-income figures of the Department of Commerce for the same year. His intricate statistical studies and adjustments lead to two conclusions: there is no great disparity in income distribution, since 90 per cent of the national income goes to the group whose incomes are under $5,000 and most of the income of the wealthy group (over $25,000) is in the form of labor payments, since they receive only 3.5 per cent of total interest, dividends, and rent. It would take more space than is available here to give an adequate appraisal of these conclusions. Some general observations on methodology, however, might be useful.

Since it is not contended here that grossly uneven income distribution after taxes obtains in the United States today, there will be no need for extended consideration of the problem. Some points of method might be noted for the sake of completeness. Thus, it is important to note what percentage of income receivers are in each income level. If 0.1 per cent of those reporting income obtained a total of 10 per cent of income reported, there would be some disparity, even though it might not be excessive in view of the need for savings. Again, even if 90 per cent of the national income went to groups under $5,000, this could well conceal situations of great poverty. These points were noted in more detail in Chapter XII. Actually current estimates indicate greater disparity than would be gathered from the Keller studies.[10]

---

[10] The 1949 report of the Joint Committee on the Economic Report, entitled "Low-Income Families and Economic Stability," indicates how extreme poverty might

Nevertheless, the answer here is an increase of the total national income, rather than further equalization of present incomes.

The use of the term "labor payments" in the Keller income studies does not accord with normal practice among economists and statisticians. He uses it as the practical equivalent of earned income, including the profits of the self-employed and like business and professional income. Such terminology is likely to be confusing, since most readers follow the usual custom of equating labor payments with wages. As a result, the hasty reader is likely to conclude that wage earners receive 90 per cent of the national income. Actually wages constitute between 60 and 70 per cent of national income in the average year.

Another possible source of confusion is the assertion that about 70 per cent of dividends and interest goes to groups with income under $5,000. This figure does not agree, of course, with the

TABLE 6

DISTRIBUTION OF INCOME BY SPENDING UNITS

| Spending units ranked from lowest to highest income | % of total money income before federal income tax | | | | % of total money income after federal income tax | | | |
| | By tenths | | Cumulative | | By tenths | | Cumulative | |
	1947	1948	1947	1948	1947	1948	1947	1948
Lowest tenth	1	1	1	1	1	1	1	1
Second tenth	3	3	4	4	3	4	4	5
Third tenth	4	5	8	9	5	5	9	10
Fourth tenth	6	6	14	15	6	7	15	17
Fifth tenth	7	7	21	22	8	8	23	25
Sixth tenth	9	9	30	31	9	9	32	34
Seventh tenth	10	10	40	41	10	10	42	44
Eighth tenth	12	12	52	53	12	12	54	56
Ninth tenth	15	15	67	68	15	15	69	71
Highest tenth	33	32	100	100	31	29	100	100

obtain, even where a large percentage of income accrued to groups under $5,000. As an indication of disparity existing in income distribution, the following table, based on the 1949 Survey of Consumer Finances as issued by the Federal Reserve Board, might be useful:

Treasury income statistics. It is obtained by imputing income received by savings banks, insurance companies, and building and loan associations to low-income groups who have savings invested in this fashion. Latest Treasury statistics show that in 1945 only about 27 per cent of dividends and interest and about 55 per cent of rents and royalties went to the group under $5,000. Thus, dividends, interest, and rents constitute an important part of the incomes of wealthy persons. When capital gains are added to this, it seems clear that such individuals do not become wealthy primarily through "labor payments." This point is not noted in a critical manner, since such investments constitute an important feature of our economy.[11]

Father Keller's studies on wealth and income, like his analysis of the encyclicals, were directed primarily at correcting popular exaggerations. Instead of engaging in direct polemics, however, he used the method of objective study to answer indirectly the views he opposed. This technique in turn left him vulnerable to certain criticisms which could have been avoided by direct controversy. Had he cited the views considered erroneous and answered them point by point, the average reader would have understood and appreciated his position. But when the studies appeared as analyses of wealth and income distribution in the United States, with no direct reference to the background controversy, there was bound to be criticism both for omissions and for selective use of statistics.

A more direct approach would have been clearer and more effective. An apologist for business today can make many telling points, without any accusation of ambiguity or overselectiveness. Thus, a direct defense of the function of capital (the word is acceptable, whereas circumlocutions such as "tools" cause uneasiness in many readers) and business enterprise is easily made. Likewise, a blunt analysis of the present tax structure would be

---

[11] The best known research work on income and wealth has been done by the National Bureau of Economic Research. By early 1950, the Bureau has published twelve monographs on these subjects. Volume 12 is entitled *Thirteen Papers on National Wealth.*

sufficient to show how difficult it is to become wealthy today. Even with income before taxes, the semiannual reports of the President's Council of Economic Advisers show that disparity is much less than was formerly the case and that it is decreasing in recent years. Moreover, a very strong case can be made against present tax laws, since they stifle incentive for private (as contrasted with corporate) investment.

Business has made notable progress in industrial and human relations within the last decade. There is widespread effort, independently of collective bargaining, to better the conditions of workers. Even the high profits of recent years have received strong defense, without the use of the percentage-on-sales method of computation. Again, while many prices have been too high in recent years, other economic groups (such as labor and the farmers) have bettered their condition at the expense of consumers. It should not be too hard to prove that business is neither better nor worse than other economic groups. It may not be above criticism, but it certainly should not be made the exclusive object of attack by Catholic groups. A defense along these lines would have been much more effective than the involved statistical analyses actually used.

It may be concluded from the data given in this chapter that the specialized approach to social problems has both merits and defects. Its value lies in focusing attention upon important but neglected aspects of the problem. Thus, both Father Furfey and Father Keller emphasized matters which had been largely understressed in Catholic social writings. The value of the extreme monetary reformers is less evident, but there is a legitimate field of study in this province as well.

At the same time, however, there are real dangers in a selective study of social problems. No matter how carefully an author qualifies his own writings, there are bound to be readers who will miss these cautions and conclude that here is the whole truth in social matters. This is inevitable for a number of reasons. Some persons seek confirmation for their predilections or prejudices. In other cases, there may be no particular leanings on the part of the reader, but rather a disposition to seek a simple and all-inclusive solution of the social problem. Many persons are impatient with complex analyses and involved remedies. They seek something which is easy and decisive, not reckoning with the complexity of human nature and the intricacy of social institutions. Hence faddists and cranks are more likely to be attracted by a specialized than by a well-rounded approach. This is the more likely when an author, carried away by the importance of the problems he considers neglected, states his case strongly. Specialized writers would be less liable to misinterpretation were they to devote a relatively lengthy space to putting their problem in perspective and even repeat qualifications and warnings at important points.

The danger to be feared from the personalist approach is twofold. One group of extremists is likely to conclude that spiritual reform is the only method of social reform. They may concentrate upon personal piety to the neglect of institutional betterment. There is also the drawback of expecting the counsels of perfection to be widely accepted in society. History shows that only a few attain the higher levels of Christian abnegation. They may be an influence in society, but they hardly set a pattern which we may confidently expect to be followed by all. The dividing line between command and counsel should not be obscured. The former is law, whereas the latter is an ideal which we urge but do not demand under pain of sin. We would not be wise in relying mainly upon a technique which is of its nature limited in appeal. It is difficult enough to secure a wide acceptance of social justice and social charity, without demanding nonparticipation in this world or abstention from all but the most elementary economic concerns.

Another group may use the stress on spiritual reform as an excuse for inaction in the social field. They may argue that nothing really constructive can be done until we make people better. Hence we should have no truck with social action programs and concentrate upon ordinary parish work. What they fail to see is that social action, properly conceived, tends to make people better in an important part of their environment. It is not enough to use general spiritual means as the only religious solution to the social problem. This is like using rest, exercise, and diet to cure disease, with no attention paid to specific drugs adapted for the illness in question. Normal parish work will build up general spiritual health, but some diseases in the social order also need specifics if they are to be cured.

There are also dangers in the approach used by Father Keller. In the effort to counter exaggerations from the left, he may be unconsciously encouraging standpattism on the right. While the Church does vindicate the moral foundation for private property and reasonable freedoms for business, at the same time it calls for profound reforms of the social order. One such reform involves much more than bettering the condition of share-croppers or similar underprivileged groups. It calls for an entirely new attitude and structure in society. Co-operation must replace conflict, not only in the field of the class struggle, but also where competition threatens the common good. Moreover, it demands a self-governing organic society, instead of present trends toward giantism and statism. Even in the narrow field of specific social problems, misunderstandings could arise from the Keller attempt to focus attention upon the South as the neglected area in the nation. Some readers might conclude that this is the only specific area of social pathology, overlooking such problems as depressions, underpaid city workers, and family incomes inadequate to support more than two children. Our national standard of living is high, but there are many far-reaching reforms needed, which call for sincere co-operative effort by all groups.

Finally, there are psychological drawbacks to any specialized and selective approach to the social problem. It tends to convince only those already predisposed to the conclusions reached. It may give them additional arguments for polemical purposes, but it rarely persuades those inclined to the other extreme. Rather the latter draw comfort from the fact that encyclical arguments and economic facts which buttress their position have been neglected by their opponents. Hence they dismiss the rebuttal as partisan and overselective. The wise bridge player concedes his losers before he embarks upon a fancy squeeze play. Likewise, the wise controversialist concedes all that his opponents may reasonably claim before beginning to attack. This enhances his arguments in the eyes of unprejudiced seekers for truth. At the same time, it makes partisan rebuttal extremely difficult, since opponents can advance no arguments which were not already treated and given proper weight. Extremes beget extremes, whereas moderation wins adherents.

In reality, the social problem is too complex for any simple solution. Many lines of approach are needed before we reach an ideal society. There must be first steps and partial programs. Serious evils must be combated and lesser goods must be improved. Spiritual reform is needed, but institutional changes on a broad front are also necessary. Moreover, the two approaches are intertwined. Some detailed suggestions as to concrete methods are offered in the concluding chapter.

READINGS

P. H. Furfey, *Fire on the Earth*.
―――― *Three Theories of Society*.
―――― *The Mystery of Iniquity*.
E. Mounier, *A Personalist Manifesto*.
E. Walsh, *The Saints and Social Work*.
C. Hollis, *The Breakdown of Money*.
J. L. Benvenisti, *The Iniquitous Contract*.
F. H. Drinkwater, *Money and Social Justice*.
D. Fahey, *Money Manipulation and Social Order*.
E. A. Keller, "The Church and Our Economic System."
―――― *A Study of the Physical Assets . . . in the United States. . . .*
―――― "The National Income and Its Distribution."
―――― *Who Gets How Much for Doing What in America?*

Chapter XIX. CONCLUSION

This concluding chapter is more than a summary of the
chapters preceding. The purpose rather is to integrate this present
volume with its predecessor, *Catholic Social Action*. From the
combined resources of both books, a plan is presented for a
Catholic contribution to American social life. Of necessity, such
an outline is tentative. In neither field have we reached the stage
of definitive knowledge. There is still work to be done both in
the clarification of principle and in its application through social
action. But we may start with what we have and go forward
until we reach our goal.

THE   GOAL   SOUGHT

Economic Society. In the most general terms, we seek an economic society which ministers to the needs of man. It should
serve as the material basis for the protection of individual freedom and dignity, a sound family life, and properly organized
civic society. Negatively, we should root out evils and abuses
which threaten human values. Positively, we should strive for
such economic balance that social institutions will of their own
nature tend to promote the general welfare. These positive and
negative aspects are rarely separated in practice, any more than
moral reform is likely in the concrete to be distinct from institutional reform. We should remove evils by replacing them
with healthy social institutions. We replace, not merely displace.
In a proper social order, the institutions of economic life

should promote both the immediate interests of the affected parties and the common good of all. This means a society organized along lines of collaboration and co-operation, rather than conflict and strife. Against individualism, we bespeak the need for organization in labor, business, industry, finance, trades, professions, and farming. Such groups must, above all, seek the common interests of all concerned in the several occupations, subordinating such concerns, however, to the general welfare of the body public. In practice, this means labor-management co-operation in industry, organized action in business and the professions to place proper limits upon competition, and collaborative action by all economic groups to handle on the highest level common problems such as depressions and unemployment. In such a society, there will be a legitimate place for special-interest groups, such as labor unions or employer associations. But their activities will likewise be subject to the demands of the common good, and should be ultimately subordinate in importance to the common-interest groups.

As a foundation for a collaborative society, there should be diffusion of economic power. This is to be sought by three main methods: encouragement of widespread ownership of productive property; the development of a partnership atmosphere between labor and management; and the transferences of many functions, now assumed by government as a result of default by private groups, into the hands of quasi-public common-interest groups in business, industry, finance, trade, the professions, and farming. Diffusion of power will check collectivist trends which threaten individual freedom. Collaborative action for the general welfare means exercise of social responsibility by free individuals and groups, thus avoiding the danger of individualism and selfish atomization of society. In this social order the first duty of government will be to promote the aims outlined above. Then the state, freed from complex problems of detailed regulation, will more efficiently perform those duties which belong to it alone, encouraging, directing, or restraining the actions of lesser groups in the interests of the community.

Through common action, the various economic groups will seek the most efficient uses of natural resources and, as a result, a national standard of living adequate to meet human needs. Production will be organized in a rational fashion, so that labor productivity will be enhanced and workers can earn a family living wage. Sound methods of distribution and other devices should keep the level of production reasonably constant, with a long-range trend toward higher output, thus avoiding depressions and unemployment. Many men will then have the independence which comes with the ownership of productive wealth. Millions more, who are wage earners, will have security in employment and dignity in work. Such a well-organized society could gradually clear up social problems in regard to housing, medical care, unsuitable employment of women and children, and even the economic factors entering into racial and other forms of discrimination. With material needs thus taken care of, man would have the opportunity to devote more time to the cultural and spiritual side of his nature.

Means Used. The fundamental means for achieving this goal involve a combination of moral reform and institutional change. We use the phrase moral reform in the broadest sense, including a replacement of secularism by the restoration of God to His proper place in society; by working against selfishness, greed, avarice, and unsound ambition for power, with the aim of making social justice and social charity dominant forces in economic life; and by using all the resources of the Church in raising man to God, so that thereby he may be truly human. But at the same time we seek to infuse the social virtues into the institutions of economic society, so that organized groups will collaborate for the common interests of their occupation and the general good of all. This means that men of good will should strive to influence their economic environment, even aspiring to positions of leadership, so that the truth of Christ will permeate these groups. "The kingdom of heaven is like unto a leaven."

In carrying out this program, the Church has a great duty of education and inspiration. In the first place, it must train and inspire its own sons to think clearly and soundly in social matters. More than this, they should be given the flaming zeal of apostles, so that they will influence others according to their stations in life. Nor should the Church overlook the opportunity of direct influence on those who do not accept its discipline. Men of good will are looking for the truth. They will not reject our message, if it is properly presented to them.

It may be necessary to distinguish between long-range and short-term objectives in working out a program of social reform. Once the desired goal is seen clearly, we must appraise the existing social order and evaluate it in terms of the ideal. Undoubtedly the result of such study will be mixed. Areas of injustice and selfish individualism will be found. Here stern measures must be taken to secure justice for workers, farmers, small businessmen, or others who are victims of economic aggression. In other regions we will find much good will and high aspiration. This must be encouraged, nurtured, guided, and integrated into a sound pattern of common welfare. Much of the economy will be found in an intermediate position — confused, uncertain, and groping. Here we can offer an outlook which some will eagerly accept and others will at least examine, sometimes skeptically, sometimes with a feeling of desperate hope. We will have enemies in our crusade. Some will be from the reactionary right, seeking to go back to nineteenth-century *laissez faire*. Others will be liberals or even radicals of the left, who seek a collectivist or at least an excessively centralized economy. Fortunately, the influence of extremists is usually slight, if only the great intermediate mass can be given a sense of unity and direction. The Church can meet this challenge, if only we have the zeal and energy to put our own ideals into effect.

THE TASK OF THE CHURCH

Social Education Needs. The first task of the Church must include an intensified study of the social problem and the training of its members in sound Christian ideals in relation to economic life. In general, education must be the prelude to action. This does not of necessity involve chronological priority, in the sense that social action must remain dormant for twenty years until we have finished our task of education. There is such a thing as education through action. Again, we can use our present trained resources, while seeking a broader program of indoctrination. But, generally speaking, we will not have much influence until our own thinking is clarified, a large body of clergy trained in the social field, our laity in turn instructed in schools and through adult-education devices, and all groups inspired with the zeal to permeate social life with justice and charity.

We need more study in the social field. The goal should be a large corps of priests and laymen, trained to high scientific excellence in the fields of economics or sociology, and equally conversant with the social ethics of the Church. It would be tragic if the social encyclicals were misapplied through shoddy economic thinking. It would be equally calamitous, were our experts in social science to ignore the place of ethics and religion in setting goals and determining values in this field. There is need for further clarification in matters of social ethics. Obligations and objectives should be made as precise as possible in terms of modern conditions. But sound principles must be applied with exactitude and with full knowledge of the scientific and practical problems involved. We stultify ourselves if we give, as an application of Catholic social theory, a program based on unsound economic analysis. Nor is it a practical solution of this difficulty to say: Let the theologians and economists consult. Men trained exclusively in either discipline find it difficult to understand the problems in the other science. The only feasible approach is to have a sufficient number of men who are experts in both fields. Such men can write for theologians in their language and for economists or sociologists in terms which carry meaning and conviction.

The training of these experts should be primarily the duty of our colleges and universities and of the religious communities or other authorities who direct them. This is not an advocacy of inbreeding. On the contrary, it would be desirable that some priests get their Ph.D. in economics at a high-class secular university and then an S.T.D. in Rome, Louvain, or some similar Catholic university. But Catholic schools might well require for their degrees in the social sciences a knowledge of social ethics as well as technical competence in the specific discipline involved. The idea of theology courses for laymen, now happily taking root, might furnish an opportunity for our lay professors to acquire a high degree of competence in both fields. Our schools might subsidize such courses and consider this training in offering academic advancement in the social sciences. The Catholic Economic Association, the Catholic Theological Society, and the American Catholic Sociological Society could be important factors in stimulating these programs.

Training the Clergy. The next step, again logically rather than chronologically, is the training of the clergy. What is needed here, more than anything else, is to capture the sense of urgency contained in papal writings on the subject. It is difficult to reconcile the quotations given in connection with Chapter XIV and elsewhere in this book with the uneven and haphazard courses offered in many seminaries. Too often the only training offered is in connection with the moral theology course in justice. The textbooks used are frequently antiquated in regard to social problems and, at times, the professors do not have the technical competence to supplement them. Regardless of this fact, it is doubtful that any incidental training in connection with the treatise on justice meets adequately the needs of the times and the commands of the popes.

For a priest to speak with even minimum assurance in this field, it would seem that at least four courses are necessary, dealing with economics, sociology, Catholic social principles, and Catholic social action. The first two could be offered in the philosophy section and the latter two given at the theology levels, with social action studied at the same time that pastoral theology is taken. Such a program would not interfere with adequate training in philosophy, dogmatic and moral theology, Sacred Scripture,

Canon Law, and Church History. Few seminaries confine their students only to these last-named courses. Most of them offer other subjects, suitable in another age, but less vital today than a careful training in social problems. Secondary studies of this nature might well yield place in these days to the social sciences. The need is equally great for religious as for diocesan priests. Even students for the foreign missions find that in most mission regions social problems are pressing concerns. If present professors are not trained to handle social subjects, there are abundant opportunities for summer courses in the field.

We cannot wait for a new generation of priests adequately trained by the seminaries. There is need for courses to be given to men already ordained. Larger dioceses, particularly in industrial areas, could spare one or two priests to get an M.A. or Ph.D. in economics or sociology. Both large and small dioceses could give interested priests the opportunity for six weeks at the Institute of Catholic Social Studies. If 3 per cent of the clergy had such training, a vigorous program of social action would be feasible. Finally, there is need for some instruction for priests who will not have the opportunity to leave the diocese for study. This would call for social action schools, lasting from two weeks to a month, held in one or more large cities of a diocese.

Priests could attend such schools without leaving their parishes overnight. They would receive a minimum training, enabling them to co-operate more readily with diocesan social action programs staffed by men who had a more extensive preparation. Teachers in these diocesan courses could be obtained from local colleges and universities, from religious orders, or from nationally recruited staffs who would tour the country. If held during the summer, they could command a wider variety of trained teachers from other regions, but it may often be feasible to have such schools throughout the year, with experts who are not confined to teaching duties. A large-scale program of this nature would call for sacrifices on the part of all concerned, but the results would be worth the effort. Diocesan schools or even one-day meetings also serve as recruiting agencies for priests who desire more thorough training in these subjects.[1]

Training the Laity. A trained clergy could give moral instructions to the laity in social matters. The task of social education of the laity must be carried out on many levels. In the first place, there should be a social emphasis in our schools. The task of preparing a curriculum for this purpose has been brilliantly achieved for elementary schools by the Commission on American Citizenship, at the Catholic University. The Commission is currently proceeding with the high school curriculum. Moreover, many of the more recent Catholic textbooks in social sciences and in religion bring the Church teaching on social questions to high school students. Indeed, the problem now is to train teachers to use the newer texts in an adequate manner. Social institutes for teachers as well as for the clergy are a pressing need.

On the other hand, our social program has been quite uneven in colleges, universities, and professional schools. Many Catholic colleges require all students to study ethics, but only a few offer courses in social ethics and the papal encyclicals. The ideal would be a required course in Catholic social principles to be taken by all students in Catholic colleges. This should be supplemented in professional schools by a special course applying these principles to the needs of doctors, lawyers, businessmen, teachers, and even chemists and engineers. It often happens that engineers or similar technicians advance to managerial positions in industry. Accordingly, they should receive the same social training offered (if the ideal were realized) in schools of business and commerce. Quite apart from future business or professional opportunities, our Catholic college graduates normally attain to some position of leadership or civic responsibility. They need commensurate social training.

Once again, however, we cannot wait for a new generation to emerge from the schools. The social problem is with us today. Hence there is need for general and specialized adult social

---

[1] Further details on this subject and suggestions for diocesan social action organization are contained in *Catholic Social Action*.

education. This involves use of all the media for adult education, such as lectures, forums, schools, discussion and study clubs, the radio, the press, sermons, and similar devices. Nearly all the techniques named have been mentioned explicitly in papal encyclicals in connection with the social training of the laity. Moreover, there is an important place for specialized forms of adult education. These would include labor schools and forums for employers. Likewise, farmers and all the various professions should be reached, preferably through Catholic organizations in each field. In this way, Catholic laymen would be trained and inspired to the work of the apostolate, so vitally needed if we are to permeate our society with justice and charity. This training could be given by parish priests, by diocesan social action groups, and by various specialized groups of Catholic action. Whether the work be done by older groups, such as the Confraternity of Christian Doctrine and various Catholic societies, or by newer groups such as the Young Christian Workers and similar Jocist-inspired movements or the Christopher movement, the important point is that it be done. Experience will determine which techniques insure the best results. In all likelihood, it will be found that any of several approaches may be equally successful. The main point is to keep the goal clear: the thorough training of the laity in the social teaching of the Church, so that they will be apostles in their respective fields of work.[2]

As the work progresses, the need will be felt for various teaching aids, such as simple books, pamphlets, specialized studies, films, radio scripts, and the like. We have adequate resources in the way of trained personnel to meet these needs. Here the main problem will be one of co-ordination and direction of activity. This should be a challenge to national Catholic groups, such as learned societies in the social field and the various departments and affiliated organizations of the National Catholic Welfare Conference. These national groups could visualize needs and map out a suitable program. The execution of these writing and

---

[2] Several chapters of *Catholic Social Action* are devoted to the subject of social education.

related projects could then be entrusted to teachers, specialists in religious orders, and lay experts in various walks of life. For current applications, Catholic periodicals and newspapers would be of service. Ultimately it would be desirable to set up a national research and information service, as has already been done in the social field by several Protestant groups. We would then be doing a full job of teaching and applying the social principles of the Church in the light of current problems.

INFLUENCE ON AMERICAN ECONOMIC LIFE

Principles. Since Catholics are a minority in this country, the question might legitimately be asked: Could our social program affect American economic life? In reply to this query, there are solid reasons to feel that we may be influential. Some may be prejudiced against our ideas in view of their source, but those ideas, properly presented, should carry considerable appeal on the basis of intrinsic merit. Here is a middle ground between statism and individualism which should be acceptable to those who are groping for sound solutions. Moreover, Catholics are not seeking their own selfish interests in promoting these ideals. We would gain by their adoption only to the extent that we participate in the public economic good and share the common benefits accruing to everyone.

We should not meet opposition from Jewish or Protestant religious groups, since we have often discussed social questions with such groups in a friendly and harmonious atmosphere. There will be, of course, objections to any Church organization's mingling in the economic field, but this type of prejudice is now lessening among businessmen. Many are more receptive than formerly to the notion that religion can offer a positive contribution to the world of affairs. Accordingly, there is no inherent reason why the Catholic social program would not be of service to the general American public. Our task is to present our views in the proper language and with arguments designed to convince those not of our faith. We ask them to accept our principles, not because they are Catholic, but because they are true.

In the action field, Catholic lay apostles and priests engaged in social action will be working side by side with businessmen, industrialists, workers, professional men, and farmers — all men of varying principles and religious convictions. Our task will be to use the diverse techniques of influence and persuasion, adapted to concrete situations, to bring about a more social attitude in particular environments. In doing this, it is necessary to have both a clear view of long-range aims and sound ideas as to immediate objectives. The latter will normally be controlled by the former. Short-range programs should leal to the ultimate goal, although at times the course may be indirect and devious. Thus, justice may call for social legislation as the means for meeting a particular problem, although in the long run we may aim to decentralize economic authority and remove many regulatory burdens from government. Prudence and good sense will dictate the answers in this field.

Concrete Steps. One of the first problems to be met is the establishment of justice where injustice prevails today. It may sometimes happen that good results may be secured by relatively direct and isolated action. This is the case where the evil in question is likewise isolated. An example would be exploitation of workers by a single employer, motivated by selfishness rather than driven to such an extreme by unfair competition. Here the unionization of workers would be the obvious answer. But, in other cases, a wage problem may be industry-wide. The remedies may range from extensive organization and minimum-wage legislation to even drastic measures in the case of sick industries. In most cases, it is necessary for economic groups to organize so as to meet their common problems and needs. Such organization in the United States is fairly well advanced, even though there are areas where labor, business, or similar groups are not adequately united. Without overlooking the need for promoting unions or business or professional associations, the major task ahead is the encouragement of common-interest in contrast to special-interest groups.

Here we face a choice between creating new organizations or

transforming existing ones. As a rule, the latter approach is preferable. It is usually easier to adapt and modify what already exists than to promote something entirely new. Hence the immediate task is to minimize selfishness and stimulate concern for the common good in present-day trade unions, employers' associations, professional groups, and farmers' organizations. This is a task of education and persuasion. Thus, to promote labor-management co-operation, case histories of successful plans should be studied with great care. An effort should be made to draw general principles from these cases and to apply the principles to immediate problems in particular plants or industries. Both groups should be persuaded that it is to their common interest to find means of working together on mutual problems. In such instances, it is often helpful to work from the problem to the solution, rather than to propose ready-made solutions at the beginning. Here the clergy and trained laymen can perform valuable functions, not only as teachers of these ideals, but also as mediators in the effort to restore trust where hostility has prevailed.

The methods used on the local level may also be applied nationally. To the extent that we can influence national organizations of economic groups, directly as a Church, through our trained laity, or merely by the force of sound ideas, we can promote the cause of unity and collaboration. Here likewise, the problem approach is preferable to the blueprint technique. All economic groups are interested in higher standards of living, steady and full employment, maintenance of individual freedom, and avoidance of depressions. Unceasing efforts should be made to promote common discussion of common problems, in the hope of gradually enlarging the area of agreement. Many will still seek selfish, short-term interests, but the overwhelming importance of the problems listed should conduce to sober thought and concern over long-range results. On this level likewise, the Church can exercise an important mission of mediation and conciliation. This is best done when our representatives gain the confidence of all groups because they recognize our competence, integrity, and sincere interest in the general welfare. The mediation approach is particularly valuable for toning down hostility based on past conflicts and securing the abandonment of positions held through stubborn adherence to previous stands.

What began as conferences or discussions of immediate problems on local, industrial, regional, or national levels could, with the passage of time, develop into firm institutions designed to seek the common good in each area. Successful handling of particular issues leads to increased confidence and a broadening of the area of mutuality. All would work toward the common objective of steadily increasing production and employment. There might still be special-interest conflicts over the distribution of the national product. Even here, however, the degree of strife might well be minimized. Workers' interest in higher wages is often paralleled by employers' concern for mass consumption. Employers' desire for adequate profits and opportunities for investment and expansion meets the workers' need for more jobs for an expanding population. There might be gradual agreement upon a body of sound economic principles which all groups would accept.

It is to be expected that some problems will not admit of solution in terms of mutual interest. Thus, the promotion of small business in contrast to large business, or of family farms in preference to huge commercial farms, is a matter of general national welfare rather than of mutual interest of the affected parties. This would be an appropriate field for government action, since the state is primarily concerned with the common good of the entire nation. The role of the state would not be limited merely to conflict situations. It may need to intervene so as to protect the interests of groups which are not able to defend themselves. Present reform legislation may need modification or even extension. Illustrations of this would be an upward revision of minimum-wage levels and social-security payments, with broadening of the coverage of both laws. But the general trend of government action should be in the direction of promoting self-government by the affected parties, always subject to the superior claims of the common good of all.

The promotion of collaboration will not automatically solve our problems. It is a means to an end, not an all-sufficient goal. Definite technical and economic obstacles must be removed, if we are to have full employment and increasing living standards. Some industries must increase efficiency drastically in order to pay a living wage to their workers. Farm problems will continue to be difficult. We must make many changes to encourage small business, investment, and job expansion. But these problems will be solved much more readily by collaborative effort than by conflict.

The work of the Church in encouraging a sound reorganization of society will not be easy. We face a tremendous problem of scholarship in bridging the gap between sound principles and detailed applications which will gain wide acceptance. Once this is done, the educational task of spreading these ideas will reach considerable proportions. If we are to perform the duty of mediation, we must gain influence and respect in business and professional groups comparable to that which we already have with organized labor. At the same time, we must use all available media to promote a concept of government which is neither statist nor individualist. The magnitude of these aims might well be considered overwhelming and discouraging. But we can gain courage and resolution from the powerful teachings of the popes. We might also look around the world and consider the alternatives to success in our task. With the threat of communism or statism hovering before our eyes, and knowing the fearful price in terms of souls paid for a faulty organization of society and material life, we simply cannot acknowledge the possibility of failure. Time and again, the present Holy Father has called for courage and resolution in the face of the present crisis. He considers those who isolate themselves from the fray or who minimize the social duties of Christians as virtual traitors in the face of the enemy. He calls us to a crusade more urgent and vital than those of old. To such a task we must give our all.

A SUMMARY

What We Seek. Justice and charity, where injustice and strife now exist. Justice sought through education, organization, and, where necessary, legislation.

An organic society, based on collaboration and co-operation among the social and economic groups. The common good at all levels of economic and political life, to replace class struggle and ruthless competition.

Diffusion of economic power, through widespread ownership of productive property, as the best guarantee of freedom. At the same time, co-operative action of owners and workers for the highest possible level of production and the soundest methods of distribution.

What the Church Can Do. Educate lay apostles who will in turn influence their environment so that the ideals of social justice and social charity may prevail.

Promote intensified study of social problems by experts who know both moral and social science. Train students to the priesthood by a thorough study of the social question. Give special education to selected priests and some general training to all parish priests.

Bring social education to the schools at all levels, including universities and professional schools. Where necessary, train teachers and encourage the preparation of curricula and text-books for this purpose.

Use all the media of adult education, such as lectures, radio, press, and so forth, to reach the adult laity, both in general and in their specialized work as businessmen, workers and professional men.

How to Influence American Life. Develop lay apostles to work in their own fields, promoting a middle ground between statism and anarchic individualism. Give special stress to encouragement of common-interest, in contrast to special-interest, social groups. Foster harmony between capital and labor. Develop a sense of common problems and needs, to be met by joint action. Permeate existing groups with this new spirit, rather than seek to create entirely new organizations.

Stress the importance of such problems as depressions. Promote discussions with the hope that the need for common action will be felt. Advocate government intervention where necessary, but seek self-governing mutual-interest groups where possible.

Realize that attitudes and approaches are more important than techniques. Men working together for common goals will find the technical means for securing the best results. Divided they will fail. When they fail, government must step in, thus increasing the trend toward statism. The middle way is the only hope. Properly presented, it will be accepted by all but the most extreme Americans.

Appendix I. THE SOCIAL ETHICS OF
RT. REV. MSGR. JOHN A. RYAN

The late Msgr. Ryan offered an excellent summary of his social ethics in Chapter 24 of the 1942 edition of Distributive Justice. *Copyright 1916, 1917, 1942 by the Macmillan Company and used with their permission.*

THE LANDOWNER AND RENT

We began this inquiry with the landowner and his share of the product, i.e., rent. The arguments of Henry George against it are invalid because they do not prove that labor is the only title of property, nor that men's equal rights to the earth are incompatible with private landownership, nor that the so-called social production of land values confers upon the community a right to rent. Private ownership is not only socially preferable to the Socialist and the Single Tax systems of land tenure, but it is, as compared with Socialism certainly, and as compared with the Single Tax probably, among man's natural rights.

Nevertheless, the present system of land tenure is not perfect. Its principal defects are: The promotion of certain monopolies, as anthracite coal, steel, natural gas, petroleum, water power, and lumber; the diversion of excessive gains to landowners and the very large holdings by individuals and corporations; and the exclusion of large masses of men from the land because the owners will not sell it at its present economic value. The remedies for these evils fall mainly under the heads of ownership and taxation. All mineral, timber, gas, oil, grazing, and water-power lands that are now publicly owned, should remain the property of the states and the nation, and be brought into use through a system of leases to private individuals and corporations. Cities should purchase land, and lease it for long periods to persons who wish to erect business buildings and dwellings. By means of taxation the State might appropriate a part of the future increases of land values; and it could transfer the taxes on improvements to land, provided that the process were sufficiently gradual to prevent any substantial decline in land values. In some cases a supertax might with advantage be applied to exceptionally large and valuable holdings and to farms in absentee ownership.

THE CAPITALIST AND INTEREST

The Socialist contention that the laborer has a right to the entire product of industry, and therefore that the capitalist has no right to interest, is invalid unless the former alleged right can be effectuated in a reasonable scheme of distribution; and we know that the contemplated Socialist scheme is impracticable. Nevertheless, the refutation of the Socialist position does not automatically prove that the capitalist has a right to take interest. Of the titles ordinarily alleged in support of such a right, productivity and service are inconclusive, while abstinence is valid only in the case of those capital owners to whom interest was a necessary inducement for saving. Since it is uncertain whether sufficient capital would be provided without interest, and since the legal suppression of interest is impracticable, the State is justified in permitting the practice of taking interest.

The only available methods of lessening the burden of interest are a reduction in the rate, and a wider diffusion of capital through cooperative enterprise. The second proposal contains great possibilities of betterment in the fields of banking, agriculture, stores, and manufacture. Through cooperation the weaker farmers, merchants, and consumers can do business and obtain goods at lower costs, and save money for investment with greater facility, while the laborers can slowly but surely become capitalists and interest-receivers, as well as employees and wage-receivers.

THE BUSINESS MAN AND PROFITS

Just remuneration for the active agents of production, whether they be directors of industry or employees, depends fundamentally upon five canons of distribution; namely, needs, efforts and sacrifices, productivity, scarcity, and human welfare. In the light of these principles it is evident that business men who use fair methods in competitive conditions, have a right to all the profits that they can obtain. On the other hand, no business man has a strict right to a minimum living profit, since that would imply an obligation on the part of consumers to support superfluous and inefficient directors of industry. Those who possess a monopoly of their products or commodities have no right to more than the prevailing or competitive rate of interest on their capital, though they have the same right as competitive business men to any surplus gains that may be due to superior efficiency. The principal unfair methods of competition, that is, discriminative underselling, exclusive-selling contracts, and discrimination in transportation, are all unjust.

The remedies for unjust profits are to be found mainly in the action of government. The State should either own and operate all natural monopolies, or so regulate their charges that the owners would obtain only the competitive rate of interest on the actual investment, and only such surplus gains as are clearly due to superior efficiency. It should prevent artificial monopolies from practicing extortion toward either consumers or competitors. Inasmuch as overcapitalization has frequently enabled monopolistic concerns to obtain unjust profits, and always presents a strong temptation in this direction, it should be legally prohibited. A considerate part of the excessive profits already accumulated can be subjected to a better distribution by progressive income, excess profits, and inheritance taxes. Finally, the possessors of large fortunes and incomes could help to bring about a more equitable distribution by voluntarily complying with the Christian duty of bestowing their superfluous goods upon needy persons and objects.

THE LABORER AND WAGES

None of the theories of fair wages that have been examined under the heads of "the prevailing rate," "exchange-equivalence," or "productivity" is in full harmony with the principles of justice. The minimum of wage justice can, however, be described with sufficient definiteness and certainty. The adult male laborer has a right to a wage sufficient to provide himself and family with a decent livelihood, and the adult female has a right to remuneration that will enable her to live decently as a self-supporting individual. At the basis of this right are three ethical principles: All persons are equal in their inherent claims upon the bounty of nature; this general right of access to the earth becomes concretely valid through the expenditure of useful labor; and those persons who are in control of the goods and opportunities of the earth are morally bound to permit access thereto on reasonable terms by all who are willing to work. In the case of the laborer, this right of reasonable access can be effectuated only through a living wage. The obligation of paying this wage falls upon the employer because of his function in the industrial organism. And the laborer's right to a living wage is morally superior to the employer's right to interest on his capital.

Laborers who put forth unusual efforts or make unusual sacrifices have a right to a proportionate excess over living wages, and those who are exceptionally productive or exceptionally scarce have a right to the extra compensation that goes to them under the operation of competition.

The methods of increasing wages are mainly four: A minimum wage by law, labor unions, profit-sharing, and ownership. The first has been fairly well approved by experience, and is in no wise contrary to the

principles of either ethics, politics, or economics. The second has likewise been vindicated in practice, though it is of only small efficacy
in the case of those workers who are receiving less than living wages.
The third and fourth would enable laborers to supplement their wage
incomes by profits and interest, and would render our industrial system
more stable by giving the workers an influential voice in the conditions
of employment, and by laying the foundation of that contentment and
conservatism which arise naturally out of the possession of property.

CONCLUDING OBSERVATIONS

No doubt many of those who have taken up this volume with the
expectation of finding therein a satisfactory formula of distributive justice,
and who have patiently followed the discussion to the end, are dis-
appointed and dissatisfied at the final conclusions. Both the particular
applications of the rules of justice and the proposals for reform must
have seemed complex and indefinite. They are not nearly so simple
and definite as the principles of Socialism or the Single Tax. And yet,
there is no escape from these limitations. Neither the principles of
industrial justice nor the constitution of our socioeconomic system is
simple. Therefore, it is impossible to give our ethical conclusions anything
like mathematical accuracy. The only claim that is made for the discussion is that the moral judgments are fairly efficacious. When both have
been realized in practice, the next step in the direction of wider
distributive justice will be much clearer than it is to-day.

Although the attainment of greater justice in distribution is the
primary and most urgent need of our time, it is not the only one that
is of great importance. Neither just distribution, nor increased production, nor both combined, will insure a stable and satisfactory social order
without a considerable change in human hearts and ideals. The rich
must cease to put their faith in material things, and rise to a simpler
and saner plane of living; the middle classes and the poor must give up
their envy and snobbish imitation of the false and degrading standards
of the opulent classes; and all must learn the elementary lesson that
the path to achievement worthwhile leads through the field of hard
and honest labor, not of lucky "deals" or gouging of the neighbor, and
that the only life worth living is that in which one's cherished wants are
few, simple, and noble. For the adoption and pursuit of these ideals the
most necessary requisite is a revival of genuine religion.

Appendix II. ANNOTATED READING LISTS

The reading list to follow complements in many ways the material treated in the present book. To a certain degree it indicates sources which inspired the views given here. More important, however, is its possible use for further study and research. It offers suggestions for more detailed scrutiny of problems than was possible in these pages. The scope of Catholic thinking in the socioeconomic field is so broad that of necessity only brief outlines of solutions and programs could be offered in a single volume. It is hoped that those who are interested in particular problems will find these suggestions an aid for further study.

This list is obviously much more comprehensive than the brief readings given at the end of each chapter. The chapter readings might be considered as student aids. They offer references to a relatively few sources which might be consulted in connection with the chapter topic. Usually these sources are textbooks or manuals whose aims parallel to some degree those of the present book. By contrast, the volumes listed here are usually book-length studies of a particular topic. As such, they are more likely to interest the student preparing a dissertation or term paper. Likewise, the general reader may secure leads for deeper study of a topic which interests him.

The selections are generally biased in favor of more recent books. Since the economic and social climate of the United States has changed so drastically as a result of the New Deal, the Fair Deal, and World War II, the probabilities are that newer treatments more closely correspond to present-day realities. At the same time, many of the better older works have been included. Even volumes which are out of print have been listed, on the theory that most of them can be found in the better libraries. A few foreign-language publications are given, either because they were important sources or because they reflect current European Catholic thinking. No attempt was made, however, to give a comprehensive list of German, French, Spanish, or Italian Catholic publications on social matters.

Comments are descriptive rather than evaluative. The fact that a book was selected is in itself an endorsement of its reference value. Naturally no automatic approval of the author's views is implied in these listings. Likewise, the giving of several books on the same topic does not necessarily indicate that each has a substantially different treatment of the subject. Rather the assumption is that most readers will consult books in libraries, so that plural listing would increase the chances that at least one recommended volume would be available. Because of this fact, it is not advised that any of these lists be followed literally in building up personal or institutional libraries. Where duplication seems probable, it is suggested that the lists be supplemented by consultation of the better book-review sources.

The present book list has been constructed independently of the twenty-page list in *Catholic Social Action*. Where topics overlap, the list given here will naturally contain more recent volumes. As far as possible, however, the recommendations are made in view of the main topics treated in these pages. The order of presentation is roughly the same as that followed in the chapters. The headings and subheadings, however, are not always the same as those used in the body of the text, mainly because of the plethora of books in some fields and the scarcity in others. The availability of titles, rather than the plan of the present book, was controlling in determining subject headings.

For keeping information current and noting newer volumes on the several subjects, standard periodicals should be consulted. A listing of recommended sources is given in *Catholic Social Action*, pp. 208–210.

1. SOURCES FOR CATHOLIC SOCIAL PRINCIPLES

The main source material for Catholic social principles is, naturally, the teaching of the sovereign pontiffs. Major encyclicals are normally available in English, either in book-length collections or in pamphlets or periodicals. The primary American pamphlet sources for encyclicals are the Paulist Press, the National Catholic Welfare Conference, and the America Press. The *Catholic Mind* also carries many papal addresses, letters, and radio discourses, but for a full coverage foreign sources must be used. The N.C.W.C. reprints statements by the American hierarchy. In addition to such authoritative material, the following list gives some of the more important commentaries and historical sources.

Papal Encyclicals

Husslein, J. (ed.), *Social Wellsprings* (Milwaukee: Bruce, 1940–1942).
These two volumes contain the main social encyclicals of Popes

Leo XIII and Pius XI. Paragraph numbering differs from that used in many N.C.W.C. and Paulist Press pamphlet editions of the same encyclicals.

Koenig, H. C. (ed.), *Principles for Peace* (Milwaukee: Bruce, 1943). Selections from papal documents dealing with peace, arranged chronologically from 1878 to 1942. Excerpts are generous and include many documents dealing with socioeconomic problems.

Hughes, P., *The Popes' New Order* (New York: Macmillan, 1943). A summary of papal documents, with occasional quotations. Deals mainly with social problems. Covers period 1878–1941. Out of print.

Two Basic Social Encyclicals (New York: Benziger, 1943). Contains the Latin text and the newest English translation of *Rerum Novarum* and *Quadragesimo Anno.*

Kothen, R., *L'enseignement social de l'Église* (Louvain: Warny, 1949). A topical arrangement of excerpts from social writings of the popes, from 1878 to 1948. Introductory and explanatory material is brief but valuable.

Sherbno, J. C. (ed.), *A Handbook of Papal Statements on Economic Society* (Norwood, Ohio: Mt. St. Mary Seminary, 1949). A compilation in topical order of brief excerpts from papal documents arranged under 74 headings. Less inclusive than Kothen since only eleven documents have been used by the editor.

The Pope and the People (London: Catholic Truth Society, 1937). Selected papal writings on the social question in a broad sense. Main value is inclusion of documents of Pope Pius X not easily secured in English.

Acta Sanctae Sedis (Rome: Typographia Vaticana, 1878–1908). Contains major documents issuing from the popes during the period in question.

Acta Apostolicae Sedis (Rome: Typographia Vaticana, 1909–). Replaced the *Acta Sanctae Sedis.* Same coverage.

Leonis XIII Pontifici Maximi Acta (Rome: Typographia Vaticana, 1881–1905). More inclusive than the *Acta Sanctae Sedis.*

Pius X Pontificis Maximi Acta (Rome: Typographia Vaticana, 1905–1914). Also contains material not found in the *Acta Sanctae Sedis* and the *Acta Apostolicae Sedis.*

Actes de S. S. Pie XI (Paris: Bonne Presse, 1932–1940). Contains all the public documents of Pope Pius XI. The original text and a French translation are given in each case.

Discorsi e Radiomessagi di sua Santita Pio XII (Rome: Tipographia Poliglotta Vaticana, 1939–). The best single source for the complete utterances of the present Holy Father. Like the *Acta,* all documents are given in the language of the authentic original document.

Colleción de Enciclicas y Cartas Pontificias (Madrid: Junta Técnica Nacional de la A.C.E., 1948). A Spanish collection of encyclicals, valuable for its 261-page analytical index.

Carlen, Sr. M. C., *A Guide to the Encyclicals of the Roman Pontiffs from Leo XIII to the Present Day (1878–1937)* (New York: Wilson, 1939). Gives full title, subjects, sources for text, and main commentary material for papal encyclicals issued during the period covered. Out of print.

La Hiérarchie Catholique et le problème social (1891–1931) (Paris: Editions Spes, 1931). A listing and generally a description of papal and episcopal statements on social questions, with sources indicated in the appendix. All documents are listed in chronological order, with episcopal statements grouped under 17 countries or regions. Out of print.

Ryan, J. A., and Husslein, J. (edd.), *The Church and Labor* (New York: Macmillan, 1924). A collection of papal and episcopal statements on the social question. Valuable for documents of Popes Pius X and Benedict XV not easily available in English.

The Great Encyclical Letters of Pope Leo XIII (New York: Benziger, 1903). Selection differs from that of Husslein. Includes some documents not contained in *Social Wellsprings*.

English-Language Commentaries

Alter, K. J., *A Bishop's Rostrum* (Milwaukee: Bruce, 1946). Occasional addresses by the Bishop of Toledo, with considerable emphasis upon social problems. Out of print.

Bruehl, C., *The Pope's Plan for Social Reconstruction* (New York: Devin-Adair, 1939). A somewhat philosophical discussion of the social teaching of Pope Pius XI.

Cahill, E., *The Framework of a Christian State* (Dublin: Gill, 1932). This volume covers a broad social field in applying ethics to modern problems, with special reference to Irish conditions. The historical sections are also valuable. A good summary. Less profound than Messner (see List No. 4, *infra*); less detailed than Clune.

Clune, G., *Christian Social Reorganization* (Dublin: Browne & Nolan, 1940). A careful study of Christian social ethics as applied to economic and political life. While written for Irish readers, it has a much broader field of usefulness. Out of print.

McKevitt, P., *The Plan of Society* (Dublin: Catholic Truth Society, 1944). A brief work applying Catholic social principles to Irish conditions.

Code of Social Principles (Oxford: Catholic Social Guild, 1937). A work of international scholarship expressing in pithy form the major tenets of Catholic social ethics.

Doboszynski, A., *The Economics of Charity* (London: Mildner, 1945). An application of social principles to English economic life, with emphasis on distributist ideals.

Husslein, J., *The Christian Social Manifesto* (Milwaukee: Bruce, 1939). A popular interpretation of the major ethical principles enunciated in *Rerum Novarum* and *Quadragesimo Anno.* Out of print.

Michel, V., *Christian Social Reconstruction* (Milwaukee: Bruce, 1937). A popular exposition of the ideas contained in *Quadragesimo Anno.*

Miller, R. J., *Forty Years After* (St. Paul: Radio Replies Press, 1948). An interpretation of *Quadragesimo Anno* in the light of American economic life. The author follows the order of *Q.A.* in his commentary.

Nell-Breuning, O., *Reorganization of Social Economy* (Milwaukee: Bruce, 1936). A careful commentary on the general principles of *Quadragesimo Anno.* The translator, Rev. Bernard Dempsey, S.J., has given an English bibliography. Out of print.

Osgniach, A. J., *Must It Be Communism?* (New York: Wagner, 1950). A treatise on Catholic social ethics with some emphasis upon communism and some economic application. Includes a reprint of three articles by Rev. Jerome Toner, O.S.B.

Ryan, John A., *A Better Economic Order* (New York: Harper, 1935). Contains much of Msgr. Ryan's economic thought. Out of print.

——*Social Doctrine in Action* (New York: Harper, 1941). The autobiography of America's pioneer Catholic social thinker. Out of print.

Foreign-Language Commentaries

Banchi, J., *Principi dell' ordine sociale Cristiano* (Rome: A.V.E., 1944). Main points of social ethics applied to the modern world. Brief bibliography.

Brucculeri, A., *Le dottrine sociale del Cattolicismo* (Rome: Civiltá Cattolica, 1944–1948). A series of fifteen brochures, reprinted from *Civiltá Cattolica,* dealing with a wide range of social problems.

——*Intorno al corporativismo* (Rome: Civiltá Cattolica, 1934). Philosophical studies of a functional society.

Deploige, S., *Le conflit de la morale et de la sociologie* (Paris: Nouvelles Lit. Nat., 1900). A standard study of the relationships between ethics and social science.

Gonella, G., *Principi di un ordine sociale* (Rome: Tipographia Poliglotta Vaticana, 1944). A commentary on the Christmas Message, 1942, of Pope Pius XII.

Haessle, J., *Arbeitethos der Kirches nach Thomas von Aquin und Leo XIII*

(Freiberg: Herder, 1923). A basic study in labor ethics. Quite influential in German social Catholicism.

Hitze, F., *Die Arbeiterfrage und die Bestrebungen zu Ihrer Lösung* (Munster: 1894) and *Die Sozialefrage und die Bestrebungen zu Ihrer Lösung*. These works influenced strongly the destinies of the Catholic Center Party in Germany.

Hubatka, P. C., *Soziale fragen* (Luzern: Raeber & Giex, 1948). Brief but well-documented outline of the social teaching of the Church.

Lopez, U., *et al.*, *Il pensiero sociale Cattolico* (Rome: Gregorianum, 1945). Six Jesuit authors discuss varied problems of social ethics.

Lubac, H. de, *Catholicisme, les aspects sociaux du dogme* (Paris: Éditions du Cerf, 1947). Christian doctrine viewed in its social aspects by a scholarly Jesuit.

Montcheuil, I. de, *L'Église et le monde actuel* (Paris: Éd. de Tém. Chrét., 1945). The social problem in the light of Christian teaching.

Rutten, G. C., *La doctrine sociale de l'Église* (Paris: Éditions du Cerf, 1932). This volume gives a brief, but carefully thought out, summary of Catholic social teaching.

—— *Manuel d'Étude et d'Action sociales* (Paris: Éditions du Cerf, 1945). Planned as a two-volume work guiding the Belgian clergy in social study and action. Only the volume on social study is currently available.

Schaup, Fr., *Die Eigentumslehre nach Thomas von Aquin und der Modernen Sozialismus* (Freiberg: Herder, 1898). A classic study on the Catholic doctrine concerning property.

Steinbüschel, T., *Der Sozialismus als Sittliche Idee* (Dusseldorf: Schwann, 1921). A critique of socialism from the aspect of social ethics.

Strider, J. (ed.), *Die Soziale Frage und der Katholicizmus* (Paderborn: Schöningh, 1931). A symposium by a score of distinguished authors, issued on the fortieth anniversary of *Rerum Novarum*. Considered a standard work on Catholic social thought.

Taviani, P. E., *La proprietá* (Rome: Editrice Studium, 1946). Property considered in its historical and social aspects.

Del Vecchio, G., *La guistizia* (Rome: Editrice Studium, 1946). This treatment of justice is highly philosophical and well documented.

Vito, F., *Economia e personalismo* (Milan: Vita e Pensiero, 1949) and *La Riforma sociale secondo la dottrina Cattolica* (Milan: Vita e Pensiero, 1946). Brief but thoughtful studies of modern social problems in the light of Christian ethics.

Welty, E., *Gemeinschaft und Einzelmensch* (Salzburg: Pustet, 1935). Social metaphysics in the Thomistic tradition. Treats of relationships between the community and society.

See also: H. Pesch, *Lehrbuch der Nationalökonomie* (List No. 8).

History of Catholic Social Thought

Giordani, I., *The Social Message of Jesus* (Paterson, N. J.: St. Anthony Guild Press, 1943) and *The Social Message of the Early Christian Fathers* (1944). Two volumes of a trilogy dealing with origins of Catholic social thought. *The Social Message of the Apostles* has not yet been translated.

Lugan, A., *Social Principles of the Gospel* (New York: Macmillan, 1928). Treats Gospel principles on major social issues. Out of print.

Schumacher, J., *Social Message of the New Testament* (Milwaukee: Bruce, 1937). Explains social message in the Gospels and Epistles. Out of print.

Husslein, J., *Bible and Labor* (New York: Macmillan, 1924). Emphasizes the position of labor in the Old Testament. Out of print.

Troeltsch, E., *The Social Teaching of the Christian Churches* (London: Allen and Unwin, 1949). A monumental two-volume study covering the period from the Gospels to the nineteenth century.

Ryan, J. A., *The Alleged Socialism of the Church Fathers* (St. Louis: Herder, 1913). Studies passages alleged to prove early Christian socialism and shows from context that they were not socialistic. Out of print.

O'Brien, E. G., *Essay on Mediaeval Economic Teaching* (New York: Longmans, 1920). The social ethics of great medieval theologians, applied to economic problems. Valuable, but out of print.

Moon, P. T., *The Labor Problem and the Social Catholic Movement in France* (New York: Macmillan, 1926). Well-documented study of French social Catholicism, with reference to related movements elsewhere. Out of print.

McEntee, G. T., *The Social Catholic Movement in Great Britain* (New York: Macmillan, 1927). English social Catholicism up to the end of World War I. Out of print.

Somerville, H., *The Catholic Social Movement* (London: Burns, Oates, 1933). Modern social Catholicism in the nineteenth century and early twentieth. Out of print.

Kothen, R., *La pensée et l'action sociales des Catholiques, 1789–1944* (Louvain: Warny, 1945). Discusses social Catholicism, country by country, before and after *Rerum Novarum*.

Hogan, W. E., *The Development of Bishop Wilhelm Emmanuel von Ketteler's Interpretation of the Social Problem* (Washington: Catholic University Press, 1946). A doctorate on the great German leader in the field of social reform.

Fitzpatrick, P. J. and Dirksen, C., *Bibliography of Economic Books and Pamphlets by Catholic Authors, 1891–1941* (Washington: Catholic University Press, 1941). Alphabetical listing.

2. SOURCES FOR ECONOMIC FACTS

The present author has compiled two relatively recent bibliographical essays on source material for economic facts. There is no point in duplicating here material covered in the appendix to *Economic Analysis and Problems* and in Chapter 12 and the Appendix to *Catholic Social Action*. Accordingly, the listing under the present heading will deal only with sources for statistics and with a few useful economics texts or compilations.

Statistical Material

Statistical Abstract of the United States (Washington: Government Printing Office, annually). Basic compilation of government statistics.

Handbook of Economic Statistics (Washington: Economic Statistics Bureau, monthly). A current compilation of government statistics in the economic field.

The Economic Almanac (New York: National Industrial Conference Board, annually). Contains privately gathered statistics in addition to government figures. Glossary at end.

The World Almanac (New York: World Telegram and Sun, annually). Less comprehensive than government collections of economic data, but often more generally available.

The Economic Report to the President (Washington: Government Printing Office, semiannually). These reports contain, in addition to the analyses of the Council of Economic Advisers, selected statistics on national production and income.

Coman, E. T., *Sources of Business Information* (New York: Prentice-Hall, 1949). Lists and evaluates sources of information on broad business problems. Several chapters highly useful for students of social questions.

Mills, F. C., and Long, C. D., *The Statistical Agencies of the Federal Government* (New York: National Bureau of Economic Research, 1949). A report to the Hoover Commission. Evaluates government statistical work.

Hauser, P. M., and Leonard, W. R. (edd.), *Government Statistics for Business Use* (New York: Wiley, 1946). A listing and description of statistical services available through government research.

The following periodicals also contain economic statistics: *Economic Indicators* (Council of Economic Advisers), general statistics; *Monthly Labor Review* (Department of Labor), employment, prices, and similar labor material; *Survey of Current Business* (Department of Commerce), national income, trade, and like commercial figures; and *Federal Reserve Bulletin* (Federal Reserve System), financial information, also income studies. All the above should be ordered from the Superintendent of Documents, except the *Federal Reserve Bulletin,* which is ordered directly from the Federal Reserve Board of Governors. Census Bureau studies are also very useful for statistical information.

Selected Economics Texts

Cronin, J. F., *Economic Analysis and Problems* (New York: American Book Company, 1945). Emphasizes social problems more than has been customary in prewar economics textbooks. Contains brief history of Catholic social thought and also a chapter on Protestant and Jewish social thought.

Bowen, H. R., *Toward Social Economy* (New York: Rinehart, 1949). An economics text which considers the place of economics in the entire social fabric.

Samuelson, P. A., *Economics, An Introductory Analysis* (New York: McGraw-Hill, 1948). A readable text with full emphasis upon modern theories.

Whittaker, E., *A History of Economic Ideas* (New York: Longmans, 1940). Differs from usual pattern of histories of economic thought. Chapters deal with central ideas rather than historical periods.

Ellis, H. W. S. (ed.), *A Survey of Contemporary Economics* (Philadelphia: Blakiston, 1948). Thirteen experts aided by twenty-six critics survey the state of economic theory as it appeared in 1948. An excellent refresher work for advanced students or specialists who wish to broaden their horizons.

Spann, O., *The History of Economics,* (New York: Norton, 1930). Brief. Contains some reference to Catholic schools of thought.

Horton, B. J., and others, *Dictionary of Modern Economics* (Washington: Public Affairs Press, 1948). Contains definitions, digests of laws and court decisions, and citations of reference books.

3. THE SOCIAL QUESTION

Two main classes of books are included in this heading, namely, those dealing with historical phases of the social question and general works on the American scene. This latter group obviously will also treat of many detailed problems included in later lists.

Medieval Economic Life

Carlyle, R. W. and A. J., *A History of Medieval Political Theory in the West* (New York: Putnam, 1903–1936). Two non-Catholic authors devote six volumes to a documented study of medieval institutions.

They hold that medieval political life was basically democratic. Out of print.

Clune, G., *The Medieval Gild System* (Dublin: Browne & Nolan, 1943). The social effects of the guild system in medieval Europe. Out of print.

Husslein, J., *Democratic Industry* (New York: Kenedy, 1919). A sympathetic appraisal of the guild system. Out of print.

Penty, A. J., *A Guildsman's Interpretation of History* (New York: Sheed, 1939). The author favors a distributist society and interprets history in a way favorable to the medieval guilds. Out of print.

Pirenne, H., *Economic and Social History of Medieval Europe* (New York: Harcourt, 1937). Balanced in treatment. Generally favorable picture of medieval society. Less critical than Thompson.

Thompson, J. W., *Economic and Social History of the Middle Ages* and *Economic and Social History of Europe in the Later Middle Ages* (New York: Appleton-Century, 1928–1931). Scholarly and documented study of economic development of medieval Europe during the years 300–1530.

Stephenson, C., *Mediaeval Feudalism* (Ithaca, N. Y.: Cornell University Press, 1942). This brief study is accurate and sympathetic.

Origin and Growth of the Social Problem

Fanfani, A., *Catholicism, Protestantism, and Capitalism* (New York: Sheed, 1936). Traces individualist spirit to the eleventh century and shows how it led to rise of modern capitalism.

Tawney, R. H., *Religion and the Rise of Capitalism* (New York: Harcourt, 1926). Brilliant in style and incisive in thought. Studies breakdown of medieval ethical controls and the rise of individualism.

Weber, M., *The Protestant Ethic and the Spirit of Capitalism* (London: Allen & Unwin, 1930). Holds that ethical teachings of Protestantism contributed to the rise of modern capitalism.

Sorokin, P. A., *The Crisis of Our Age* (New York: Dutton, 1941). The underlying spiritual crisis of our age described by a keen sociologist.

Polanyi, K., *The Great Transformation* (New York: Farrar & Rinehart, 1944). An evaluation of modern capitalism in terms of its effect on human welfare. One of the great books of our time. Extensive bibliographical note.

Hughes, E. J., *The Church and the Liberal Society* (Princeton: Princeton University Press, 1944). This Catholic author offers a critical and well-documented evaluation of individualism in terms of its historical development and in the light of Church principles. Out of print.

Ware, N., *Wealth and Welfare* (New York: Sloane, 1949). Well-written and even witty discussion of historical background of modern economic life. Compares present system with predecessors and currently competing systems.

Cunningham, W., *The Growth of English Industry and Commerce* (Cambridge, England: Cambridge University Press, 1915, 1929, 1938). This monumental study documents many of the facts surrounding the growth of modern capitalism and the rise of the social question.

Dixon, R. A., and Eberhart, E. K., *Economics and Cultural Change* (New York: McGraw-Hill, 1938). Discusses the social effects of various economic societies, from primitive cultures to modern industrialism.

Hammond, J. L. and B., *The Rise of Modern Industry* (New York: Harcourt, 1937). Emphasizes the social effects of the commercial and industrial revolutions. Out of print.

Toynbee, A., *The Industrial Revolution of the Eighteenth Century in England* (New York: Longmans, 1908). Includes economic theories, technical developments, and the social problem. Out of print.

Mantoux, P., *The Industrial Revolution in the Eighteenth Century* (New York: Macmillan, 1947). Scholarly treatment of this important period.

Packard, L. B., *The Commercial Revolution* (New York: Holt, 1927). Brief but intelligent survey of the expansion of commerce prior to the industrial revolution.

Dietz, F. C., *The Industrial Revolution* (New York: Holt, 1927). Brief but clear. Bibliographical note at end.

Briefs, G. A., *The Proletariat* (New York: McGraw-Hill, 1937). A thorough study of the proletariat as connected with modern wage-earner status. Out of print.

Cochran, T. C., and Miller, W., *The Age of Enterprise* (New York: Macmillan, 1942). A well-written social history of industrial America. Good bibliography.

Greer, T. H., *American Social Reform Movements: Their Pattern Since 1865* (New York: Prentice-Hall, 1949). Notes influence of reform movements in changing American economic life.

Myers, G., *History of the Great American Fortunes* (New York: Modern Library, 1936). A reprint of a classic depiction of the greed and corruption attendant upon the rise of industrialism in the United States.

Josephson, M., *The Robber Barons* (New York: Harcourt, 1934). Studies the great American capitalists during the period 1861–1901. An exposé of various evils which characterized this period.

Allen, F. L., *The Lords of Creation* (New York: Harper, 1935). Same theme as *The Robber Barons,* but carries the story from 1901 to 1935. Out of print.

The Autobiography of Lincoln Steffens (New York: Harcourt, 1931).

The period from Cleveland to Wilson, seen through the eyes of an acute reporter.

Wecter, D., *The Age of the Great Depression* (New York: Macmillan, 1948). A survey of the period 1929–1941. Valuable for background of the New Deal.

Rauch, B., *The History of the New Deal* (New York: Creative Age Press, 1944). Outlines the major developments of this significant period.

Proposed Programs for America

Burnham, J., *The Managerial Revolution* (New York: John Day, 1941). Upholds the thesis that business and government administrators are main centers of power today, displacing stockholders, labor, and voters.

Dewhurst, J. F., and others, *America's Needs and Resources* (New York: Twentieth Century Fund, 1947). A major study of the possibilities for raising our standards through full use of resources.

Carskadon, T. R., and Modley, R., *U.S.A.: Measure of a Nation* (New York: Macmillan, 1949). Summarizes in a more popular manner the thesis contained in *America's Needs and Resources.*

Clark, J. M., *Guideposts in Time of Change* (New York: Harper, 1949). Economic policies for a free society resisting a totalitarian threat. Harmonizes with industry-council idea.

Drucker, P. F., *The Future of Industrial Man* (New York: John Day, 1942). The author pleads for industrial self-government as the only safe foundation for freedom.

Heron, A. R., *Beyond Collective Bargaining* (Stanford, California: Stanford University Press, 1948). Emphasizes the scores of common interests between workers and employers. Good material for industry-council study.

Johnson, R. W., *Or Forfeit Freedom* (New York: Doubleday, 1947). Challenging call for enlightened business leadership, written by a public-spirited corporation executive. Out of print.

Lauterbach, A., *Economic Security and Individual Freedom* (Ithaca: Cornell University Press, 1948). Argues that economic insecurity is a threat to democracy. Favors moderate social controls.

Moulton, H., *Controlling Factors in Economic Development* (Washington: Brookings, 1949). A middle-of-the-road analysis of our economy, optimistic about the future. Opposes government controls and favors price reduction as a means of increasing living standards.

Nourse, E. G., *Price Making in a Democracy* (Washington: Brookings, 1944). Argues for progressive lowering of prices as means for securing economic stability and higher living standards.

Raymond, F. I., *The Limitist* (New York: Norton, 1947). Argues for limits on economic concentration in the interests of more widely diffused property ownership.

Ross, I., *Strategy for Liberals* (New York: Harper, 1949). Argues for a mixed economy of capitalism, socialism, and co-operation, with emphasis upon the political strategy needed by liberals.

Schlesinger, A. M., *The Vital Center* (New York: Houghton Mifflin, 1949). The philosophy of an American liberal.

Slichter, S. S., *The American Economy* (New York: Knopf, 1948). A concise study of current economic problems with suggested solutions.

Wright, D. M., *Democracy and Progress* (New York: Macmillan, 1948). A good study of a middle road between statism and monopoly capitalism. This competent economist advocates basic freedom with some over-all controls.

4. ETHICS AND ECONOMIC LIFE

Many of the subjects covered by books listed below are also treated in the works given in List No. 1 above. In the present list, the emphasis is upon natural ethics, whereas in the earlier list reference is frequently made to the social encyclicals and hence to theology in addition to ethics.

Messner, J., *Social Ethics* (St. Louis: Herder, 1949). A learned study of social ethics with emphasis on political and economic problems. More profound than most English studies on the subject.

Ryan, John A., *Distributive Justice* (New York: Macmillan, 1942). Social ethics studied in relation to the distribution of the products of economic life.

Haas, F. J., *Man and Society* (New York: Appleton-Century, 1930). While this text deals mainly with sociology, there is considerable socioeconomic emphasis. At this writing, a new and revised edition is being prepared.

Cronin, M., *The Science of Ethics* (Dublin: Gill, 1939). The second volume of Canon Cronin's learned text deals with many social problems.

Ferree, W., *The Act of Social Justice* (Washington: Catholic University Press, 1942). An excellent doctoral study on the nature of social justice. Out of print.

Maritain, J., *The Person and the Common Good* (New York: Scribner, 1947). The eminent French philosopher shows that society should serve the individual person and that the common good is not a totalitarian concept.

Rommen, H. A., *The Natural Law* (St. Louis: Herder, 1947). The history of natural-law ethics.

Cleary, P., *The Church and Usury* (Dublin: Gill, 1914). A study of the problem, with emphasis on the medieval period. Out of print.

Shewring, W. (ed.), *Rich and Poor in Christian Tradition* (London: Burns, Oates, 1947). Excerpts from the Church Fathers and theologians on poverty and riches.

Kelly, J. P., *Aquinas and Modern Practices of Interest Taking* (Brisbane, Australia: Aquinas Press, 1945). This brochure offers a spirited defense of the medieval interest theory in the light of modern problems.

Dempsey, B. W., *Interest and Usury* (Washington: American Council on Public Affairs, 1943). Studies teaching of late medieval theologians in the light of modern theory. Technical.

Knight, F. H., and Merriam, T. W., *The Economic Order and Religion* (New York: Harper, 1945). A debate on the place of religion in economic life. Out of print.

Dirksen, C., *Economic Factors of Delinquency* (Milwaukee: Bruce, 1948). Brief study of economic influences in social pathology.

LaFarge, J., *The Race Question and the Negro* (New York: Longmans, 1944). Penetrating observations from an experienced priest.

Frazier, E. F., *The Negro in the United States* (New York: Macmillan, 1949). Traces the slow and painful integration of the Negro into American society.

Myrdal, G., *An American Dilemma* (New York: Harper 1944). One of the basic works on Negro problems, based on an extensive survey by a Swedish sociologist.

Rose, A., *The Negro in America* (New York: Harper, 1948). A summary of Myrdal's two-volume work.

5. INDIVIDUALISM AND CAPITALISM

This list deals with topics treated in the first parts of Chapters V and VIII. It is obvious that the present author does not endorse the theme of several of the works given, insofar as they favor economic individualism of an amoral type.

Dixon, R. A., *Economic Institutions and Cultural Change* (New York: McGraw-Hill, 1941). Studies such institutions as property, price, free enterprise, and the corporation, with bibliography following each chapter.

Devane, R. S., *The Failure of Individualism* (Dublin: Browne & Nolan, 1948). Treats of religious, political, and economic individualism as the roots of modern life.

Pirou, G., *Economié libérale, economie dirigée* (Paris: Societé de l'Enseignment Sup., 1946). A two-volume study of economic liberalism and its degeneration into economic dictatorship.

The American Enterprise System: Its Nature, Evolution, and Future

(New York: McGraw-Hill, 1946). Fifteen authors associated with the National Association of Manufacturers present a case for *laissez faire*. Out of print.

Sombart, W., *Quintessence of Capitalism* (New York: Dutton, 1915). One of the pioneer studies in the field. Authoritative.

Griffin, C. E., *Enterprise in a Free Society* (Chicago: Irwin, 1949). A defense of free enterprise in contrast to the welfare state.

Hayek, F. A., *The Road to Serfdom* (Chicago: University of Chicago Press, 1944). This much-quoted and challenging book argues that economic planning leads of necessity to totalitarianism.

Mises, L. von, *Human Action* (New Haven: Yale, 1949). A plea for a free economy in contrast to a controlled system.

Schumpeter, J. A., *Capitalism, Socialism, and Democracy* (New York: Harper, 1942). The author is pessimistic as to the possibility of capitalist survival. Discusses various forms of socialism which may succeed present-day capitalism.

Siever, A. M., *Has Market Capitalism Collapsed?* (New York: Columbia University Press, 1949). Argues against Polanyi's thesis that economic liberalism has failed.

Snyder, C., *Capitalism the Creator* (New York: Macmillan, 1940). A defense of capitalism because of its productive achievements. Out of print.

Viereck, P., *Conservatism Revisited* (New York: Scribner, 1949). A plea for an ethical approach to politics, in contrast to power philosophies.

Arnold, T. W., *The Bottlenecks of Business* (New York: Harcourt, 1940). Explains the workings of the antitrust laws as means for securing economic prosperity. Out of print.

Brady, R. A., *Business as a System of Power* (New York: Columbia University Press, 1943). Shows that business throughout the world has concentrated immense power into the hands of a few persons.

Burns, A. R., *The Decline of Competition* (New York: McGraw-Hill, 1936). A masterly study of price control. Extensive bibliography.

Edwards, C. D., *Maintaining Competition: Requisites of a Governmental Policy* (New York: McGraw-Hill, 1949). While rejecting the idea that competition can automatically guide the entire economy, the author explores useful areas where it should be promoted.

Lynch, D., *The Concentration of Economic Power* (New York: Columbia University Press, 1946). A critical study of the Temporary National Economic Committee's data on economic concentration.

Stocking, G. W., and Watkins, M. W., *Cartels or Competition* (New York: Twentieth Century Fund, 1948). Analyzes the effect of cartels and recommends policies.

See also the following authors cited in earlier lists:

Tawney, R. H., *Religion and the Rise of Capitalism* (List No. 3);

Weber, M., *The Protestant Ethic and the Spirit of Capitalism* (List No. 3);

Polanyi, K., *The Great Transformation* (List No. 3);

Hughes, E. J., *The Church and the Liberal Society* (List No. 3).

6. SOCIALISM AND STATISM

This list is not extensive, since the general subject of statism is treated incidentally in other lists, especially Nos. 1, 4, 5, 7, 8, and 12.

Socialism

Harris, S. E., *Economic Planning* (New York: Knopf, 1949). Plans of fourteen countries analyzed and discussed sympathetically.

Jewkes, J., *Ordeal by Planning* (New York: Macmillan, 1948). Opposes all centralism, whether by business or by government. Moderately liberal.

Mises, L. von, *Omnipotent Government* (New Haven: Yale, 1944). Holds that statism leads to war and destruction of liberty.

Loucks, W. N., and Hoot, J. W., *Comparative Economic Systems* (New York: Harper, 1948). A balanced study of capitalism, socialism, communism, fascism, and the co-operative movement.

Laidler, H. W., *Social-Economic Movements* (New York: Crowell, 1947). Survey of various systems of social reform. Author is a Socialist.

Gray, A., *The Socialist Tradition* (New York: Longmans, 1946). Socialist ideas traced from Old Testament days to modern times.

Beckwith, B. P., *The Economic Theory of a Socialist Economy* (Stanford, California: Stanford University Press, 1949). An effort by an advocate of socialism to spell out how a socialist economy could work.

Lange, O., and Taylor, F. M., *On the Economic Theory of Socialism* (Minneapolis: University of Minnesota Press, 1948). Argues that economic calculation and free consumer choice are possible under socialism.

Sweezy, P. M., *Socialism* (New York: McGraw-Hill, 1949). A sympathetic study by a Marxist economist.

See also: Schumpeter, J. A., *Capitalism, Socialism, and Democracy* (List No. 5).

Statism

Metz, H. W., and Thomson, C. A. H., *Authoritarianism and the Individual* (Washington: Brookings, 1949). The impact of authority upon the freedom of the individual is studied, with special reference to historical background as well as modern statism.

Welk, W. G., *Fascist Economic Policy* (Cambridge: Harvard University Press, 1938). An objective study of the economics of the fascist experiment in Italy. Out of print.

Murphy, R. E., and others, *National Socialism* (Washington: Government Printing Office, 1943). The basic principles of National Socialism, heavily documented by the State Department authors.

Cotta, F., *Economic Planning in Corporative Portugal* (London: King & Staples, 1937). A sympathetic study of the Portuguese dictatorship.

7. COMMUNISM

The literature on communism today is immense, largely because its fields of activity have been so widespread. While the list given here is rather lengthy, it would be difficult to cover such a vital subject adequately with a smaller list.

Theory of Communism

Communism: Its Plans and Tactics (Washington: Infantry Journal Press, 1948). The report on the Bolton congressional subcommittee on the theory and tactics of world communism.

McFadden, C. J., *The Philosophy of Communism* (New York: Benziger, 1939). An analysis and criticism of the philosophical theory of communism.

Mauriac, F., and others, *Communism and Christians* (London: Paladin Press, 1938). Six distinguished Christian authors discuss communism from various aspects.

Orwell, G., *Animal Farm* (New York: Harcourt, 1946). Satire describing the transformation of communism into an exploitive system, in terms of a fable of animal life. A highly superior treatment.

—— *Nineteen Eighty-Four* (New York: Harcourt, 1949). The impact of statism on human personality is discussed in novel form.

Sheed, F. J., *Communism and Man* (New York: Sheed, 1939). The nature of communism and the nature of man compared, showing that they do not harmonize.

Shub, D., *Lenin, A Biography* (New York: Doubleday, 1948). Penetrating study, revealing much of the psychology and tactics of communism.

See also: Osgniach, A. J., *Must It Be Communism?* (List No. 1).

Sources Favorable to Communism

Lenin, N., *Left Wing Communism: An Infantile Disorder* (Detroit: Marxian Educational Society, 1921) and *Religion* (New York: International Publishers, 1933). Two brochures by the major modern theoretician of communism.

Marx, K., and Engels, F., *Communist Manifesto* (New York: International Publishers). The classic statement of communist aims, written over a century ago.

Marx K., *Capital* (New York: Modern Library reprint). An inexpensive edition of the first authentic exposition of communism.

Peters, J., *The Communist Party: A Manual on Organization* (New York: Workers' Library, 1936). A basic document by a Comintern agent, telling Communists how to organize most effectively. Out of print from communist sources, but available from William F. Mitchell, 50 Broad St., Columbus, Ohio.

Stalin, J., *Foundations of Leninism* (New York: International Publishers, 1939). The Stalinist interpretation of Leninism. One of the basic texts for Communists.

Sweezy, P. M., *The Theory of Capitalist Development* (New York: Oxford, 1942). A study of Marxist theory by an author favorable to these ideas.

Communism in Action

Ebon, M., *World Communism Today* (New York: McGraw-Hill, 1948). Postwar communist strength assayed country by country, with names of principal leaders and important organizations.

Rindl, J., and Gompers, J. (Ypsilon pseud.), *Pattern for World Revolution* (New York: Ziff-Davis, 1947). Two former Comintern agents discuss the evolution and function of the Comintern. Out of print.

Foote, A., *Handbook for Spies* (New York: Doubleday, 1949). Confessions of a former Soviet spy, illustrating Comintern tactics.

Counts, G. S., and Lodge, N., *Country of the Blind* (New York: Houghton Mifflin, 1949). Addressed mainly to intellectuals, showing how Soviet policies have prevented independent thought in Russia.

Barmine, A., *One Who Survived* (New York: Putnam, 1947). Former Soviet executive describes inner workings of Soviet administration.

Kravchenko, V., *I Chose Freedom* (New York: Scribner, 1946). A diplomat and industrial official describes Russian life and tells why he fled Soviet tyranny.

Koestler, A., and others, *The God That Failed* (New York: Harper, 1950). Four former Communists and two former fellow travelers tell a typical story of disillusionment.

Deane, J. R., *The Strange Alliance* (New York: Viking, 1947). The story of our efforts at wartime co-operation with Russia. Useful for answering the argument that reason on our side would bring about peace with communism.

Timasheff, N. S., *The Great Retreat* (New York: Dutton, 1946). Argues that the early ideals of communism have now been replaced by an iron party dictatorship.

Dallin, D. J., *The Real Soviet Russia* (New Haven: Yale, 1944). A penetrating study of internal conditions in Russia, by one of the best scholars in the field.

———— *The Rise of Russia in Asia* (New Haven: Yale, 1949). An eminent historian shows Russia's perennial interest in the Far East. Useful for background on the fall of China.

———— *Soviet Russia and the Far East* (New Haven: Yale, 1948). Explains Russian policy of penetration in northeast Asia.

Dallin, D. J., and Nicolaevsky, B. I., *Forced Labor in Soviet Russia* (New Haven: Yale, 1947). Restrained but detailed study of Soviet slavery.

Baykov, A., *The Development of the Soviet Economic System* (Cambridge, England: Cambridge University Press, 1946). Emphasizes planning and shows the historical development of the Soviet economy.

Schwartz, H., *The Soviet Economy* (Syracuse: Syracuse University Press, 1949). An annotated and topically divided bibliography. Emphasizes economic studies, but also lists many general works.

Shore, M. J., *Soviet Education: Its Psychology and Philosophy* (New York: Philosophical Library, 1949). How Soviet rulers train youth in ideology.

Bienstock, G., and others, *Management in Russian Industry and Agriculture* (Ithaca: Cornell University Press, 1944). The economic system in the Soviet Union described in terms of management functions.

The Report of the Royal Commission (*To Investigate Disclosure of Secret and Confidential Information to Agents of a Foreign Power*) (Ottawa, Canada: The King's Printer, 1946). A carefully documented story of Soviet espionage. Reveals both motivation and technique of communist traitors.

Rossi, A., *A Communist Party in Action* (New Haven: Yale, 1949). A profound study of the workings of a communist party, based on French experience. Applies equally well to the United States.

Nagy, F., *The Struggle Behind the Iron Curtain* (New York: Macmillan, 1948). Hungary's prime minister under communist occupation depicts the story of gradual but inexorable communist seizure of absolute power.

Fotitch, C., *The War We Lost* (New York: Viking, 1948). The Yugoslav ambassador to Washington explains how his country was betrayed by its allies during the war.

Ciechanowski, J., *Defeat in Victory* (New York: Doubleday, 1947). The story of Poland's betrayal, as told by the former ambassador to Washington. Out of print.

Mikolajczyk, S., *The Rape of Poland* (New York: McGraw-Hill, 1948). The former Polish premier tells of his country's betrayal to Russia.

Lane, A. B., *I Saw Poland Betrayed* (Indianapolis: Bobbs-Merrill, 1948).
Our former ambassador to Poland explains the perfidy at Yalta.

Markham, R., *Rumania Under the Soviet Yoke* (Boston: Meador, 1949).
The final work of a distinguished correspondent. Shows considerable
insight into developments behind one segment of the Iron Curtain.

Martin, D., *Tito: The Story of a Fraud* (New York: Prentice-Hall, 1946).
The story of American and British diplomatic blunders which imposed
Tito upon Yugoslavia. Formerly published under title *Ally Betrayed*.

Communism and American Policy

Burnham, J., *The Struggle for the World* (New York: John Day, 1947).
Incisive analysis of the Soviet menace and suggestions for a strategy
which will defeat imperial communism.

———— *The Coming Defeat of Communism* (New York: John Day,
1950). Emphasizes strategy for exploiting weaknesses of the Soviet
system.

Bullitt, W. C., *The Great Globe Itself* (New York: Scribner, 1946). Soviet
plans for world conquest, outlined by an experienced diplomat.

Smith, W. B., *My Three Years in Moscow* (Philadelphia: Lippincott,
1949). The memoirs of an American ambassador to Russia. Moderate
and effective analysis.

Baarslag, K., *Communist Trade Union Trickery Exposed* (Chicago: Argus
Publishing Company, 1949). Brilliant psychological and tactical analysis
of communist trade union policy by one of America's top experts in the
field of communist psychology.

Budenz, L. F., *This Is My Story* (New York: McGraw-Hill, 1947). The
story of a Catholic who returned from communism. Good for understanding communist psychology.

Gitlow, B., *The Whole of Their Lives* (New York: Scribner, 1948) and
I Confess (New York: Dutton, 1940). These exposés by a former Communist are valuable but the earlier work is superior in quality.

Lyons, E., *The Red Decade* (Indianapolis: Bobbs-Merrill, 1941). Prewar
communism in the United States. While dated and out of print, this
book remains the best study of American communism. Superior to more
recently published works.

Dies, M., *The Trojan Horse in America* (New York: Dodd, Mead, 1940).
The much criticized head of the Dies Committee writes a fairly objective
study of American communism. Out of print.

Toledano, R. de, and V. Lasky, *Seeds of Treason* (New York: Funk &
Wagnalls, 1950). A gripping account of the Hiss-Chambers episode,
with an analysis of the motivation of both principals.

Reports, House Committee on Un-American Activities. This controversial organization has improved the quality of its various reports starting with 1948. Actually, the earlier reports were of more value than has been generally realized. In evaluating the earlier work, a distinction should be made between full hearings and the offhand political statements which caused so much adverse reaction.

8. THE IDEAL SOCIAL ORDER

There are not many English-language Catholic books dealing exclusively with the ideal social order. On the other hand, most of the commentaries given in List No. 1 and several of the ethical treatises given in List No. 4 treat this subject at length. Moreover, many secular works given in the final section of List No. 3 and in List No. 9 are basically sympathetic to the broad principles embodied in papal teaching on the subject.

Arès, R., *What Is Corporative Organization?* (St. Louis: Central Bureau Press, 1939). Gives the theory of functional economic society and tells how it might work in practice.

Report, Commission on Vocational Organization (Dublin: The Stationery Office, 1943). The functional society idea applied to Irish conditions by an official commission.

Munier, J. D., *Some American Approximations to Pius XI's "Industries and Professions"* (Washington: Catholic University Press, 1943). Applies the idea of a functional society to selected American attempts at social control. Out of print.

Trehey, H. F., *Foundations of a Modern Guild System* (Washington: Catholic University Press, 1940). A doctorate on the functional organization of society. Valuable. Out of print.

Mueller, F., *Heinrich Pesch and His Theory of Christian Solidarism* (St. Paul: College of St. Thomas, 1941). A pamphlet study of this important but little-known philosopher.

Brauer, T., *Economy and Society* (St. Paul: Wanderer Press, 1940). A philosophical study of the social problem.

Pesch, H., *Lehrbuch der Nationalökonomie* (Freiburg: Herder, 1905–1924). This five-volume study is considered a definitive presentation of Catholic socioeconomic philosophy as embodied in papal encyclicals.

O'Shaughnessy, M., *Economic Democracy and Private Enterprise* (New York: Harper, 1945). An interpretation of the industry-council plan, which favors total planning through these groups. Out of print.

See also:

Edwards, C. D., *Maintaining Competition: Requisites of a Governmental Policy* (List No. 5);

Clark, J. M., *Guideposts in Time of Change* (List No. 3);

Drucker, P. F., *The Future of Industrial Man* (List No. 3);

Heron, A. R., *Beyond Collective Bargaining* (List No. 3);

Bakke, E. W., *Mutual Survival: The Goal of Management and Labor* (List No. 9);

Chamberlain, N. W., *The Union Challenge to Management Control* (List No. 10);

Wright, D. M., *Democracy and Progress* (List No. 3).

9. CAPITAL-LABOR RELATIONSHIPS

The literature in this field is quite extensive. It is also of exceptional importance as a starting point for the ideal social order.

Human Relations

Human Relations in Modern Business (New York: Prentice-Hall, 1950). A blending of social ethics with business practice. Developed by a representative committee and signed by seven corporation executives. Useful for social action work with employers. Bibliography.

Mayo, E., *The Social Problems of an Industrial Civilization* (Boston: Harvard Graduate School of Business Administration, 1945). Argues that our social organization has lagged behind technological progress. A very important book.

Gardner, B. B., *Human Relations in Industry* (Chicago: Irwin, 1945). Individual and group relationships as affecting the social structure of industry.

Hoslett, S. D. (ed.), *Human Factors in Management* (New York: Harper, 1946). The competent writers of this symposium discuss the human problem in the relationship between the executive and the worker.

Selekman, B. M., *Labor Relations and Human Relations* (New York: McGraw-Hill, 1947). Social changes enforced by collective bargaining analyzed, with special stress on need for leadership on both sides. Excellent.

Heron, A. R., *Why Men Work* (Stanford, California: Stanford University Press, 1948). Argues that workers must be given some share in managerial functions, if they are to do their best work.

Tootle, H. K., *Employees Are People* (New York: McGraw-Hill, 1947). Counsels employers on treating workers as human beings. A study in the Industrial Organization and Management Series, a collection of manuals on sound management methods.

Hacker, L. M., and others, *The New Industrial Relations* (Ithaca, New York: Cornell University Press, 1948). A series of lectures given at the New York School of Labor Relations. Most of the speakers emphasize the human aspect in industrial relations.

Nyman, R. C., *Foundations for Constructive Industrial Relations* (New York: Funk & Wagnalls, 1949). A sociologist works out a pattern of labor-management co-operation.

Blum, M. L., *Industrial Psychology and Its Social Foundations* (New York: Harper, 1949). The human dignity of workers and method of co-operation studied from a psychological aspect.

Yoder, D., *Personnel Management and Industrial Relations* (New York: Prentice-Hall, 1948). A good textbook, with ample bibliography and references.

Business Leadership

Barnard, C. I., *Organization and Management* (Cambridge: Harvard University Press, 1948). A selection of papers dealing with good human relationships in industry.

—— *The Function of the Executive* (Cambridge: Harvard University Press, 1938). Studies the techniques of business organization, with stress on the ability to develop co-operation.

Leighton, A. H., *The Governing of Men* (Princeton: Princeton University Press, 1946). A psychological study of leadership, based on experiences in Japanese relocation camps, but universal in application. Useful for study of business leadership.

McCormick, C. P., *The Power of People* (New York: Harper, 1949). The multiple-management plan for giving lower management levels real power in directing a firm.

Merrill, H. F. (ed.), *Responsibilities of Business Leadership* (Cambridge: Harvard University Press, 1948). Business responsibility to the public, employees, government, consumers, stockholders, and the world. Brief but cogent.

Moore, W. E., *Industrial Relations and the Social Order* (New York: Macmillan, 1946). Industry's relationship with society and its responsibility toward workers.

Roethlisberger, F. J., *Management and Morale* (Cambridge: Harvard University Press, 1942). One of the pioneer studies in human relations, calling for co-operation between management and workers.

Tead, O., *The Art of Leadership* (New York: McGraw-Hill, 1935). Still considered a classic in its field of defining the functions of a leader.

Whitehead, T. N., *Leadership in a Free Society* (Cambridge: Harvard University Press, 1947). A social theory of industrial society, based on its adequacy to meet human wants.

Whyte, W. F., *Industry and Society* (New York: McGraw-Hill, 1947). Emphasizes the social responsibilities of modern industry.

Noland, E. W., and Bakke, E. W., *Workers Wanted* (New York: Harper,

1949). Discusses proper procedures for hiring workers, so that the right man will be secured for a job.

Bowler, E. M., and Dawson, F. T., *Counseling Employees* (New York: Prentice-Hall, 1948). Explains need for employee counseling and best methods for getting results.

Cantor, N., *Employee Counseling* (New York: McGraw-Hill, 1945). Industrial psychology applied to industrial relations in a pioneer field.

Heron, A. R., *Sharing Information with Employees* (Stanford, California: Stanford University Press, 1942). First volume of a valuable trilogy on making workers effective partners in industry.

Planty, E. G., and others, *Training Employees and Managers for Production and Teamwork* (New York: Ronald Press, 1948). One of the most comprehensive and enthusiastic books in the field. Gives detailed suggestions for building teamwork in a plant.

Leiter, R. D., *The Foreman in Industrial Relations* (New York: Columbia University Press, 1948). Unionization problems in relation to foremen and the impact of labor legislation upon this group.

Gardiner, G., *When Foreman and Steward Bargain* (New York: McGraw-Hill, 1945). Suggests guiding principles at a crucial point in union-management relations.

Charm, S. D., *Wage Policy for Management* (New York: Funk & Wagnalls, 1949). A nontechnical survey of wage negotiation and determination, by a personnel expert. Emphasizes human relations.

Smyth, R. C., and Murphy, J. J., *Bargaining with Organized Labor* (New York: Funk & Wagnalls, 1949). Emphasizes good faith and understanding as keys to successful labor relations on the part of businessmen.

Cheyfitz, E. T., *Constructive Collective Bargaining* (New York: McGraw-Hill, 1947). A former union official offers suggestions as to the improvement of free collective bargaining.

Labor-Management Co-operation

Bakke, E. W., *Mutual Survival, the Goals of Unions and Management* (New York: Harper, 1946). A brochure-sized book, giving reasons for labor-management difficulties and suggestions as to reaching understanding.

Braun, K., *Union-Management Co-operation* (Washington: Brookings, 1947). A thorough study of co-operation in the clothing industry, with some analysis of implications for other industries.

Cooke, M. L., and Murray, P., *Organized Labor and Production* (New York: Harper, 1946). Suggests common grounds for understanding and techniques for implementing agreements.

Greater Productivity Through Labor-Management Co-operation (New

York: American Management Association, 1949). Discusses concrete experiences in the field and recommends policies.

Golden, C. S., and Ruttenberg, H. J., *The Dynamics of Industrial Democracy* (New York: Harper, 1942). Basic principles of collaboration between workers and employers, with illustrations from the steel industry.

Lever, E. J., and Goodell, F., *Labor-Management Co-operation and How to Achieve It* (New York: Harper, 1948). A guide to the organization and functioning of joint-production committees.

Mooney, P., *Profitable Labor Relations and How to Develop Them* (New York: Harper, 1946). Emphasizes effective leadership and employee participation in industry.

Partners in Production (New York: Twentieth Century Fund, 1949). Shows how major goals of labor and management can be reconciled in their mutual interest to the furthering of the common good.

Seward, W., *Teamwork in Industry* (New York: Funk & Wagnalls, 1949). Offers constructive proposals for better labor-management cooperation.

Schweinitz, D. de, *Labor and Management in a Common Enterprise* (Cambridge: Harvard, 1949). A factual study on labor-management collaboration as found in wartime production committees.

See also: Heron, A. R., *Beyond Collective Bargaining* (List No. 3); *Causes of Industrial Peace Under Collective Bargaining* (List No. 10).

Profit Sharing

Hartman, R. S. (ed.), *Profit Sharing Manual* (Columbus, Ohio: Council of Profit Sharing Industries, 1948). Factual material on profit sharing, coming from a group whose growth is a significant move in the direction of social justice.

Stewart, B. M., and Couper, W. J., *Profit Sharing and Stock Ownership for Wage Earners and Executives* (New York: Industrial Relations Counselors, 1945). Reviews past experience in the field based on study of 209 plans and 15 American studies on the subject. Out of print.

Thompson, K. M., *Profit Sharing* (New York: Harper, 1949). An up-to-date study of this important problem. Concrete and informative. Bibliography, references, and appendix material.

10. LABOR PROBLEMS

Books in this section deal directly with the problems of workers, in contrast to those in the preceding section which were largely addressed to business executives, treating workers' problems only indirectly. The literature on labor problems is immense, as befits labor's enhanced position in the national economy. Moreover, the type of publication is changing as a result of labor's maturity. Instead of the impassioned pleas for the rights of workers, we now have more sober appraisals of union responsibility for community welfare. The works of Slichter, Chamberlain, and Lindblom reflect this new trend.

General Books on Labor

Bloom, G. F., and Northrup, H. R., *Economics of Labor and Industrial Relations* (Philadelphia: Blakiston, 1950). An excellent, up-to-date labor textbook, which emphasizes economics of labor problems.

Baerwald, F., *Fundamentals of Labor Economics* (New York: D. X. McMullen, 1947). Stresses economic principles rather than factual material.

Lester, R. A., *Economics of Labor* (New York: Macmillan, 1941). Emphasizes economic aspects of the labor problem, with stress on wages and employment.

Peterson, F., *Survey of Labor Economics* (New York: Harper, 1947). A labor textbook with emphasis upon economic aspects.

Reynolds, L. G., *Labor Economics and Labor Relations* (New York: Prentice-Hall, 1949). Collective bargaining studied with special reference to the economics of wage determination.

Shister, J., *Economics of the Labor Market* (Philadelphia: Lippincott, 1949). This textbook on labor reflects postwar problems and issues.

Taft, P., *Economics and Problems of Labor* (Harrisburg, Pa.: Stackpole & Heck, 1948). One of the better labor textbooks.

Hopkins, W. S., *Labor in the American Economy* (New York: McGraw-Hill, 1948). A good textbook, with sound recommendations.

Handbook of Labor Statistics (Washington: Government Printing Office, 1948). Essential statistical material on labor and related problems. Same material currently available in *Monthly Labor Review*.

A Trade Union Library, 1949 (Princeton: Industrial Relations Section, Princeton University, 1949). An extensive, annotated, and topically arranged reading list on labor topics.

Dickerman, M., and Taylor, R. (edd.), *Who's Who in Labor* (New York: Dryden Press, 1946). Authorized biographies of persons in the labor field, with other miscellaneous labor information.

Cohen, S., *State Labor Legislation, 1937–1947* (Columbus, Ohio: Ohio State University, 1948). Both laws and judicial decrees concerning labor unions are studied.

Gregory, C. O., *Labor and the Law* (New York: Norton, 1949). Gives both the basic laws and the most important judicial decisions affecting labor.

Miller, G. W., *American Labor and the Government* (New York: Prentice-Hall, 1948). A good textbook on labor legislation and judicial decisions.

Taylor, G. W., *Government Regulation of Industrial Relations* (New York: Prentice-Hall, 1948). Major government intervention in labor-management relations during the period 1935–1948.

The American Story of Industrial and Labor Relations (Albany, N. Y.: Williams Press, 1943). Prepared by the New York State Joint Legislative Committee on Industrial and Labor Conditions. A balanced, simple survey of labor problems.

Austin, A., *The Labor Story* (New York: Coward-McCann, 1949). Brief, impressionistic history of American Labor.

Dulles, R., *Labor in America: A History* (New York: Crowell, 1949). An excellent brief history of the labor movement viewed against the background of national development.

Commons, J. R., and others, *History of Labor in the United States* (New York: Macmillan, 1918–1935). A four-volume, definitive study of labor history up to 1932. Out of print.

Wages

Dickinson, Z. C., *Collective Wage Determination* (New York: Ronald Press, 1941). Factors affecting wage rates, especially collective bargaining and federal laws.

Dunlop, J. T., *Wage Determination Under Trade Unions* (New York: Macmillan, 1944). How union policies affect labor costs. Out of print.

Ross, A. M., *Trade Union Wage Policy* (Berkeley: University of California Press, 1948). Stimulating study of collective bargaining considered as a political activity.

Snider, J. L., *The Guarantee of Work and Wages* (Boston: Harvard Graduate School of Business Administration, 1947). A critical study of guarantee plans, with proposals for extension of sound plans.

Latimer, M. W., *Guaranteed Wages* (Washington: Government Printing Office, 1947). A report by the United States Office of War Mobilization and Reconversion, giving a detailed study of guaranteed wages.

Guaranteed Wage Plans in the United States (Washington: Government Printing Office, 1948, BLS Bulletin No. 925). Data on 62 plans, with study of clauses in collective-bargaining agreements dealing with wage guarantees.

Kaplan, A. D. H., *The Guarantee of Annual Wages* (Washington: Brookings, 1947). Emphasizes the difficulties faced in securing guaranteed wages.

Heller Committee, *Annual Budgets* (Berkeley: University of California Press). Annual budgets for families and individuals at different income levels, based on San Francisco prices. Useful for determining suitable wage standards.

Patton, J. A., and Smith, R. S., *Job Evaluation* (Chicago: Irwin, 1949). Studies job evaluation and merit rating in the attempt to secure a scientific appraisal of a worker's contribution to the enterprise.

Louden, J. K., *Wage Incentives* (New York: Wiley, 1944). Analyzes reasons for success or failure of incentive plans.

Kennedy, D. V., *Union Policy and Incentive Wage Methods* (New York: Columbia University Press, 1945). Based on actual experience ascertained through direct inquiries to both management and labor.

Gomberg, W., *Trade Union Analysis of Time Study* (Chicago: Science Research Associates, 1948). A critical but competent survey of time-study methods, written by a union official.

——— *A Labor Union Manual on Job Evaluation* (Chicago: Roosevelt College, Labor Education Division, 1947). A brief study by a labor official who favors job evaluation as a means of increasing productivity.

Mundel, M. E., *Systematic Motion and Time Study* (New York: Prentice-Hall, 1947). A good text on a problem related to the fields of industrial efficiency and wage determination.

See also: Charm, S. D., *Wage Policy for Management* (List No. 9).

Health and Housing

Abrams, C., *The Future of Housing* (New York: Harper, 1946). A comprehensive study of the problem in the light of sound community planning.

Colean, M. L., *American Housing: Problems and Prospects* (New York: Twentieth Century Fund, 1944). Factual material on housing with recommendations for better production and marketing of houses.

Straus, N., *The Seven Myths of Housing* (New York: Knopf, 1945). Deals with misconceptions in regard to housing and offers plans for postwar housing.

Goldmann, F., *Voluntary Medical Care Insurance in the United States* (New York: Columbia University Press, 1948). Favors both group prepayment and group practice as the best methods for voluntary medical insurance.

The Nation's Health (Ewing Report) (Washington: Government Printing Office, 1948). The controversial study arguing for a system of national health insurance.

Rothenberg, R. E., and others, *Group Medicine and Health Insurance in Action* (New York: Crown Publishers, 1949). Stresses advantages of group medical practice within framework of voluntary national health insurance.

Social Insurance

Beveridge, W., *Social Insurance and Allied Services* (New York: Macmillan, 1942). The basis in part for the British social-insurance policy. Out of print.

Burns, E. M., *The American Social Security System* (New York: Houghton Mifflin, 1949). Up-to-date factual study with recommendations for improvements in our present system.

Gagliardo, D., *American Social Insurance* (New York: Harper, 1949). A concise textbook on social security and related problems, including proposed improvements.

Haber, W., and Cohen, W. J., *Readings in Social Security* (New York: Prentice-Hall, 1948). Selected and mostly recent readings on this vital problem.

Meriam, L., and others, *The Cost and Financing of Social Security* (Washington: Brookings, 1950). A critical survey, in terms of costs, of the social security system.

Meriam, L., *Relief and Social Security* (Washington: Brookings, 1946). Lengthy, critical study of social insurance and relief programs here.

Callaghan, H. C., *The Family Allowance Procedure* (Washington: Catholic University Press, 1947). A doctoral dissertation exploring the field with great thoroughness and insight.

Full Employment

Bakke, E. W., *The Unemployed Worker* (New Haven: Yale, 1940) and *Citizens Without Work* (New Haven: Yale, 1940). Sociological studies of unemployment, stressing the effect upon the individual and his community relations.

Beveridge, W. H., *Full Employment in a Free Society* (New York: Norton, 1945). Inasmuch as this book influenced the policy of a nation, it is important for understanding the ideas underlying British socialism.

Hansen, A. H., *Economic Policy and Full Employment* (New York: McGraw-Hill, 1947). Emphasizes need for compensatory government spending to secure full employment.

—— *Monetary Theory and Fiscal Policy* (New York: McGraw-Hill, 1949). Advocates flexible tax and public spending policies as means to counteract depressions.

Wright, D. M., *The Economics of Disturbance* (New York: Macmillan, 1947). A study of the theory and practical problems connected with depressions.

National and International Measures for Full Employment (New York: Columbia University Press, 1950). A United Nations report submitted by five experts. Deals with measures to be taken individually and jointly by nations in order to achieve full employment.

Wernette, J. P., *Financing Full Employment* (Cambridge: Harvard Uni-

versity Press, 1945). A competent economist advocates controlled monetary inflation as a means of preventing or counteracting depressions. Out
of print.

Chandler, L. V., *Introduction to Monetary Theory* (New York: Harper,
1940). A simple but very competent work.

────── *The Economics of Money and Banking* (New York: Harper,
1948). A more extensive and more recent treatment by the same author.

Goldenweiser, E. A., *Monetary Management* (New York: McGraw-Hill,
1949). A review of Federal Reserve policy, 1914–1948, and a discussion
of current problems. Authoritative.

Feldman, H., *Stabilizing Jobs and Wages Through Better Management*
(New York: Harper, 1940). Discusses practical plans for securing business stability. Out of print.

Labor Unionism

Peterson, F., *Handbook of Labor Unions* (Washington: American Council
on Public Affairs, 1944). Reference book on American unions.

────── *American Labor Unions* (New York: Harper, 1945). Factual
material on union organization and activities.

Brooks, R. R., *When Labor Organizes* (New Haven: Yale, 1937). Excellent
on the psychology of labor organization, even though business environment has changed for the better since this book was written.

Tannenbaum, F., *A Philosophy of Labor* (New York: Knopf, 1950). A
non-Catholic Columbia University professor elaborates a philosophy of
labor which is quite similar to that of the encyclicals.

Barbash, J., *Labor Unions in Action* (New York: Harper, 1948). Discusses
the structure and function of unions and also present-day union
leadership.

Roe, W., *Juggernaut: American Labor in Action* (Philadelphia: Lippincott,
1948). A critical study of union leadership by a former union officer.

Mills, C. W., *The New Men of Power* (New York: Harcourt, 1948). This
collective picture is a composite of 500 labor leaders in terms of backgrounds and attitudes.

Lens, S., *Left, Right, and Center* (Hinsdale, Ill.: Regnery, 1949). Discusses
conflicting ideological forces in American labor, also racketeering and
like unsavory activities. The author is a union official.

Ginzberg, E., *The Labor Leader* (New York: Macmillan, 1948). The
psychology of labor leadership, based on a study of leaders in ten
national unions.

Howe, I., and Widick, B. W., *The UAW and Walter Reuther* (New York:
Random House, 1949). Describes one of America's most dynamic unions
and its leader as forces influencing our social structure.

Bakke, E. W., and Kerr, C., *Unions, Management, and the Public* (New York: Harcourt, 1948). Uses many sources to show impact of trade unionism on workers, management, and the public.

Chamberlain, N. W., *The Union Challenge to Management Control* (New York: Harper, 1948). A penetrating analysis of the thorny problem of union functions versus management rights.

Lindblom, C. E., *Unions and Capitalism* (New Haven: Yale, 1949). The author sees the vices as well as the virtues of unionism. Fears monopoly tendencies and interference with essential freedom of enterprise.

Slichter, S. H., *Union Policies and Industrial Management* (Washington: Brookings, 1941). Detailed study of policies worked out in collective bargaining with analysis of their economic import.

—— *The Challenge of Industrial Relations* (Ithaca: Cornell University Press, 1947). Economic implications of trade unionism. Suggestions for a sound labor policy.

Chamberlain, N. W., *Collective Bargaining Procedures* (Washington: American Council on Public Affairs, 1944). Suggests methods most likely to succeed in producing mutual agreement.

Causes of Industrial Peace Under Collective Bargaining (Washington: National Planning Association, 1948–). A series of fifteen studies of various firms and industries where labor-management peace has prevailed, in the effort to determine policies which lead to harmonious co-operation.

Smith, L. J., *Collective Bargaining* (New York: Prentice-Hall, 1946). Issues and techniques in collective bargaining. Annotated bibliography.

Taylor, G. W. (ed.), *Industry-Wide Collective Bargaining Series* (Philadelphia: University of Pennsylvania Press, 1949). The problem of industry-wide bargaining examined in a series of brochures.

Williamson, S. T., and Harris, H., *Trends in Collective Bargaining* (New York: Twentieth Century Fund, 1945). Problems and issues are discussed, with recommendations given.

Millis, H. A. (ed.), *How Collective Bargaining Works* (New York: Twentieth Century Fund, 1942). The subject is studied in terms of major industries, describing collective bargaining practices in each. Out of print.

Collective Bargaining Provisions (Washington: Government Printing Office, 1947–). A series of booklets digesting detailed provisions found in union contracts. Valuable for contract-negotiation study in labor schools.

Braun, K., *The Settlement of Industrial Disputes* (Philadelphia: Blakiston, 1944). Examines underlying issues, with frequent reference to foreign experience, especially German labor courts. Out of print.

Copelof, M., *Management-Union Arbitration* (New York: Harper, 1949). Practical, well-documented study of theory and technique of arbitration.

Updegraf, C. M., and McCoy, W. P., *Arbitration of Labor Disputes* (Chicago: Commerce Clearing House, 1946). A comprehensive and modern treatment of the subject, based on extensive experience.

Seidman, J., *Union Rights and Union Duties* (New York: Harcourt, 1943). Duties to employers, members, and public, with suggestions for reform.

Labor Unrest and Dissatisfaction (Albany, N. Y.: International Brotherhood of Paper Makers, 1944). Another brochure on a similar subject. Suggestions for improvements.

Democracy in Trade Unions (New York: American Civil Liberties Union, 1943). The problem of union civil liberties surveyed in a brief brochure. Out of print.

Democracy in Trade Unions (New York: American Civil Liberties Union, 1949). A briefer form of the earlier document of the same name.

Bollens, L. F., *White Collar or Noose?* (New York: North River Press, 1947). An argument for the unionization of white-collar workers.

Northrup, H. R., *Organized Labor and the Negro* (New York: Harper, 1944). Racial policies of various unions and the factors influencing these policies.

Cayton, H. R., and Mitchell, G. S., *Black Workers and the New Unions* (Chapel Hill: University of North Carolina Press, 1939). Organization problems of Negro workers.

Toner, J. L., *The Closed Shop* (Washington: American Council on Public Affairs, 1942). Father Toner's doctorate is still the best English-language study of the problem. Out of print.

See also:

Gardiner, G., *When Foreman and Steward Bargain* (List No. 9);

Smyth, R. C., and Murphy, J. J., *Bargaining with Organized Labor* (List No. 9);

Cheyfitz, E. T., *Constructive Collective Bargaining* (List No. 9);

Dickinson, Z. C., *Collective Wage Determination* (*supra*);

Dunlop, J. T., *Wage Determination Under Trade Unions* (*supra*);

Ross, A. M., *Trade Union Wage Policy* (*supra*);

Kennedy, V. D., *Union Policy and Incentive Wage Methods* (*supra*);

Briefs, G. A., *The Proletariat* (List No. 3).

Miscellaneous

Anderson, N., *Men on the Move* (Chicago: University of Chicago Press, 1940). Migratory labor viewed in its social and economic effects. Treats efforts to solve the problem. Out of print.

McWilliams, C., *Factories in the Field* (Boston: Little, Brown, 1939) and *Ill Fares the Land* (Boston: Little, Brown, 1942). Studies of migratory labor by a leftist author. Out of print.

Ross, M., *All Manner of Men* (New York: Harcourt, 1948). The story of the federal Fair Employment Practices Commission, written by a former chairman.

Weaver, R. C., *Negro Labor, A National Problem* (New York: Harcourt, 1946). Discussed in terms of wartime gains for Negroes and probable postwar changes.

Warne, C. E. (ed.), *Labor in Postwar America* (Brooklyn: Remsen Press, 1949). Thirty-one authors discuss major problems facing labor after World War II. A good reference book.

See also:

Rose, A., *The Negro in America* (List No. 4);

Myrdal, G., *An American Dilemma* (List No. 4).

11. PROPERTY, WEALTH, AND INCOME

In addition to the books dealing directly with the problem of property, there are many in Lists Nos. 1 and 4 which have fairly extensive treatments of the subject as part of general social or ethical studies. The books on distributism in List No. 14 treat of the subject of property. Moreover, the economic source material given in List No. 2 gives statistical information on wealth and income.

McDonald, W. J., *The Social Value of Property According to St. Thomas Aquinas* (Washington: Catholic University Press, 1939). Excellent for general medieval ethics as well as for the topic considered in this doctorate. Out of print.

Schumacher, L. S., *The Philosophy of the Equitable Distribution of Wealth* (Washington: Catholic University Press, 1949). A doctorate applying Thomistic ideals of property to modern wealth distribution.

Crofts, A. M., *Property and Poverty* (Dublin: Irish Rosary Office, 1948). Private ownership according to the principles of St. Thomas Aquinas. The book was written in 1938, but only published in 1948.

Hoffman, R. J., *Tradition and Progress* (Milwaukee: Bruce, 1935). Stresses property as a basis for freedom.

Berle, A. A., and Means, G. C., *The Modern Corporation and Private Property* (New York: Macmillan, 1933). The authors study the social implications of power concentration through narrow control of corporate wealth. A masterly treatment.

Fletcher, J. F. (ed.), *Christianity and Property* (Philadelphia: The Westminster Press, 1947). Eight Protestant-Episcopal leaders set forth their views on property.

Kaplan, A. D. H., *Small Business: Its Place and Problems* (New York: McGraw-Hill, 1948). Both analysis and corrective programs are given in this excellent study.

George, H., *Progress and Poverty* (New York: Schalkenbach Foundation, 1940). The classic formulation of the single-tax theory of social reform. See also:

Arnold, T. W., *The Bottlenecks of Business* (List No. 5);
Brady, R. A., *Business as a System of Power* (List No. 5);
Raymond, F. I., *The Limitist* (List No. 3);
Lynch, D., *The Concentration of Economic Power* (List No. 5).

12. GOVERNMENT AND ECONOMIC LIFE

As in the preceding list, it will be found that the social and ethical treatises given in Lists Nos. 1 and 4 deal with the Christian philosophy of the state. Other material is found in Lists Nos. 3, 5, 6, 7, and 8.

The State

Dawson, C., *Religion and the Modern State* (New York: Sheed, 1935). Penetrating philosophy of history and study of modern ideologies. Out of print.

Democracy: Should It Survive? (Milwaukee: Bruce, 1943). Thirteen Catholic leaders contribute essays on various forms of democracy.

Maritain, J., *Christianity and Democracy* (New York: Scribner, 1944). A study of the close interrelationship between the two.

Osgniach, A. J., *The Christian State* (Milwaukee: Bruce, 1943). Presents basic political ethics, as well as a discussion of major modern problems in political theory. Out of print.

Rommen, H. A., *The State in Catholic Thought* (St. Louis: Herder, 1945). Applies social ethics to government.

Orton, W. A., *The Economic Role of the State* (Chicago: University of Chicago Press, 1950). Argues that the criteria of state action should be moral rather than economic. Fundamental principles of morality are the only sound basis for freedom.

The Hoover Commission Report (New York: McGraw-Hill, 1949). The main outlines of our most recent and most ambitious plan for reforming government.

Benson, C. G. S., *The New Centralization* (New York: Farrar & Rinehart, 1941). Studies the new relationships brought about by changing functions of federal, state, and local governments.

MacIver, R. M., *The Web of Government* (New York: Macmillan, 1947). A sociopolitical study of government. Warns against excessive concentration of power in the state.

Dimock, M. E., *Business and Government* (New York: Holt, 1949). The mixed economy of private enterprise under some government control analyzed from economic and political aspects.

Allen, E. D., and Brownlee, O. H., *Economics of Public Finance* (New York: Prentice-Hall, 1947). A textbook treatment of taxation and public spending.

Groves, H. M., *Postwar Taxation and Economic Progress* (New York: Committee for Economic Development, 1946). Suggests tax policies which will aid business expansion and high, stable employment levels.

Our National Debt: Its History and Meaning Today (New York: Harcourt, 1949). The Committee on Public Dept Policy analyzes the economic implications of our national debt, particularly in terms of its effect on economic life.

See also: Mises, L. von, *Omnipotent Government* (List No. 6).

International Ethics and Economics

Eppstein, J., *The Catholic Tradition and the Law of Nations* (London: Burns, Oates, 1935). Christian principles on peace. Out of print.

Code of International Ethics (Oxford: Catholic Social Guild, 1937). A compilation of the basic principles of international relations, by the Malines Union.

Gonella, G., *A World to Reconstruct* (Milwaukee: Bruce, 1944). Explanation of the ethical principles involved in papal peace messages, particularly the Christmas messages of Pope Pius XII.

Pamphlet studies by the Catholic Association for International Peace, 1312 Massachusetts Ave., N.W., Washington 5, D. C. A series of timely studies on both ethical principles and current problems.

Buchanan, N. S., and Lutz, F. A., *Rebuilding the World Economy* (New York: Twentieth Century Fund, 1947). Advocates multilateral world trade and discusses means for achieving it.

Condliffe, J. B., *The Commerce of Nations* (New York: Norton, 1949). Economic history of foreign trade, leading up to current problems.

Heilperin, M. A., *The Trade of Nations* (New York: Knopf, 1947). A discussion of world trade theory and policies, supporting the ideal of more freedom of trade.

Wilcox, C., *A Charter for World Trade* (New York: Macmillan, 1949). The author defends the International Trade Organization as the best method for restoring world trade.

See also: *National and International Measures for Full Employment* (List No. 10).

13. SOCIAL REFORM AND SOCIAL ACTION

The studies on Catholic social principles in List No. 1 often contain suggestions for social reform and social action. Since there were few books dealing explicitly with this subject, most of the titles given below deal with specialized Catholic action.

Cronin, J. F., *Catholic Social Action* (Milwaukee: Bruce, 1948). Manual by present author dealing with techniques for social action in fields of education, labor, and community relations. Lengthy bibliography.

Plater, C. D., *The Priest and Social Action* (New York: Longmans, 1914). Studies work of clergy in European social reform movements. Out of print.

Suhard, E., *Growth or Decline* (South Bend: Fides Publishers, 1948). A powerful analysis of the Church's problem in the modern world, by the late Cardinal Archbishop of Paris.

Anderl, S., and Ruth, Sr. M., *The Religious and Catholic Action* (La Crosse, Wis.: St. Rose Convent, 1947). Emphasizes part played by religious in Catholic action. Reprints many papal and episcopal documents.

Studies in Catholic Action (Melbourne: Australian National Secretariat of Catholic Action, 1948). A practical approach to the problems of Catholic Action, written on the basis of the excellent Australian experience in the field.

Charbonneau, J., *Catholic Action* (South Bend: Fides Publishers, 1943). The former Archbishop of Montreal explains the basic principles of Catholic action.

Civardi, L., *A Manual of Catholic Action* (New York: Sheed, 1936). The philosophy of Catholic action and papal teaching on the subject.

Fitzsimons, J., and McGuire, P., *Restoring All Things* (New York: Sheed, 1938). A practical guide to Catholic action, based on English and Australian experience.

Geissler, E. S., *Training of Lay Leaders* (South bend: Fides Publishers, 1944). Prepared especially for the student movement. An excellent study.
—— *The Young Christian Farmer* (South Bend: Fides Publishers, 1948). Application of Catholic action principles to the rural apostolate.

Hesburgh, T. M., *The Theology of Catholic Action* (South Bend: Fides Publishers, 1948). The dogmatic and moral principles behind Catholic action.

Lelotte, S. M., *Fundamental Principles of Catholic Action* (South Bend: Fides Publishers, 1943). One of the best works. Practical, with helps for discussion groups.

Kothen, R., *The Priest and the Proletariat* (New York: Sheed, 1948). A brief book, describing French priest-workmen.

Furfey, P. H., *Fire on the Earth* (New York: Macmillan, 1936); *Three Theories of Society* (New York: Macmillan, 1937); *The Mystery of Iniquity* (Milwaukeee: Bruce, 1944). Emphasizes the spiritual aspect of social reform. A specialized approach which could be misleading if not carefully studied.

Weaver, R. M., *Ideas Have Consequences* (Chicago: University of Chicago Press, 1948). Shows far-reaching influence of ideology.

14. DISTRIBUTISM AND CO-OPERATIVES

Catholics have shown a considerable interest in distributism and the co-operative movement both here and abroad. It is only natural that a substantial percentage of the books listed below are written by Catholic authors.

Distributism

Belloc, Hilaire, *The Restoration of Property* (New York: Sheed, 1936). A blueprint for a distributist society.

────── *The Servile State* (London: Foulis, 1913; American edition, New York: Holt, 1946). One of the first arguments for distributism. Holds that ownership by the few means a servile state.

Chesterton, G. K., *What's Wrong With the World?* (New York: Dodd, Mead, 1910; reprinted by Sheed, 1942). A searching attack on industrialism by one of the keenest minds of modern Catholicism.

Marx, W. J., *Mechanization and Culture* (St. Louis: Herder, 1941). Argues that excessive devotion to the technical is undermining higher values.

Mumford, L., *The Culture of Cities* (New York: Harcourt, 1938). Opposes the corrosive effects of excessive urbanization.

Peterson, E. T. (ed.), *Cities Are Abnormal* (Norman, Okla.: University of Oklahoma Press, 1946). Likewise attacks urban life as a method of normal human living.

Hewes, T., *Decentralize for Liberty* (New York: Dutton, 1947). One of the more recent distributist pleas, by a former government official.

Robbins, H., *The Sun of Justice* (London: Heath Cranton, 1938). Argues that distributism best meets the social ideas of the Catholic Church.

Nutting, W. D., *Reclamation of Independence* (Nevada City, Calif.: Berliner & Lonigan, 1947). A mixture of personalism, distributism, and agrarianism, by a thoughtful Catholic writer.

See also:

Penty, A. J., *A Guildsman's Interpretation of History* (List No. 3);

Doboszynski, A., *The Economics of Charity* (List No. 1);

Nourse, E. G., *Price Making in a Democracy* (List No. 3).

The Co-operative Movement

Bergengren, R. F., *Credit Union, North America* (New York: Southern

Publishers, 1940). History of the movement, with practical hints on running a successful credit union. Out of print.

Giles, R., *Credit for the Millions: the Story of Credit Unions* (New York: Harper, 1950). Not yet published at this writing. Should substitute for Bergengren, noted above as out of print.

Coady, M. M., *Masters of Their Own Destiny* (New York: Harper, 1939). Firsthand accounts of the co-operative movement in Antigonish, Nova Scotia. Out of print.

Cowling, E., *Co-operatives in America* (New York: Harper, 1944). A thorough study of the principles and practice of American co-operatives.

Fowler, B. B., *The Co-operative Challenge* (Boston: Little, Brown, 1947). History of the co-operative movement in the United States and Canada. Out of print.

———— *The Lord Helps Those* (New York: Vanguard, 1938). How the people of Nova Scotia are solving their problems through co-operation.

Schmiedeler, E., *Co-operation, A Christian Mode of Industry* (St. Nazianz, Wis.: Salvatorian Fathers, 1941). Studies the whole co-operative movement, including credit unions.

"Co-operatives," *Law and Contemporary Problems,* Summer, 1948. A symposium with emphasis upon the economic and legal aspects of co-operatives.

Warbasse, J. P., *Co-operative Democracy* (New York: Harper, 1942). The philosophy of the movement described.

Ward, L. R., *Ourselves, Inc.* (New York: Harper, 1945). Interesting narratives of experiences with the co-operative movement. Out of print.

Ward, L. R. (ed.), *United for Freedom* (Milwaukee: Bruce, 1945). Nearly a score of authors discuss various phases of the co-operative movement, with emphasis upon its contribution to Christian Democracy.

15. RURAL PROBLEMS

In addition to the books listed here, there is a considerable amount of pamphlet literature available from the National Catholic Rural Life Conference, Des Moines, Iowa. The Conference also publishes a monthly paper, *The Christian Farmer.*

Manifesto on Rural Life (Milwaukee: Bruce, 1939). A co-operative statement by leading Church authorities giving a philosophy of rural life.

Howard, T. E., *Agricultural Handbook for Rural Pastors and Laymen* (Des Moines: National Catholic Rural Life Conference, 1947). A brief manual of social action, with quotations from Church authorities.

Ligutti, L. G., and Rawe, J. C., *Rural Roads to Security* (Milwaukee: Bruce, 1940). Emphasizes ideals of farm life, with suggestions as to how they may be preserved and enlarged.

Les valeurs humaines dans le domaine rural (Montreal: L'Oeuvre des Tracts, 1950). A declaration of principles from the Malines International Union of Social Studies (issued September, 1949).

Black, J. D., and Kiefer, M. E., *Future Food and Agriculture Policy* (New York: McGraw-Hill, 1948). American and world food problems in the next decade.

Fryer, L., *The American Farmer* (New York: Harper, 1947). Emphasizes the problems of small farmers and farm workers.

Lindstrom, D. E., *American Rural Life* (New York: Ronald Press, 1948). A study of rural sociology, with emphasis on methods for bettering conditions in the country.

Schultz, T. W., *Agriculture in an Unstable Economy* (New York: McGraw-Hill, 1945). This earlier work by Professor Schultz discusses farm problems in the light of national economic welfare.

—— *Production and Welfare of Agriculture* (New York: Macmillan, 1949). A thoroughly up-to-date study of farm problems and policies.

Taylor, C. C., and others, *Rural Life in the United States* (New York: Knopf, 1949). Eight U. S. Department of Agriculture experts write an excellent text on rural sociology.

Waring, P. A., and Golden, C. S., *Soil and Steel* (New York: Harper, 1947). A labor leader and a practical farmer collaborate in explaining common interests of farmers and union workers.

Appendix III. CORRELATION OF MAIN AUTHORITIES WITH CHAPTERS OF PRESENT TEXT

As a service to readers who may be interested in a detailed study of a particular document, the following table correlates individual documents with the chapters of the present book. Arabic numerals refer to the paragraph numbers of the source material in the edition cited. The Roman numerals which follow indicate the chapters of the present book which comment on the particular text.

RERUM NOVARUM
(*N.C.W.C. Edition*)

5. I	20. VII, XII	38. VIII, XI	60. IX
6. I	21. XII	39. VIII, XI	61. X
7. V	22. XII	40. XIV	62. IX, X
8. V	23. XII	42. II, XIV	63. X
9. V	24. II	48. IV, XIII	65. XII
10. XII	25. II, XI	49. IV	66. I, XII
11. XII	26. III, VIII	50. IV	67. XII
12. XII	28. VII, VIII, XI	51. X, XIII	71. III
13. XII	30. XI	52. IV, XIII	72. III, XI
14. IV, XII	31. VIII, IX	53. XIII	75. XIII, XIV
15. XII	32. VIII	54. XIII	76. VII, XI
16. XII	33. VIII, XI	55. XII	78. XI
17. XII	35. XII	56. XI	79. XI
18. XII	36. XII	57. IX	83. IV
19. XII	37. VIII, XI	59. IX	

QUADRAGESIMO ANNO
(*N.C.W.C. Edition*)

3. I	14. V	22. XIV	26. XIV
4. IV	19. XIV	23. XIV	27. V, XIV
5. I	20. XIV	24. XIV	28. XIII, XIV
10. V	21. XIV	25. IV, V, XIII, XIV	29. XIV

30. XI, XIV	59. I, XII	88. IV, V	117. V
31. XIV	60. I, XII	89. XIII	118. V
32. XIV	61. X, XII	90. IV	119. V
33. III, XI, XIV	62. I, VI, VIII	91. V	120. V
34. XIV	63. XII	92. V	125. II, XIV
35. XI, XIV	64. VIII, IX	93. V	127. XIV
36. XIV	65. VIII, IX	94. V	129. XIV
37. III, XIV	66. X	95. V	130. II
38. XIV	67. X	96. V, XIV	131. XIV
39. VII, XIV	68. X	97. VII	132. I, XIV
41. II	69. X	98. XIV	133. V
42. II, III	71. IV, IX, X	101. IV, VIII	134. I
43. II, III	72. X	102. XII	135. I, IX
45. XII	73. X	103. VIII	136. VIII, XIV
46. XII	74. IV, X	104. II	137. IV
47. IV, XII	75. III, X, XII	105. I, V	138. XIV
48. XII	78. V, XIII	106. V	140. XI, XIV
49. IV, XII, XIII	79. VII, XIII	107. V	141. XIV
50. IV, XII	80. VII, XIII	108. V	142. XIV
51. XII	81. VII	109. I, V	143. XIV
53. VIII, X	82. VII	110. III, IV, XIII	144. II
54. I, VIII	83. I, VII, IX	112. I, VI	146. XIV
55. VIII	84. IV, VII	113. V	147. XIV
56. XII	85. IV, VII	114. V, XIII	
57. IV, VIII, XII	86. VII	115. V, XIII	
58. I, IV, VIII, XII	87. VII	116. V	

ON ATHEISTIC COMMUNISM
(*N.C.W.C. Edition*)

8. I, VI	32. V, VII, X, XIII	49. IV, X	63. XIV
9. VI	33. III	50. VIII, XII	64. XIV
10. VI	34. II, III	51. IV	65. XIV
12. VI	35. XIV	52. X	66. XIV
14. VI	37. XIV	53. IV, X	68. XIV
15. VI	38. V	54. IV, VII	69. XIV
17. VI	39. XIV	55. XIV	72. XIV
22. VI	41. XIV	56. XIV	75. XII, XIII
23. VI	44. XIV	57. VI	76. XIII
27. III	45. XIV	58. VI	77. XIV
29. III	46. IV	59. XIV	
30. III, XIII	47. I, IV	61. XIV	
31. IV	48. IV, XII	62. XIV	

LA SOLENNITÀ DELLA PENTECOSTE (*Principles for Peace*)	CHRISTMAS BROADCAST, 1942 (*Principles for Peace*)	CHURCH AND SOCIAL ORDER (*N.C.W.C. Edition*)	
1675. II, XIII	1831. III	9. II	31. XII
1676. II	1832. III	18. II	32. X, XII
1683. XII	1833. IV, XIII	20. XII	35–38. X
1684. XII	1834. XIII	22. XII	40–47. X
1685. III, IV, XIII	1839. I	25. XII	58. VII
1686. III	1840. XII	26. XI, XII	59. VII
1688. IX	1844. III	27. X	60. VII
1689. IX, XIII	1845. III	28. XI	63. IV
1690. XIII	1846. IX		
1692. XII	1847. III		
1693. XII, XIII	1850. IX		
1694. XIV	1851. III, X, XII		
	1852. XIII		

CODE OF SOCIAL PRINCIPLES

(*Catholic Social Guild*)

1. III	66. VII	108. XIII	143. XII
2. III	67. VII	109. XIII	144. XII
3. III	68. VII	110. XIII	145. XII
4. III	70. II	111. XIII	146–149. XII
5. III	72. II	117. XI	150. XIII
7. II	73. II	118. XI	151. XIII
8. II	94. XII	119. XI	152. XIII
57. VII	95. XII	120. XI	153. XIII
58. VII	96. XII	135. X	154. XIII
59. VII	97. XII	136. X	155. XIII
60. VII	98. XII	137. X	156. XIII
61. VII	103. XIII	138. X	157. XIII
62. VII	104. XIII	139. X	158. XIII
63. VII	105. XIII	140. X	159. XIII
64. VII	106. XIII	141. X	160. IV
65. VII	107. XIII	142. VIII	161. IV

Appendix IV. FULL TABLE OF CORRELATION

In the following table, the reader will be able to correlate all references to authoritative documents in the present book. The vertical lines indicate the references in each of the fourteen chapters which cite Church sources. Reading horizontally for a given document, the reader will note which chapters contain excerpts from this particular source. Where numbered paragraphs are available, these were used to indicate the exact citation. Editions cited are those listed in the authoritative references given after the Table of Contents. Where no paragraph number is available, an asterisk is used to indicate that the document was cited.

	CHAPTERS				
	1	2	3	4	5
POPE LEO XIII					
Quod Apostolici Muneris					
Diuturnum Illud			7, 8, 9		17
Immortale Dei			2	22	23
Libertas Praestantissimum					32
Sapientiae Christianae			2		
Rerum Novarum	5, 6, 66	24, 25, 42	26, 71, 72	14, 48, 49, 50, 52, 83	7, 8, 9
In the Midst of Solicitudes, February 16, 1892					•
Letter to Bishop of Grenoble, June 22, 1892					
Longinque Oceani					
Graves de Communi		10		11	6
Letter to Italian Bishops, December 8, 1902					
POPE PIUS X *Il Firmo Proposito*					
POPE BENEDICT XV *Letter to Bishop of Bergamo,* March 11, 1920					
POPE PIUS XI *Ubi Arcano*		60			
Mens Nostra					
Divini Illius Magistri					
Casti Connubii					
Quadragesimo Anno	3, 5, 54; 58, 59, 60, 62, 83, 105, 109, 112, 132, 134, 135	41, 42, 43, 104, 125, 130, 144	33, 37, 42, 43, 75, 110	4, 25, 47, 49, 50, 57, 58, 71, **74, 84,** 85, 88, 90, 101, 110, 137	10, 14, 25, 27, 78, 88, 91–96, 105–109, 113–120, 133
Non Abbiamo Bisogno					49, 57
Caritate Christi Compulsi	2, 3, 28		30		
Ad Catholici Sacerdotii					
Mit Brennender Sorge			35		
On Atheistic Communism	8, 47	34	27, 29, 30, 33, 34	31, 46, 47, 48, 49, 51, 53, 54	32, 38
Firmissiman Constantiam		19			

CHAPTERS

6	7	8	9	10	11	12	13	14
	9							
							3, 4, 5, 12	
							2	
								2
	20, 28, 76	26, 28, 31, 32, 33, 37, 38, 39	31, 57, 59, 60, 62	51, 61, 62, 63	25, 28, 30, 33, 37, 38, 39, 56, 72, 76, 78, 79	10–17, 18–23, 35, 36, 55, 65, 66, 67	48, 51, 52, 53, 54, 75	40, 42, 75
							*	
								*
		15			*			10
								*
	*							*
								*
							20	17, 30, 55, 56
								23
.							41	
				123, 126, 127			126, 127	
62, 112	39, 79, 80, 81, 82, 83, 84, 85, 86, 87, 97	53, 54, 55, 57, 58, 62, 64, 65, 101, 103, 136	64, 65, 71, 83, 135	53, 61, 66, 67, 68, 69, 71, 72, 73, 74, 75	30, 33, 35, 140	45, 46, 47, 48, 49, 50, 51, 56, 57, 58, 59, 60, 61, 63, 75, 102	25, 28, 49, 78, 79, 80, 89, 110, 114, 115	19–39, 96, 98, 125, 127, 129, 131, 132, 136, 138, 140, 141, 142, 143, 146, 147
						15	4	13, 14, 16, 19, 20, 25, 27, 29, 30
								8
8, 9, 10, 12, 14, 15, 17, 22, 23, 57, 58	32, 54	50		32, 49, 52, 53		48, 50, 75	30, 32, 75, 76	35, 37, 39, 41, 44, 45, 55, 56, 59, 61, 62, 63, 64, 65, 66, 68, 69, 72, 77
								19, 23

CHAPTERS

	1	2	3	4	5
POPE PIUS XII *Summi Pontificatus*				1419, 1437	1420, 1429
Sertum Laetitiae				37	
La Solennità della Pentecoste		1675, 1676	1685, 1686	1685	
Nell' Alba	1748, 1749		1751		
Christmas Broadcast, 1942	1839		1831, 1832, 1844–5, 1847, 1851	1833	
Address to Italian Workers, June 13, 1943			*		
Christmas Message, 1943		*			
Radio Address, September 1, 1944	*		*		
Letter to French Episcopate, January 6, 1945					
Address to Italian Workers, March 11, 1945					
Address to College of Cardinals, June 2, 1945					*
On Women's Duties	*				
Christmas Broadcast, 1945					
Discourse to Members of Italian Electric Industry, January 24, 1946					
Letter to Semaines Sociales, 1946					
Discourse to Italian Farmers, November 15, 1946					
Address to Members of Renascita Cristiana, January 22, 1947		*			
Allocution to Sacred College of Cardinals, June 2, 1947		*			
Letter to Semaines Sociales, 1947					
Discourse to Catholic Action Men, September 7, 1947					
Allocution to International Union of Leagues of Catholic Women, September 12, 1947					
Address to Small Craftsmen, October, 1947					
Christmas Broadcast, 1947					
Address to Congress of International Exchange, March 7, 1948					
Discourse to International Institute for Unification of Private Rights, May 20, 1948					
Allocution to Sacred College of Cardinals, June 2, 1948					
Discourse to Christian Association of Italian Workers, June 29, 1948					
Address to Young Men, September 12, 1948			*		
Discourse on Public Finance, October 2, 1948					

CHAPTERS

6	7	8	9	10	11	12	13	14
							1418, 1419, 1420, 1424, 1429	1398, 1400, 1402, 1437, 1444
			1465, 1466			1464		1468
			1688, 1689			1683, 1684, 1692, 1693	1675, 1685, 1689, 1690, 1693	1694
							1758, 1760	
			1846, 1850	1851		1840, 1851	1833, 1834, 1852	
			*			*	*	
						*		
								*
	*						*	
							*	
		*	*				*	
*								
						*	*	*
	*						*	
						*		
	*					*	*	*
						*		
								*
						*		
								*
							*	
						*		
	*							*
					*			
						*		

CHAPTERS

	1	2	3	4	5
POPE PIUS XII (Continued)					
Discourse to Members of Fiat Automobile Plant, October 31, 1948			●		
Christmas Message, 1948					
Address to Catholic Employers, May 7, 1949				●	
Address to Minister From India, July 6, 1949					
Address to Women of Italian Catholic Action, July, 1949					
Letter to Semaines Sociales, 1949		*			
Message to German Catholics, September 4, 1949		*			
Allocution to Belgian Workers, September 11, 1949					
AMERICAN HIERARCHY *Social Reconstruction*, 1919					
Pastoral Letter, 1919					
Bishops' Statement, 1933					
The Church and Social Order, 1940		9, 18		63	
Secularism, Statement, November, 1947					
The Christian in Action, November, 1948					
The Christian Family, November, 1949					
OTHER AUTHORITIES *Summa Theologica, St. Thomas Aquinas*				*	
Sacred Congregation of the Council, to Bishop of Lille, June 5, 1929					
Socialization, Australian Bishops, 1948					
Pattern for Peace, Australian Bishops					
Peace in Industry, Australian Bishops					
Congregation of the Holy Office, July 13, 1949					
Pastoral Letter, French Cardinals, September 8, 1949					
Pastoral Letter, Hierarchy of Quebec, February, 1950					
Code of Social Principles		7, 8, 70, 72–73	1–5	160–161	

6	7	8	9	10	11	12	13	14
POPE PIUS XII (Continued)								
							*	*
	*	*			*		*	
*								
								*
					*			*
					*			
				*	*			*
	*				*			
*						*		*
	58–60			27, 32, 40–47, 35–38	26, 28	20, 22, 25–26, 31–32		
								*
	*							
				*				
					*			
						*	*	
	*							
					*			
*								
		*						
				131	179–181			
	57–68	142		135–141	117–120	94–98, 143–149	103–111, 150–159	

INDEX OF AUTHORITIES

Inequality, 4 ff; natural, 257; in wealth, 470

Insecurity, causes of, 349 f; and ownership, 473

Instability, economic, 562

Institutions, social, and living wage, 341; and social justice, 97, 98

Interfaith co-operation, 569, 573 f, 575

International trade, 526 ff; principles of, 529 f

Internationalism, false, 136

Isolationism, spiritual, 563

Justice, 94 ff; and charity, 100 ff, 341; commutative, 94; commutative, and property, 466; distributive, 94 f; distributive, and taxation, 464; need for, 562; neglect of, 7; social, see Social justice; and wages, 339 ff

Labor, 303 ff; basis for social unity, 203 f; and capital, 200 ff, 257, 409 ff, 472 f; chaplains of, 568; and the clergy, 568; condition of, 3 ff; dignity of, 262, 303 ff, 412; duties of, 412 ff; exploitation of, 6, 9; hours of, 306 f; men degraded by, 304; and moral reform, 563; necessary to men, 337 f; not a commodity, 304; personal nature of, 337 f; perverted today, 7; and property, 459; rights of, 261 f, 304; value of, 72

Labor-management co-operation, 200 ff, 257, 409 ff

Labor unions, 404 ff; abuses of, 204, 414 f; activities of, 414; Catholic, 405; and Catholic action, 577; duties of, 412 ff; and economic stability, 350; necessary, 405 f; need for, 473; not complete answer, 207 f; obligation to join, 406; principles governing, 404, 413 f; product of capitalism, 405 f; and workers' rights, 407 f

Laity, apostolate of, 570 f, 573; leadership by, 576; and social reform, 569 ff

Leo XIII, appraisal of past achievements, 576; on capitalism, 257 f; on child labor, 305; on Church and government, 133, 134; on the Church and the social problem, 33 ff; on civil authority, 68 f; on class struggle, 3, 200; on the clergy and social reform, 564; on the common good, 95; on communism, 137; on dignity of labor, 257 f, 262, 303; on distribution of property, 467; on duties of government, 513 f; on duties of property owners, 261 f, 465; on duties of workers, 412 f; on forms of government, 133 f, 512, 513; on guilds, 3; on hours of labor, 306 f; on human dignity, 303; on human rights, 68; on justice, distributive, 94; on labor management co-operation, 409 f; on the laity and social reform, 569; on Liberalism, 134; on living wage, 337 f; on man in society, 67, 68 f; on morality and economic life, 456; on natural inequality, 257 f; on nature of man, 65; on need for society, 69; on nihilism, 137; on origin of society, 69; on poverty, 257 f; on private and public societies, 67 f; on religion and the social question, 555 f; on right of association, 210 f; on right to organize, 404; on right of ownership, 458 f; on rights of labor, 138, 262; on social charity, 99 f; on social co-operation, 200; on social legislation, 524 f; on the social problem, 3; on socialism, 137 f; on source of public authority, 512 f; on strikes, 406 f; on subsidiarity, 212; on taxation, 461 f; on usury, 3; on women workers, 305; see also General Index

Liberalism, 4, 514; economic, 134 f; see also Individualism

Liberty under communism, 167 f

Living wage, 337 ff, 473; and profits, 563

Machines and men, 471

Man, and civil society, 515; dignity of, 64 ff, 140 f, 262, 303 ff, 412, 568; dignity of, under communism, 167; dignity of, see also Dignity, human; equality of, 65; nature of, 64 ff; and ownership, 458 ff, 468 ff; rights of, 64 ff; and society, 66 ff; spiritual education of, 562

Management, rights of, 263; sharing of, 263

Manchester School, 4, 260

Materialism, 8, 140 f; and communism, 167; condemned, 65, 259; dialectical, 167

GENERAL INDEX

788 GENERAL INDEX

Berridge, W. A., cited, 402 n
Beveridge, W. H., cited, 758, 759
Bienstock, G., cited, 749
Bigness, see Giantism
Bishops, authority of, 604
Black, J. D., cited, 671 n, 680, 769
Black Death, 15
Bloom, G. F., cited, 336, 756
Blum, M. L., cited, 753
Boland, F. L., cited, 554
Bollens, L. F., cited, 762
Bolles, J. K., cited, 652
Bonds, payments for, 275
Borsodi, R., cited, 633, 652
Bowen, H. R., cited, 739
Bowler, E. M., cited, 754
Boycotts, 442
Boyle, G., cited, 653
Brady, R. A., cited, 745, 764
Brannan Plan, 675 f, 676 n
Brauer, T., cited, 751
Braun, K., cited, 754, 761
Briefs, G. A., cited, 741, 762
Brooks, R. R., cited, 452 n, 760
Browder, E., cited, 177
Brownlee, O. H., cited, 765
Brucculeri, A., cited, 113 n, 735
Bruehl, C., cited, 165, 253, 511, 554, 734
Buchanan, N. S., cited, 765
Buckley, L. F., cited, 388 n
Budenz, L. F., cited, 750
Budget, family, 362 ff; for woman, 329 f
Bullitt, W. C., cited, 750
Burnham, J., cited, 742, 750
Burns, A. R., cited, 154 n, 241 n, 244 n, 253, 745
Burns, E. M., cited, 759
Business, appraisal of, 707; big, 300; and Church intervention, 42; and collective bargaining, 431; common good in, 216; common interests in, 228 ff; defended by Catholics, 699 ff; and distributive justice, 111; duties of, 288 ff; duties of labor regarding, 444 ff; duties in social justice, 358; and ethics, 54; fostering of small firms, 503 ff; and human relations, 126 f; and labor unions, 417 f, 421 ff, 447; and a living wage, 353 ff; psychology of, 299; rejects price fixing, 239; size of, 498 f; small, 300; small, aid to, 507 f, 641; small, and freedom, 634 f; social aspect of, 45; and strikes,

436; under statism, 160 f; and union officials, 450 f; and union security, 427 f; and wage increases, 374 f
Business cycle, see Depressions
Business groups, and industry councils, 223 f
Butters, J. K., cited, 498 n

Cahill, E., cited, 32, 63, 93, 132, 165, 457, 491 n, 554, 600, 734
Callaghan, H. C., cited, 759
Cantor, N., cited, 754
Capital, 264 ff; definitions of, 269; duties of, 288 ff; and labor, 214 ff; physical, 267 f; productivity of, 269, 286
Capitalism, 264 ff; American, 22 f; and communism, 173 f; condemned, 264 f; defended, 265 f; definition of, 264 f
Caritate Christi Compulsi, 608
Carlen, Sr. M. C., cited, 734
Carlyle, A. J., and R. W., cited, 13 n, 739
Carr-Saunders, A. M., cited, 653
Carskadon, T. R., cited, 742
Casti connubii, 366, 534
Catholic action, 719; bishops on, 609; and the clergy, 592 f; meaning of, 593 f; papal ideal of, 594 f; and the social apostolate, 594 ff
Catholic Church, see Church
Catholic Conference on Industrial Problems, 614
Catholic Economic Association, 250, 627, 716
Catholic Mind, 591
Catholic social action, and charity, 128
Catholic Social Action, 565 n, 592, 593, 596, 597; discussed, 711 ff
Catholic social movement, 21, 41
Catholic Theological Society, 716
Catholic Worker, appraised, 691
Catholics, and agriculture, 510, 654 ff; 676 ff; and American business, 699 ff; and business, 301; and communism, 195; and co-operatives, 633, 644, 649 ff; discrimination against, 318 ff; and distributism, 633; and family standards, 365, 366 f; and human-relations programs, 292; and labor-management co-operation, 448; and labor unions, 423 f; and a living wage, 360; and medical care, 384; and monetary reform, 692 ff; and nationalization, 537 f;

Farming, bishops on, 609 f
Farms, commercial, 660; disadvantages of,
657; economic problems, 22; family,
657 ff, 680; family, NCRLC on, 664;
tenancy in, 659, 664
Fascism, 49; condemned, 162
Father Keller, appraisal of, 706 ff, 709
Federal Council of Churches, 62
Federal Reserve Act, 24, 542
Federal Reserve Board, 699
Federal Reserve System, 234, 396, 400,
539, 697, 698
Federal Trade Commission, 234, 640; on
economic concentration, 497 f, 504
Federal Trade Commission Act, 543
Feldman, H., cited, 760
Ferree, W., cited, 113 n, 122, 132, 632,
743; views of, 628
Feudalism, 12 f
Fire on the Earth, analyzed, 684 ff
Fitzpatrick, P. J., cited, 627 n, 737
Fitzsimons, J., cited, 766
Fletcher, J. F., cited, 763
Food, Drug, and Cosmetic Act, 543
Foote, A., cited, 748
Foremen, abuses by, 312; rights of, 294 f
Fotitch, C., cited, 749
Foundations of a Modern Guild System,
analyzed, 629
Fowler, B. B., cited, 653, 768
Frazier, E. F., cited, 744
Free enterprise, Fr. Keller on, 700 f
Free trade, 550 f
Freedom, and collectivism, 217 f; and co-
operatives, 645; economic basis of, 27;
. and organic society, 217 f; and owner-
ship, 634 ff; and property ownership,
302, 494 f; and socialism, 159; threats
to, 50; under communism, 184 f
Fryer, L., cited, 769
Full employment, *see* Employment, full
Furfey, P. H., cited, 682 ff, 685 n, 686 n,
710, 766

Gagliardo, D., cited, 759
Gardiner, G., cited, 754, 762
Gardner, B. B., cited, 752
Gee, W., cited, 681
Geissler, E. S., cited, 766
General Motors, wage agreement of, 379
George, H., cited, 764
Giantism, 496, 634 ff, 640 f; and co-

operatives, 645 f; remedies for, 507 f; a
social evil, 219
Gibbons, J., cited, 598, 607
Giles, R., cited, 768
Ginzberg, E., cited, 760
Giordani, I., cited, 60 n, 737
Gitlow, B., cited, 750
God, in economic life, 41 ff, 121 f; source
of political power, 531 ff; and the uni-
verse, 77 f
Goldberg, J. P., cited, 433 n
Golden, C. S., cited, 229 n, 253, 448 n,
680, 755, 769
Goldenweiser, E. A., cited, 760
Goldmann, F., cited, 758
Gomberg, W., cited, 758
Gompers, J., cited, 748
Gonella, G., cited, 554, 735, 765
Goodell, F., cited, 755
Gosplan, 183
Government, and agriculture, 676 ff; aid
for housing, 380; aid to migrant labor,
323; centralization in, 638 f; and de-
pressions, 396 f; economic influence of,
277; in economic life, 533 ff, 723;
economy in, 357 f; and farming, 663;
Fr. Munier on, 630; and medical care,
383; and small business, 504 f; and
small farms, 659; source of power,
531 ff; *see also* State
Grange, 677
Gray, A., cited, 766
Greed, 585; *see also* Avarice
Greer, T. H., cited, 741
Gregory, C. O., cited, 756
Griffin, C. E., cited, 745
Groves, H. M., cited, 491 n, 765
Guilds, craft, 13; medieval, 13 f; me-
dieval, decay of, 19; merchant, 13 f

Haas, F. J., cited, 237 n, 589, 743
Haber, W., cited, 759
Hacker, L. M., cited, 752
Haessle, J., cited, 735
Hall, F., cited, 653
Hammond, B., and J. L., cited, 20 n, 741
Haney, L. H., cited, 17 n
Hansen, A., cited, 275, 455, 622
Hansen, A. H., cited, 759
Harmel, J., and L., cited, 47, 598
Harris, H., cited, 761
Harris, S. E., cited, 746

N.C.W.C., 618; and profit-sharing, 289
Labor relations, psychology of, 313 f
Labor unions, 415 ff; admission to, 425 ff;
Catholic, 424 f; and Catholic employers,
423 f; civil rights of members, 451 f;
and the closed shop, 427 ff; and collective bargaining, 429 ff, 455 f; discipline by, 428; discrimination by, 425 ff;
duties of members, 448 ff; duties of officers, 449 ff; duties toward public,
452 ff; duty to join, 418 ff; and economic analysis, 455 f; and health plans,
382; and industry councils, 223 f; and
a living wage, 373 ff; and migrant
labor, 323 f; in public jobs, 422 f; and
racial discrimination, 320; recognition
of, 421 ff; right to organize, 416 ff;
security for, 427 ff; social function of,
416 ff; and wage demands, 456 f; and
women workers, 332
Labor's Monthly Survey, cited, 215, 228 n,
377
LaFarge, J., cited, 744
Laidler, H. W., cited, 746
Laissez faire, advocated, 17; condemned,
150
Laity, apostolate of, 725; leadership by,
bishops on, 609; social action by, 593 ff;
social training of, 718 ff
Lammenais, F. de, cited, 533
Land, *see* Property
Lane, A. B., cited, 750
Lange, O., cited, 746
Lapp, J., cited, 615
Lasky, V., cited, 750
Latimer, M., cited, 402 n, 757
Lauterbach, A., cited, 742
Laux, J. J., cited, 476 n
Law, penal, 532
Lazarus, H., cited, 433 n
Leadership, value of, 118 f
Lee, Wm. J., cited, 618 n
Leighton, A. H., cited, 753
Leiter, R. D., cited, 754
Lelotte, S. M., cited, 766
Lenin, N., cited, 177, 179, 182, 747
Lens, S., cited, 760
Leo XIII, cited, 41, 56, 58, 109, 508, 533,
608, 702; on living wage, 352; on
natural inequality, 268; on property,
480, 494; on right of association,, 221;
on taxation, 489; on usury, 287; *see also*

Index of Authorities
Leonard, W. R., cited, 738
Lerhinan, J. P., cited, 199
Lester, R. A., cited, 375 n, 457, 756
Lever, E. J., cited, 755
Liberalism, economic, *see* Individualism
Liberality, 130 f
Libertas Praestantissimum, 533
Liberty, and the social question, 18; and
socialism, 159; *see also* Freedom
Ligutti, L. G., cited, 661 n, 680, 768
Lindblom, C. E., cited, 456 n, 761
Lindstrom, D. E., cited, 681, 769
Lintner, J., cited, 498 n
Living wage, 351 ff; bishops on, 607, 611;
and Catholic employers, 360; and child
labor, 326; economics of, 367 ff; how
achieved, 373; Msgr. Ryan on, 620 f,
729 f; a moral right, 352 ff; obligation
of, 108; and profits, 358 f, 370; and
restitution, 359 f; standards for, 354 f,
361 ff; types of, 353 f; and women
workers, 331
Lodge, N., cited, 748
Long, C. D., cited, 738
Lopez, U., cited, 736
Loucks, W. N., cited, 746
Louden, J. K., cited, 758
Lubac, H. de, cited, 736
Lugan, A., cited, 737
Lutz, F. A., cited, 765
Lynch, D., cited, 745, 764
Lyons, E., cited, 180 n, 181 n, 750

Machines and men, 76, 314, 637 f, 641,
667
MacIver, R. M., cited, 764
Maimonides, M., cited, 493
Malthus, T. R., cited, 17
Man, dignity of, 73 ff, 126, 291, 307 ff,
352; dignity of, and hours of work, 333;
and economic life, 32, 88 ff; equality
of, 80 ff, 268, 320 f; nature of, 73 ff,
149 f; political nature of, 531 f; and
property, 480; rights of, 76 ff; rights
of, and labor unions, 417 f; and rural
life, 656, 662 f; social nature of, 531 f;
and society, 74, 83 ff, 121 f, 149 f;
under industrialism, 76, 85, 314; *see
also* Dignity, human
Management, economic function of, 269 ff;
salaries of, 271 f; sharing of, 290 ff, 295,

political, 85 f; and property, 479 f; reform of, 214; and the state, 531

Sociology, supernatural, 684 ff

Solidarity, co-operative, 642 f

Sombart, W., cited, 265, 745

Some American Approximations to Pius XI's Industries and Professions, analyzed, 629 ff

Somerville, H., cited, 599 *n*, 737

Sorokin, P. A., cited, 10, 740

Soviet Union, communism in, 181 ff; Communist Party in, 185; economic life, 183 f; economics, 193 f; and family life, 185; farming, 184; foreign policy, 187 f; freedom in, 184 f, 193; and international communism, 176, 186 ff, 194; labor conditions in, 183 f; slave labor in, 183 f

Spann, O., cited, 739

Speculation, control of, 542; economic, 19, 23; economic function of, 269 f

Speed-up, 312 f

Speltz, G. H., cited, 659 *n*

Spengler, O., cited, 10

Spiritual problems in modern society, 582 ff

Spiritual reform and communism, 197

Spiritualism, excessive, 50, 88, 119, 579 f, 683

Stability, economic, 91; and international trade, 551 f

Stalin, J., cited, 179, 182, 186, 748

Standards of living, 636

State, and the Church, 144 ff; and common good, 121 f; and communism, 174; duties of, 535 f; economic function of, 530 ff; and economic life, 161 f; and economic planning, 244; and industry councils, 219 f, 223 f, 250; intervention by, 26, 124; and monetary policy, 538 f; and property, 479, 484 f; and social legislation, 541 ff; and social reform, 92 f; and society, 531; *see also* Government

Statement on Present Crisis (1933), analyzed, 608 ff

Statism, 160 ff; and the Church, 49; condemned, 75 f, 120, 164 f; and co-operatives, 643; Fr. Keller on, 701; a present danger, 216; remedy for, 219, 236, 252; and welfare state, 548; *see also* Collectivism

Status, medieval, 13

Steffens, L., cited, 741

Steinbüschel, T., cited, 736

Stephenson, C., cited, 740

Stewart, B. M., cited, 755

Stockholders, obligations of, 487 f

Stocking, G. W., cited, 745

Stocks, payments for, 275

Straus, N., cited, 758

Stretch-out, 312 f

Strider, J., cited, 736

Strikes, 433 ff; bishops on, 607; and collective bargaining, 438 ff; conditions for, 434 ff; duties regarding, 443; evils of, 440 f; general, 436; jurisdictional, 437; justice in, 435 f; and labor unions, 452 f; moral means in, 441 f; national emergency, 437 f; sit-down, 442 f; sympathy, 436; types of, 436; in the United States, 444; violence in, 441 f; and workers' rights, 434

Suarez, F., cited, 85, 477 *n*, 532; on property, 477

Subsidiarity, 534 f; principle of, 124, 219

Suhard, E., cited, 582, 766

Supernatural, importance of, 684 ff

Supernaturalism, misguided, 688

Surplus value, 174, 352

Sweezy, P. M., cited, 746, 748

Taft, P., cited, 336, 457, 756

Taft-Hartley Act, *see* Labor Management Relations Act

Tannenbaum, F., cited, 760

Tariffs, 552

Tate, A., cited, 652

Taviani, P. E., cited, 736

Tawney, R. H., cited, 12 *n*, 16 *n*, 32 *n*, 740, 746

Taxation, 489 ff; bishops on, 606; and depressions, 391, 397 ff; distributists on, 639; economic effects of, 277; and economic size, 498 f, 507; effects of, 490 f; incentive, 398; principles regarding, 489 f; and profits, 279; reform of, 131; Msgr. Ryan on, 729; and small business, 505 f

Taylor, C. C., cited, 769

Taylor, F. M., cited, 746

Taylor, G. W., cited, 757, 761

Taylor, R., cited, 756

Tead, O., cited, 753

Technology, 636, 641; and living stand-

ards, 372; NCRLC on, 667; and un-
employment, 394 f, 402 f; value of, 90
Tennessee Valley Authority, 651, 652
Thompson, J. W., cited, 20 *n*, 740
Thompson, K. M., cited, 294 *n*, 755
Thomson, C. A. H., cited, 165, 746
Three Theories of Society, analyzed, 684 ff
Thrift, 493
Timasheff, N. S., cited, 748
Toledano, R. de, cited, 750
Toner, J. L., cited, 429 *n*, 762
Tootle, H. K., cited, 752
Totalitarianism, and the Church, 49; con-
demned, 161
Tour du Pin, R. de la, cited, 598
Toynbee, A., cited, 10, 20 *n*, 740, 741
Trehey, H. F., cited, 93, 124, 132, 223 *n*,
224 *n*, 225 *n*, 226 *n*, 227 *n*, 253, 632,
751; views of, 628 f
Troeltsch, E., cited, 16 *n*, 32, 737
Trotsky, L., cited, 184, 186
Turgot, A. R., cited, 17

Unearned increment, 482
Unemployment, bishops on, 609; causes of,
389 ff; compensation for, 385; evils of,
388; and labor restrictions, 445 f; remedies for, 395 ff; and the social problem,
19; technological, 394 f, 402 f; types of,
389
Unions, *see* Labor unions
United Nations, and communism, 197;
problems of, 550
United States, agricultural problems in,
510; attitude toward papal program,
220; capitalist abuses in, 271 f; Catholic social action in, 590 ff, 720 ff; Catholic social movement in, 42; and Catholic social teaching, 59 f, 603 ff; Catholic
social thought in, 599; child labor in,
326 ff; communism in, 178 f, 186 f,
188 ff; competition in, 297; co-operatives in, 647 ff; cost of living in, 362 ff;
defense of business in, 699 ff; distribution of wealth in, 496 ff; economic dictatorship in, 154 ff; economic needs in,
276; farm problems in, 22, 668 ff; and
free trade, 551; frontier in, 22; government intervention in, 536 f; income
distribution in, 364 f, 499 ff; individualism in, 115; and industry-council
plan, 227 ff; interest rates in, 287;

labor problem in, 22; labor-management co-operation in, 294; living
wage in, 356 f; medical care in, 381 f;
migratory labor in, 322 ff; monopoly in,
297; physical resources, 368; prices in,
154 ff; productivity in, 371 f; profit levels in, 277 ff, 283; profit-sharing in,
289; property diffusion in, 503 ff; real
wages in, 267; reform movements in,
23 f; social legislation in, 541 ff; social
policy in, 251 f; social problem in, 21 ff;
social program for, 711 ff; social reform
in, 218 f; strikes in, 444; taxation in,
489 ff; wages in, 364; welfare state in,
548 f; women workers in, 328 ff
United States Employment Service, approved, 605
Updegraf, C. M., cited, 762
Usury, 14, 106 f; condemned, 285; and
monetary reformers, 695; and the popes,
287

Venture capital, 506
Viereck, P., cited, 745
Villeneuve-Bargement, V. de, cited, 598
Virtue and social reform, 587 f
Virtues, social, 104 ff; subsidiary, 129 ff
Vito, F., cited, 736
Vocational groups, *see* Industry councils

Wage contract, 267 ff
Wages, bishops on, 611; and depressions,
393; economics of, 456 f; equalization
of, 378; guaranteed, 401 f; and incen-
tives, 289; increases in, 373 ff; and in-
dustry councils, 232 ff; Iron Law of,
351; living, *see* Living wage; and man-
agement returns, 272; and productivity,
369 ff; in the United States, 364; and
women workers, 329
Waggaman, M. T., cited, 402 *n*
Walsh, E., cited, 686 *n*, 710
War Labor Board, 242, 439
War Price and Rationing Board, 242
War Production Board, 242
Warbasse, J. P., cited, 653, 768
Ward, B., cited, 241 *n*
Ward, J. R., cited, 652
Ward, L. R., cited, 768
Ware, N., cited, 740
Waring, P. A., cited, 680, 769
Warne, C. E., cited, 763

Watkins, M. W., cited, 745
Watkins, W. P., cited, 653
Wealth, acquisition of, 491 f; Christian attitude toward, 588; distribution of, 30, 89 f, 266, 293 f; distribution of, bishops on, 611; distribution of, in the United States, 496 ff; distribution of, Fr. Keller on, 703 ff; and money, 697; remedies for concentration of, 503 ff; superfluous, 130, 492
Weaver, R. C., cited, 320 n, 763
Weaver, R. M., cited, 12 n, 599 n, 767
Weber, M., cited, 265, 740, 746
Wecter, D., cited, 742
Welcker, J. W., cited, 281 n, 283
Welfare plans and social charity, 129
Welfare state, 547 ff; and agriculture, 678 f
Welk, W. G., cited, 747
Welty, E., cited, 736
Wernette, J. P., cited, 759
Whitehead, T. N., cited, 753
Whittaker, E., cited, 17 n, 739
Whyte, W. F., cited, 753

Widick, B. W., cited, 760
Wilcox, C., cited, 553 n, 765
Williams, M. J., cited, 600 n
Williamson, S. T., cited, 761
Wolfbein, S., cited, 320 n
Wolfe, C., cited, 402 n
Women, economic oppression of, 20, 29 f; and a living wage, 365 f; as workers, 328 ff
Work, conditions of, 309 ff; conditions of, and collective bargaining, 430; conditions of, and women workers, 329; duty to, 315 ff; right to, 315 ff; satisfaction in, 316
Workers, see Labor
World citizenship, impractical, 550
World Federation of Trade Unions, 188
Woytinsky, W. S., cited, 456 n
Wright, D. M., cited, 743, 752, 759

Yoder, D., cited, 753
Young Christian Workers, 594, 719